CW00923625

8th May 1996

The Yimas Language
of New Guinea

The Yimas Language
of New Guinea

William A. Foley

Stanford University Press
Stanford, California

Stanford University Press
Stanford, California

Copyright © 1991 by the Board of Trustees of the
Leland Stanford Junior University

Printed in the United States of America

CIP data appear at the end of the book

For the Yimas people
as they find their way in the modern world

Preface

This book is the result of a research project spread over some ten years and funded largely by the Australian Research Grants Scheme (Grant A176/15655), with some supplementary funding in 1985 from the Faculties Research Fund of the Australian National University. The goal of the project was a complete study of the Yimas language, its grammar and lexicon, the social and cultural contexts of the use of the language, its history and genetic relations, and its interactions with neighboring languages. Some of the results of this project have been reported in previous works, notably Foley (1986, 1988), but this book represents the most complete document on the language to date. Still to come are a Yimas dictionary and a volume of traditional legends, presented in Yimas with Tok Pisin and English translations. Further, the result of the Yimas language project will play a central role in a long term research project I have just commenced—a reconstruction of the prehistory of the Sepik-Ramu basin, using largely linguistic data.

The following grammar is not written in any set theoretical framework. I wanted the organization of the grammar to reflect the structure of the language as closely as possible. Hence, I have deliberately chosen to be eclectic, choosing various ideas from different theories when these seem to elucidate the structure of the language best. Thus, the reader will find that the phonology is largely cast in an autosegmental framework, while the syntax reflects a rather broad structuralist/functionalist perspective. Still, these frameworks are not rigidly adhered to, but are adapted as needs be in order to make the grammar widely accessible. This seemed to me to be the best approach, because this work is likely to be the only documentation ever of the grammar of the Yimas language, and hence it is essential that it be intelligible to the widest possible audience. Those who find in the labyrinth of Yimas grammar, facts which are confirmations (or disconfirmations!) of their favorite linguistic hypotheses are welcome to make whatever use they like of this grammar and restate it in whatever theoretical model they fancy.

This book is the last I will write at the Australian National University, and I would like to take this opportunity to thank my colleagues and the general staff of the University for their help and kindnesses over the years, which have made my twelve years here such a pleasant time. The conditions at the Australian National University must be among the very best in the world, and whatever value the reader may find in this work is due in no small part to the excellent support provided by the University over the years.

For the completion of this work, I owe a great debt to several people. The two most important are Mrs. Ellalene Seymour, who patiently and uncomplainingly typed the manuscript from untidy handwritten drafts, and Rosemary Butt, whose electronic wizardry made the correcting and editing of the manuscript much less painful than it otherwise would have been. Thanks also go to Val Lyons, who drew the maps.

Finally, a simple thanks is inadequate to express my debt to my main language teacher Stephen Yakayapan Mambi and my other language helpers at Yimas: Paul Api, Pius Taki, Marikin, Malkior Yumbwi, and Bruno Yumbwi. It was their hard work and patience which made this book possible. Finally, I hope the dedication of this book to the Yimas people goes part of the way in repaying their kindness and trust in me over the last ten years.

Contents

List of Maps and Tables

Abbreviations

A — subject of transitive verb
ACC — accusative
ADJ — adjective
ADV — adverbial
AGR — agreement
ALL — allative
ASP — aspect
BEN — benefactive
CAUS — causative
COM — comitative
COMP — completive
CONT — continuative
COP — copula
D — dative of ditransitive verb
DAT — dative
DEF — definitive
DEP — dependent
DL — dual
DR — different referent
DUR — durative
ELEV — elevational/directional
ERG — ergative
F — feminine
F — [front] autosegment
FOL — following
FR DIST — far distal verb
FR PAST — far past
FUT — future

HAB — habitual
HORT — hortative
IMM — immediate
IMP — imperative
IMPERF — imperfective
INCH — inchoative
INDIC — indicative
INVIS — invisible
IRR — irrealis
KIN — kinetic
L — low
LIKE — likely
LOC — locative
M — masculine
MOD — modifier
MOT — motion
N — noun
NEG — negative
NFN — non-finite
NIGHT — nightime
NOM — nominative
NP — noun phrase
NR DIST — near distal
NR FUT — near future
NR PAST — near past
NUM — numeral
O — object of transitive verb
OBL — oblique

P — preposition
PC — paucal
PERF — perfective
PL — plural
POSS — possessive
POSSR — possessor
POT — potential
PP — postpositional phrase
PRES — present
PRO — pronominal
PROG — progressive
PROX — proximal
PURP — purposive
Q — quote
R — [round] autosegment
RCP — reciprocal
RED — reduplication
RM FUT — remote future
RM PAST — remote past
S — subject of intransitive verb
S — sentence
SEQ — sequential
SG — singular
SIM — simultaneous relation
SOV — actor-object verb

sp — species
T — theme of ditransitive verb
TNS — tense
TR — transitive
V — verb
V_0 — verb root
V_1 — verb stem
V_2 — verb theme
VAL — valence
VIS — visual
VIS — visible
VOC — vocalized
1 — first person
2 — second person
3 — third person
I — class I
II — class II
III — class III
IV — class IV
V — class V
VI — class VI
VII — class VII
VIII — class VIII
IX — class IX
X — class X

The Yimas Language
of New Guinea

1

The Language and Its Speakers

1.1 Linguistic Type

Yimas belongs to the grouping of languages spoken in the Pacific known as Papuan languages. Languages of the New Guinea area are generally divided into two large groupings: Austronesian languages and Papuan languages. The Austronesian languages all belong to the far-flung Austronesian language family, stretching east to west from Southeast Asia to Hawaii, and north to south from Formosa to New Zealand. Most of the roughly 250 Austronesian languages of the New Guinea area (and all of those in Papua New Guinea) belong to a single subgroup of the family known as the Oceanic subgroup.

Papuan languages are quite different in this respect. The 750 or so Papuan languages do not constitute a single, genetically unified language family, but rather are organized into about sixty different language families averaging ten member languages each. With much more careful and detailed comparative work, some of these language families will undoubtedly be combined into larger genetic groupings, as the Celtic, Germanic, and Slavic language families among others have been combined to form the Indo-European language family. Wurm (1982) presents some hypotheses in this direction, but at this point nearly all of these need to be verified by careful comparative work.

With so many Papuan language families composed of so many distinct languages, it is very difficult to describe what a 'typical' Papuan language is, as all generalizations will be contradicted by one language or indeed one language family. Nonetheless, I attempted just this in Foley 1986, and I will summarize here how Yimas fits with the characterizations of Papuan languages proposed in that work. Yimas is one of six member languages of the Lower Sepik family (see Section 1.4 for more discussion of the family, as well as Foley 1986, 214–29). As with the other languages of the family, it is morphologically agglutinative, employing both prefixes and suffixes. Word order is highly variable and quite free, although some other languages in the family have a weak preference for Subject/Object/Verb.

The phonological inventory of Yimas is small, even by the standards of Papuan languages, having only 12 consonants and 4 vowels. The phonology exhibits many features typical of Sepik area languages. There are no fricative phonemes; [s] is just an allophonic realization of the voiceless palatal stop /c/. The language distinguishes four places of articulation: bilabial, dental, palatal, and velar, with a corresponding voiceless stop and nasal in each position. There is no voiced/voiceless distinction for stops, the voiced stops being allophonic realizations of the voiceless stops in certain positions, such as following nasals. Unusually for a Papuan language, Yimas has an r/l distinction, but the /l/ is always palatal(ized), i.e., [lʸ] or [ʎ], and the /r/ is always dental-alveolar, to a large extent varying freely between [l] and [ɾ] as phonetic realizations. The vocalic system is typically—one might say prototypically—Sepik. There is a dearth of vowel phonemes, both abstractly and as the segmental phonemes of particular words. Many words lack underlying vowel phonemes altogether, and the string of underlying consonants is broken up in phonetic realization by epenthetic vowels inserted by a phonological rule. The only clear unambiguous underlying vowel in the language is the low central vowel /a/. The three high vowels /i, ɨ, u/ are often the result of vowel epenthesis, the /ɨ/ almost invariably so. The semivowels /y/ and /w/, especially the latter, interact closely with the phonological rules involving vowels, such that their phonetic realization is often the result of these rules. Stress is predictable and generally occurs initially.

Yimas has two major word classes, noun and verb. In addition to these, there are eight minor categories: adjective, quantifier, locational, temporal, pronoun, deictic, conjunction, and interjection. There are only three true adjectives in Yimas; other roots corresponding to adjectives in English belong to the major classes of verb and noun. Quantifiers must be treated as a separate word class from adjectives in Yimas due to their highly divergent morphology. Locationals and temporals are two adverb-like parts of speech, expressing the spatial and temporal orientations of events. They both share some of the features of nouns, such as the occasional ability to pluralize. The number distinctions of Yimas pronouns are much richer than in most other Papuan languages. In addition to the usual three persons, Yimas pronouns distinguish four numbers: singular, dual, paucal (a few), and plural (more than a few). Deictics exhibit a three-way distinction: place near the speaker, place near the addressee, and place near neither of these. There are over sixty of these deictic forms; besides deictic distance, they distinguish noun class and number of the nominal designating the object whose position they describe. Like most Papuan languages, Yimas has a very restricted set of conjunctions (some languages in the central highlands of Papua New Guinea lack them entirely). There are no subordinating conjunctions and only two coordinating conjunctions, equivalent to 'and' and 'but'.

Nouns in Yimas are characterized by being divided into ten major classes, plus a few idiosyncratic classes. The criteria for assignment to noun class are both semantic and phonological. Nouns are obligatorily inflected for three numbers (singular, dual, and plural), with the morphemes indicating number highly variable according to noun class. Suppletion of the noun stem in the plural form is common. The only other inflection available to nouns is case, and for this there is only a single oblique case inflection, which marks nouns functioning in an instrumental or locative role. Possession is marked by a particle postposed to the possessor.

Verbs are the most morphologically complex word class in Yimas, and they are highly so; about half of this grammar is devoted to verb morphology. Because of this complexity, Yimas can properly be characterized as an agglutinative polysynthetic language, equal in most respects to the much discussed polysynthetic languages of the Americas. The verb can occur with many prefixes and suffixes, with the former predominating. The suffixes largely express notions of tense, aspect, and mood. The language is very rich in this area, marking, for example, eight distinct tenses. There are five potentially filled suffixal slots to the verb. The prefixes are more numerous, with eight potentially filled positions. The prefixes express notions like modality; agreement for noun class, person and number of core nominals like subject, direct object, and indirect object (this information can also be expressed by suffixes in some environments); adverbial notions like place, direction, duration and manner; and finally, valence alternations to the verb like reciprocal formation, causativization and applicative verb formation (see Comrie 1985). Another common feature of verbs is verb compounding, or serialization. This is done at the word level, as shown by the fact that the whole set of verbal prefixes and suffixes flank these compounded verbal forms.

Pronouns in Yimas are not inflected. True pronouns only exist for first- and second-persons; the so-called third-person independent pronouns are actually deictics, and distinguish noun class and number. Pronouns are actually rather infrequently used in Yimas, for the simple reason that the verb has pronominal affixes for the subject, direct object, and indirect object of the clauses. These affixes exhibit a very complex person-based split for their case-marking schema. First- and second-person forms follow an underlying nominative/accusative pattern, and third-person forms, something like an ergative/absolutive one.

Word order in Yimas is remarkably free, even in comparison to the relative freedom exhibited by other Papuan languages. Within the clause, there is no set word order pattern at all (in fact, the majority of clauses consist of just a verb, so word order is not much of a question in these cases anyway). The verb has a slight tendency to occur last in a pragmatically unmarked context, with the preceding nominals in any order, but it is common for a nominal to occur after the verb with a slightly marked pragmatic force. Word order in Yimas is so free that noun phrases need not even form a constituent. Yimas exhibits the 'scrambled' pattern of noun phrases, well known from Australian languages, in which a noun and its modifiers can be separated from one another within the clause. In these cases, the modifiers obligatorily take concord affixes for the noun class and number of the noun they modify.

Yimas contrasts with many other Papuan languages in making less extensive use of clause chaining (Foley 1986). Yimas completely lacks a productive morphological system of switch reference: the same form of a medial dependent verb form can be used before another verb regardless of whether they share the same subject or not. The most common type of clause linkage in Yimas involves nominalization, both finite and non-finite. Finite nominalizations in Yimas correspond to relative and adverbial subordinate clauses in more familiar languages, while non-finite nominalizations are like infinitive complements and gerunds. Yimas can also link clauses through coordination, by simple juxtaposition, or by using one of its two conjunctions.

Yimas discourse strikes an English speaker as very dense. Because of the pronominal agreement affixes, overt nominals are rare and carry strong contrastive emphasis. This results in the text often consisting of little more than verbs over long stretches. The highly incorporating, agglutinative morphology of the verb further contributes to this impression of density: much information is carried by the bound affixes of the verb, in contrast to the independent words of a language like English. This can put heavy processing loads on the hearer in trying to decipher a verb consisting of ten morphemes.

Yimas is spoken in two villages, totaling about 250 people. One village is the original village site, and the other has only recently hived off from that village, since 1970 or so. There is constant traveling back and forth between the two villages, most people spending some time each year in both. Only a small minority live exclusively in one or the other village, but even these make day trips between the two, which are separated by about 15 km. Because of this situation, there is no geographically based dialect differentiation in the Yimas language. There is, however, significant socially based differentiation according to age. All speakers under 40 have grown up bilingual in Tok Pisin, and this has influenced their Yimas to a greater or lesser extent. Even older male speakers who grew up monolingually in Yimas and learned Tok Pisin while serving stints as recruited plantation labor show this influence to some extent. Older women speak the least affected Yimas and show the lowest degree of fluency in Tok Pisin.

Tok Pisin is the prestige language and its influence on Yimas has two effects. First, Tok Pisin words are borrowed into Yimas. This borrowing may be so heavy that the speaker's talk may resemble a code switching-like discourse, containing snatches of Yimas followed by Tok Pisin. In other cases, Tok Pisin forms are borrowed into what is otherwise pure Yimas. These may be nativized to such an extent that speakers are unaware of the words' ancestry. Second, the very complex morphology of Yimas is subject to simplification. Verbs have fewer morpheme slots filled, and irregular and suppletive forms are regularized. In some cases these irregular forms may be lost altogether. For example, almost no speakers under 40 can completely control the highly complex and irregular numeral system. In daily use these are replaced by the Tok Pisin numbers. The whole impression of the Yimas of younger speakers is its simplicity and regularity relative to the highly complex and irregular language of older (especially female) speakers. The language described principally in this grammar is of men now in their late thirties, who grew up in an almost purely monolingual Yimas environment, and who speak a relatively rich and elaborate version of the language. Regularizations and changes in the speech of younger speakers will be noted when relevant.

The influence of Tok Pisin on Yimas is now reaching its logical outcome among the very young. Many young children in the Yimas communities, especially those under seven years of age, are not learning Yimas at all and are certainly growing up with Tok Pisin as their first language. Whether they will learn Yimas as a second language around ten years of age or slightly older is not clear at the moment, but this seems unlikely, given the status attached to Tok Pisin (Foley 1986, 27–8) and the great morphological complexity of Yimas, which puts a great burden on simple memory in language acquisition. In traditional times, the single greatest intellectual task facing a Yimas child was probably learning his language. But now with schooling and other Western accoutrements, there are other claims on his time. It is perhaps too early to say that the Yimas language is dying, but it must be admitted that the prognosis is not good.

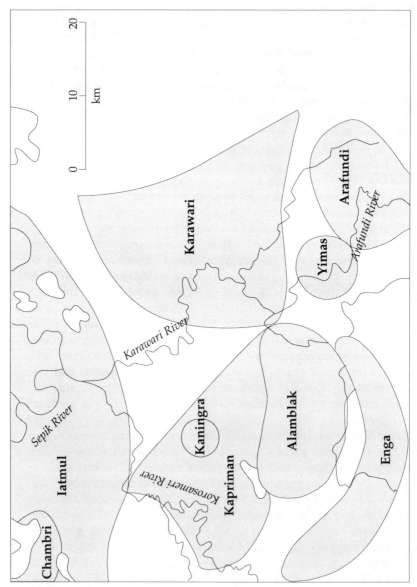

Map 1. Yimas and neighboring languages

1.2 Neighboring Languages

The Yimas language is found in the Sepik river basin area of Papua New Guinea. It is spoken in two villages along the lower reaches of the Arafundi river, a tributary of the Karawari river, which in turn is a tributary of the main Sepik river, the great pulsing cultural artery of this region of New Guinea. Map 1 depicts the linguistic situation in this general area. Yimas is the southernmost language of the Lower Sepik family, so that most of the surrounding languages are genetically unrelated to it. Only directly to the north is a related language, Karawari.

Karawari and Yimas are rather closely related, on the order of Dutch and German, and form a subgroup within the Lower Sepik family. The family as a whole will be discussed in some detail in Section 1.4, so only a few points of close similarity between the two languages will be noted. Phonologically the two languages are very close, except that Karawari lacks the palatal lateral, having /r/ as its only liquid. Thus, Yimas /lʸ/ corresponds to /ri/ in Karawari (Y: palʸapa, K: pariapa 'front porch'). Other correspondences are Yimas /r, t/ to Karawari /s/ (Y: triŋ, K: sisiŋ 'tooth'); word initially, Yimas /n/ to Karawari /y/ (Y: nam, K: yam 'house'); and Yimas /ŋ/ for Karawari ∅ (Y: ŋarwa, K: arwo 'penis'). Finally, in the environment of the low vowel /a/, Yimas /r, t/ correspond to Karawari /y/ (Y: patn, K: payn 'betelnut'; Y: numpran, K: yimbyan 'pig').

Morphologically, the two languages are quite similar, but generally Karawari exhibits a greater simplicity than Yimas. Both languages have inherited the complex noun class system of Proto-Lower Sepik, but whereas Yimas has preserved a three-way contrast in number (singular, dual, and plural) in all classes, Karawari has merged the dual with the plural in half of its classes, resulting in a simple singular/plural contrast for these. Verbs in Karawari are also less elaborate than in Yimas. Karawari has fewer tense distinctions than Yimas (which has eight), and also lacks the paucal number suffix of Yimas. Still, the languages are remarkably similar, even to fine points of detail. For example, instead of the expected prefix sequence ma-ka for a first-person singular subject and a second-person singular object, both languages have a suppletive form kampan-.

To the east of Yimas, along the upper reaches of the Arafundi river, and in the mountains which constitute its source, lie the villages speaking the Arafundi language. This is spoken by around a thousand people in ten villages. Dialect differentiation within the Arafundi language is significant. Until very recently, it was thought to be a language isolate, but it now seems fairly likely that it is genetically related to the Harwai, Hagahai and Pinai languages spoken in the mountains further to the

east in the head waters of the Yuat river. Although there has been some
borrowing of words from Yimas because of long-standing trading contact
(even basic vocabulary like Yimas *apwi* 'father' into the Wambramas-
Yamandim dialect of Arafundi), Yimas and Arafundi are clearly not
genetically related and are contrastive on all levels. In contrast to the
two-height vowel system of Yimas, Arafundi distinguishes three vowel
heights and adds a length distinction (*yampa* 'his fire', *ya·mpa* 'door'.
The palatal consonants of Yimas seem to be a relatively recent addition
and most are derived by a productive phonological rule of palatalization (see rule (2-3) in Chapter 2). This claim is buttressed by their
restricted distribution: they cannot occur at the ends of words. Palatals
in Arafundi are strongly established in the phonological system; there
are even two series, lamino-palatals and palatalized velars. The palatals
are basic, underived consonants and occur in most positions of the word,
including finally (*niɲ* 'you (DL)').

Morphologically, Arafundi is much simpler than Yimas. Nouns are
not inflected for gender, noun class or number. There is an optional
nominative case marker for nouns, -*n*, and an accusative case marker
for pronouns, -*i*. The only other feature for which a noun may be
inflected is its possessor (*kot-k* hand/foot-1SG POSS 'my hand/foot').
Yimas, like Lower Sepik languages generally, lacks this possibility. All
person/number suffixes in Arafundi fail to distinguish between second-
and third-person in the non-singular numbers. Arafundi verbs are also
much simpler than those of Yimas: there are no prefixes at all (prefixes
being diagnostic of Lower-Sepik family languages), and suffixes are used
for tense and to indicate subject and object (*pok-nanci-na-cik* hit-2SG
O-FUT-1SG A 'I will hit you'). (A marks the subject of a transitive verb
and O, its object. I will also employ the abbreviation S for the subject of
an intransitive verb. These are Dixon's (1979) suggestions.) The subject
suffixes are also portmanteau, representing basic tense/aspect/mood distinctions, a common feature of the languages of the neighboring central
highlands (*ow-k* wash-1SG S PERF 'I washed' versus *ow-ŋ* wash-1SG S
IRR 'let me wash' versus *ow-p-cik* wash-PROG-1SG S IMPERF 'I am
washing'). This never occurs in Lower Sepik languages. Finally, most
dialects of Arafundi have the typical clause-chaining structures of central highlands languages, involving morphologically distinct dependent
verb forms, and make extensive use of switch-reference morphology, as
in this example from the Auwim dialect.

(1-1) ɲiŋ   nam   yep-tum-uŋ   aɲ
       1SG   woman see-DEP.DR-1SG   go.3SG S PERF
       'I saw the woman and she left.'

Southwest of Yimas in the foothills of the central highlands is spoken the Iniai dialect of the Enga language, which in terms of speakers, is the largest of Papuan languages. This belongs to the Engan language family and is in most respects typical of the languages of highland New Guinea. One respect in which Enga diverges from other highland languages, however, is in the presence of palatal consonants, otherwise uncommon in the languages of the central highlands. In fact, like Yimas, Enga possesses a palatalized liquid and a voiceless palatal stop with the usual allophone [s]. This reflects areal diffusion of a palatal series among the unrelated languages of the area. Palatals are well established in Enga and appear to have been inherited from Proto-Engan (Franklin 1975). Enga contrasts with both Yimas and Arafundi in that it has a voiced series of stops (including one in the palatal position), which are always prenasalized. In Yimas such sequences are best analyzed as nasal plus stop clusters, but in Enga they are unit phonemes. Enga also lacks the high central vowel so characteristic of Sepik languages generally and Yimas in particular. Rather it has the standard five-vowel system of highlands languages.

Morphologically, Enga fits the general highlands pattern. As in Arafundi, nouns are not inflected for gender or number, but they are inflected for case, and rather richly so: Enga has seven distinct case suffixes, including an ergative. One area is which Enga does parallel Yimas is in the marking of a possessor. Both languages use a remarkably similar form: Yimas *na*, Enga -*nya*. Enga verbs are like those of Arafundi and contrast with those of Yimas in that they are nearly exclusively suffixing (there is only one prefix, the negative, in the entire language). Verbal suffixes in Enga mark tense and the person and number of the subject, but unlike the situation in Arafundi, there is no object suffix. A further feature shared with Arafundi is that the subject suffixes do not distinguish between second- and third-person in the non-singular numbers. While there is some variation in form of the subject suffixes due to tense variation, they clearly are all derived from a single form (Lang 1973) (*l-é-ó* say-FR PAST-1SG S 'I said long ago', *lá-p-ú* say-NR PAST-1SG S 'I said', *lé-ly-o* say-PRES-1SG S 'I am saying'). Finally, Enga makes heavy use of morphologically distinct dependent verb forms and switch-reference morphology (Lang 1973).

(1-2) nambá   p-e-ó-pa   baa-mé   kalaí
       1SG   go-FR PAST-1SG S-DR 3SG-ERG work

       p-i-a
       do-FR PAST-3SG S

       'I went and he worked.'

To the west of Yimas along the upper reaches of the Karawari river and along the Wagupmeri river, lies the Alamblak language, spoken by about 1200 people in a dozen villages. This is the easternmost language of the Sepik Hill family, stretching away to the west to the West Sepik provincial border and the south to the Southern Highlands provincial border. This family is composed of 14 languages and is quite possibly related to the languages of the middle Sepik area, such as the Ndu languages, Iatmul and Abelam. The evidence for this is merely suggestive, however, and any conclusive proof of genetic relationship remains to be produced.

Alamblak has exactly the same three-height vowel system as Arafundi, but is phonetically very similar to Yimas in the heavy preponderance of the epenthetic high central vowel. It also parallels Yimas in the relatively recent appearance of the palatal series and in having a productive synchronic rule of palatalization. It contrasts with Yimas, Arafundi, and Enga in having a somewhat richer inventory of fricatives, including those at the bilabial and velar positions. A further difference from Yimas and Arafundi is the presence of a distinctive voiced stop series, which, contra Enga, is not prenasalized.

Morphologically, Alamblak is most like Yimas, in spite of the lack of any genetic affiliation. This seems to be the result of extensive diffusion of structural traits over the centuries, which probably also accounts for some of the phonological similarities. It must be emphasized that Yimas and Alamblak share traits of general morphological structure; they do not share any actual morphological cognates. Alamblak nouns are inflected for gender and number. There is a three-way number distinction and a two-way gender distinction between masculine and feminine. Gender in Alamblak is determined by biological sex or shape: long thin objects are masculine and short squat objects are feminine. There is no neutralization of person distinctions in the non-singular numbers, as in Arafundi and Enga. Nouns functioning in core roles like subject and object are not inflected for case, but there is a rather rich array of case suffixes for oblique functions like instrumentals or locatives. Verbs are again largely suffixing (in contrast to prefixing Yimas), the main prefixes being those marking mood, like imperative and hortative. The main suffixes are for tense, subject agreement and object agreement, in that order. This contrasts with Arafundi, in which the object agreement suffix precedes the tense suffix which in turn is followed by the subject agreement morpheme. Like Yimas and Enga, Alamblak has a rich tense system, distinguishing a number of past tenses according to the number of days removed from today. The subject and object agreement suffixes encode person and number, and for third-person singular, they encode gender as well, using the same affixes which code the gender and number of nouns. Alamblak further shares with Yimas a very productive process of verb-compounding or serialization. Clause linkage is typically achieved by nominalization and coordination, as in Yimas, but Alamblak does make sparing use of switch-reference morphology (Bruce 1984).

(1-3) na   ningna-më-t-a   mëfha-t
       1SG   work-RM PAST-DR-1SG S   head-F
       fa-më-t-a
       eat-RM PAST-3SG F A-1SG O
       'I worked and (my) head hurt me.'

1.3 Ethnographic Sketch
The Yimas people can best be described as sedentary hunter-gatherers. That is, while they live in permanent established villages, they do not practice subsistence agriculture, but rather collect their food from the surrounding forest and wetlands. The Yimas lands are very rich: the main village is surrounded by a great expanse of swamp and eight major lakes. These supply the staple protein source of the Yimas, fresh fish, the most common species being *tilapia*, *mosambia*, called *makau* in Tok Pisin and Yimas. The word is a loan into Yimas from Tok Pisin because this fish species is not native to New Guinea, but South America. They were introduced into the Sepik as the result of an accident at an experimental agricultural station in Maprik. By the mid-sixties they were well established in the Yimas lakes. They seem to have largely replaced indigenous species, and now constitute the largest proportion of any fish catch. Second to *makau* in percentage of catch are native specifies of catfish (*mawnta*). Fishing is largely the province of the women, who use nets purchased in towns and traditional traps woven from reeds in this task. Men provide a relatively minor supplement of fish by spear fishing, using multiple-prong spears.

Hunting is exclusively the domain of men. While fishing is done daily by nearly all the women, hunting is a rather irregular, more infrequent activity. The male members of the tribe vary greatly in their enthusiasm for hunting, some going out on a hunt a couple of times a week, some never going. The major animals hunted are wild pigs (*numpran*) and possums (*tuŋkntuma*), but cassowaries (*awa*), which are extremely dangerous large flightless birds, and wallabies (*warkawpwi*), smaller relations of kangaroos, are also taken, albeit rarely. Men also shoot ducks (*manpakwarŋ*) and other wild birds, such as the large crowned pigeon or gouria (*mpuŋkan*). Crocodiles (*manpa*) are also eaten, but they are never hunted as food per se. They are hunted for their skins, which are dried and sold as a source of cash. The carcass of the crocodile is then eaten. Meat from hunting is a much less important protein source in the Yimas diet than fish, but it does provide a much-desired respite from a constant bland fare of fish.

The staple carbohydrate for Yimas is sago derived from the sago palm tree, *Metroxylum rumphii* (*tnum*). The gathering of sago is a cooperative effort involving both men and women. The men cut down the sago palm, strip off its bark (*kaɲwa*), and pulverize (*pan-*) the pith of the tree with blunt adzes (*awi*). The pulverized pith (*tki*) is placed in large woven baskets (*pantimpram*) and passed to the women. The women set up a canoe with a small wooden frame at one end as the catchment for the washed sago pith. The women wash (*tuk-*) the sago pith by placing it in another type of woven basket (*walamuŋ*), filling it with water and squeezing the basket over the wooden frame. The sago flour (*wampunŋ*) flows out through the holes in the basket and, being very heavy, collects in the bottom of the canoe. The women finish washing the sago pith and then scoop out all the water from the canoe. They then collect the sago flour and place it in clay storage pots (*yaŋi*).

Sago flour is cooked in two ways, either in flat, rather dry pancakes (*tpuk*) or in a porridge (*kalk*) made by adding sago flour to boiling water until it gels. A Yimas meal typically consists of sago (*tpuk*) and a meat (*naŋkpuk*), usually fish, but occasionally other animals. Meats are often also supplemented with various types of edible green plants gathered by the women; the most common type is a fern of the lake shores (*namlan*). One of the great delicacies in Yimas cuisine are sago grubs (*wun*) which are cultivated by felling and opening a sago palm which is allowed to decay. A large black beetle lays its eggs in the tree, and these hatch into the sago grubs. The tree is allowed to lie for a month or so until the grubs become large and fat. They are then collected and eaten.

Yimas divide their year into two seasons, dry and wet, or dry water (*kaŋm*) and high water (*arm kparm*). The dry season, which is at its height around September, is a time of plentiful food. As the lakes dry out due to lack of rain, the fish get trapped in the shrinking pools and float to the surface for lack of oxygen. Further, as the forest dries out, animals come closer to the lakes for water and are easier to hunt. This is a time of gluttonous feasting on fish and hence is a good time for rituals requiring feasts. The wet season, which runs from November through May and peaks around February, is exactly the opposite. This is a time of scarcity of food, although the Yimas with their rich lands never suffer real hardship in this regard. With the lakes at a high level and the river in flood, fish find many hiding places from the net, trap, and spear. Pigs and other animals retreat deeper into the rain forest and, as much of the low lying forest is flooded anyway, hunting is seriously disadvantaged. There may be as much as a seven meter difference in water levels between the dry and wet seasons.

As many anthropologists have noted, exchange and trade is a pervasive feature of the life of most New Guineans, and the Yimas are no exception in this regard. Indeed, Yimas life is so structured by exchange that people conceive of their relations to others primarily in terms of exchange potential and responsibilities. All major rituals require an exchange of valuables. For example, when a villager dies, his relatives are compensated by other villages with small payments of money; this is regarded as part of the mourning ritual. Links with other villages are almost exclusively structured in terms of exchange, and an important trade network with Yimas as a pivotal link has existed for some time in this area. As Gewertz (1983) has so clearly pointed out, a central theme in Sepik societies is the asymmetrical exchange relationship between water and bush peoples. The bush peoples produce sago and trade this with the water people for fish. As is typical throughout the world, fish being a protein food is more prestigious, so that the exchange rate favors the water people. As a water people, the Yimas enter into this asymmetrical exchange relationship with the bush peoples speaking the Arafundi and Alamblak languages to the east and west. These are long-standing and important trade links, as demonstrated by the existence of pidginized forms of Yimas which were used in these transactions (their function has now been usurped by Tok Pisin).

These trading links persist today, but traditionally, Yimas was involved in an even more extensive trading network. The flat, swampy lands of the Yimas are especially valuable in that they produce strong large strands of grass. These are collected, pounded flat, and woven by the women into highly prestigious items throughout the middle and lower Sepik: mosquito bags (*arŋ*) (absolutely necessary in the mosquito infested Sepik basin), various types of baskets, and sleeping mats (*irwa*). In the past, men would fashion spears (*iŋkay*) and bows (*parmpan*) and arrows (*piam*) and would collect birds of paradise plumes (*warwarŋkat*) from the nearby foothills to trade. These would be traded for clay pots (*yaŋi*), plates (*aprm*), and hearths (*nuŋkp*) through the middlemen of the middle Sepik, the Iatmul. This network has ceased to function since World War II, but as far as I can reconstruct it from reports of older villagers, it worked as follows. The Iatmul people of the villages at the mouth of the Korosmeri and Karawari rivers, Mindimbit and Angriman, grew tobacco and other goods and traded these with the people in the Aibom village in Lake Chambri for the plates, pots, and hearths fashioned there from the plentiful clay. The Iatmul then carried these to Yimas to trade for the Yimas produced goods. My older informants assure me that a special pidginized form of Iatmul was used in these transactions. Although the pidgin is no longer known, this report is consistent with Mead's (1935) claim of the widespread use of a jargon Iatmul for intervillage trade in the middle Sepik. Further, both the Yimas language and culture show unmistakable traces of importations from Iatmul (Foley 1989).

Yimas, like Sepik societies generally, is strongly egalitarian in its social structure and ideology. There is no institutionalization of power and authority, and the people are very resistant to any attempt to impose someone else's will or decisions on them. The concept of advantageous exchange remains the ideal even in interpersonal relationships. With the lack of any institutionalized differences in status, social life is characterized by incessant competition between individuals and clans, often resulting in quarrels and even brawls. Individuals of both sexes are proud, assertive, and demonstrative, but there are significant differences in the social character of men and women which bear mentioning.

There is a strong sex-based differentiation of tasks in Yimas society, and from a very early age boys and girls are separated. The life of the women revolves around cooperative tasks such as fishing or making sago thatch for roofing. Reflecting this, Yimas women tend to have a practical, cooperative approach to life, and are interested primarily in caring for their children. They lack the love of competitive display so characteristic of the men, but exhibit a down-to-earth self-confidence. It is important to note that Yimas women, in contrast to their sisters of the highlands and western regions, are economically independent; they produce the prestigious trade goods like fish and woven objects, and they hold the rewards of this production.

In contrast, Yimas men are boastful, individually competitive, and prone to aggression. They jealously guard their prerogatives and constantly gossip, attempting to run down the reputation of rivals. Any perceived status gain or economic reward is likely to be a cause of a quarrel or worse. Yimas men find it virtually impossible to engage in large-scale cooperative activities. What cooperation there is among them is generally the activity of close kin. If it were not for the activities of the women, Yimas society would probably be subject to constant fissions, as Bateson (1936) claims the Iatmal are, or would end up like the picture of Mundugumor society that Mead (1935) draws.

Traditionally, the life of Yimas men, like so many Sepik societies, revolved around the male cult house or house tambaran (*manm*). These houses were destroyed during World War II and never rebuilt, with the result that all the important ritual life associated with these ceased before 1950. It is quite likely that the activities of the male cult house provided a powerful integrating force in the life of the men, counterbalancing the divisive effects of their competitive strivings, as appears elsewhere in the Sepik (Tuzin 1974), and their disappearance might have left a serious cultural vacuum. The male cult houses were the places where the initiated men of the village spent most of their time, gossiping, chewing betelnut, and doing small odd jobs. They were closed to women and uninitiated boys under pain of death. Men typically slept in their clan's cult house, not with their wives or children, who slept together in the large family houses. Young boys were initiated into the life of the male cult house in early puberty. They were secluded in the cult house for several months and only allowed to go outside to bathe in the dead of night so that they would not be seen by the women. Within the cult house they were plastered with mud, beaten regularly and only given the foulest of food to eat, which they were forbidden to touch, being fed by their mother's brothers. In the final act of initiation, their backs were cut transversely with sharp rocks, leaving permanent scars.

All traditional Yimas religious life centered on the male cult house (they are now baptized Roman Catholics, but many of the traditional beliefs in spirits still persist). The male cult house held carvings and bark paintings depicting the spirits of totemic ancestors, as well as fetishes, such as stones that housed spirits. Religious rituals entailed making entreaties to these spirits of totemic ancestors to provide benefits for the living. Most of these rituals required the playing of paired bamboo flutes *(taŋkut)*, which were said to be the voices of the spirits. These were kept in the cult house and hidden from women. Rituals would typically go on all night or even for several nights in a row. Elaborate rituals would precede all important male activities, such as raiding a neighboring village. The Yimas were both headhunters and cannibals, the former playing an especially important role in the culture of the village. For example, only boys who had killed in a headhunting raid were permitted to wear a pubic covering of a flying fox skin and hence be eligible to take a wife. During the frenzied, all-night rituals which preceded a headhunting raid, a man would often fall into trance, taken by other men to be possession by a totemic spirit. He would then be interviewed as to the prospects and proper procedures for a successful raid. The most popular targets for Yimas raids were the Arafundi villages of Imanmeri and Wambramas-Yamandim and the Alamblak village of Chimbut. Their only ally was the Arafundi speaking Auwim village.

Yimas society is built up out of kinship ties. In fact, unlike our

western society, there are no other institutionalized social ties. The
largest kinship groups in the village are the patrilineal clans, each with
its own totemic ancestor(s) and totemic animal. For example, my main
informant's clan has the central totemic ancestor *Kikay* and the totem
the hornbill (*kaykut*). Each clan is divided into two or more lineages.
Every member of the clan is given at birth a personal name drawn from
the names of the totemic ancestors of the clan. There are no specific
names for the clans in Yimas; rather, each takes its name from that
area of the village where its male cult house stood. There is also no
generic word for 'clan', the word *anti* 'land' being used instead. So to
say 'we are of the same clan', one would actually say 'we are of one land'.
The clans are the unit of marriage within the village. The Yimas are
largely endogamous (marrying inside the village), and marriage is across
clans. Tradition has long prescribed which clans are linked together in
marriage arrangements, and from a very early age, children are aware
as to who are permissible spouses within this schema. Within recent
years this has weakened somewhat, with couples occasionally marrying
according to personal choice, against the traditional arrangements. This
is frowned on by older villagers, but they shrug their shoulders and say
'this is another time'. There are also some traces of what may have
been a dual organization of the clans into two moieties. This seems to
have been involved in the initiation of boys in the male cult house and
other rituals associated with this, but as these had completely ceased
for over 25 years before I went to Yimas for the first time, it has proved
impossible to verify this.

The Yimas kinship system, like that of many Sepik societies, is a
Crow-Omaha variant (or, to be more precise, an Omaha system given
the patrilineal bias). Crow-Omaha systems are those which exhibit a
conflation of generations along the main line of descent. In Yimas, this
occurs because the paternal grandfather (father's father) is classified as
older brother (*kpan*) i.e., of the same generation as ego instead of two
generations above. This also has the peculiar effect of placing one's
own father in the class of one's son, because his father is one's older
brother (sons of a group of brothers are sons of each). Thus, one's
father is simultaneously one's son and one's son is simultaneously one's
father. I have often witnessed the event of a father addressing his five
year old son as *api* 'father' because of this generational collapsing. This
tallies well with Bateson's (1936, 38–41) point about the identification
of father and son in Iatmul society (also having a Crow-Omaha variant
for kinship terminology), but as far as I know, Yimas is the only culture
in which this identification finds articulation in the kinship terminology.
In the maternal clan, one's most important relation is mother's brother

(*away*). He is always ready to provide support and take one's side in an argument. Whereas there is some tension in the father/son relationship, there is none in this maternal uncle/nephew kin link.

Yimas recorded history only stretches back about 50 years. Prior to that, we must rely on oral history in the form of myths and legends (a small amount of archeological work was very recently done at Yimas, but no results are available just yet). The Yimas legends indicate that it is largely an immigrant village (see Harrison 1989 for a similar claim about the prehistory of Manambu-speaking villages of the Sepik river). The ancestors of the various clans came to Yimas from different areas: from the Sepik river near the mouth of the Korosmeri-Karawari, from the extensive swamps of the Blackwater river, a tributary of the Korosmeri, from the foothills beyond the large southern group of Yimas lakes, and from the mountainous country which forms the source for the Arafundi river. The last group called their homeland *Manki* and today say that it was also the homeland of the Chambri and Murik peoples. The myth relates that after a quarrel with their menfolk over food, the women of *Manki* drifted in a hollow log down the Arafundi river. At the junction of the Arafundi and Karawari rivers, the log got tied up in some debris. The women went ashore and climbed up the hill there and saw the mountain behind the present Chambri village. Some determined to go there. They reboarded their log and floated down the Karawari river until it joins the Sepik. Here some of the women separated and went to Lake Chambri, where they perfected the art of pottery making. The rest remained on the log and floated down the Sepik to its mouth where they married the men there. This legend is especially interesting in that it provides a historical account for the clear genetic relationship between the Yimas, Chambri and Murik languages.

The Yimas also have legends concerning a flooding of the site of the village and the creation of land out of endless expanse of water, both of which correlate quite closely with recent speculations on the prehistory of the Sepik area (Swadling 1984). Other legends give explanations for natural phenomena, such as why flying foxes sleep hanging upside down in trees, or for cultural themes, like the origin of bamboo flutes. Many of the legends related by men show a deep distrust and fear of the power of women, a not unusual theme in New Guinea.

Yimas contact with the western world only came in the 1930s, and then it was only marginal. Their major induction into the modern world was the Japanese invasion of northern New Guinea in World War II. This was a very traumatic period for the Yimas, as the Japanese stationed a small garrison in the village and irrevocably disrupted much of their life and culture. The male cult houses were destroyed, and all their associated rituals abandoned. The entire village was burned during a bombing raid. The massive technological superiority of the western world left a deep impression on the Yimas, and following the war they determined to follow European practices with a view to acquiring European made goods. They moved down from the original village site on the hill above the river (a good defensive position) and built their houses along the river, hoping to attract European interests. They abandoned their traditional religion of the male cult house, converted to Roman Catholicism and built a church. Yimas children of both sexes have gone to school since the mid-1960s. But western type development and western-made goods have been slow in coming. The only source of work in the area is a tourist lodge which employs about a half dozen Yimas. In spite of the appearance of goods like outboard motors and cassette players, Yimas life still largely revolves around subsistence hunting and gathering. For most Yimas, daily life is pretty much as it was 50 years ago, although a little easier. The major casualty of western contact has been their ritual and spiritual life. (Virtually no traditional legends are known by anyone under 30.) The young have no interest in them, preferring electrified music from Port Moresby and New York.

1.4 Sepik Area Languages in General and the Lower Sepik Family in Particular

Excluding the languages of the upper Sepik and the Torrecelli mountains which are very diverse, but are beyond the purview of this study, the languages of the Sepik-Ramu basin number about 80 in over a dozen language families. In spite of such great genetic diversity, the languages of many different families often share a number of structural traits. This diffusion is a linguistic reflection of the pronounced consciousness of trade and exchange discussed in the previous section. Because of trade and other cultural links, a village's language is subject to strong influences from the outside. Further, shared linguistic allegiance is insufficient as a basis for intercommunity solidarity. The Karawari language is spoken by around 1,500 people in ten villages. Dialect differentiation is not great, but there is little feeling of a larger community composed of the villages speaking Karawari. Some Karawari villages have closer cultural links to villages speaking other languages such as Iatmul or Angoram, than to those speaking Karawari. Iatmul villages provide another example; they often raided and headhunted in other Iatmul villages, the shared language being no hindrance in this regard. Clearly, in the Sepik region, shared linguistic allegiance is not a rallying point for cultural cohesion.

Given this situation, it is not surprising that frequent shifting of language boundaries is common in this area of New Guinea. Like other cultural artifacts, language is a trade item. Villages on the border between two language groups may shift their linguistic allegiance if their shifting cultural and economic links would seem to warrant this. Some border villages may be so precariously balanced linguistically that it is difficult to determine their affiliation. Some individuals and families are bilingual; others speak only one of the two languages. Mead (1938, 159) mentions the case of Ulup village on the border between the Arapesh and Abelam languages. These two languages are structurally very different and belong to different language families. Neither the Arapesh, nor the Abelam, nor the inhabitants of the village themselves were sure of Ulup's affiliations. In a shifting situation like this the final result may be that small language groups are gradually assimilated and disappear entirely. (See Foley 1989 for further discussion of the points of this and the previous paragraph.)

Given a sociolinguistic situation like this, it comes as no surprise that genetically unrelated languages over a wide area often display remarkably uniform structural features. Phonologically, for example, nearly all languages of the area are characterized for a short high to mid-central vowel, non-phonemic and epenthetically introduced to separate impermissible consonant clusters. A common consonantal pattern is to have stops in four places of articulation (labial, dental, palatal, and velar), with a corresponding nasal in each position. This is attested, for example, in such widely geographically separated languages as Yimas, Abelam (Maprik area), and Mikarew (Ramu river). Prenasalized stops are common, but are sometimes best analyzed as clusters consisting of a stop preceded by a homorganic nasal. Unlike other areas of New Guinea, a phonemic contrast between two liquids, /r/ and /l/, is not uncommon. Suprasegmental phenomena are limited to stress; languages with phonemic tone are unattested, in contrast to their common occurrence in the central highlands.

With the notable exception of the Lower Sepik family and a few others, languages of the Sepik-Ramu region are morphologically rather simple. What affixation there is is largely suffixal, but again, the Lower Sepik family is an exception. All languages make a sharp distinction between noun and verb. Nouns are simpler morphologically than verbs; in some languages the only common nominal inflections are suffixes to mark oblique cases, as in Iatmul (Staalsen 1972) (*ŋkəy-mpa* house-LOC 'in the house'). Languages of the lower Sepik and Ramu rivers area commonly have complex, highly irregular plural formations. Compare these forms from Miyak (Yuat river), Angoram (lower Sepik river) and Kaian (Ramu river; Z'graggen 1971):

		Miyak	Angoram	Kaian
'man'	SG	avɨt	pondo	namot
	PL	awutu	pandaŋ	namtair
'betelnut'	SG	siman	pariŋ	mboʔ
	PL	simandu	pariŋgli	mbuk
'nose'	SG	mumut	naŋim	iindup
	PL	mumuta	naŋimbɨr	iindpar
'pig'	SG	vre	imbar	markum
	PL	viru	imbarŋgar	markump
'back'	SG	mbɨtaŋ	wunɨm	kupik
	PL	mbɨtaŋgi	wunɨmbɨr	kupkar

Although the plural allomorphs of the three languages are not cognate, the overall plural-marking system of the three languages is quite similar and clearly an areal feature.

Another areal feature of the region concerns the possessive morpheme. In all languages this is a suffix or postposition and occurs in one of two forms: -kV or -nV. Unrelated, geographically widely separated languages will often show agreement in the morpheme form chosen for this function. For example, Miyak (Yuat river) and Tangu (Ramu river; Z'graggen 1971) both employ -kV (M: ŋa-kə ken 1SG-POSS dog 'my dog', T: ku-ka riei 1SG-POSS dog 'my dog'), while Yimas, like all Lower Sepik languages, and Kaian (Z'graggen 1971) both use -nV (Y: ama-na mamay 1SG-POSS brother 'my brother', K: ʔʌ-na yakay 1SG-POSS brother 'my brother'). While the possessor precedes the possessed in these cases (and this is the usual pattern), it is not always so (Emerum (upper Ramu river: Z'graggen 1971): isam ya-ka brother 1SG-POSS 'my brother'). Proto-Ndu and most of the languages of this family have an interesting variant on this theme; they use -nV if the possessor is first- or second-person and -kV if it is third-person.

Verbal morphology of Sepik region languages is on the whole rather simple. In many languages the only affixation is suffixation for tense/aspect/mood (Yessan-Mayo (middle Sepik; cf. Foreman 1974): yi-we go-NR PAST 'went', Miyak (Yuat river): som-b-a cook-PRES-INDIC 'cooking', Bosman (between the Sepik and Ramu rivers; cf. Capell 1951): vas-et see-PAST 'saw', Abelam (Maprik area; cf. Wilson 1980): k-ək eat-PAST 'ate'). In addition to tense/aspect/mood suffixes, a minority of languages have subject agreement suffixes, cross-referencing the person and number of the subject of transitive and intransitive verbs (Iatmul (Staalsen 1972): yɨ-kə-wɨn go-PRES-1SG 'I am going'). More complex verbal morphology than this in the area is rare, although quite common elsewhere in New Guinea. Only the languages of the Lower Sepik family and some contiguous languages in the region (Gapun, Alamblak, and Arafundi) have both subject and object agreement. The relevant affixes are prefixes in Lower Sepik languages (Yimas: *pu-ka-tay-ɲcut* 3PL O-1SG A-see-RM PAST 'I saw them') but suffixes in Alamblak (Bruce 1984) (*fayk-r-m* get-3SG M A-3PL O 'he got them') and Arafundi (*yep-ŋgi-na-cɨk* see-3PL O-FUT-1SG A 'I will see them').

All Papuan languages of the Sepik-Ramu region have typological characteristics of verb final languages. Many, perhaps most, of these have rather rigid subject/object/verb word order.

(1-4) a. Yessan-Mayo: an   toma mati-ye
      (Foreman 1974) 1SG talk   hear-NR PAST
      'I heard the talk.'

    b. Bosman: ŋgɔ-t   dupu vas-et
      (Capell 1951)   1SG-NOM snake see-PAST
      'I saw a snake.'

    c. Miyak: ŋə-n   wu-nu   ɲjit-b-a
                    1SG-NOM he-ACC see-PRES-INDIC
      'I see him.'

    d. Iatmul: ntɨw nyan vɨ-ntɨ
      (Staalsen 1972) man child see-3SG M
      'The man saw the child.'
      *'The child saw the man.'

Note that the Bosman and Miyak examples show case-marking on the core arguments of the verb. This is a sporadic feature of Sepik languages, cropping up here and there, although many are like Iatmul and Yimas in lacking case suffixes. One fairly common feature of Sepik languages is the use of the dative case suffix to mark animate, particularly human, direct objects.

(1-5) a. Yessan-Mayo: an ti-ni   aki-ye
      (Foreman 1974) 1SG 3SG F-D fear-NR PAST
      'I feared her.'

    b. Abelam: wɨnə nyan-ət   kəynək-gwə
      (Laycock 1965) 1SG child-DAT scold-PRES
      'I scold the child.'

Compare the Abelam example (1-5b) with that of Iatmul (1-4d) above. Sepik languages with rather richer morphology, including nominal gender or noun classes and subject and object agreement, are not so rigid. Yimas, for example, is extremely free in its word order, as seems to be true of the other Lower Sepik languages.

(1-6) krayŋ   k-n-tay   kalakn
       frog VI SG   VI SG O-3SG A-see   boy I SG
       'The boy saw the frog.'

Any permutation of these three words in Yimas produces a grammatical sentence. Alamblak tends to have the verb last, although oblique
constituents commonly follow it, with subject and object preceding the
verb, but in either order (Bruce 1984).

(1-7) fëh-m   yima-r   fayk-r-m
       pig-3PL   person-3SG M   get-3SG M A-3PL O
       'A man got pigs.'

All Sepik area languages attested make use of dependent medial verb
forms, but in almost all these are restricted to the case in which the
subjects of the linked clauses are the same (but see Section 7.3.1 for a
discussion of the complications in this regard in Yimas). Consider these
examples of clauses linked with dependent medial verb forms:

(1-8) a. Bosman: wuru   ŋgɔ-t   lakam laŋ-ga
          (Capell 1951) yesterday 1SG-NOM   pig   hit-DEP
                         wetk-at
                         cook-PAST
                         'Yesterday I killed the pig and ate it.'
       b. Iatmul: waalə klə-laa   yə-ntɨ
          (Staalsen 1972) dog   get-DEP come-3SG M
                         'He got the dog and came.'
       c. Yessan-Mayo: nim ak   ya-n   la-ya
          (Foreman 1974) 1PL then come-DEP   see-NR PAST
                         'We came then and saw.'
       d. Yimas: kalakn   ŋayuk   tay-mpi
                         child I SG mother-II SG   see-DEP
                         na-na-kuck-n
                         3SG S-DEF-happy-PRES
                         'The child sees his mother and is happy.'

If the subjects of the two linked clauses are different, then two fully
inflected independent verbs must be conjoined as in this Iatmul example
(Staalsen 1972):

(1-9) klə-ntɨ   maa yə-ntɨ
       get-3SG M   and come-3SG M
       'He₁ got it and he₂ came.'

in which the person getting and the person coming must be different
individuals. The only languages in the region attested to have depen-

dent medial verbs with switch-reference morphology, permitting clauses
with different subjects to be linked in this manner, are Alamblak and
Arafundi, discussed in Section 1.2. I repeat the Arafundi example for
comparative purposes here.

(1-10) Arafundi: ɲɨŋ   nam   yep-tum-uŋ   aɲ
               1SG   woman   see-DEP.DR-1SG   go.3SG S PERF
               'I saw the woman and she went.'

When compared to the general picture of the linguistic scene of the
Sepik-Ramu region just sketched, the languages of the Lower Sepik family emerge as a great anomaly in many grammatical respects. Phonologically they fit quite well, but morphologically they are very divergent.
Lower Sepik languages are highly elaborated morphologically, and most
are just as heavily prefixing as suffixing, if not more so. They tend to
have quite free word order at the clausal level and a weak development
of dependent verb forms.

The languages of the Lower Sepik family are relatively closely related, roughly on the order of the Germanic family. There are six member languages in the family: Yimas (250 speakers), Karawari (1,500
speakers), Angoram (7,000 speakers), Chambri (1,200 speakers), Murik
(1,500 speakers) and Kopar (250 speakers). Map 2 gives the relative
positions of these languages. Murik and Kopar are very closely related,
almost dialects of the same language, so I will treat them as one for the
purposes here. The 25 cognate sets in Table 1 demonstrate this close
relationship of the languages. (K after a form indicates that it is Kopar,
not Murik). In Foley (1986, 215–20), I attempted a careful, somewhat
detailed, reconstruction of the phonology of the protolanguage; I will
simply summarize the results here. Proto-Lower Sepik had a phonemic
system of consonants like the following:

*p	*t	*k
(*b)	*d	(*g)
*mp	*nt	*ŋk
*mb	*nd	*ŋg
	*s	
*m	*n	*ŋ
	*r	
*w	*y	

This system is rather tentative; only Chambri preserves the distinction
between the voiceless and voiced prenasalized stops, the other languages
merging them. Further, the plain voiced series is established on the basis
of a single sound correspondence establishing *d in one cognate set. If

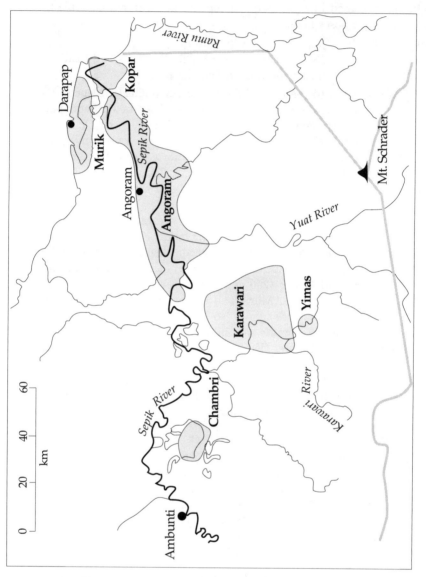

Map 2. The Lower Sepik Family

TABLE 1

Lower Sepik Cognate Sets

		Yimas	Karawari	Angoram	Chambri	Murik
1	'one'	mba-	mba-	mbia-	mbwia-	abe
2	'male'	panmal	panmari	pondo		puin
3	'water'	arɨm	arɨm	alɨm	arɨm	arɨm
4	'fire'	awt	awi	aluŋ	ayɨr	awr
5	'canoe'	kay	kay	ke	ke	gain
6	'village'	num	imuŋga	num	num	nomot
7	'breast'	niŋay	ɲjay	ŋge	niŋke	niŋgen
8	'blood'	yat	yay	ayakone	yari	yaran
9	'tongue'	mɨɲɨŋ	mumɨɲɨŋ	mɨnɨŋ	tɨbulanɨŋk	menɨŋ
10	'ear'	kwandumɨŋ	kwandukas	kwandum	kukunam	karekep
11	'egg'	awŋ	yawŋ	awŋ	awŋk	gaug
12	'tree'	yan	yuwan	lor	yuwan	yarar
13	'yesterday'/					
	'tomorrow'	ŋarɨŋ	arɨŋ	nakɨmɨn	namasɨnɨŋ	ŋarɨŋ
14	'betelnut'	patn	payn	parɨŋ	muntɨkɨn	porog
15	'lime'	awi	as	awer	ayɨr	ayr
16	'pig'	numbran	imbian	imbar	numpran	(nɨm)bren
17	'mosquito'	naŋgun	yaŋgun	wawarɨn	naŋgun	nauk/ naŋgɨt(K)
18	'pound sago'	pan-	pan-	pan-	pun-	pon-
19	'wash sago'	tuku-	suku-	tuku-	tuku-	tokun-
20	'hear'	andɨ-	andu-	andɨ-	andɨ-	dɨn-
21	'hit'	tupul-	kurar-	tɨ-	dii-	di-
22	'eat'	am-	am-	am-	am-	mɨn-
23	'feces'	mɨlɨm	mɨndi	mɨndi	muɲjar	mɨndɨn
24	'spine of leaf'	kɨnɨŋ	kɨnɨŋ	kɨnɨŋ	kɨnɨŋk	kɨnɨŋ
25	'big'	kɨpa-	kupa-	kupa-	wupa-	apo-

further research should prove this to be incorrect, then the system will reduce to a system like that of Karawari and not too different from Yimas:

$$
\begin{array}{lll}
{}^{*}\text{p} & {}^{*}\text{t} & {}^{*}\text{k} \\
{}^{*}\text{mb} & {}^{*}\text{nd} & {}^{*}\text{ŋg} \\
& {}^{*}\text{s} & \\
{}^{*}\text{m} & {}^{*}\text{n} & {}^{*}\text{ŋ} \\
& {}^{*}\text{r} & \\
{}^{*}\text{w} & {}^{*}\text{y} &
\end{array}
$$

Typologically, the vowel systems of the Lower-Sepik languages divide into two groups. One group, composed of Murik, Angoram, and Chambri consists of six-vowel languages; the other, consisting of just Yimas and Karawari, has four-vowel languages:

TABLE 2
Cognate Sets for Class VI

		Yimas	Karawari	Angoram	Chambri
	NOUN	tiriŋ 'tooth'	sisiŋ 'tooth'	sisiŋ 'tooth'	sraŋk 'tooth'
SG	POSS	tiriŋ ama-na-ŋ	sisiŋ ama-na-k	sisiŋ amɨ-na-ŋga	sraŋk amɨ-na-ŋk
	ADJ	tiriŋ kipa-ŋ	sisiŋ kupa-ŋ	sisiŋ kupa-ŋga	sraŋk wupa-ŋk
	NUM	tiriŋ mba-ŋ	sisiŋ mba-ŋ	sisiŋ mbia-ŋ	sraŋkmbwia-ŋk
	VERB	tiriŋ kɨ-tumukit	sisiŋ ŋgipuŋgiar	sisiŋ ikolondika-ŋ	sraŋk aŋkɨ-kibran
	NOUN	tiriŋgi	sisiŋgri		sraŋkikri
DL	POSS	tiriŋgil ama-na-ŋgil	sisiŋgri ama-na-kŋgri		sraŋkikri amɨ-na-ŋkikri
	ADJ	tiriŋgil kipa-ŋgil	sisiŋgri kupa-ŋgri		sraŋkikri wupa-ŋkikri
	NUM	tiriŋgil kɨ-rpal	sisiŋgri k-ripay		sraŋkikri k-ri
	VERB	tiriŋgil kila-tumukit	sisiŋgri ŋgri-puŋgiar		sraŋkikri arɨ-kibran
	NOUN	tiriŋgi	sisiŋgi	sisiŋ	sraŋkir
PL	POSS	tiriŋgi ama-na-ŋgi	sisiŋgi ama-na-kŋgi	sisiŋ amɨ-na-ŋglia	sraŋkir amɨ-na-ɾ
	ADJ	tiriŋgi kipa-ŋgi	sisiŋgi kupa-ŋgi	sisiŋ kupa-ŋglia	sraŋkir wupa-ɾ
	NUM	tiriŋgi k-ramnawt	sisiŋgi k-rianmaw	sisiŋ kɨ-elim	sraŋkir kia-ram
	VERB	tiriŋgi kia-tumukit	sisiŋgi ŋgi-puŋgiar	sisiŋ ikolondika-ŋgli	sraŋkir aɾ-kibran

```
        M, A, C:                  Y, K:

 i       ɨ      u          i       ɨ      u
    e        o
         a                         a
```

Proto-Lower Sepik appears to have been like Murik, Angoram, and Chambri, Yimas and Karawari having merged the relatively rare mid vowels to /a/. Yimas and (to a lesser extent) Karawari have also undergone an extensive process of vowel centralization, the peripheral high vowels being attracted to the central /ɨ/. In phonemic terms this amounts to vowel deletion, for the /ɨ/ is typically epenthetic in these languages, breaking up impermissible clusters.

All the Lower Sepik languages have complex morphologies, with Yimas being the most elaborate in this regard. All the languages except Murik-Kopar have an extensive system of noun classes with assignment to class being determined by a mix of semantic and phonological criteria. For example, in Karawari, there are three semantically-based classes—class I (male humans), class II (female humans), and class III (higher animals)—and six phonologically based classes—class V (ending in -*mb*), class VI (ending in (-*ŋg*), and class VII (ending in -*i* or -*y*), etc. Proto-Lower Sepik had seven noun classes, as follows:

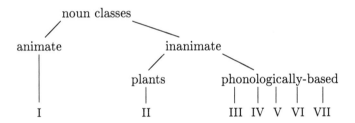

This system is essentially preserved in Angoram and Chambri, but Yimas and Karawari have added to it by distinguishing humans from other animates, and within humans, distinguishing male and female. A further innovation in Karawari is the merger of the functional plants class with the phonologically based class of nouns ending in -*i* or -*y*. These noun classes are manifested in the grammars of all four languages by concord suffixes on all nominal modifiers and agreement prefixes (or suffixes in Angoram) on the verb for subject and object, as illustrated by this example for Karawari:

(1-11) sɨsɨŋgi   kupa-ŋgi   ama-na-kŋgi   k-rianmaw
        tooth VI PL big-VI PL   1SG-POSS-VI PL   VI-three

ŋgi-puŋia-r
VI PL-break-PERF
'My three bad teeth have broken.'

The cognate system for class VI in the four languages is presented in
Table 2 (the relevant agreement prefixes and suffixes are underlined).
The reconstructed affixes for this class are Class VI: class marker *ŋk:

	SG	DL	PL
NOUN	*ŋk	*ŋk-ri	*-ŋk-i
POSSESSOR	*-ŋk	*ŋk-ri	*-ŋk-i
ADJECTIVE	*-ŋk	*ŋk-ri	*-ŋk-i
NUMERAL	*-ŋk	*k-	*k-
VERB	*k-	*k-ri-a-	*k-i-a-

For the methodology by which these affixes were reconstructed as well
as the reconstruction for a couple of other noun classes, see Foley 1986
(pp. 222–9).

As mentioned above, Murik today lacks noun classes, but it does
have traces of them. First of all, both the numerals for 'two' and 'three'
begin in k, an unmistakable fossilization of the class VI concord prefix
for numerals *k-: kompari (K) 'two' and kerongo 'three' from *k- class
VI marker plus *pa- 'two' or *ram- 'three' plus *-ri DL or *-ŋk PC.
Second, Murik nouns, while not marked for noun class, are inflected for
number, and nominal modifiers take suffixes indicating number agreement, both vestiges of the earlier noun class system. These suffixes are
given below,

	N	ADJ
SG	Ø	-o
DL	-mbo	-abo
PC	-gi/-moara	-ara
PL	-mot	-k

and exemplified in the following: 'big person' SG nor apo, DL norimbo
apaabo, PC norigi apaara, PL normot apak. Murik is the only Lower
Sepik language to distinguish a paucal number for nouns; most (Yimas,
Chambri and Karawari) only distinguish three numbers, singular, dual
and plural, and Angoram has only a simple singular/plural contrast.
Yet there is reason to believe that Murik is conservative in this respect.
Most of the languages (Murik, Yimas and Chambri) distinguish a paucal
number in their personal pronouns. Also, the plural allomorphs for
nouns in most of the languages are highly irregular (in contrast to the

dual inflections) and some of these allomorphs end in /r/ (Yimas /t/), close to the Murik paucal forms in -r. This suggests the proto-Lower Sepik may have inflected nouns for all four numbers, but that in most languages the paucal and plural merged, some noun classes and words taking the old paucal suffix as their plural marker and others taking the old plural. This would account for the unusually complex allomorphs for plural marking of nouns in most of the languages.

The verbal morphology of all Lower Sepik languages is very elaborate, and all follow a basically agglutinative model. All languages but Angoram are predominately prefixing, although tense is generally a suffix (Murik is the exception here). All languages make at least a tense distinction between past, present and future, but most are more complicated than that. Yimas and Murik (Abbott 1978) distinguish two future tenses (near and remote), while Yimas has multiple past tenses (near, far and remote). A typical tense form for each of the languages is illustrated below:

Yimas: ama-wa-nan   Chambri: am-wa-i
           1SG S-go-NR PAST   1SG S-go-PAST
           'I went.'   'I went.'

Karawari: ama-kurayk-nan   Angoram: ama-kal-ka-m
           1SG S-walk-PAST   1SG S-go-PRES-1SG
           'I walked.'   'I'm going.'

           Murik: ti-min-arakuma
           (Abbott 1978)   PAST-1SG S-walk
                           'I walked.'

At this stage of investigation, it has not proved possible to reconstruct tense suffixes for Proto-Lower Sepik, but one morpheme which does appear reconstructible is the imperative suffix *-ka attested in Chambri, Angoram, and Murik (Abbott 1978).

Chambri: dii-ka   Angoram: w-aməŋ-ka
          hit-IMP   (Laycock 1959)   IMP-eat-IMP
          'Hit him!'   'Eat!'

          Murik: ko-dii-ka
                   IMP-kill-IMP
                   'Kill!'

Yimas -na IMP and Karawari -ra IMP are innovations.

All Lower Sepik languages have verbal pronominal affixes for subject and object, and all make a sharp morphological distinction between

those with a single pronominal affix (intransitive verbs) and those with
both (transitive verbs). In all of these languages but Angoram, the prefix
form for the subject of an intransitive verb (S prefix) is different in most
person-number combinations from that of the subject of a transitive verb
(A prefix):

	S prefix	A prefix
Yimas:	*ama*-wa-t	na-*ka*-tu-t
	1SG S-go-PERF	3SG O-1SG A-kill-PERF
	'I went.'	'I killed him.'
Karawari:	*ama*-kurayk-nan	ya-*ka*-krar
	1SG S-walk-PAST	3SG O-1SG A-hit
	'I walked.'	'I hit him.'
Chambri:	*ami*-wa-n	an-*o*-dii-n
	1SG S-go-PRES	3SG O-1SG A-hit-PRES
	'I'm going.'	'I'm hitting him.'
Murik:	*min*-arakuma	di-k-*wa*-ra-kera
(Abbott 1978)	1SG S-go	PL O-TR-1SG A-NR FUT-dig
	'I'm going.'	'I will dig them.'

Angoram uses the same prefix form for S and A, but has in addition a
suffix indicating an S but not an A (the same suffixal position marks the
object in transitive verbs), so that the same thoroughgoing dichotomy
between transitive and intransitive verbs is preserved, albeit in a different way.

Angoram:	*ama*-kal-ka-*m*	*ama*-paniŋ-ka-ne
	1SG S-go-PRES-1SG S	1SG A-pound-PRES-VI SG O
	'I'm going.'	'I pounded it (sago).'

It is also possible in Angoram to dispense with the prefix and just use
the suffix.

ya-klea-*ndu*
come-PERF-2 PL
'You all came.'

A morphological curiosity characteristic of most Lower Sepik languages is homophony between the second- and third-person A forms.
Karawari may be an exception to this generalization; the picture in this
language is still confused. This homophony of 2/3 SG may be diagnostic
of a language in this family, as it is unattested elsewhere in the Sepik
region.

	Second-person	Third-person
Yimas:	na-*n*-tu-t	pu-*n*-tu-t
	3SG O-2SG A-kill-PERF	3SG O-3SG A-kill-PERF
	'You killed him.'	'He killed them.'
Chambri:	*man*-o-dii-n	kɨba-*man*-dii-n
	2SG A-1SG O-hit-PRES	2DL O-3SG A-hit-PRES
	'You are hitting me.'	'He is hitting you two.'
Angoram:	na-*n*-ti-k-an	pa-*n*-ti
	3SG O-2SG A-hit-PRES-2	3PL O-3SG A-hit
	'You are hitting him.'	'He is hitting them.'
Murik:	bo-t-*o*-tabii-rɨn	bɨ-tɨ-k-*o*-tabii-rɨ
	DL O-PAST-2SG A-blow-2	DL O-NR FUT-TR-3SG A-blow-3
	'You blew two.'	'He will blow two.'

Another intriguing feature shared by Yimas, Karawari, Chambri, and Angoram, as against Murik, concerns the order of the subject and object pronominal affixes. In Murik the order is fixed: the object agreement prefix precedes the subject prefix (Abbott 1978).

dɨ-bɨ-takwat-ara
PL O-3DL A-hit-3
'They two are hitting them.'

But in the other four languages, the order of the subject and object suffixes varies. The conditioning factors for this variation are different across the languages. For Yimas and Karawari, the causal factor is a topicality hierarchy of first-person > second-person > third-person, with the stipulation that the highest ranked prefix must occur closest to the verb stem. These two languages typically have distinct prefix forms for subject and object.

	Subject with higher topicality	Object with higher topicality
Yimas:	na-*ka*-tu-t	na-*ŋa*-tu-t
	3SG O-1SG A-kill-PERF	3SG A-1SG O-kill-PERF
	'I killed him.'	'He killed me.'
Karawari:	ya-*ka*-krar	ya-*ŋa*-krar
	3SG O-1SG A-hit	3SG A-1SG O-hit
	'I hit him.'	'He hit me.'

Chambri is more rigid in that in most cases the object prefix precedes the subject prefix.

an-o-dii-n   am-(m)an-dii-n
3SG O-1SG A-hit-PRES 1SG O-3SG A-hit-PRES
'I am hitting him.'   'He is hitting me.'

However, if the two prefixes are first- and second-person, the order is reversed.

am-nan-dii-n   man-o-dii-n
1SG A-2SG O-hit-PRES 2SG A-1SG O-hit-PRES
'I am hitting you.'   'You are hitting me.'

Note that the prefix forms in Chambri do not code syntactic functions like subject or object directly, but merely linear order: *am*- occurs initially and *o*- internally. There is some of this in the Yimas prefixes as well (see Section 5.1.1).

Angoram is the most distinctive language in this regard. It employs a topicality hierarchy like that of Yimas and Karawari. If both participants are of the same rank (i.e., both third-person) they occur as prefixes in the order object/subject, as would be the case in Yimas or Karawari too (the following Angoram examples are from Laycock 1959, but the analysis is mine).

na-pwa-ti   pa-n-ti
3SG O-3PL A-hit   3PL O-3SG A-hit
'They are hitting him.' 'He is hitting them.'

If the object is third-person and the subject first- or second-person, they will again appear in that order, but the subject will additionally be expressed by a suffix.

na-n-ti-ka-ndu   pa-m-ti-ka-nde
3SG O-2-hit-PRES-2PL A 3PL O-l-hit-PRES-1 PL A
'You all are hitting him.' 'We are hitting them.'

Or they may both appear as suffixes again in the order object/subject (the factors determining this choice are unknown).

sali-ka-na-ndu   sali-k-umba-nda
see-PRES-3SG O-2PL A see-PRES-3PL O-1PL A
'You all see him.'   'We see them.'

If the subject is third-person and the object first- or second-person, the subject appears as a prefix (not distinguishing number, but varying allomorphically according to the person of the object), while the object is a suffix.

opwa-ti-ka-ndu   pa-ti-ka-ŋge
3-hit-PRES-2PL O   3-hit-PRES-1 DL O
'He/they are hitting you.' 'He/they hit us two.'

The syntactic cohesion of sentences in all Lower Sepik languages is remarkably loose. Although the verb tends to occur finally, word order is quite free in most of them (Murik may be an exception, but information is insufficient to decide). For example, in these Chambri and Yimas sentences, any permutation of the three words will produce a grammatical sentence, although a sentence with the verb first would sound a bit stilted and awkward:

(1-12) a. Chambri: noranan   numpranasïm empï-m-dii-n
               man I SG   pig II DL   3DL O-3SG A-hit-PRES
               'The man is killing two pigs.'
     b. Yimas: numprantrm impa-n-tu-t   panmal
               pig III DL   3PL O-3SG A-kill-PERF man I SG
               'The man killed two pigs.'

There is no case marking for core nominals in any Lower Sepik language, but there is a general oblique suffix of the form *-n(a) found in Yimas, Karawari and Chambri: Y: *nam-n* house-OBL 'in the house', K: *upuniŋg-na* lake-OBL 'in/to the lake', C: *oro-n* stone-OBL 'on the stone'. All of the languages use postpositions, but the only cognate among all is *na* POSS.

Yimas:	kay	ama-*na*-y
	canoe VIII SG	1SG-POSS-VIII SG
	'my canoe'	
Karawari:	kay	ama-*na*-ki
	canoe VII SG	1SG-POSS-VII SG
	'my canoe'	
Chambri:	ke	amï-*na*-ke
	canoe VI SG	1SG-POSS-VI SG
	'my canoe'	
Angoram:	ke	ami-*na*-ki
	canoe VI SG	1SG-POSS-VI SG
	'my canoe'	
Murik:	gain-mot	ma-*na*-k
(Schmidt 1953)	canoe-PL	1SG-POSS-PL
	'my houses'	

At this stage of our knowledge it is difficult to fully subgroup the Lower Sepik family. While Murik and Kopar form one clear, low-level subgroup, as do Yimas and Karawari, beyond that the picture is less clear. The balance of the evidence presented above seems to favor grouping Chambri with Yimas-Karawari, but Angoram is very problematic. It shows many features which are uniquely its own, some it shares with Murik-Kopar and some with Chambri-Yimas-Karawari. The following very tentative family tree of the Lower Sepik seems the most acceptable:

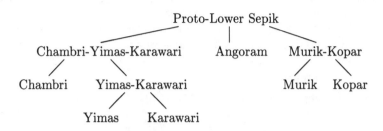

1.5 Sources for This Study

The Yimas language has never been studied before, so there was no material to consult before I began work on it. The first field trip was undertaken in 1977 and lasted seven months. Since then there have been five additional shorter trips: 1978–9 (2 months), 1981–2 (2 months), 1983–4 (2 months), 1985–6 (3 months), and 1988 (1 month). The total time spent in the field amounted to 17 months. The great bulk of that time was devoted to the in depth study of Yimas, but the study of the neighboring language Arafundi and other languages of the Lower Sepik family for comparative purposes was also pursued.

By far the greater part of the language work in Yimas was conducted with a single very fine informant, Stephen Yakayapan Mambi, a man now (1988) in his late thirties. He is far and away the best speaker of Yimas in his age group, and indeed, has a richer and more sophisticated knowledge of the language than most men twenty years his senior. He is also exceptionally well versed in traditional Yimas lore and legends. This is all due to the upbringing by his father, a very traditional man, already in his late forties at the time of Stephen's birth, who had reached adulthood in the precontact time and spoke only a rudimentary Tok Pisin. Stephen was very close to his father and as a child spent much of his time with him, in contrast to the typical pattern of young Yimas boys, who congregate in age groups and spend most of their time with each other. As a result of his father's tutelage, Stephen has an exceptional knowledge of his language and culture, and is sometimes referred to in the village by people his age and younger as *tumbuna man*, literally 'ancestor man', one familiar with the traditional life.

My other informants were two men now (1988) in their late twenties, Pius Tapi and Paul Api. They were the major sources of my information on the somewhat regularized and simplified Yimas of younger speakers. Pius and I worked together in my first 3 months of field work in 1977. When I first went to Yimas, I could not speak Tok Pisin, and I needed to work with someone who spoke English. Pius had completed six years of English language medium schooling and was very helpful in this transitional period. My sessions with Paul Api were in 1984. Paul's special gift is the ability to elucidate the meanings of complex constructions and propose alternative examples (a task Stephen Mambi has little patience with). He is also the source of much of my data on changes in the language among younger speakers.

There were a few other people, mostly older men in their fifties, that I worked with sporadically. My sessions with them were almost exclusively concerned with the recording and transcribing of traditional legends. The man who stands out in this group is Bruno Yumbwi, who taught me many valuable legends (really oral history), such as the story concerning the migration of the Chambri and Murik. He is also the source of my information on pidginized Yimas, the highly simplified and conventionalized jargon derived from Yimas used in trading contacts with the Arafundi speaking villages upriver (Foley 1988).

Most of the data in this grammar comes from spontaneous spoken texts, narratives, conversations, or expository prose. Some examples come from elicitation sessions, but these have all been carefully and doubly checked with informants, as have even those coming from spontaneous texts. The texts were recorded on tape and then transcribed with the informant, who constantly monitored my oral repetition of what was on the tape. I also got good data from speaking with the villagers in Yimas, as they would quite gleefully correct me whenever I made a mistake! Elicitation sessions were mostly restricted to the collection of paradigms and the like, but there were many of these, for, as the reader will soon discover, the structure of the language required it.

The language being described here is essentially that of Yimas speakers in their late thirties and older in 1988. Younger speakers show significant simplifications and regularizations in their speech, many of which will be noted where relevant in the grammar. Very young speakers, under seven, rarely know the language at all, having learned Tok Pisin as their first language. It remains to be seen whether they will learn Yimas later, but the long term prognosis for the language is not good. It is very likely that in 30 years or so it would not prove possible to write a grammar of the language described herein.

2

Phonology

For a Papuan language Yimas has a fairly complex phonology, with
a significant inventory of phonological rules, especially those involving
vowels. Many morphemes exhibit a number of different phonetic forms
depending on the environment in which they appear. In order to provide significant generalizations about these morphemes, it is necessary
to propose abstract underlying forms which are converted into their actually occurring phonetic forms in each environment by the operation
of phonological rules. Many of these phonological rules are general and
will be treated in this chapter; those rules which are restricted to one or
a few morphemes will be discussed when those morphemes are treated
in later chapters. I will be employing a theoretical framework in this
chapter based loosely on autosegmental phonology (Goldsmith 1979), in
which phonological features are associated with the segments in a basic consonant-vowel phonotactic schema in a number of hierarchically
organized tiers (see, for example, Goldsmith 1985, on the treatment of
vowel harmony). I have also adapted some ideas of Kiparsky's (1982,
1985) framework of lexical phonology, which proposes that there are two
major types of phonological rules: lexical phonological rules, which are
internal to the lexicon and apply when new, lexically specified stems are
derived from roots by morphological derivational processes; and postlexical phonological rules, which apply to all forms generated by the morphological processes of the language, not just those which are lexically
specified. The form of this theory necessarily stipulates that lexical
phonological rules precede postlexical ones. The form of this theoretical framework and its usefulness in the analysis of Yimas will become
apparent as the description proceeds.

In this chapter I will follow the following conventions: a form enclosed in slashes, i.e., /x/, denotes a systematic phonemic or underlying morphophonemic form; a form enclosed in square brackets, i.e., [x],

represents a systematic phonetic surface form; and any form in italics indicates a taxonomic phonemic ('classical phonemic') representation.

2.1 Consonants

2.1.1 Segmental Phonemes

Yimas has one of the simplest phonological inventories of any Papuan language. It has only twelve underlying consonantal phonemes, and even three of these are suspect. The consonant phonemes are

- four stops and their corresponding nasals for four places of articulation,

	stop	nasal
bilabial	p	m
dental-apical	t	n
palatal-laminal	c	ɲ
velar	k	ŋ

- two liquids,

palatal lateral	l^y
apical rhotic	r

- and two semivowels,

high, front, unrounded	y
high, back, rounded	w

The problematic underlying phonemes are the palatal sounds, /c/, /ɲ/ and /l^y/. These often arise by transparent phonological rules involving the palatalization of an adjoining dental-apical consonant by a high front vowel or semivowel: for example, *kay* 'canoe' + -*nan* LOC > *ka(y)ɲan* 'in the canoe', and *tay-* 'see', reduplicated becomes *tacay* 'see repeatedly, stare'. A number of older speakers pronounce /ri/ instead of /l^y/ or show variation between these two realizations. Clearly some occurrences of the palatals must be regarded as derived from underlying dental-apical sounds. However, for those cases of palatals which never show alternation with a dental-apical there seems no compelling reason for treating these other than as underlying palatals. These are always internal to stems, for with the exception of /l^y/, which can occur finally, a palatal may not occur stem initially or finally. These stem internal palatals, which never alternate with dental-apicals, are taken as underlying palatals. Examples of these are *akul^y im* 'wrist', *iɲcit* 'urine', *akipiɲan* 'behind', and *wacakin* 'small'. Not surprisingly, many of these palatals correspond to dental-apicals plus high front vowels in the cognates of the related language Karawari (*awkurim* 'hand', *sindi* 'urine').

A stop and its corresponding nasal generally have the same articulatory position, but other than this they often exhibit a wide divergence of articulatory features. This is because the stops have a rather wide range of allophonic variation, while the nasals have very little.

The nasals have no audible allophonic variation and are always articulatorily realized with the phonetic quality of the conventional symbol chosen to represent them. There is a tendency for younger speakers to merge /n/ and /ŋ/ in initial position. So, while older speakers say [ŋáɾwʌ] for *ŋarwa* 'penis', many younger speakers would say [náɾwʌ]. The only major allophonic rule concerning nasals syllabifies them in final position after a homorganic stop (*irɨpm* [íɾəp°m̩] 'coconut palm', *patn* [pʰát°n̩] 'betelnut'), or word internally between two stops, at least one of which must be homorganic (*yaracukŋkwi* [yáɾʌsùk°ŋgwi] 'white (PL)').

Stops, on the other hand, are much more varied. Following nasals, they are generally voiced, though this is optional (*kumpwi* [kʰúmbwi] 'flying fox', -*ntut* [-ndut] RM PAST, *ɨŋcɨt* [íɲjIt] 'urine', *pamki* [pámgi] 'legs'). The stops also have voiceless aspirated allophones. These occur in initial position and before stressed vowels (*tɨkay* [tʰəkʰáy] 'nose', *pɨkam* [pʰəkʰám] 'skin o'f back', *triŋ* [tʰɾə́ŋ] 'tooth'). Finally, stops are not orally released preceding a nasal (*irɨpm* [íɾəp°m̩]] 'coconut palm', *watn* [wát°n̩] 'ironwood', *wacakŋ* [wʌsák°ŋ̩] 'small', *atmpi* [át°n̩bi] 'cutting'.

The peripheral stops /p/ and /k/ are also subject to allophonic rules of lenition. /p/ is likely to be voiced before a high back vowel (*irpulʸɨk* [íɾbulʸIk] 'black ants', *kuput* [kʰʊbút] 'rain'). Before a /w/, it is likely to be both voiced and lenited to [β] (*ipwa* [iβá] 'you (PL)'). Lenition is even more common with /k/. Intervocalically before an unstressed vowel, /k/ optionally becomes voiced and spirantized to [ɣ] (*wakɨntɨt* [wáɣindɨt] 'snakes', *amanakɨn* [ʌmʌnáɣin] 1 SG POSS). In final syllables, this lenited /k/ often disappears completely with compensatory vowel lengthening; so, for example, the second example above would be pronounced [ʌmʌná·n].

The palatal-laminal stop /c/ has the most complex allophony of the four stops. Intervocalically, it is often realized simply as the voiceless slit dental fricative [s̪], but this varies according to age, with younger speakers preferring [s̪], while older speakers prefer the palatal-laminal stop [c].

		Older	Younger
'small'	*wacakɨn*	[wʌcáɣin]	[wʌsáɣin]
'send'	*acak*	[ácʌk]	[ásʌk]
'break'	*kumpracak*	[kʰumbrácʌk]	[kʰumbrásʌk]

Following a consonant, /c/ is invariably a stop for all speakers, voiced when following a nasal, as is the rule for all stops (*kwalcak* [kʰwálcʌk]

TABLE 3

Distinctive Features of Yimas Consonants

	p	t	c	k	m	n	ɲ	ŋ	r	l	y	w
consonantal	+	+	+	+	+	+	+	+	+	+	−	−
liquid	−	−	−	−					+	+		
peripheral	+	−	−	+	+	−	−	+				
nasal	−	−	−	−	+	+	+	+				
labial	+		−		+		−					
front (i.e., F)		+				−	+			−	+	+	
round (i.e., R)												+

'get up', *iɲcit* [íɲjIt] 'urine'). Unlike /p, t, k/, /c/ must always occur stem internally, never initially or finally, with a couple of exceptions like *arc* 'grandparent'. This must be a borrowed word, because in addition to the aberrant final /c/, the consonant cluster /rc/ is also disallowed in Yimas, as all such clusters must agree in palatality, i.e., Yimas demands /lc/. The presence of both these aberrant features marks this word as outside the normal system of Yimas phonology.

The palatalized lateral /lʸ/ has two phonetic realizations, which are seen in free variation: a strongly palatalized apical lateral [lʸ] or a palatal-laminal lateral [ʎ]. Examples are *walʸ* [wa^ᶜlʸ] ∼ [wa^ᶜʎ] 'wind', *mikilʸ* [məkIlʸ] ∼ [məkIʎ] 'monitor lizard', and *walʸamuŋ* [wá^ᶜlʸʌmɒŋ] ∼ [wá^ᶜʎʌmɒŋ] 'basket'. Note that as in the above examples, vowels are quite fronted preceding the phoneme /lʸ/. This applies somewhat to all palatal consonants, but is most apparent with /lʸ/. In some cases the fronting of /a/ may be so pronounced that it becomes a low front vowel or takes on the character of a diphthong (*walʸamuŋ* [wælʸʌmɒŋ] ∼ [wáylʸʌmɒŋ] 'basket').

The apical rhotic /r/ varies freely in most environments between an apical lateral [l] and an alveolar tap [ɾ] (*irak* [ilák] ∼ [iɾák] 'dance', *pramuŋ* [pʰlámɒŋ] ∼ [pʰɾámɒŋ] 'sleep'). But following the dental-apical stop /t/, only the tap articulation is allowed (*triŋ* [tʰɾə́ŋ] *[tʰlə́ŋ] 'tooth', *amtra* [ámdɾʌ] *[amdlʌ] 'food', *trukwa* [tʰɾúkwʌ] *[tʰlúkwʌ] 'knee'). Elsewhere, some speakers prefer one articulation over the other, but there is no hard and fast rule, both being acceptable. The [l] articulation is most favored intervocalically and the [ɾ] elsewhere, but this is just a tendency. /r/ may not occur word initially or finally and is subject to some complex phonological rules which convert it to /t/ (see Section 2.3.2).

Yimas has two semivowels, a high front unrounded /y/ and a high back rounded /w/. I have defined these in terms of vocalic features like *front* rather than consonantal features like *palatal*, because as we shall see, they interact in fundamental ways with the vowel system of Yimas. I will therefore defer further discussion of these features until treating vowels in Section 2.2.

The distinctive features of the consonants of Yimas are represented in Table 3. Some of the features chosen may seem strange at this point, but the reasons for their selection will become apparent as the vowel system and phonological rules are presented. They have been chosen to provide the maximally simple and transparent statement of the phonological rules. Henceforth, I will represent the palatal lateral phoneme /lʸ/ simply as /l/.

2.1.2 Consonant Clusters

At the phonetic level, initial and final consonant clusters in Yimas are strongly constrained, but they are rather freer word-medially. Yimas words can begin in a vowel (_aŋkayapan_ 'afternoon', _i̱ncɨt_ 'urine') or any consonant other than /r/ or the palatals /c/, /ɲ/ or /l/. Clusters of no more than two consonants can begin a word. The permissible combinations are any stop (other than /c/) plus /r/ (_pramuŋ_ 'sleep', _tri̱ŋ_ 'tooth', _kramnawt_ 'three') or /p, k/ plus /w/ (_pwi̱ncɨni̱ŋ_ 'cross beams', _kwarkwa_ 'today'). Finally, initial clusters of homorganic nasal plus stop are permitted (_mpum_ 'large crayfish', _ŋkak_ 'go'). Palatal nasal plus stop initial clusters are, of course, prohibited by the general ban on initial palatals.

This last possibility might be seen to argue for unit phonemes of pre-nasalized voiced stops, abrogating the need to posit these ad hoc /mp/ initial clusters. There are a number of arguments against this analysis. First of all, as pointed out in Section 2.1.1, homorganic nasal plus stop clusters following another stop are realized with the nasal as syllabic. This would be very difficult to account for if the entire cluster nasal plus stop were a unit phoneme. Second, non-homorganic nasal plus stop clusters are common in the language, such as _namtampara_ 'foot' or _manpa_ 'crocodile'. The language provides no evidence for distinguishing non-homorganic nasal plus stop clusters from homorganic ones, and it is simplest to treat all as clusters. Third, the language has a highly productive rule of nasal truncation, reducing sequences of nasals to one, which is simplest to state if the nasals are always treated as separate segments (see Section 2.3.5), as in _pamuŋk+i_ > [pámgi], where the cluster /m+ŋ/ reduces to [m]. Finally, I have been able to discover fewer than ten stems in the entire language which begin in nasal plus stop clusters, the great majority of which begin in /mp/. There is only one example of /nt/ and one of /ŋk/, and both are verb stems normally preceded by prefixes. This set of stems with initial nasal plus stop clusters is

/mp/:   *mpan* 'one', *mpa* 'now, already', *mpum* 'large crayfish',
        mpunawŋ 'elbow', *mpuŋkan* 'crowned pigeon',
        mpiŋam 'navel', *mpatnpara* 'few', *mpɨmtak* 'cross river'
/nt/:   *ntakɨk* 'leave'
/ŋk/:   *ŋkak* 'go by land'

This small inventory is much more in keeping with an analysis of these
as initial consonant clusters, all examples of which are quite rare, rather
than as a single initial consonant.

In summary, Yimas words can begin with up to two consonants,
summarized in the following formula:

$$\# \ (C_1) \ (C_2) \ V$$

Both consonants are optional, i.e., a word can begin in a vowel. If (C_2)
is missing, then C_1 may be any consonant except the palatals and /r/.
If C_1 and C_2 are both present, only the following three possibilities are
allowed:

(a) C_1 = non-palatal stop C_2 = /r/
(b) C_1 = /p,k/ C_2 = /w/
(c) C_1 = nasal C_2 = homorganic stop

Permissible final clusters are even more restricted. Yimas words can
end in vowels: *manpa* 'crocodile', *awakɨ* 'stars'. They can also end in
any consonant except the palatals /c/ and /ɲ/ (/l/ may end a word),
and /r/. The only final consonant clusters allowed are a stop plus a
homorganic nasal (always syllabic as discussed in Section 2.1.1) (*irɨpm*
'coconut palm' *patn* 'betelnut' and *wasakŋ* 'small'). The finals of Yimas
words can be summarized in the following formula:

$$V(C_1) \ (C_2) \ \#$$

$$C_1 = \begin{bmatrix} p \\ t \\ k \end{bmatrix} \qquad C_2 = \begin{bmatrix} m \\ n \\ \eta \end{bmatrix}$$

Medial clusters are much more varied than both initials and finals.
Clusters of up to three consonants are permitted in this position. All
Yimas consonants can occur intervocalically, but need not occur, as
vowel clusters are allowed (*kɨaŋ* 'cough'). Medial clusters of two elements
are of three types, depending on the initial consonant. Yimas does not
permit geminates; so, for example, clusters of nasal plus nasal may not
be homorganic.

Type 1: C_1C_2 where C_1 = nasal and
        C_2 = stop: *manpa* 'crocodile', *ŋɨmkiŋɨn* 'below'
        C_2 = nasal: *kramnawt* 'three', *panmal* 'male'

C_2 = semivowel: *manwa* 'fish', *kaciɲyakin* 'dry'
but not *C_2 = liquid

Type 2: C_1C_2 where C_1 = stop and
 C_2 = nasal: *awtmayɲi* 'sugarcane', *alakmal* 'place name'
 C_2 = liquid (*/l/): *waprim* 'hair', *pikriŋ* 'mouth'
 C_2 = semivowel: *warkapwi* 'wallaby', *trukwa* 'knee'
 but not *C_2 = stop

Type 3: C_1C_2 where C_1 = liquid and
 C_2 = stop: (/l/ only with /c/ and */rt/): *warkapwi* 'wallaby',
  malcawkwa 'lower back'
 C_2 = nasal: (/l/ only with /ɲ/ and */rn/): *narmaŋ* 'woman',
  walɲakin 'light'
 C_2 = semivowel (only /rw/): *ŋarwa* 'penis'
 but not *C_2 = liquid

Medial clusters of three consonants are much more restricted. Most
of those involve a nasal plus stop cluster. The first type of cluster with
three consonants is a nasal plus stop cluster, followed by a liquid or
semivowel,

Type 1: $C_1C_2C_3$ where C_1 = nasal, C_2 = stop, and
 C_3 = /r/:   *awantrim* 'cassowaries (DL)', *numpran* 'pig',
  tantayŋkraym 'spider'
 C_3 = /w/:   *tumpwik* 'yellow', *nuŋkwara* 'hand'
Examples in which C_3 = /w/ require the nasal and stop to be homorganic
and peripheral (i.e., labial or velar).

Type 2: $C_1C_2C_3$ where C_2 = peripheral nasal, C_3 = peripheral stop,
 and
 C_1 = liquid: *ilŋk apuk* 'go down', *alŋkat* 'machete (PL)',
  tikirŋkat 'chair (PL)'
 C_1 = stop: *matɲci* 'bird (sp)', *atnpi* 'cutting',
  yaracikŋki 'white'
The medial nasals in these last cluster types are always syllabic, as
discussed in Section 2.1.1. Other clusters of three consonants are formed
with /r/ followed by a stop,

Type 3: $C_1C_2C_3$ where C_1 = /r/, C_2 = peripheral stop and
 C_3 = nasal   *irpmul* 'two coconut palms'
 C_3 = /w/:   *kwarkwa* 'today', *tarpwa* 'belly'

Combining the statements of permissible consonant clusters in initial, medial and final position, we may state that a Yimas word has the following consonant-vowel (CV) skeletal structure:

(2-1) # $(C_1)(C_2)$ V_1 $([(C_3)C_4(C_5)]^n)$ V_2 $(C_6)(C_7)$ #

where the constraints on the initial, medial and final clusters are those described above. Both affixes and roots conform to this CV skeletal structure. According to this skeleton, the simplest Yimas word would be a vowel, and there is such a form, the verb stem *i-* 'say'. The superscript n over the medial syllable allows it to iterate this syllable a number of times to produce syllables of more than two syllables. The longest roots are around five or six syllables, for example *mamantakarman* 'land crab' or *tiŋkimpiɲawa* 'bird (sp)'; but words can be much longer, as in these tongue twisters: *naɲanaŋkanampanɨra* 'you all give those to them few' or *kampupaymatakatnampanɨm* 'let them paint them all inside first'.

Syllabification in Yimas is generally transparent. If a single consonant occurs between two vowels, the syllable boundary precedes it (V.CV). With clusters of two consonants, it falls between the two consonants $(VC_1.C_2V)$, unless $C_1 =$ stop and $C_2 = /r/$, in which case it precedes the cluster $(V.C_1C_2V)$. For clusters of three consonants, the syllable boundary follows the first consonant $(VC_1.C_2C_3V)$.

2.2 Vowels

In terms of phonetic contrasts, Yimas presents a system of four vowels, /i/, /ɨ/, /u/, and /a/ as documented by the following minimal pairs: *mum* 'they', *mɨm* 'it', *mam* 'another', *mi* 'you(SG)'; *pikrɨŋ* 'fart', *pikrɨŋ* 'mouth'. However, a simple list of minimal pairs such as these disguises some important facts about the Yimas vowel system. Not all these vowels are equally common. Together /ɨ/ and /a/ account for the overwhelming percentage of vowel tokens in Yimas, over 90%, with /u/ coming next and /i/ decidedly rare, perhaps 1%–2% of all vowel tokens. Furthermore, /ɨ/ and /a/ have extensive allophonic variation, varying widely over the vowel space, but /u/ and especially /i/ have a very narrow range.

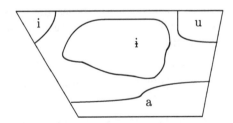

The allophones of the four vowels can be stated in the following rules:

/ɨ/ → [I] / [+front]

    akipɨɲan   [ʌkəpÌɲan]   'behind'

    kalɨk   [kʰá<lʸIk]   'sago pudding'

    [ɨ] / __ [-peripheral, -front, -liquid]

        mɨn   [mɨ́n]   'he, she, it'

    [ə] / elsewhere

        nɨnɨkɨnɨŋ   [nínəkʰɨ̀nəŋ]   'chin'

        tɨkɨt   [tʰə́kɨt]   'chair'

        mɨrɨm   [mə́ɾəm]   'they (DL)'

/a/ → [ɛ] / [+front] __ [+front]

    yacɨrɨm   [yɛ́səɾəm]   'daga: betel chewing
                                      accessory'

    [a<] / [-front] __ [+front]

    (This rule only applies if the [+front] C is in the same syllable
    as the /a/.)

        malcakwa   [má<l.cɔkwʌ]   'lower back'

    [ɔ] / __ C_1^2 X
             [+peripheral]   [+round]

        wɨŋkapuk   [wíŋgɔpuk]   'go up'

        malcakwa   [má<l.cɔkwʌ]   'lower back'

    [ʌ] / elsewhere [-stress]

        wantakampa   [wándʌkàmbʌ]   'door'

    [a] / elsewhere [+stress]

        patn   [pʰát°n̩]   'betelnut'

        yanara   [yánʌɾʌ]   'bark of clove tree'

/u/ → [ɯ<] / __ m $\left\{ \begin{matrix} C \\ \# \end{matrix} \right\}$

    mum   [mɯ́<m]   'they (PL)'

    tɨnum   [tʰɨnɯ́<m]   'sago palm'

    kumprak   [kʰɯ<mbrák]   'break'

    [ɷ] / __ ŋ

        muŋ   [mɷ́ŋ]   'it'

        irpuɲi   [írpɷɲì]   'coconut palms'

    [u] / elsewhere

        tuk   [tʰúk]   'kill'

        nampunɨm   [námbunɨm]   'wing'

/i/ → [i] / everywhere

kaŋki	[kʰáŋgi]	'shells'
irak	[iɾák]	'dance'

Yimas has only two diphthongs, /ay/ and /aw/. Both have a strong tendency to be raised, i.e., realized phonetically as /ey/ and /ow/. In addition, /aw/ is commonly monophthongized to [ɔ], thus merging /aw/ with /a/ for one of its allophones. Some speakers actually make a minimal pair between *pay* 'be in flat, reclining position' and *pey* '(human being) sleep'. This latter verb may never be realized as [pʰáy]; but since it is clearly a semantic specialization of one of the phonetic realizations of *pay* 'be in a flat, reclining position', it seems unnecessary to propose a distinct phonemic diphthong for this one example. Yimas lacks all other diphthongs; there are no /iw/, /uy/, and most importantly, no /ɨw/ or /ɨy/. When /ɨ/ comes in contact with /w/ or /y/ through morphological processes, it becomes /u/ or /i/ respectively (*antɨ*- 'hear' + -*wat* HAB > *antuwat* 'usually hear' and *kampɨ*- LIKE 3DL + *yan* 'come' > *kampiyan* 'let them both come'). This suggests that the high vowels do not have the same status in the phonology as the low vowel /a/.

The problematic status of /ɨ/ among Sepik area languages has been well documented (see Laycock 1965, Pawley 1966, Foley 1986), and Yimas is no exception. The problem arises because of the epenthetic function of ɨ to break up impermissible consonant clusters, as in these examples:

am-	'eat'	+	-*n* IMP	>	*amɨn*	'eat'
al-	'cut'	+	-*k* IRR	>	*alɨk*	'cut'
k-	class V SG	+	-*k* PROX	>	*kɨk*	'this'
k-	class V SG	+	*tumukut* 'fell down'	>	*kɨtumukut*	'it fell down'

This is a pervasive feature of Yimas; any extensive sample of Yimas text will present hundreds of examples of epenthetic ɨ. (Vowels not enclosed in slashes indicate contrastive, taxonomic phonemes, not underlying, systematic ones.) However, not all examples of ɨ can be analyzed away as epenthetic. There are a few clear examples of /ɨ/ separating two consonants which would form a permissible consonant cluster and so must be analyzed as underlyingly present,

patɨn	'betelnut'	versus	*amanatɨn*	'I feel'
kaŋkan-	'shooting'	versus	*ninɨkɨnɨŋ*	'chin'

The problem can be stated summarily as follows: How do we know when a /ɨ/ is really there and not epenthetic? Unfortunately, there is no straightforward answer to this question and I will adopt the following conventions in this analysis:

1. Any ɨ which alternates with ∅ will be treated as epenthetic:

'stick' SG: *yanɨŋ* PL: *yan<u>k</u>i* underlying form: /yanŋ/
'bone'   SG: *tanɨm* PL: *tan<u>p</u>at* underlying form: /tanm/

2. Any ɨ which occurs in an otherwise impermissible cluster will be treated as epenthetic. All others are underlying:

'chin' *nɨnɨkɨnɨŋ* underlying form: /nnɨkinŋ/
'nose' *tɨkay*   underlying form: /tkay/

Epenthetic ɨ is inserted according to convention 2 from left to right. Consider /mkrayŋ/ 'cane'. /mk/ is a prohibited initial cluster, so /ɨ/ is inserted, while /kr/ is a permissible medial cluster resulting in *mɨkrayŋ*.

3. If an ɨ phoneme is not established as underlying by conventions 1 and 2, it will be treated as epenthetic. This will result, in many cases, in vowelless words, roots and affixes.

Consider *tɨkɨt* 'chair'. Both tokens of ɨ in this word should be considered as epenthetic, because both break up impermissible clusters. Treating both as such then results in the vowelless root /tkt/. ɨ insertion applies twice from left to right, first to break up the impermissible initial cluster /tk/, and then again to break up the impermissible final cluster /kt/.

Now consider the more complex underlying form /tŋkntk/ 'blacken'. Again, ɨ-insertion will apply from left to right. /tŋ/ is not an acceptable initial cluster by the phonotactic statement of Section 2.1.2, so ɨ insertion will apply to form *tɨŋ*. The next cluster /ŋk/ is a permissible medial cluster but */ŋkn/ is not, so ɨ insertion must apply. The problem is to decide exactly where it will apply, and for this the principles of syllabification given at the end of Section 2.1.2 are crucial. Remember that for clusters of two consonants the syllable boundary falls between them $(VC_1.C_2V)$, so that for /ŋk/ we have /ŋ.k/ (i.e., /ŋ/ belongs to the previous syllable). A basic constraint on the operation of the ɨ insertion rule is that it may not apply at a syllable break, because its whole function is to create syllable peaks where there are none. By default, ɨ would appear between /k/ and /n/. Note, however, that /n/ now falls between two stops /k/ and /t/, one of which is homorganic. This is the environment for syllabic nasals, as discussed in 2.1.1, and /n/ will be realized syllabically, although alternatively, an epenthetic ɨ may occur in this environment because, like nasal syllabification, ɨ-insertion functions to provide lacking syllabic peaks. In fact, I view the nasal syllabification rule in these environments as nothing but a phonetic variant of the ɨ insertion rule. Finally, /tk/ is not a permissible final cluster, resulting in another application of ɨ insertion and the final form *tiŋ.kn̩.tɨk* or *tiŋ.kin.tɨk*, with syllable boundaries marked. Other examples of words which would be vowelless if not for convention 3 are

/ŋmkŋn/	*ŋɨmkɨŋɨn*	'below'
/ɲclŋ/	*ɨɲcilɨŋ*	'betelnut type'
/klkt/	*kilɨkɨt*	(place name)
/trŋ/	*trɨŋ*	'tooth'
/mɲŋ/	*miɲɨŋ*	'tongue'
/mml/	*mimɨl*	'Javan file snake'
/klklk/	*kilɨkilɨk*	'mosquito (sp)'
/pkrŋ/	*pɨkrɨŋ*	'mouth'
/tmpt/	*tɨmpɨt*	'palm tree like betelnut palm'

We are now ready for a more explicit statement of the ɨ insertion rule as follows:

(2-2)   ɨ insertion: $\emptyset \rightarrow$ ɨ

between all underlying clusters which do not meet the structural conditions of permissible consonant clusters presented in Section 2.1.2. ɨ is never inserted at a syllable boundary. A sequence of ɨ plus nasal which would result from the rule of ɨ insertion may be realized as a syllabic nasal, provided it is flanked by two stops one of which must be homorganic.

The rule of ɨ insertion (2-2) clearly indicates that ɨ is the unmarked vowel in Yimas. However, all three high vowels show examples of epenthesis. Phonological rules of *a* epenthesis are unknown. Examples of *u* insertion are rather less common than for ɨ, and those of *i* insertion are decidedly rare, but all three do occur. Examples follow:

1. *u* insertion, when an adjoining syllable contains /u/ or /w/:

    maŋkum 'vein' + -*l* DL   → *maŋkumul* 'veins (DL)'
    antir- 'heard' + -*mpwi* 'words' → *antirumpwi* 'heard words'

2. *i* insertion, when an adjoining syllable contains /i/ or /y/ (very restricted application between verb stem and suffixes):

    nakatimayk 'I call him' + -*kiak* PAST → *nakatimaykikiak* 'I call him'

To summarize the insertion rules we may say that a high vowel is inserted to break up impermissible consonant clusters. Normally, this is the neutral, central vowel ɨ unless the adjoining syllable contains a rounded vowel /u/ or semivowel /w/, in which case the inserted vowel is *u*; if the adjoining syllable contains a front vowel /i/ or semivowel /y/, Fit is *i*. Furthermore, ɨ changes to *u* or *i* before a /w/ or /y/ respectively. Finally, the diphthongs /aw/ and /ay/ are common in the language, while */iy/ and */iw/ do not exist. All of this suggests a close relationship between /i/ and /u/ and /i/. In fact, I will now propose an analysis where /u/ and /i/ are nothing other than /i/ with associated autosegments of rounding (R) and fronting (F), respectively.

In this analysis, Yimas has only two underlying vowels: /i/ and /a/. The vast majority of tokens of i are, of course, not underlying /i/ but are the result of i insertion, while all examples of a correspond to underlying /a/. /i/, as befits its neutral status, is defined simply as V, but /a/ is represented as having a feature low (L), associated as an autosegment over the CV skeleton, as in the following examples:

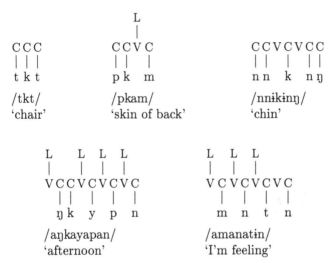

i insertion can now be simply restated as 'insert V,' subject to the same constraints.

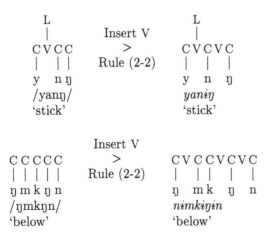

/u/ and /i/ are now restated as V with the autosegments round (R) and front (F), respectively:

/aw/ and /ay/ are V̩ associated with R and F:

The rules of *u* and *i* insertion can now be collapsed with that of *i* insertion, i.e., insert V, with consequent spreading of the autosegments.

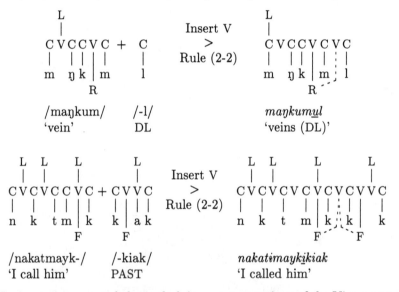

/maŋkum/   /-l/   *maŋkumul*
'vein'   DL   'veins (DL)'

/nakatmayk-/   /-kiak/   *nakatimaykikiak*
'I call him'   PAST   'I called him'

Having now presented the underlying representations of the Yimas vowels, I am now ready to turn to the more complex phonological rules of the language.

2.3 Segmental Phonological Rules

Yimas has a fairly rich system of phonological rules which interact in interesting ways. Perhaps the most common rule is that for palatalization, so it seems a good place to start.

2.3.1 Palatalization

Consider the following examples:

arkwi 'vine' + *-ntimpɨt* PL > *arkwiɲcimpɨt* ~ *arkwiɲcimpɨt* 'vines'

tay- 'see' + *-nak* IMP > *tayɲak* ~ *taɲak* 'look at it'

niŋay 'breast' + *-ntimpɨt* PL > *niŋayɲcimpɨt*
$$\sim niŋaɲcimpɨt \text{ 'breasts'}$$

awŋkwi 'sink' + *tipaŋ-* 'wash' > *awŋkwicipaŋ* ~ *awkwicipaŋ*
$$\sim awŋkucipaŋ \text{ 'bathe'}$$

pampay- KIN + *tipalɨk* 'descend' > *pampaycipalɨk*
$$\sim pampacipalɨk \text{ 'carry down'}$$

All these examples illustrate the palatalization of a following apical-dental by a preceding front vowel or semivowel. In all cases of palatalization the preceding /i/ or /y/ may be retained or disappear entirely. The *ɨ* in the examples involving /i/ is, of course, merely epenthetic, to break up the impermissible consonant clusters produced by palatalization. Whether the palatalizing high front segment remains after the application of the rule, or disappears, can be analyzed as the choice between the spreading versus the shift of the autosegment F to the right.

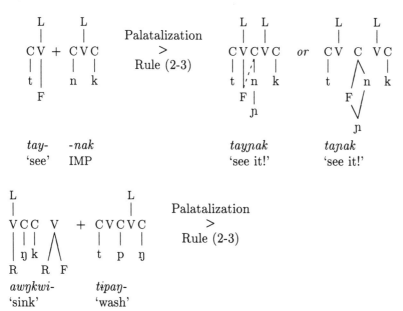

tay-   -nak   tayɲak   taɲak
'see'   IMP   'see it!'   'see it!'

awŋkwi-   tipaŋ-
'sink'   'wash'

52   PHONOLOGY

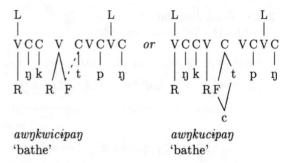

awŋkwicipaŋ   *awŋkucipaŋ*
'bathe'   'bathe'

Note that the fronting autosegment can spread beyond a single segment.
If the first member of a consonant cluster is palatalized, so is the second;
in other words, the rule applies twice,

L
|
V C V + C C V C C V C   Palatalization
 | | | | | | | >
 w | n t   m p   t   Rule (2-3)
   F
awi   *-ntimpit*
'axe'   PL

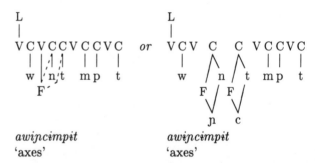

awiɲcimpit   *awiɲcimpit*
'axes'   'axes'

This palatalization rule can be formalized as follows (where X indicates
any segment, either a consonant or vowel):

(2-3) Palatalization

$$X + \begin{bmatrix} +\text{consonantal} \\ -\text{peripheral} \end{bmatrix} \rightarrow X \begin{bmatrix} +\text{consonantal} \\ -\text{peripheral} \end{bmatrix} \; or \; X \begin{bmatrix} +\text{consonantal} \\ -\text{peripheral} \end{bmatrix}$$
| | |
F   F   F

I have as yet not given examples of palatalization involving /l/. This
is because its behavior can only be understood within the context of the
rules involving /r/, so let us consider those next.

2.3.2 Liquid Strengthening

There is a set of rules which convert /r/ into t in a number of environments. /r/ is a restricted phoneme in Yimas; it may only occur word internally. When an underlying /r/ occurs word finally, it becomes t, as in these examples:

/tkr/	'chair'	SG:	*tɨkɨt*	PL:	*tɨkɨrŋkat*
/tar/	'needle'	SG:	*tat*	PL:	*tarɨt*
/apur/	'green skink'	SG:	*aput*	PL:	*apurŋkat*

This rule only applies to /r/; the front liquid /l/ may occur word finally.

/mkl/	'monitor lizard'	SG:	*mɨkɨl*	PL:	*mɨkɨlŋkat*
/mml/	'Javan file snake'	SG:	*mimil*	PL:	*mimilŋkat*
/al/	'machete'	SG:	*al*	PL:	*alŋkat*

This rule of final /r/ strengthening can be stated formally as follows:

(2-4) Final /r/ strengthening

$$r \rightarrow t \;/\; \_\_ \#$$

The second rule of liquid strengthening applies to both /r/ and /l/. This rule converts a liquid to t preceding a [-peripheral] nasal, as illustrated in these examples by adding the oblique suffix *-nan* to noun stems with final liquids:

/tkr/	'chair'	*tɨkɨtnan*	'in the chair'
/tar/	'needle'	*tatnan*	'with a needle'
/tmal/	'sun/day'	*tɨmatɲan*	'during the day'
/al/	'machete'	*atɲan*	'with a machete'

This rule may be formalized as follows:

(2-5) Prenasal liquid strengthening

$$\text{liquid} \rightarrow t \;/\; \_\_ \begin{bmatrix} \text{nasal} \\ \text{[-peripheral]} \end{bmatrix}$$

The final rule of liquid strengthening to be considered here is liquid dissimilation. Yimas does not permit two liquids to appear in adjacent syllables separated only by a vowel. If this is to be the case, the second becomes t. The application of this rule can best be seen in reduplication. Reduplication is only a peripheral feature of Yimas and is mainly used with verb roots to mark iterative actions (see Section 6.2.4). There are two different patterns of reduplication, the choice depending on the individual verb root (see Section 2.4). I am only interested here in the pattern of partial reduplication which reduplicates an internal consonant to the left. If the consonant adjoins a low vowel, it (with the vowel) is reduplicated.

a̲w̲k̲ura-	awkawkura-	'gather'
a̲p̲an-	apapan-	'spear'
a̲r̲p̲al-	arpapal-	'go out'
ti̲p̲a̲ŋ-	tipapaŋ-	'bathe'

If the consonant involved is /r/, the second /r/ is dissimilated to t following the application of reduplication.

i̲r̲a̲ŋ-	irataŋ-	'cry'
wa̲r̲k-	waratɨk-	'make'
pa̲r̲k-	paratɨk-	'cut up'
ya̲r̲a̲-	yarata-	'pick up'

If the consonant involved is /l/, not only is there dissimilation to t, but the /l/ loses its F autosegment as well and reverts to r.

wu̲l̲-	wurɨt-	'put down'
ta̲l̲-	tarat-	'hold'
mu̲l̲-	murɨt-	'run'

The rule of liquid dissimilation can be formalized as follows:

(2-6) Liquid dissimilation

   liquid → t / r V __

The associated subrule of F loss for reduplication is then as follows:

(2-7) Dissimilative F loss (reduplication)

                RED

   (V) r   >   (V) r (V) r
      | |
      F   F

Naturally, rule (2-7) stands in a feeding relation (Kiparsky 1968) to rule (2-6), but there is no need to stipulate intrinsic rule order between the two rules. Stated as part of the reduplication process, rule (2-7) has to be regarded as a rule of the lexical phonology (Kiparsky 1985), for reduplication is a verbal derivational process specified for the verb root in its lexical entry (see Sections 2.4 and 6.2.4). Rule (2-6), on the other hand, is a postlexical rule, applying to the outputs of the general morphological processes of the language. The ordering difference follows logically from a view of phonology in which rules involved with lexically specified derivational processes apply in the lexicon, while others associated with general morphological and phonological patterns of word formation apply after these lexical formations.

2.3.3 Palatalization Again

The alert readers will have already noticed an interaction between the rule of prenasal liquid strengthening (2-5) and palatalization (2-3). Yimas has a strict constraint that *c* and ɲ may occur not stem- or word-finally. Consider the following examples:

/tmal/ 'sun/day'   + /-nan/ OBL > *ti̵matɲan* 'during the day'
/al/   'machete'   + /-nan/ OBL > *atɲan*   'with a machete'
/wul-/ 'put down' + /-nak/ IMP > *wutɲak*   'put it down'
/tal-/   'hold'   + /-nak/ IMP > *tatɲak*   'hold it!'

In these examples F shifts from the final liquid to the following nasal by the palatalization rule (2-3), and the resulting *r* becomes *t* by the prenasal liquid strengthening rule (2-5), as in the following derivation:

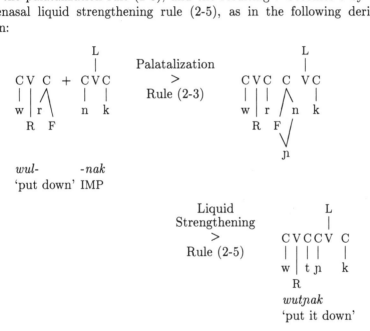

wul-   *-nak*
'put down' IMP

But note that if we apply the rules in the opposite order, we will still get the same result; no extrinsic ordering between the rules is necessary.

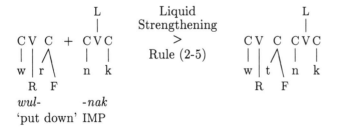

wul-   *-nak*
'put down' IMP

Palatalization
>
Rule (2-3)

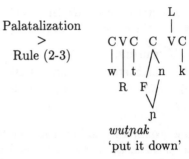

wutɲak
'put it down'

Consider an example with two applications of the palatalization rule:

Palatalization

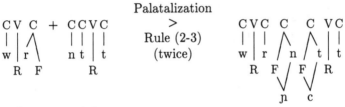

Rule (2-3)
(twice)

wul-   *-ntut*
'put down' RM PAST

Liquid Strengthening
>
Rule (2-5)

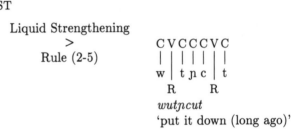

wutɲcut
'put it down (long ago)'

The data clearly support the analysis of /l/ as ṛ. There is no need

to propose a more abstract analysis than this, i.e., there is no need for a phonological rule which generates /l/ from underlying sequences of /r/ plus a high front vowel or semivowel, as there is with /c/ and /ɲ/. /l/ never derives synchronically from /r/ in Yimas. Consider the following derivation, which includes a process of reduplication involving the /l/:

RED
>
Rule (2-7)

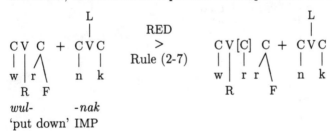

wul-   *-nak*
'put down' IMP

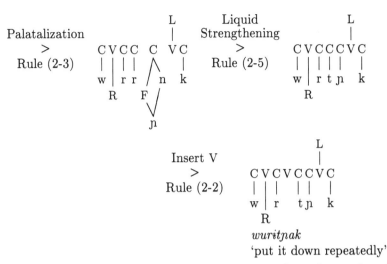

Insert V
>
Rule (2-2)

wuritɲak
'put it down repeatedly'

Again, the ordering of the phonological rules is free. Any order of application will produce the same result, except that reduplication as a lexical rule must come first. But that need not be stated explicitly; the principle that phonological rules associated with lexically specified derivations precede all others is part of the general theory adopted here.

A final point concerns the interaction of the palatalization rule and the prohibition on word-final palatal stops and nasals. If an iterative application of the palatalization rule would potentially apply to a word-final alveolar stop or nasal, converting it to a palatal, the rule is simply blocked. Consider the following example:

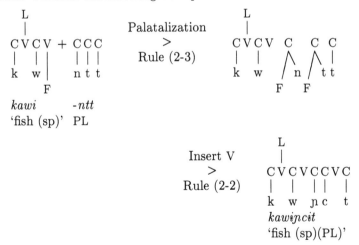

Insert V
>
Rule (2-2)

kawiɲcɨt
'fish (sp)(PL)'

Note that the autosegment F does not spread to the word-final *t*.

2.3.4 The Spreading of the Autosegment R [round]
This is a pervasive phonological feature of Yimas, in which the autosegment R is spread from one vowel to that of an adjoining syllable, provided
they are only separated by a peripheral consonant or consonant cluster.
Its operation can best be seen in combination with the rule of V insertion, for the autosegment R of an adjoining vowel will spread in either
direction to a V inserted by this rule.

/awŋk/ 'egg'   + /-l/ DL   > *awŋkul* 'eggs (DL)'
/num/ 'village'   + /-n/ OBL   > *numun* 'in the village'
/nakaŋak/ 'I gave it' + /-mpun/ 3PL D > *nakaŋakumpun* 'I gave
                                          it to them'
/takantɨk/ 'I didn't + /-mpwi/ 'talk' > *takantɨkumpwi* 'I didn't
       hear'   hear it'

The consonants separating the vowels must be peripheral. If they are
[-peripheral] the rule does not apply.

/wun/ 'sago grub'   + /-t/ PL > *wunɨt* 'sago grubs (PL)'
/takul/ 'brother-in-law' + /-t/ PL > *takulcɨt* 'brothers-in-law'

We can illustrate the application of this rule in autosegmental terms as
follows:

```
                  Insert V                Spread R
C V C + C            >       C V C V C        >        C V C V C
| | |   |   Rule (2-2)       | | | |  Rule (2-8)       | | | ¦ |
n | m   n                    n | m  n                  n | m ¦ n
  R                            R                         R
num      -n                                           numun
'village' OBL                                         'in the village'


  L  L  L                                      L  L  L
  |  |  |               Insert V               |  |  |
C V C V C V C + C C V C    >        C V C V C V C V C C V C
| | | | | | |   | | | |  Rule (2-2)  | | | | | | | | | | |
n k  ŋ  k       m p | n               n  k  ŋ  k   m p | n
                  R                                       R
nakaŋak         -mpun
'I gave it'      3PL D
```

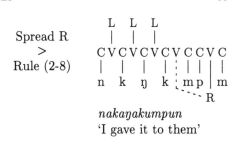

$$nakaŋakumpun$$
'I gave it to them'

R spreading can be formalized as follows:

(2-8) R spreading (mirror image rule)

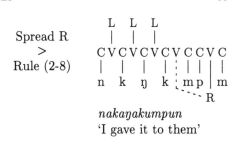

(The parentheses around the association line of the autosegment R indicates that it need not be anchored to a V slot for the rule to apply, but may be free floating. This is essential to handle the cases of R spreading following unstressed /u/ deletion discussed below.) The optional L is to indicate that the rule applies to /aw/ $\begin{bmatrix} (L) \\ V \\ R \end{bmatrix}$ as well as to /u/ $\begin{bmatrix} V \\ R \end{bmatrix}$. This rule needs to apply after the rule of V insertion, but it does not seem necessary to stipulate extrinsic ordering between them. R spreading can simply be an 'anywhere rule' that applies whenever its structural conditions are met. Obviously, before the application of V insertion, no environment for R spreading exists, but once it has occurred, R spreading will follow naturally. It must also be pointed out that application of this rule is subject to lexically and grammatically specified exceptions. It applies in most cases that meet its structural description, but fails to do so in some. Those grammatical environments which block it will be noted as appropriate in sections of the morphology.

The spreading of rounding is a pervasive feature of Yimas stems, so that one may profitably speak of vowel harmony for roundedness for Yimas. The statement for R spreading in Yimas stems is quite complex and requires specifying both the vowels and consonants involved. Again, only peripheral consonants and consonant clusters permit R spreading. As for the vowels, ɨ always accepts rounding from an adjoining syllable, while a occasionally resists it. Consider the following examples:

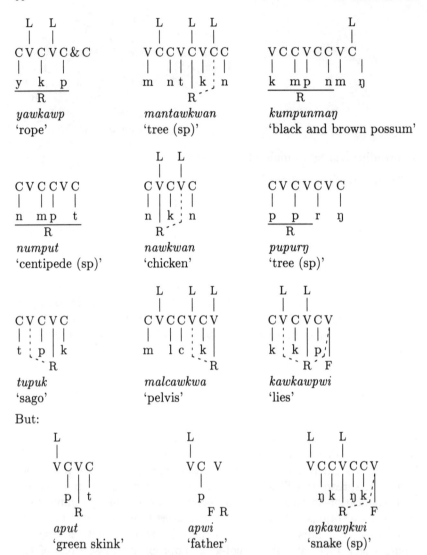

But:

Note that /a/ optionally resists R spreading if it is in initial position (these last three words do have an alternate pronunciation with the initial diphthong *aw*). There is a further constraint on the rounding of /a/ in that it refuses R from the right if its syllable contains /w/, so *wapwi* 'hair', not **wawpwi*. ɨ never resists R spreading, but given that it never occurs in an initial position where the environment for the rule is met, it is impossible to determine whether this is a particular feature of /a/ or of vowels in general. As these examples show, /a/ has a different phonetic realization depending on the direction of R spreading. If R spreads from the left, it is realized as rounding on the consonant (i.e., *pw*, *kw*). If it spreads from the right, it appears as *aw*. The high front vowel /i/ only allows R spreading from the left, and in this case the R is realized on the preceding consonant. Yimas presents no examples of /i/ permitting R to spread from the right, which may be the effect of the feature F; F acts as a barrier for the spread of R. Yimas has no diphthong **iw*, so any rounding on /i/ must be realized on the previous consonant. But this would entail the feature R necessarily crossing F. This possibility the language does not permit (nor does the general theory of autosegmental phonology; association lines may not cross). It is also worth noting that F is only associated with [-peripheral] consonants, exactly that set of consonants which block R spreading.

ɨ plus R is realized phonetically as [u], regardless of the direction of spread. Hence it is impossible in some cases to determine the actual direction of R spreading directly from the phonetic form of a word. Other principles, such as phonological alternations, must be considered. Look at *tupuk* 'sago' above. In this example, the R is shown as spreading from the right. This is determined from the dual form *tupukul*, which shows a harmonized *u* in the suffix. This is easiest to account for without any rule ordering if the adjoining syllable is associated with the underlying R. This spreads to the suffix by rule (2-8).

Now consider words which, if the surface vowels present were ɨ, would be underlyingly vowelless. When the vowels are in fact *u*, similar considerations should apply. Take the example above *numput* 'centipede (sp)'; this word is composed of impermissible clusters and would underlyingly be vowelless. I adopt the convention here of not attaching the autosegment R to either syllable, but spreading it prosodically over the word unanchored. This is indicated by a line extended right and left from R over the word. Both vowel slots in the word arise by rule (2-2), epenthetic vowel insertion. The autosegment R would then be anchored to these:

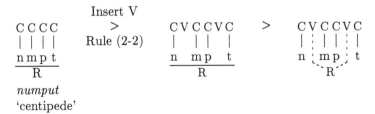

numput
'centipede'

Similar considerations apply to the first two syllables of *kumpunmaŋ* 'black and brown possum'. This word does have an underlying vowel,

/a/ in the final syllable. But this vowel is unrounded, and, furthermore, being separated from the previous vowels by a [-peripheral] consonant /n/, could not possibly spread R to them anyway. But the first two syllables contain vowels that would have arisen from epenthesis, as the consonant clusters would otherwise be impermissible. Thus, the same derivation as that for *numput* 'centipede' applies to these two syllables:

$$
\begin{array}{ccc}
\overset{\displaystyle L}{\underset{\displaystyle |}{}} & & \overset{\displaystyle L}{\underset{\displaystyle |}{}} \\
\underset{\underset{\displaystyle R}{\text{k m p n m} \quad \text{ŋ}}}{\text{C C C C C V C}} & \overset{\text{Insert V}}{\underset{\text{Rule (2-2)}}{>}} & \underset{\underset{\displaystyle R}{\text{k} \quad \text{m p} \quad \text{n m} \quad \text{ŋ}}}{\text{C V C C V C C V C}}
\end{array}
$$

$$
>\quad
\begin{array}{c}
L \\
| \\
\text{C V C C V C C V C} \\
\text{k \; m p \; n m \quad ŋ} \\
R
\end{array}
$$

kumpunmaŋ
'black and brown possum'

A particular feature of Yimas R spreading that argues strongly for an autosegmental approach as opposed to a more traditional segmental one is what might be termed 'floating roundedness', in imitation of the floating tone problem of African languages (Clements and Ford 1979). In Yimas, a high vowel bearing R can be deleted at the level of the segmental CV skeleton, but its associated R autosegment remains and will spread to new vowels inserted by the rule of V insertion. In traditional segmental approaches to phonology, this would be impossible to state without appealing to rule ordering, but in autosegmental approach this is entirely unnecessary. Let us see how it is done.

Yimas has a minor, and somewhat optional, rule which deletes unstressed /u/ at morpheme boundaries in environments that will produce certain acceptable consonant clusters. The clusters which favor this are the following:

(1) any cluster of /r/ plus a stop or nasal

/pu-/ 'go'   + -*ra* REVERSE > *pra* 'come'
/turu-/ 'killing' + -*mat* AGENT > *turmat* 'killers'

(2) any cluster of a stop followed by a homorganic nasal

/yarack/ 'white' + -*uŋ* CLASS IX SG > *yaracukŋ* 'white'

(3) any cluster of nasal plus nasal followed by a stop (in these cases the second nasal deletes as well, see Section 2.3.5)

/pramuŋ/ 'sleep' + -t PERF > *pramut* 'slept'
/pamuŋk/ 'leg' + -l DL > *pamkil* 'legs (DL)'

This rule (which only applies at the segmental level, the autosegment R remaining) can be formalized as follows:

(2-9) Unstressed /u/ deletion

$$
\begin{matrix} \text{V} \\ | \\ \text{R} \end{matrix} \rightarrow \emptyset \quad / \quad \left\{ \begin{matrix} \% & r\begin{matrix} \text{C} \\ \underline{\quad} \text{[-liquid]} \end{matrix} \\ \begin{Bmatrix} \text{stop}\underline{\quad}\text{nasal} \begin{Bmatrix} \# \\ \text{stop} \end{Bmatrix} \\ \text{nasal}\underline{\quad}\text{nasal stop} \end{Bmatrix} \end{matrix} \right\}
$$

This rule commonly operates in tandem with R spreading, as in the following derivation:

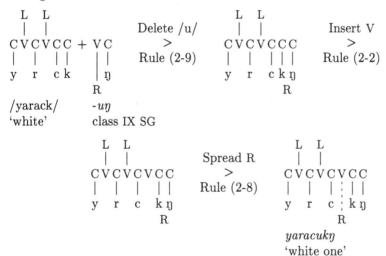

Or as in this example:

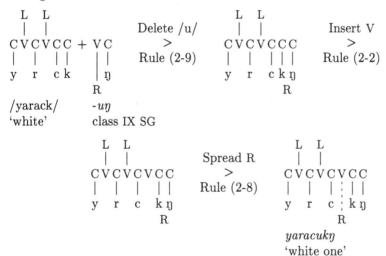

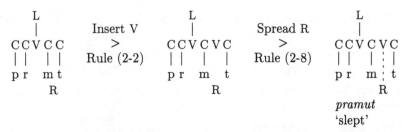

There is a small class of nominal roots, represented by /pamuŋk/ 'leg' which undergo unstressed /u/ deletion (2-9), but do not exhibit R spreading. This set of words is anomalous and must be marked as such in the lexicon (see Section 4.1.10).

This analysis abrogates again any need for rule ordering, as the above derivations are the most problematic ones, in that /u/ deletion was applied first. Yet the correct output is assured. As with R spreading generally, a floating R can spread in both directions, as in the plural of the above form.

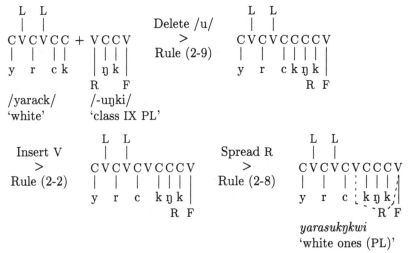

This rule also applies to /a/:

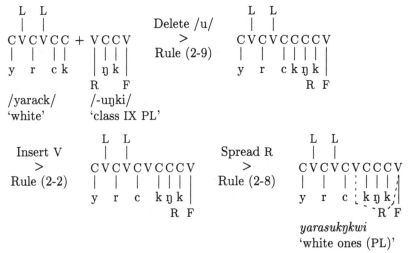

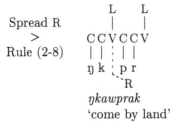

Spread R
>
Rule (2-8)

ŋkawprak
'come by land'

Having presented the basic features of R spreading, it is now necessary to view its interactions with other rules of the language, specifically the rule of palatalization. An interesting feature to note is that those segments which are susceptible to palatalization, the [-peripheral] consonants, are barriers to R spreading; and those which are transparent to R spreading, the [+peripheral] consonants, do not palatalize. Hence, the potential and actual hosts of F are opaque to R, and those which are transparent to R are not potential hosts of F. There seems no way to explicitly represent this correlation, but it does seem noteworthy.

As further illustrations of the interaction of palatalization and R spreading, consider the following:

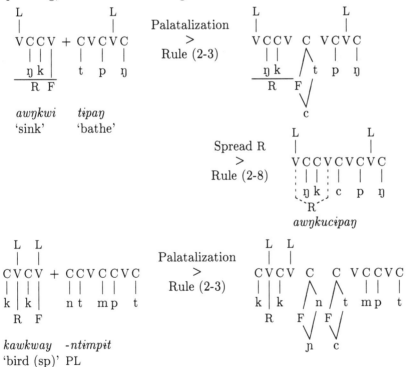

awŋkwi   *tipaŋ*
'sink'   'bathe'

Spread R
>
Rule (2-8)

awŋkucipaŋ

kawkway   *-ntimpit*
'bird (sp)' PL

$$
\begin{array}{l}
\text{Spread R} \\
> \\
\text{Rule (2-8)}
\end{array}
\qquad
\begin{array}{c}
\text{L} \quad \text{L} \\
| \quad | \\
\text{C V C V C C V C C V C} \\
| \; | \; | \; \vdots \; | \; | \quad | \; | \quad | \\
\text{k} \; | \; \text{k} \; \text{j} \; \text{ɲ} \; \text{c} \quad \text{m p} \quad \text{t} \\
\text{R}
\end{array}
$$

kawkwaɲcimpɨt

'birds (sp)'

The reader is advised to try the opposite order of rule application and will discover that the same result is obtained. Again, this analysis works without any extrinsic rule ordering.

The final problem I wish to consider in this section concerns the phonetic realizations of the autosegments. We have seen that the basic realizations are

$$
V = i \qquad V = u \qquad
\begin{array}{c}
\text{L} \\
| \\
\text{V} = ay \\
| \\
\text{F}
\end{array}
\qquad
\begin{array}{c}
\text{L} \\
| \\
\text{V} = aw \\
| \\
\text{R}
\end{array}
$$

with V over F for $V=i$ and V over R for $V=u$.

$\overset{V}{\underset{R}{|}}$ is always realized as u, regardless of the direction of the spreading of R. $\overset{\text{L}}{\underset{R}{\overset{|}{V}}}$, on the other hand, has different realizations depending on the direction of the spread. R spreading from the right is realized as /aw/, as below,

$$
\begin{array}{c}
\text{L} \\
| \\
\text{V} \qquad = aw \\
\vdots \\
\text{R}
\end{array}
$$

while R spread from the left is realized as /wa/.

$$
\begin{array}{c}
\text{L} \\
| \\
\text{V} \qquad = wa \\
\vdots \\
\text{R}
\end{array}
$$

/i/ only allows R spreading from the left. The combination of F and R on a single vowel nucleus is always realized as *wi*.

$$\begin{array}{c} V \\ \wedge \\ R \ F \end{array} = wi$$

Other rules involve the realization of the autosegments as semivowels. Yimas shows free variation in initial position between *i* and *u* and *yi* and *wu*, respectively.

urakatay	~ *wurakatay*	'turtle'
ulɨk	~ *wulɨk*	'put down'
unamara	~ *wunamara*	'centipede'
impram	~ *yimpram*	'basket type'
irɨpm	~ *yirɨpm*	'coconut palm'

This semivowel onset seems to be favored with /u/ and the vowel onset with /i/, but both are acceptable in all cases. This rule can be formalized as follows:

(2-10) Initial semivowel formation

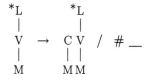

Where M can be either autosegment, F or R. The asterisk on L indicates that the rule does not apply if this feature is attached, i.e., initial $\overset{\text{L}}{\underset{\text{F}}{\text{V}}}$ and $\overset{\text{L}}{\underset{\text{R}}{\text{V}}}$ are realized as *ay* and *aw* respectively, not **yay* and **waw*. This use of the asterisk in phonological rules parallels its use in syntax, to mark unpermitted combinations. The operation of this rule can be illustrated autosegmentally as follows:

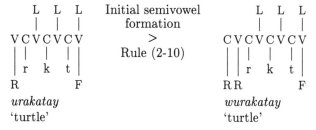

The strong psychological reality of this rule is also indicated by the fact that Yimas people often spell the official name of their village as *Imas*.

This rule also provides evidence to support the earlier claim that some palatal consonants should be taken as underlying palatals, rather than deriving all from the palatalization rule (2-3). Consider *icin* 'salt' and *iciŋan* 'plant (sp)'. These forms freely alternate with *yicin* 'salt' and *yiciŋan* 'plant (sp)'. If the palatal stops /c/ in these forms were derived from the rule of palatalization (2-3), we would get the following incorrect derivation:

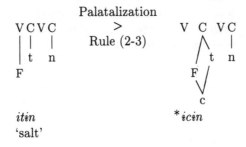

If, on the other hand, we accept the palatal stops as underlying, the free variants are derived easily by the rule of initial semivowel formation (2-10):

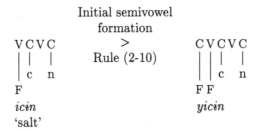

Two similar rules apply word internally before /a/. When a vowel with an associated autosegment precedes /a/, the corresponding semivowel is inserted between the vowel and the /a/. This rule can be formalized as follows (where M = either autosegment):

(2-11)   Medial semivowel formation (I)

$$
\begin{array}{c} \\ V \\ | \\ M \end{array}
\;\rightarrow\;
\begin{array}{c} \\ V\,C \\ |\ | \\ M\,M \end{array}
\;/\;\#\ (C_0 V)^n C_0 \underset{\displaystyle \overset{|}{L}}{\_\_} V
$$

It is illustrated in this example:

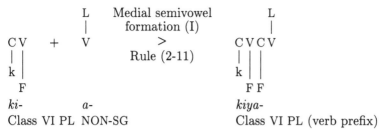

The second rule of medial semivowel formation applies when a morpheme ending in /a/ precedes a morpheme beginning in a vowel associated with an autosegment. Again the corresponding semivowel is inserted between the two vowels.

naka-	+	ul	>	nakawul
1SG/3SG		'put in water'		'I put it in water'

amana-	+	iran	>	amanayiran
1SG PROG		'dance'		'I am dancing'

This rule can be formalized in parallel fashion to (2-11) as follows:

(2-12) Medial semivowel formation (II)

$$
\begin{array}{ccc}
^{*}\text{L} & ^{*}\text{L} & \text{L} \\
| & | & | \\
\text{V} & \to & \text{C V} \quad / \text{ V} + \_\_\ \text{C}^{n} \ (\text{VC}_{0})^{n} \ \# \\
| & | & | \\
\text{M} & \text{M} & \text{M}
\end{array}
$$

The rule is illustrated autosegmentally below:

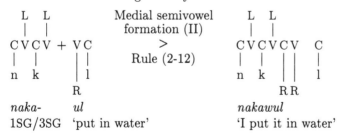

The final rule to consider involving vowels is that of vowel truncation. This occurs at morpheme boundaries when two vowels lacking either autosegment come together. In this case, an optimal rule applies to delete one of these.

amana-	+	amin	>	amanaamin or amanamin
1SG PROG		'eat'		'I am eating'

taka-	+	amit	>	takaamit or takamit
NEG 1SG		'ate'		'I didn't eat'

This rule can be formalized as follows:

(2-13) Vowel truncation (optional)

$$V \rightarrow \emptyset \; / \; V \; + \; \_\_$$
$$\underset{*M}{|} \qquad\qquad \underset{*M}{|}$$

2.3.5 Consonant Truncation

The last set of Yimas phonological rules to be discussed are those involving simplification of clusters consisting of nasals and stops. The first of these rules is obligatory and is the cause of common Yimas alternations in which a final nasal alternates with a medial nasal plus stop cluster.

impram	'basket type'	DL:	*imprampɨl*
wakɨn	'snake'	PL:	*wakɨntɨt*
kaŋ	'shell'	DL:	*kaŋkɨl*
trɨŋ	'tooth'	DL:	*trɨŋkɨl*
ŋarɨm	'branch'	DL:	*ŋarɨmpɨl*

The rule which generates these alternations is one which deletes a final stop after a homorganic nasal.

(2-14) Final nasal + stop cluster simplification

$$\text{stop} \qquad\quad \rightarrow \; \emptyset \; / \qquad \text{nasal} \qquad \_\_ \; \#$$
$$\begin{bmatrix} \alpha \text{ peripheral} \\ \beta \text{ labial} \end{bmatrix} \qquad\qquad\qquad \begin{bmatrix} \alpha \text{ peripheral} \\ \beta \text{ labial} \end{bmatrix}$$

So:

/impramp/	'basket type'	+	∅	SG	>	*impram*
		+	/-ɫ/	DL	>	*imprampɨl*
/trŋk/	'tooth'	+	∅	SG	>	*trɨŋ*
		+	/-ɫ/	DL	>	*trɨŋkɨl*

The second truncation rule is optional, but is a very pervasive feature of Yimas phonology. This involves the deletion at a morpheme boundary of one of two nasals in adjoining syllables, if they are followed by a stop. Note the following alternations:

/tanmp/	'bone'	+	/-ɫ/	DL	>	*tanpɨl* or *tanɨmpɨl*
/nampunmp/	'wing'	+	/-ɫ/	DL	>	*nampunpɨl* or *nampunɨmpɨl*
/kawkrapanŋk/	'red ant'	+	/-ɫ/	DL	>	*kawkrapankɨl* or *kawkrapanɨŋkɨl*
/pamuŋk/	'leg'	+	/-ɫ/	DL	>	*pamkɨl* or *pamuŋkɨl*
/kan-/	'shoot'	+	-*mpi*	SEQ	>	*kanpi* or *kanɨmpi*
/klŋ-/	'remove'	+	-*mpi*	SEQ	>	*kilɨŋpi* or *kilɨŋɨmpi*

Note that it is always the second nasal which drops. For the nominal examples this is the nasal of the underlying final homorganic nasal + stop cluster of the stem, but for the verbs it is the initial nasal of -mpi

SEQ. This rule only applies at morpheme boundaries: for the nominals, the morpheme boundary follows the stop, while for the verbs, it precedes. It will be necessary to represent this difference explicitly in the formal statement of the rule.

While strictly speaking this rule is optional, it does apply in most cases, especially with verb stems + /-mpi/ combinations. This rule only applies if the vowel is high, for words in which the nasals are separated by /a/ do not undergo it.

/paramaŋ/	'large spear'	+ /-l/ DL >	*paramaŋkɨl* *paramkɨl*
/kawknaŋ/	'bird (sp)'	+ /-l/ DL >	*kawkunaŋkɨl* *kawkunkɨl*
/antmaŋ/	'sulphur crested cockatoo'	+ /-l/ DL >	*antamaŋkɨl* *antamkɨl*

So the rule must be formalized in a way to exclude the low vowel. I suggest the following representation:

(2-15) Nasal truncation

$$\overset{*\text{L}}{\underset{\pm}{\text{nasal} \rightarrow \emptyset / \text{nasal (V)} + \underline{\quad} \text{stop} +}}$$

The use of the convention └─┴─┘ is borrowed from tagmemics (Elson and Pickett 1962). It indicates that one of the two units must be present, but not both. This will handle the varying position of the morpheme boundary for this rule.

This completes the presentation of the general segmental phonological rules of Yimas. There are a number of other minor rules, which involve one or two morphemes and will be treated when these particular morphemes are discussed in the relevant sections of the morphology (Chapters 3 to 6). Now I will turn to the suprasegmental phonology, but before that, I offer a short aside on the phonology of reduplication.

2.4 Reduplication

Reduplication is a rather uncommon feature of Yimas and mainly applies productively for verb stems to express repeated action over a short period of time. Reduplications can be full, in which the whole stem (minus the final stop in a few cases) is reduplicated, or partial, in which a non-initial consonant plus an adjoining low vowel are reduplicated. There are no meaning differences between these two, but different verb roots choose either full or partial reduplications in essentially the same construction. Which type of reduplication a verb favors must be stated in its lexical entry. Examples of full reduplications follow:

ark-	'break'	arkark-
kan-	'shoot'	kankan-
kwaɲca-	'cut up'	kwaɲcakwaɲca-
tay-	'see'	tacay-
arɨm-	'jump down'	arɨmarɨm-
am-	'eat'	amam-
way-	'turn'	wayway-
ant-	'hear'	antant-
tɨkak-	'pull'	tɨkatɨkak-
aykwara-	'jump'	aykwaraykwara-

There are a couple of cases of completely irregular full reduplication for common verbs.

| taw- | 'sit' | tantaw- |
| pay- | 'carry' | pampay- |

These forms will need to be stipulated in the lexicon for these verbs.

Note that, as in the example of *tacay* < *tay* 'see', phonological rules such as palatalization apply to the forms produced by reduplication. Forms such as *tɨkatɨkak* < *tɨkak* 'pull' indicate that reduplication in Yimas is to the left, i.e., the copied stem precedes the base stem, for in cases like these the first stem is lacking the final consonant.

Further evidence that Yimas reduplication is leftward is provided by partial reduplication. In these cases a non-initial consonant or homorganic nasal plus stop cluster and an adjoining low vowel is reduplicated to the left. If there is no adjoining low vowel, only the consonant is reduplicated. Consider the following examples in which the reduplicated segments of the base are underlined for convenience:

<u>a</u>pi-	'put in'	apapi-
<u>apan</u>-	'shoot'	apapan-
<u>awk</u>ura-	'gather'	awkawkura-
w<u>ark</u>-	'make'	waratɨk-
p<u>ark</u>-	'cut up'	paratɨk-
y<u>ara</u>-	'get'	yarata-
<u>ira</u>y-	'cry'	iratay-
ar<u>pal</u>-	'go out'	arpapal-
i<u>rm</u>-	'stand'	irɨtɨm-
wu<u>l</u>-	'put down'	wurɨt-
ta<u>l</u>-	'hold'	tarat-
pam<u>paŋ</u>-	'fix'	pampampaŋ-
wam<u>pak</u>i-	'throw'	wampampaki-

There is also one verb root irregularly reduplicated with partial reduplication.

ira- 'dance' *iranta-*

In examples of partial reduplication involving /r/, the second /r/ becomes *t* by the /r/ dissimilation rule (2-6). The fact that the final /l/ of *wul-* 'put down' and *tal-* 'hold' appears as /r/ in their reduplications is the result of the rule of dissimilative F loss (2-7). Note that only the vowel /a/ occurs in reduplications. We find *park* 'cut up' > *paratik*, but *wul* 'put down' > *wurit*, **wurut*. This can be accounted for by claiming that reduplication copies the C's of the CV skeletal structure, plus any vowel with the upper feature L, but not the vowel autosegments F and R. So we have

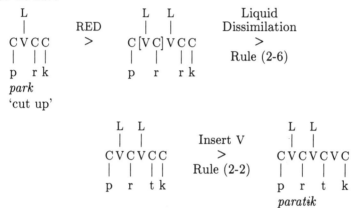

but

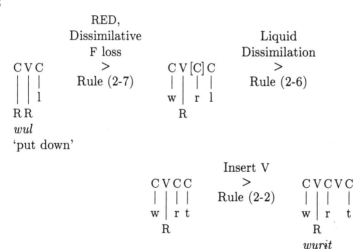

Accepting the argument that autosegments associated with vowels cannot be copied, then *awkura-* > *awkawkura-* provides additional evidence for leftward reduplication. The R autosegment on the first syllable would not be present in the basic reduplicated form, but would be the result of R spreading from the adjoining syllable on the right. Note that the form *aw* is the proper realization for R spreading from the right. The following derivation is then proposed:

```
  L     L             L   L     L                    L  L      L
  |     |    RED       |   |     |    Spread R        |  |      |
V C V C V    >      [V C] V C V C V       >         V C V C V C V
| | | |            | | | | | |       Rule (2-8)     : | | | | |
| k | r            k   k | r                        : k | k | r
R   R              R   R                            : `R   R
awkura-                                             awkawkura-
'gather'
```

This analysis is confirmed by a form like *timayk-* 'call', with partial reduplication *timamayk*, not **timaymayk*. Note that F does not occur in the reduplicated syllable. Further, as F does not normally spread, the vowel in this syllable remains /a/.

```
L
|           RED                   Insert V
C C V C     >      C [C V] C V C     >        C V C V C V C
| | | |           | |   | | |    Rule (2-2)   | | | | | |
t m | k           t m   m | k                 t m   m | k
    F                   F                           F
timayk                                        timamayk-
'call'
```

Other examples supporting this analysis are *warpayn* 'close' reduplicated as *warpapayn* not **warpaypayn*, and most strikingly *tumwik* 'to smoke (fish)' reduplicated as *tumumwik* not **tum(w)imwik*. The latter example has the following derivation:

```
                    RED                   Insert V
    C V C V C       >      C V [C] C V C     >
    | | | | |             | | | | | |    Rule (2-2)
    t | m | k             t | m m | k
    R   F                 R     F
tumik                     tumik
'smoke (fish)'
```

tumumwik

The reduplication of *tay* > *tacay* is not a counterexample to this claim, as this must be a full reduplication, there being no medial consonant. Full reduplications are just that, copied in full, without the diagnostic autosegment truncation of partial reduplication. These facts would suggest that the feature L on the upper tier is in fact much more intimately associated with the CV skeletal structure than the autosegments F and R. Given that these other two, especially the latter, also show such prosodic tendencies, this conclusion would indeed seem warranted.

2.5 Suprasegmentals

The suprasegmental feature that Yimas presents is stress. Stress is marked phonetically by a higher pitch on the syllable and a somewhat lengthened vowel. Stress is not distinctive in Yimas, i.e., there are no pairs of words which are distinguished from each other only in terms of which syllable carries stress, parallel to English examples like désert (noun) versus desért (verb), próduce (noun), prodúce (verb), présent (noun), presént (verb). Rather, Yimas stress is essentially predictable by a simple rule: assign primary stress to the first syllable of the word and secondary stress to the third syllable, if the word is longer than three syllables. Some examples are given in the table at the top of the next page.

The rules which supply stress can be stated formally as follows:

(2-16) Primary stress rule

$$V \rightarrow [1\ stress]\ /\ \#\ C_0 \_\_$$

(2-17) Secondary stress rule

$$V \rightarrow [2\ stress]\ \#\ C_0VC_0VC_0 \_\_ ([C_0V]^n)C_0VC_0\ \#$$

It is important to note that the input to these rules specify V. These stress rules apply to the underlying forms of words, hence it is the first underlying vowel of the word which takes primary stress. Thus, if the first phonetic vowel of the word is epenthetic, it will not affect stress, and the actual stress bearing syllable will be that which is phonetically second. The following words of varying lengths illustrate this.

Disyllabic roots:

wáŋkaŋ	'bird (sp)'	*ácan*	'send'
áwak	'star'	*ŋárwa*	'penis'
wárpayn	'close'	*múraŋ*	'paddle'
kíaŋ	'cough'	*núŋkraym*	'toe'
kwálcan	'arise'		

Trisyllabic roots:

áwtmayŋi	'sugarcane'	*námarawt*	'person'
málcawkwa	'lower backside'	*páɲcamuŋ*	'pillow'
wárkapwi	'wallaby'	*táŋkarmaŋ*	'young girl'
tántayŋkraym	'spider'	*yámparan*	'stand up'
wálamuŋ	'type of basket'	*kúlanaŋ*	'walk'

Tetrasyllabic roots:

máraŋàpa	'type of basket'	*wúratàkay*	'turtle'
wánkanàwi	'insect (sp)'	*tápukànɨŋ*	'type of green fruit'
wúnamàra	'large centipede'	*kámantàrɨm*	'bamboo'
ímpɨnpàra	'basket for serving fruit'	*námaràwi*	'bird of paradise (sp)'

Pentasyllabic roots:

mámantàkarman	'land crab'	*náŋkranùmpunɨŋ*	'tree (sp)'
árakukunawt	'bird of paradise (sp)'	*yáwkawpùnumprum*	'yellow possum'
yámpukàɲumpuk	'caterpillar'		

/pkam/	*pɨkám*	'skin of back'
/tkay/	*tɨkáy*	'nose'
/tmal/	*tɨmál*	'sun'
/tpuk/	*tupúk*	'sago pancake'
/tmi/	*tɨmí*	'say'
/mpnawŋ/	*mpunáwŋ*	'elbow'
/tnum/	*tɨnúm*	'sago palm (sp)'
/mkrayŋ/	*mɨkráyŋ*	'cane'
/tnwantŋ/	*tɨnwántɨŋ*	'2 days removed from today'
/kcakk/	*kɨcákɨk*	'cut'
/tparpuŋ/	*tɨpárpuŋ*	'fish (sp)'
/tmarmaŋ/	*tɨmármaŋ*	'possum'
/kpanmaŋ/	*kɨpánmaŋ*	'older sister' (♀ ego)
/nmpanmara/	*nɨmpánmara*	'stomach'
/klakyanŋ/	*kɨlákyanɨŋ*	'parrot (sp)'

There is a further twist to this. Yimas has a surface phonetic constraint that one of the first two syllables of the phonetic form of the word must carry primary stress. If both vowels of the first two syllables are epenthetic, then the first one carries stress.

/tkt/	*tɨkɨt*	'chair'
/mɲŋ	*mɨɲɨŋ*	'tongue'
/nmprm/	*nɨmprɨm*	'leaf'
/nmkŋn/	*nɨmkɨŋɨn*	'below'
/wɲcmpt/	*wɨɲcɨmpɨt*	'name'
/tpnm/	*tɨpɨnɨm*	'spear point'
/krmknawt/	*krɨmkɨnawt*	'wasp'
/klwa/	*kɨlɨwa*	'flower (sp)'
/klŋpaŋ/	*kɨlɨŋpaŋ*	'worm'
/pwɲcnŋ/	*pwɨɲcɨnɨŋ*	'rafters of house'
/ɲclŋ/	*ɨɲcɨlɨŋ*	'palm tree (sp)'
/tŋkntkn/	*tɨŋkɨntɨkɨn*	'heavy'
/tmpnawkwan/	*tɨmpɨnàwkwan*	'sago palm (sp)'

There is a slight irregularity in pentasyllabic words of this type: when the vowel of the third syllable is also epenthetic, stress is retracted to the penultimate syllable, as in these examples:

/kntkcki/	*kɨntɨkɨcɨki*	'bird (sp)'
/tŋkmpɲawa/	*tɨŋkɨmpɨɲàwa*	'wild fowl'

An interesting problem concerns words in which the first two vowels in the phonetic form of the word are [u]. Note the contrast between [tupúk] 'sago pancake' and [túmpun] 'clouds'. The stress difference between these can be accounted for by proposing the following underlying forms:

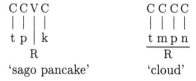

The form for 'sago pancake' contains an underlying vowel to which the autosegment R is anchored. Because the word contains an underlying vowel, this receives primary stress. The surface phonetic form is derived by vowel epenthesis (2-2) to break up the impermissible initial cluster, followed by R spreading (2-8). The form for 'cloud', on the other hand, is simply a sequence of consonants associated with the autosegment R, which is not anchored to any specific V position. Because it lacks any underlying vowels, primary stress will be applied to the first syllable of the surface phonetic form, which is derived as follows. Vowel epenthesis

(2-2) applies, breaking up the impermissible initial and final consonant clusters. The autosegment R is then associated with the epenthetic vowels. Other examples of words like *tuÍmpuŋ* 'cloud' are

núŋkup	'stove'
túmpuntut	'morning'
túpunɨŋ	'firefly'
púpurɨŋ	'tree (sp)'
túmpukut	'cane (sp)'
úpuntàmpɨŋ	'heart'
kúmpunkàmanuŋ	'buttock'

Yet another complication to stress assignment in Yimas is found with many disyllabic or trisyllabic words with underlying vowels in the first two syllables, especially when these vowels are /a/. In such cases, the primary stress varies freely between the first or second syllable.

áwa	∼ *awá*	'cassowary'
píam	∼ *piám*	'arrow'
yáwran	∼ *yawrán*	'pick up'
kíka	∼ *kiká*	'rat'
mácawk	∼ *macáwk*	'father-in-law'
yúan	∼ *yuán*	'good'
áwtmayŋi	∼ *awtmáyŋi*	'sugarcane'
yánara	∼ *yanára*	'bark of clove tree'
pámpaŋin	∼ *pampáŋin*	'correct'
wámpakin	∼ *wampákin*	'throw'
kúnapa	∼ *kunápa*	'mushroom'

To handle such forms, the following supplementary rule must be added to the primary stress rule (2-16):

(2-18)　Variant primary stress rule

$$V \rightarrow [1 \text{ stress}] \ / \ \# \ C_0V \quad C_0 \_\_ (C_0V)^n C_0VC_0 \ \#$$
$$[-\text{stress}]$$

Thus, if the primary stress rule (2-16) does not apply to disyllabic or trisyllabic words, then rule (2-18) obligatorily applies. Otherwise, the resulting phonetic form would be unstressed and hence unacceptable.

　　Morphologically complex forms with suffixes also require some additional stipulations. The number suffixes of nouns (and the corresponding adjectival/possessive concord suffixes, as these formally derive nominals; see Section 4.6) typically occur with secondary stress.

	SG	DL	PL
'leg'	*pámuŋ*	*pámkìl*	*pámkì*
'paddle'	*múraŋ*	*múraŋkìl*	*múraŋkì*
'nose'	*tɨkáy*	*tɨkáɲcrɨm*	*tɨkákyŋkàt*
'chair'	*tɨkɨt*	*tɨkɨtntrɨm*	*tɨkɨrŋkàt*
'big'	*kɨpáŋ*	*kɨpáŋkɨl*	*kɨpáŋkì*
'grasshopper'	*wánwanɨŋ*	*wánwankɨl*	*wánwankì*
'fruit (sp)'	*núŋkrumùnɨŋ*	*núŋkrumùnkɨl*	*núŋkrumùnkì*
'land crab'	*mámantàkarman*	*mámantàkarmantrɨm*	*mámantàkarmankàt*

This can be stated formally as follows:

(2-19) Nominal suffix stress rule

$$V \rightarrow [2 \text{ stress}] \; / \; C_0 \; V \; C_0 \,] \quad + \quad [C_0 \underline{\quad} C_0]$$

$$\text{Noun} \qquad \text{Noun Class}$$
$$\text{Number}$$

Another morphologically induced stress peculiarity concerns adjectival verbs (see Section 3.3). The final vowel of the root of these always take secondary stress when followed by the irrealis tense suffix -*k* and a nominal concord marker, regardless of the number of syllables of the stem. Examples follow. (The concord marker is -*n* for class V singular).

wálɲàkɨn	'light'
káwŋkràkɨn	'long'
wácàkɨn	'small'
tíŋkɨntɨkɨn	'heavy'
yáracìkɨn	'white'
kántamàkɨn	'new'
úrkupwicàkɨn	'black'
áraŋalcàkɨn	'stubborn, proud'

The rule assigning secondary stress to these forms can be stated explicitly as follows:

(2-20) Adjectival verb root stress rule

$$V \rightarrow [2 \text{ stress}] \; / \; \underline{\quad}] \quad + \quad -k] \quad + \quad [C_0 \; V \; C_0]$$

$$\text{Adjectival} \quad \text{TNS} \qquad \text{Concord}$$
$$\text{Verb}$$

Note that this rule blocks the operation of the secondary stress rule (2-17) for the pentasyllabic words. Normally, these would have secondary stress on the antepenultimate syllable by rule (2-17), but rule (2-20) is more restricted in its domain and hence overrides it, so that the secondary stress appears on the penultimate syllable, the final syllable of the roots.

The final morphologically induced peculiarity of stress concerns verbs inflected with pronominal prefixes (see Section 5.1.1). These are nor-

mally unstressed, and the primary and secondary stress rules apply to
the root (in the glosses, A marks the subject of a transitive verb and O
its object).

(2-21) a. pia-ka-timí
         words O-1SG A-say
         'I talked.'

      b. na-mpu-wapát-ɲcut
         3SG O-3PL A-climb-RM PAST
         'They climbed it (the tree).'

      c. nan-áwkura-na   amtra
         PL IMP-gather-IMP   food V PL
         'Collect food!'

In each of these cases the primary stress assigns stress to the verb root
as if there were no prefixal syllables; in other words, they are ignored
for the purposes of the stress rules.

2.6 Boundaries and the Notion of the Word

If one approaches the notion of word from a formal perspective, it is
clear that it can be defined in either of two ways: either by phonological
criteria or by morphosyntactic ones. (Di Sciullo and Williams (1987)
have recently proposed that this latter actually disguises two distinct
types of criteria for the word, morphological ones versus syntactic ones.
They propose some very useful and interesting ideas, but for the purposes here we will treat both of these types under the single category
of morphosyntactic criteria). A word can be determined by phonological criteria in terms of the rules, both segmental and suprasegmental,
whose domain is specified with respect to this notion. For example,
Yimas provides a number of rules which help us to determine words.
The final nasal plus stop cluster simplification rule (2-14) only applies
at the ends of words; initial semivowel formation (2-10) only applies at
the beginning of words; and most of the other rules, such as R spreading
(2-8), (but not, notably, palatalization (2-3)) occur internally to a word.
In addition, the stress rules of Yimas discussed in the previous section
also help to define the word, for they supply to every word unit at least
a primary stress and possibly one or more secondary stresses. Thus, any
string of phonemes which behave as a unit with respect to these rules can
be designated as a word and set off by the word boundaries before and
after it. So because the underlying phoneme sequence /awklmp/ 'wrist'
is realized phonetically as [áwkulɨm] (from initial syllable primary stress
(2-16), vowel epenthesis (2-2), R spreading (2-8), and final nasal plus

stop cluster simplification (2-14)), we know that it constitutes a single word with the placement of word boundaries thus /# awklmp #/.

Turning now to morphosyntactic criteria, we can state analogously that a word is a string of morphemes that behaves as a single unit with respect to morphological processes in the language. The strictly morphological processes of a language, of course, are a language-specific fact: some languages such as Vietnamese may have no morphological processes at all; others, like Yimas, have an exuberance of these. Let me first consider the morphological patterns of nouns in Yimas. Nouns are marked for number in Yimas, as well as case. Thus, consider the above noun 'wrist' inflected for these two categories: /awklmp + l + nan/ wrist + DL + OBL realized phonetically as [áwkulɨmbìtɲan] 'on the two wrists'. The plus sign here is used conventionally to mark a morpheme boundary, i.e., a boundary between morphemes internal to a word. This form is morphologically a single composite unit. The morphemes must occur in this order and no other:

/awklmp + l + nan/ wrist + DL + OBL,
*/awklmp + nan + l/ wrist + OBL + DL,
*/l + awklmp + nan/ DL + wrist + OBL, etc.

Further, no other morphemes may be inserted internal to this sequence:

*/awklmp + kpa + l + nan/ wrist + big + DL + OBL,
*/awklmp + l + kpa + nan/ wrist + DL + big + OBL,
*/awklmp + prpal + l + nan/ wrist + two + DL + OBL,
*/awklmp + l + prpal + nan/ wrist + DL + two + OBL.

From the grammatical point of view, this noun forms a composite unit, a word, and should therefore be represented as /# awklmp + l + nan #/, with both the internal morpheme boundaries + and the external word boundary # indicated.

Note that the grammatical criteria in this case coincide with the phonological criteria in defining this as a single word-level unit. Whereas the uninflected form /awklmp/ undergoes final nasal plus stop cluster simplification (2-14) to surface as [áwkulɨm], thus indicating a word boundary, this rule fails to apply to /awklmp + l + nan/, which is realized as [áwkulɨmbìtɲan]. This leaves no doubt that there is no word boundary between the root for 'wrist' and the DL suffix in this form. This is buttressed by the fact that the /p/ is voiced to [b] following the nasal. Postnasal voicing of stops in Yimas is all but obligatory internal to a word. Further, the liquid strengthening rule (2-5) applies in this form between the /-l/ DL and the initial /n/ of the oblique suffix /-nan/. This rule, like most phonological rules treated earlier, is restricted to applying internally to the word across morpheme boundaries. (Palatalization (2-3) is the one exception here: it does commonly apply across word boundaries.) Clearly, then, both the grammatical criteria and the phonological criteria unambiguously identify /awklmp + l + nan/ wrist + DL + OBL [áwkulìmbítɲan] as a single word.

Similar considerations apply to adjectives. Consider the form of the adjective 'big' which would modify the inflected noun above: /kpa + mp + l/ big + class VII + DL, realized as [kìpámbìl]. This demonstrates that adjectives are inflected for the class and number of their modified noun. Again the ordering of morphemes is rigid.

*/kpa + l + mp/ big + DL + class VII,
*/mp + kpa + l/ class VII + PL + big;

and nothing may be inserted between the morphemes.

*/kpa + prpal + mp + l/ big + two + class VII + DL,
*/kpa + mp + prpal + l/ big + class VII + two + DL,
*/kpa + plak + mp + l/ big + this + class VII + DL,
*/kpa + mp + plak + l/ big + class VII + this + DL.

All this indicates that /kpa + mp + l/ big + class VII + DL is a composite unit, a single word. Again the phonological criteria bring down the same verdict. The class VII concord marker /-mp/ appears phonetically as [mp], rather than as its word final allomorph [m] derived by final nasal plus stop cluster simplification (2-14). Clearly there is no word boundary between the class VII concord marker and the DL suffix, so that the form can be established as /# kpa + mp + l #/.

The coincidence between phonological and grammatical criteria for determining word boundaries vanishes, however, when we turn to verbs. They are by far the most morphologically complex part of speech in Yimas, but here I will concern myself only with negation and valence-increasing, both of which are marked by prefixes. Negation is an especially good diagnostic of words, for it affects both the first morpheme of a word and the last. Negation is marked by a prefix *ta-*. which occupies the first prefixal slot of the verb, usurping the normal occupier of this slot, a pronominal prefix, and shifting this to the final suffixal slot of the word. Thus, consider the following pair:

(2-22) a. tampaym   p-ka-apca-t
         hook VII SG   VII SG O-1SG A-hang up-PERF
         'I hung up the hook.'
      b. tampaym   ta-ka-apca-r-m
         hook VII SG   NEG-1SG A-hang up-PERF-VII SG O
         'I didn't hang up the hook.'

Example (b) corresponds to (a) as negative to positive. Note that the pronominal prefix *p-* in (a) appears as the corresponding suffix *-m* in the negative example (b), as a result of its position being usurped by the initial negative prefix *ta-*. Thus, we define the string flanked on both sides by these affixes as a word, using the behavior of negation as a grammatical criterion for determining words.

Unfortunately, this grammatical criterion is often at odds with phonological ones. Consider this example with an incorporated nominal (S marks the subject of an intransitive verb):

(2-23) mamam   p-na-waca-k-m-tɨ-n
        sore VII SG   VII SG S-DEF-small-IRR-VII SG-become-PRES
        'The sore is getting smaller.'

waca-k-m small-IRR-VII SG is a derived nominal incorporated into the verb and forming a grammatical unit with it (see Section 6.2.3.1.3). This is clearly demonstrated by the fact that when rule (2-23) is negated, the usurped pronominal prefix *p-* becomes the suffix *-m* at the end of the word, following the tense suffix *-nt* PRES.

(2-24) a. mamam
           sore VII SG

           ta-na-waca-k-m-tɨ-nt-m
           NEG-DEF-small-IRR-VII SG-become-PRES-VII SG S

           'The sore isn't getting smaller.'

        b.*mamam
           sore VII SG

           ta-na-waca-k-m-m-tɨ-n
           NEG-DEF-small-IRR-VII SG-VII SG S-become-PRES

Other pieces of evidence that this is a single grammatical word are the behavior of valence-increasing prefixes. For example, if a causative is derived from (2-23), the causative prefix *tar-* ~ *tal-* can precede the incorporated nominal.

(2-25) marasin   mamam
        medicine V SG   sore VII SG

        p-n-na-tar-waca-k-m-tɨ-n
        VII SG O-3SG A-DEF-CAUS-small-IRR-VII SG-become-PRES

        'The medicine made the sore smaller.'

The whole sequence *waca-k-m-tɨ-* small-IRR-VII SG-become 'become small' is causativized by *tar-* CAUS, again demonstrating that it functions as a grammatical unit.

While the verbs in (2-23) and (2-24) are single words by grammatical criteria, they are not so on phonological grounds. Consider the incor-

porated nominal *waca-k-m* small-IRR-VII SG again. Note that the class
and number concord marker appears as the word final allomorph -*m*
and not the word medial (and underlying) form -*mp*. This indicates a
word boundary between -*m* and the verb *ti̇-* 'become'. Stress patterns
also indicate two words, as the stress pattern for the verb in (2-23) is
p-na-wácà-k-m-ti̇-n, with both *waca-k-n* and *ti̇-* being assigned stress
independently (remember as discussed above, the pronominal prefixes
are unstressed and ignored by the stress rules when assigning stress).
So on phonological criteria, the word would be represented as /# p-
na-waca-k-m # ti̇-n #/, while on grammatical criteria it would be /#
p-na-waca-k-m-ti̇-n #/. Clearly, this is contradictory, and in order to
solve this dilemma, it is necessary to appeal to two different notions of
word, a phonological word and a grammatical word. With the earlier
discussion of nouns and adjectives, this was not necessary, as the two
criteria types coincided (although in treating noun compounds a similar
distinction would need to be invoked in English as well as Yimas; see
Di Sciullo and Williams 1987). But with verbs, this distinction is clearly
needed. Phonological words are those word units defined by phonological
criteria, while grammatical words are those determined by grammatical
criteria. Units defined as words in Yimas by the segmental phonological
rules and stress rules are phonological words; I will henceforth use the
word boundary symbol to indicate the boundaries of phonological words.
Sequences which behave as integrated units with respect to grammatical
processes like valence changing and negative (among others) are grammatical words. The boundaries of grammatical words have no special
symbol. Rather, I will use the practical orthography to indicate these.
Sequences of verbal morphemes that I write as single words correspond
to grammatical words (they may, of course, also correspond to phonological words), and the sub-word morphological units will be set off from
each other by hyphens.

Another interesting example of the contrast between phonological
and grammatical words involves the very common Yimas construction
of verb compounding or serialization, in which two or more verb roots
join to form a complex verb, as seen in examples such as these:

(2-26) a. uraŋknut
         coconut meat IX PL

         ura-mpu-nták-mpi-ɲá-ntut
         IX PL O-3PL A-leave-SEQ-stay-RM PAST
         'They left the coconut meat.'

      b. mamparŋkat
         branches V PL

ya-mpu-párk-mpi-kápik-mpi-wárk-t
V PL O-3PL A-split-SEQ-break-SEQ-tie-PERF
'They split the branches, broke (them) and tied (them).'

Each of these verbs corresponds to more than one phonological word, as shown by the number of primary stresses marked in each example. Yet they each clearly correspond to one grammatical word. First of all, negation applies to the verb as a whole, demoting the first pronominal prefix to the end of the full sequence of morphemes.

(2-27) a. uraŋknut
    coconut meat IX PL

    ta-mpu-nták-mpi-ɲá-ntuk-ut
    NEG-3PL A-leave-SEQ-stay-RM PAST-IX PL O
    'They didn't leave the coconut meat.'

  b. mamparŋkat
    branch V PL

    ta-mpu-párk-mpi-kápik-mpi-wárk-ra
    NEG-3PL A-split-SEQ-break-SEQ-tie-V PL O
    'They didn't split the branches, break (them) and tie
    (them).'

Further, valence increasing also applies to the verb compound as a whole. Consider the examples above in (2-26) in combination with *taŋ-* COM, indicating an action done for the benefit of someone present (see Section 6.2.3.3).

(2-28) a. uraŋknut
    coconut meat IX PL

    ura-mpu-kra-taŋ-nták-mpi-ɲá-ntut
    IX PL T-3PL A-1PL D-COM-leave-SEQ-stay-RM PAST
    'They left the coconut meat with us.'

  b. mamparŋkat
    branch V PL

    ya-mpu-ŋa-taŋ-párk-mpi-kápik-mpi-wárk-t
    V PL T-3PL A-1SG D-COM-split-SEQ-break-SEQ-tie-PERF
    'They split branches, broke (them) and tied (them) for me.'

Interestingly, it is in the area of compounds where nouns also show a split between the phonological and grammatical word, albeit not as extreme as that for the verbs. Yimas has a productive system of noun compounding employing the oblique case suffix on the first member of the compound, rather like the use of the genitive case in German noun compounds.

(2-29) a. kálk-n   ápra
           sago pudding V SG-OBL   plate VII PL
           'plates of sago pudding'
        b. núm-n   númpran
           village SG-OBL pig III SG
           'domesticated pig'

Each of the nouns in these compounds constitute a phonological word in
themselves, as shown by the individual primary stresses. Yet they form
one grammatical word in that there is only one inflection for number,
and this on the head (rightmost) noun:

(2-30) a. num-n   numpray
           village SG-OBL pig III PL
           'domesticated pigs'
        b.*numkat-n   numpray
           village PL-OBL pig III PL

Further, the noun class and number of the whole compound is that of
the head noun; modifiers of the compound exhibit only its specifications
for their concord suffix.

(2-31) a. kalk-n   apra   kpa-ra
           sago pudding V SG-OBL   plate VII PL big-VII PL
           'big plates of sago pudding'
        b.*kalk-n   apra   kpa-n
           sago pudding V SG-OBL   plate VII PL big-V SG

The latter is ungrammatical because the adjective registers concord with
the internal noun *kalk* 'sago pudding'. The prohibition on number inflection for the internal noun and the impermissibility of concord with
it is explicable if we conclude that these are single grammatical words
with grammatical features being determined by the head noun (see also
discussion of nominal compounding in Di Sciullo and Williams 1987).

As the nominal complexes in (2-29) have been established as single
grammatical words, according to the writing conventions propounded
above, strictly speaking they should be written all together as a single word. I do not do this in noun compounds for two reasons. First,
they are closely paralleled by many productive English noun compounds,
which by the conventions of English phonology are typically written as
separate words (see Palmer 1984). But more significantly, this differential application of my conventions to nouns and verbs as grammatical
words reflects an important difference between them. With the exception of the oblique suffix, the units which make up noun compounds are
words in their own right, both phonological and grammatical, and can

be used as independent nouns in other constructions. I use the convention of writing them separately to indicate this freedom of occurrence. But this is definitely not true of most of the types of units which come together to form a verbal grammatical unit. Consider this example:

(2-32) na-mpɨ-yákal-cántaw-ánt-ntut
        3SG O-3DL A-CONT-sit-hear-RM PAST
        'They both sat listening to him.'

This is a single grammatical word, but three phonological words, as indicated by the primary stresses. Of the six formal units which make up this word, only two (*tantaw-* 'sit down' and *ánt-* 'hear', as verb roots) can independently occur in a wide range of constructions, parallel to the nouns in the above noun compounds. The other four are grammatical morphemes like inflectional affixes in more familiar languages. Of special interest is the continuative aspect marker *yakal-*. While a phonological word, it can never function as a verb root or on its own. It is restricted to occurring before a following verb or verb compound as the means of expressing its aspectual character. The great majority of morpheme types which constitute a verbal grammatical word are like this, and for this reason I follow the convention of writing these as a single orthographic word.

2.7 A Note on Orthography

In the remainder of this book I will use a standardized practical orthography for writing Yimas. (I have already used this in the final examples of the previous section.) It is essentially a compromise between the underlying systematic phonemic representations and the taxonomic phonemic forms, but with a closer approach to the latter. For example, final stops which are deleted by the final nasal plus stop cluster simplification rule (2-14) will not be written. Thus, the underlying /awklmp/ 'wrist' will be written as awklm. This reflects a surface phonemic representation. Vowels, on the other hand, reflect more closely the underlying representations. Epenthetic vowels will not be written, but *u* (i.e., $\underset{R}{\text{y}}$) presents

some problems. Because of R spreading, it is not always possible to determine which syllable, if any, is linked to the autosegment R (see Section 2.3.4). A case in point is *tupuniŋ* 'firefly'. Underlyingly this would be represented as

$$
\begin{array}{cccc}
\text{C} & \text{C} & \text{C} & \text{C} \\
| & | & | & | \\
\text{t} & \text{p} & \text{n} & \text{ŋ} \\
\hline
\multicolumn{4}{c}{\text{R}}
\end{array}
$$

with R hovering over the first two syllables (it cannot spread further to the right, because /n/, a [-peripheral] consonant, blocks R spreading).

However, in reducing this underlying representation to a practical orthography, the problem remains: in which syllable do we write the u? In these cases, I adopt the convention of writing the $u$in the first, the stressed, syllable.

Note that no such problem applies to *tumpukut* 'cane (sp)'. Because R spreading applies in both directions, but to only one syllable, either of the following are possible as underlying representations for this word:

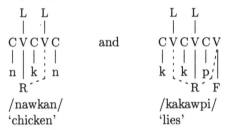

Because the latter provides an unambiguous orthographic representation, I will use this and write the word as tmpukt. All results of R spreading with other vowels such as *aw, wa* or *wi* will be reflected in the practical orthography, as illustrated below:

```
    L  L                          L  L
    |  ·|                         |   |
    C V C V C         and         C V C V C V
    | | | : |                     | : | | |
    n | k ; n                     k ; k | p;|
    R ̆                          ̆R ́ F
  /nawkan/                      /kakawpi/
  'chicken'                     'lies'
```

will be written as nawkwan and kawkawpwi, respectively. This seems necessary because R spreading in these cases produces a segment *w* rather than just rounding the vowel. Finally, initial *w* as a result of initial semivowel formation (2-10) will also be orthographically represented; thus /ut/ 'night' becomes orthographic wut. This will not be done with initial *y* resulting from the same rule. This difference in orthographic convention reflects the more common pronunciation.

Consonants contrast with vowels in the orthography in that their writing conventions approach their surface phonetic realizations more closely. This was already mentioned with the case of final stops following nasals. Any underlying consonant which undergoes a phonological rule of Section 2.3, such as palatalization (2-3) or liquid strengthening (2-4, 2-5), will be written as the derived segment, not the underlying one. Thus /taŋkway + takal + k/ 'look after' will be written as taŋkwaycakalk (palatalization), /apur/ 'green skink' as aput (final liquid strengthening), and /tal + na + k/ 'hold it' as tatɲak (palatalization plus prenasal liquid strengthening).

3

Word Classes

Yimas has only two major, open classes of words, nouns and verbs; all other classes are small and closed. The inventory of the closed classes is the following:

adjectives	pronouns
quantifiers	deictics
locationals	conjunctions
temporals	interjections

We can distinguish these word classes by a variety of criteria; both semantic and formal. Often the semantic content of a word class will determine its range of morphological possibilities. For example, nouns commonly denote objects. Hence number, the morphological category for the expression of multiple tokens of an object, and case, the category which indicates the role an object plays in a given event, are general inflectional possibilities for nouns. Verbs, on the other hand, denote states or events. A common morphological category for them is tense, which expresses the time at which the event occurs. But not all inflectional categories can be explained so straightforwardly: Yimas verbs are assigned to just one word class, but the language has a rich system of derivational morphology by which verbs are derived into nouns and adjectives. Adjectives in turn may be derived into adverbs and verbs. No other parts of speech are derivable. Some choices are just an arbitrary feature of a particular language. For example, in Yimas number is an inflectional category of verbs as well as nouns. Consequently, word classes cannot be defined in terms of semantic content alone, but we must use in their definitions a combination of semantic content, morphological possibilities, and syntactic behavior. This is the procedure that I will follow in defining each of the Yimas word classes in the sections that follow.

3.1 Nouns

Nouns are the word class which provides an inventory of the objects
of interest in the world (or imagination) of the speakers of a language.
Nouns are employed in discourse to introduce props, entities, and participants relevant to the progression of the discourse. They accomplish this
because by the conventions of the language they are symbols associated
with their referents, the real world or imaginary objects which are called
into mind when the noun is uttered in discourse.

The natural world, as well as the human creations of the social and
cultural worlds, presents a vast array of entities which may be conventionally expressed by nouns. Each language group, according to its
interests, its ecological niche, its social and cultural forms, selects from
this range and codes a subset of it in its system of nouns. However, the
system of nouns is still always large and is invariably the largest word
class in a language. This is undoubtedly true of Yimas, in which the set
of nouns is much larger than the next largest word class, verbs.

Because nouns are typically employed in discourse to introduce or
mention props or participants, they are associated with syntactic functions which describe these participants or express their roles. Nouns fill
the functions of grammatical relations such as subject and object and are
associated with the category of case, which expresses the syntactic roles
of participants. For example, Yimas has a single case marker, an oblique
case suffix -n ~ -nan, which indicates locations, times or instruments
(see Section 4.2). This is a common inflection for noun stems:

(3-1) nam-n   ma   tmat-ɲan   wanwa-n
       house-OBL   other sun-OBL   knife-OBL
       'in the house'   'on another day'   'with a knife'

Nouns also function as the subject and object of a verb. Nouns in
these functions are not inflected for case, but do agree in person and
number with the verb. Their agreement is indicated by a set of verb
prefixes (O indicates the object of a transitive verb and A, its subject;
see Section 5.1.1).

(3-2) a. narmaŋ namat pu-n-tu-t
          woman   men   3PL O-3SG A-kill-PERF
          'The woman killed the men.'
       b. narmaŋ namat na-mpu-tu-t
          woman   men   3SG O-3PL A-kill-PERF
          'The men killed the woman.'

The word order of the nouns in Yimas is free, so order does not signal their syntactic functions as it does in English (compare the English
translations of the above examples). Rather this is indicated by the pre-

fixes to the verb. The sequence of prefixes in (3-2a) *pu-n-* indicates a
singular subject and a plural object, so the plural noun in the sentence
namat 'men' is the subject, and the singular noun *narmaŋ* 'woman' is
the object. The opposite situation obtains in (3-2b) where the prefix
sequence *na-mpu-* indicates a singular object and a plural subject.

The morphology of nouns will be treated in greater detail in Chapter
4, so I will only mention here some basic morphological defining characteristics. All nouns except for proper names are inflected for three
numbers—singular, dual and plural—and are assigned to a single noun
class. It is this last feature which distinguishes nouns from adjectives
or deictics. Adjectives and deictics vary over the whole range of noun
classes, co-occurring with all possible number/class suffixes. Nouns differ in being uniquely assigned to a class and taking the number/class
suffixes specific to that class. Contrast the adjective *ma* 'other', occurring with a number of different number/class suffixes, with the class VI
noun *kaŋ* 'shell':

	SG	DL	PL
VI	maŋ	maŋkl	maŋki
VII	mamp	mampl	mara
IX	ma	mawl	mawt
VI	kaŋk	kaŋkl	kaŋki
VII	*kamp	*kampl	*kara
IX	*ka	*kawl	*kawt

A salient feature of nouns, lacking in all other word classes, is that
many common nouns have suppletive forms to mark number, i.e., the
singular and plural forms have different stems (in all these cases the dual
form is derived regularly from the singular stem). This generally applies
to nouns referring to human beings, some animals and other important
objects. Consider the following small sample:

	SG	PL
'woman'	narmaŋ	ŋaykum
'man'	panmal	payum
'child'	kalakn	kumpwi
'mother'	ŋayuk	ŋaykumpam
'bird'	paypra	paypratawi
'pig'	numpran	numpray
'sago palm'	tnum	tpwi
'leaf'	nmprm	nmpi
'meat'	naŋkpuk	naŋkpt

This suppletion for number in noun stems is a common feature of all

the Lower Sepik languages, especially for kin terms. Consider these
Angoram and Chambri examples:

Angoram:		SG	PL
	'man'	pondo	pandaŋ
	'father'	apa	anont
	'woman'	aŋɨno	akum

Chambri:		SG	PL
	'woman'	nɨmenan	mɨntamar
	'man'	noranan	noramp
	'daughter'	pisanim	pisamtamp

Nouns are morphologically much simpler than verbs, having only
two possible inflections, the number/class markers and the oblique case
suffix -*n* ~ -*nan*. The morphology of nouns is exclusively suffixal, while
that of verbs is both prefixal and suffixal. Nouns are inherently assigned
to a given class and are marked for number by a set of number suffixes
which vary for class.

		SG	DL	PL
Class V	'snake'	wakn	wakntrm	wakntt
Class VI	'tooth'	trŋ	trŋkl	trŋk
Class IX	'penis'	ŋarwa	ŋarwawl	ŋarut

Verbs also take affixes for number/class by agreeing with nouns functioning as subject or object. These, however, are typically prefixes. The
verbal prefixes for the above number/class combinations are

	SG	DL	PL
Class V	na-	tma-	ya-
Class VI	k-	kla-	kia-
Class IX	wa-	ula-	ura-

3.2 Verbs

Verbs contrast with nouns in that they are the word class which denote
events or states. While objects, especially those in the natural world,
exist in their own right, this is not true of events or states. These only
manifest themselves by virtue of some object or objects undergoing or
performing them. The set of verbs in a language may be viewed as a
script outlining the various modes in which objects denoted by the set
of nouns may interact.

Because verbs function as the script of a language, it is they which
lay out the basic plot of a discourse. Verbs prototypically fill the syntac-
tic/semantic function of the predicate of the clause, which denotes the

nature of the state or event participated in by a set of objects referred to by the nouns in the clause. Thus, the verb *hit* functioning in *John hit Peter* tells us the manner in which John and Peter interacted. Verbs like *hit* indicating a transaction between two or more objects are transitive. Other verbs function as predicates denoting an event or state performed or undergone by some object; these are intransitive verbs, and examples are *run* as in *John ran in the race*, or *sleep* as in *John slept in the barn*.

The morphology of verbs will be treated in detail in Chapters 5 and 6, so I will only discuss some basic defining features here. The morphological feature most characteristic of verbs, and the only obligatory one, is tense. All finite verbs must be inflected for tense, and non-finite verbs must have a suffix *-ru* in the normal inflectional position for tense. No other part of speech is ever inflected for tense, so it can be regarded as a necessary and sufficient condition on the word class verb.

A second defining characteristic of verbs is that only they can occur with the modal prefixes, such as *ta-* NEG, *ant-* POT and *ka-* LIKELY. These are not necessary inflections on a verb, as most verbs are unmarked for modality. But the potential occurrence of one of these prefixes on a word always identifies it as a verb, for no other word class is inflectable for modality.

A third morphological characteristic of verbs is the presence of prefixes to indicate the person, number, and noun class of core nominal arguments, i.e., subject, object, and indirect object. I have already pointed out how nouns are uniquely assigned to noun classes and inflected for number by *suffixes*, varying allomorphically according to noun class. Verbs parallel this variation for noun class and number by indicating these features for the nouns functioning as their core arguments, but do so by means of *prefixes*. Examples of such verbal prefixes corresponding to the noun suffixes were presented at the end of Section 3.2.

3.3 Adjectives

Adjectives are the word class that expresses a state, quality, or defining characteristic of some object. As such, they most commonly function syntactically as the modifier of some noun in a noun phrase. Some languages seem to have no word class of adjectives at all, assigning all words denoting states or qualities of objects to the word classes verb or noun (Dixon 1977). Other languages have a very small and restricted class of adjectives. Yimas is one of these. There are only three true unambiguous examples of adjectives in the language. They are *kpa* 'big', *yua* 'good', and *ma* 'other'. These are distinguished from other Yimas words denoting qualities of objects in that they are uninflected for the verbal category tense and may occur with a following noun in a tightly knit noun phrase (see Section 4.6).

(3-3) a. kpa nam   b. *nam kpa
           big   house   house big
           'a big house'

No other word can occur between the adjective and the head noun. If this should occur, the adjective must then be suffixed with a number class suffix agreeing in these features with the modified noun. Its position is now free and can occur on either side of the noun.

(3-4) a. kpa-nm   nam
           big-house SG   house
           'a big house'
       b. nam   kpa-nm
           house big-house SG
           'a big house'

In fact, the inflected adjective need not even adjoin the noun, but may occur anywhere in the clause.

(3-5) ama-na   nam
       1SG-POSS   house SG

       ant-ka-na-war-kiant-nm   kpa-nm
       POT-1SG A-DEF-build-NR FUT-house SG big-house SG

       'Tomorrow I will be able to build my big house.'

Other words denoting qualities are morphologically verbs. These occur with the suffix -k, the tense suffix for irrealis (IRR). This suffix is normally used to remove the action denoted by the verb from the continuum in real time and thus mark it as timeless. It is therefore used for events in the legendary past, unrealized events in the future whose time of occurrence cannot be fixed, and states whose duration cannot be bound (see Section 5.2.1.1). It is this last meaning which accounts for its use with words denoting qualities. These adjectival-like verbs suffixed with -k also require a number/class suffix, agreeing in these features with a modified noun. As such they may occur on either side of the noun, or may not even adjoin it. These tensed adjectival verbs never occur in the construction characteristic of true adjectives, i.e., immediately preceding the head noun in a close-knit noun phrase without the number/class suffixes. Examples of these adjectival verbs follow:

(3-6) a. apak   tŋkŋt-k-nmaŋ
           sister heavy-IRR-II SG
           'a fat sister'

b. urkpwica-k-n   numpran
   black-IRR-III SG pig III SG
   'a black pig'

c.*urkpwica numpran
   black   pig III SG

The adjectival verbs comprise the largest class of words denoting qualities in Yimas. Besides the first *stems* already illustrated, we have the following non-exhaustive list:

'white'	yarac-	'sharp'	wapi-
'long'	kawŋkra-	'whole'	munta-
'short'	parmpa-	'hollow'	urmpwi-
'hard/strong'	kalc-	'stubborn'	araɲalca-
'light'	walɲa-	'empty, clear'	kamta-
'new'	kantma-	'dry'	kacɲa
'straight'	kratŋk-		

A further indication that these so-called adjectival verbs are really verbs shows up in the formation of inchoatives, expressing changes of state. The adjectival verbs can do this directly, by changing the tense inflection to one within the real temporal continuum, and changing the number/class suffixes to the more typically verbal number/class prefixes (S indicates the subject of an intransitive verb).

(3-7) a. na-tŋknt-t
         II SG S-become heavy-PERF
         'She got fat.'

     b. narm   p-urkpwica-t
         skin VII SG   VII SG S-blacken-PERF
         '(My) skin darkened.'

The examples in (3-7) clearly indicate that these stems in their basic meaning are process verbs; they only assume the stative meaning by virtue by the IRR suffix -k, which stipulates that the event is unbounded in time.

The true adjectives may not form inchoatives in this fashion. Rather they must occur with the verb *ti*- 'do, become, feel', which carries the tense suffix. The adjective may occur as a separate word or may be incorporated into the verb, but in both cases it must co-occur with the proper number/class suffix for the subject of the verb.

(3-8) a. irpm   kpa-m   mu-ti-t
         coconut palm IV SG big-IV SG IV SG S-become-PERF
         'The coconut palm got big.'

    b. irpm   mu-kpa-m-ti-t
        coconut palm IV SG IV SG S-big-IV SG-become-PERF
        'The coconut palm got big.'

    c. watn   yua-n   na-ti-t
        ironwood V SG good-V SG V SG S-become-PERF
        'The ironwood became good.'

    d. watn   na-yuwa-n-ti-t
        ironwood V SG V SG S-good-V SG-become-PERF
        'The ironwood became good.'

Constructions such as these are also possible for the adjectival verbs, provided they are suffixed with -*k* IRR.

(3-9) apak   na-tŋknt-k-nmaŋ-ti-t
       sister-II SG II SG S-heavy-IRR-II SG-become-PERF
       'Sister got fat.'

The fact that both true adjectives and adjectival verbs occur in this construction shows that, although they are of different word classes, they have much in common. This is further demonstrated by two adjectives 'bad' and 'small', which belong to both classes.

(3-10) a. waca nam   *or*   nam   waca-k-nm
          small house   house small-IRR-house
          'a small house'

      b. mama patn   *or*   patn   mama-k-n
          bad   betelnut V SG   betelnut V SG bad-IRR-V SG
          'a bad betelnut'

Note that these two stems differ from the true adjectives and resemble the adjectival verbs in requiring the tense suffix -*k* when suffixed with number/class markers. The true adjectives may never occur with this suffix. They contrast with the adjectival verbs and parallel the true adjectives in requiring the auxiliary verb *ti*- 'do, become, feel' in change of state meanings.

(3-11) a. mamam   p-waca-k-m-ti-t
          sore-VII SG VII SG S-small-IRR-VII SG-become-PERF
          'The sore got small (dried up).'

      b.*mamam   p-waca-t
          sore-VII SG VII SG S-small-PERF

Although adjectival verbs belong to the class of verbs by virtue of taking tense, they contrast with true verbs in that when modifying a noun they do not form relative clauses as do the true verbs. Consider the following examples:

(3-12) a. irpuŋ   tŋknt-k-ŋ
           stone-VI SG   heavy-IRR-VI SG
           'a heavy stone'
       b.*irpuŋ   m-tŋknt-k-ŋ
           stone-VI SG   NR DIST-heavy-IRR-VI SG

(Example (3-12b) is grammatical in the sense 'it is heavy like a rock' but not in the intended sense 'a heavy rock'.)

(3-13) a. numpran   m-na-ya-n-∅
           pig-III SG   NR DIST-DEF-come-PRES-III SG
           'the pig which is coming'
       b.*numpran   ya-k-n
           pig-III SG   come-IRR-III SG

Note that true verbs form tensed relative clauses by attaching a fully inflected verb to the near distal deictic base m- 'that', as in (3-13a). This construction is blocked for adjectival verbs (3-12b). On the other hand, the noun modifying construction using -k and the number/class suffixes so typical of adjectival verbs (3-12a) is blocked for true verbs (3-13b). All this demonstrates that the adjectival verbs must be regarded as a quite distinct sub-class from the true verbs.

Additional evidence for the distinctness of the adjectival verbs from true verbs can be seen in the treatment of the suffix -k. As I have already argued this is a tense suffix potentially available to every verb stem. For a number of adjectival verb stems, the suffix -k has become permanently attached to the stem, occurring in both adjectival and verbal uses.

(3-14) a. apak   kawŋkra-k-nmaŋ
           sister-II SG   long-IRR-II SG
           'a tall sister'
       b. apak   na-kawŋkra-k-t
           sister-II SG   II SG S-lengthen-IRR-PERF
           'Sister grew tall.'
       c.*kawŋkra-k   apak
           long-IRR   sister

(3-14b) suggests that the -k has been re-analyzed as part of the stem and perhaps is no longer a tense marker. This is probably true, but it by no means shifts these adjectival verbs into the class of true adjectives, for they may still not occur in the tightly knit adjective + noun construction of true adjectives (3-14c). Other stems like *kawŋkra-k* 'long' are *kantma-k* 'new', *kamta-k* 'clear' an *urmpwi-k* 'hollow'. These stems could be analyzed as ending in /k/ and taking a zero allomorph of the tense suffix -k, but this ad hoc analysis adds no explanatory power. What clearly is going on here is that the adjectival verbs are recognized as being divergent from true verbs and are gradually moving toward the true adjectives. As the adjectival verbs are like the true adjectives in denoting qualities, while the true verbs denote events or actions, this reassignment of class membership is understandable semantically. The bleaching of the meaning of the irrealis suffix so that it actually appears as part of the stem is an indication of this reassignment of the adjectival verbs to a separate adjective class. This process is obviously not complete as yet, but it will be complete when -k gets reanalyzed as part of the stem for all adjectival verbs, and they become indistinguishable in grammatical behavior from true adjectives. The adjectival verbs already have as much in common with the true adjectives as with the true verbs. For example, while both adjectives and adjectival verbs form inchoatives with ti- 'feel, become, do' (see examples (3-8) and (3-9)), this is not available for true verbs.

(3-15) *muŋkawŋ   ku-wul-k-uŋ-ti-t
       post X SG   X SG S-put down-IRR-X SG-become-PERF

So far we have seen the class of words corresponding to adjectives in English divided up in Yimas between true adjectives (3 stems), adjectival verbs (about 15 stems) and words corresponding to both (2 stems). This does not complete the inventory, however, for there are some Yimas words denoting qualities which are structurally like nouns. Therefore I refer to these as 'adjectival nouns'. These stems occur with the postposition kantk- 'with', often used to express possession or accompaniment. Consider the following examples:

(3-16) a. amtra   kunti kantk-ra   arak
          food-V PL   tasty with-V PL   COP V PL
          'The food is tasty.'

       b. narm   upwi   kantk-m   papk
          skin VII SG   hot   with-VII SG COP VII SG
          'I'm hot.'

Words like kunti 'tasty' and upwi 'hot' must be analyzed as nouns in Yimas, for only nouns may normally be the object of the postposition kantk-. This is further supported by the fact that some of these adjectival nouns can function syntactically as nouns.

(3-17) a. kalakn   tamana   kantk-n   anak
          child-I SG   sick IX SG   with-I SG COP I SG
          'The child is sick.'

       b. tamana   wa-ŋa-tal
          sick IX SG   IX SG A-1SG O-hold
          'I became sick.'

tamana 'sick' functions as an adjectival noun in a phrase with *kantk-* in (3-17a), but as a nominal subject agreeing with the verb in number/class in (3-17b). Only a noun could function as *tamana* does in (3-17b). The postposition *kantk-* is used in these adjectival noun constructions to carry the normal adjectival concord suffixes for the modified noun. Other examples of the class of adjectival nouns are:

'cold'	tark	'sad'	yapan
'happy'	wapun	'dirty'	wurk
'ashamed'	irmut		

Because these stems are basically nouns, they do not form inchoatives in the same way as the true adjectives or adjectival verbs. Consider the stative construction and the inchoative construction for the adjectival noun *wapun* 'happy'.

(3-18) a. wapun   kantk-n   amayak
          happy V SG   with-V SG   COP 1SG
          'I'm happy.'

      b. wapun   kantk-n   ama-na-ti-n
          happy V SG   with-V SG   1SG S-DEF-become-PRES
          'I'm becoming/feeling happy.'

The first sentence means something like 'I have or am feeling something which is good, so I am happy'. The second goes like 'I am doing/experiencing something good, and I'm becoming/feeling happy because of that.' The first sentence would be uttered when a person is happy because of the property or clothes he owns, while the second is appropriate to contexts of, say, just finishing a carving or house. Thus, the form with the copula is appropriate for longer duration or relatively permanent states and the form with *ti-* for transitory states or changes of state. But there are other inchoative constructions available to adjectival nouns by virtue of their status as nouns.

(3-19) a. wapun   ama-na-pay-n
          happy V SG   1SG S-DEF-lie/carry-PRES
          'I'm feeling happy.'

      b. wapun   na-ŋa-na-ti-n
          happy V SG   V SG S-1SG O-DEF-do/feel-PRES
          'I'm feeling happy.' (literally 'happiness does/feels on me')

In these examples the adjectival noun functions as a nominal core argument of the verb—an object in (3-19a) and a subject in (3-19b). These two sentences contrast in meaning. (3-19a) means 'I'm doing something good and I'm feeling happy because of that', i.e., very close in meaning to (3-18b). The difference between (3-18b) and (3-19a) is that the lat-

ter is appropriate in contexts describing something about the speaker's
demeanor and appearance. For example, if the speaker has just dressed
up in new clothes and thinks he looks very handsome and smart, he
will likely utter (3-19a). (3-18b), on the other hand, is more appropriate when just having finished a difficult task. The final construction
(3-19b) contrasts with both (3-18b) and (3-19a) in that one feels happy
not because of anything one has done, but because of something that has
happened, often without any input from the experiencer. (3-19b) then
would be an appropriate utterance on just winning the lottery or receiv-
ing an unsolicited gift. Constructions such as (3-19b) are only possible
for adjectival nouns denoting human sensations (see (3-17b) also). Consider their construction with *upwi* 'hot' (compare with (3-16b) above):

(3-20) a. narm   upwi p-ŋa-na-wampaki-n
            skin VII SG hot   VII SG A-1SG D-DEF-throw-PRES
            'I'm feeling hot.' (literally 'skin throws heat on me'
            'my skin throws heat')

       b. narm   upwi p-ŋa-na-tɨ-n
            skin VII SG hot   VII SG A-1SG D-DEF-do/feel-PRES
            'I'm feeling hot.' (literally 'skin does heat on me' or
            'my skin does/feels heat')

Again, these constructions express an involuntary change of state which
the experiencer does nothing to bring about. It is something which *happens* to him, rather than something he does. This contrast between vol-
untary actions and involuntary changes in state, especially of sensations,
is a pervasive feature of Papuan languages and is realized morphologically and syntactically in many of them (see Foley 1986, 121–7).

    The final stems expressing qualities which I wish to consider in this
section are those denoting speed. In Yimas, these are not adjectives,
verbs, or nouns; they are adverbs, normally bound morphemes incorporated directly into the verbal complex.

(3-21) a. kay   i-na-mamaŋ-ya-n
            canoe VIII SG   VIII SG S-DEF-slow-come-PRES
            'The canoe is slow.'

       b. kay   i-na-kaykaykay-ya-n
            canoe VIII SG   VIII SG S-DEF-fast-come-PRES
            'The canoe is fast.'

       c.*kaykaykay kay
            fast   canoe VIII SG

       d.*kay   kaykaykay-k-i
            canoe VIII SG   fast-IRR-VIII SG

Stems denoting speed can only modify nouns as part of a verb complex as in (3-21a, b). Used as adjectives stems, either without -*k* (3-21c) or with (3-21d), they produce ungrammatical constructions.

3.4 Quantifiers

The numeral system of Yimas is quite complex, but is based fundamentally on the fingers and toes of a human being. It operates simultaneously with three bases: base twenty, base ten and base five. The stems denoting these bases are invariable, but all other numerals vary for noun class depending on the features of the noun which are being counted. Further, not all numerals agreeing for noun class do so in the same way: the numbers 'one' and 'four' (and higher numbers ending in these units) agree like adjectives using suffixes, while 'two' and 'three' (and again higher numbers ending in these units) take the verbal agreement prefixes. Thus, for the class VII noun *tanm* 'bone', *mpa-* 'one' takes the adjectival agreement suffix -*m* (*tanm mpa-m* 'one bone'), but -*rpal* 'two' takes the verbal agreement prefix *p-* (*tanpl p-rpal* 'two bones'). Although 'two' and 'bones' are obviously not singular, only the singular noun class affixes are used on the numerals. Interestingly, this generalization is not true of other Lower Sepik languages like Chambri, which do employ the non-singular concord markers on numerals. Yimas also presents a considerable degree of suppletion in its number system, which will be discussed in the sections on the noun classes in Chapter 4.

The first three numerals are monomorphemic stems which vary for the class of the noun counted: *mpa-* 'one', -*rpal* 'two' and -*ramnawt* 'three'. 'Four' is derived from the adjective stem *ma-* 'other' plus the relevant number/class suffix for dual number reduplicated, i.e., 'other two and other two' equals 'four'. 'Four' is the one exception to the rule that only the singular gender class suffixes are used on the Yimas numerals. So for a class VII noun like *tanm* 'bone', we have the following paradigm:

tanm	mpa-m	'one bone'
tanpl	p-rpal	'two bones'
tanpat	p-ramnawt	'three bones'
tanpat	ma-mpl+ama-mpl	'four bones'

'Five' is the invariable base *tam*, while 'six' through 'nine' are formed from this invariable base plus *mawŋkwat* 'other side' plus 'one' through 'four'. So:

tanpat tam	'five bones'
tanpat tam mawŋkwat mpa-m	'six bones'
tanpat tam mawŋkwat p-rpal	'seven bones'

tanpat tam mawŋkwat p-ramnawt   'eight bones'
tanpat tam mawŋkwat ma-mpl+ama-mpl   'nine bones'

'Ten' is another invariable base: *nuŋkara-wl* hand-DL 'two hands'.
'Eleven' through 'nineteen' are formed from this base plus *arm-tap-mpi*
jump.down-COMP-SEQ 'and then jump down' plus *pamk-n* leg-OBL 'on
the leg' plus the numbers 'one' through 'nine'. For example:

tanpat   nuŋkarawl   arm-tap-mpi
bone VII PL   hand DL   jump down-COMP-SEQ

pamk-n   mpa-m
leg-OBL   one-VII

'eleven bones'

tanpat nuŋkarawl armtapmpi pamkn tam mawŋkwat mpam
'sixteen bones'

tanpat nuŋkarawl armtapmpi pamkn tam mawŋkwat
mamplamampl   'nineteen bones'

'Twenty' is the invariable base *namarawt munta-k-n* person whole-IRR-I
SG 'a whole person'.

tanpat namarawt muntakn   'twenty bones'

Numbers above 'twenty' are simply 'twenty' plus 'one' through 'nineteen'. These higher numerals are in practice never used, Tok Pisin being
the invariable choice here, but the system does make them possible. The
following is acceptable, although I have never heard it spontaneously uttered:

tanpat namarawt muntakn nuŋkarawl armtapmpi pamkn tam
mawŋkwat mpam   'thirty-six bones'

Following this logic, 'forty' would be *namaraw-rm muntak-rm impu-mpal*
person-I DL whole-I DL I DL-two 'two whole men.' The numeral system
can continue producing numbers infinitely with this logic. For higher
numbers, simply divide by base twenty, then base ten, and then base
five, with the remainder realized as 'one' through 'four'. So again the
following is acceptable, but never actually spontaneously said:

tanpat   namat   muntak-um   manpamarm
bone VII PL   person I PL   whole-I PL   four I

nuŋkarawl   arm-tap-mpi   pamk-n
hand DL   jump down-COMP-SEQ   leg-OBL

tam   mawŋkwat   mamplamampl
five   other side   four VII

'ninety-nine bones'

Given the extreme complexity of an example like this it is pretty clear why it is never used: it is far too difficult both to construct and to process. In a sense this comment applies to the whole numeral system in Yimas. The complex paraphrases for any number above 'five' and the great variations in form for numbers below 'five' make the whole system quite unwieldy. It is not surprising then that as a whole it is giving way and most younger speakers control it poorly, if at all. These speakers just substitute the simple numerals of Tok Pisin.

In addition to the cardinal numerals, Yimas possesses a defective set of ordinal numerals. These only go as far as 'fourth'. The forms for 'second' through 'fourth' are derived from the cardinal numerals for classes I and II by suffixing a form -ɲawt, except for 'third' which is derived in the same way from the form for 'three' in classes III and V.

cardinal numeral		*ordinal numeral*	
'two'	impumpal	'second'	impumpatɲawt
'three'	tamunum	'third'	tamunumputɲawt
'four'	manpamarm	'fourth'	manpamarmputɲawt

The form for 'first' is suppletive; it is *kaŋkran*, which also has the meaning 'before'. 'Last' is expressed by the invariable word *nawt*, which in other circumstances expresses 'prototypical, the most common or typical exemplar of a category, real, true'. For example *nawt-ɲaŋkun* 'prototype-mosquito' refers to the most common ordinary brown mosquito in the area. This Yimas correlation of 'last' and 'prototypical' is not too dissimilar from the English ambiguity in the word *ultimate*. When used specifically in the meaning 'last', *nawt* is normally compounded with the cardinal numeral for one *mpa-*, so the result for class VII is *nawt mpa-m* 'last one', 'last'. It is also commonly compounded with the other cardinal numerals to express concepts such as 'the last two'.

> nawt p-ral
> last VII-two
> 'the last two'

These ordinal numerals are never inflected with agreement suffixes for the nouns they modify; they are simply juxtaposed and may occur on either side of the noun. Further, with the exceptions of *kaŋkran* 'first' and *nawt* 'last', they are restricted to modifying animate, particularly human, nouns. For inanimate nouns, circumlocutions such as the following are necessary; compare (a) and (d) with (b) and (c):

(3-22) a. irpm   kaŋkran wul-k-um
          coconut palm IV SG first   put down-IRR-IV SG
          amuk
          COP IV SG
          'This is the first coconut palm planted.'

    b. irpm
          coconut palm IV SG

          m-mpu-na-kanta-mpi-wul-k-um
          NR DIST-3PL A-DEF-follow-SEQ-put down-IRR-IV SG
          amuk
          COP IV SG
          'This is the second coconut palm planted.'

    c. irpm
          coconut palm IV SG

          m-mpu-na-mampi-kanta-mpi-wul-k-um
          NR DIST-3PL A-DEF-again-follow-SEQ-put down-IRR-IV SG
          amuk
          COP IV SG
          'This is the third/fourth coconut palm planted.'

    d. irpm   nawt tampin
          coconut palm IV SG last   after
          mu-kay-wut-ɲcut
          IV SG O-1PL A-put down-RM PAST
          'We planted the last coconut palm.'

The final type of numerals to consider are the adverbial numbers
'once', 'twice', etc. These are formed for 'three' and above by modifying
the plural noun kŋki 'times', belonging to class VI, with the corresponding cardinal numeral.

    kŋki   k-ramnawt
    times-VI PL VI-three
    'three times'

    kŋki   ma-ŋkl-ama-ŋki
    times-VI PL other-VI DL-other-VI PL
    'four times'

'Once' and 'twice' are suppletive, as in English (mparuŋkut 'once' and
tukrpatn 'twice'). However, 'twice' does have a regularly formed alternate, using the dual form kŋkl 'times' plus the proper cardinal number.

kŋkl   k-rpal
times VI DL VI-two
'twice'

Other quantifiers in Yimas besides numerals are *mpatnpa-* 'few,' and
muntak 'many, all'. *muntak* is invariable, but *mpatnpa-* varies according
to the noun class of the modified noun by suffixing the plural adjectival
number/class suffixes (*tanpat mpatnpa-ra* 'a few bones'). There is also
the interrogative quantifier *ntuknti* 'how much, how many', which is also
invariable.

3.5 Locationals

Locationals are words which describe the location of an object with respect to that of another object or the speech event. In Yimas there are
two types of locationals: free locationals, corresponding to English locational adverbs, and locational postpositions, corresponding to English
locational prepositions. Locationals end in *n*, undoubtedly a fossilized
occurrence of the oblique suffix -*n* ~ -*nan*.

Free locationals never occur in the postpositional phrase construction
consisting of a noun plus postposition that is diagnostic of locational
postpositions. Free locationals normally occur as independent words in
a sentence, modifying the copula or a positional verb. Examples of free
locationals are given below:

'far'	kwantayn	'left'	payŋkan
'near'	warpayn	'right'	ampan
'alone'	tantukwan		

Examples of their usage are:

(3-23) a. num   kwantayn numa-na-pay-n
          village far   village S-DEF-lie-PRES
          'The village is far.'

      b. taki   warpayn na-na-irm-n
          stone V SG   near   IV SG S-DEF-stand-PRES
          'The stone is near.'

While these stems semantically modify nouns, they are not adjectives.
They may never occur with the typical adjectival number/class suffixes,
nor may they precede the head noun in a tightly knit noun phrase.
Closely related in form and behavior to these free locationals and not
too dissimilar in meaning is *pawin* 'plain, naked, unadorned'. This too
ends in *n* and occurs as an independent word, modifying a verb. Note
the exact parallelism in these two examples:

(3-24) a. panmal   tantukwan na-na-awŋkcpa-n
          man-I SG alone   3SG S-DEF-bathe-PRES
          'The man is bathing alone.'

     b. panmal   pawin na-na-awŋkcpa-n
          man-I SG naked 3SG S-DEF-bathe-PRES
          'The man is bathing naked.'

The stems *tantukwan* and *pawin* are not adjectives because they may
never be inflected with the adjectival class/number suffixes. *Pawin*, but
not *tantukwan*, does, however, possess one distinctive feature of true
adjectives: it may form a close-knit noun phrase with a following noun,
e.g., *pawin tpuk* 'plain sago pancake', 'sago pancake with no meat or
embellishments'. *Pawin* seems to be a stem intermediate in behavior
between the word classes true adjective and free locational. Its form
and most of its grammatical behavior mark it as a free locational, but
its occurrence in noun phrases indicate that it is a true adjective. Given
that along its full range of meaning, *pawin* denotes qualities, it is not
surprising that it would take on some adjectival features. A plausible
scenario for the development of *pawin* would be starting out as a free
locational and gradually being reanalyzed as a member of the adjective
class. It is now in an intermediate stage. Although *tantukwan* 'alone'
would also seem to English speakers to denote a quality, it is also fairly
easy to see its locational meaning, i.e., something is in a location without
anyone/anything else. This word so far has resisted any move toward
reanalysis as an adjective, as in **tantukwan panmal* 'alone man'. Rather
one must say

(3-25) panmal   tantukwan na-na-pay/taw/irm/-n
       man I SG alone   3SG S-DEF-lie/sit/stand-PRES
       'The man is alone.'

Locational postpositions contrast with free locationals in not always
being independent words. They most commonly occur as postpositions
to a noun or noun phrase, and in these constructions they require the
noun to be inflected with oblique case suffix -*n* ~ -*nan*.

(3-26) a. panmal   ya-nan   wampuɲan
          man I SG tree V SG-OBL in front of

          na-na-irm-n
          3SG S-DEF-stand-PRES
          'The man is in front of the tree'

     b. panmal   nam-n   wampuŋn na-na-taw-n
          man I SG house-OBL inside   3SG-DEF-stand-PRES
          'The man is inside the house.'

Examples of these locational postpositions are given below:

'underneath' (trees)	pawmpn				
'at the bottom, below'	ŋmkŋn				
'above, at the top'	mawn				
'behind'	akpɲan				
'in front of'	wampuɲan				
'inside'	wampuŋn	< wampuŋ	'heart'	+ -n OBL
'outside'	tapukapn	< tapukap	'outside'	+ -n OBL
'at the side of'	ayŋkn	< ayŋk	'outside'	+ -n OBL

Some of these are transparently derived from nouns by affixing the oblique suffix. A few other locational words are still nouns because they can be pluralized. Examples are *kcpn* 'space underneath a house', PL: *kcpnkat* 'the spaces underneath houses'; and *mawŋkwat* 'the other side', PL: *mawŋkwara* 'the spaces on or at the sides of a dwelling or object'.

Although these locational postpositions most commonly occur in postpositional phrases, they may also be used as free locationals. In this sense, they are like English prepositions, as in *John slept inside* versus *John slept inside the house*. So compare the following examples:

(3-27) a. akrŋ   yampaŋk-n   mawn k-na-taw-n
            frog VI SG head VI SG-OBL   above VI SG-DEF-sit-PRES
            'The frog is on top of (his) head.'

        b. akrŋ   mawn k-na-taw-n
            frog VI SG above VI SG S-DEF-sit-PRES
            'The frog is on top.'

In the second example, the location which the frog is above is left unspecified. It is either the position of some object inferred from the context or may be taken to be the position of the speech event itself or some event reported in the discourse.

Yimas has four other postpositions which may perhaps be treated here and squeezed into the class of locationals, although they contrast from those postpositions treated thus far in some important respects. These postpositions are

'toward, for, because of'	nampan
'like'	nampayn
'toward, at the house/residence/property of (French *chez*)'	naŋkun
'with, together'	kantk

These grammatical postpositions contrast with the locational postpositions in that the preceding noun is never marked with the oblique case suffix. Hence, these grammatical postpositions function like case markers themselves, and this explains why they have more abstract relational meanings in contrast to the concrete locational meanings of the locational postpositions. Besides being postpositions, another feature shared by members of both types is their ability to become specified through prefixes to the verb. When this happens with a locational postposition, the associated noun remains oblique, but with a grammatical postposition, it becomes a core argument cross-referenced by a verbal agreement prefix. Consider the following examples:

(3-28) a. panmal   numpk-n   mawn
         man I SG   mountain V SG-OBL   above

         na-na-taw-n
         3SG S-DEF-sit-PRES

         'The man is on top of the mountain.'

       b. panmal   numpk-n   na-na-wi-caw-n
          man-I SG   mountain V SG-OBL   3SG S-DEF-above-sit-PRES
          'The man is on top on the mountain.'

(3-29) a. panmal   ŋaykum   kantk na-na-wa-n
          man I SG   woman-II PL   with   3SG-DEF-go-PRES
          'The man is going with the women.'

       b. panmal   ŋaykum   pu-na-taŋ-wa-n
          man I SG   woman II PL   3PL O-3SG A-DEF-COM-go-PRES
          'The man is going with the women.'

In (3-28a) the oblique noun *numpuk-n* 'mountain' is followed by the postposition, *mawn* 'above', while in (3-28b) the oblique noun occurs by itself, and the notion of 'above' is expressed by the verbal elevational prefix *wi-* 'above', which triggers palatization of the following /t/. (For a detailed discussion of elevational prefixes, see Section 6.3.3.) Sentences (3-28) (a) and (b) are not perfectly synonymous in all senses. (3-28a) would normally be taken to mean 'the man is at the top of the mountain'. Although the reading 'the man is above (us, where the speech act occurs) on the mountain' is possible, it is definitely not preferred. (3-28b) has the exact opposite ranking of preferred readings. It would normally be taken to mean 'the man is above (us, where the speech act occurs) somewhere on the mountain'. The reading 'the man is at the top of the mountain' could only be a special case of the former reading, a discourse-based inference. Thus, the structural difference between a locational postposition and a verbal elevational prefix reflects a difference in the preferential readings of the scope of 'above'. As a locational postposition, it is primarily taken as a modifier of its oblique head noun, while as a verbal elevational prefix, it is taken as a modifier of the verb and, more widely, the speech act. Note that this same contrast is carried in English by the choice of the prepositions *of* versus *on* (see the English translations of (3-28a, b)).

The examples (3-29a, b) are different in two respects. The noun *ŋaykum* 'women' is not case marked by the oblique suffix, but is directly followed by the postposition *kantk* 'with'. When the concept of 'with' is expressed by the comitative verbal prefix *taŋ-*, *naykum* is necessarily a core argument. This is demonstrated by its corresponding verbal prefix *pu-*, which agrees with the noun in terms of number/class features. (For a detailed discussion of the notion of core arguments and the function of valence-increasing verbal affixes like *taŋ-* COM, see Section 6.2.3.3. These two examples also contrast with the previous two in that they are absolutely synonymous. As far as can be determined, there is no difference in sense whatsoever between (3-29) (a) and (b). There are pragmatic differences, however, concerning the contrastiveness of *ŋaykum* 'women' (see Section 5.1.6).

In their true postpositional use, all four grammatical postpositions require human (or at least higher animate) nouns or pronouns as their objects. *kantk* has another adjectival-like use to express possession and then is often found with inanimate object nouns, but that is not of concern here (see Section 4.5). *nampan*, *naŋkun*, and *nampayn* contrast with *kantk* in that their objects, when pronouns, must be in the form of the bound possessive prefixes (see Section 4.5). This is prohibited for *kantk*, whose pronoun objects must be the free forms.

mpu-nampan	mpu-naŋkun	mpu-nampayn	pun kantk
3PL-for	3PL-toward	3PL-like	3PL with
'for them'	'toward their house'	'like those'	'with them'

3.6 Temporals
Temporals express the time setting of an action. Temporals are of two types in Yimas, basic temporals and nouns metaphorically used as temporals. Basic temporals are themselves of several types:

General temporals:	muntawktn	'at first'
	kaŋkran	'before, early'
	tampin	'after, later'
	mpa	'now, already'
Parts of the day:	kratut	'twilight' (5:00–6:00)
	tumpntut	'morning' (6:00–9:00)
	aŋkayapan	'late afternoon' (17:00–19:00)
	wut	'night' (19:00–5:00)

There is no specific word to refer to the main part of the day from about 9:00–17:00 hours. The general word *tmal* 'sun, day' can be used for this period, and more specifically, the phrase *kpa tmal* 'big sun' can be used for the middle, hottest part of the day. In parallel fashion, *kpa wut* 'big night' can be used to refer to the period around midnight. In addition speakers often use the Tok Pisin word *belo* 'noon' for the very specific period between 12:00-13:00, when government offices are closed, and people would have lunch in the towns.

Day counters:	kwarkwa	'today'
	ŋarŋ	'one day removed'
		(i.e., 'yesterday, tomorrow')
	urakrŋ	'two days removed'
	tnwantŋ	'three days removed'
	kampraɲcŋ	'four days removed'
	manmaɲcŋ	'five days removed'

Yimas has the interesting, but not unusual, Papuan system of reckoning time from the point 'now' Janus-like in both directions, so that one day in the past (yesterday) and one day in the future (tomorrow) are both denoted by the same term *ŋarŋ*. The actual time referred to by *ŋarŋ* is distinguished by the choice of tense on the verb, near past (yesterday) versus near future (tomorrow) (see Section 5.2.1).

Yimas also has two basic nouns used metaphorically as temporals. These nouns contrast with all previous temporals in that when they are used as temporals, they must be suffixed with the oblique case suffix.

tmat-ɲan	mlantrm-nan
sun, day V SG-OBL	moon, month V DL-OBL
'during the day'	'in two months'

They are, however, not the only temporals which some morphological features of nouns. A few temporal words from all types except the general temporals may form close-knit noun phrases with the adjective *ma-* 'other' to mean 'on another ___'. Such noun phrases formed with the temporal nouns or the words for parts of the day occur with the oblique suffix.

ma	tmat-ɲan	ma	wut(-ɲan)
other	sun, day V SG-OBL	other	night(-OBL)
'on another day'		'on another night'	

The oblique suffix is optional with *wut*, but required with *tmal*. *ŋarŋ* from the class of day counters also forms this construction, but is prohibited from taking the oblique suffix.

> ma   ŋarŋ   *ma   ŋarŋ-n
> other   1 day removed   other   1 day removed-OBL
> 'next day'

Stems occurring in these constructions may pluralize. *tmal* and *wut* do
so directly in a normal inflectional pattern.

> ma   tmalŋkat-n   ma   wurŋkat-n
> other   sun, day V PL-OBL   other   night PL-OBL
> 'on many other days'   'on many other nights'

Words from the set of day counters may not pluralize directly. They
must be followed by the pluralizing morpheme *mpŋkat-*, to which is
added the oblique suffix.

> ma   ŋarŋ   mpŋkat-n
> other   1 day removed   PL-OBL
> 'on a number of successively following days'

3.7 Pronouns

Yimas has a very rich inventory of pronominal forms, but most of these
are bound morphemes and will be discussed in the relevant sections of
the morphology. I will only be concerned here with pronouns which
are free independent words. True pronouns in Yimas only belong to
the first- and second-persons, i.e., refer to the speaker and addressee.
The so-called third-person pronouns refer to participants absent, or not
directly interacting in the immediate, ongoing speech act, and belong
to the word class of deictics in Yimas, to be treated in the following
section.

Besides two persons, Yimas distinguishes four numbers in its pronouns: singular, dual, paucal (a few: from three up to about seven,
but variable depending on context), and plural. The basic independent
pronouns are

	SG	DL	PC	PL
1	ama	kapa	paŋkt	ipa
2	mi	kapwa	paŋkt	ipwa

It should be noted that for the non-singulars, the second-person forms
are derived from the first by an infix -*w*- (this goes back to Proto-Lower
Sepik; see Foley 1986, 220–1). In fact, in the paucal there is no difference
whatsoever; the two forms are homophonous, the distinction being made
by cross-referencing verbal person/number prefixes.

Compared to English, these pronouns are used relatively infrequently,
their basic categories being normally expressed by prefixes to the verb
(see Section 5.1). The free pronouns can be used in combination with

the verbal prefixes, but then the pragmatic effect is generally contrastive, i.e., *'it's me (not you or anyone else) who ...'* (see Section 5.1.6).

3.8 Deictics

As with many languages, deictics are a rather elaborated part of Yimas grammar. The basic function of a deictic is to locate the position of an object in space (or in some languages, in time (Becker 1974)) with respect to the positions of the participants in the speech act. The basic participants in a speech act are the speaker, the addressee, and the person spoken about (absent from the immediate speech act, but nonetheless one of its topics). Yimas has a deictic stem corresponding to each of these three positions. There is a deictic stem -*k* 'this (near me)' to refer to things close to the speaker, a stem *m*- 'that (near you)' for those close to the addressee and a stem -*n* 'that yonder (near neither you nor me)'. All deictics agree in number and noun class with the noun denoting the objects whose location they are specifying. The proximal deictic -*k* and the far distal deictic -*n* take the set of verb prefixes, while the near distal deictic *m*- takes the adjectival suffixes. So for class VII we would have the following set of nine forms:

	-*k* PROX	*m*- NR DIST	-*n* FR DIST
SG	p-k	m-n	p-n
DL	pla-k	mpl	pla-n
PL	pia-k	m-ra	pia-n

mpl 'those two' is a contraction from *m*- the near distal stem plus -*mpl* the adjectival class VII dual suffix.

These deictic forms can be used as modifiers of head nouns (like adjectives) or as noun phrases in their own right (like pronouns). When used like adjectives they most commonly occur after the head noun, as in *impram pk* 'this basket', but this is by no means obligatory, and the opposite order is also found, *pk impram*. The former are sometimes elliptical versions of predicative uses of the deictics with the usual copula deleted. So we would have examples like the following

(3-30) impram   p-k   papk
        basket VII SG   VII SG-PROX   COP VII SG
        'This is a basket.'

The copula in Yimas is a highly complex verb form with many irregularities (see Section 5.1.5). It agrees for person, number, and class with the noun it predicates (in the above example, class VII SG). The forms of the copula with different person, number, and class combinations are presented in Section 5.1.5. In the singular (and only for some classes) the copula makes an additional distinction usually associated with de-

ictics in a number of languages. In these classes, there are two forms in
the singular for the copula, one used for objects which are visible and
one for things invisible.

(3-31) a. anti   aykk
           ground VIII SG COP VIII SG VIS
           'It's ground (seen).'
       b. anti   ayk
           ground VIII SG COP VIII SG INVIS
           'It's ground (unseen).'

(3-32) a. awruk   ku-k   kawk
           bandicoot X SG X SG-PROX COP X SG VIS
           'This is a bandicoot (seen).'
       b. awruk   akuk
           bandicoot X SG COP X SG INVIS
           'It's a bandicoot (unseen).'

The (a) examples above use the visible copula forms and identify objects seen by the speaker. These are largely identificational uses of the
copula, rather than predicational: the (a) examples would be uttered in
a context when the speaker is holding up a bandicoot or a lump of dirt
and identifying what it is. The (b) examples are used when describing
objects unseen by the speaker and largely correspond to predicational
uses of the copula. For example, (3-32b) would be uttered if on walking
through the bush one heard a rustling sound in the grass, while (3-
31b) would be said if on swimming through the lakes one stood up and
touched bottom. (3-30), with a visible copula form, also corresponds to
a predicational usage and would be a likely answer to a question like
'what are you making?', asked while watching someone weaving. As the
object being woven is visible to both parties in this context, this demonstrates that the semantic contrast of visible versus invisible is more basic
than that between identificational and predicational uses. In most cases
the two meanings coincide, so it is in fact difficult to extricate them.
As mentioned above, the visible/invisible contrast is only found in the
singular and only with some classes; for further discussion of the uses of
the copula and a complete listing of all forms, see Section 5.1.5.

These deictics also function in Yimas as the third-person pronouns.
The unmarked form in this usage is the near distal deictic. In ongoing
narrative discourse, it is this set of forms which are most commonly
used as free pronouns. But in direct quotes in and in normal everyday
conversational discourse, all three basic forms are employed with the
following meanings. Forms based on the proximal deictic stem -k are
used to refer to participants or objects within the immediate context

of the speech act. So in talking about a child sitting next to the two interlocutors, one would use the form *na-k*, the proximal form for class I and II singular, the classes for human beings. The choice between the near distal and the far distal stems is more subtle. If one wishes to emphasize the position of the participant or object as being near the addressee, one could use the near distal stem. Similarly, if one wishes to emphasize its distance from both major participants, one could use the far distal form. But both of these reasons for their use would be unusual and would result in a quite emphatic reading on the deictic, i.e., 'that thing right here near you' or 'that thing which is certainly far away, not near you or me'. More commonly, the choice of the near or far distal deictic stem reflects the centrality of the participant in the discourse or the speaker's empathy toward it. So, for example, one would talk about a child using *m-n*, the near distal form for classes I and II singular, if he was a central participant in the discourse or we felt good feelings toward him. The far distal form *na-n*, on the other hand, is likely to be used if we are angry at the child or if he is of only passing, secondary interest.

Corresponding to each of the deictic stems is deictic adverb of place. These are formed from the same stems plus an affix.

ta-k	'here (near me)'
m-nti	'there (near you)'
ta-n	'there (near neither me nor you)'

Again the stems *-k* and *-n* occur with a prefix in this case *ta-*, while *m* has a suffix *-nti*. These forms are closely related to the interrogative deictic, meaning 'where'. Yimas has a stem *ŋka*, meaning 'where?', to which is added the same set of prefixes found on the deictic stems *-k* and *-n*. The basic form is *ta-ŋka* 'where', which is used when the location of an action is queried or when the speaker wishes to be vague about the object whose location is requested. In all other cases in which the location of a known object is being sought, the stem *-ŋka* must be prefixed with the proper verbal prefix for the class of the object. Quite clearly, in Yimas the word 'where?' is a verb. Consider the following question in (a) with its answer in (b), employing the class VII singular noun *impram* 'basket'.

(3-33) a. impram   p-ŋka?
         basket VII SG VII-where
         'Where is the basket?'

       b. impram   tampaymp-n
          basket VII SG hook VII SG-OBL

p-na-apca-mpi-irm-n
VII SG S-DEF-hang-SEQ-stand-PRES
'The basket is hanging on the hook.'

In the interrogative (a) sentence, the -*ŋka* 'where?' functions as the main verb, taking the normal verbal prefix for its nominal argument. -*ŋka* is a rather defective verb. It cannot be inflected for any typically verbal categories like tense, mood, or aspect, nor can it mark the number of its nominal argument by the prefix; it can mark only class.

Other interrogative words in Yimas are:

naw-n	(who-SG)	'who (SG)'
naw-rm	(who-DL)	'who (DL)'
naw-ŋkt	(who-PC)	'who (PC)'
naw-m	(who-PL)	'who (PL)'
wa-ra	(what-PL)	'what, something'
wara pucmp-n	(what time VII SG-OBL)	'when'
wara-t-nti	(what-NFN-action)	'why/how'
wara-wal	(what-manner)	'how'
wara-mpwi	(what-talk)	'what talk'
wara-wampuŋ	(what-heart)	'what want'
wara-t-awt	(what-NFN-SG)	'what kind'
ntuk-nti	(how many-act)	'how much, how many'
ntuk-mpat	(how many-VII PL)	'when'

As can be clearly seen many of these interrogative words are based on the stem *wara* 'what' plus suffixes of nominalizations and complements. This suggests that like -*ŋka* 'where', *wara* also has verbal characteristics.

Another set of words to be considered in this section are adverbs of manner derived from the deictics of place. These are formed by adding the adverbial suffix -*mpi* to the proximal and near distal adverbs:

tak   'here'   +   -mpi   >   takmpi 'like this'
mnti 'there'   +   -mpi   >   mntmpi 'like that'

Interestingly, this suffix can be added to the word *taŋka* 'where?' to form a derived verb (further demonstrating its status as a verb), as in the following example:

(3-34) taŋka-mpi   ya-n-ntak-t   mnta
        where-ADV   V PL O-2SG A-leave-PERF   then

        ma-ya-t
        2SG S-come-PERF

        'You left (things) where and now you came?'

Here the things left behind are left unspecified, cross-referenced by the vague, unmarked plural prefix *ya-* (probably understood as referring to the noun *maramara* 'things, possessions'). There is no real semantic contrast between this sentence and one with the underived *taŋka*, although the *taŋkampi* form is more likely to be used with action verbs (especially motion verbs) and *taŋka* with stative or position verbs. Perhaps a more accurate translation, then, of *taŋkampi* would be 'in a where-ing manner?'.

Finally, there are two stems, which on morphological and to a certain extent semantic grounds, seem best assigned to the deictic word class. These are *kawŋkwan-* 'something like __' and *mntn-* 'this sort of __'. Like the near distal deictic stem *m-*, these take the adjectival concord suffixes indicating the class and number of their modified noun.

(3-35) a. anti   kawŋkwan-i
            land VIII SG   something like-VIII SG
            'something like land.'

        b. ŋaykum   mntn-put
            woman II PL   this sort-II PL
            'these sorts of women.'

        c. yara   mntn-ra
            tree V PL   this sort-V PL
            'these sorts of trees.'

3.9 Conjunctions

Yimas has only three conjunctions *tay* 'and then', *mnta* 'and then' and *kanta* 'but'. The second two are obviously built on a stem -*nta*, to which is added the near distal deictic stem *m-* or a negative prefix *ka-*. Both of these are coordinating conjunctions. Yimas lacks a disjunctive coordinating conjunction, i.e., 'or', and all subordinating conjunctions. The meanings of the latter are expressed through bound affixes to verbs, sometimes in combination with temporal stems. The conjunction *tay* normally introduces a new sentence, but may function to conjoin clauses within a single sentence. The other two conjunctions *kanta* and *mnta* normally occur after the first element of the second clause they are conjoining, rather than between the two clauses (as do their English equivalents), although that position is also possible. Consider this example:

(3-36) i-kay-api-wat   kaɲut   mnta
        VIII SG O-1PL A-put in-HAB   black palm X PL   then

        ura-kay-mampi-api-wat
        X PL O-1PL A-again-put in-HAB

        'We put in (the floor supports) and again we put in the (pieces of) black palm.'

Note that *mnta* occurs following *kaɲut* 'black palm', the object of the second clause it is conjoining. If, as in most cases, the two clauses just consist of verbs, *mnta* will occur between them:

(3-37) ya-n-kaprak-t   mnta ya-n-am-t
        V PL O-3SG A-cut up-PERF   then   V PL O-3SG A-eat-PERF
        'He cut (the food) up and then ate it.'

Clause boundaries are sometimes difficult to determine with these conjunctions. If a nominal is shared by the two conjoined clauses, the conjunctions will often follow it, especially if it is oblique.

(3-38) impa-l-ŋka-pra-kia-k 7 parwa-n   kanta
        3DL S-down-walk toward-NIGHT-IRR   dock IX SG-OBL   but

        kamta-k-wa   impa-tay-kia-k
        empty-IRR-IX SG   3DL S-see-night-IRR

        'They walked down to the dock, but they saw it was empty.'

For more discussion of the grammar of conjunctions, see Section 7.3.2.

3.10 Interjections

Interjections are a small class of uninflected words used to express emotional states or reactions, yes or no, or greetings. The following are interjections in Yimas:

yaw	'yes'
kayak	'no'
ay	'wow, really, heh, what!'
aw	'hello, farewell' (social greeting)
apa	'OK'

Interjections typically form an utterance by themselves, constituting a separate intonation group.

4

Nouns and Noun Phrases

Nominals are those words which can stand on their own as referring expressions. Besides nouns, other word classes which can function as nominals are adjectives, quantifiers, some temporals, pronouns, and deictics. A general morphological feature of nominals is specification for number and noun class. These are inherent to each common noun, but are assigned to other nominal types according to the noun they modify or refer to. Because number and class are inherent features of common nouns, and only acquired features of other nominal types, it is best to organize the study of these features around the various classes of nouns. The number inflection of nouns varies with class, so these two features will be treated together. Yimas also has a set of proper nouns, which function as names for people and places. These are never assigned to any noun class and are not inflectable for number.

4.1 Noun Classes

Yimas has ten basic noun classes with a reasonably large number of members and a half dozen or so minor classes with a single member each. The basic noun classes are of two types: those with a semantic basis for the assignment of members to the class, and those for which the assignment is strictly phonological. There is one class that combines both of these features. The assignment of nouns to classes is determined by the system of adjectival agreement: all nouns with the same set of agreement suffixes for adjectives belong to the same noun class, and any noun with a different set belongs to another noun class.

4.1.1 Class I

This class includes male humans and human beings whose sex is not highlighted. It is therefore the unmarked class for human beings. Many

of the nouns in this class show great irregularity and suppletion in their
formation of plurals. The dual is normally formed from the singular
by suffixing -*rm*, although there are some irregularities among its allomorphs. Consider the following examples of nouns from class I:

SG	DL	PL	
namarawt	namarawrm	namat	'person'
panmal	panmalɲcrm	payum	'man/husband'
apwi	apwicrm	apwiam	'father'
matn	matntrm	matnum	'brother (♀ ego)'
mamay	mamacrm	mamayam	'brother'
kalakn	kaymampan	kumpwi	'son, child, boy'
taŋkarawt	taŋkarawrm	taŋkat	'adolescent boy'
away	awacrm	ŋawaɲct	'mother's brother'
takul	takulɲcrm	takulct	'brother-in-law'
macawk	macawkrm	macawkwi	'father-in-law'
maypŋknawt	maypŋknawrm	maypŋki	'sister's son' (♂ ego)
apuk	apukrm	apukwi	'father's sister's husband'
akay	akacrm	akayam	'grandparent/cousin/ grandchild'
yanaw	yanawntrm	yanawntt	'ceremonial companion'
apanwakn	apanwakntrm	apanwakntt	'old man'
kayantaki	kayantakcrm	kayantakiŋkat	'spirit'
wuntumpnawt	wuntumpnawrm	wuntum	'ghost'
wuntumaŋ	wuntumaŋtrm	wuntumaŋkat	'mask carving'

From these examples it can be seen that there is no distinctive mark
for the singular in class I, but that the dual, with the exception of
'son, child', is marked by the suffix -*rm*, added to the singular forms,
which function as the stems. However, only in the stems ending in /k/,
'father-in-law' and 'father's sister's husband', is the formation simply
the stem plus the dual suffix -*rm*. All other stems, except those ending
in *t* (underlying /r/), require an intrusive /t/ between the stem and
the dual suffix, which is then subject to palatalization (rule (2-3)) if the
stem ends in a segment with F.

> matn + -rm > matntrm   'brothers (DL)'
> away + -rm > awaytrm > awacrm 'mother's brothers (DL)'

The second example can be represented diagrammatically as follows:

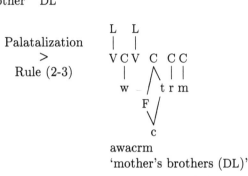

awacrm
'mother's brothers (DL)'

Palatalization will not shift further to the right to effect /r/, as rule (2-3) is specified in such a way so as to only affect [-peripheral] segments. /r/ is not specified for peripherality (see Table 3). All palatalized liquids (i.e., /l/), are underlying, not derived. We can propose the following rule to handle these cases of /t/ epenthesis:

(4-1) /t/-epenthesis

$$\emptyset \rightarrow t \,/\, \underline{\quad} + rm_{\{DL\}}$$

This rule will not apply if the stem ends in /k/ or /t/. Finally, stems ending in /l/ as well as a few other sporadic cases (e.g., 'ceremonial companion') add an epenthetic /n/ as well.

takul + -rm > takulntrm > takuljncrm 'brother-in-law'
yanaw + -rm > yanawntrm   'ceremonial companions'

This rule can be stated as follows:

(4-2) /n/-epenthesis

$$\emptyset \rightarrow n \,/\, \underline{\quad} + t + rm_{\{DL\}}$$

As we shall see later in the forms for classes III and V, both rule (4-1) and rule (4-2) are frequently encountered in Yimas. (Both rules can apply to form optional variants of all class I nouns; thus, an alternative dual form for *apuk* 'father's sister's husband' is *apukntrm*.)

The plurals of class I are much more complicated than the duals. A number of forms, 'person', 'man', 'son, child', 'mother's brother', 'sister's son', have suppletive forms for the plural stems. In addition, there are three basic forms for the plural endings for class I nouns, grouped as follows:

-t forms	-m forms	-i form
-(ŋk)at	-am	-i
-(n)tt	-um	

It is clearly impossible to collapse all of these allomorphs under a single underlying form. Rather, we must recognize both morphologically conditioned (i.e., stem conditioned) allomorphs and phonologically conditioned ones. That the former are absolutely necessary is established by *away* 'mother's brother', PL: *ŋawaɲct*; but *akay* 'grandparent, grandson', PL: *akayam*. Clearly, there is no phonological conditioning which could account for this contrast, and the proper plural allomorphs must be entered lexically, as morphologically conditioned. Other allomorphic choices are conditioned phonologically. For example, -*i* is the plural allomorph following the peripheral stops /p/ and /k/ (the /w/ is provided by the spreading of rounding from the previous syllable).

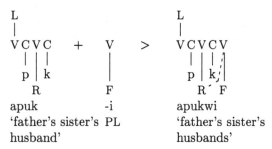

apuk	-i	apukwi
'father's sister's	PL	'father's sister's
husband'		husbands'

-*am* can be treated as the result of the contraction of -*a* + -*um*, taking -*um* as the basic allomorph, a position which will be supported by the agreement affixes below. This analysis does require us to claim that forms like 'father' and 'brother' have irregular plural stems, i.e., *apwia*- and *mamaya*-, so it may seem that we have just exchanged complexity in the plural allomorphs for complexity in the stems. But as we shall see below, a productive contraction of -*um* > -*m* after /a/ is a basic rule of Yimas so this analysis is in fact warranted.

It must be noted here that the underlying form of -*um* is in fact -*ump*, with the rule of final nasal + stop cluster simplification (2-14) applying to convert -*ump* to -*um* in final position. The /p/ will surface when the plural suffix is protected by another suffix (*payump-n kumpwi* man I PL-OBL child I PL 'boys'). Thus the basic morphologically conditioned allomorphs for plural for class I plurals are -(ŋk)*at*, -(n)*tt*, and -*ump*

(-*i* being basically a phonologically conditioned variant). There seems no way to predict which will be used for a given noun and this must be indicated lexically. Compare, as a final example, *matn* 'brother', PL: *matnum* with *apanwakn* 'old man', PL: *apawakntt*. Both stems end in /n/, but take different plural allomorphs.

As discussed in Chapter 3, all noun classes have a set of agreement suffixes and another set of agreement prefixes. The agreement suffixes are used with adjectives to mark them for the same number/class features of their modified noun and also with possessive pronouns for the same function. For most noun classes, exactly the same set of suffixes are used for both adjectives and possessive pronouns. Class I is aberrant in that in the singular and dual, it has distinct suffixes for adjectival versus possessive agreement. The adjectival agreement suffixes for class I are as follows:

SG	DL	PL
-n	-mampan	-ump

The plural agreement suffix -*ump* (which will of course surface as -*um* in final position) again loses its /u/ following /a/. Examples of the usage of these suffixes follow:

(4-3) a. kalakn   yua-n
      child I SG good-I SG
      'a good child'

    b. namarawrm   urkpwica-k-mampan
      person I DL black-IRR-I PL
      'two black persons'

    c. payum   kpa-m
      man I PL big-I PL
      'big men'

These non-singular agreement suffixes are always used for class I nouns regardless of the dual or plural allomorphs on the noun itself, with the single exception of the suppletive plural *kumpwi* 'children' for *kalakn* 'child'. This noun takes the adjectival suffix -*i* and in all formal particulars behaves like a class VIII singular noun (see Section 4.1.8). Contrast (4-4) with (4-3c) above:

(4-4) kumpwi   waca-k-i
      child I PL small-IRR-I PL
      'small children'

In fact, the form *wacaki* 'kids' is often used as a noun, as a synonym for *kumpwi*. Adjectives or adjectival verbs suffixed with class I adjectival suffixes often function as nouns in Yimas. Other examples appear below:

yarac-k	+ -ump	> yarackum	'Europeans'
white-IRR	I PL		
kpa-	+ -n	> kpan	'big brother' (♂ ego)
big	I SG		
waca-k	+ -mampan	> wacakmampan	'two little brothers'
small-IRR	I DL		(♂ ego)
kpa-	+ -ump	> kpam	'big men, elders'
big	I PL		

The possessive suffixes for class I contrast with the adjectival set in both singular and dual. They are as follows:

SG	DL	PL
-kn	-rm	-ump

Possessive pronouns in Yimas are formed by suffixing the possessive marker -na to the bound possessive form of the pronoun (see also Section 4.5). Following -na are the agreement suffixes, such as those for class I above. Examples with a first person singular possessor follow:

(4-5) a. apwi   ama-na-kn
           father I SG 1SG-POSS-I SG
           'my father'

       b. matntrm   ama-na-rm
           brother-I DL 1SG-POSS-I DL
           'my two brothers'

       c. takulct   ama-na-m
           brother-in-law I PL 1SG-POSS-I PL
           'my brothers-in-law'

Note that here the dual suffix -rm appears without the epenthetic /t/, further evidence that it is the basic form (the noun modified in (4-5b) does have the epenthetic /t/, but this does not effect the possessive agreement suffix). The plural suffix -ump appears as -m because of the preceding /a/.

Both class I and class II, the two classes referring to human beings, have the same set of verbal prefixes. Further, these prefixes correspond to the basic set of intransitive verbal person/number prefixes used for third person (for a full explication of basic person and number affixes to the verb see Sections 5.1.1 and 5.1.2). The verbal prefixes for classes I and II are as follows:

SG	DL	PL
na-	impa-	pu-

Note that these verbal prefixes are fairly closely related in form to the adjectival suffixes, and may be viewed as being essentially derived from

them, by metathesizing their sequence of phonological segments. So the
plural adjective suffix -*ump* becomes the verbal prefix *pu*- by this process
of metathesis. This is a general feature of noun classes in Yimas, and
for most, it is more regular than for class I, which exhibits a number
of complications. The singular and dual verbal prefixes *na*- and *impa*-,
while clearly relatable to the adjectival suffixes -*n* and -*mampan*, cannot
be claimed to be derived from them transparently by this same process
of metathesis.

These verbal prefixes are used to express the subject of an intransitive verb and the object of a transitive verb, but not the subject of a
transitive verb. This then is an ergative-absolutive system of argument
marking (see Section 5.1.1). Examples of their use with intransitive
verbs follow:

(4-6) a. panmal   na-tmuk-t
           man I SG   I SG S-fall-PERF
           'The man fell down.'
       b. apanwakntrm impa-na-kulanaŋ
           old man I DL I DL S-DEF-walk
           'The two men are walking.'
       c. ŋawaɲct   ama-na-m   pu-wa-t
           mother's brother I PL 1SG-POSS-I PL I PL S-go-PERF
           'My mother's brothers went.'

The following summarizes the agreement affixes for class I:

	SG	DL	PL
Adjectival	-n	-mampan	-ump
Possessive	-kn	-rm	-ump
Verbal	na-	impa-	pu-

The numerals used with class I nouns show a number of complications.
The normal agreement pattern of adjectival suffixes for 'one' and 'four'
and verbal prefixes for 'two' and 'three' still applies, but the forms produced are not regular. In fact, that for 'three' is completely suppletive.
It is best to just list them and enter them lexically.

mpa-n	'one'	yamprantpat	'three'
impu-pal	'two'	manpamarm	'four'

The numerals above 'four' are formed as outlined in Section 3.4. Of the
forms above, only 'one' is regularly formed. 'Three' is totally suppletive, while 'two' has an unexpected prefix form *impu*- instead of *impa*-.
'Four', if regular, would be something like *ma-mampan-ama-mampan*,
but obviously this is not the case. Rather there is an unusual dual form
-*npa* following the first instance of *ma*- 'other'. This may be a spo-

radic contraction of -*mampan*, i.e., *ma+mampan* > *ma-npa*. Also, the
final suffix is the possessive dual suffix -*rm*, rather than the expected
-*mampan*. This may reflect an analogy with the form for 'four' in classes
III and V, which is not too dissimilar from this form.

Finally, the deictic stems for class I are formed almost totally regularly. The verbal prefixes are added to the proximal and far distal stems
and the adjectival suffixes to the near distal stem. The following gives
the deictic forms for class I for each of the three deictic stems:

	SG	DL	PL
PROX	na-k	impa-k	pu-k
NR DIST	m-n	m-rm	m-um
FR DIST	na-n	impa-n	pu-n

The only irregularity here is the dual form for the near distal deictic in
which the possessive concord suffix is found, rather than the adjectival
form: *m-rm*, rather than **m-mampan*.

4.1.2 Class II

Class II is the class of female humans. A majority of words in this class
are marked with the suffix -*maŋ*, a distinctive badge of the female sex.
Examples of class II nouns include the following:

SG	DL	PL	
narmaŋ	narmprum	ŋaykum	'woman/wife'
ŋay(u)k	ŋaykrm	ŋaykumpam	'mother'
apak	apakrm	apaki	'sister' (♂ ego)
kaywi	kaywcrm	ŋaykumpn	'daughter, girl'
		kumpwi	
taŋkarmaŋ	taŋkarmprum	taŋkarmput	'adolescent girl'
ŋaki	ŋakcrm	ŋakɲct	'father's sister'
warkwarmaŋ	warkwarmprum	warkwarmput	'sister-in-law' (♂ ego)
macawkmaŋ	macawkmprum	macawkmput	'mother-in-law'
marmaŋ	marmprum	marmput	'sister-in-law' (♀ ego)
pranmaŋ	pranprum	pranput	'daughter-in-law'
			(♀ ego)
kacanmaŋ	kacanprum	kacanput	'son-in-law's mother'
			(♂ ego)
awaymaŋ	awaymprum	awaymput	'mother's brother's
			wife'
apanwaknmaŋ	apanwaknprum	apanwaknput	'old woman'
kayantakimaŋ	kayantakimprum	kayantakinput	'female spirit'

This class is nearly as irregular as class I. The dual is formed in two
ways. If the singular noun has the distinctive marker of class II, -*maŋ*,
then the dual is formed with the distinctive class II dual suffix, -*mprum*,

often with nasal truncation (rule (2-15)) if the singular stem ends in a nasal. For example, the singular form *kacan-maŋ* son-in-law's mother-II SG becomes *kacan-prum* in the dual, with the loss of the nasal /m/ after the stem final /n/, according to rule (2-15). Singular class II nouns lacking -*maŋ* form their duals exactly as do class I nouns, employing the suffix -*rm*, with or without epenthetic /t/. The /t/ is inserted—this is done according to the same rule (4-1) as for class I nouns.

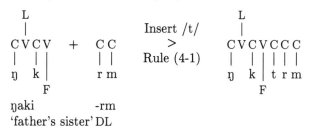

ŋaki   -rm
'father's sister' DL

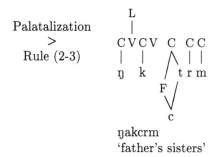

ŋakcrm
'father's sisters'

The second V in the phonetic form is, of course, realized as ɨ, but since it would be predictable anyway between the cluster /kc/, it is omitted orthographically.

As with class I, the plurals of class II are more complicated. With the single exception of 'woman', the forms in -*maŋ* form their plural regularly by the suffix -*mput*, again subject to the nasal truncation rule (2-15). The plural of 'woman' is clearly formed from the stem of 'mother' plus the class I plural suffix -*ump*. This in turn has required a new form for the plural of 'mother', which is this plural form of 'woman' plus -*am*, perhaps on analogy with the plural of 'fathers' *apwiam*. The word *apak* 'sister' forms its dual and plural exactly as do class I stems ending in /k/, so these variants are probably phonologically conditioned. The plural of *kaywi* 'daughter, girl' is clearly a compound made up of the plural of 'woman' plus the oblique suffix and the plural of the class I noun *kalakn* 'son, child, boy' (*ŋaykump-n kumpwi* woman II PL-OBL child I PL 'daughters, girls'). Finally, the plural of *ŋaki* 'father's sister', *ŋakɲct*, is completely unpredictable. It shows the same kind of irregular plural formation as class I nouns like 'brother-in-law' and 'ceremonial companion', and would simply need to have its plural specified in the lexicon.

Unlike class I, class II has the same set of suffixes for both adjectival and possessive forms. They are as follows:

SG	DL	PL
-nmaŋ	-nprump	-nput

(The final /p/ of *-nprump* DL is normally deleted by rule (2-14). Only when the oblique suffix *-n* ∼ *-nan* follows will the stop appear.) These are derived by compounding the typical class II suffixes *-maŋ*, *-mprum*, *-mput*, and the suffix *-n* (possibly from singular class I) with the usual nasal truncation in the dual and plural. The same agreement suffixes are used for possessives, but are always preceded by an epenthetic /k/, probably on analogy with the class I singular possessive suffix *-kn*. Examples of class II nouns with possessives and adjectives are offered below:

(4-7) a. apak   yua-nmaŋ
           sister-II SG   good-II SG
           'a good sister'

       b. kaywcrm   waca-k-nprum   ama-na-knprum
           daughter II DL   small-IRR-II DL   I SG-POSS-II DL
           'my two small daughters'

       c. ŋaykum   ma-nput
           woman II PL   other-II PL
           'other women'

As with the class I suffixes, these are often added to adjectives or adjectival verbs to form nouns.

yarac-k	+ -nmaŋ	> yaracknmaŋ	'European woman'
white-IRR	II SG		
waca-k	+ -nprum	> wacaknprum	'two little sisters' (♀ ego)
small-IRR	II DL		
kpa-	+ -nput	> kpanput	'big sisters' (♀ ego)
big	II PL		

The verbal prefixes, numerals, and deictics for class II are identical to those of class I, with the single exception of the word for 'one'. Here the typical adjectival agreement suffix for class II singular is suffixed to the stem for 'one' to produce *mpa-nmaŋ* one-II SG.

4.1.3 Class III

Class III is the class for higher animals, such as pigs, dogs, and crocodiles, and as such has grammatical features halfway between those of class I,

the unmarked human class, and class V, the unmarked class for inanimate nouns and the one which includes the majority of lower animals.
Examples of nouns belonging to class III follow:

SG	DL	PL	
numpran	numprantrm	numpray	'pig'
yura	yurantrm	yuray	'dog'
awa	awantrm	awawi	'cassowary'
manpa	manpantrm	manpawi	'crocodile'
nawkwan	nawkwantrm	nawkawi	'chicken'
paypra	payprantrm	paypratawi	'bird'
kika	kikantrm	kikawi	'rat'
warkawpwi	warkawpwɲcrm	warkawpwiŋkat	'wallaby'
yaka	yakantrm	yakawi	'black possum'
tmarmaŋ	tmarmaŋtrm	tmarmaŋkat	'red possum'
tuŋkntuma	tuŋkntumantrm	tuŋkntamawi	'possum (general)'
wantat	wantatntrm	wantarŋkat	'mixed color possum'
namarawi	namarawɲcrm	namarawiŋkat	'type of bird of paradise'
namakat	namakatntrm	namakarŋkat	'Count Raggi's bird of paradise'
wakrapak	wakrapakntrm	wakrapakawi	'large eel'

This class only includes higher animals, those important to humans,
such as pets, domesticated livestock, other sources of food, ceremonial
accoutrements or mythological figures. There is not a sharp boundary
between the animals of this class and those included in class V or the
other inanimate classes. Depending on the role an animal plays in a
particular discourse it may be upgraded from class V and occur with
the typical affixes of class III. This upgrading may even sporadically
occur with class III nouns. I have a few cases of *numpran* 'pig', a clear
class III noun, with the forms of class I, the unmarked human class.
Furthermore, some of the nouns listed above as class III may also belong
to class V, especially the names of the lower mammals, like the possums,
and the birds. In fact, the word for 'white possum' *irwan* is not included
above, in spite of the fact that it belongs to the general class *tuŋkntuma*
'possum', because it takes -*ra*, the typical class V plural suffix following
/n/ (*irwan-ra* 'white possums') and would normally be associated with
class V agreement affixes. However, the other words for types of possum
may also be seen with these affixes. Clearly, the boundary between
classes III and V is anything but sharp for these lower animals.

The formation of non-singulars in class III is much less complicated
than in classes I and II. All duals are formed with the suffix -*ntrm*; in
other words, the rules of /t/ and /n/ epenthesis (rules (4-1) and (4-2))

are obligatory for nouns of this class. The /n/ is, of course, subject to nasal truncation (rule (2-15)) if the stem should end in a nasal (*tmarmaŋ* 'red possum' + -*ntrm* DL > *tmarmaŋtrm*). The plural is slightly more complex. There are two allomorphs, -(*w*)*i* and -*ŋkat*. The former is restricted to nouns where singular forms end in /a/ (*numpran* 'pig' and *nawkwan* 'chicken' are exceptions, but note that the plural is irregular in the loss of the final /n/, again producing a stem ending in /a/). The epenthetic /w/ in many nouns with this plural allomorph probably reflects an earlier stem form ending in /aw/. (Karawari has the singular form *manpo* for 'crocodile', with contraction of /aw/ to /o/. Yimas has a productive rule which simplifies word-final /aw/ diphthongs to /a/; see Section 4.1.9). The plural suffix -*i* would protect the final /w/ so that it surfaces in the plural forms. However, this rule cannot be set up as productive for class III nouns (as opposed to class IX nouns), because a glance at the dual forms above shows that they have the simple vowel /a/ rather than the expected */aw/. The duals have probably been re-formed by analogy on the basis of the singulars, but the difference between the dual and plural forms demonstrates that the allomorphy of -*wi* ∼ -*i* cannot be put down to productive phonological rules, but again must be entered as a morphologically conditioned variant. The second plural allomorph for class III nouns, -*ŋkat*, is used with nouns not ending in /a/. This is a common plural marker for class V nouns; in fact, it is the unmarked one, and may have spread from class V to class III, replacing earlier plural endings.

The adjectival/possessive suffixes for class III nouns are closely related to those of class I and class V, but are distinct from both.

	SG	DL	PL
class I	-n(ADJ), -kn(POSS)	-mampan/-rm	-ump
class III	-n(ADJ), -kn(POSS)	-ntrm	-ump
class V	-n(ADJ), -kn(POSS)	-ntrm	-ra

All three classes have the same singular suffix, but in the dual, class III goes with class V in having -*ntrm* (i.e., -*rm* with obligatory /n/ and /t/ epenthesis), while in the plural it is similar to class I in having -*ump*. Examples of the usage of adjectival/possessive suffixes follow:

(4-8) a. ama-na-m   numpray   kpa-m
         1SG-POSS-III PL   pig III PL big-III PL
         'my big pigs'

      b. tmarmaŋtrm   ama-na-ntrm   waca-k-ntrm
         red possum III DL 1SG-POSS-III DL   small-IRR-III DL
         'my two small red possums'

The verbal prefixes of class III exhibit the same pattern as the adjectival/possessive suffixes: the dual is shared with class V, and the plural with class I.

	SG	DL	PL
class I	na-	impa-	pu-
class III	na-	tma-	pu-
class V	na-	tma-	ya-

The only new form is the dual prefix for class III, *tma-*. This is clearly related to the adjectival/possessive suffix *-rm*, where /r/ becomes *t* in initial position (/r/ may not occur word-initially in Yimas). Unlike the other forms, there is no metathesis of consonant and vowel in the derivation of this verbal prefix from the corresponding adjectival/possessive suffix. The suffix *-rm* is simply converted to a prefix *tma-*. The final /a/ is not completely explicable, but may be the result of analogy with all the other classes, for which the dual verbal prefix always ends in an /a/. The following are examples of the usage of verbal prefixes for class III nouns:

(4-9) a. numprantrm tma-na-tampulanta-n
pig III DL   III DL S-DEF-run-PRES
'The two pigs are running.'

b. manpawi   pu-awŋkwi-kia-ntut
crocodile III 1PL III PL S-sink-NIGHT-RM PAST
'The crocodiles went down.'

The numerals of class III generally are very different from those of class I and are identical in form to those of class V.

mpa-n	'one'	tamunum	'three'
tm-pal	'two'	maramarm	'four'

'One' and 'two' are formed regularly, 'two' by prefixing the verbal prefix *tm-* minus the final /a/. 'Three' is totally suppletive; this suppletion is ancient, going back to Proto-Lower Sepik, as Chambri has the cognate form for 'three' *samnenamp*. The form for 'four' is still based on *ma-* 'other', but in this case probably derives from contraction of a form with *-rm* (*ma-rm+ama-rm > maramarm*).

The deictics of class III are formed in the regular way by adding the verbal prefixes to the proximal and far distal deictic stems and the adjectival/possessive suffixes to the near distal stem, resulting again in forms which are a mix of classes I and V.

	SG	DL	PL
PROX	na-k	tma-k	pu-k
NR DIST	m-n	m-rm	m-ump
FR DIST	na-n	tma-n	pu-n

The near distal forms are identical to those of class I, as are the plural proximal and far distal forms with the prefix *pu-*. The dual proximal and far distal forms, on the other hand, take the same prefix *tma-* as their class V equivalents, rather than the class I prefix *impa-*.

4.1.4 Class IV

This class is restricted almost completely to plants and trees, many of them important to human activities. Not all words for plants and trees are in this class, but many are. Its diagnostic marker is a stem-final *-um*, and in many ways this class is similar to the phonologically based classes VI through X. Consider the following examples from this class:

SG	DL	PL	
irpm	irpmul	irpuɲi	'coconut palm'
tnum	tnumul	tpwi	'canonical sago palm'
tmarum	tmarmul	tmaruɲi	'sago palm with short spikes'
tŋklum	tŋklumul	tŋklŋkat	'sago palm with very short spikes'
maɲcrum	maɲcrmul	maɲcruɲi	'vine type'
maŋkum	maŋkumul	maŋkuɲi	'vein, tendon'
nŋkrum	nŋkrumul	nŋkruɲi	'tree (sp)'
pawnum	pawnumul	pawnuɲi	'tree (sp)'
tapukam	tapukamul	tapukaɲi	'tree (sp)'
kwarum	kwarmul	kwaruɲi	'tree (sp)'
tarkumpiam	tarkumpiamul	tarkumpiaɲi	'tree (sp)'
maripm	maripmul	maripuɲi	'wild coconut palm'
plum	plmul	pluɲi	'bush (sp) in swamp'
tuanum	tuanumul	tuanumkat	'black beetle'

The word *maŋkum* 'vein, tendon', of course, does not denote a plant or tree, but the physical similarity of these to a vine is clearly the basis for the assignment of this noun to class IV. The assignment of *tuanum* 'black beetle' to this class is quite unexpected. The only explanation is the people's observation that it comes up from the ground like grass. The singular forms of all class IV nouns end in *-m*, underlying *-um*. The /u/ deletes according to rule (2-9) between a stop and a homorganic nasal in the final syllable (/irp-um/ > *irpm* 'coconut palm') and idiosyncratically, for this suffix, following an /a/ (/takupa-um/ > *tapukam* 'tree (sp)'). This deletion of /u/ following /a/ also applies to the very similar class I plural marker *-ump*, but as we shall see when considering the markers for class X, this is not a general feature of noun class markers beginning in /u/. That the /u/ is in fact underlyingly present is demonstrated by the operation of roundedness dissimilation.

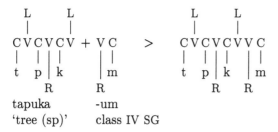

tapuka   -um
'tree (sp)'   class IV SG

Remember that /u/ deletion (2-9) only applies to the CV skeleton and leaves the R autosegment floating on the syllable. Applying rule (2-9) to the above, we get the following:

Since R is still associated with the syllable, it prevents the R in the previous segment from spreading across the peripheral stop, deriving the correct form *tapukam*, rather than the erroneous *tapukwam, which would be produced by R spreading. A similar explanation applies to *tarkumpiam* 'tree (sp)', instead of *tarkumpwiam.

The distinctive marker of the dual for class IV is -*l* and this it has in common with classes VI through X. As the final cluster formed by suffixing -*l* to the singular form ending in -*um* is an impermissible one, a *i* is naturally inserted. This *i* is subject to R spreading from the previous syllable, but often the /u/ of the previous rule disappears subject to rule (2-9) (and also idiosyncratically for a number of stems in this class; see the above examples), so that the *u* resulting from vowel insertion is the only carrier of R. Furthermore, it is invariably the case that this vowel carries primary stress in the dual form. Consider the following derivations:

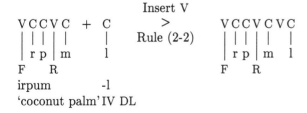

irpum   -l
'coconut palm' IV DL

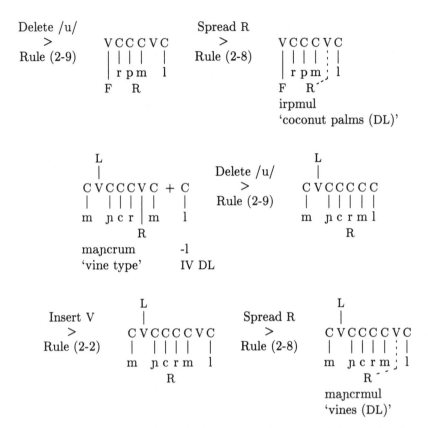

Delete /u/
>
Rule (2-9)

Spread R
>
Rule (2-8)

'coconut palms (DL)'

Delete /u/
>
Rule (2-9)

maɲcrum   -l
'vine type'   IV DL

Insert V
>
Rule (2-2)

Spread R
>
Rule (2-8)

maɲcrmul
'vines (DL)'

The plurals are formed regularly by replacing -*um* with -*uɲi* (again with loss of /u/ after /a/). The only irregularities are the suppletive plural *tpwi* for *tnum* 'canonical sago palm' (this is also the plural form for *tpuk* 'sago pancake', the discussion of which appears in Section 4.1.10) and the -*ŋkat*-based plural for *tŋklum* 'sago palm with very short spikes' and *tuanum* 'black beetle'. An interesting feature of the plural suffix -*uɲi* is that the /ŋ/ is opaque to R spreading, i.e., -*uɲwi* is completely unacceptable. This may be to avoid confusion with the class X plural suffix -*uŋkwi*, but in fact there are no examples anywhere in Yimas of **ŋwi*, only *ŋkwi*. The reason for this gap is unclear, especially in view of the fact that the sequence *mwi* does exist (*tumwikwa* 'smoked fish').

The adjectival/possessive endings of class IV are closely related to the noun markers; only the plural is divergent.

SG	DL	PL
-um	-mul	-ra

Again, the dual is derived from -*um* + -*l*, but the plural is a completely unpredictable suppletive form, -*ra*. This is the plural form for the unmarked class V and presumably spread from it to class IV by analogy. Examples of usage of these suffixes follow:

(4-10) a. tnum   ama-na-m   kawŋkra-k-um
    sago palm IV SG 1SG-POSS-IV SG long-IRR-IV SG
    'my tall sago palm'

   b. nŋkruŋi kalc-k-ra
    tree (sp) IV PL strong-IRR-IV PL
    'strong trees'

The verbal prefixes for class IV are derived in a parallel fashion to those of classes VI through X and are as follows:

SG	DL	PL
mu-	mula-	ya-

The basic verbal prefix, that of the singular, is derived regularly from the corresponding adjectival/possessive suffix by metathesizing the vowel-consonant sequence: -*um* > *mu*-. The dual prefix is formed by adding the dual marker *l*- to the singular verbal prefix *mu*- and following this with a further non-singular morpheme *a*- (we have already seen this final *a*- in other dual verbal prefixes, e.g., *tma*- < -*rm* in class III). *ya*- is the verbal prefix always associated with the adjectival/possessive suffix -*ra* (besides class IV other classes which have adjectival/possessive -*ra* are classes V, VII, VIII, and X). *ya*- actually has no overt class marker and is made up of a plural marker *i*- plus the non-singular verbal prefix *a*-, i.e., *ya*- < ∅ (class marker) + *i*- (plural) + *a*- (non-singular). Examples of the use of these verbal prefixes are given below:

(4-11) a. tnumul   mula-tmuk-t
    sago palm IV DL IV DL S-fall-PERF
    'The two sago palms fell over.'

   b. maŋkuŋi ya-na-kkt-n
    tendon IV PL IV PL S-DEF-hurt-PRES
    'The tendons are sore.'

The numerals and deictics for class IV are formed perfectly regularly: by suffixing the adjectival/possessive suffixes to 'one', 'four', and the near distal deictic, and the verbal prefixes to 'two', 'three', and the proximal and far distal deictics.

   Numerals:

mpa-m	mu-ramnawt
one-IV SG	IV SG-three
'one'	'three'

mu-rpal   ma-mul-ama-mul
IV SG-two   other-IV PL-other-IV DL
'two'   'four'

Deictics:

	SG	DL	PL
PROX	mu-k	mula-k	ya-k
NR DIST	m-um	mu-mul	m-ra
FR DIST	mu-n	mula-n	ya-n

The first *u* in the dual near distal form comes from R spreading to the left to an inserted V. This form actually commonly alternates with a contracted form *mul*.

4.1.5 Class V

This is by far the largest class in the language and contains close to 50% of all nouns. There is no semantic basis for this noun class; it is the first for which assignment is determined phonologically, by the final segment(s). If a noun does not belong to one of the previous noun classes by virtue of its meanings (or, in the case of class IV, its meaning and diagnostic ending -*um*), it belongs to class V when it terminates in one of the following segments: /p, k, m, n, ŋ, nt, r, l/. Furthermore, if a word ends in /i/ or /y/ and is arbitrarily not assigned to class VIII, the normal class for such nouns, it too is assigned to class V. Study the following examples of nouns of class V, presented according to underlying final segments:

SG	DL	PL	
Final /p/:			
nuŋkp	nuŋkpntrm	nuŋkpŋkat	'hearth'
yawkawp	yawkawpntrm	yawkawpŋkat	'rope'
awkp	awkpntrm	awkpŋkat	'wild sago palm'
Final /k/:			
numpk	numpkrm	numpkat/ numpkmpt	'mountain'
amk	amkrm	amkat	'uvula'
awak	awakrm	awaki	'star'
muntuk	muntukrm	muntukat	'neck'
ŋaŋkmpak	ŋaŋkmpakrm	ŋaŋkmpaki	'vine (sp)'
majck	majckrm	majckat	'rope to climb coconut palm'
awaklak	awaklakntrm	awaklaki	'florescent moss'
kampramak	kampramakntrm	kampramaki	'black ant'
kkrak	kkrakrm	kkraki	'brown toad'
wik	wiktrm	wikat	'gecko'

klak	klakntrm	klaki	'large green parrot'
lukayk	lukaykntrm	lukaykat	'tree (sp)'
yarakrak	yarakrakntrm	yarakraki	'tree (sp)'
trk	trkrm	trkat	'gills of fish'

Final /m/:

aŋkaŋkam	aŋkaŋkamtm	aŋkaŋkamkat	'black water python'
mpiŋam	mpiŋamtm	mpiŋamkat	'navel'
mpum	mpumtm	mpumkat	'large crayfish'
naykam	naykamtm	naykamkat	'clavicle'
tkum	tkumtm	tkumkat	'black bird (sp)'

Final /n/:

muŋkn	muŋkntm	muŋkunra	'earring'
mpuŋkan	mpuŋkantm	mpuŋkanra	'crowned pigeon'
wurmpn	wurmpntm	wurmpnra	'tree (sp)'
yampn	yampntm	yampnra	'tree (sp)'
pian	piantm	piankat	'fish (sp)'
wun	wuntm	wunt	'sago grub'
tamun	tamuntm	tamut	'big mouth fish'
nawran	nawrantm	nawray	'armband'
awn	awntm	awnra	'pitpit'
tmun	tmuntm	tmunra	'cane type'
yan	yantm	yara	'tree, wood'
tampan	tampantm	tampanra	'liver'
waŋkn	waŋkntm	waŋknra	'hourglass drum'
taŋkun	taŋkuntm	taŋkunra	'cassowary bone dagger'
wamun	wamuntm	wamura	'owl'
klwan	klwantm	klwanra	'lotus'
yukn	yukntm	yuknra	'tree (sp)'

Final /ŋ/:

klmpaŋ	klmpaŋtm	klmpaŋkat	'worm'
irmpŋ	irmpŋtm	irmpŋkat	'slit drum/garamut'
wuntumaŋ	wuntumaŋtm	wuntumaŋkat	'carved mask'[1]
wampuŋ	wampuŋtm	wampuŋkat	'heart'
mumunmaŋ	mumunmaŋtm	mumunmaŋkat	'large turtle'

Final /nt/ (cluster simplifies to /n/ in word-final position
by rule (2-14)):

makun	makuntrm	makuntt	'anus'

---

[1] These last two words, *irmpŋ* and *wuntumaŋ*, often co-occur with agreement affixes of class I because of mythological beliefs that they are men.

| kapun | kapuntrm | kapuntt | 'freshwater prawn' |
| wakn | wakntrm | wakntt | 'snake' |

Final /r/ (becomes *t* in word-final position and before /n/ by rules (2-4) and (2-5)):

tat	tatntrm	tart	'spikes on sago palm'
kat	katntrm	karŋkat	'sago palm bark'
tkt	tktntrm	tkrŋkat	'chair'
makut	makutntrm	makurŋkat	'tree (sp)'
tmpt	tmptntrm	tmprŋkat	'spine for sago thatch'
tmpukt	tmpuktntrm	tmpukrŋkat	'cane type'
kaykut	kaykutntrm	kaykurŋkat	'hornbill'
aput	aputntrm	apurŋkat	'green skink'
takt	taktntrm	takrŋkat	'clitoris'
yakut	yakutntrm	yakurŋkat	'net bag'
numpt	numptntrm	numprŋkat	'small centipede'

Final /l/:

mml	mmlcrm	mmlŋkat	'Javan file snake'
mkl	mktɲcm	mklŋkat	'monitor lizards, goanna'
al	atɲcrm	alŋkat	'bushknife, machete'
tmal	tmatɲcrm	tmalŋkat	'sun, day'[2]

Final /i/ or /y/ (i.e., the autosegment F):

kawi	kawɲcrm	kawɲct	'fish (sp)'
kawi	kawɲcrm	kawiŋkat	'large red parrot'
taki	takcrm	takiŋkat	'rock'
walŋkawi	walŋkawcrm	walŋkawiŋkat	'cane type'
kmpi	kmpcrm	kmpiŋkat	'lime gourd'
wampaŋkawi	wampaŋkawcrm	wampaŋkawiŋkat	'palm tree (sp)'
aŋkawŋkwi	aŋkawŋkwcrm	aŋkawŋkwiŋkat	'large white snake'
waŋkanawi	waŋkanawcrm	waŋkanawiŋat	'green grasshopper insect'
pakaray	pakaracrm	pakarayŋkat	'short, brown snake'
tkay	tkaɲcrm	tkayŋkat	'nose'
wuratakay	wuratakaɲcrm	wuratakayŋkat	'turtle'
mapray	mapraɲcrm	mamprayŋkat	'fish (sp)'
aŋkiamay	aŋkiamaɲcrm	aŋkiamayŋkat	'black cockatoo'

---

[2]Note that neither liquid strengthening (rule (2-5)) nor palatalization (rule (2-3)) necessarily apply in the dual forms; sample alternatives are *alntrm* and *tmalntrm*.

Lastly, there are two Yimas words ending in /c/, a segment which is normally prohibited from occurring word-finally. There may be recent loans from neighboring languages, but in any case they are assigned to class V.

SG	DL	PL	
mac	mactrm	macŋkat	'beetle (sp)'
wumprkac	wumprkacntrm	wumprkacŋkat	'white heron'

With such a large, heterogeneous class, it is not surprising that the marking for number exhibits a considerable degree of allomorphy. The dual is much simpler than the plural: all class V nouns take the suffix -*rm* (-*tm* following a nasal, as in *yampn-tm* tree (sp)-DL). The rules of /n/ and /t/ epenthesis obligatorily apply only in some forms. They apply universally to stems ending in /p/ and /r/ and may never apply to those ending in /nt/, presumably because the output of the rules, the cluster /nt/, is already present. As the above examples clearly demonstrate, stems ending in other segments exhibit some variation. All dual forms with obligatory /n/ and /t/ epenthesis, of course, exist in those forms only, but those without have hypercoristic alternative forms in which these rules apply. So, alternating with *awak-rm* star-DL 'two stars', there is the acceptable, albeit less common, *awak-ntrm*. Further, there are generational differences in the application of the epenthesis rules in this class. Younger speakers, i.e., under thirty, have a much greater tendency to use the epenthesized forms than not. This undoubtedly reflects a process of regularization in the system, for the epenthesized forms are the most common, and are equivalent to the form of the dual adjectival/possessive suffix for this class, i.e., -*ntrm*.

The stems ending in nasals never have overt /n/ epenthesis, merely /t/ epenthesis. This is a likely reflection of the nasal truncation rule (2-15): *irmpŋ* 'slit drum' + -*rm* DL would become **irmpŋntrm* by /n/ and /t/ epenthesis, and finally *irmpŋtrm*, an acceptable form, by nasal truncation. Note that if neither epenthesis rule applies to stems ending in nasals, the initial /r/ of -*rm* DL strengthens to *t* following the nasal (*irmpŋ-tm* 'slit drum (DL)').

The plural allomorphs are much more complex. These class V nouns present not less than four distinct plural allomorphs. They are classified below according to final segments of the nouns they occur with:

-*ŋkat* ~ -*kat* (after nasals)
         ~ -*at* (after /k/):   /p, k, m, n, ŋ, r, l, i, y, c/
-*i* ~ -*y* (after vowels):   /k, n/
-*ra*:   /n/
-*t*:   /n, nt, r/

This chart clearly indicates that -*ŋkat* is the unmarked plural allomorph for class V, as it occurs with all final segments except /nt/. This conjecture is further supported by the fact that when a speaker is unsure of the proper suffix, he will invariably correct to -*ŋkat*, provided the final segment is anything but /n/. The plural allomorph -*ra* is so uniquely associated with final /n/ that this is always the choice for nouns ending in this consonant. However, loan words into Yimas from Tok Pisin which fit into class V phonologically are also pluralized with -*ŋkat*, even if they do end in /n/ (Tok Pisin *sospen* 'saucepan' > Yimas *tcpn*, PL: *tcpn-kat*).

The allomorph -*i* is predominately associated with stems ending in /k/, although it occurs with one noun ending in /n/ (*nawran* 'armband', PL: *nawray*). This suffix is, of course, the primary plural formative for class III nouns, and this demonstrates again the close relation between class III and class V. Nouns ending in /k/ which do not take -*i* use -*ŋkat*, almost always in the form -*at*. The difference between -*i* and -*ŋkat* for /k/ final stems may be phonological: all examples of -*i* plurals have the vowel /a/ in the previous syllable. As mentioned previously, the plural formative -*ra* is uniquely associated with /n/-final nouns, but there are exceptions. In addition to the examples of -*ŋkat* and -*i* plurals, there are also /n/ final nouns with the plural -*t*, e.g., *wun* 'sago grub', PL: *wunt*. Sporadically, nouns ending in /n/ lose this segment before adding the plural suffix (*yan* 'tree, wood', PL: *ya-ra*; *tamun* 'big mouth fish', PL: *tamu-t*). The plural suffix -*t*, besides being occasionally found in these /n/-final stems, is the unexceptional choice for nouns ending in /nt/ and also occurs with monosyllabic /r/-final stems containing the vowel /a/ (*tat* 'spikes on sago palm', PL: *tart*).

The adjectival/possessive agreement suffixes for class V nouns are close to those of classes I and III.

SG	DL	PL
-n(ADJ), -kn(POSS)	-ntrm	-ra

Only the plural diverges from the suffixes of class III. It is the same form as the plural suffix for class IV. Note that the dual form is -*rm* with obligatory /n/ and /t/ epenthesis. This is invariable, regardless of whether the noun modified has /n/ or /t/ epenthesis in its dual form. The following examples illustrate the use of these suffixes:

(4-12) a. tnknt-k-ntrm   tktntrm   ama-na-ntrm
        heavy-IRR-V DL   chair V DL   1SG-POSS-V PL
        'my two heavy chairs'

       b. nawray   ama-na-ra   urkpwica-k-ra
        armband V PL   1SG-POSS-V PL   black-IRR-V PL
        'my black armbands'

As with the adjectival/possessive suffixes, the verbal prefixes for class V are close to those of classes I and III, again with a divergence in the plural. (As mentioned in the discussion of class IV affixes, a plural adjectival/possessive suffix -ra is always correlated with a verbal prefix ya-.) The verbal prefixes for class V are given below:

SG	DL	PL
na-	tma-	ya-

(4-13) a. tkt   na-tmuk-t
        chair V SG V SG S-fall-PERF
        'The chair fell over.'
     b. kkraki   ya-aykwara-t
        toad V PL V PL S-jump-PERF
        'The toads jumped.'

The numerals of class V are identical to those of class III, and the deictics are very close, with only the plural affixes -ra and ya- in place of the class III forms -ump and pu-.

Numerals:

mpa-n	'one'	tamunun	'three'
tm-pal	'two'	maramarm	'four'

Deictics:

	SG	DL	PL
PROX	na-k	tma-k	ya-k
NR DIST	m-n	m-rm	m-ra
FR DIST	na-n	tma-n	ya-n

4.1.6 Class VI

Nouns are assigned to class VI by ending in /ŋk/, which is simplified in word-final position to /ŋ/ by the final nasal plus stop cluster simplification rule (2-14). This is the most regular of all noun classes in its formations. Consider the following examples of class VI nouns:

SG	DL	PL	
antmaŋ	antmaŋkl	antmaŋki	'sulphur crested cockatoo'
kaŋ	kaŋkl	kaŋki	'kina shell'
yampaŋ	yampaŋkl	yanpaŋki	'head'
pamuŋ	pamkl	pamki	'leg'
trŋ	trŋkl	trŋki	'tooth'
pantaŋ	pantaŋkl	pantaŋki	'buttocks'
krayŋ	krayŋkl	krayŋki	'swamp frog'
iraŋ	iraŋkl	iraŋki	'venomous snake (sp)'
yarmuraŋ	yarmuraŋkl	yarmuraŋki	'black eel'

muraŋ	muraŋkl	muraŋki	'paddle'
akrŋ	akrŋkl	akrŋki	'green tree frog'
iciŋaŋ	iciŋaŋkl	iciŋaŋki	'plant (sp)'
naŋkranumpnŋ	naŋkranumpnkl	naŋkranumpnki	'tree (sp)'
upntampŋ	upntampŋkl	upntampŋki	'heart'
yampunŋ	yampunkl	yampunki	'small reddish bird'
muntanŋ	muntankl	muntanki	'kidney'
wampunŋ	wampunkl	wampunki	'sago flour'
walamuŋ	walamkl	walamki	'sago carrying basket'
wuntŋ	wuntŋkl	wuntŋki	'fish (sp)'
yanŋ	yankl	yanki	'stick, twig'
karŋ	karŋkl	karŋki	'glans penis'

The formations here are regular and pretty straightforward. The stems end underlyingly in /ŋk/. As the singular has no overt affixation, this cluster appears word-finally and becomes /ŋ/ by rule (2-14). The dual is formed by suffixing -*l*, as in class IV, but there is no spread of R for class VI nouns, even if the vowel of the final syllable of the stem is /u/. Note that the dual form of *pamuŋ* 'leg' is *pamkl*, pronounced [pamgil], not *[pamgul]. The deletion of /u/ in the dual forms is of course the result of the /u/ deletion rule (2-9), but it appears that with this class (and only with this class), there is no compensatory R spreading. As will be discussed in Section 4.1.10, there are two ways to deal with this problem: as a morphologically conditioned exception to R spreading, or as a stipulation on the /u/ deletion rule for class VI nouns that functions to delete the R autosegment as well as the V slot in the CV skeleton. Contrast the derivations of the dual forms of class IV *irpm* 'coconut palm' with class VI *pamuŋ* 'leg':

Class IV:

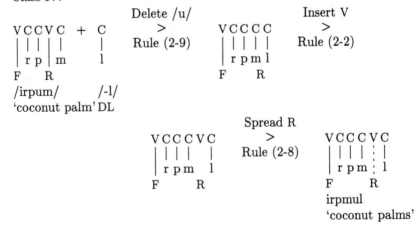

Class VI:

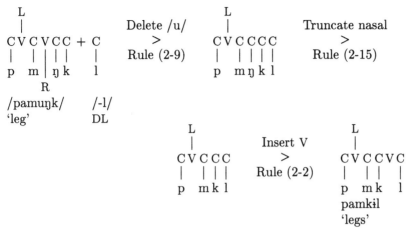

L
|
CVCVCC + C   Delete /u/
| | | | | | >
p m | ŋ k   l   Rule (2-9)
     R
/pamuŋk/   /-l/
'leg'   DL

This behavior of class VI nouns cannot be put down to phonological reasons, i.e., the differences in stem-final /m/ and /ŋk/. As we shall see later in Section 4.1.10, there is another class, class X, which is like class VI in having stems ending in /ŋk/, but for which /u/ deletion and R spreading operate normally. (It needs to be pointed out that *pamkul* is in fact a possible variant for some speakers, although *pamkil* is the preferred form. This would suggest that the operation of /u/ deletion with this form, and others like it, is in fact variable, sometimes deleting just the V slot, and sometimes deleting the autosegment R as well).

The plural of class VI nouns is formed by suffixing -*i*, with the same battery of phonological rules such as /u/ deletion (2-9) and nasal truncation (2-14). Again, /u/ deletion is typically exhaustive so that there is no R spreading. Hence the normal plural of *pamuŋ* 'leg' is *pamki* (*pamkwi* is, however, a marked alternate).

The adjectival/possessive agreement suffixes for class VI are transparently derived from the noun inflections. As with the nouns, they are the class marker -*ŋk* plus the number marker Ø for the singular, the number marker -*l* for the dual, and the number marker -*i* for the plural, as follows:

	SG	DL	PL
	-ŋk	-ŋkl	-ŋki

The singular form will of course be realized as *ŋ* in word-final position by rule (2-14). Examples of these suffixes follow:

(4-14) a. trŋ   ama-na-ŋ   urkpwica-k-ŋ
       tooth VI SG 1SG-POSS-VI SG black IRR-VI SG
       'my black tooth'

b. muntankl   mama-ŋkl   ama-ŋkl
   kidney VI PL   bad-IRR-VI PL   1SG-POSS-VI DL
   'my two bad kidneys'

The verbal prefixes for class VI are also derived from the noun inflections. The basic class marker -ŋk sheds its nasal and becomes a prefix
for the verbal class marker. The singular verbal prefix is simply that,
i.e., k-, from k- (class VI verbal marker) plus ∅ (singular). The dual
is kla- from k- (class VI) plus l- (dual marker) plus a- (non-singular
marker), constructed in parallel fashion to the verbal prefixes of classes
IV and V. The plural verbal prefix kia- is much the same: k- (class VI)
plus i- (plural marker) plus a- (non-singular).

SG	DL	PL
k-	kla-	kia-

(4-15) a. yampaŋ   k-ŋa-na-kkt-n
         head VI SG   VI SG S-1SG D-DEF-hurt-PRES
         'I have a headache.'

   b. muraŋki   kia-tmuk-t
      paddle VI SG   VI SG S-fall-PERF
      'The paddles fell over.'

The numerals and deictics for this class are formed as expected, by
adding the adjectival/possessive suffixes to 'one' and 'four' and the near
distal deictic stem and the verbal prefixes to 'two', 'three', and the proximal and far distal deictic stems.

Numerals:

mpa-ŋ	'one'	k-ramnawt	'three'
k-rpal	'two'	ma-ŋkl+ama-ŋki	'four'

This last form is slightly irregular. Note that it is formed by adding the
dual suffix to the first instance of ma- 'other', but by adding the plural
suffix to the second (ma-ŋkl+ama-ŋki other-VI DL+other-VI PL 'four').

Deictics:

	SG	DL	PL
PROX	k-k	kla-k	kia-k
NR DIST	m-ŋ	m-ŋkl	m-ŋki
FR DIST	k-n	kla-n	kia-n

4.1.7 Class VII

This class is marked by final /mp/, again simplified by rule (2-14) to m
in word-final position. It is similar in a number of respects to class VI,
but is not quite as regular in its formations.

SG	DL	PL	
tanm	tanpl	tanpat	'bone'
akm	akmpl	akmpat	'sword grass (kunai)'
impram	imprampl	imprampat	'basket type'
tampaym	tampaympl	tampaympat	'food hanger'
nampunm	nampunpl	nampunpat	'wing'
tantayŋkraym	tantayŋkraympl	tantayŋkraympat	'spider'
yaym	yaympl	yaympat	'vagina'
paym	paympl	paympat	'black beetle'
pawm	pawmpl	pawmpat	'black bird (sp)'
tpnm	tpnmpl	tpnmpat	'spear point'
manm	manpl	manpat	'men's cult house'
karm	karmpl	karmpat	'lip, language'
akakrm	akakrmpl	akakrmpat	'green grasshopper'
piam	piampl	piampat	'arrow'
pkam	pkampl	pkampat	'back'
paŋklm	paŋklmpl	paŋklmpat	'small mantis'
narm	narmpl	narmpat	'skin'
ŋarm	ŋarmpl	ŋarmpat	'branch'
muntam	muntampl	muntampat	'swamp'
naŋklm	naŋklmpl	naŋklmpat	'finger'
waprm	waprmpl	wapwi	'hair'
nuŋkraym	nuŋkraympl	nuŋkray	'toe'
ŋaŋkm	ŋaŋkmpl	ŋaŋki	'swamp grass (for making baskets, roofing and mats)'
antkm	antkmpl	antki	'sago thatch'
nmprm	nmprmpl	nmpi	'leaf, letter'
kampurm	kampurmpl	kampwi	'grass'
aprm	aprmpl	apra	'plate'

This class is completely parallel to class VI in the singular and dual. The class marker for class VII is /mp/. The singular is simply this (i.e., -mp plus ∅ for singular), and the dual is the class marker plus -l, the dual suffix. Nasal truncation (rule (2-15)) will apply to resulting nasal clusters (SG: *tanm* 'bone', DL: *tanpl* 'two bones'). The plurals, unlike those of class VI, show some variation. The unmarked plural is -*at*, possibly a contraction of -*ŋkat* after the final /mp/ cluster of the stem, but there are two other allomorphs. One allomorph, -*a*, is very rare, found only in *aprm* 'plate', PL: *apra*. This form has a regularized alternative *aprmpat* in common use, especially with younger speakers, i.e., under thirty-five. The other allomorph, -*i*, is a little more common:

there are perhaps a half dozen forms in all. The -*i* plural of class VII differs from the morpheme of the same form in class VI in that the class marker for class VII is deleted before it is suffixed (*ŋaŋkum* 'swamp grass', PL: *ŋaŋki*). This deletion does not occur when -*i* is added to class VI nouns (*trŋ* 'tooth', PL: *trŋki*). Some of the -*i* plurals of class VII have regularized alternate forms in -*at*, but others do not.

SG	PL	
waprm	wapwi, *waprmpat	'hair'
nuŋkraym	nuŋkray, nuŋkraympat	'toe'
ŋaŋkm	ŋaŋki, ŋaŋkmpat	'swamp grass'
nmprm	nmpi, *nmprmpat	'leaf'
kampurm	kampwi, kampurmpat	'grass'
antkm	antki, ?antkmpat	'sago thatch'

While the two plural forms for 'toe' are clearly acceptable alternatives, with the regularized -*at* form favored by younger speakers, the -*at* form for 'leaf' is still stigmatized and, if used, would elicit a corrective response from most speakers.

The adjectival/possessive agreement suffixes for class VII are:

SG	DL	PL
-mp	-mpl	-ra

The singular will, of course, be pronounced as /m/ word-finally. The formation of the singular and dual suffixes are exactly like those of class VI. The singular is the class marker -*mp* plus the number marker $\emptyset$ for singular, while the dual is the same class marker -*mp* plus -*l*, the dual number marker. The plural agreement suffix is the unexpected -*ra*, but this reflects the divergent plural inflection for class VII nouns. Examples of the usage of these suffixes follow:

(4-16) a. impram   ama-na-m   kpa-m
            basket VII SG   1SG-POSS-VII SG   big-VII SG
            'my big basket'

        b. nmpi   yua-ra   ama-na-ra
            leaf VII PL   good-VII PL   1SG-POSS-VII PL
            'my good leaves, letters'

The verbal prefixes are formed similarly: the singular and the dual parallel those of class VI, but not the plural. The verbal class marking prefix is again formed by dropping the initial nasal. So while class VI -*ŋk* becomes *k*-, class VII -*mp* becomes *p*-. The singular is simply *p*-, the class marker, plus $\emptyset$ for singular; the dual is, as expected, *pla*-, from *p*- (class VII marker) plus *l*- (dual) plus *a*- (non-singular). The plural is, of course, *ya*- from $\emptyset$ (class marker) plus *i*- (plural) plus *a*-

(non-singular). As mentioned earlier in the discussion of classes IV and
V, the adjectival/possessive suffix -*ra* is invariably associated with the
verbal prefix *ya*-.

	SG	DL	PL
	p-	pla-	ya-

(4-17) a. tanm   ama-na-m   p-kumprakara-t
bone VII SG 1SG-POSS-VII SG VII SG S-break-PERF
'My bone broke.'

   b. tampaympat   ya-na-apica-mpi-irm-n
food hanger VII PL VII PL-DEF-hang-SEQ-stand-PRES
'The food hangers are hanging up.'

The numerals and deictics for class VII are totally regular: the ad-
jectival/possessive suffixes are added to 'one', 'four', and the near distal
deictic, and the verbal prefixes to 'two', 'three', and the proximal and
far distal deictics.

Numerals:

mpa-m	'one'	p-ramnawt	'three'
p-rpal	'two'	ma-mpl+ama-mpl	'four'

Deictics:

	SG	DL	PL
PROX	p-k	pla-k	ya-k
NR DIST	m-m	mpl	m-ra
FR DIST	p-n	pla-n	ya-n

The near distal dual form is derived regularly by nasal truncation (2-15):
m-, near distal stem, plus -*mpl*, class VII dual becomes *mpl*.

4.1.8 Class VIII
Only nouns ending in /i/ or /y/, i.e., the autosegment F, may belong to
this class. The majority of such nouns actually belong to class V, and
class VIII has steadily decreased in size by ceding its members to class
V. Today class VIII is smallest of the ten major noun classes, with under
twenty members. Some examples of class VIII nouns follow:

SG	DL	PL	
kay	kal ~ kayl	kacmpt ~ kaycmpt	'canoe'
nŋay	nŋal ~ nŋayl	nŋaɲcmpt ~ nŋayɲcmpt	'breast'
kawkway	kawkwal ~ kawkwayl	kawkwaɲcmpt ~ kawkwayɲcmpt	'small black bird'
tŋay	tŋal ~ tŋayl	tŋaɲcmpt ~ tŋayɲcmpt	'shark'

yaŋi	yaŋl ~ yaŋil	yaŋɲcmpt	'clay pot'
matɲci	matɲcl ~ matɲcil	malcmpt	'white water bird'
katɲci	katɲcl ~ katɲcil	kalci	'black hawk'
mayŋi	mayŋl ~ mayŋil	mayŋɲcmpt	'beetle (sp)'
	~ mayɲl	~ mayɲɲcmpt	
	~ mayɲil	~ mayŋiɲcmpt	
		~ mayɲiɲcmpt	
tarpi	tarpl ~ tarpil	tarpɲmpt	'tree (sp)'
		~ tarpiɲmpt	
arakwi	arakul	arakwɲcmpt	'vine (sp)'
		~ arakuɲcmpt	
awi	awɨl ~ awil	awiɲcmpt	'sago pounding
	~ awl	~ awɲcmpt	adze'
awtmayŋi	awtmayŋl	awtmayŋɲmpt	'sugarcane'
	~ awtmayŋil	~ awtmayɲɲmpt	
	~ awtmayɲl	~ awtmayŋiɲmpt	
	~ awtmayɲil	~ awtmayɲiɲmpt	
anti	—	—	'ground, land'
kumpwi	kumpul ~ kumpwɨl	kumpwia	'flying fox'
	~ kumpwil		
waŋki	waŋkl ~ waŋkil	waŋkia	'cross beams'

All nouns in this class end in a segment representable as $\overset{(L)}{\underset{F}{V}}$. In the

dual forms, the suffix -*l* is added, represented as $\underset{r\;\;F}{C}$. In other words,

the dual forms in this class contain two adjacent segments linked to
the autosegment F. The dual suffix cannot accept F from the adjoining
$\overset{(L)}{\underset{F}{V}}$ by palatalization, because it is itself already associated with F and

therefore does not fit the structural description of the palatalization rule
(2-3). The language allows two possibilities in this case. The sequence
can be realized as is, with the two adjoining segments linked to their
own F features, as follows, yielding /il/ or /ayl/.

Or an optional rule of dissimilative F loss, similar to that involved in

reduplication (rule (2-7)) can apply (but here restricted to the dual suffix
-*l*), in which the first segment loses its F autosegment.

(4-18) Dissimilative F loss (DL) (optional)

$$
\begin{array}{c}
\text{(L)} \\
\mid \\
\text{V} \\
\mid \\
\text{F}
\end{array}
\rightarrow
\begin{array}{c}
\text{(L)} \\
\mid \\
\text{V} \quad / \ \_\_ + \ \text{C} \\
\qquad\qquad\qquad \wedge \\
\qquad\qquad\quad \text{r} \quad \\
\qquad\qquad\qquad\quad \text{F}_{\{DL\}}
\end{array}
$$

That is, any vowel associated with F loses this autosegment immediately
before -*l*. This rule is optional, but is especially favored for class VIII
noun stems ending in /i/.

$$
\begin{array}{c}
\text{L} \\
\mid \\
\text{C V C V} + \ \text{C} \\
\mid \ \mid \ \mid \quad\ \ \wedge \\
\text{y} \ \text{ŋ} \ \mid \quad \text{r} \\
\qquad\ \text{F} \qquad \text{F}
\end{array}
\quad > \quad
\begin{array}{c}
\text{L} \\
\mid \\
\text{C V C V} \ \text{C} \\
\mid \ \mid \ \mid \text{r} \wedge \\
\text{y} \ \text{ŋ} \ \text{r} \\
\qquad \text{F} \ \text{F}
\end{array}
$$

yaŋi   -l   yaŋil
'clay pot' PL

Or:

$$
\begin{array}{c}
\text{Lose F} \\
> \\
\text{Rule (4-18)}
\end{array}
\qquad
\begin{array}{c}
\text{L} \\
\mid \\
\text{C V C V} \ \text{C} \\
\mid \ \mid \ \ \ \wedge \\
\text{y} \ \text{ŋ} \ \text{r} \\
\qquad\quad \text{F}
\end{array}
$$

yaŋl

One of the variant dual forms for 'sago pounding adze' *awɨl* contains a
distinctive /ɨ/ which must be written, because it forms a minimal pair
with *awl* 'to get'. The derivation of this form, though, proceeds just as
the above.

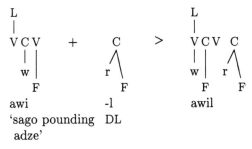

awi   -l   awil
'sago pounding DL
 adze'

Or:

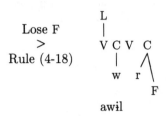

This form results because the /w/ is an underlying consonant, and so it is not a possible source for the R spreading, which applies only to vowels (see rule (2-8)). Also, if the /w/ were treated as part of the realization of the structural description of $\overset{L}{\underset{R}{V}}$, the environment for the application of R spreading would still not be met because there would then be no [-peripheral] consonant separating the two vocalic nuclei. Consequently, no R spreading is possible for this dual form, and it can be realized as *awïl*.

Now consider the dual form *kumpul* for 'flying fox'. The following derivation applies:

```
                            Lose F
C V C C V  +  C               >          C V C C V C
| | | |       |           Rule (4-18)    | | | |   |
k | m p |     l                          k | m p   l
  R     F                                  R
kumpi         -l
'flying fox'  DL
```

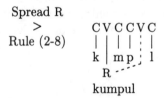

```
                        Spread R
                           >          C V C C V C
                       Rule (2-8)     | | | | : |
                                      k | m p : l
                                        R ----'
                                      kumpul
```

In this example a [-peripheral] consonant separates the vocalic nuclei, and the source of R is a vowel, so the specifications for R spreading are met.

As a final example, take *arakul*, the dual form of *arakwi* 'vine (sp)'. Its derivation would go as follows:

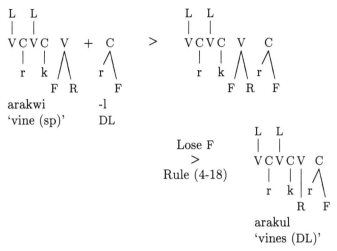

arakwi   -l
'vine (sp)'   DL

                              Lose F
                                >
                              Rule (4-18)

arakul
'vines (DL)'

This form has no need of R spreading (rule (2-8)). The loss of F by rule
(4-18) above produces the desired phonetic forms, changing /wi/ C̣ to
/u/ y̦.

The plural allomorphs for nouns of class VIII are rather irregular.
The great majority of these nouns have a plural allomorph -C*mpt*, but
the choice of the initial consonant shows up variously as /c/ (*kacmpt*
'canoes'), /ɲ/ (*tarpɲmpt* 'trees (sp)'), or /ɲc/ (*yaɲɲcmpt* 'clay pots').
The initial consonants do not seem predictable, but they are always
palatal and are derived from underlying alveolars by the palatalization
rule (2-3). This accounts for the variation in the form of the final vowel
of the stem, i.e., whether it is associated with the autosegment F or not.
The forms without it have simply shifted it to the following alveolar by
the palatalization rule (2-3). An alternative analysis here would be to
treat the plural allomorphs as beginning in underlying palatals and the
vowels preceding them as subject to the same rule of dissimilative F loss
as the dual forms. At present, there is no evidence to decide between
these alternatives. In addition to this very common plural allomorph,
there is one example of -*i* (*kalci* 'black hawks') and two of -*a* (*kumpwia* 'flying foxes', *waŋkia* 'cross beams'). It is also to be noted that
stems with medial /ŋ/, surrounded by segments which have the feature
F (*mayŋi* 'beetle (sp)' and *awtmayŋi* 'sugarcane') have alternative forms
in the dual and plural in which the /ŋ/ is palatalized to ɲ (*mayɲɲcmpt*
'beetles (sp)' and *awtmayɲl* 'two pieces of sugarcane').

The adjectival/possessive agreement suffixes for class VIII are derived
similarly to those of classes VI and VII. They are formed with the class

marker *i* (more abstractly, the class marker for VIII is simply F, the front autosegment, attached to a V slot), plus the associated number markers, -∅ for singular and -*l* for dual. The plural is the irregular -*ra*, as with class VII.

SG	DL	PL
-i	-l ~ -il	-ra

The dual form is again subject to the optional rule of dissimilative F loss, accounting for the alternation -*l* ~ -*il*. Some examples involving the class VIII affixes follow:

(4-19) a. nŋal   kpa-l   ama-na-l
          breast VIII DL big-VIII DL 1SG-POSS-VIII DL
          'my two large breasts'

     b. kacmpt   kawŋkra-k-ra   ama-na-ra
          canoe VIII PL long-IRR-VIII PL   1SG-POSS-VIII PL
          'my long canoes'

The verbal prefixes are derived similarly. As the plural adjectival/possessive suffix is -*ra*, the verbal prefix is, as expected, *ya-*, from ∅ (class marker) plus *i-* (plural) plus *a-* (non-singular). As the class marker for class VIII is F, the singular prefix is *i-*, from the class VIII marker plus ∅ (singular), and the dual is *ila-*, from *i-* (class VIII marker) plus *l-* (dual) plus *a-* (non-singular).

SG	DL	PL
i-	ila-	ya-

(4-20) a. kay   i-ɲa-ampu-n
          canoe-VIII SG VIII SG S-DEF-float-PRES
          'The canoe is floating.'

     b. awɲcmpt   ya-tmuk-t
          sago axe VIII PL VIII PL S-fall-PERF
          'The sago axes fell over.'

The numerals and deictics for class VIII are formed completely regularly: the adjectival/possessive suffixes are added to 'one', 'four', and the near distal deictic stem, and the verbal prefixes to 'two', 'three', and the proximal and far deictic stems.

Numerals:

mpa-y	'one'	i-ramnawt	'three'
i-rpal	'two'	ma-yl+ama-yl	'four'
		~ ma-l+ama-l	

The alternative forms for 'four' derive from the optional rule of dissimilative F loss (4-18).

Deictics:	SG	DL	PL
PROX	i-k	ila-k	ya-k
NR DIST	m-i	m-il	m-ra
FR DIST	i-n	ila-n	ya-n

4.1.9 Class IX

Class IX is the class of nouns ending in a segment with the autosegment
R. As /ɨ/ and its R counterpart /u/ do not occur finally, this amounts
to a de facto class of nouns ending in underlying /aw/, i.e., $\overset{\text{L}}{\underset{\text{R}}{\text{V}}}$.

Examples of class IX nouns follow:

SG	DL	PL	
tarpwa	tarpawl	tarput	'belly'
ŋarwa	ŋar(w)awl	ŋarut	'penis'
trukwa	trukawl	trukut	'knee'
yaw	yawl	yawt	'road'
malcawkwa	malcawkawl	malcawkut	'lower back'
yanara	yanarawl	yanarut	'bark chewed with betelnut'
namtampara	namtamparawl	namtamparut	'foot'
wantakampa	wantakampawl	wantakamput	'doorway'
napra	naprawl	naprut	'membranes'
nmpanmara	nmpanmarawl	nmpanmarut	'stomach'
kampraŋkwa	kampraŋkawl	kampraŋkut	'cockroach'
krpa	krpawl	krput	'sago beetle'
wunamara	wunamarawl	wunamarut	'large centipede'
irwa	irwawl	irwut	'mat'
tumpa	tumpawl	tumput	'death adder'
krukwa	krukawl	krukut	'swamp grass'
kwikwa	kwikawl	kwikut	'fish (sp)'
kaɲwa	kaɲwawl	kaɲut	'flooring'
maywa	maywawl	maywut	'side of abdomen'
nuŋkwara	nuŋkarawl	nuŋkarut	'hand'
kawkwa	kawkwal	kawkut	'branch of sago palm'

The underlying forms of these class IX nouns can be isolated simply by
removing the dual suffix -l from the dual form; what remains is the true
base form. The plural is derived from this base form by dropping the
final diphthong /aw/ and suffixing the plural allomorph -ut. There are
a couple of additional complications. Forms in which a /w/ precedes the
final /aw/ also usually lose that /w/ (*kaɲwaw-* 'flooring', DL: *kaɲwawl*,
PL: *kaɲut*), but there are two exceptions: *irwaw-* 'mat', PL: *irwut*; and

maywaw- 'side of abdomen', PL: *maywut*. A second exception is the
plural of 'road', *yawt* from a base *yaw-*. Here there is no deletion of
/aw/, but rather the /u/ of the plural morpheme *-ut* elides.

Unusually, it is the singular which is the most irregular form in this
class. Only for 'road' *yaw* is the singular identical to the base form. In
all other words the diphthong or the final /aw/ $\overset{\text{L}}{\underset{\text{R}}{\text{V}}}$ is realized as /a/, that
is, the R segment is deleted entirely.

$$
\begin{array}{ccc}
\begin{array}{cc} \text{L} & \text{L} \\ | & | \\ \text{C V C C V} \\ | & | | \\ \text{n} & \text{p r} \\ & \quad\;\;\text{R} \end{array}
& > &
\begin{array}{cc} \text{L} & \text{L} \\ | & | \\ \text{C V C C V} \\ | & | | \\ \text{n} & \text{p r} \end{array}
\end{array}
$$

napraw   napra
'membrane'

For such examples, the rule can be stated as follows:

(4-21) R deletion:

$$
\begin{array}{c} \text{L} \\ | \\ \text{V} \\ | \\ \text{R} \end{array}
\quad > \quad
\begin{array}{c} \text{L} \\ | \\ \text{V} \end{array}
\quad / \underline{\;\;} \#
$$

However in other forms, the R gets realized as a consonantal /w/ preceding the /a/.

$$
\begin{array}{ccc}
\begin{array}{cc} \text{L} & \text{L} \\ | & | \\ \text{C V C C V} \\ | & | | \\ \text{t} & \text{r p} \\ & \quad\;\;\text{R} \end{array}
& > &
\begin{array}{cc} \text{L} & \text{L} \\ | & | \\ \text{C V C C C V} \\ | & | | \\ \text{t} & \text{r p} \\ & \qquad\text{R} \end{array}
\end{array}
$$

tarpaw   tarpwa
'belly'

These forms undergo a rule which may be stated formally as follows:

(4-22) Leftward R-shift:

$$
\begin{array}{c} \text{L} \\ | \\ \text{V} \\ | \\ \text{R} \end{array}
\quad > \quad
\begin{array}{c} \text{L} \\ | \\ \text{C V} \\ | \\ \text{R} \end{array}
\quad / \underline{\;\;} \#
$$

It does not seem possible to predict on phonological grounds which form will undergo which rule. For example, *krpaw* 'sago beetle' is subject to rule (4-21), but the phonologically similar word *tarpaw* 'belly' undergoes rule (4-22). One generalization that does hold is that the forms in which the consonant preceding /aw/ is a velar always undergo rule (4-22): (*kampaŋkwa* 'cockroach'). Perhaps the most interesting example of this predilection of velars for rule (4-22) is in the form for 'hand', in which the /w/ formed by rule (4-22) actually jumps a syllable to attach to /k/.

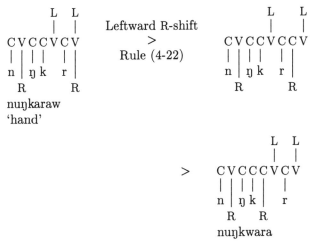

Rules (4-21) and (4-22) interact frequently with R spreading. Consider the derivation of *trukwa* 'knee' or *tumpa* 'death adder'.

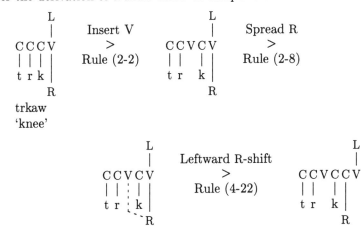

```
    L                                  L
    |        Insert V                  |        Spread R
 C C C V        >                  C V C C V        >
 | | | |      Rule (2-2)           |   | | |      Rule (2-8)
 t m p |                           t   m p |
      R                                   R
```

```
            L                                       L
            |           R deletion                  |
        C V C C V           >                   C V C C V
        | ⋮ | | |       Rule (4-21)             | | | |
        t ⋮ m p |                               t | m p
         `---- R                                   R
                                                 tumpa
```

This last example may present the very rare example of necessary rule ordering in Yimas phonology. The rule of R spreading must precede rule (4-21). Otherwise, the feature which triggers R spreading is deleted before it is able to do so. An alternative to this rule ordering would be to claim that the underlying forms of such words as *tumpa* already contain the /u/ and that it is not the result of R spreading from the following syllable. There is no obvious way to decide between these two alternatives at this point; neither are completely satisfactory.

The adjectival/possessive agreement suffixes of class IX are closely related to the noun inflections. They are as follows:

SG	DL	PL
-aw	-awl	-ut

The singular suffix is subject to both rules (4-21) and (4-22). Consider these examples:

(4-23) a. namtampara ama-na-∅   kpa-∅
        foot IX SG   1SG-POSS-IX SG big-IX SG
        'my small foot'

       b. nuŋkwara   ama-na-∅   waca-k-wa
        hand IX SG 1SG-POSS-IX SG   small-IRR-IX SG
        'my big hand'

When used with words ending in /a/, like *ama-na-* 'my' and *kpa-* 'big', the singular agreement suffix is subject to rule (4-21), which reduces it to -*a*. The resulting vowel cluster is then subject to the vowel truncation rule (2-13), resulting in what is, in essence, a ∅ allomorph. The adjectival verbs ending in the irrealis suffix -*k*, on the other hand, undergo rule (4-22) (as is typical of velars), converting -*aw* to -*wa*, as with 'small' in (4-23b). Examples with the dual and plural allomorphs are straightforward.

(4-24) a. trukawl   ama-na-wl   mama-k-awl
        knee IX DL 1SG-POSS-IX DL bad-IRR-IX DL
        'my two bad knees'

     b. kampraŋkut   urkpwica-k-ut
        cockroach IX PL black-IRR-IX PL
        'black cockroaches'

The loss of the initial /a/ in the dual agreement suffix here reflects the vowel truncation rule (2-13).

The verbal prefixal class marker for this class is derived similarly to those of classes IV through VIII. As in class IV, the singular adjective/possessive agreement suffix of the form -VC is metathesized to form the verbal prefixal class marker. So -aw becomes wa-. The singular is simply wa- (class IX marker) plus ∅ (singular), but the dual and plural are the unexpected forms given below:

SG	DL	PL
wa-	wɨla- ~ ula-	ura-

If the dual and plural were formed regularly, one would expect *wa-l-a and *wa-y-a- respectively, but they clearly are not, and there is no obvious explanation for the aberrations. The two dual forms are in free variation. Examples involving these verbal prefixes follow:

(4-25) a. namtamparawl wɨla-na-kkt-n
        foot IX DL   IX DL S-DEF-hurt-PRES
        '(My) feet hurt.'

     b. ŋarwa   wa-ŋa-kwalca-t
        penis IX SG IX SG S-1SG D-rise-PERF
        'I have an erection.'

The numerals and deictics are formed in the usual way: adjectival/possessive suffixes attach to 'one', 'four', and the near distal deictic, and verbal prefixes attach to 'two', 'three', and the proximal and far distal deictics.

    Numerals:

mpa-∅	'one'	wu-ramnawt	'three'
wu-rpal	'two'	ma-ul+ama-ul	'four'

The forms for 'two' and 'three' are irregular in that the prefix is wu- rather than the expected *wa-; this wu- is undoubtedly related to the dual verbal prefix wɨla- ~ ula-. The form for 'one' is the result of rule (4-21) and the vowel truncation rule (2-13).

Deictics:

	SG	DL	PL
PROX	wa-k	ula-k	ura-k
NR DIST	m-a	m-ul	m-ut
FR DIST	wa-n	ula-n	ura-n

4.1.10 Class X

This class is closely related to class VI and seems to be a diachronic specialization of it. The nouns in class X end in $\overset{(L)}{\underset{R}{V}}$ followed by the velar stop or homorganic nasal plus stop cluster. This difference in choice of final segments reflects a division of class X into two distinct subclasses. Examples follow:

Sub-class A (ends in /k/):

SG	DL	PL	
antuk	antukul	antukwat	'voice'
awruk	awrukul	awrukwat	'bandicoot'
kawnɲcmpruk	kawnɲcmprukul	kawnɲcmprukwat ~ kawnɲcmpt	'brain'
mawruk	mawrukul	mawrukwat	'ginger'
tpuk	tpukul	tpwi	'sago pancake'
naŋkpuk	naŋkpukul	naŋkpt	'meat'

Sub-class B (ends in /ŋk/):

SG	DL	PL	
awŋ	awŋkul	awŋkwi	'egg'
kawŋ	kawŋkul	kawŋkwi	'bark of sago palm'
aympanuŋ	aympankul	aympankwi	'heavy piece of wood for pounding grass'
mŋkawŋ	mŋkawŋkul	mŋkawŋkwi	'house post'
tmpuŋ	tmpuŋkul	tmpuŋkwi	'headdress'
mpnawŋ	mpnawŋkul	mpnawŋkwi	'elbow'
paɲawŋ	paɲawŋkul	paɲawŋkwi ~ paɲawŋkwat	'scrotum'
plaɲcmpuŋ	plaɲcmpuŋkul	plaɲcmpuŋkwi ~ plaɲcmpuŋkwat	'butterfly'
kmpunkamanuŋ	kmpunkamankul	kmpunkamankwat	'buttock'

This is a small class, with most members listed above. Many potential members, i.e., nouns meeting the phonological specifications, actually are assigned to classes V and VI. What distinguishes class X from these is the regular feature of R spreading. This rule does not apply to the phonologically similar members of classes V and VI. Contrast the behavior of class V *muntuk* 'neck' with class X *antuk* 'voice', and class VI *walamuŋ* 'basket type' with class X *kmpunkamanuŋ* 'buttock':

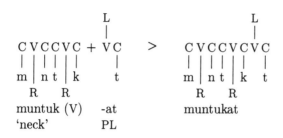

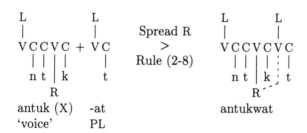

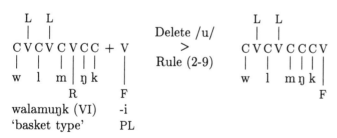

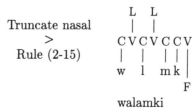

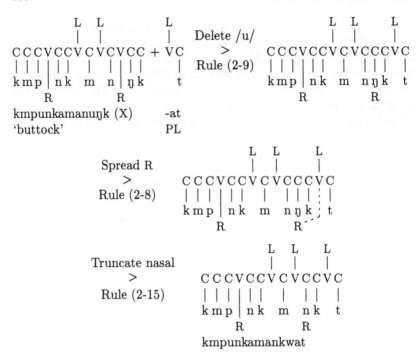

```
  L  L              L                              L  L       L
  |  |              |      Delete /u/              |  |       |
C C C V C C V C V C V C C  +  V C        >     C C C V C C V C V C C C V C
| | | | | |   |   | | | |      |      Rule (2-9) | | | | | |   |   | | |   |
k m p | n k   m   n | ŋ k      t               k m p | n k   m   n ŋ k   t
      R       R                                      R       R
kmpunkamanuŋk (X)             -at
'buttock'                    PL
```

```
                                       L  L       L
              Spread R                 |  |       |
                 >                 C C C V C C V C V C C C V C
              Rule (2-8)           | | | | | |   |   | | | ⋮ |
                                   k m p | n k   m   n ŋ k ⋮ t
                                         R       R⁀
```

```
                                       L  L       L
            Truncate nasal             |  |       |
                 >                 C C C V C C V C V C C V C
              Rule (2-15)          | | | | | |   |   | |   |
                                   k m p | n k   m   n k   t
                                         R       R
                                   kmpunkamankwat
```

The class X nouns always exhibit R spreading, but those of the other two classes do not. The handful of class V nouns will simply have to be marked [-rule (2-8)], i.e., [-R spreading], but the difference in behavior in classes VI and X could be handled in the statement of the rule of /u/ deletion (rule (2-9)), because all examples of class VI nouns which fail to spread R are subject to this rule. As mentioned in Section 4.1.6, one can simply stipulate that /u/ deletion remove R as well as the V slot in the CV skeleton for class VI nouns, but only the V slot for class X nouns. This would, of course, require rule ordering, /u/ deletion before R spreading for class VI nouns, which seems counter-intuitive in view of the symbiotic relationship of these two rules for classes IV and X. So perhaps it is ultimately more attractive to treat the irregular examples in class VI in parallel fashion to class V, as a morphologically based exception to the rule of R spreading.

Note that the major morphological difference between sub-classes A and B is in the plural. Both form the dual by suffixing the usual dual suffix -*l*. In the plural, all but one noun in subclass A have plurals with -*(a)t*. The one exception is *tpuk* 'sago pancake' which has the suppletive plural *tpwi*. Note that the plural of *naŋkpuk* 'meat' is also suppletive (*naŋkpt*), but the plural still takes -*t* in this case.

Sub-class B nouns have plurals in -*i*, again with one exception: the plural of *kmpunkamanuŋ* 'buttock' takes -*at*, *kmpunkamankwat*. Two other sub-class B nouns have competing plurals in -*at*: *paɲawŋ* 'scrotum', PL: *paɲawŋkwi* ~ *paɲawŋkwat*, and *plaɲcmpuŋ* 'butterfly', PL: *plaɲcmpuŋkwi* ~ *plaɲcmpuŋkwat*. While both forms are acceptable, the -*i* plurals are clearly regarded as better, even by younger speakers.

As the contrast between sub-classes A and B is largely manifested in the plural, it is these agreement suffixes which differ. The adjectival/possessive agreement suffixes for both sub-classes are set out as follows:

	SG	DL	PL
Sub-class A:	-uŋk	-uŋkl	-ra
Sub-class B:	-uŋk	-uŋkl	-uŋkwi

The class marker for both sub-classes is -*uŋk*. The singular is simply that—*uŋk* (class X marker) plus ∅ (singular marker). In final position, this suffix will be subject to the nasal plus stop cluster simplification rule (2-14) and will be realized simply as *uŋ*, just as in the singular forms of class X nouns. The dual consists of the class marker plus -*l*, the dual suffix. The plural agreement suffixes show the contrast between the two classes. Sub-class A takes -*ra*, as do class V nouns which have the same final consonant, while sub-class B nouns occur with -*uŋk*, the class X marker plus -*i* (plural), with consequent R spreading (rule (2-8)). The sub-class B nouns are very similar to class VI nouns, which, of course, have items ending in the same final consonant cluster. Finally, there are a couple of exceptions. The plural agreement suffix of the sub-class A noun *tpwi* 'sago pancake' is not the expected *-*ra*, but -*i*, and that of the sub-class B noun *kmpunkamankwat* 'buttocks' is -*ra*, rather than *-*uŋkwi*. In fact all sub-class B nouns, when suffixed with the typically sub-class A plural allomorph -*at*, take its associated agreement suffix -*ra*. Examples of these suffixes with class X nouns follow:

(4-26) a. antuk   ama-na-wŋ   kpa-wŋ
          voice X A SG   1SG-POSS-X SG   big-X SG
          'my loud voice'

       b. awŋkul   ama-naw-ŋkl   yua-wŋkul
          egg X B PL   1SG-POSS-X DL   good-X DL
          'my two good eggs'

       c. mawrukwat   mama-k-ra   ama-na-ra
          ginger X A PL   bad-IRR-X A PL   1SG-POSS-X A PL
          'my bad (pieces of) ginger'

d. awŋkwi   mama-k-ŋkwi   ama-na-wŋkwi
   egg X B PL bad-IRR-X B PL 1SG-POSS-X B PL
   'my bad eggs'

The /u/ in the class X B PL suffix -uŋkwi is often removed by /u/ deletion (rule (2-9)). The nasal is then realized syllabically.

e. tpwi   ama-na-y   wasa-k-i
   sago pancake X PL   1SG-POSS-X PL   small-IRR-X PL
   'my small (bits of) sago pancake'

The verbal agreement prefixes are derived in parallel fashion to the other classes. The forms are as follows:

	SG	DL	PL
Sub-class A:	ku-	kula-	ya-
Sub-class B:	ku-	kula-	kwia-

The verbal prefixal class marker is derived by metathesizing the segments in the -VC agreement suffix, as in classes IV and IX, but also by deleting the homorganic nasal, as in classes VI and VII. So from the -uŋk form of the class marker in the agreement suffixes, we derived ku- for the verbal prefixes. Again, the singular is simply this: ku- (class X verbal prefix) plus ∅ (singular). The dual is kula-, from the class marker plus l- (dual) plus a- (non-singular). Again, the plurals contrast for the two sub-classes. Because sub-class A has the adjectival/possessive agreement suffix -ra, its verbal equivalent is the ubiquitous ya-, from class marker ∅ plus i- (plural) plus a- (non-singular). The plural of sub-class B is formed regularly on the class marker: kwia- from ku- (class X verbal prefix) plus i- (plural) plus a- (non-singular). Note that the /u/ of the class marker ku- becomes the semivowel w before the plural morpheme i-. This is probably the result of medial semivowel formation (I) (rule (2-11)) followed by idiosyncratic /u/ deletion (*ku-i-a- > kuw-i-a- > kwia-). Again, the plural form tpwi 'sago pancakes' is irregular: its verbal prefix is i-.

(4-27) a. paɲawŋ   ku-ŋa-na-kkt-n
          scrotum X SG   X SG S-1SG D-DEF-hurt-PRES
          'My scrotum hurts.'

       b. awrukat   ya-na-tampulanta-n
          bandicoot X A PL   X A PL S-DEF-run-PRES
          'The bandicoots are running.'

       c. awŋkwi   kwia-tumuk-t
          egg X B PL   X B PL S-fell-PERF
          'The eggs fell.'

d. tpwi   i-kalc-k-i-tɨ-t
sago pancake X PL   X PL S-strong-IRR-X PL-become-PERF
'The sago pancakes got hard.'

The numerals and deictics of this class are formed regularly: adjectival/possessive suffixes for 'one', 'four', and the near distal deictic, and verbal prefixes for 'two', 'three', and the proximal and far distal deictic.

Numerals:

mpa-wŋ	ku-ramnawt
ku-rpal	ma-wŋkul+ama-wŋkwi

The word for 'three' is an interesting exception to the rule of /u/ deletion (rule (2-9)). It fits its structural description, but if it were to apply, the resulting form would be homophonous with the numeral for 'three' for class VI. Hence, its application is blocked. The word for 'four' has the dual suffix for the first instance of *ma-* 'other', but the plural suffix for the second. This is exactly parallel to the equivalent form for class VI.

Deictics:

	SG	DL	PL
PROX	ku-k	kula-k	ya-k(A)/kwia-k(B)
NR DIST	m-uŋ	m-uŋkul	m-ra(A)/m-uŋkwi(B)
FR DIST	ku-n	kula-n	ya-n(A)/kwia-n(B)

4.1.11 Minor Classes

In addition to the ten major classes already discussed there are a few very common nouns that form classes unto themselves. These are listed below:

SG	DL	PL	
nam	naml	nampt	'house'
num	numul	nmkat	'village'
wut	wutntrm	wurŋkat	'night'
arm			'water'
awt			'fire'
awi			'lime'

The last three only exist as mass nouns; they have no dual or plural forms.

The adjectival/possessive agreement suffixes for each of these nouns are given below:

SG	DL	PL	
-nm	-nml	-ra	'house'
-num	-numul	-ra	'village'
-ut	-ntrm	-ra	'night'
-rm			'water'
-ut (i.e., IX PL)			'fire'
-ra (i.e., V PL)			'lime'

Examples of a few of these follow:

(4-28) a. arm   kpa-rm
          water big-water
          'a high tide'

     b. nam   ama-na-nm   mpa-nm   kpa-nm
        house SG   1SG-POSS-house SG one-house SG   big-house SG
        'my one big house'

     c. numkat   m-ra
        village PL NR DIST-village PL
        'those villages'

Some of the corresponding verbal prefixes are regular, i.e., *-ra* still always pairs with *ya-*, but there are also idiosyncrasies.

SG	DL	PL	
nma-	nmla-	ya-	'house'
numa-	numula-	ya-	'village'
ura-	tma-	ya-	'night'
ima-			'water'
ura- (i.e., IX PL)			'fire'
ya- (i.e., V PL)			'lime'

(4-29) a. nampt   nm-ramnawt ya-k
          house PL   house-three   house PL-PROX
          ya-mntk-t
          house PL S-finish-PERF
          'These three houses are finished.'

     b. arm   ima-k   ima-na-awkpc-n
        water water-PROX   water S-DEF-boil-PRES
        'This water is boiling.'

     c. num   kpa-num   numa-n   kwantayn
        village SG big-village SG village SG-FR DIST far
        numa-na-pay-n
        village SG S-DEF-lie-PRES
        'That big village is far away.'

In addition to these minor class nouns, there are two sets of agreement affixes which have no overt noun corresponding to them. These are given below:

ADJ/POSS	VERB	
-mpwi	pia-	'talk, words, language'
-nti	tia-	'actions, deeds'

The affixes for 'talk, words, language' may possibly go back to the affixes for a now non-existent plural form *karmpi* from *karm* 'lip, language', but that is of little help in the synchronic analysis. Both of these affixes sets are heavily used in the system of Yimas complementation (see Section 7.1.2) and are a pervasive feature of natural discourse. Some examples follow:

(4-30) a. pia-k   ama-na-mpwi   yua-mpwi apiak
        talk-PROX   1SG-POSS-talk   good-talk   COP talk
        'This talk of mine is good.'

     b. tia-n   mama-nti   antiak
        action-FR DIST   bad-action   COP action
        'That action is bad.'

     c. ma-mpwi   pia-ŋa-i
        other-talk   talk-1SG D-say
        '(He) said something else to me.'

Finally, Table 4 provides a summary of the basic morphology of classes I through X.

4.2 The Oblique Suffix -*n* ∼ -*nan*

This is the single nominal case marker in Yimas and is used to mark a range of peripheral, adverbial-like case uses, such as instruments, locatives and temporals.

(4-31) a. tktntrm-nan   namarawt   na-ŋa-tpul
        chair V DL-OBL   person I SG   3SG A-1SG O-hit
        'The person hit me with two chairs.'

     b. tnumut-ɲan   ama-na-irm-n
        sago palms IV PL-OBL   1SG S-DEF-stand-PRES
        'I'm standing at the two sago palms.'

     c. tpuk   ku-ka-pay-pra-t
        sago pancake X SG   X SG O-1SG A-carry-toward-PERF
        maraŋapawl-ɲan
        basket IX DL-OBL
        'I carried the sago pancake in the two baskets.'

As the (c) example shows, the initial /n/ in the allomorph -*nan* is subject to the rule of palatalization (rule (2-3)) following a segment carrying F (the /l/ is only optionally subject to liquid strengthening (rule (2-5))). Essentially, the allomorphic choice between -*n* and -*nan* is determined by the following basic rule: use -*n* with singular forms and -*nan* with non-singular forms. But this rule is subject to a number of irregularities and complications. The dual is completely regular: all dual forms take -*nan*. The variation between -*n* and -*nan* is not statable in strictly phonological terms. Minimal pairs such as *tktmtrm-nan* chair V DL-OBL versus *arm-n* water-OBL clearly show this to be the case. Rather, as with many of the variants in Yimas morphology, the choice is governed partly by morphological features and partly by phonological ones.

The plural forms are more complex. The allomorph -*nan* is used with nouns whose plurals end in -*i*, and -*n* is found elsewhere. But again there are exceptions. The plurals of classes VIII and IX, both of which end in /t/ (i.e., -*mpt* and -*ut*) always take -*nan*, while the plurals of other classes which end in /t/, like V and VII (e.g., -*ŋkat* and -*mpat*) occur with -*n*.

(4-32) a. kaŋk-ɲan   na-ka-warapa-kia-k
            shell VI PL-OBL 3SG O-1SG A-cut-NIGHT-IRR
            'I cut him with shells.'

Note that the rule of palatalization (rule (2-3)) applies following the -*i* plural, copying the F feature onto the initial /n/ of -*nan* and converting /i/ to *i*, which of course being predictable, is not written. Another example is given below:

   b. ŋaŋk-ɲan   ama-na-irm-n
         grass VII PL-OBL 1SG S-DEF-stand-PRES
         'I'm standing in the grass.'

Further examples showing the contrast of -*n* with -*nan* in plurals follow:

   c. namarawt   awtmayɲɲ-nan   na-ɲa-tpul
         person I SG sugarcane VIII PL-OBL 3SG A-1SG O-hit
         'The person hit me with (stalks) of sugarcane.'

   d. tanpat-n   na-ka-kacakapi
         bone VII PL-OBL 3SG O-1SG A-hide
         'I hide it in the bones.'

The singular forms almost always take -*n*, but those ending in a segment associated with F (i.e., /i/, /ay/ or /l/) take -*nan*, as do nouns ending in the other liquid, underlying /r/ (of course, realized as *t* in word-final position and before /n/). Words ending in /n/ or /ŋ/ also

TABLE 4
Yimas Noun Classes

		I	II	III	IV
		male humans	female humans (-maŋ)	higher animals	plants (-um)
SG	NOUN				
	ADJ/POSS	-n(ADJ)/-kn(POSS)	-(k)nmaŋ	-n(ADJ),-kn(POSS)	-um
	VERB	na-	na-	na-	mu-
DL	NOUN	-(nt)rm	-(nt)rm ~ -mprum	-(n)trm	-mul
	ADJ/POSS	-mampan(ADJ)/-rm(POSS)	-(k)nprum	-ntrm	-mul
	VERB	impa-	impa-	tma-	mula-
PL	NOUN	-um,-i,-ŋkat, -ntt	-um,-i,-mput, -ntt	-i,-ŋkat	-uŋi, -ŋkat
	ADJ/POSS	-ump	-(k)nput	-ump	-ra
	VERB	pu-	pu-	pu-	ya-

TABLE 4 *continued*

		V	VI	VII	VIII	IX	X
SG	NOUN	-p, -k, -m. -n, -ŋ, -nt, -r, -l, -i, -y, -c	-ŋk	-mp	-i, -y $\begin{smallmatrix}L\\V\\F\end{smallmatrix}$	-aw $\begin{smallmatrix}L\\V\\R\end{smallmatrix}$	-uk(A)/-uŋk(B)
	ADJ/POSS	-n(ADJ)/-kn(POSS)	-ŋk	-mp	-i	-aw	-uŋk
	VERB	na-	k-	p-	i-	wa-	ku-
DL	NOUN	-(nt)rm	-ŋkl	-mpl	-l ~ -il, -l ~ -yl	-awl	-ul(A)/-uŋkl(B)
	ADJ/POSS	-ntrm	-ŋkl	-mpl	-l ~ -il	-awl	-uŋkl
	VERB	tma-	kla-	pla-	ila-	wila- ~ ula-	kula-
PL	NOUN	-ŋkat, -i, -ra, -t	-ŋki	-mpat,-i,-a	-Cmpt, -i, -a	-ut	-at(A)/-uŋkwiB
	ADJ/POSS	-ra	-ŋki	-ra	-ra	-ut	-ra(A)/-uŋkwiB
	VERB	ya-	kia-	ya-	ya-	ura-	ya-(A)/kwia-(B)

take -*nan*, but with degemination of the resulting /nn/ cluster. First, consider some examples with -*n*.

(4-33) a. trŋk-n/tanp-n/wanwa-n
tooth VI SG-OBL/bone VII SG-OBL/knife IX SG-OBL
na-ŋa-kra-t
3SG A-1SG-cut-PERF
'He cut me with a tooth/bone/knife.'

b. numpk-n   na-na-wi-caw-n
mountain V SG-OBL 3SG S-DEF-up-sit-PRES
'He is up on the mountain.'

Nouns from classes IV and X cause R spreading (rule (2-8)), so the V inserted to break up the impermissible final cluster formed by adding the -*n* is realized as /u/.

c. irpm-un/kawŋk-un   akpɲan
coconut palm V SG-OBL/wall X SG-OBL behind
na-na-irm-n
3SG S-DEF-stand-PRES
'He is standing behind the coconut palm/wall.'

Now consider the contrasting examples with -*nan* (the initial /n/ is, of course, always subject to palatalization (rule (2-3)) following segments bearing F):

d. kay-ɲan/tkt-nan/ant-ɲan
canoe VIII SG-OBL/chair V SG-OBL/ground VIII SG-OBL
na-na-taw-n
3SG S-DEF-sit-PRES
'He is sitting in/on the canoe/chair/ground.'

e. tmat-ɲan   nma-kay-wark-wat
sun/day V SG-OBL house O-1PL A-build-HAB
'We always build a house during the day.'

f. yan-an   akpɲan ama-na-irm-n
tree V SG-OBL behind 1SG S-DEF-stand-PRES
'I'm standing behind a tree.'

4.3 Proper Nouns

Proper nouns correspond to names for persons and places in Yimas. All inhabitants of Yimas village are given a traditional Yimas name at birth, which stays with them throughout life, although they may acquire additional names as they mature. This traditional name is generally that of a legendary or mythological ancestor, usually belonging to the same clan as the conferee. As with many Sepik societies (Bateson 1936; Gewertz 1983), knowledge of long lists of names for totemic ancestors is a valued resource for Yimas clans, so there is an enormous pool of available names to draw on for any newborn child. As Yimas is a missionized, Catholic village, almost all inhabitants also have a Christian name, bestowed by the priest at baptism. These are names of saints or other Biblical characters. In daily social intercourse in the village, the great majority normally go by these Christian names; the traditional names are more commonly used in ceremonial indigenous contexts. Traditional names are also commonly associated with contexts for Yimas vernacular, while Christian names are almost invariably employed in contexts for Tok Pisin. For official, governmental purposes, Yimas people go by their Christian name plus the traditional name of their father, following the Anglo-Saxon convention in this regard. Thus, my primary language helper, whose traditional name is *Yakayapan*, is found on the electoral rolls as *Stephen Mambi*, his Christian name plus the traditional name of his (adopted) father.

All significant areas in the territory of the Yimas have names which designate them. Within the immediate area of the village, a separate name may cover areas as small as a hundred square meters, but outside of this area, the regions enclosed by a particular name are usually much larger. Still, all hills, mountains, or even sub-parts of mountains, parts of lakes, and lake shorelines, sections of the river, and canals have separate names. Sometimes, these names are based on common nouns, coining a proper noun from these to name the place according to some salient physical feature. But this is rather rare. More commonly, a place takes the name of some legendary person who died or performed an important action there. But most commonly, the name is unanalyzable and has no personal legendary precursor.

Proper nouns contrast with common nouns in that they are assigned to no noun class and they never take number inflections. Proper nouns designating the names of persons are also completely prohibited from occurring with the oblique suffix. The proper nouns denoting place names are more complicated. A few place names based on a common noun, such as *Kpa-upnk-n* big-lake-OBL 'the largest of the eight major lakes in the Yimas territory', have the oblique suffix as part of the name. But in these cases it is semantically and syntactically empty, for it is always present, regardless of the syntactic function of the nominal. It is simply fossilized as a constituent in the compound which makes up the name of the lake. Other than these fossilized cases, proper nouns denoting place names generally cannot occur with the oblique suffix. When being used locatively they appear simply in their stem form. There is one exception: proper nouns denoting the names of villages do generally take the oblique suffix when being used locatively. Some examples are *Tamprakmat-n* Yimas-OBL 'at Yimas', *Kapakampt-n* Imanmeri-OBL 'at Imanmeri', and *Kaywal-ɲan* Kaiwaria-OBL 'at Kaiwaria'. Note that the morphological forms with these village names can be quite exceptional. The proper name for Yimas village is *Tamprakmal*, so by the usual allomorphic rules for *-n* ~ *-nan*, the form chosen should be *-nan*, rather than *-n*.

4.4 Noun Compounds

Both nouns and verbs, the major, open word classes in Yimas, compound freely. Verbal compounds are an extremely common and pervasive feature of Yimas (see Section 6.3.1). Noun compounds are rather less common, but still are not infrequently encountered. Noun compounds by definition always have nouns as their heads, and it is the noun class and number of the head noun which determines these features for the compound as a whole. The other member of the compound (there are no examples with more than two basic constituents) may be either a verb or another noun or noun phrase (see Section 4.6).

Compounds made up of two noun roots are the most common type. The language has a few examples of lexical compounds formed directly by juxtaposing two stems. This is non-productive, and sometimes the non-head stem is not an isolatable morpheme in the language, i.e., these are examples of 'cranberry' morphemes (Nida 1949). Examples of this kind of non-productive compounding follow:

(4-34) a. wala-kput
            wind(*wal*)-rain V SG
            'heavy storm'

        b. kampat-paympan
            ?-eagle V SG
            'small brown and white hawk'

        c. Parampt-paympan
            name-eagle V SG
            'totemic ancestor'

        d. kayan-taki
            spirit-stone/spirit I SG
            'spirit'

        e. anti-ɲam-n
            ground-house-OBL
            'cave'

   f. yal-campan
      blood?(*yat*)-liver V SG
      'spleen'

   g. irwan   pkam
      white possum V SG skin of back
      'hide of white possum'

The much more common and productive way of forming noun plus noun compounds in Yimas is to suffix the first (the non-head) noun with the oblique suffix. The oblique suffix occurs in the allomorph proper to that noun. Examples follow:

(4-35) a. muca-n   marm
        flower (sp) IX SG-OBL smell V SG
        'smell of muca flower'

     b. puratuŋk-n   tampan
        bile VI SG-OBL liver V SG
        'gall bladder'

     c. num-n   numpran
        village-OBL pig III SG
        'domesticated pig'

     d. narmaŋ-n   wurm
        woman-OBL flute VII SG
        'female (i.e., smaller) flute'

     e. kalk-n   apra
        sago pudding V SG-OBL plate VII PL
        'plates of sago pudding'

     f. pŋkmp-n   yaw
        guts VII SG-OBL road IX SG
        'intestines'

     g. yanan   yanŋ
        tree V SG-OBL stick VI SG
        'tree branch'

     h. namtamparawt-ɲan api-c-awt
        foot IX DL-OBL   put inside-NFN-SG
        'sock' (i.e., something into which the two feet are put)

The last example is interesting in that the head noun is actually a verb which has been nominalized by -*ru* (realized as -*c*) and -*awt* (see Section 7.1.1 on nominalizations of verbs). The semantic relations between the nouns in these compounds are part/whole (e,g), characteristic property (a,b,c), and location or goal (c,f,h).

Generally in these compounds, the noun marked by the oblique suffix may not be inflected for number: (4-35h) is one of the few examples that shows that this is indeed possible, though such cases are rather rare. Other cases are the words 'male' and 'female' from *panmal* 'man' and *narmaŋ* 'woman', which seem to vary freely between singular and plural in some cases,

(4-36) a. narmaŋ-n   wurm
       woman II SG-OBL   flute VII SG
       'female flute'

      b. ŋaykump-n   wurm
         woman II PL-OBL   flute VII SG
         'female flute'

but not in others.

(4-37) a. ŋaykump-n   kumpwi
       woman II PL-OBL   child I PL
       'girls'

      b.*narmaŋ-n   kumpwi
        woman II SG-OBL   child I PL

This difference may simply reflect the fact that (4-37a) is actually a lexical entry, the plural form of *kaywi* 'girl, daughter'.

Proper nouns may also occur in noun compounds, as the non-head noun, but as usual they occur without the oblique suffix.

(4-38) a. Malŋkawt   yaw-n
       place of the dead   road IX SG-OBL
       'on the road to Malŋkawt'

      b. Kapakampt   kaywi
         Imanmeri   girl II SG
         'girl from Imanmeri'

      c. Kamrat   namat
         place in big lake   person I PL
         'people of Kamrat'

      d. Wamut   num
         Wambramas   village
         'Wambramas village'

As mentioned above, noun plus noun compounds may consist of exactly two major constituents (see Section 4.6). Compounds as a whole may be modified by other elements, in which case the resulting constituency may at first seem ambiguous.

(4-39) a. [ama-na   [[num-n]   [karm]]]
       1SG-POSS   village-OBL   lip/language VII SG
       'my native language' (i.e., my village language')

b. [[ama-na   num-n]   [karm]]
   1SG-POSS village-OBL lip/language VII SG
   'my native language' (i.e., 'the language of my village')

This string could be analyzed at first as having either the constituency of
(4-39) (a) or (b); it is impossible to determine this from the meanings in
these cases, as they are identical. As soon as the head noun is switched
from *karm* 'lip/language' to *numpran* 'pig', however, it becomes possible
to determine that the constituency of (a) is correct for (4-39).

(4-40) [ama-na   [[num-n]   [numpran]]]
        1SG-POSS   village-OBL   pig III SG
        'my domesticated pig' (i.e., 'my village pig')

If one wanted to express the equivalent of the constituency outlined in
(4-39b), i.e., 'the pig of my village', a compound construction would not
be possible. Rather we would need a construction something like (4-41)
in which a finite relative clause modifying *numpran* 'pig' is employed:

(4-41) numpran [num-n   ama-na-num-n
        pig III SG   village-OBL 1SG-POSS-village-OBL

        m-ya-t]
        NR DIST-come-PERF

        'a pig which came from my village'

Further evidence that the constituency diagrammed in (4-39a) and (4-
40) is correct for nominal compounds comes from the behavior of adjectival modifiers. These always modify the compound as a whole and
have the number/class features of the second (i.e., head) noun. They
are prohibited from ever agreeing with these features for the first noun.

(4-42) a. [kpa-n   [num-n   numpran]]
          big-III SG   village-OBL pig III SG
          'my big domesticated pig'

       b.*[kpa-nm   num-n]   numpran]
          big-village SG village-OBL pig IV SG

The impossibility of (4-42b) clearly demonstrates that the actual constituency for nominal compounds is that of (4-42a).

    These noun plus noun compounds bear a superficial similarity to
noun plus postposition constructions. Compare these noun plus postposition constructions with the noun compounds in (4-35):

(4-43) a. nam-n   wampuŋn
          house-OBL inside
          'inside of the house'

      b. yan-an   akpɲan
         tree V SG-OBL behind
         'behind the tree'

As with noun compounds, the first noun bears the oblique suffix. But this similarity is more apparent than real, for the constituency of these noun plus postposition constructions is quite different. When a modifier is added, it modifies only the noun, not the whole construction, which argues for the constituency in (4-44):

(4-44) [[[kawŋkra-k-n   yan]-an]   akpɲan]
       long-IRR-V SG tree V SG-OBL behind
       'behind the tall tree'

In this example, the whole noun phrase *kawŋkra-k-n yan-an* is embedded under the postposition. Also, the noun and the postposition can be separated by modifiers, something not possible within noun compounds:

(4-45) [[[yan   kawŋkra-k-n]-an]   akpɲan]
       tree V SG long-IRR-V SG-OBL behind
       'behind the tall tree'

Noun compounds are also formed with a verb root functioning as the non-head constituent. The verb roots occur in the same pre-head position, but are suffixed with the nonfinite suffix -*ru* (for the rules for the allomorphic variation of this suffix, see Section 7.1.1).

(4-46) a. araka(l)-t   muraŋ
         paddle-NFN paddle VI SG
         'a paddle for paddling'

      b. pan-t   impram
         pound sago-NFN basket VII SG
         'a basket used for carrying pounded sago pith to the washing place'

      c. ayk-t   yaw
         marry-NOM road IX SG
         'rule for a proper marriage'

Verbs occurring in these noun compounds obligatorily lack tense suffixes and the cross-referencing affixes for core arguments. However, a noun functioning as the object of the verb in the compound can appear overtly.

(4-47) [[tamana tu-t]   [kalk]]
       sickness kill-NFN sago-pudding V SG
       'sago pudding for curing sickness'

In these cases the complex consisting of the noun object plus verb functions as the first constituent of the noun compound.

    It is also possible for a verb plus noun compound to occur as the first constituent of a noun plus noun compound. These structures fit well into the overall structure of Yimas complex nominals, for the language has a structural principle requiring heads on the right. When verb plus noun compounds occur as non-head members of noun plus noun compounds, this target is met serially; the two noun heads are adjacent to each other to the right of the verb as follows:

> [[verb -*ru* noun] noun]

Examples of such compounds follow:

(4-48) a. [[[aw(l)-t]   [ɲum]-n]   kay]
          take-NFN   village-OBL   canoe VIII SG
          'dinghy' (i.e., 'foreigner's boat')

     b. [[[[aw(l)-t]   [ɲum]]-n]   nmkat]-n
           take-NFN   village-OBL   village PL-OBL
           'at the outstations/patrol posts' (i.e., 'at foreign places')

4.5 Possession

As in many languages, possession in Yimas is best characterized as an oblique relation, i.e., the semantic relation between possessor and possessed is paraphrasable by English prepositions like 'with', 'to', or 'at'. This is most transparently indicated in Yimas when possession is expressed clausally, in examples like 'I/you/etc. have a chair'. In these cases the possessor functions as the subject of the clause whose predicate is the copula, and the thing possessed appears as the object of a postpositional construction with *kantk-* 'with, along with' (*tak-* is an alternative when the possessed noun is a body part). The postposition *kantk-* occurs with an agreement suffix of the adjectival suffix set, indicating the number and class of the possessor. Consider these examples:

(4-49) a. ama tkt   kantk-n   amayak
          1SG   chair V SG   with-I SG   COP 1SG
          'I have a chair.'

     b. impa-n   arm   kantk-nprum   aympak
          3DL-FR DIST   water   with-II PL   COP 3DL
          'Those two (females) have kerosene.'

     c. ipwa tawra   kantk-um   aypwak
          2PL   money   with-I PL   COP 2PL
          'You have money.'

These uses of *kantk-* 'with' to express possession are no different from its other uses, such as comitative.

Nouns marked by *kantk-* and hence functioning as oblique nominals may under certain semantic conditions (see Section 6.2.3.3.1) become

core nominals by increasing the valency of the verb with *taŋ-* COM, i.e.,
kantk- peripheral nominals correspond to *taŋ-* core nominals. Compare
(4-49a) above with (4-50):

(4-50) arm   ma-na-taŋ-taw-n
        water   2SG S-DEF-COM-sit-PRES
        'Do you have kerosene?'

This use of *kantk* 'with' to indicate possession is obviously closely
related to its use with the adjectival nouns (see Section 3.3). Since
these function syntactically as nouns, the relationship to the nouns they
modify is close to one of possession, and so it is no surprise that the
same construction is available, among others (see Section 3.3).

(4-51) a. ama   tamana   kantk-n   amayak
           1SG   sickness IX SG with-I SG   COP 1SG
           'I am sick.'

        b. ipa   wapun   kantk-um   aypak
           1PL   happiness V SG with-I PL   COP 1PL
           'We are happy.'

These examples with adjectival nouns contrast with examples involving
true possessives, in that when the adjectival noun becomes a core argument it does so directly; *taŋ-* COM is completely unacceptable in the
same meaning.

(4-52) a. wapun   ama-na-pay-n
           happiness V SG   1SG S-DEF-carry-PRES
           'I'm feeling happy.'

        b.*wapun   ama-na-taŋ-pay-n
           happiness V SG   1SG S-DEF-COM-carry-PRES

(Example (4-52b) is acceptable in the meaning 'My clan is happy' where
taŋ- COM marks the members of one's clan, literally 'I (with my clan)
am happy'. This is a true comitative usage). Further, when adjectival
nouns become core arguments, they often function as subjects of their
clauses. This is impossible for truly possessed items.

(4-53) a. wapun   na-ŋa-na-ti-n
           happiness V SG   V SG A-1SG O-DEF-do/feel-PRES
           'I'm feeling happy.'

        b. tamana   wa-ŋa-tal
           sickness IX SG   IX SG A-1SG O-hold
           'I got sick.'

        c.*tkt   na-ŋa-na-ti-n
           chair V SG   V SG A-1SG O-DEF-feel/do-PRES

Not only can possession be expressed clausally with *kantk-* 'with' plus the copula, it can also be indicated nominally, often as part of a noun phrase. If a noun phrase is formed of the possessor plus possessed, the possessor precedes the possessed item and is followed with the possessive marker *na*.

(4-54) a. ama-na   apak   na-mal
          1SG-POSS sister II SG 3SG S-die
          'My sister died.'

     b. na-k   ama-na-kn   tkt   anak
         V SG-PROX 1SG-POSS-V SG chair V SG COP V SG
         'This is my chair.'

     c. Yakayapan na   ka-ɲan   ama-wa-k
         name   POSS canoe VIII SG-OBL 1SG S-go-IRR
         'I will go in Yakayapan's canoe.'

The possessive marker *na* normally is a particle rather than a bound affix. It takes stress, although not full primary stress. Rather like English *'s* POSS, it can follow and have scope over whole phrases or clauses.

(4-55) [awt m-nanaŋ-pampay-taw-na-ntut]   na
       fire NR DIST-DUR-carry-sit-DUR-RM PAST   POSS
       kalakn
       child I SG
       'The one who looks after the fire's child'

The embedded structure is a finite relative clause (see Section 7.2.1).

Possessive constructions consisting of possessor plus *na* plus possessed form tightly knit noun phrases. The word order is rigid: no permutations are possible and nothing may be inserted between the two constituents. The head of the construction is the possessed noun, as demonstrated by the fact that it is this noun which is cross-referenced on the verb (see example (4-54a)). In all these features, possessor plus possessed noun phrases are exactly like noun plus noun compounds, and the close similarity between the possessive suffix *na* and the oblique suffix *-n ∼ -nan* would seem not to be coincidental. We have already documented above the claim that the relation of possession in Yimas is an oblique one, like the relationship between the nouns marked by the oblique suffix. It appears then that the fundamental relationships between the nouns in a nominal compound and a possessive noun phrase are very closely related, if not identical. Further evidence for this view is provided by examples like the following:

(4-56) a. tuŋkntuma   na-kn   marm
          possum III SG   POSS-V SG   smell V SG
          'smell of a possum'

      b. mlmp-n   marm
          feces VII SG-OBL smell V SG
          'smell of feces'

(4-56a) is a possessor-possessed construction while (4-56b) is a noun
plus noun compound. The head noun *marm* 'smell' is identical in both
cases, and it could hardly be claimed that the basic relationship between
the nouns is very different in the two examples. However, there is a
subtle semantic difference between these two, which is responsible for
the difference in construction. The smell of a possum may be important
in a particular discourse, but is not normally taken as a permanent,
pervading characteristic of the animal, while the smell of feces is. The
difference between transitory qualities and characteristic properties is an
important semantic contrast throughout Yimas grammar and realized in
a number of different ways and constructions, as we shall see in Chapters
6 and 7. It is this contrast which is being realized here in the choice
between a possessive noun phrase construction or a noun compound.
Another factor probably relevant here is that *na* POSS is restricted to
the animate nouns, the only possible true possessors.

Common and proper nouns functioning as possessors are simply suffixed with *na* POSS. First and second person possessors use the independent pronoun forms (see Section 3.7), while the forms for third person
are closely related to the verbal prefixes for third person (see Section
5.1.2.1).

	SG	DL	PC	PL
1	ama-	kapa-	paŋkra-	ipa-
2	mi-	kapwa-	paŋkra-	ipwa-
3	m-/na-	mpɨ-	kra-	mpu-

mi- 2SG will, of course, cause palatalization of the initial /n/, so that the
combination will appear as *m-ɲa* 2SG-POSS. These possessive pronouns
are always bound to *na* POSS as prefixes. It is *na* which carries word
stress (*ama-na* [ʌmʌ-ná] 1SG-POSS). Examples of these follow:

(4-57) a. kra-na   ŋayuk   na-wa-t
          3 PC-POSS   mother II SG   3SG S-go-PERF
          'Their mother left.'

      b. m-ɲa   apak   na-ayk-ntut
          2SG-POSS   sister-II SG   3SG S-marry-RM PAST
          'Is your sister married?'

c. i-n   kapa-na-i   anti
   VIII SG-FR DIST   2DL-POSS-VIII SG   ground VIII SG
   aykk
   COP VIII SG VIS
   'Over there is our land.'

In the third person singular, the language makes a distinction between what might be called proximative and obviative pronouns. The proximative form *m-* (the near distal deictic stem) is used when the possessor is coreferential with a core argument in the clause, generally the subject, while obviative *na-* is used when it is not.

(4-58) a. *m*-na-kn   patn   na-wayk-t
          3SG-POSS-V SG   betelnut V SG   3SG S-buy-PERF
          'He bought his (own) betelnut.'

       b. *na*-na-kn   patn   na-wayk-t
          3SG-POSS-V SG   betelnut V SG   3SG S-buy-PERF
          'He bought his (someone else's) betelnut.'

This contrast is only found in the singular; to get the same distinction in the other numbers, the normal possessor form must be modified by the adjective *ma* 'other' to express unambiguously the non-coreferential reading. Otherwise, the form remains ambiguous.

(4-59) a. mpu-na-kn   patn   pu-wayk-t
          3PL-POSS-V SG   betelnut V SG   3PL S-buy-PERF
          'They bought their (own/someone else's) betelnut.'

       b. ma   mpu-na-kn   patn   pu-wayk-t
          other   3PL-POSS-V SG   betelnut V SG   3PL S-buy-PERF
          'They bought their (someone else's) betelnut.'

The latter construction, it must be admitted, was obtained only by elicitation; I have never heard it used spontaneously. The speaker was content to live with the ambiguity of (4-59a).

4.6 Nominals and Noun Phrases
From some of the above examples the alert reader will have noted two constructions for possessor-possessed relations, illustrated again in the following examples.

(4-60) a. ama-na   matn
          1SG-POSS   brother I SG
          'my brother'

       b. ama-na-kn   patn
          1SG POSS-V SG   betelnut V SG
          'my betelnut'

Superficially these two constructions only differ formally in the presence or absence of the possessive agreement suffix -*kn*, but syntactically there is a world of difference between them. The construction without the possessive agreement suffix for the noun class and number of the possessed noun is a tightly knit noun phrase. Its word order is rigid and nothing may intervene between the two constituents.

(4-61) a.*matn   ama-na
         brother I SG 1SG-POSS

      b.*ama-na   mpa-n   matn
         1SG-POSS   one-I SG   brother I SG

However, neither of these prohibitions apply to the construction with the agreement suffix.

(4-62) a. patn   ama-na-kn
         betelnut V SG   1SG-POSS-V SG
         'my betelnut'

      b. ama-na-kn   mpa-n   patn
         1SG-POSS-V SG   one-V SG   betelnut V SG
         'my one betelnut'

In fact, when the possessor is suffixed with an agreement marker, any word order is possible.

(4-63) a. patn   ama-na-kn   mpa-n
         betelnut V SG   1SG-POSS-V SG   one-V SG

      b. mpa-n   patn   ama-na-kn
         one-V SG   betelnut V SG   1SG-POSS-V SG

      c. mpa-n   ama-na-kn   patn
         one-V SG   1SG-POSS-V SG   betelnut V SG

      d. patn   mpa-n   ama-na-kn
         betelnut V SG   one-V SG   1SG-POSS-V SG

      e. ama-na-kn   patn   mpa-n
         1SG-POSS-V SG   betelnut V SG   one-V SG
         'my one betelnut'

In such cases the possessor need not even adjoin the possessed noun, nor its other modifiers.

(4-64) patn   wayk-k   ama-na-kn   wa-n
        betelnut V SG   buy-IRR   1SG-POSS-V SG   go-PRES
        'Go buy my betelnut.'

If the possessed noun is understood from context, it need not even be mentioned.

(4-65) ama-na-kn   wayk-k   wa-n
       1SG-POSS-V SG buy-IRR go-IMP
       'Go buy my (betelnut).'

The obvious conclusion to be drawn from the contrast in syntactic behavior between (4-60a) and (4-60b) is that (4-60a), without possessive agreement, is a noun phrase, but (4-60b), with it, is not. The latter construction is a scrambled paratactic construction, with the two nominals in apposition to each other (as we will argue below). In addition to these structural differences there is a semantic difference between the (a) and (b) constructions, as demonstrated by the choice of nouns in (4-60a) and (4-60b). The unaffixed (a) construction is largely restricted to possessed kin terms. These are the only possessed nouns for which it is commonly heard spontaneously and indeed is highly favored for them. The (a) construction with other types of nouns, while grammatical, is only marginally so and is rarely encountered. The (b) construction with the possessive agreement suffix is much preferred with non-kin nouns. It could be argued that this difference reflects a distinction between alienable and inalienable possession, but, since classically inalienably possessed nouns such as body parts occur in the (b) construction (as well as the possessor raising construction with verbs, see Section 6.2.3.2), this claim does not seem entirely warranted. The (a) construction seems reserved for kin terms only.

The (a) construction, i.e., the noun phrase structure, is restricted to possessor-possessed phrases and true adjective plus noun constructions. Phrases composed of *kpa* 'big', *yua* 'good', and *ma* 'other' have the same restrictions as possessors lacking agreement.

(4-66) a. ma   patn
          other betelnut V SG
          'Another betelnut'
      b.*patn   ma
          betelnut V SG other
      c.*ma   kpa patn
          other big betelnut V SG

As soon as these adjectives are suffixed with the adjectival agreement suffixes for the modified nouns, all these restrictions disappear.

(4-67) a. patn   ma-n
          betelnut V SG other-V SG
          'another betelnut'
      b. ma-n   kpa patn
          other V SG big betelnut V SG
          'another big betelnut'

When the adjectives are suffixed with the proper agreement affixes, all
word order permutations are possible.

(4-68) a. patn   kpa-n   ma-n
          betelnut V SG big-V SG other-V SG

    b. ma-n   patn   kpa-n
          other-V SG betelnut V SG big-V SG

    c. kpa-n   ma-n   patn
          big-V SG other-V SG betelnut V SG

    'another big betelnut'

Unlike possessive-possessed phrases, there is no semantic restriction for
true adjectives concerning the type of noun which can occur in either
the tightly knit noun phrase or the scrambled pattern. Common nouns
like *patn* 'betelnut' occur freely in both structures. Adjectival verbs
which require in all contexts the adjectival agreement suffixes are only
encountered in the scrambled pattern. The tightly knit noun phrase
structure is ungrammatical for them.

(4-69) a.*walɲa impram
          light   basket VII SG

    b. walɲa-k-m   impram
          light-IRR-VII SG basket VII SG

       ~ impram   walɲa-k-m
              basket VII SG light-IRR-VII SG

    'a light basket'

    c. walɲa-k-m   kpa impram
          light-IRR-VII SG big   basket VII SG

       ~ kpa impram   walɲa-k-m
              big   basket VII SG light-IRR-VII SG

    'a light big basket'

The two stems, *mama* 'bad' and *waca* 'small', which are simultaneously
members of the class of true adjectives and adjectival verbs, are especially interesting. When they have the morphological properties of true
adjectives, they only occur in the tight noun phrase structure; with
the morphological properties of adjectival verbs, they are found in the
scrambled patterns.

(4-70) a. mama patn
          bad   betelnut V SG

    b.*patn   mama
          betelnut V SG bad

      c.*mama mpa-n   patn
         bad   one-V SG betelnut V SG

(4-70) shows *mama* without the *-k* IRR or adjectival agreement suffixes. Hence, it occurs in the tightly knit noun phrase structure, as in (4-70a), and the variants (4-70b,c) are ungrammatical.

(4-71) mama-k-n   patn
       bad-IRR-V SG betelnut V SG

     ~ patn   mama-k-n
       betelnut V SG bad-IRR-V SG

    'bad betelnut'

(4-72) a. mama-k-n   mpa-n   patn
        bad-IRR-V SG one-V SG betelnut V SG

     b. patn   mama-k-n   mpa-n
        betelnut V SG bad-IRR-V SG one-V SG

     c. mpa-n   patn   mama-k-n
        one-V SG betelnut V SG bad-IRR-V SG

     'one bad betelnut'

In (4-71) and (4-72), *mama* 'bad' is suffixed with *-k* IRR plus an agreement affix, demonstrating its membership in the class of adjectival verbs. As such, it can occur in any position and be freely separated from the noun it modifies by other words.

We may summarize the behavior of these two constructions in the following table (where AGR indicates any adjectival/possessive agreement suffix):

Noun modifier constructions

Tight noun phrase	*Scrambled pattern*
Possessor *na* N	N+Possessor *na*-AGR
Adjective+N	N+Adj/Adj verb-AGR

The constructions in the first column are clear examples of noun phrases and should be generated explicitly by phrase structure rules. An important generalization about noun phrases in Yimas is that they may consist of only two constituents, a modifier and a head, in that order. If more than two modifiers are present for a given noun, one must take an agreement suffix and occur in the scrambled pattern.

(4-73) a.*yua kpa impram
       good big   basket

    b. [yua-m   [kpa impram]]
       good-VII SG big   basket VII SG

    ~ [[yua   impram]   kpa-m]
        good basket VII SG big-VII

    'a good big basket'

This constraint, of course, does not apply if the head noun is a compound
noun, for such behave as a single complex word, which is derived through
morphological, not syntactic rules.

(4-74) a. [ama-na   [num-n   karm]]
       1SG-POSS   village-OBL lip/language VII SG
       'my native language'

Although interestingly, this is not possible if the modifier is an adjective.

    b.*kpa num-n   numpran
       big   village-OBL pig III SG

What accounts for the difference between possessors and adjectives for
nominal compound heads is unknown. The constraint against complex
heads also applies to heads consisting of conjoined nouns, as conjoining
is done by syntactic means.

(4-75) a.*yua   [panmal   narmaŋ]
       good   man I SG woman II SG

    b. [yua   panmal] [yua   narmaŋ]
       good man I SG   good woman II SG
       'a good man and woman'

    c. panmal   yua-n   narmaŋ   yua-nmaŋ
       man I SG good-I SG woman II SG good-II SG
       'a good man and a good woman'

    d. panmal   narmaŋ   yua-mampan
       man I SG woman II SG good-I DL
       'a good man and woman'

    e.*panmal   narmaŋ   yua-nput
       man I SG woman II SG good-II DL

A noun phrase with a head noun composed of conjoined nouns, as in
(4-75a), is ungrammatical. One uses either a conjoined construction of
two noun phrases, each consisting of an adjective plus a head noun, as
in (4-75b), or a scrambled structure in which the adjective occurs with
an agreement suffix and has no restrictions as to its position, as in (4-
75c,d). Note that the gender resolution in (4-75d,e) is to the masculine
class I with the agreement suffix -*mampan* I DL. Using the corresponding
female suffix -*nput* II DL, as in (4-75e) results in ungrammaticality. This

illustrates the general gender/class resolution rule always neutralizes to
the unmarked class, class I for animates and class V for inanimates.

Clearly, the phrase structure rules needed to generate Yimas noun
phrases must produce structures of no more than two constituents, the
rightmost of which must be a noun, not another noun phrase, in order
to block structures like (4-75a). In other words, unlike English noun
phrases, those of Yimas are non-recursive, and the phrase structure rules
must reflect this. The following is suggested:

(4-76)   NP   →   (M) + N

         M   → $\left\{ \begin{array}{l} \text{ADJ} \\ \text{POSSR} \end{array} \right\}$

N, of course, covers simple nouns like *patn* 'betelnut' as well as noun
compounds like *numn karm* 'native language'. ADJ covers all members of the class of true adjectives, i.e., those which may occur without
agreement suffixes. POSSR consists of a noun or pronoun plus *na* POSS.
There is a selectional restriction concerning noun phrases with POSSR
to the effect that they are highly preferred when N is a noun, and disfa-
vored (but grammatical) elsewhere. The constituent preceding *na* POSS
in the POSSR slot is either a noun or a pronoun. As these are nominals,
it could be the case that a noun phrase precedes *na* and this would be
potential source for recursion. This possibility is more theoretical than
actual, however, for the language has general ways to avoid such possibilities. For example, if we wanted to say 'my mother's brother's child'
with recursive in the POSSR constituent, one might expect the following:

(4-77) ?ama-na   ŋayuk   na   matn   na
       1SG-POSS   mother II SG   POSS   brother I SG   POSS
       kalakn
       child I SG
       'my mother's brother's child'

This is a possible structure but would, in fact, very rarely if ever be
uttered. There is a perfectly good kin term for 'mother's brother's child',
akay, just like 'cousin' in English, which would be used instead.

(4-78)   ama-na   akay
         1SG-POSS   mother's brother's child
         'my mother's brother's child'

Since the overwhelming use of possessives in noun phrases is with kin
terms, this effectively almost excludes recursion in the POSSR slot. But
even in cases with non-kin terms recursion may be avoided. Consider,
for example, the following phrase:

(4-79) ama-na   matn   na   kay
       1SG-POSS brother-I SG POSS canoe VIII SG
       'my brother's canoe'

This contains a recursive POSSR slot and is grammatical. But an alternative, and preferred, way to express (4-79) is to treat the complex POSSR constituent as a single noun phrase and attach the possessive agreement suffix for *kay* 'canoe' to it, thus generating a scrambled structure overall.

(4-80) kay   [ama-na   matn]   na-y
       canoe VIII SG   1SG-POSS brother I SG POSS-VIII SG
       'my brother's canoe'

It is important to note that noun phrases generated by the rules in (4-76) typically inflect as if they were single nouns. We have already seen that noun class and number are obligatory inflections for nouns; they cannot be carried solely by adjoining modifiers.

(4-81) a. m-ŋkl   tuŋkurŋkl
        NR DIST-VI DL eye VI DL
        'those eyes'

      b. m-ŋkl   *tuŋukrŋ
        NR DIST-VI DL eye

(4-82) a. mu-m   payum
        NR DIST-I PL man I PL
        'those men'

      b. m-um   *panmal
        NR DIST-I PL man

The (b) examples are ungrammatical because the nouns appear in their base forms (equivalent to the singular), but are modified by non-singular pronouns. This is impossible. Nouns which are non-singular must be inflected as such, e.g., in the (a) examples, number and noun class inflection may not be carried by adjoining modifiers. As the (a) examples further demonstrate, the modifiers themselves must be inflected for the same features of noun class and number.

But this is not the case with modifiers in noun phrases. In these constructions, the adjective or possessor remains completely uninflected for noun class and number (if they are so inflected the scrambled pattern results), and the head noun is the sole carrier of these features. In other words, the noun phrase is assigned the features of noun class and number as a whole.

(4-83) a. ama-na   tuŋkurŋkl
        1SG-POSS eyes VI DL
        'my two eyes'

      b. yua   payum
        good   man I PL
        'good men'

The claim that grammatical features are assigned to the noun phrase as a whole is further borne out by the behavior of the oblique suffix. It follows the head noun, but has scope over the whole noun phrase.

(4-84) a. [ma   ka]-ɲan
         other canoe VIII SG-OBL
         'in another canoe'

      b.*ma-nan   ka-ɲan
         other-OBL canoe VIII SG-OBL

(4-84b) shows that the modifier in a noun phrase cannot be affixed with the oblique suffix even if its head noun already is indicating that the domain of the oblique suffix is the whole noun phrase not just the head noun.

    The modifiers which freely form noun phrases are possessors and true adjectives, but there are sporadic instances of other word types occurring in noun phrases without their normal adjectival/possessive agreement suffixes. An interesting example is the following:

(4-85) [[mpa ant]-ɲan   namat]   aypak
        one   ground VIII SG-OBL person I PL COP I PL
        'We are one clan.' ('people of one ground')

The numeral *mpa* 'one' almost always takes adjectival agreement suffixes, but here it occurs as modifier of a noun phrase which is the first constituent of a compound. If *mpa* 'one' were to take an agreement suffix in the above example, it would no longer form a noun phrase with the following noun. Because nouns and noun phrases are the only possible first constituents in this compound it would then be ill formed. Consequently, an agreement suffix for *mpa* is blocked in this case.

    The scrambled structures have very different properties from the tight noun phrases. They are not single noun phrases at all, but rather two noun phrases in apposition, one consisting of a noun, the other a modifier, nominalized by the agreement suffix. They are joined together as a single semantic unit (but two syntactic units) by the agreement suffix, for it is this marker on the modifier which links it to the noun being qualified. In no sense, though, is this noun the head of the modifier; they are only joined at the level of semantic interpretation to form a conceptual unit. Rather, there is evidence to suggest that the actual head of the modifier is the agreement suffix itself.

(4-86) a. ama-na   matn   anak
             1SG-POSS brother I SG   COP I SG
             'It's my brother.'

    b. matn   ama-na-kn   anak
             brother I SG   1SG-POSS-I SG   COP I SG
             'It's my brother.'

    c. m-n   matn   ama-na-kn   anak
             NR DIST-I SG brother I SG 1SG-POSS-I SG   COP I SG
             'That's my brother.'

    d.*matn   ama-na   m-n   anak
             brother I SG   1SG-POSS   NR DIST-I SG   COP I SG

(4-87) a. yua   imprampat   arak
             good   basket VII PL COP VII PL
             'They're good baskets.'

    b. imprampat   yua-ra   arak
             basket VII PL   good-VII PL   COP VII PL
             'They're good baskets.'

    c. ya-n   imprampat   yua-ra   arak
             VII PL-FR DIST   basket VII PL good-VII PL   COP VII PL
             'Those baskets are good.'

    d.*imprampat   yua   ya-n   arak
             basket VII PL   good VII PL-FR DIST   COP VII PL

The (a) examples are typical noun phrases, while (b) and (c) are scrambled structures, with and without an overt deictic, respectively. The (d) examples are the ones relevant here. They demonstrate that a deictic cannot serve as the head of a noun phrase. Note the close parallelism between the (b) and (d) examples. The agreement suffix in (b) corresponds to the deictic in (d). This suggests that the agreement suffix could be analyzed as the realization of the deictic, as follows:

(4-88) [[yua]   m-ra]
      good   NR DIST-VII PL

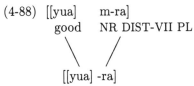

     [[yua] -ra]

In other words, modifiers affixed with the adjectival/possessive agreement suffixes are noun phrases in miniature, with the agreement suffix functioning as the head. A noun and a modifier affixed with an agreement suffix are simply noun phrases in apposition to each other. There is no strong syntactic relationship between them, merely a loose paratactic link, established by the coreference in noun class and number. This accounts for the completely unconstrained permutations of word order observed between a noun and a modifier with an agreement suffix. So the structural relationships in a sentence like (4-86b) are as shown below:

(4-89) [imprampat]   [[yua-]ra]   [ya-n-ampa-wat]
      basket VII PL   good-VII PL   VII PL O-3SG A-weave-HAB
      'She weaves good baskets.'

or more literally:

      'She weaves baskets, good ones.'

There is no closer *syntactic* relationship in (4-89) between *imprampat* 'baskets' and *yua-ra* 'good' than there is between *imprampat* and the verb. The linking between them is done at the semantic level; they are interpreted as denoting the same real world objects because of the coreference in the noun class and number specifications.

     Further evidence that modifiers with agreement suffixes are noun phrases in miniature is demonstrated by their behavior with the oblique suffix, even when there is no overt noun in the clause.

(4-90) [[[ma]-m]-un]   na-wapal
      other-IV SG-OBL   3SG S-climb
      'She climbed on another (sago palm).'

The understood noun is *tnum* 'sago palm', indicated only by the class IV singular adjectival suffix *-(u)m*. The claim is that the stem *ma-m* other-IV SG is a noun phrase and, as expected, it may be affixed with the oblique suffix.

     A more interesting example is given below:

(4-91) [anti]   [kanta]   [[[[waca-k]-i]-ɲan]
      ground VIII SG   but   small-IRR-VIII SG-OBL
      [kapa-taw-wat]]
      1DL S-sit-HAB
      'But we two live on a little land.'

As mentioned in Section 3.9, Yimas conjunctions like *kanta* 'but' have a strong tendency to occur in the second position of the clause, as in this example; but here it intervenes between a noun and an adjectival verb modifier. The adjectival verb is nominalized and functions as a noun phrase because of the suffix *-i* VIII SG (triggering the palatalization rule (2-3) for the following /n/). It is clear that it modifies *anti* 'ground' because of their agreement in noun class and number features. The really interesting detail is the position of the oblique suffix. While *anti* 'ground' is obviously under the scope of the oblique suffix, it is only indirectly linked to it, by having the same noun class and number specifications as the noun phrase *waca-k-i* small-IRR-VIII SG, which is in turn affixed by the oblique suffix. Note that the oblique suffix is here attached to what would seem at first view to be a modifier rather than the head, but given the claim that such modifiers are in fact noun phrases themselves, the construction is quite straightforward.

5

Basic Verbal Morphology

The verb is by far the most morphologically complex word class in Yimas. Much of this complexity derives from elaborate processes of derivation and root compounding which will be the focus of the next chapter. In this chapter I will discuss what would in traditional terms be described as verbal inflection, although as we shall see, a sharp line between verbal inflection and verbal derivation is very difficult to draw in Yimas. Specifically, this chapter will deal with the inflectional system for tense, aspect, and mood, as well as the pronominal affixes for the core arguments. Because Yimas lacks any case marking on nominals functioning as core arguments, these pronominal affixes serve as the primary device signalling grammatical relations in the language. Since the pronominal affixes can cause allomorphic variation in the tense/aspect/mood system, I will begin with them. As the exposition will demonstrate, the inflection of Yimas verbs with pronominal affixes is very complex. The possibilities are summarized in Tables 5–7 at the end of Section 5.1.3.

5.1 The Pronominal Affix System for Core Nominals
5.1.1 The Basic Schema for Role Marking
As mentioned above, it is the verbal pronominal affixes on a Yimas verb which indicate the semantic roles of its associated core nominals. These function like case marking in languages like Latin or Sanskrit or word order in languages like English or Indonesian. Consider the following two examples:

(5-1) a. payum   narmaŋ   na-mpu-tay
      man I PL   woman II SG   3SG O-3PL A-see
      'The men saw the woman.'

    b. payum   narmaŋ   pu-n-tay
      man I PL   woman II SG   3PL O-3SG A-see
      'The woman saw the men.'

Note that the word order in both these sentences is exactly the same, and further that neither of the nouns have any case marking affixes. Yet their meanings are contrastive. This meaning difference is carried by the different choice of verbal prefixes. In the first example, the prefixes indicate a singular object and a plural subject. The associated plural noun *payum* 'men' must therefore be the subject, and the singular noun *narmaŋ* 'woman' the object, resulting in 'the men saw the woman'. In the (b) example, the inflectional pattern of the prefixes is the opposite, indicating a singular subject and a plural object. Hence, the singular noun *narmaŋ* 'woman' must now be the subject and the plural noun *payum* 'men', the object, expressing the meaning 'the woman saw the men'. Note that the verbal affixes signal the grammatical relations of core nominals rather indirectly: they associate a grammatical relation with a certain person/number combination. The noun which matches this person/number combination is then interpreted as filling the grammatical relation. If the person/number combinations of the pronominal affixes are the same, ambiguous sentences may result.

(5-2) panmal   narmaŋ   na-n-tay
       man I SG   woman II SG   3SG O-3SG A-see
       'The man saw the woman.' *or*
       'The woman saw the man.'

Noun class distinctions may come to the rescue in many cases. This does not help in (5-2) because, although the two nouns belong to different classes (classes I and II) the verbal prefixes for these clauses are identical. If, however, the object were a class VI noun, the ambiguity would disappear.

(5-3) krayŋ   narmaŋ   k-n-tay
       frog VI SG woman II SG   VI SG O-3SG A-see
       'The woman saw the frog.'
       *'The frog saw the woman.'

The prefix *k-* VI SG is unambiguously associated with *krayŋ* 'frog', which thereby must function as the object. The subject *narmaŋ* 'woman' is similarly identified by the prefix *n-* 3SG A. Hence (5-3) is unambiguous and can only mean 'the woman saw the frog'.

I have been using the terms subject and object thus far in the exposition in a pre-theoretical and undefined way. These notions as understood from the prism of English grammar are not entirely straightforward when extended to Yimas. The notion of subject in English conflates the subject of an intransitive and a transitive verb and contrasts these to the object of a transitive verb. Note, for example, that for the third person singular masculine pronoun, English uses the same form for the subject of a transitive and an intransitive verb, but a different form for the object of a transitive verb:

(5-4) a. *He* runs.

       b. *He* hit *him*.

This English way of marking grammatical relations is called a nominative-accusative system, in which the nominative is the form for the subject of the intransitive and transitive verb, and the accusative is the form of the object of the transitive verb. In a system like this, subject is a well defined notion in that it always corresponds to the nominative form. Object is equally well defined, always corresponding to the accusative form.

Yimas is not so straightforward, and the system of grammatical relations as assigned by the prefixes cannot be so simply characterized. Different person/number combinations work in different ways, but none align grammatical relations exactly as in English. The prefixes associated with third person participants vary in form according to their position in the verb. There is one form for initial position and another for non-initial position, as in (5-5):

(5-5) a. *pu*-wa-t
        3PL S-go-PERF
        'He went.'

     b. *pu*-n-tay
        3PL O-3SG A-see
        'He saw them.'
       *'They saw him.'

     c. na-*mpu*-tay
        3SG O-3PL A-see
        'They saw him.'
       *'He saw them.'

Note that when both prefixes refer to third person participants, this schema based on linear order amounts in essence to an ergative-absolutive marking system. The form *pu*- 3PL is used for the subject of an intransitive verb (5-5a) and also functions for the object of a transitive verb (5-5b). On the other hand, the subject of the transitive verb has the unique form *mpu*- 3PL. (I adopt Dixon's (1979) symbolism of S for the subject of an intransitive verb, A for the subject of a transitive verb and O for its object). We may diagram this contrast in the alignment of grammatical relations between English and Yimas in the following terms:

English: S: *he*   Yimas: S: *pu-*

        A: *he*   O: *him*   A: *mpu-*   O: *pu-*

    nominative-accusative   ergative-absolutive

The ergative form is that for the A, the subject of the transitive verb—in this Yimas example, *mpu-* 3PL. The absolutive corresponds to the S, the subject of the intransitive verb, and the O, the object of the transitive verb—in this case, the prefix *pu-* 3PL. Note that at least in these morphological terms, the notion of subject as employed in English is not applicable to Yimas, for it fails to align A, S, and O in the way in which this term is normally understood.

In fact the situation is more complex than this, for with the first and second person prefixes, A, S, and O typically do not conflate at all, each one of them having a distinct form, as in these examples of the first person singular prefixes:

(5-6) a. *ama*-wa-t
           1SG S-go-PERF
           'I went.'

       b. pu-*ka*-tay
           3PL O-1SG A-see
           'I saw them.'

       c. pu-*ŋa*-tay
           3PL A-1SG O-see
           'They saw me.'

For the first person singular, *ama-* is the form for the S, *ka-* for A, and *ŋa-* for O. (The alert reader will have noted the form *pu-* for A instead of the expected *mpu-*; this is because it occurs initially. As mentioned above, the form of the third person pronominal prefixes is largely determined by linear order, as will be discussed in detail below.) These forms for first singular contrast with those of third plural presented earlier in that they do not display an ergative system. Instead of aligning S and O as against A as do the third plural forms (*pu-* S, O; *mpu-* A), all three are distinct. This presents an equally difficult problem for extending the English notion of subject to Yimas, for again the S fails to align with A, the morphological defining characteristic of the notion subject for English and for languages generally with nominative-accusative marking conventions for grammatical relations.

Having said this, however, there is in fact some morphological evidence in Yimas for a notion of subject along the lines of English. This evidence appears in secondary verbal forms, particularly those with one of the modal prefixes (see Section 5.2.2). When one of these modal prefixes is added to a verb which normally would occur with the S prefix form, the prefix actually appears as the A form.

(5-7) a. *ama*-tmuk-t
           1SG S-fall-PERF
           'I fell down.'

       b. ant-*ka*-tmuk-t
           POT-1SG A-fall-PERF
           'I almost fell down.'

       c.*ant-*ŋa*-tmuk-t
           POT-1SG O-fall-PERF

(5-7a) is a straightforward verbal form with no modal prefixes in which the S argument is indicated by the normal S form *ama*-. (5-7b) is a verb inflected with the prefix for potential modality *ant*-, and the S argument is inflected with the normal A form *ka*- instead of the expected S form *ama*-. As (5-7c) indicates, the O prefix *ŋa*- is ungrammatical in this construction. Thus, in this construction the S argument surfaces with the A prefix, rather than the O form, demonstrating a clear conflation of S and A, that is, a nominative-accusative alignment reflecting a notion of subject much like that of English.

The third person prefixes diverge here. When a modal prefix is added to a verb with a third person S form prefix, this remains and does not convert to an A prefix.

(5-8) a. *pu*-tmuk-t
           3PL S-fall-PERF
           'They fell down'

       b. a-*pu*-tmuk-r-um
           POT-3PL S-fall-PERF-PL
           'They almost fell down.'

In (5-8a), a verbal form without any modal prefix, the normal absolutive form *pu*-, is used to indicate S. When the verb is inflected with the potential modal prefix *ant*- (with the allomorph *a*- for third plural), the S form *pu*- is still used to indicate the S argument, unlike the comparable situation for first and second person S arguments, which would be indicated with the A prefix forms (compare (5-7b)). So while the first and second persons betray in their modally inflected verbs an underlying nominative-accusative argument alignment, the third person does not, the absolutive form being used in both normal and modally inflected verbs.

It has already been mentioned that linear order imposes the primary constraints on the form of verbal prefixes, particularly the third person ones. The pronominal prefixes are normally the initial prefixes to a verb. The only prefixes which may ever precede them are the modal prefixes. For third person participants, Yimas requires the order O prefix-A prefix: for example, for two third plural participants, *pu-mpu-* 3PL O-3PL A. Yimas has an additional stipulation (to be discussed in detail in the following section) that the highest participant on a person hierarchy 1 > 2 > 3 should appear to the right, closest to the verb stem. Thus, in constructions involving a third person A and a first or second person O, the A will actually appear on the left, in initial position, outranked for the rightmost position by the O. Whenever this happens, the third person A will actually surface in what is typically the O prefix form, as in the following example:

(5-9)   *pu*-nan-tay
      3PL A-2SG O-see
      'They saw you.'

The prefix *pu-* 3PL is actually the usual S/O prefix form, being used for A because it is in initial position. The normal corresponding A form would be ungrammatical in this environment.

(5-10) a.**mpu-nan-tay
       3PL A-2SG O-see

Interestingly, for some unknown reason, the third plural A form and only this form may optionally appear in initial position if the O is first person singular.

     b. mpu-ŋa-tay
       1PL A-1SG O-see
       'They saw me.'

There is no explanation forthcoming for this anomaly, but it does demonstrate that the rules determining the forms of the prefixes cannot be completely put down to linear order. Clearly, (5-10b) supports the contention that the basic underlying alignment for the third person prefixes is ergative-absolutive, or A (*mpu-*) versus S, O (*pu-*).

Now when modal prefixes occur, they always occupy the initial prefix position. Any co-occurring third person prefix must occur in the second position, the position normally associated with the A form. Yet any third person participant functioning as S will still surface with the S prefix form in a verb inflected with a modal prefix.

(5-11) a-*pu*-tmuk-r-um
      POT-3PL S-fall-PERF-PL
      'They almost fell down.'

This example demonstrates that the basic underlying ergative-absolutive basis of the third person prefixes weighs more heavily in determining their form than the constraints imposed by linear order. Here the third person plural S participant is still coded by the S form *pu-* and not the A form *mpu-*, in spite of the fact that it occurs in the normal second position of the A prefix. Thus, for third person prefixes, linear order can cause an A participant to be coded by a S or O prefix form if outranked by a first or second person O participant, as in (5-9) (although that is only optional if the O participant is first person). But it will not cause an S participant to be indicated by an A prefix form even if its pronominal prefix occurs in second position, the normal position of A, as a result of a modal prefix preceding it.

This does happen, however, with first and second person participants. There, the accusative pattern with modally inflected verbs really does reflect the underlying pattern, for there are no linear order constraints prohibiting the A or the O prefix from occurring in second position (look back at examples (5-6b,c)). The S prefix forms for first and second person participants are closely related to the corresponding independent pronoun forms (see Section 5.1.2), and in most cases simply seem to be these pronouns bound to the verb stem. No other prefixes are allowed to precede these normal S forms. The other two prefixes for first or second person participants—those for A and O—do allow prefixes to precede them, typically a prefix for a third person core participant (again see examples (5-6b,c)). When a verb with an associated S participant is inflected with a modal prefix, one of the two prefix forms which allow a preceding prefix must be chosen, and it must be that which would normally mark an A.

(5-12) a. ant-*ka*-tmuk-t
            POT-1SG A-fall-PERF
            'I almost fell down.'

        b.*ant-*ŋa*-tmuk-t
            POT-1SG O-fall-PERF

Both examples illustrate first person singular S participants, but this participant must be realized by the A prefix form *ka-* (5-12a) and not the O form *ŋa-* (5-12b). Given what has been presented about the language so far, either option could be expected, but the fact that the language chooses the A form to reference an S participant clearly identifies an accusative pattern. S and A are conflated here rather than the ergative pattern of S and O. This fact clearly argues that underlying the usual three-way split of role marking for first and second person participants, i.e., treating all three distinctly (as is found with verbs without modal

inflection), is a basic nominative-accusative schema, which conflates S
and A and opposes this to O. We will see more evidence for this claim
as the exposition proceeds.

5.1.2 The Prefixes and Their Combinations

The pronominal prefixes in Yimas for each of the three functions A,
S, and O and for all person-number combinations are presented below.
The independent pronouns for first and second persons also appear for
comparison with the S forms (there are, of course, no true pronouns for
third person, that function being simply filled by the various deictics for
the different noun classes discussed in Chapter 4).

	A	O	S	Pronoun
1DL	ŋkra-	ŋkra-	kapa-	kapa
1PL	kay-	kra-	ipa-	ipa
1SG	ka-	ŋa-	ama-	ama
2DL	ŋkran-	ŋkul-	kapwa-	kapwa
2PL	nan-	kul-	ipwa-	ipwa
2SG	n-	nan-	ma-	mi
3SG	n-	na-	na-	
3PL	mpu-	pu-	pu-	
3DL	mpɨ-	impa-	impa-	

The person-number combinations are arranged in what seems to be a
rough Silversteinian hierarchy of feature markedness (Silverstein 1976).
Only the highest ranked combination, first dual, fails to distinguish A
and O. It uses the same prefix *ŋkra-* 1DL for both A and O and contrasts
this to an S form *kapa-*, derived in the typical fashion from the independent pronoun *kapa* 1DL. Verbs using this *ŋkra-* 1DL are ambiguous
between the A and O interpretation.

(5-13) pu-*ŋkra*-tay
        3PL A/O-1DL A/O-see
        'We two saw them.' *or*
        'They saw us two.'

Note that the 3PL prefix is of no help in disambiguating the construction,
because, since it occupies the initial position, it must appear in the S/O
form regardless of whether it is functioning as A or O.

The remaining combinations for first and second person all have distinct forms for A and O and, with a distinct form for S, (which is transparently the bound form of the corresponding independent pronoun),
all exhibit a three-way split in their role marking schema. Only for the
second singular S form *ma-*, is there any difference from the independent

pronoun, in this case *mi* 2SG. Transitive verbs involving these prefixes are always unambiguous in their role indications.

(5-14) a. pu-ka-tay
            3PL O-1SG A-see
            'I saw them.'

        b. pu-ŋa-tay
            3PL A-1SG O-see
            'They saw me.'

Finally, all third person prefixes operate on an ergative-absolutive role-marking schema, conflating S and O and opposing this to the A form, as in the following:

(5-15) a. pu-n-tay
            3PL O-3SG A-see
            'He saw them.'

        b. na-mpu-tay
            3SG O-3PL A-see
            'They saw him.'

A curious anomaly in the Yimas paradigm of verbal pronominal pre-fixes is the coincidence in form of the A prefix for second and third singular. This coincidence only applies in combinations of second singular with third person, for in combinations with first person, other consid-erations are operative, as we shall see below. But this coincidence does create ambiguity in a number of verbal forms as seen in the examples below.

(5-16) a. pu-n-tay
            3PL O-2/3 SG A-see
            'You/he saw them.'

        b. na-n-tay
            3SG O-2/3SG A-see
            'You/he saw him.'

A similar problem of ambiguity afflicts the O prefix for second singular. Notice that its form *nan-* is homophonous with the A prefix for second plural, so that again verbal forms involving third person participants are ambiguous.

(5-17) a. pu-nan-tay
            3PL A-3SG O-see
            'They saw you.'

        b. pu-nan-tay
            3PL O-2PL A-see
            'You all saw them.'

If the combination of participants is third singular A and second singular O, the prefix *na-* functioning as A may be optionally deleted, resulting in homophony with (5-16b) and a further ambiguity.

(5-18) a. na-nan-tay
               3SG A-2SG O-see
               'He saw you.'

          b. ∅-nan-tay
               3SG A-2SG O-see
               'He saw you.'

          c. na-n-tay = (5-16b)
               3SG O-2/3SG A-see
               'You/he saw him.'

I should point out that there are ways to disambiguate most of these forms either by the use of independent pronouns or by nominalizing them. See the discussion of finite nominalizations in Section 7.2.

It is now necessary to turn to the major principles which determine the linear order of the A and O prefixes on transitive verbs. There are two, sometimes conflicting, principles involved here. The first is a person hierarchy in which first person outranks second which outranks third. The second is a role hierarchy which states that for first and second persons O outranks A, but for third person, A outranks O.

Let us start with the simplest case, a verb with two third person participants. In such a case, the first principle is irrelevant, for there is no difference in person. Because both participants are third person, by the second principle the higher ranked prefix will be the A. Rank is indicated in the Yimas verb by a position to the right, closer to the verb stem. Thus, for a verb with two third person participants, the O will occur first and be followed by the higher ranked A, as in these examples:

(5-19) a. pu-n-tay
               3PL O-3SG A-see
               'He saw them.'

          b. na-mpɨ-tay
               3SG A-3DL A-see
               'They two saw him.'

In (5-19a) the A is third singular and the O third plural, so the prefixes must occur in the order O-A or *pu-n-* 3PL O-3SG A. Similarly, in (5-19b) there is a third dual A and a third singular O, and again the prefixes must occur in the order O-A or *na-mpɨ-* 3SG O-3DL A.

So far, all third person participants we have considered have referred to humans, that is, members of noun classes I and II. One may have in fact noted that the S/O prefixes given for third person correspond to the verbal agreement prefixes for classes I and II. These two are in fact one and the same. But the vast majority of potential third person participants, the nouns of Yimas, refer to animals, plants or inanimate objects. These too may be marked on the verb by the corresponding verbal prefixes for noun classes given in Chapter 4. Like the prefixes for classes I and II, these verbal prefixes are the forms used to mark S and O.

(5-20) a. tampaym   p-na-apica-mpi-irm-n
          food hanger VII SG   VII SG S-DEF-hang-SEQ-stand-PRES
          'The food hanger is hanging up.'

       b. tampaym   p-ka-apica-t
          food hanger VII SG   VII SG O-1SG A-hang-PERF
          'I hung up the food hanger.'

(5-20a) contains an intransitive verb for which *tampaym* 'food hanger' functions as the S nominal and is marked on the verb by the corresponding class VII verbal prefix *p-*. (5-20b) illustrates the corresponding transitive verb for which the same nominal now functions as the O argument, but again it is indicated by the prefix *p-*. Thus, these verbal prefixes for noun classes exhibit the same ergative-absolutive pattern found throughout the forms for third person. Examples from other classes follow:

(5-21) a. wut   ura-na-irm-kia-k
          night night S-DEF-stand-night-IRR
          'It's getting dark.'

       b. wanwa   wa-ka-tar-wapi
          knife IX SG   IX SG O-1SG A-CAUS-sharp
          'I sharpened the knife.'

       c. muraŋkl kla-ka-yamal
          paddle VI DL VI DL O-1SG A-carve
          'I carved the two paddles.'

   Only occasionally can an inanimate noun be referenced by an A prefix. The A prefixes have no differentiation for noun class: all nouns regardless of noun class are indicated by one of the three A prefixes for third person given above. Inanimate nouns may be expressed by an A prefix if they are associated with a transitive verb indicating a change of state or location, and they function as the force or instrument causing the change. For example:

(5-22) al   pu-n-kra-t
       machete V SG   3PL O-3SG A-cut-PERF
       'The machete cut them.'

Here *al* 'machete' functions as the instrument responsible for the cutting. There is no responsible agent mentioned in the sentence, so it is the instrument which is coded by the A prefix. Note that although the O is animate and the A inanimate, the A still occurs closer to the verb stem, in the higher ranking position. Now consider the following two examples:

(5-23) a. arm   i-mpu-tal-cŋknt-t   kay
         water VIII SG O-3PL A-CAUS-heavy-PERF canoe VIII SG
         'The water made the canoe heavy.'

     b. ikn   antki
         smoke V SG thatch VII PL

         ya-n-tar-urkpwica-t
         VII PL O-3SG A-CAUS-blacken-PERF
         'The smoke blackened the roof (thatch).'

It is worth pointing out that *arm* 'water', which constitutes a noun class by itself and is normally referenced by an S/O verbal prefix *ima-*, is treated as a plural noun when an A argument and indicated by the third plural A prefix *mpu-*. In both examples, the verbs are overtly causative, as expressed by the causative prefix *tar-* ~ *tal-* (see Section 6.2.3.1.3), and the inanimate nouns which express the forces functioning as the causes are referenced by the corresponding A prefix. While constructions like those of (5-23) are certainly grammatical in Yimas, such constructions with an overtly causativized verb have an alternative in which the verb is intransitive and associated with an S argument expressing the entity undergoing the change of state and an oblique noun for the causing force. So compare the examples in (5-23) to the corresponding intransitive examples in (5-24):

(5-24) a. arm-n   kay   i-cŋknt-t
         water-OBL canoe VIII SG VIII SG S-heavy-PERF
         'The canoe got heavy from the water.'

     b. ikn-an   antki   ya-urkpwica-t
         smoke-OBL thatch VII PL VII PL S-blacken-PERF
         'The roof (sago thatch) blackened from the smoke.'

These later constructions obviate the need to code the inanimate causers with an A prefix, instead marking them as peripheral nouns with the oblique suffix. The constructions of both (5-23) and (5-24) are equally grammatical and there is no significant meaning difference between them, although perhaps the examples (5-23), in which the causing functions are marked as A, reflect a more direct causation, focusing on the causer, rather than the change of state. This seems to be true of the corresponding English translations.

Having now discussed in some detail verbs associated with two third person participants, let me turn to the next most straightforward cases, those with one third person participant and one first or second person participant. According to principle one, the first or second person participant outranks the third person, so it must occupy the position closer to the verb stem. Now the second principle must be considered: A outranks O for third person, but O outranks A for first and second. So if the A is third person and the O is first or second, there is no conflict between the two principles: the first or second person O will occupy the ranking position closer to the verb stem, and the third person A will precede it.

(5-25) a. pu-ŋa-tay
          3PL A-1SG O-see
          'They saw me.'

       b. impa-ŋkul-cay
          3DL A-2DL O-see
          'They two saw you two.'

       c. na-kra-tay
          3SG A-1PL O-see
          'He saw us.'

       d. naŋkm   p-ŋa-kra-t
          grass VII SG VII SG A-1SG O-cut-PERF
          'The grass cut me.'

Note that because of the constraints on the form of the third person prefixes imposed by linear order, the third person A's in these examples actually appear in the form for S and O, the only permissible form for initial position. Also, because the A prefix must occur initially in an S/O form, it is now possible to indicate the noun class of inanimate A's as in (5-25d). This is not possible for verbs with two third person participants, in which the A prefix must be the A form in the ranking second position (5-23).

If the A is first or second person and the O third person, the two principles for ranking are now in conflict with each other. In this situation, principle one provides, and the first or second person participant occupies the higher ranked position, even though it is an A (compare these with examples in (5-25)):

(5-26) a. pu-ka-tay
          3PL O-1SG A-see
          'I saw them.'

> b. impa-ŋkran-tay
>   3DL O-2DL A-see
>   'You two saw them two.'
>
> c. na-kay-cay
>   3SG O-1PL A-see
>   'We saw him.'

Now let us turn to the most complex cases, verbs with a first person participant and a second person participant. By principle one, the first person participant, will always outrank the second. But principle two poses a potential dilemma. Remember that for first and second persons O outranks A, so that if the first person participant is the O and the second person the A, there is no problem: both principles select the same participant, the first person O, as the higher ranked. If, on the other hand, the first person participant is the A and the second person the O, the two principles are in conflict: principle one selects the first person A as the higher ranked, while principle two chooses the second person O. As we shall see below, Yimas has evolved a clever solution to this dilemma.

Let us start with the simpler of the two cases, that in which the principles are in harmony. These involve a first person O and a second person A. By both principles the higher ranked will be the first person O, and therefore the prefix for this participant will occur closer to the verb stem:

(5-27) a. ma-ŋa-tay
          2SG A-1SG O-see
          'You saw me.'

       b. ma-kra-tay
          2SG A-1PL O-see
          'You saw us.'

       c. kapwa-ŋkra-tay
          2DL A-1DL O-see
          'You two saw us two.'

       d. ipwa-ŋkra-tay
          2PL A-1DL O-see
          'You all saw us two.'

Because the second person A is the lower ranked participant, it would have to appear in the verb-initial position. But as we have seen with third person prefixes, there is a constraint which prohibits the A prefix forms from appearing there. Hence, the second person A is actually realized with the S prefix form, as with the third person examples discussed earlier. For example, in (5-27a,b), the second singular A is marked by the prefix *ma-* 2SG S. The same constraint causes the S prefixes for non-singular second person participants to be employed in examples (5-27c, d), although in these cases it is a little more difficult to be sure that there are in fact bound S prefixes, for they are completely homophonous with the independent pronouns. Evidence that there are in fact bound prefixes will be presented below in Section 5.1.4 on paucal marking and again in Section 5.2.2.1 on negation.

Let us now look at the case in which the two principles fixing the linear order of A and O prefixes are in conflict, those involving a first person A and a second person O. By principle one, the first person A should be the higher ranked, but by principle two, the second person O should be. For a second person singular O, the language avoids the problem entirely by having a suppletive portmanteau morpheme *mpan-* ~ *kampan-* (whose allomorph occurs word-initially) which is used whenever a first person A of any number acts on a second singular O.

(5-28) a. kampan-tay
　　　　　1A/2SG O-seé
　　　　　'I saw you.'

　　　 b. kapa kampan-tay
　　　　　1DL   1A/2SG O-see
　　　　　'We two saw you.'

　　　 c. ipa   kampan-tay
　　　　　1PL   1A/2SG O-see
　　　　　'We saw you.'

To distinguish the number of the first person A, an independent pronoun must be used, as in (5-28b, c). Without a pronoun, first singular is assumed, unless context determines otherwise (5-28a).

If the second person O is non-singular, the language copes by simply prohibiting both participants from being realized as bound prefixes to the verb. The second person O occupies the ranking position of the prefix to the verb, and the first person A must appear as an independent pronoun. These independent pronouns are, of course, again homophonous with the corresponding S prefixes (as with the examples of the non-singular second person A's in (5-27c, d), but in this situation the first person A's are flatly prohibited from being bound to the verb).

(5-29) a. ŋkul-cay
　　　　　2DL O-see
　　　　　'I saw you two.'

　　　 b. kapa kul-cay
　　　　　1DL   2PL O-see
　　　　　'We two saw you all.'

c. ipa   ŋkul-cay
   1PL   2DL O-see
   'We saw you two.'

Evidence that the non-singular second person A's in (5-29c, d) are bound
to the verbs, but that these first person A's are not is presented in
the discussion of negation (see Section 5.2.2.1). As (5-29a) shows, a
first singular A is assumed in the absence of an overt pronoun. These
examples indicate that in the conflict between principles one and two for
the ordering of the first and second person A and O prefixes, the second
is the more important, for it is the O which is realized as the verbal
prefix, as principle two would require, in spite of the fact that it is the
lower ranking participant by principle one.

5.1.3 Ditransitive Verbs and the Expression of the Dative
So far I have been using the notions of transitive and intransitive in a
descriptive and rather pre-theoretical manner. As we shall see in Section
5.1.6, these notions are not without their problems when applied to Yimas, but for the time being I will continue to use them as I have defined
above. In addition to the many intransitive and transitive verbs, Yimas
has four inherently ditransitive verbs, although many basic transitive
verbs can be made ditransitive through the valence increasing prefixes
(see Section 6.2.3). These four basic ditransitive verbs are ŋa- 'give', i-
'tell someone', tkam- 'show', and pul- 'rub on'. Ditransitive verbs are
distinctive in Yimas by allowing three pronominal affixes, the third one
being used to express what is called in traditional grammar the indirect
object or dative case, as *boy* in *the girl gave the snake to the boy*. The
range of this third affix in Yimas is much wider than simply the indirect
object in English and corresponds to many uses of the dative case in
classical languages like Latin, so I will refer to these affixes as the dative
affixes (abbreviation: D). For first and second person, these dative affixes are, in fact, homophonous with the O prefixes, but for third person
there is a distinct set of dative *suffixes*.

(5-30) a. uraŋ   k-mpu-*ŋa*-tkam-t
           coconut VI SG VI SG O-3PL A-1SG D-show-PERF
           'They showed me the coconut.'

      b. uraŋ   k-mpu-tkam-r-*mpn*
           coconut VI SG VI SG O-3PL A-show-PERF-3DL D
           'They showed them two the coconut.'

Note that the dative affixes are the same as the O forms only in the
first and second persons, the persons that align participant roles according to a nominative-accusative schema. In the third person forms,

which follow an ergative-absolutive alignment, the dative suffixes are distinct from both the A and O prefix forms. This suggests that the first and second persons follow not so much a nominative-accusative schema, as a nominative-dative one, in accord with Silverstein's (1976, 1980) claim of the underlying salience of the nominative-dative case opposition. Although the O and D prefixes for first and second person are homophonous, they must be regarded as distinct because of their different substitution possibilities: O prefixes by third person absolutive prefixes and D prefixes by third person dative suffixes. This claim is further buttressed by their behavior in relativization (see Section 7.2.1).

The data on the verbal pronominal suffixes presented so far demonstrates a fundamental split between the first and second persons on the one hand and third person on the other. First and second person have a three way split between S, A, and O, with D equivalent formally to O. This is of course, underlaid by a nominative-accusative system (or nominative-dative) with S = A and opposed to O/D. Third person forms exhibit an ergative-absolutive system with S = O opposed to A and with a distinct D series. The differences between the persons can be summarized as follows:

	A	S	O	D
1/2	ka-	ama-	ŋa-	
3	mpɨ-	impa-		-mpn

In the accusatively marking persons O collapses with D, but in the ergatively marking person, it collapses with S. Is there a unified notion of O that lies behind these different encodings? This question parallels the earlier one whether there is a unified notion of subject underneath the nominative-accusative/ergative-absolutive split based on person. Both questions are far too complex to answer completely here, and data bearing on them will be continually presented when I treat the syntax of clauses and complex sentences in Chapters 6 and 7. The vast majority of syntactic processes in Yimas are realized through morphological devices, and the grammatical relations involved in these processes are those reflected in the morphology. Hence when the morphology reflects this person-based split, there is scant evidence to support the claim of a unity underlying that split. There are, however, a few syntactic constructions which do provide evidence for unified notions of subject and object, and this will be noted when they are discussed. But at this point I will stick closely to the various categories that the morphology justifies.

Now let me return to the examples in (5-30). Even though I have rejected the idea of a morphologically coherent notion of O for ditransitive verbs, equivalent to the O of transitive verbs, I can still propose rather straightforward analyses. In (5-30a), the verb *tkam* 'show' is associated with three core arguments. The initiating participant, the A, is third person plural and is realized by the proper prefix *mpu-* 3PL A. The next participant is the dative nominal, the participant to whom the coconut is shown. Because the dative participant is first singular, a person-number combination whose marking of participant relations follows a nominative-dative schema, it will be realized by the prefix *ŋa-*, the O form, or perhaps more precisely, the non-nominative form. Because the first person participant outranks the third person participant by the first hierarchical principle, its prefix will occupy the ranking position closer to the verb stem. Finally, the remaining core participant, *uraŋ* 'coconut', a class VI singular noun, is realized on the verb by the corresponding prefix of that class and number, *k-*. Because it is the lowest ranking prefixed participant, its prefix will occur first. Now consider (5-30b). Again the verb is the ditransitive *tkam* 'show', and the first of the three arguments is the third plural A marked by the prefix *mpu-* 3PL A. But in the example, the dative participant is third dual, and this is a person/ number combination which follows an ergative-absolutive schema. In these cases there is a distinct set of suffixes for dative participants and the proper form here is -*mpn* 3DL D. Finally, the remaining core participant *uraŋ* 'coconut' is realized by its prefix *k-*, which as the lower ranking of the two prefixes, occurs initially.

In these analyses, the underlying participant relations of (5-30a,b) are identical. The differences in structure are accounted for by the same general split in case marking schema that we saw with transitive verbs: first and second person work accusatively (nominative-dative schema) and third person works ergatively (ergative-absolutive-dative schema). The main point with ditransitive verbs is that the dative participants marked with the prefixes identical in form to the O prefixes are not in an O relation; that is, the grammatical relationship between such a prefix and its governing ditransitive verb differs from that of the same prefix with a governing transitive verb. The notion of O is an applicable and useful notion for transitive verbs, but is not extendable to ditransitive verbs in Yimas. We may summarize the core arguments with the three basic types of verbs in Yimas as follows,

intransitive verb:		S	
transitive verb:		A	O
ditransitive verb:	A	T	D

where T refers to the theme core argument, that which is shown, given, etc., i.e., whose location is at issue (Foley and Van Valid 1984). These can only be third person in Yimas and must always be realized by the first agreement prefix. A final point to be noted from these examples is the form of the A prefix in (5-30a). Compare this to the corresponding transitive verb in (5-14b). In spite of its preceding the prefix *ŋa-* 1SG O, the A actually must appear in the A prefix form *mpu-* rather than being optionally neutralized to the S/O form *pu-*, as in (5-14b). This is because it does not occur initially in (5-30a), but follows another prefix *k-*. This is conclusive proof that the neutralization to the S/O form initially for third person prefixes (e.g., (5-14b)) is, as claimed, simply a surface reflex of being in initial position, and nothing more. When not in initial position, the true A form emerges.

Now we are ready to look in more detail at the morphology of ditransitive verbs and the dative suffixes. The forms of the dative suffixes for the three numbers in third person are as follows:

SG	DL	PL
-(n)akn	-mpn	-mpun

(5-31) a. k-ka-tkam-r-*akn*
        VI SG T-1SG A-show-PERF-3SG D
        'I showed him (the coconut).'

        b. k-ka-tkam-tuk-*nakn*
        VI SG T-1SG A-show-RM PAST-3SG D
        'I showed him (the coconut) long ago.'

        c. k-nan-tkam-r-*mpun*
        VI SG T-2PL A-show-PERF-3PL D
        'You all show them (the coconut).'

As (5-31a,b) demonstrate, there is some allomorphic variation for the third singular dative suffix. -*akn* occurs following a [-peripheral] consonant and -*nakn* occurs elsewhere.

A salient feature of all three dative suffixes is the final -*n*. This, of course, bears a transparent relationship to the oblique suffix -*n* ~ -*nan*. The dative is in many ways a transitional relation between the true core relations, represented by A, S, and O, and the oblique, peripheral relations of location and time (see Foley 1986, 96–8), and these Yimas dative suffixes clearly seem to be formerly independent pronominal elements followed by the oblique suffix which have become bound to the verb and reanalyzed as suffixes. These forms must always occur in absolute final position in the verb. If another suffix should follow them, there are suppletive variants of these suffixes which must be used.

SG	DL	PL
-(n)ak	-rmpan	-mpan

(5-32) a. ta-ka-tkam-r-*ak*-ŋ
　　　　　 NEG-1SG A-show-PERF-3SG D-VI SG T
　　　　　 'I didn't show him (the coconut).'

　　　 b. ta-nan-tkam-r-*mpan*-ŋ
　　　　　 NEG-2PL A-show-PERF-3PL D-VI SG T
　　　　　 'You all didn't show them (the coconut).'

These suppletive variants may represent the earlier basic forms of the D
suffixes, which were replaced in verb final position by the present day
verb final D suffixes when they became bound to the verb.

　　　 These D suffixes almost invariably reference human participants, but
one of the ditransitive verbs, *pul-* 'rub on', does allow inanimate nouns
to be marked by the dative suffixes. In these cases the noun class of the
inanimate D noun is never indicated, just its number.

(5-33) kacmpt　　　　　 anti
　　　　 canoe VIII PL   ground VIII SG
　　　　 i-kay-pul-c-*mpun*
　　　　 VIII SG T-1PL A-rub-PERF-3PL D
　　　　 'We rubbed ground on the canoes.'

kacmpt 'canoes' is a class VIII plural noun functioning as the D argument
of the ditransitive verb *pul-* 'rub on'. But because the D suffixes only
indicate number, it is impossible to mark its class, and so only its number
is indicated by the D suffix -*mpun* 3PL D.

　　　 Generally the conjugations of ditransitive verbs follow the rules given
earlier for transitive verbs—with the added complication, of course, of
another core argument. Ditransitive verbs associated only with third
person participants differ from the corresponding transitive verbs (5-19)
only in the presence of the D suffixes.

(5-34) a. anti　　　　　　 i-n-pul-c-mpun
　　　　　 ground VIII SG   VIII SG T-3SG A-rub-PERF-3PL D
　　　　　 'He rubbed ground on them.'

　　　 b. na-mpɨ-tkam-r-akn
　　　　　 3SG T-3DL A-show-PERF-3SG D
　　　　　 'They two showed it to him.'

　　　 c. makaw　　　　　　 wa-mpu-ŋa-r-mpun
　　　　　 fish (sp) IX SG   IX SG T-3PL A-give-PERF-3PL D
　　　　　 'They gave makau to them.'

The fourth inherently ditransitive verb, *i-* 'tell someone', is constrained
in that its theme argument must always be filled by the verbal prefix
pia-, referring to 'talk, language':

(5-35) a. pia-mpu-i-c-akn
            talk T-3PL A-tell-PERF-3SG D
            'They told him.'
        b. pia-n-i-c-mpun
            talk T-3SG A-tell-PERF-3PL D
            'He told them.'

Ditransitive verbs with a third person participant and a first or second person participant are formed in two ways, depending on which is A and which is D (we can ignore the theme argument here and in the following because it is almost invariably inanimate or of relatively low animacy status and never plays any role in determining the conjugation of a ditransitive verb). Because the first or second person participant is higher ranking by hierarchical principle one, it will occupy the ranking position of the pronominal prefix closest to the verb. If it functions as A, it will appear in its proper A prefix form and the third person D will appear as a D suffix.

(5-36) a. uraŋ   k-ka-tkam-r-mpun
            coconut VI SG VI SG T-1SG A-show-PERF-3PL D
            'I showed them the coconut.'
        b. makaw   wa-ŋkran-ŋa-r-mpn
            fish (sp) IX SG IX SG T-2DL A-give-PERF-3DL D
            'You two gave them both makau.'
        c. pia-kay-i-c-akn
            talk T-1PL A-tell-PERF-3 SG D
            'We told him.'

If, on the other hand, the first or second person participant is the D argument, it will be realized by the same prefix form as the O of a transitive verb. It will still be the inner prefix because it is the highest ranked, but the third person A will precede it in the A prefix form, preceded in turn by the lowest ranking prefix, that for the T argument.

(5-37) a. uraŋ   k-mpu-ŋa-tkam-t
            coconut VI SG VI SG T-3PL A-1SG D-show-PERF
            'They showed me the coconut.'
        b. makaw   wa-mpɨ-ŋkul-ŋa-t
            fish (sp) IX SG IX SG T-3DL A-2DL D-give-PERF
            'They two gave you two makau.'

There is no example parallel to (5-37a,b) in which the A is third singular. We have seen earlier with the transitive verbs that the third singular form in Yimas is completely homophonous with second singular and that is the case here. The rules which apply to second person A's

for ditransitive verbs apply to third singular as well. Ditransitive verbs
with first and second person participants differ in certain respects from
the corresponding transitive verbs. With the exception of verbs with a
first person A and a second singular D, it is not possible to mark both A
and D participants with pronominal prefixes. If the D argument is first
person and the A second person (or third singular), the D argument will
occur as the verb prefix for it is higher ranked. The A, if present at
all, must occur as an independent pronoun. This is in contrast to the
situation with transitive verbs, in which second person A's surface with
the S prefix forms (see (5-27)).

(5-38) a. uraŋ   k-ŋa-tkam-t
           coconut VI SG VI SG T-1SG D-show-PERF
           'You/he showed me the coconut.'

       b. kapwa makaw   wa-ŋkra-ŋa-t
           2DL   fish (sp) IX SG T-1DL D-give-PERF
           'You two gave us two makau.'

       c. ipwa pia-kra-i
           2PL   talk T-1PL D-tell
           'You all told us.'

       d. pia-ŋa-i
           talk T-1SG D-tell
           'You/he told me.'

As can be gleaned from examples (5-38a,d), verbs without associated
independent pronouns are ambiguous between a second or third person
singular A. These sentences can, of course, be disambiguated by adding
the independent pronoun *mi* 2SG for second singular or the near distal
deictic form *m-n* NR DIST-I/II SG 'he, she' for third singular.

Finally, for ditransitive verbs with a first person A and a second
person D, only the situation in which the D argument is second singular
allows marking of both participants on the verb. This is again done by
the suppletive form *kampan-* ~ *mpan-*. Number of the first person A
must be indicated by an independent pronoun; without such, singular is
assumed.

(5-39) a. irpm   mu-mpan-tkam-t
           coconut palm IV SG IV SG T-1A/2SG D-show-PERF
           'I showed you a coconut palm.'

       b. kapa makaw   wa-mpan-ŋa-t
           1DL   fish (sp) IX SG IX SG T-1A/2SG D-give-PERF
           'We two gave you makau.'

TABLE 5

Inflection with Pronominal Affixes of
Intransitive Verbs (*wa*- 'go')

	SG	DL	PL
1	ama-wa-ntut	kapa-wa-ntut	ipa-wa-ntut
2	ma-wa-ntut	kapwa-wa-ntut	ipwa-wa-ntut
3	na-wa-ntut	impa-wa-ntut	pu-wa-ntut

c. ipa   pia-mpan-i
   1PL   talk T-1A/2SG D-tell
   'We told you.'

If the second person D argument is non-singular, then the suppletive morpheme is not available. Only one of the two participants may be realized by a verbal prefix, and parallel to the situation with transitive verbs (5-29), this must be the second person D argument, rather than the first person A. The A is then expressed through an independent pronoun. Again, with no overt pronoun, a first person singular A is assumed, unless context forces otherwise.

(5-40) a. irpm   mu-ŋkul-tkam-t
          coconut palm IV SG IV SG T-2DL D-show-PERF
          'I showed you two a coconut palm.'

       b. kapa makaw   wa-kul-ŋa-t
          1DL   fish (sp)IX SG IX SG T-2PL D-give-PERF
          'We two gave you all makau.'

       c. ipa   pia-ŋkut-ɲa-i-n
          1PL   talk T-2DL D-DEF-tell-PRES
          'We are telling you two.'

Note in (5-40c) that the final /l/ of *ŋkul*- 2 DL D causes palatalization (rule (2-3)) of the following /n/ of *na*- DEF and undergoes liquid strengthening (rule (2-5)). The same verb form, but in the perfective, has a zero verb stem, because it gets absorbed by the preceding palatal.

(5-41) ipa   pia-ŋkul-∅
       1PL   talk T-2 DL D-tell
       'We told you two.'

Tables 5–7 summarize the inflection with pronominal affixes of intransitive, transitive and ditransitive verbs, respectively. (All forms are in remote past tense.)

5.1.4 The Indication of Paucal Number

If one glances back to the array of pronouns presented in Section 3.7, he will note that Yimas actually distinguishes four numbers in its independent pronouns: singular, dual, paucal, and plural. The paucal expresses a set of a few; more than two and usually less than seven, but the exact number varies quite widely according to context. Prototypically, however, it refers to a class of three to five individuals, and is always restricted to humans. So far in the exposition of the verbal pronominal affixes, I have ignored the indication of paucal number. This is because this number category works rather differently from the other three, and it seemed simplest to postpone its introduction for ease of exposition. It is now time to remedy this omission.

The expression of paucal number in a Yimas verb is, in fact, one of the more complicated parts of the verbal morphology, although its general pattern is like that outlined above for transitive and ditransitive verbs. Again, there is the pervasive split in behavior between first and second persons, on the one hand, and third person, on the other. Basically, first and second person participants with paucal number do not have distinctive person-number prefixes of their own. These use the plural prefixes functioning in their normal three way role marking contrast, in combination with the paucal suffix -ŋkt (realized as -ŋkut by R spreading (rule (2-8)) following a tense suffix containing a /u/, notably -ntuk RM PAST). The third person paucal participants have a distinct set of pronominal prefixes which follow the usual ergative-absolutive schema for this person. Thus, consider the following paucal forms for first person.

(5-42) a. *paŋkra*-wa-t
           1/2 PC S-go-PERF
           'We/you few went.'

       b. pu-*kay*-cay-c-*ŋkt*
           3PL O-1PL A-see-PERF-PC
           'We few saw them.'

       c. pu-*kra*-cay-c-*ŋkt*
           3PL A-1SG O-see-PERF-PC
           'They saw us few.'

paŋkra- is the bound S form for first and second person paucal and is transparently related to the corresponding independent pronoun *paŋkt* 1/2 PC. For the A and O forms there is no distinct paucal form. Rather the plural prefixes, *kay*- 1PL A and *kra*- 1PL O are used, in combination with the paucal suffix -*ŋkt*. This paucal suffix is in fact rather like the third person D suffixes in that it must occur in absolute final position

TABLE 6

Inflection with Pronominal Affixes of Transitive
Verbs (*tay*- 'see')

	SG	DL	PL
A=1SG			
O=1	————	————	————
2	kampan-tay-ɲcut	ama kul-cay-ɲcut	ama kul-cay-ɲcut
3	na-ka-tay-ɲcut	impa-ka-tay-ɲcut	pu-ka-tay-ɲcut
A=2SG			
O=1	ma-ŋa-tay-ɲcut	ma-ŋkra-tay-ɲcut	ma-kra-tay-ɲcut
2	————	————	————
3	na-n-tay-ɲcut	impa-n-tay-ɲcut	pu-n-tay-ɲcut
A=3SG			
O=1	na-ŋa-tay-ɲcut	na-ŋkra-tay-ŋcut	na-kra-tay-ɲcut
2	na-nan-tay-ɲcut	na-ŋkul-cay-ɲcut	na-kul-cay-ɲcut
3	na-n-tay-ɲcut	impa-n-tay-ɲcut	pu-n-tay-ɲcut
A=1DL			
O=1	————	————	————
2	kapa kampan-tay-ɲcut	kapa ngkul-cay-ɲcut	kapa kul-cay-ɲcut
3	na-ŋkra-tay-ɲcut	impa-ŋkra-tay-ɲcut	pu-ŋkra-tay-ɲcut
A=2DL			
O=1	kapwa-ŋa-tay-ɲcut	kapwa-ŋkra-tay-ɲcut	kapwa-kra-tay-ɲcut
2	————	————	————
3	na-ŋkran-tay-ɲcut	impa-ŋkran-tay-ɲcut	pu-ŋkran-tay-ɲcut
A=3DL			
O=1	impa-ŋa-tay-ɲcut	impa-ŋkra-tay-ɲcut	impa-kra-tay-ɲcut
2	impa-nan-tay-ɲcut	impa-ŋkul-cay-ɲcut	impa-kul-cay-ɲcut
3	na-mpɨ-tay-ɲcut	impa-mpɨ-tay-ɲcut	pu-mpɨ-tay-ɲcut
A=1PL			
O=1	————	————	————
2	ipa kampan-tay-ɲcut	ipa nykul-cay-ɲcut	ipa kul-cay-ɲcut
3	na-kay-cay-ɲcut	impa-kay-cay-ɲcut	pu-kay-cay-ɲcut
A=2PL			
O=1	ipwa-ŋa-tay-ɲcut	ipwa-ŋkra-tay-ɲcut	ipwa-kra-tay-ɲcut
2	————	————	————
3	na-nan-tay-ɲcut	impa-nan-tay-ɲcut	pu-nan-tay-ɲcut
A=3PL			
O=1	pu-ŋa-tay-ɲcut	pu-ŋkra-tay-ɲcut	pu-kra-tay-ɲcut
2	pu-nan-tay-ɲcut	pu=ngkul-cay-ɲcut	pu-kul-cay-ɲcut
3	na-mpu-tay-ɲcut	impa-mpu-tay-ɲcut	pu-mpu-tay-ɲcut

of the verb. If another suffix should follow it, it too has a suppletive
variant -*ŋkan*. Thus, compare (5-42b) with the following:

(5-43) ta-kay-cay-c-*ŋkan*-um
        NEG-1PL A-see-PERF-PC-3PL O
        'We few didn't see them.'

TABLE 7

Inflection with Pronominal Affixes of Ditransitive
Verbs (ŋa- 'give') T = ŋa- V SG

	SG	DL	PL
A=1SG			
D=1	————	————	————
2	na-mpan-ŋa-ntut	ama na-ŋkul-ŋa-ntut	ama na-kul-ŋa-ntut
3	na-ka-ŋa-ntuk-nakn	na-ka-ŋa-ntuk-mpn	na-ka-ŋa-ntuk-mpun
A=2SG			
D=1	mi na-ŋa-ŋa-ntut	mi na-ŋkra-ŋa-ntut	mi na-kra-ŋa-ntut
2	————	————	————
3	na-n-ŋa-ntuk-nakn	na-n-ŋa-ntuk-mpn	na-n nga-ntuk-mpun
A=3SG			
D=1	na-ŋa-ŋa-ntut	na-ŋkra-ŋa-ntut	na-kra-ŋa-ntut
2	na-nan-ŋa-ntut	na-ŋkul-ŋa-ntut	na-ŋkul-ŋa-ntut
3	na-n-ŋa-ntuk-nakn	na-n-ŋa-ntuk-mpn	na-n-ŋa-ntuk-mpun
A=1DL			
D=1	————	————	————
2	kapa na-mpan-ŋa-ntut	kapa na-ŋkul-ŋa-ntut	kapa na-kul-ŋa-ntut
3	na-ŋkra-ŋa-ntuk-nakn	na-ŋkra-ŋa-ntuk-mpn	na-ŋkra-ŋa-ntuk-mpun
A=2DL			
D=1	kapwa na-ŋa-ŋa-ntut	kapwa na-ŋkra-ŋa-ntut	kapwa na-kra-ŋa-ntut
2	————	————	————
3	na-ŋkran-ŋa-ntuk-nakn	na-ŋkran-ŋa-ntuk-mpn	na-ŋkran-ŋa-ntuk-mpun
A=3DL			
D=1	na-mpɨ-ŋa-ŋa-ntut	na-mpɨ-ŋkra-ŋa-ntut	na-mpɨ-kra-ŋa-ntut
2	na-mpɨ-nan-ŋa-ntut	na-mpɨ-ŋkul-ŋa-ntut	na-mpɨ-kul-ŋa-ntut
3	na-mpɨ-ŋa-ntuk-nakn	na-mpɨ-ŋa-ntuk-mpn	na-mpɨ-ŋa-ntuk-mpun
A=1PL			
D=1	————	————	————
2	ip na-mpan-ŋa-ntut	ipa na-ŋkul-ŋa-ntut	ipa na-kul-ŋa-ntut
3	na-kay-ŋa-ntuk-nakn	na-kay-ŋa-atuk-mpn	na-kay-ŋa-ntuk-mpun
A=2PL			
D=1	ipwa na-ŋa-ŋa-ntut	ipwa na-ŋkra-ŋa-ntut	ipwa na-kra-ŋa-ntut
2	————	————	————
3	na-nan-ŋa-ntuk-nakn	na-nan-ŋa-ntuk-mpn	na-nan-ŋa-ntuk-mpun
A=3PL			
D=1	na-mpu-ŋa-ŋa-ntut	na-mpu-ŋkra-ŋa-ntut	na-mpu-kra-ŋa-ntut
2	na-mpu-nan-ŋa-ntut	na-mpu-ŋkul-ŋa-ntut	na-mpu-kul-ŋa-ntut
3	na-mpu-ŋa-ntuk-nakn	na-mpu-ŋa-ntuk-mpn	na-mpu-ŋa-mtuk-mpun

The paucal suffix can also occur optionally with the S form. Corresponding to (5-42a) without the paucal suffix we have the following variant:

(5-44) paŋkra-wa-r-ŋkt
        1/2PC S-go-PERF-PC
        'We/you few went.'

The paucal forms for first person exhibit the typical three-way participant marking for first and second person. But the same two-way nominative-dative system that we saw was behind this split elsewhere also applies here. If we form a modally inflected verb from (5-44), the A for first plural will appear and the O prefix will be ungrammatical.

(5-45) a. ant-*kay*-wa-r-*ŋkt*
POT-1PL S-go-PERF-PC
'We few almost went.'

b.*ant-kra-wa-r-*ŋkt*
POT-1PL O-go-PERF-PC

Because the S form neutralizes to the A form rather than the O form in these modally inflected verbs, the underlying accusative schema is clearly demonstrated for these paucal forms.

But the third person forms are quite different; they are truly and fundamentally ergative-absolutive in their participant marking. There is a distinct A prefix for third person paucal, *ŋkl*- and another prefix *kra*- for S and O. The paucal suffix -*ŋkt* is not used.

(5-46) a. *kra*-wa-t
3PC S-go-PERF
'They few went.'

b. *kra*-n-tay
3PC O-3SG A-see
'He saw those few.'

c. na-*ŋkl*-cay
3SG O-3PC A-see
'Those few saw him.'

This is a clear ergative-absolutive system and follows the pattern of the other number categories in third person. In addition to these paucal prefixes, Yimas also has a set of paucal deictics which are clearly related to these. They commonly function like independent pronouns and are restricted in reference to humans (members of classes I and II). They are formed on the same deictic stems discussed in Chapter 3.

PROX	kra-k
NR DIST	m-ŋkt
FR DIST	kra-n

Typically, the PROX and FR DIST forms are composed with the verbal prefix, *kra*- 3 PC S/O. The NR DIST is formed with the paucal suffix, -*ŋkt*, which does seem transparently related to *ŋkl*- 3PC A. These may function as pronouns as deictics generally do in Yimas.

The conjugations of verbs with paucal participants in which all are

third person follow the same principles enunciated earlier for transitive
and ditransitive verbs.

(5-47) a. kra-mpɨ-tay
           3PC O-3DL A-see
           'Those two saw those few.'

       b. kra-ŋkl-kankantakal
           3PC O-3PC A-ask
           'Those few asked those few.'

       c. na-ŋkl-cay
           3SG O-3PC A-see
           'Those few saw him.'

       d. makaw   wa-ŋkl-ŋa-r-akn
           fish (sp) IX SG IX SG T-3PC A-give-PERF-3SG D
           'Those few gave him makau.'

       e. makaw   wa-n-ŋa-r-ŋkan
           fish sp IX SG   IX SG T-3SG A-give-PERF-3PC D
           'He gave those few makau.'

Because the paucal number resides directly in the verbal pronominal
prefixes, these third person forms are quite straightforward and follow
exactly the patterns outlined for transitive and ditransitive verbs: the
O prefix always precedes the A prefix. The only new point is the ditransitive example (5-47e), in which the third person paucal D suffix -ŋkan
is introduced.

When paucal first and second persons are present, the paucal suffix
-ŋkt must be used. The simplest cases are those involving a third person
participant and a first or second person participant. In these cases the
suffix -ŋkt PC always references the number of the first or second person
participant, whether it is A, O, or D. Because the first or second person
prefix is the higher ranked, it must always occur closer to the verb stem.
As with other number categories, the third person A must actually be
realized in the S/O form kra- for transitive verbs, because it occurs in
initial position.

(5-48) a. pu-kay-cay-c-ŋkt
           3PL O-1PL A-see-PERF-PC
           'We few saw them.'

       b. pu-kra-tay-c-ŋkt
           3PL A-1PL O-see-PERF-PC
           'They saw us few.'

       c. na-nan-tay-c-ŋkt
           3SG O-2PL A-see-PERF-PC
           'You few saw him.'

    d. na-kul-cay-c-ŋkt
       3SG A-2PL A-see-PERF-PC
       'He saw you few.'

    e. kra-kay-cay-c-ŋkt
       3PC O-1PL A-see-PERF-PC
       'We few saw them few.'

    f. kra-kra-tay-c-ŋkt
       3PC O-1PL O-see-PERF-PC
       'They few saw us few.'

Note that -*ŋkt* PC is only used if the first or second person participant is paucal. If it is some other number, and the third person participant is paucal, then -*ŋkt* is blocked, and the paucal is marked by the corresponding third person paucal affix for A, O, or D.

    g. kra-ŋkul-cay
       3PC A-2DL O-see
       'They few saw you two.'

    h.*kra-ŋkul-cay-c-ŋkt
       3PC A-2DL O-see-PERF-PC

    often in its variant -*ŋkan* if a third person dative suffix follows.

(5-49) a. pia-mpu-kra-i-c-ŋkt
       talk T-3PL A-1PL D-tell-PERF-PC
       'They told us few.'

    b. pia-kay-i-c-ŋkan-mpun
       talk T-1PL A-tell-PERF-PC-3PL D
       'We few told them.'

    c. uraŋ   k-ŋkl-kra-tkam-r-ŋkt
       coconut VI SG VI SG T-3PC A-1PL D-show-PERF-PC
       'Those few showed us few the coconut.'

    d. uraŋ   k-kay-tkam-r-ŋkan-akn
       coconut VI SG VI SG T-1PL A-show-PERF-PC-3SG D
       'We few showed him the coconut.'

When we come to transitive and ditransitive verbs with both a first and second person participant, the use of the paucal suffix becomes more complex, because it is now potentially (albeit, in practice, almost never) ambiguous as to what participant it is linked to. To grasp clearly the basic system let me first present examples which are not potentially ambiguous, involving a paucal and a dual or singular participant. Following the pattern of exposition established for transitive and ditransitive verbs above, let us begin with the case of a second person A and a first person O. Consider the case in which the second person A is paucal:

(5-50) a. pa-ŋa-tput-c-ŋkt
            2PC-1SG O-hit-PERF-PC
            'You few hit me.'

        b. pa-ŋkra-tput-c-ŋkt
            2PC-1DL O-hit-PERF-PC
            'You few hit us two.'

Because the first person O is the higher ranked prefix, it occurs in the inner position. The second person paucal A is realized by the prefix *paŋ-* (appearing as *pa-* before an /ŋ/), presumably a contraction from the S form, *paŋkra-*. Although unnecessary because the prefix *paŋ-* uniquely marks paucals, the suffix *-ŋkt* is also used. This second person prefix *paŋ-* only occurs in combination with first person participants, never third person.

Now consider the opposite case, with a singular or dual second person A and a paucal first person O.

(5-51) a. ma-kra-tpul-c-ŋkt
            2SG A-1PL O-hit-PERF-PC
            'You hit us few.'

        b. kapwa-kra-tupul-c-ŋkt
            2DL A-1PL O-hit-PERF-PC
            'You two hit us few.'

Here the suffix *-ŋkt* is necessary to distinguish these forms from the corresponding verbs with plural O, for there is no unique first person paucal prefix parallel to *paŋ-*. As with transitive verbs generally, the S forms are used to mark the second person A in both examples (compare (5-27)).

Switching the assignment of participant roles to a first person A and a second person O and considering the case of a paucal second person first, I present the following:

(5-52) a. paŋ-kul-cpul-c-ŋkt
            2PC-2PL O-hit-PERF-PC
            'I hit you few.'

        b. kapa paŋ-kul-cpul-c-ŋkt
            1DL 2PC-2PL O-hit-PERF-PC
            'We two hit you few.'

Again, the prefix *paŋ-* 2PC is found, but this time in combination with *kul-* 2PL O and *-ŋkt* PC, although *-ŋkt* PC seems to be somewhat optional in these examples. Note that, as we saw with transitive verbs earlier (see (5-29)), the first person A may not occur as a bound affix in these forms, but only as an independent pronoun; absence of a pronoun (5-52a) is again interpreted to mean first singular.

Finally, there is the case of a paucal first person A and a singular or dual second person O. If the O is second singular the ubiquitous *kampan-* ~ *mpan-* appears.

(5-53) a. uraŋ   paŋkt   k-mpan-tkam-r-ŋkt
           coconut VI SG 1PC   VI SG T-1A/2SG D-show-PERF-PC
           'We few showed you a coconut.'

       b. paŋkt   ŋkul-cpul
          1PC   2DL-hit
          'We few hit you two.'

As usual, the number of the first person A must be indicated by an independent pronoun, in this case, *paŋkt* 1PC, and only one pronominal prefix is permitted, referencing the person and number of the O. Note that the paucal suffix is not present in (5-53b); in fact, its occurrence will result in an ungrammatical construction.

(5-54) *paŋkt   ŋkul-cpul-c-ŋkt
        1PC 2DL-hit-PERF-PC

The explanation for this is related to a claim made in Section 5.1.2. There I asserted that non-singular second person A's are bound to their verbs as the S prefix forms, while first person A's are not, but are simply the independent pronouns. This is in spite of the fact that in both cases the S prefix forms and the independent pronouns are completely homophonous. Their differential behavior with respect to the paucal suffix is a strong argument for this analysis, for a second person paucal A occurs with it.

(5-55) a. pa-ŋa-tpul-c-ŋkt
          2PC-1SG O-hit-PERF-PC
          'You few hit me.'

       b. pa-ŋkra-tpul-c-ŋkt
          2PC-1DL O-hit-PERF-PC
          'You few hit us two.'

But a first person paucal A does not:

(5-56) a. paŋkt   ŋkul-cpul-*(ŋkt)
          1PC   2DL O-hit-PC
          'We few hit you two.'

       b. paŋkt   kul-cpul-*(ŋkt)
          1PC   2PL O-hit-PC
          'We few hit you all.'

This prohibition on -ŋkt PC is explained by the fact that *paŋkt* is an

independent pronoun, not a bound affix, and that -*ŋkt* must be linked
to a bound person affix in its verb. Interestingly, (5-56b) with -*ŋkt* might
be expected to be grammatical if it were linked to *kul-* 2PL O. But that
is not the case; in fact, if the second person is to be paucal, the prefix
paŋ- must be used.

(5-57) paŋkt paŋ-kul-cpul-c-ŋkt
        1PC   2PC-2PL O-hit-PERF-PC
        'We few hit you few.'

Again, -*ŋkt* is necessarily linked to a bound affix. The final very strong
piece of evidence for this analysis is provided by examples of verbs with
kampan- ∼ *mpan-*, expressing a first person paucal A. This allows the
paucal suffix.

(5-58) uraŋ   paŋkt k-mpan-tkam-r-ŋkt
        coconut VI SG 1PC   VI SG T-1A/2SG D-show-PERF-PC
        'We few showed you a coconut.'

This example conclusively demonstrates that it is not the person of the
A which controls the distribution of -*ŋkt* PC, but whether it is expressed
through a bound verbal affix or not. As a first person A is indicated in
the bound portmanteau morpheme *kampan-* ∼ *mpan-* 1A/2SG O,D, the
paucal suffix expressing its number is permitted.

Now let me turn to a few potentially ambiguous cases, verbs inflected
with the paucal suffix and having two plural or paucal participants. This
ambiguity is largely theoretical, for these verbs in practice almost never
truly are ambiguous. Verbs in which the paucal participant is second
person are often disambiguated by the prefix *paŋ-* 2PC.

(5-59) paŋkt paŋ-kul-cpul-c-ŋkt
        1PC   2PC-2PL O-hit-PERF-PC
        'We few hit you few.'

Here *paŋ-* indicates second paucal and in combination with the prefix
kul- 2PL O forces the reading of the O as second paucal and the pronoun
paŋkt as the first person paucal A. Consider the alternative participant
arrangement:

(5-60) paŋkt kra-tpul-c-ŋkt
        2PC   1PL O-hit-PERF-PC
        'You few hit us few.'

Here the verbal prefix is the first person O, *kra-* 1PL O, indicated as
paucal by the suffix -*ŋkt*. This clearly establishes the potentially ambiguous independent pronoun *paŋkt* as second person. Although the A is
therefore second person paucal, the prefix *paŋ-* 2PC is in fact prohibited

in this example, for its presence would result in homophony with the verb expressing a first person dual O (see (5-50b)).

As a final example consider the following set of examples with a paucal participant and a plural participant:

(5-61) a. ipa   paŋ-kul-cpul-c-ŋkt
           1PL 2PC-2PL O-hit-PERF-PC
           'We hit you few.'

       b. paŋkt kul-cpul
          1PC   2PL O-hit
          'We few hit you all.'

       c. ipwa-kra-tpul-c-ŋkt
          2PL A-1PL O-hit-PERF-PC
          'You all hit us few.'

       d. paŋkt kra-tpul
          2PC   1PL-hit
          'You few hit us.'

Note that the verb form in (5-61a) is exactly the same as that of (5-59): only the choice of the independent pronouns *paŋkt* 1PC versus *ipa* 1PL disambiguates the two. (5-61b) is unambiguous because the lack of any paucal marking on the verb identifies the prefix *kul-* 2PL O as truly plural and by elimination *paŋkt* must be first person. (5-61c) is also unambiguous because *ipwa-* is unambiguously plural and therefore -*ŋkt* must be associated with *kra-* 1PL O. Finally, (5-61d) has no paucal suffix, so *kra-* 1PL must be plural and the pronoun *paŋkt* second person. (5-61d) has a second person paucal A, and we would perhaps have expected it to be realized on the verb by the prefix *paŋ-*, producing the following:

(5-62) *paŋ-kra-tpul-c-ŋkt
        2PC-1PL O-hit-PERF-PC
        'You few hit us.'

This, while a possible form, is in fact impossible in this meaning. This is because (5-62) is completely homophonous with (5-55b) which is a grammatical form expressing a first person dual O.

5.1.5 The Forms of the Copula
The copula is used in equational, identificational and possessive statements (for its function in the last type, see Section 4.5). The copula always expresses a relation between two noun phrases, either establishing its identity or ascribing a quality to it. Consider these two examples:

(5-63) a. k-n   akrŋ   akk
         VI SG-FR DIST tree frog VI SG COP VI SG INVIS
         'That's a tree frog.'

     b. m-n   kpa-n   anak
        NP DIST-I SG big-I SG COP I SG
        'He's big.' (literally 'he's a big one')

The first example would be in answer to the question 'what's that?' on
hearing a noise in the woods. The second ascribes the quality of bigness
to a human referent represented by *m-n* 'he'. Although *kpa-* 'big' is an
adjective base, when the concord marker *-n* is added it becomes a noun,
as discussed in Section 4.6; so again, (5-63b) demonstrates that copula
always connects two noun phrases.

The copula is the only truly irregular verb in Yimas, and it is highly
so. The underlying basic stem is (*a*)*ya-* to which the S prefix forms are
attached. But these prefixes generally metathesize to become infixes,
with often highly unpredictable results, so it seems best to simply list
the variant forms of the copula.

		Number			
		SG	DL	PC	PL
Person	1	amayak	kapayak	paŋkrayak	aypak
	2	amyak	kapwayak		(p)aypwak
	3	anak	aympak	akrak	(p)apuk

The third plural copula form (*p*)*apuk* only begins with /p/ if the preceding noun ends underlyingly in /mp/ (realized as phonetic [m] by final
nasal plus stop cluster simplification (rule (2-14)). This may suggest
that the copula forms a single phonological word with the preceding
noun, thereby blocking the operation of the phonological rule. Each of
the ten noun classes has copula forms particular to it, a distinct form
for singular, dual and plural. Those for classes I and II are those for the
third person above. Those of the other classes are given below:

	SG	DL	PL
class III	anak	antmak	(p)apuk
class IV	amuk	amulak	arak
class V	anak	antmak	arak
class VI	kak/akk	aklak	akiak
class VII	papk/apk	aplak	arak
class VIII	aykk/ayk	alak	arak
class IX	ayak/yak	awlak	awrak
class X	kawk/akuk	akulak	arak

The two forms in the singular column for classes VI through X represent the contrast between visible and invisible discussed in Section 3.8, the former being the visible form and the latter the invisible. The nouns forming classes by themselves also have distinct copula forms,

		SG	DL	PL
nam	'house'	anmak	anmlak	arak
num	'village'	anumak	anumlak	arak
wut	'night'	awrak	antmak	arak
arm	'water'	aymak		
awt	'fire'	awrak		
awi	'lime'	arak		

as do the two classes which have no overt nouns but only correspond to bound affixes.

'talk, words, language'	apiak
'actions, deeds'	antiak

It should be noted that every form of the copula ends in -*k*. This is none other than the irrealis suffix and is obligatory on the copula because the statements in which it occurs are not bound in time. These statements of identity or ascription of qualities are not held to a particular temporal frame of reference, but are held to be true generally, or at least without clearly defined temporal limits. If the statement is bound within some stable temporal limits, then the verb *ti*- 'become, feel, do' must be used with a tense suffix.

(5-64) m-n   kpa-n   na-ti-nan
        NR DIST-I SG big-I SG   3SG S-become/do-NR PAST
        'He was big yesterday.'

5.1.6 The Grammatical Status and Pragmatic Functions of the Pronominal Affixes

Having now expended a great deal of effort to understand the complexity to which Yimas has elaborated its system of pronominal affixes, the reader will probably be surprised to discover that they are not obligatory. This is not to say that they are not very common; they certainly are. The great majority of transitive verbs in discourse, for example, have both an A and an O prefix attached to them. But the fact remains that they are an option, and it is the purpose of this section to outline what are the factors which determine these choices and, further, what is the grammatical status of these affixes on verbs which contain them.

To borrow terminology from Bresnan and Mchombo (1987), the Yimas pronominal affixes are examples of pronominal agreement rather than grammatical agreement. The idea behind this contrast is not new:

it is basically the analysis of Aztec that Wilhelm von Humboldt presented 150 years ago (Humboldt 1836). In essence, the claim is that the pronominal affixes actually fill the argument positions of the verb and that any noun phrases filling what seem to be the core argument positions of the verb are actually only indirectly linked to it, by being in apposition to a pronominal affix which bears the same noun class, person, and number specifications as the noun phrase. Consider some examples:

(5-65) a. kacmpt   payum   ya-mpu-yamal-wat
          canoe VIII PL   man I PL   VIII PL O-3PL A-carve-HAB
          'The men usually carve the canoes.'

     b. ŋaykum   makaw   panmal
         woman II PL   fish (sp) IX SG   man I SG
         wa-mpu-ŋa-r-akn
         IX SG T-3PL A-give-PERF-3SG D
         'The women gave the man makau.'

The verb *yamal* 'carve' is a simple transitive verb with two core arguments, A and O. The prefixes to the verb identify the A as third person singular and the O as class VIII plural. As pointed out earlier, the A prefixes do not normally distinguish noun class and are almost always restricted to human nouns, or at least higher animates. Now the processing task is to search for the noun phrases which have the same person, number and class specifications as the verbal prefixes, so as to fill out the interpretation of the clause. The class VIII plural noun *kacmpt* 'canoes' has the same class and number specifications as the O prefix *ya-* VIII PL; the nominal is therefore integrated with the prefix and interpreted as carrying the O role. The human plural class I noun *payum* 'men' has the same number specifications as the A prefix *mpu-* 3PL A. Being human, it is a potential A, unlike the other noun, and hence is interpreted with the role of A in the clause. The two nouns are not themselves filling argument positions in the verb; those are simply the pronominal affixes. The nouns are, however, linked to these affixes by virtue of having the same category specifications and through this indirect route are interpreted as having the same participant roles. The word order of the noun phrases is free and plays no role in their interpretation.

    Example (5-65b) is similar, but in this case the verb is ditransitive. Its affixes indicate a class IX singular T (*wa-*), a third plural A (*mpu-*) and a third singular D (*-nakn*). The singular class IX noun *makaw* 'fish (sp)' is clearly linked to *wa-* and thereby receives the theme interpretation. The other two nouns, the class II plural *ŋaykum* 'women' and the class I singular *panmal* 'man' are both human and hence both potentially A and D. But the number contrast here is sufficient to disambiguate.

As the A prefix is plural, the plural *ŋaykum* 'women' is linked to it and interpreted as the A. The singular D prefix then links to the singular noun *panmal* 'man' which assumes a D participant relation. Note that if there was no number distinction between these two nouns, the clause would be ambiguous.

(5-66) ŋaykum   makaw   payum
        woman II PL   fish (sp) IX SG   man I PL

        wa-mpu-ŋa-r-mpun
        IX SG T-3PL A-give-PERF-3PL D

        'The men gave the women makau.'
        'The women gave the men makau.'

As mentioned previously, the word order among noun phrases is free, so that it does not play a role in disambiguating this clause. Taken out of context, it must remain ambiguous.

It must be emphasized again that it is the pronominal affixes which fill the argument positions of the verb, not the noun phrases, and these latter only receive a participant role interpretation by being in a paratactic relationship with a pronominal affix of the same categorical specifications. Given this fact, it is not surprising that in the large majority of Yimas clauses in ongoing discourse, there are no independent noun phrases at all. The participant roles are simply filled by the pronominal affixes; so the following then correspond to (5-65a,b):

(5-67) a. ya-mpu-yamal-wat
            VIII PL O-3PL A-carve-HAB
            'They usually carve them.'

        b. wa-mpu-ŋa-r-akn
            IX SG T-3PL A-give-PERF-3PL D
            'They gave it to them.'

These Yimas verbs would be used in contexts very similar to those of their English clausal translations: when the referents of the pronominal affixes had been established in the discourse or context. The noun phrases are suppressed and their referents tracked simply by the pronominal affixes in Yimas, as the pronouns do in English. However, because of the difference in grammatical status between the Yimas pronominal affixes and the English pronouns, and because of the great range of distinctions made in its affixes, through the systems of noun class, person, and number, Yimas allows much greater latitude in this feature than English. For example, in some recitations of traditional legends, important props and characters are not introduced through overt nouns, but only with pronominal affixes. It seems to be assumed that the story line

and characters are so familiar and well known that that is all that is
necessary. Also, the established, old information status of a participant
may persist much longer in Yimas discourse than in English. For example, in the Yimas creation legend, there is an important prop which is
introduced and then ignored for a reasonably long stretch of discourse,
about 3 pages; it is then reintroduced, but only through the use of its
corresponding pronominal prefix! This is because, being class VII dual,
a relatively rare combination, there is no chance of confusion with any
other referent. English with its undifferentiated *it* is too impoverished
morphologically to allow this kind of free pronominalization over such a
long stretch of discourse.

An interesting difference between Yimas and English in this area
concerns translation strategies. I have very often been surprised by the
frequency with which Yimas speakers reference a participant simply by
a pronominal prefix when asked to translate a sentence from Tok Pisin.
For example, when asking for a translation of the Tok Pisin version of
'I bought betelnut', one may very well get:

(5-68)   na-ka-wayk-t
         V SG O-1SG A-buy-PERF
         'I bought it'

in which *na-* V SG O is the only overt indication of the class V singular
noun *patn* 'betelnut'. I have made no study of this, but I conjecture that
if English speakers were asked to translate the same Tok Pisin sentence
into English it is highly unlikely the noun would be omitted. I believe
this again reflects the basic difference between these pronominal affixes
and English pronouns: the pronominal affixes fill the argument slots of
the verb, and a clause is complete with just them. The noun phrases
are indirectly and paratactically linked to the verb through these affixes.
They may be omitted freely if they correspond to established referents.
On the other hand, in English the noun phrases themselves, whether
they be nouns or pronouns, fill these argument slots of the verb. So in
parroting back a clause in translation, it is straightforward and expected
that the speaker will simply repeat the nouns of the prompt sentence,
given that the noun phrase positions of an English clause must be filled
if it is to be complete.

An additional argument for regarding the affixes as filling the verbal
argument positions concerns the indication of paucal number. Paucal
number is predominantly a verbal category; with the exception of the
pronouns and deictics for humans, no noun phrases exhibit overt inflection for paucal, i.e., the plural number covers the range of paucal as well.
Consider the following example:

(5-69) namat   patn   na-ŋkl-wayk-t
        men I PL betelnut V SG V SG O-3PC A-buy-PERF
        'The few men bought betelnut.'

Assuming that the pronominal affixes fill the argument positions, this example is easy to analyze. The A prefix *ŋkl-* 3PL A is third person and paucal. Searching for a noun phrase which shares these features we come across the class I plural noun *namat* 'men'. Knowing that the equation paucal = plural holds for all nouns, we conclude that *namat* 'men' is linked to *ŋkl-* 3PL A, and it is interpreted to function in the A role.

Now consider an analysis with the opposite assumption: that the noun phrases really fill argument slots of the verb and the pronominal affixes are just automatic copies of these onto the verb. Example (5-69) now becomes problematic because *namat* is morphologically plural and should therefore be copied by the plural A prefix, *mpu-*. One could argue, of course, that *namat* is actually specified as paucal, and that it just happens that paucal and plural are homophonous. But this seeming harmless coincidence happens throughout the language: no Yimas noun distinguishes paucal from plural number. This analysis requires us to posit a morphological category for Yimas nouns which never has any overt realization for them. The previous analysis, with the pronominal prefixes only filling argument positions, has no such requirement and is therefore to be preferred.

Still another piece of evidence concerns verbal pronominal prefixes with conjoint reference. Consider this example:

(5-70) panmal   narmaŋ   impa-wa-ntut
        man I SG woman II SG 3DL S-go-RM PAST
        'The man and woman went.'

I have already presented arguments that Yimas does not permit noun phrases composed of conjoined nouns in Section 4.6. Hence *panmal* 'man' and *narmaŋ* 'woman' cannot form a constituent in this example to trigger the dual number specification for the S prefix on the verb *impa-* 3 DL S. Rather this is specified independently and fills the S argument position for this verb. This is then linked to both singular nouns paratactically, integrating both of them to fill out the dual specification of the S prefix.

A final argument concerns the phenomenon of possessor raising to be discussed in detail in Section 6.2.3.2. In this construction, a human possessor of a core argument of the verb is promoted to function in its own right as a core argument marked by a D affix.

(5-71) a. wampuŋ   mama-k-n   na-tɨ-k-nakn
heart V SG   bad-IRR-V SG   V SG S-feel-IRR-3SG D
'His heart felt bad.' (i.e., 'He was angry.')

b. yampaŋ   k-mpu-ŋa-kra-t
head VI SG   VI SG O-3PL A-1SG D-cut-PERF
'They cut my hair.'

tɨ- 'become, fell' is normally an intransitive verb, but in (5-71a) it has
two affixes, S and D; *kra-* 'cut' is a transitive verb, but in (5-71b) it has
three pronominal affixes, S, O, and D. These D affixes mark fully core
arguments: whatever processes are available to D affixes on ditransitive
verbs are available to these as well, e.g., relativization, anaphoric control
over non-finite modifiers, etc. (see Chapter 7). By assuming that the
pronominal affixes directly fill the core argument positions of the verb,
this is easily explicable. But otherwise it is not, for the nouns which
these affixes reference are only possessors of other core arguments, the
S in (5-71a) and the O in (5-71b). While these may be coded as core
arguments through the verbal prefixes, they may not appear as core
arguments in their own right:

(5-72) a.*wampuŋ   mama-k-n   m-n   na-tɨ-k
heart V SG NR   bad-IRR-V SG   DIST-V SG   V SG S-feel-IRR

b.*ama yampaŋ   k-mpu-kratw
I   head VI SG   VI SG O-3PL A-cut-PERF

These examples are ungrammatical because these possessors may
not be treated as core (i.e., lacking the oblique suffix) unless linked to
a pronominal affix. The contrast in grammaticality between (5-71) and
(5-72) clearly demonstrates that it is the pronominal affixes which confer
core status and, in fact, fill the argument slots of a verb.

Thus far, I have been discussing referents which are old or established
information and can therefore be indicated by a pronominal affix. What
about new information, characters or props now just being introduced
in the discourse? These can appear with or without a pronominal affix
so that in essence we have the three following structural patterns:

Pattern 1:   Ø   PRO-verb   established referent
Pattern 2:   NP   PRO-verb   established/new referent
Pattern 3:   NP   verb   new referent

where Ø means no overt noun phrase and PRO any pronominal affix.
Pattern 1 has already been illustrated and discussed elsewhere (examples (5-67a,b) and discussion thereof), as has pattern 2 for established
referents (examples 5-65a,b). In considering how new referents are intro-

duced, let me consider the unambiguous case, pattern 3, first. Examples
of this follow:

(5-73) a. num-n-mat   Kampramanan wapal-k
        village-OBL-PL hill name   climb-IRR
        'The villagers climbed Kampramanan.'

     b. m-n   impa-tay-k   paympan
       NR DIST-III SG 3PL O-see-IRR eagle III SG
       'It, the eagle, saw those two.'

     c. patn   pu-nan-ŋa-t
       betelnut V SG 3PL A-2SG D-give-PERF
       'They gave you betelnut.'

(5-73a) has an intransitive verb, *wapal-* 'climb', with no pronominal
affixes; (5-73b) a transitive verb, *tay-* 'see', with only one pronominal
affix, that of the O argument; and (5-73c) a ditransitive verb, *ŋa-* 'give',
with only two pronominal affixes, A and D. In each case, the missing
core argument is provided by an overt noun in the clause: *numunmat*
'villagers' in (5-72a), *paympan* 'eagle' in (5-73b), and *patn* 'betelnut' in
(5-73c). These examples all come from running texts in which these
nouns are just being introduced or re-introduced after a longish gap.
They are new information.

Given the earlier claim that the pronominal affixes fill the argument
positions of the verb, an important question is what is the relationship
to the verb of these nouns without coreferent agreement affixes? The
simple answer is just the same, but in this case they are linked to a
zero pronominal affix. In other words, Yimas has much in common
with the feature of uncontrolled 'pronoun drop' in East Asian languages
like Japanese, Thai, and Indonesian. To see how this analysis would
work, consider (5-73b) again. The transitive verb *tay-* 'see' has two core
arguments, A and O (I am here considering the notion of transitivity and
associated arguments to be a straightforward notion in Yimas. This
is not entirely the case, but it is best to postpone the discussion of
this until Section 6.2.1.). This transitive verb only has a single overt
agreement prefix, the prefix *impa-* 3DL O, but, as it is a transitive verb,
it must have an A participant. Because of pragmatic reasons, i.e., the
referent of the A is a new participant, this is realized by a zero prefix.
A zero prefix is exactly that, one which has no specifications for class,
person and number and may therefore be linked to any noun which is
morphologically marked as core, i.e., is not suffixed with the oblique
suffix *-n* ∼ *-nan*. Both noun phrases in (5-73b) meet this requirement,
m-n NR DIST III SG and *paympan* eagle III SG. But as they have the
same noun class and number specifications, they clearly have the same

234 BASIC VERBAL MORPHOLOGY

referent, which is linked to the zero A prefix and interpreted with the A role.

Example (5-73c) is similar, except that it contains a ditransitive verb *ŋa-* 'give' with overt agreement prefixes for A and D, but a zero prefix for T. The clause contains a morphologically core noun *patn* 'betelnut' which is linked to the verb through the zero T prefix and interpreted as the theme.

Now consider example (5-73a). This sentence contains an intransitive verb, *wapal* 'climb', with no agreement prefixes and two associated noun phrases. One of these, *numnmat* 'villagers', is morphologically a core argument; the other, *Kampramanan* 'place name', is morphologically oblique, with the oblique suffix *-n ~ -nan*. Hence only *numnmat* 'villagers' may be linked to the zero S prefix on the verb and interpreted in the S role.

This last example points up a very important constraint on the grammaticality of Yimas clauses which I will call the completeness constraint (Foley and Van Valin 1984, 183). It states that a noun may be realized morphologically as a core argument (i.e., without the oblique suffix *-n ~ -nan*) if and only if it is linked to a pronominal affix on the verb (which may be zero). In other words, a noun without the oblique suffix must be linked to a pronominal affix and a noun with it never can. The verb *wapal-* 'climb' is a good one to illustrate this principle with. Although basically intransitive, as in (5-73a), it is actually ambitransitive like its English equivalent. English *climb* is intransitive in *the child climbed to the top of the tree* but formally transitive in *the child climbed the tree*. Yimas behaves identically.

(5-74) a. irpm-un   na-wapal
            coconut palm IV SG-OBL   3SG S-climb
            'He climbed up on the coconut palm.'

        b. irpm   mu-n-wapal
            coconut palm IV SG   IV SG O-3SG A-climb
            'He climbed the coconut palm.'

(5-74a) contains *wapal-* 'climb' used intransitively with a single S prefix. The noun *irpm-un* coconut palm IV SG-OBL is not a core argument and therefore occurs with the oblique suffix. In (5-74b), the verb *wapal* is used transitively and has both the A prefix *n-* 3SG A and the O prefix *mu-* IV SG O. Now *irpm* 'coconut palm' must be realized morphologically as a core argument and lack the oblique suffix. The use of the oblique suffix in (5-74b) will result in ungrammaticality.

(5-75) *irpm-un   mu-n-wapal
        coconut palm IV SG-OBL   IV SG O-3SG A-climb

Having discussed in some detail examples of pattern 3 (i.e., NP verb), used to express new referents, let me return briefly to the case of pattern 2 constructions (i.e., NP PRO-verb), which may also express new referents. It is important to remember that pattern 2 is potentially ambiguous; it can also express established referents, as illustrated in (5-65). Pattern 2, (noun phrase plus PRO-verb) commonly has a strong contrastive component to its meaning. For example, it is generally used in answer to an information question when the question word functions as O or D.

(5-76) a. Q: nawn ma-tpul
           who   2SG S-hit
           'Who did you hit?'

       b. A: ŋaykum   pu-ka-tpul
           woman II PL 3PL O-1SG A-hit
           'I hit the women'

Here, *ŋaykum* 'women' is the focus of the answer. This is indicated both by an independent noun and the verbal agreement affix *pu-* 3PL O.

In other cases, new referents are introduced through pattern 2 if they are especially important new props in the development in the discourse around which its progression turns, as in this example from a traditional legend:

(5-77) ɲct   mnta   ya-n-awa-ta-k-nakn
        urine V PL and then V PL O-3SG-excrete-put-IRR-3SG D
        'And then she urinated on him.'

Although *ɲct* 'urine' is a new participant here, it is an important one, because by noticing the urine, the man locates his daughter, and the remaining plot of the story unfolds.

These examples are meant to give the reader a general feel for the pragmatic, discourse-based differences which determine the choices of pattern 1, 2 or 3. Because they are pragmatic and discourse-based, it is impossible to write hard and fast, all-encompassing rules. Rather, there are devices left open to the speaker to use creatively as he frames the text. Some of the general principles involved I have discussed here, but a more complete account will have to remain for a later more detailed study of Yimas discourse structures. The reader who is especially interested is invited to study the texts at the end of this grammar and try to work out some of these principles himself.

5.2 Tense, Aspect, and Mood

Yimas has a very rich system of tense, aspect, and mood distinctions. Some aspectual distinctions are expressed through incorporated adver-

bials and compounded verb stems and will be discussed in the relevant
sections in the next chapter (Sections 6.3.1 and 6.3.2). In this section, I
will only treat the aspect distinctions which are indicated in the suffixal
slots. Mood really corresponds to two separate inflectional categories in
Yimas: modality and illocutionary force. Modality is expressed through
a set of modal prefixes which occur verb-initially, before the pronominal prefixes, while illocutionary force distinctions such as imperatives or
hortatives are indicated by distinctive inflectional patterns with specific
pronominal affixes.

5.2.1 The Tense/Aspect System

The only affixal position of a finite verb which is obligatorily occupied is
that of tense. This is a suffixal position following the verb stem(s) and
preceding the paucal and dative suffixes. If these latter are lacking, it
will occur in word final position.

(5-78) a. patn   na-kay-ŋa-ntuk-mpun
            betelnut V SG   V SG T-1PL A-give-RM PAST-3PL D
            'We gave betelnut to them long ago.'

        b. tan   ipa-wa-ntut
            there   1PL S-go-RM PAST
            'We went there long ago.'

Note the alternation between the non-final form of the RM PAST tense
suffix, *-ntuk*, and the final form, *-ntut*. This pattern of alternation between non-final and final forms is a common feature of the tense suffixes
in Yimas.

The tense/aspect system of Yimas makes nine distinctions. The primary distinction is strictly not one of tense, but a modal one. But since
this is realized in the same suffixal slot as all the other tense distinctions,
it will be treated as part of the same paradigmatic system here. Thus,
the basic distinction in the Yimas tense/aspect system is between unreal
and real events. Unreal events are marked by the irrealis suffix $-k \sim -\eta k$,
which indicates that the event so marked is outside the continuum of real
time, e.g., in the legendary past or in the indefinite future (see Section
5.2.1.1). Real events must be marked by one of the other tense/aspect
suffixes. These express an eight way contrast. Yimas has two basic past
tenses: a near past, for events which occurred yesterday; and a remote
past, for events which occurred any time since the legendary past up
to about five days ago. In addition there is a far past, composed of
the remote past suffix plus the suffix *-kia*, discussed in Section 5.2.1.2,
which is used for events occurring from two days ago to five days ago,
although the boundary between this and the remote past is flexible, and

a switch from the remote past to the far past is often used for nuances of vividness in narratives. The present tense is used to express events which occurred today, but is divided according to aspectual contrasts. There is a three-way aspectual contrast for present tense: perfective, for events which are completed; imperfective, for events which are ongoing; and habitual, for events which recur regularly according to the normal expectations of life patterns in the community. Finally, there are two future tenses: a remote future, for events which are fully expected to occur the day after tomorrow or later; and a near future, for events expected to occur tomorrow. The contrasts in the Yimas tense-aspect system may be summarized in the following schema:

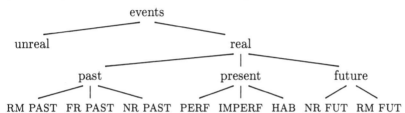

5.2.1.1 Irrealis

The irrealis suffix is used in Yimas to indicate events which are located outside of the continuum of real time: they must be completely timeless, in the legendary past or in the indefinite future. In other words, it marks events whose temporal coordinates cannot clearly be fixed by the speaker in what he regards as experiential time. Because the irrealis occurs at both ends of the temporal continuum, it may be conjectured that Yimas speakers view time not as an open infinitely expandable line, but as a closed circle.

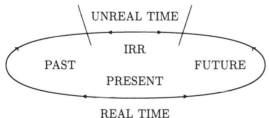

This is a tempting speculation, but there is no evidence at present, other than the distribution of the irrealis suffix to affirm or deny it.

The use of the irrealis to express timeless events is prototypically indicated by its use with the copula. If the reader will glance back at the forms of the copula in Section 5.1.5, he will note that all forms terminate in the irrealis -*k*. The copula is used in statements which hold true generally and are not bound to particular periods of time. In fact the use of any other tense/aspect/mood inflection with the copula is ungrammatical.

The irrealis suffix is probably most commonly found in traditional legends, where it is almost invariably used, although the remote past would also be an option. Consider the following:

(5-79) a. tan   impa-ampu-mpi-awl-k
            there   3DL S-float-SEQ-take-IRR
            'They both drifted there.'

        b. impa-mpu-yakal-irm-tay-ɲcut
            3DL O-3PL A-CONT-stand-see-RM PAST
            'They stood watching them both.'

These two examples come from the same text and are separated only by a single sentence. Both take place in exactly the same time period, the legendary past, yet one is marked with the irrealis and the other with the remote past suffix. In terms of absolute time reference, there is no difference in this text between the irrealis and the remote past. But the use of the remote past implies that events occurred in the stream of real, albeit remote, time, while the irrealis removes them from the continuum of real time altogether and situates them in the period before real time as apprehended by men began. The use of the remote past in such traditional legends is actually rather less common. In the text from which the sentences in (5-79) were drawn, that of the creation myth, less than 20% of all sentences in the legendary past are inflected with the remote past suffix, the rest occur with the irrealis. Quite commonly, a speaker will start a legend with the remote past suffix, but by the third or fourth sentence will switch to the irrealis and remain with that through the rest of the text. Also, it is sometimes the case that a speaker will switch from the irrealis to the remote past in the denouement of a text: this provides a vivid or immediate coloring to the events described.

The irrealis may also mark as yet unrealized future events. In this case, it contrasts with the remote future tense. Consider these examples:

(5-80) a. ama   patn   wayk-k
            1SG   betelnut V SG buy-IRR
            'I want to/will buy betelnut.'

        b. patn   na-ka-wayk-kt
            betelnut V SG   V SG O-1SG A-buy-RM FUT
            'I will buy betelnut after tomorrow.'

The remote future suffix -kt, as in (5-80b), commits the speaker to the belief that the event described will definitely or at least is highly likely to occur in the future. The irrealis suffix requires no such commitment.

Rather, as in (5-80a) it simply expresses the speaker's wishes or desires that the event will occur. Hence, it is the normal way to form a desiderative construction when the speaker is the experiencer, as in (5-80a). These desiderative constructions are curious in that they never allow the use of the bound pronominal agreement affixes. For example, the following is ungrammatical:

(5-81) *patn   na-ka-wayk-k
       betelnut V SG V SG O-1SG A-buy-IRR

(5-81) can only be interpreted as a grammatical sentence if the irrealis is interpreted as indicating the legendary past. This, then, is an important structural difference between the legendary past use of the irrealis and its desiderative use. A plausible explanation for the impossibility of pronominal affixes in desiderative constructions like (5-80a) is that these are elliptical versions of constructions with purpose clauses (see Section 7.1.3) and the main verb *ti̵-* 'feel, become', as in (5-82).

(5-82) ama patn   way-k   ama-na-ti̵-n
       1SG betelnut V SG buy-IRR 1SG S-DEF-feel/become-PRES
       'I feel like buying betelnut.'

(5-80a) arises from (5-82) by ellipsis of the main verb. This accounts for the prohibition on pronominal affixes with desiderative verbs in *-k*, for these affixes are also barred from purpose clauses, as with all non-finite constructions.

Because the irrealis expresses unrealized future events, for which the speaker is uncommitted as to whether they will or will not occur, it is commonly used with hypothetical conditional clauses:

(5-83) m-na-ya-nt-mp-n
       NR DIST-DEF-come-PRES-VII SG-OBL

       na-ka-apan-ŋ
       3SG O-1SG A-spear-IRR

       'If he comes, I'll shoot him.'

Just as in English, the protasis of these hypothetical conditional clauses is marked with the present, but the apodosis is realized by the irrealis (in English, the future). This pattern only occurs with true hypothetical conditional clauses in Yimas, in which there is no commitment as to whether the events will occur or not. Other types of conditionals and counterfactuals are quite different (see Section 7.2.3).

As the reader is probably aware by now from perusing the above examples, the irrealis occurs in two allomorphs *-k* ~ *-ŋk* (with resulting cluster simplification to *ŋ* in word final position). The latter occurs when the preceding consonant is a nasal and *-k* occurs elsewhere. The

allomorph -*ŋk* also has an optional subvariant ∅ when the preceding
nasal is also /ŋ/.

5.2.1.2 The Suffix -*kia*

This is one of the more mysterious, yet ubiquitous suffixes in Yimas.
Unlike -*k* IRR, which has cognates in other Lower Sepik languages, -*kia*
may be a borrowing from Iatmul, the prestige language of the middle
Sepik, in which -*kiyǝ* marks future tense. Whatever its origin -*kia* is now
fully integrated into the verbal morphology of Yimas.

Like its probable Iatmul source, one of the basic usages of -*kia* is to
mark future tense. In combination with the definitive prefix *na-* DEF,
discussed in Section 5.2.1.4.2, and the irrealis -*k*, -*kia* marks the near
future, i.e., events which are fully expected to occur tomorrow.

(5-84) a. ŋarŋ   na-kay-ɲa-awl-kia-k
          1 day removed   V SG O-1PL A-DEF-get-NR FUT-IRR
          'We will get them tomorrow.'

       b. num-n   ama-na-waraca-mpi-wa-kia-k
          village-OBL   1SG S-DEF-return-SEQ-go-NR FUT-IRR
          'I'm going back to the village tomorrow.'

The other uses of -*kia* seem to be derivative from this near future
meaning. A very important fact to be noted about Yimas traditional
time reckoning in that a full day is seen to elapse from sunset to sunset,
rather than from sunrise to sunrise as in English or Tok Pisin. Because
of the influence of Tok Pisin or English-based schooling, there is some
confusion about the proper reckoning of a full day among most younger
present day Yimas speakers, but sunset to sunset is the traditional view.
Thus, if someone is speaking at noon about an event which is going to
occur in that evening or night, those events must be talked about as
occurring in the next day, and hence marked with -*kia* NR FUT. Because
of this, -*kia* has become associated with the idea of nighttime, and can be
used with a number of tense/aspect morphemes to indicate specifically
that the events occur at night.

(5-85) a. tpuk   ku-k   am-kia-na-uŋ
          sago X SG   X SG-PROX   eat-NIGHT-IMP-X SG O
          'Eat this sago pancake.'

       b. Maŋ-ɲan   ama-pay-kia-wat
          Maɲi-OBL   1SG S-lie-NIGHT-HAB
          'I usually sleep at Maɲi.'

       c. wut   am-kia-k   na-ma-ŋka-pu-kia-k
          night   eat-NIGHT-IRR   3SG S-inside-go-away-NIGHT-IRR
          'That night he went inside to eat.'

d. irmpŋ   na-nan-l-ant-kia-ntut
slit drum V SG V SG O-2PL A-below-hear-NIGHT-RM PAST
'Did you all hear the slit drum down below?'

The use of -*kia* with imperatives as in (5-84a) clearly demonstrates that it may not be a tense morpheme, for imperatives are tenseless. Rather, this command and the expected action were performed at night so that -*kia* is used. The verb of (5-85b) is marked with the habitual suffix -*wat*, but this action, sleeping, is one that is normally done at night, so again the suffix -*kia* is present. (5-84c) is drawn from a traditional legend and exhibits the typical usage of the irrealis -*k* in such texts. But this sentence occurs at a particular point in the text when the scene switches from day to night. Thus, the suffix -*kia* now appears, although it was not used in the previous sentences of the text. Note that -*kia* is not only used on the main verb, but also occurs on the preceding nonfinite purpose clause, again demonstrating that it is not strictly a tense morpheme. Finally, consider the last example (5-84d). This comes from a story describing events which occurred a year previously, hence the use of -*ntut* RM PAST. The particular event of (5-84d) occurred at night, so -*kia* is used, while in most of the other sentences in the text, which describe daytime events, it is absent. (There is yet a further specialized use of -*kia* with -*ntut* RM PAST, which does not actually specify night time, but functions to express far past, i.e., events from the day before yesterday and back. This will be discussed in detail in Section 5.2.1.3.2.)

5.2.1.3 The Past Tenses

5.2.1.3.1 The Remote Past. The remote past occurs in two basic allomorphs -*ntut* and -*ntuk*, the former in word-final position and the latter elsewhere. Both allomorphs are subject to the truncation rule (rule (2-15)) which deletes the initial nasal when the previous morpheme ends in a nasal (*klŋ*- 'cut and dispose of' + -*ntut* RM PAST > *klŋtut* or *am*- 'consume' + -*ntut* RM PAST > *amtut*). Both allomorphs are, of course, also subject to the palatalization rule (rule (2-3)) if the previous morpheme ends in a segment with the F autosegment, as in *tay*- 'see' + -*ntut* RM PAST > *taɲcut* or *awl*- 'get' + -*ntut* RM PAST > *awtɲcut* (the second example also illustrates rule (2-5), liquid strengthening). The non-final allomorph -*ntuk* always triggers R spreading into a following V. The final /k/ of this allomorph is subject to loss before the paucal suffix -*ŋkt*, as in -*ntuk* RM PAST + -*ŋkt* PC > -*ntuŋkut* (by /k/ loss and R spreading).

The remote past is used to describe events in the continuum of real time, but most removed from the present now. The actual time span which it covers, however, is quite sensitive to contextual differences. Minimally, an event must be five days removed from today, but even events of a few years or more ago may be presented in the far past, rather than the remote past, if they seem especially near, important, or vivid to the narrator. Perhaps the best way to describe the time span covered by the remote past is as the period between the far past, which covers relatively near or vivid past events, and the legendary past, which is outside of real time and is best expressed via the irrealis. It is not uncommon for texts to begin in the remote past, but to switch in mid-stream to either the irrealis or the far past, depending on the pragmatic effects the speaker wishes to achieve. The irrealis distances the events further, making them timeless, while the far past brings them closer to the present and makes them more vivid.

A couple of examples of the use of the remote past follow:

(5-86) a. ma   ŋarŋ   na-n-way-mpi-
          other 1 day removed 3SG O-3SG A-turn-SEQ-
          ira-ya-ntut
          toward-come-RM PAST
          'Next day she came back to him.'

       b. kumpwia   kaŋkran kcpŋkat-n
          flying fox VIII PL before   underneath of house V PL-OBL
          wa-nanaŋ-irm-tut
          VIII PL-DUR-stand-RM PAST
          'Before flying foxes always hung from the underneath of houses.'

5.2.1.3.2 The Far Past. The far past is used for events viewed as closer in time or more vivid than those expressed in the remote past. It is formed by compounding -*kia* with the remote past, thus -*kiantut* ∼ -*kiantuk*, and the latter is subject to the same phonological rules as the remote past allomorph -*ntuk*.

The first and most obvious question concerning -*kiantut* FR PAST is why is it formed with the suffix -*kia*? This again finds an explanation of the traditional Yimas reckoning of the day from sunset to sunset. Remember that any given night is always the same day as the following noon. Hence any previous night in the past is actually in a time period closer to the present now than is the day preceding that night. Hence the re-analysis of -*kia-ntut* NIGHT-RM PAST to CLOSER-RM PAST > FR PAST finds a ready explanation.

The far past -*kiantut* ∼ -*kiantuk* covers past events from the day before yesterday to a year or even a few years ago. The boundary between the remote past and the far past is vague and is exploited by speakers for stylistic effect. The use of the remote past distances the events in time and feeling, while the far past brings them closer, enhancing them and adding a more vivid coloring. Thus, events of two years ago could quite easily be narrated in either the remote or far past, but with these pragmatic, stylistic differences noted. Interestingly, -*kia* can also be used with -*k* IRR when this replaces the remote past in legends and myths. Again this provides a closer, more vivid coloring to the events thus presented. Examples involving the far past follow:

(5-87) a. paŋkra-kwalca-mpi-cu-ŋka-pu-kiantu-ŋkt
           1PC S-get up-SEQ-out-go-away-FR PAST-PC
           'We few got up and went outside.'

       b. trawsistm   tma-mpu-ŋa-ŋa-kiantut
           trousers V DL V DL T-3PL A-1SG O-give-FR PAST
           'They gave me two pairs of trousers.'

5.2.1.3.3 The Near Past. The near past is that with the most clearly defined temporal limits: it marks events which occurred yesterday. If one is talking at noon about an event which occurred on the previous noon, that event will always be presented in the near past. But because of the conflict between the traditional Yimas reckoning of a day from sunset to sunset and the modern English/Tok Pisin based one of sunrise to sunrise, there is some confusion about last night and the night before last. Generally, a speaker talking at noon about events of the previous night will describe them as occurring during (*kwarkwa*) *wut* '(today) night' and will use the perfective suffix on the verb, equivalent to a present tense suffix for events which have already occurred today. This is the expected result if the day is calculated from sunset to sunset. There are, however, some younger speakers who follow the sunrise to sunrise pattern and will describe such events as occurring during *ŋarŋ wut* '1 day removed night', but they will still use the perfective suffix on the verb. The near past in this usage is completely unacceptable by all speakers.

   The night before last is more problematic, and younger speakers are unsure as to whether to describe it as *ŋarŋ wut* '1 day removed night' or *urakrŋ wut* '2 days removed night', although older speakers more consistently used *ŋarŋ wut* '1 day removed night'. All speakers use the far past, rather than the expected near past to describe this time period. The near past is never used to describe events which occur red at night, and it is important to note that the suffix -*kia* is never used in combination with the near past.

   The basic form of the near past is -*nan*, but the final nasal disappears whenever it is followed by a suffix. The initial /n/ is subject to palatalization rule (2-3) when it follows a segment associated with the autosegment F. Examples of the near past follow:

(5-88) a. ŋarŋ   pia-ka-i-ɲa-mpun
          1 day removed talk T-1SG A-tell-NR PAST 3PL D
          'I told them yesterday.'

       b. antki   ya-kay-klŋ-nan
          thatch IV PL   IV PL O-1PL A-cut and dispose-NR PAST
          'We cut off and disposed of the thatch yesterday.'

5.2.1.4 The Present Tenses

The present tense covers events which have occurred or are occurring today or could occur on any day including today (i.e., habitual actions). Because of the traditional reckoning of the day from sunset to sunset, when a speaker is talking at noon about events which are fully expected to occur in the coming night, these are always expressed in the near future, the tense of tomorrow, which, of course, commences with the coming sunset. Generally, events of the previous night are described in the present tense. Strictly speaking, there is no straightforward present tense morpheme in Yimas; rather there are three different aspectual categories expressed within the overall present tense category: perfective, imperfective, and habitual.

5.2.1.4.1 The Perfective. This marks events which have already occurred and been completed during today, including last night. It may also occasionally be used to mark completed events, especially changes of state, when the time of completion is unknown or irrelevant. Because last night is the same day as today according to the traditional Yimas reckoning, this is the inflection typically used to describe events which occurred then. If one is speaking at noon about events of last night one would simply use *wut* 'night' plus the perfective. The night suffix *-kia* is never used in combination with the perfective.

The basic form of the perfective is *-r*, but it is subject to extensive allomorphic variation. In word-final position it is realized as *t* by the rule of final *r* strengthening (rule (2-4)). Thus, *wu-* 'take in hand' + *-r* PERF > *wut*. The perfective is also realized in non-final position as *t* if the previous syllable contains a /r/ by the rule of *r* dissimilation (rule (2-6)) as follows: *kra-* 'cut' + *-r* PERF + *-akn* 3SG D > *kratakn*. The perfective has the allomorph Ø in word-final position following the palatalizing segments /i/, /l/, and /y/ (*awl-* 'get' + *-r* PERF > *awl*; and *tay-* 'see' + *-r* PERF > *tay*). This is probably the result of a prohibition on /c/ in word-final position, as this would be the expected realization.

If the perfective is not word-final, but is followed by another suffix, the /c/ then surfaces, as in *i*- 'say' + *-r* PERF + *-akn* 3SG D > *icakn* and *pul*- 'rub' + *-r* PERF + *-mpun* 3PL D > *pulcmpun*. Finally, it disappears before a suffix beginning with an /r/ (*wu*- 'take in hand' + *-r* PERF + *-ra* V SG > *wura*).

Examples of the use of the perfective follow:

(5-89) a. siot   na-araŋ-ara-t
        shirt V SG V SG S-tear-INCH-PERF
        'The shirt tore.'

      b. yampaŋ   k-ka-kra-t-akn
        head VI SG VI SG T-1SG A-cut-PERF-3SG D
        'I cut his hair.'

      c. wut   Kampramanan na-ka-tay-∅
        night Kampramanan 3SG O-1SG A-see-PERF
        'Last night I saw her on Kampramanan.'

5.2.1.4.2 The Imperfective. The imperfective is used to express events ongoing at the moment of speaking. If one is speaking at night, again *-kia* is blocked, the simple imperfective being used.

The imperfective is formed with the definitive prefix *na*- DEF and the suffix *-nt*, which I will gloss as present (PRES). It is possible to omit the present suffix, although this is not common. The initial /n/ of *na*-DEF disappears following a suffix ending in /n/, e.g., *n*- 3SG A.

Both of these suffixes are also present in the near future, but in that tense, in combination with *-kia*. The basic meaning of *na*- DEF is to posit a definite action which is occurring or will occur close to the present now. With the suffix *-nt* PRES, it expresses an action definitely in progress right now, the imperfective; with the suffix *-kia* and either the irrealis *-k* or the present *-nt*, it expresses an action definitely expected to occur in the near future, i.e., tomorrow (see Section 5.2.1.5.1). The prefix *na*- DEF is undoubtedly a contraction and specialization of *nanaŋ*-DUR, an incorporated adverbial within the verbal theme (see Section 6.3.2.1.2).

Both the definitive suffix *-na* and the present suffix *-nt* are subject to the palatalization rule (2-3) when following a palatalizing segment, i.e., /i/, /y/, or /l/. If the present suffix occurs word-finally, it is realized simply as *n* by the nasal + stop cluster simplification rule (2-14). In this position the palatalization rule is blocked, because it would result in a word final *ɲ*, which is, of course, prohibited by the phonotactic rules of the language. If it is not word-final and occurs after a morpheme ending in a nasal, it loses its own initial nasal, by the nasal truncation rule (2-15) (*am*- 'eat' + *-nt* 'PRES' + *-ra* V PL > *amtra*).

Examples of the use of the imperfective follow:

(5-90) a. kumpwi   i-kay-ɲa-tput-n
           children I PL   I PL O-1PL A-DEF-hit-PRES
           'We are hitting the children.'

       b. ya-r-mpwi   pia-mpu-na-i-ɲc-mpun
           come-NFN-talk   talk-3SG A-DEF-tell-PRES-3PL D
           'They are telling them to come.'

5.2.1.4.3 The Habitual. The habitual is used to express actions which
occur regularly and as a matter of course as a result of planned human
actions or natural cycles. It is most commonly encountered in procedu-
ral or expository discourse styles. It is being treated here as one of the
three aspectual contrasts within the present tense because any event it
marks could potentially occur today, but the event cannot be specifically predicated to occur in any definite period in the future nor has it
been located in any particular period of the past. In a sense any event
expressed in the habitual could be seen as timeless, but the habitual
contrasts with the other inflection of the timeless, the irrealis, in that
it predicates that the event has occurred in real time and will occur
again, while the irrealis has no such meaning component. The habitual,
however, does differ from the other aspectual contrasts in the present in
that it alone may occur with the suffix -kia, indicating an event which
generally occurs at night.

The form of the habitual is -war, with the final /r/ appearing as /t/
in word-final position according to final r strengthening (rule (2-4)), or
disappearing when followed by a suffix beginning in /r/, such as -ra V
PL O. Examples of the habitual follow:

(5-91) a. kay-ɲan   yara   ipa-na-ra
           canoe VIII SG-OBL   wood V PL   1PL-POSS-V PL

           ya-kay-at-mpi-yamal-wat
           V PL O-1PL A-cut-SEQ-carve-HAB

           'We usually cut our pieces of wood for canoes and then
           carve them out.'

       b. wurŋkat-n   panmal   kantk-nprum
           night PL-OBL   man I SG   with-II DL

           kapa-tɨ-kia-wat
           1PL S-do/feel-NIGHT-HAB

           'Nights we always have a man.'

       c. Maŋ-ɲan   na-pay-kia-wat
           Maŋi-OBL   3SG S-lie-NIGHT-HAB

           'He usually sleeps at Maŋi.'

5.2.1.5 The Future Tenses

As mentioned above, the future tenses differ from the irrealis in that, although they too describe as yet unrealized events, they commit the speaker to the belief that the events will in fact occur in the normal course of events. There are two future tenses: near future and remote future.

5.2.1.5.1 The Near Future. The near future covers events expected to happen tomorrow. If one is speaking at noon, this covers the period from the coming evening to the sunset of the following day. Most commonly the coming evening is talked about using *wut* 'night' plus the near future tense, but it is occasionally described by younger speakers as *kwarkwa wut* 'today night', again in association with the near future. Strictly speaking, *kwarkwa wut*, should be used only to refer to 'last night' according to the traditional Yimas time reckoning, but because of confusion from modern notions of time calculation, there is some variation in temporal words used to refer to 'last night' and 'tonight'. It is important to note that *ŋarŋ wut* '1 day removed night' is never used to refer to 'tonight', although it is sometimes used by younger speakers to refer to 'last night'.

The diagnostic inflection for the near future is *-kia*. We have already seen the relationship between *-kia* and the notion of closeness, and so it is altogether appropriate that it mark the near future. In the near future, *kia-* appears in combination with the irrealis suffix *-k* when in final position, but the present suffix *-nt* when followed by another suffix. These suffixes in themselves are not sufficient to specify the near future; they must also occur in combination with *na-* DEF or, more rarely, the modal prefix for likely events, *ka-* (see Section 5.2.2.3). The difference between the near future in *na-* DEF (the unmarked form) and *ka-* LIKELY is subtle, but it does seem that the use of *na-* more strongly commits the speaker to the belief that the events will occur tomorrow. Thus, one can say either *ma-na-wa-kia-k* 2SG S-DEF-go-NR FUT-IRR or *ka-n-wa-kia-k* LIKELY-2SG S-go-NR FUT-IRR 'you will go tomorrow', but with the subtle meaning difference just pointed out. The use of both prefixes on the same verb is ungrammatical.

Some examples of the near future follow:

(5-92) a. ya-ru-mpwi
 come-NFN-talk
 pia-ka-na-i-kia-nt-mpun
 talk T-1SG A-DEF-tell-NR FUT-PRES-3PL D
 '(Tomorrow) I will tell them to come.'

  b. ŋarŋ   tumpntut
    1 day removed morning
    ka-mpan-ya-ka-l-awkura-kia-k
    LIKE-1A/2SG O-come-SEQ-down-get-NR FUT-IRR
    'Tomorrow morning I will come and get you down there.'

  c. upŋk-n tpwi
    lake-OBL sago X PL
    i-kay-ɲa-pan-kia-k
    X PL O-1PL A-DEF-pound sago-NR FUT-IRR
    'Tomorrow we will pound sago over in the lakes.'

5.2.1.5.2 The Remote Future. The remote future covers the time span
from the day after tomorrow on into the indefinite future, where it ultimately merges with the irrealis in the hazy mists of unknown future
time. Of course any event within this time span may be expressed in
either the remote future or the irrealis, with the typical difference that
the remote future binds the speaker to the belief that the event will in
fact occur, while the irrealis does not.

  As with the boundary between the near and far past, the transition
between near and remote future is not sharp. The basic problem concerns the status of tomorrow night. Given the traditional reckoning of
the day from sunset to sunset, one speaking at noon about an event
happening tomorrow night should use the temporal *urakrŋ wut* '2 days
removed night' and the remote future tense, for this event is actually
occurring on the day after tomorrow. This is the most common usage in
Yimas. But an alternative in talking about events expected tomorrow
night is to use *ŋarŋ wut* '1 day removed night' with the remote future
tense. Still another an alternative is to use *ma wut* other night 'next
night' plus the remote future (this is ambiguous, but a likely interpretation is as 'tomorrow night'). To specify an event occurring at night
any time within the time span of the remote future, the suffix *-kia* in
its meaning of night time is used in combination with the remote future
tense suffix.

  The remote future tense suffix is *-kr*. The final /r/ becomes *t* in
word final position by rule (2-4), final *r* strengthening, and disappears
before suffixes beginning in /r/. Examples of the remote future follow:

(5-93) a. tmal   mpa-nan Mosbi-ɲan
     sun/day V SG one-OBL Moresby-OBL
     ama-pay-kia-kt
     1SG S-lie-NIGHT-RM FUT
     'I will sleep one night in Moresby.'

b. m-mpɨ-tɨ-ayk-kr-mp-n
NR DIST-3DL A-RCP-marry-RM FUT-VII SG-OBL

mnta   impa-wa-kt   Madaŋ-nan
and then 3DL S-go-RM FUT Madang-OBL
'When those two get married, they'll go to Madang.'

5.2.1.6 Aspectual Suffixes

The aspectual inflections presented thus far have all been restricted to
the present tense, so an obvious question is how are aspectual contrasts
in the past and future tenses expressed? Commonly, this is accomplished
by aspectual adverbials incorporated into the verbal complex, and these
will be discussed in detail in Section 6.3.2. In addition to these, there
are aspectual suffixes in Yimas which appear following the verb and in
combination with a tense inflection. These are the focus of this section.
These aspectual inflections are three in number: the completive, the
durational, and the immediate.

5.2.1.6.1 The Completive Aspect. This aspect expresses an event which
has gone to completion by totally affecting an object or by causing an entire group of individuals to undergo the same change. It is expressed by
-*rapi* ∼ -*tapi*, which are largely in free variation, except that -*tapi* must
occur after nasals and appear in its palatalized variant -*capi* after segments associated with the autosegment F. The completive aspect suffix
always precedes the relevant tense inflection as seen in the following:

(5-94) a. mi   am-tap-ɲa-rm
2SG consume-COMP-IMP-water
'Drink all of the water.'

b. katris   ya-mpu-wayk-rap-ɲcut
cartridge V PL V PL O-3PL A-buy-COMP-RM PAST
'They bought all of the cartridges.'

c. num-n-mat   pu-mal-capi-kia-k
village-OBL-PL 3PL S-die-COMP-NIGHT-IRR
'All the villagers died.'

Note that the arguments modified by the completive suffix are always
absolutive, i.e., S or O.

5.2.1.6.2 The Durational Aspect. Continuative and durational aspect
is usually expressed by incorporated adverbial prefixes inside the verbal
complex. One of these incorporated adverbials used to express duration
with stance or positional verbs is *nanaŋ*- DUR, transparently related
to the verb *naŋ*- 'live, dwell, stay at'. A contracted form of this, -*naŋ*
∼ -*na* (the final /ŋ/ disappears before a suffix beginning in a nasal) is

used as a durative aspectual suffix, most commonly with the stance or motion verbs, but is not restricted to these. This suffix normally occurs in combination with the incorporated adverbial *nanaŋ-*.

(5-95) a. kalk
        sago pudding V SG
        pu-nanaŋ-wurt-am-na-ntut
        3PL S-DUR-mix(RED: *wul-*)-eat-DUR-RM PAST
        'They kept mixing and eating sago pudding.'

    b. tantukwan   impa-nanaŋ-taw-na-ntut
       alone   3DL S-DUR-sit-DUR-RM PAST
       'The two of them were living by themselves.'

    c. ku-mpɨ-nanaŋ-yawra-kia-na-ntut
       X SG O-3DL A-DUR-get-NIGHT-DUR-RM PAST
       'Those two were getting it (the scrotum).'

5.2.1.6.3 The Immediate Aspect. This aspectual contrast results from a specialization of the temporal word, *mpa* 'just now, already'. This in combination with the present tense suffix *-nt* (realized as *-n* in word-final position) has become an enclitic, meaning 'still, now', which can follow any verb, finite or non-finite.

(5-96) a. Bil   na-na-pram-kia-k   mpan?
        Bill 3SG S-DEF-sleep-NIGHT-IRR still/now
        'Is Bill still sleeping?'

    b. yaki-marŋki
       tobacco V PL-stalk VI PL
       kia-kay-nanaŋ-kamat-kula-ntut
       V PL O-2PL A-DUR-search-walk-RM PAST
       wapapi-am-tu-mpwi   mpan
       roll(RED: *wapi-*)-eat-NFN-PURP still/now
       'We were walking around looking for stalks of tobacco to roll and smoke right then.'

mpa can also be treated as an aspectual suffix meaning 'right now, just yet' in the same affix position as *-rapi* ~ *-tapi* COMP and *-naŋ* ~ *-na* DUR, i.e., before a tense suffix or the imperative suffix. It is restricted in that it can only co-occur with the perfective and the present tense suffixes or the imperative.

(5-97) a. arm   ta-pu-n-ara-mpa-nt-rm
        water NEG-3-DEF-dry-IMM-PRES-water
        'The water isn't dry just yet.'

b. tia-n-ti-mpa-t
act O-3SG A-do-IMM-PERF
'She's just finished it.'

c. tpul-kia-mpa-na-m
hit-NIGHT-IMM-IMP-3PL O
'Hit them right now!'

d. wa-n-a-kacak-mp-n
IX SG O-3SG A-DEF-scrape-VII SG-OBL

na-na-pan-pa-n   tat-n
3SG S-DEF-pound sago-IMM-PRES   start-PRES
'Having removed (the bark), he begins to pound sago now.'

5.2.2 Modality
Modality describes the actuality of an event, whether it is realized or not (this was termed "status" in Foley and Van Valin 1984, 213–8). This is covered partially in Yimas by the contrast between the irrealis and the tense suffixes, and indeed in some languages, modality is viewed largely as a binary distinction between irrealis and realis. However, within the irrealis dimension, languages often recognized further distinctions, whether the action is necessary, likely, or merely possible. Yimas is one of these languages, and these additional modal distinctions are provided by a set of modal prefixes: *ta-* NEG, *ant-* POT, and *ka-* LIKE.

5.2.2.1 Negation
The modal prefixes are a particularly complicated area of Yimas grammar, often requiring re-arrangements of the verbal morphology. The negative prefix *ta-* is typical in this regard. The basic rule is that the lowest ranked participant, rather than being realized as the leftmost prefix, is expressed through a suffix following the tense suffix. In other words, its position is usurped by the negative prefix, so it appears as a suffix. As intransitive verbs have only a single prefix, that of the S argument, they represent the simplest case and for ease of exposition, it is best to start with them.

Consider first the contrast between the following positive and negative intransitive verbs with first person S arguments:

(5-98) a. (i)   ama-wa-t   (ii)   ta-ka-wa-t
            1SG S-go-PERF   NEG-1SG S-go-PERF
            'I went.'   'I didn't go.'

      b. (i)   kapa-wa-t   (ii)   ta-ŋkra-wa-r-(r)m
            1DL S-go-PERF   NEG-1DL S-go-PERF-DL
            'We two went.'   'We two didn't go.'

c. (i) paŋkra-wa-t   (ii) ta-kay-wa-r-ŋkt
        1PL S-go-PERF   NEG-1PL S-go-PERF-PC
        'We few went.'   'We few didn't go.'

d. (i) ipa-wa-t   (ii) ta-kay-wa-r-um
        1PL S-go-PERF   NEG-1PL S-go-PERF-PL
        'We went.'   'We didn't go.'

Note that in all cases the negative differs from the positive in that the S pronominal prefix form is replaced by the A form, reflecting the underlying nominative-accusative case-marking alignment of participants for first person participants (and second person participants which would behave identically), discussed in Section 5.1.1. In addition, the negative verb is affixed with a particular suffix which references the number of the S argument. This set of suffixes is as follows:

SG	DL	PC	PL
∅	-rm	-ŋkt	-ump

The plural -*ump* is normally realized as -*um*, as it generally occurs in final position and is subject to rule (2-14), final nasal plus stop cluster simplification. After -*na* NR PAST, the /u/ is deleted so that it is -*mp* ∼ -*m*.

The dual suffix is optional with first and second person S arguments; the others are obligatory. Note the correlation between the dual and plural of these negative number suffixes and the possessive concord suffixes for class I (see Section 4.1.1).

Now consider the forms with third person S arguments:

(5-99) a. (i) na-wa-nan   (ii) ta-pu-wa-nan
             3SG S-go-NR PAST   NEG-3-go-NR PAST
             'He went yesterday.'   'He didn't go yesterday.'

       b. (i) impa-wa-nan   (ii) ta-pu-wa-na-rm
             3DL S-go-NR PAST   NEG-3-go-NR PAST-DL
             'Those two went   'Those two didn't
             yesterday.'   go yesterday.'

       c. (i) kra-wa-nan   (ii) ta-pu-wa-na-ŋkt
             3PC S-go-NR PAST   NEG-3-go-NR PAST-PC
             'Those few went   'Those few didn't
             yesterday.'   go yesterday.'

       d. (i) pu-wa-nan   (ii) ta-pu-wa-na-m
             3PL S-go-NR PAST   NEG-3-go-NR PAST-PL
             'They went   'They didn't go
             yesterday.'   yesterday.'

The same negative number suffixes again reference the number of the
S argument, but the third person forms contrast with the first person
forms in (5-98) in that all distinctions in number in the pronominal
prefixes are lost. All four numbers in the third person are expressed
by the same prefix *pu-*, the normal S/O pronominal prefix for third
plural. Note further that whereas the negative forms for intransitive
verbs with first person S arguments reveal an underlying nominative-
accusative role-marking schema in that the S argument is realized by
the A prefix form, third person arguments continue to show an ergative-
absolutive alignment in both positive and negative forms. Thus, all third
person S arguments regardless of number are expressed in negated verbs
by the pronominal prefix *pu-* 3 PL S/O, the actual number being carried
by the negative number suffixes. I will again take up this question of
the accusative versus ergative split in negative verbs when discussing
transitive verbs below.

Second person S arguments show an interesting feature as a result
of the inflectional patterns of the positive verbs. Remember that the
pronominal prefix *n-* is homophonous for 2/3SG A, but that the other
numbers in second person show no similarity with third person. This
overlap is also exhibited in the negative verbs. Negative verbs with
second singular S arguments have *pu-* (typical of third person), and the
pronominal prefix *n-*, the normal form for second singular A, used in
this case for an S argument (demonstrating again the usual nominative-
accusative pattern for first and second person arguments). Consider the
following examples:

(5-100) a. ta-pu-n-wa-t
NEG-3-2SG S-go-PERF
'You didn't go.'

b. ta-nan-wa-r-um
NEG-2PL S-go-PERF-PL
'You all didn't go.'

Thus, although in positive verbs *n-* 2/3SG A is homophonous, the difference in negative verbs in morphological behavior of first and second
person S arguments, on the one hand, and third person, on the other,
ensures that the negative forms for verbs with second and third singular
S arguments are distinct; compare (5-100a) with (5-99a(ii)).

So far I have only considered intransitive verbs with human, pronominal S arguments. An inanimate noun, of course, can also function as
an S argument, but in this case, instead of one of the negative number
suffixes above, the possessive/adjective concord marker corresponding
to the class and number of the inanimate noun is used to reference it.

The all-purpose third person pronominal in the negative paradigm *pu*-
is still present.

(5-101) a. arm   ta-pu-na-ara-mpa-nt-rm
         water   NEG-3-DEF-dry-IMM-PRES-water
         'The water isn't dry just yet.'

      b. irpuŋi   ta-pu-tmuk-na-ra
         coconut palm IV PL   NEG-3-fall-NR PAST-IV PL
         'The coconut palms didn't fall over yesterday.'

      c. nam   ta-pu-wark-ntuk-nm
         house   NEG-3-build-RM PAST-house
         'The house wasn't built.'

Now let us turn to transitive verbs, those with two participants A
and O. The basic rule is that the lower of the two participants, i.e.,
the one which in the corresponding positive verb would be the outer
of the two prefixes, is realized by one of the negative number suffixes
above, if human or animate, or by its corresponding possessive/adjectival
concord suffix, if inanimate. The only difference between transitive and
intransitive verbs is that the singular number marker is no longer ∅, but
-*kak* (-*ak* after a [-peripheral] consonant).

Consider first the following examples with pronominal human participants:

(5-102) a. (i)   na-kay-cay   (ii)   ta-kay-cay-c-ak
             3SG O-1PL A-see   NEG-1PL A-see-PERF-SG
             'We saw him.'   'We didn't see him.'

      b. (i)   impa-ka-tay   (ii)   ta-ka-tay-c-rm
             3DL O-1SG A-see   NEG-1SG A-see-PERF-DL
             'I saw those two.'   'I didn't see those two.'

      c. (i)   kra-ŋa-tay   (ii)   ta-ŋa-tay-c-ŋkt
             3PC A-1SG O-see   NEG-1SG O-see-PERF-PC
             'Those few saw me.'   'Those few didn't see me.'

      d. (i)   pu-ŋa-tay   (ii)   ta-ŋa-tay-c-um
             3PL A-1SG O-see   NEG-1SG O-see-PERF-PL
             'They saw me.'   'They didn't see me.'

Note that when the suffixed participant is third person, it is not referenced by the negative pronominal prefix *pu*-; only the higher ranked
participant is indicated by a pronominal prefix. The pronominal prefix
may reference an A (as in the (a) and (b) examples) or an O (as in the
(c) and (d) examples), but it is always the higher ranked participant
on the person hierarchy discussed in Section 5.1.2. The lower ranked

prefix is marked only by the negative number suffix. If the lower ranked
participant is inanimate, it will, of course, be referenced for both number and noun class by the corresponding possessive/adjectival concord
suffix.

(5-103) a. takiŋkat   ya-kay-wampak-ɲan
           rock V PL V PL O-1PL A-throw-NR PAST
           'We threw the rocks yesterday.'

        b. takiŋkat   ta-kay-wampak-ɲa-ra
           rock V PL NEG-1PL A-throw-NR PAST-V PL
           'We didn't throw the rocks yesterday.'

(5-104) a. tpuk   ku-ka-am-wat
           sago pancake X SG X SG O-1SG A-eat-HAB
           'I usually eat sago.'

        b. tpuk   ta-ka-am-war-uŋ
           sago pancake X SG NEG-1SG A-eat-HAB-X SG
           'I don't usually eat sago.'

The participant which appears as the suffix is always the lower ranked
one, i.e., the one which would appear as the outer pronominal prefix in
the corresponding positive verb. Thus, the same rules which determine
the ranking of participants discussed in Section 5.1.2 determine which
participant will be prefixed and which suffixed in the negative verb. So
when both participants are third person, the O will always appear as
the suffix.

(5-105) a. (i) na-mpɨ-tpul   (ii) ta-mpɨ-tpul-c-ak
               3SG O-3DL A-hit   NEG-3DL A-hit-PERF-SG
               'Those two hit him.'   'Those two didn't hit him.'

        b. (i) impa-mpu-tpul   (ii) ta-mpu-tpul-c-rm
               3DL O-3PL A-hit   NEG-3PL A-hit-PERF-DL
               'They hit those two.'   'They didn't hit those two.'

Note that although both participants for these verbs are third person,
there is no pronominal prefix *pu-* 3. Its occurrence is rather more restricted in transitive verbs than intransitive, and it is not used when
the following prefix is a pronominal prefix representing a first person
participant, a second person dual participant, a second person plural O
participant, or a third person non-singular A participant. It is hard to
see how this grouping forms a natural class, but nonetheless, these are
the pronominal prefixes which prohibit a preceding *pu-* 3. Consider also
the following.

(5-106) a. (i)   ta-pu-n-tpul-c-ak
                  NEG-3-2/3SG A-hit-PERF-SG
                  'You/he didn't hit him.'

       (ii) ta-pu-n-tpul-c-um
                  NEG-3-2/3SG A-hit-PERF-PL
                  'You/he didn't hit them.'

Note that the difference in number of the O participant is carried by the number suffixes, -*nak* SG versus -*ump* PL.

    b. (i)   ta-kul-cpul-c-um
                  NEG-2PL O-hit-PERF-PL
                  'They didn't hit you all.'

       (ii) ta-pu-nan-tpul-c-um
                  NEG-3-2PL A-hit-PERF-PL
                  'You all didn't hit them.'

Note that *pu-* is not used when the second plural prefix refers to an O, but is used when it indicates an A participant.

    c. (i)   ta-pu-nan-tpul
                  NEG-3-2SG O-hit
                  'He didn't hit you.'

       (ii) ta-pu-nan-tpul-c-ak
                  NEG-3-2PL A-hit-PERF-SG
                  'You all didn't hit him.'

The pronominal prefix *nan-* is homophonous for 2SG O and 2PL A. The contrast between these forms is provided by the difference in the behavior of the third singular participant: the third singular A is realized as $\emptyset$, but the third singular O as -*nak*.

    d. (i)   ta-pu-nan-tpul-c-rm
                  NEG-3-2SG O-hit-PERF-DL
                  'Those two didn't hit you.'

       (ii) ta-pu-nan-tpul-c-rm
                  NEG-3-2PL A-hit-PERF-DL
                  'You all didn't hit those two.'

The examples in (d) must remain ambiguous: the number of lower ranked third person dual participant must be indicated by the dual number suffix -*rm* regardless of whether it is A (5-106d, i) or O (5-106d, ii).

    These examples of transitive verbs again bring up the question of the accusative-ergative split according to person. If we compare intransitive and transitive negative verbs having first and second person participants, we find that the S argument is indicated by the same prefix form as the A argument, a clear nominative-accusative participant role alignment.

(5-107) a. ta-*ka*-wa-t
         NEG-1SG S-go-PERF
         'I didn't go.'

      b. ta-*ka*-tay-c-um
         NEG-1SG A-see-PERF-PL
         'I didn't see them.'

      c. ta-*ŋa*-tay-c-um
         NEG-1SG O-see-PERF-PL
         'They didn't see me.'

ka- codes the first singular A and S arguments, and *ŋa*- the O argument.
On the other hand, a third person S argument of a negative verb is
realized in the same way as a third person O, and quite differently from
an A argument, i.e., an ergative-absolutive marking pattern.

(5-108) a. ta-*pu*-wa-r-*um*
         NEG-3-go-PERF-PL
         'They didn't go.'

      b. ta-*mpu*-tay-c-ak
         NEG-3PL A-see-PERF-SG
         'They didn't see him.'

      c. ta-*pu*-n-tay-c-*um*
         NEG-3-3SG A-see-PERF-PL
         'He didn't see them.'

The third plural S and O are both expressed through the morpheme combination *pu*-...-*um* 3-...-PL, while the A appears as the typical ergative
prefix *mpu*- 3 PL A. Thus, the negative verbs exhibit the typical split
for person we have seen elsewhere in the verbal morphology, nominative-
accusative for first and second persons and ergative-absolutive for third.

But this ergative-absolutive patterning for third person breaks down
in the third singular forms of negative verbs. If one surveys the previous
forms, one will discover that a third singular A is always coded by a ∅
number suffix, but an O by -*nak* (compare, for example, (5-106a(i)) with
(5-106c(i)). Additional examples are offered below:

(5-109) a. ta-kra-tpul-∅
         NEG-1PL O-hit-SG
         'He didn't hit us.'

      b. ta-kay-cpul-c-*ak*
         NEG-1PL A-hit-PERF-SG
         'We didn't hit him.'

∅ is also the morpheme to indicate singular number of a third person S
argument.

(5-110) ta-pu-wa-t-∅
NEG-3-go-PERF-SG
'He didn't go.'

Thus, the behavior of third singular forms in having ∅ marking for number of S and A, but -*nak* for O, indicates a nominative-accusative alignment, in spite of the fact that the corresponding positive verb forms are transparently ergative-absolutive.

Interestingly, this difference in behavior in negative verbs between third singular A and O allows for a distinction which cannot be made in the corresponding positive verbs. Remember that *ŋkra-* is both the A and O form for 1DL. Thus, (5-111) is ambiguous.

(5-111) na-ŋkra-tpul
3SG A/O-1DL A/O-hit
'He hit us two/we two hit him.'

But this ambiguity disappears in the corresponding negated verbs because of the difference in behavior between third person singular A and O participants.

(5-112) a. ta-ŋkra-tpul
NEG-1DL O-hit
'He didn't hit us two.'

b. ta-ŋkra-tpul-c-ak
NEG-1DL A-hit-PERF-SG
'We two didn't hit him.'

The final set of negated transitive verbs to consider are those involving both first and second person participants. The reader is advised to look back to Section 5.1.2 to review the inflectional system of positive verbs with this combination. If the A is second person and the O is first person, the A is realized simply by the negative number suffix. Thus, these negated verbs are homophonous to those with third person A participants.

(5-113) a. ta-ŋkra-tpul
NEG-1DL O-hit
'You/he didn't hit us two.'

b. ta-ŋa-tpul-c-rm
NEG-1SG O-hit-PERF-DL
'You/they two didn't hit me.'

c. ta-kra-tpul-c-um
NEG-1PL O-hit-PERF-PL
'You all/they didn't hit us.'

This ambiguity can, of course, be resolved by the use of independent pronouns.

When the A is first person and the O non-singular second person, only the O is marked on the verb. This is in keeping with the rules observed above with the positive verbs in Section 5.1.2. The negative number suffix, if present, simply redundantly specifies the number of the O.

(5-114) a. ta-ŋkul-cpul-c-rm
NEG-2DL O-hit-PERF-DL
'I didn't hit you two.'

b. kapa ta-kul-cpul-c-um
1DL   NEG-2PL O-hit-PERF-PL
'We two didn't hit you all.'

If the O is second person singular, the suppletive prefix *mpan-* 1A/2SG O is used, but no negative number suffix is allowed. The number of the A can only be indicated through the use of an independent pronoun.

(5-115) a. ta-mpan-tpul
NEG-1A/2SG O-hit
'I didn't hit you.'

b. ipa   ta-mpan-tpul
1PL   NEG-1A/2SG O-hit
'We didn't hit you.'

The latter example would be ungrammatical if the negative plural suffix -*ump* were attached.

Ditransitive verbs which code three participants on the verb through pronominal affixes present the added complication in the negative of determining which participant is to be realized as a suffix. In all cases of ditransitive verbs with three pronominal affixes, it is the theme participant which is suffixed in the negative. If the D participant is third person and hence already a suffix, the theme suffix simply follows this.

(5-116) a. uraŋ   ta-ka-tkam-r-ak-ŋ
coconut VI SG NEG-1SG A-show-PERF-3SG D-VI SG
'I didn't show him the coconut.'

b. ta-mpu-i-c-mpan-mpwi
NEG-3PL A-tell-PERF-3PL D-talk
'They didn't tell them.'

If the D participant is first or second person and the A participant third person, then both the A and D appear as prefixes following *ta-* NEG, and only the T is suffixed.

(5-117) a. ta-mpu-ŋa-tkam-r-ŋ
         NEG-3PL A-1SG D-show-PERF-VI SG
         'They didn't show me it (the coconut).'

       b. ta-mpɨ-kra-i-c-mpwi
          NEG-3DL A-1PL D-tell-PERF-talk
          'Those two didn't tell us.'

Ditransitive verbs with both first and second person participants are prohibited from marking both with pronominal affixes (see Section 5.1.3).
These are morphologically simple transitive verbs and are subject to the
same rules for negation as described for transitive verbs above. The only
exception concerns *mpan-*, which indicates a first person A and a second
singular D. In negative verbs this prefix remains unchanged, and again
the theme appears as a suffix.

(5-118) a. ta-mpan-tkam-r-ŋ
         NEG-1A/2SG O-show-PERF-VI SG
         'I didn't show you it (the coconut).'

       b. ipa   ta-mpan-tkam-r-ŋ
          1PL NEG-1A/2SG D-show-PERF-VI SG
          'We didn't show you it (the coconut).'

    When verbs with the paucal suffix are negated, the paucal suffix often
appears in its non-final form, *-ŋkan* PC, and is followed by a negative
number suffix.

(5-119) a. ta-kra-tpul-c-ŋkan-um
         NEG-1PL O-hit-PERF-PC-PL
         'They didn't hit us few.'

       b. ta-kay-cpul-c-ŋkan-rm
          NEG-1PL A-hit-PERF-PC-DL
          'We few didn't hit those two.'

       c. ta-mpɨ-kra-tkam-r-ŋkan-ŋ
          NEG-3DL A-1PL D-show-PERF-PC-VI SG
          'Those two didn't show us few it (the coconut).'

       d. ta-mpan-tpul-c-ŋkt
          NEG-1A/2SG O-hit-PERF-PC
          'We few didn't hit you.'

       e. ta-pu-nan-ŋa-r-ŋkan-um
          NEG-3-2PL A-give-PERF-PC-PL
          'You few didn't give (it) to them.'

       f. ta-kay-ckam-r-ŋkan-mpan-ŋ
          NEG-1PL A-show-PERF-PC-3PL D-VI SG
          'We few didn't show them it (the coconut).'

g. ta-nan-i-c-ŋkan-mpan-mpwi
NEG-2PL A-tell-PERF-PC-3PL D-talk
'You few didn't tell them.'

A negative verb with the paucal suffix may be potentially ambiguous as it may not be clear which participant is modified by it. The basic rule is that the paucal suffix is always interpreted as modifying a first or second person participant, rather than a third person. Thus in (5-119e, f, g), -ŋkan indicates the paucal number of the first and second person A prefix, and not the third person D prefix; these are not ambiguous. In other cases, ambiguity is avoided by removing a pronominal affix for one of the participants.

(5-120) a. kra-kul-cpul
3PC A-2PL O-hit
'Those few hit you all.'

b. kra-n   ta-kul-cpul-c-um
PC-FR DIST NEG-2PL O-hit-PERF-PL
'Those few didn't hit you all.'

c. kra-n   ta-kul-cpul-c-ŋkt
PC-FR DIST NEG-2PL O-hit-PERF-PC
'Those few didn't hit you few.'

The negative of (5-120a) is (5-120b), in which the paucal A participant is prohibited from appearing on the verb as a pronominal affix and must occur as an independent pronoun. The number suffix then references the plural number of the second plural O. If the paucal prefix is present, as in (5-120c), it is interpreted as applying to the bound pronominal prefix of the O. This principle applies even when no ambiguity is possible.

(5-121) a. kra-ŋkul-cpul
3PC A-2DL O-hit
'Those few hit you two.'

b. kra-n   ta-ŋkul-cpul-c-rm
PC-FR DIST NEG-2DL O-hit-PERF-DL
'Those few didn't hit you two.'

c.*kra-n   ta-ŋkul-cpul-c-ŋkt
PC-FR DIST NEG-2DL O-hit-PERF-PC

The proper negative of (5-121), with a third paucal A and a second dual O, is (5-121b), in which the number suffix is -rm DL, indicating the number of the O (also coded in the pronominal prefix ŋkul- 2 DL O). The presence of the paucal suffix -ŋkt as in (5-121c) results in ungrammaticality, in spite of the fact that such a construction could only unambiguously express a paucal A. The paucal suffix in negative verbs is in fact never allowed to reference the number of a third person A; it is restricted to marking a third person paucal O.

(5-122) a. ta-ka-tpul-c-ŋkt
NEG-1SG A-hit-PERF-PC
'I didn't hit those few.'

      b. ta-mpu-tpul-c-ŋkt
NEG-3PL A-hit-PERF-PC
'They didn't hit those few.'

      c. ta-ŋkl-cpul-c-um
NEG-3PC A-hit-PERF-PL
'Those few didn't hit them.'

In (5-122a,b), the suffix -ŋkt PC marks an O participant which is third paucal. Note that (5-122a) with ka- 1SG A is grammatical, while (5-121c) with ŋkul- 2DL O is not. This is because the paucal suffix is restricted in third person to O participants only. Also, note that when the third person paucal participant is an A, as in (5-122c), it is coded by the corresponding pronominal prefix ŋkl- 3PC A, and the number of the object is indicated by the negative number suffix.

The rules I have sketched above for negation apply to all verbs in the language save one, the copula. While the copula in the positive paradigm is inflected for person, number and noun class class, this does not apply in the negative. There are two forms of the copula in the negative: one used in equational statements and the other in possessive constructions.

The form of the copula in negative equational statements is *tampan*. This replaces all inflected forms of the copula presented in Section 5.1.5. Consider the following pairs:

(5-123) a. kpa-n   amayak
big-I SG   COP 1SG
'I am big.'

      b. ama   kpa-n   tampan
1SG   big-I SG   COP NEG
'I'm not big.'

(5-124) a. yaw   kawŋkra-k-wa   yak
road IX SG   long-IRR-IX SG   COP IX SG INVIS
'The road is long.'

      b. yaw   kawŋkra-k-wa   tampan
road IX SG   long-IRR-IX SG   COP NEG
'The road is not long.'

In negative possessive constructions the form of the copula is *kayak*.

This actually means 'don't have', so that the postposition *kantk-* 'with' used in the corresponding positive forms is lacking with *kayak*.

(5-125) a. ipa   tawra   kantk-um aypak
         1PL   money with-I PL COP 1PL
         'We have money.'
      b. ipa   tawra   kayak
         1PL   money COP NEG
         'We don't have money.'

(5-126) a. ama tamana   kantk-n   amayak
         1SG sickness IX SG with-1SG COP 1SG
         'I am sick.'
      b. ama tamana   kayak
         1SG sickness IX SG COP NEG
         'I am not sick.'

kayak is also the response word meaning 'no'.

The pattern of negation through verbal inflection with *ta-* NEG or the negative copula forms is the only means of negation in Yimas. All negation in Yimas is sentential, having the entire clause within the scope of the negative (but see Section 6.3.1). There is no phrasal or word level negative in Yimas, as there is in English with the prefix *un-* (see Klima 1964, Payne 1985). Only verbs can be inflected with the negative morpheme; there are no negative forms for the true adjectives, such as *kpa-* 'big'.

A final point about negation. As should be clear by now from the long and detailed exposition I have felt bound to provide, negation in Yimas is a quite complex affair, and one should not be surprised to learn that this system is now gradually being abandoned. All speakers, sometimes, and younger speakers (under 30), commonly, avoid these complexities by simply using the proclitic *ina* 'not' before a positive verb. This proclitic *ina* is a borrowing from the Tok Pisin negative *i no*. *ina* NEG is most usually encountered in equational sentences, where it is now the norm for almost all speakers, but any verb can potentially be negated by the innovation *ina* NEG instead of the traditional *ta-* NEG. The only exception is negated possessive clauses with *kayak* 'don't have'; *ina* can never replace *kayak*.

5.2.2.2 Potential Modality
This modal prefix expresses events which are viewed as possible occurrences in the normal course of events, but not likely. Perhaps its most common use is with tense suffixes expressing past tense to indicate events which almost happened in the past, but did not in fact eventuate. The

potential modal prefix has the form *ant-*, but this contracts with third
person prefixes as follows: *ant-* POT + *n-* 3SG > *anan-*, *ant-* POT +
mpɨ- 3DL > *ampɨ-*, and *ant-* POT + *mpu-* 3PL > *ampu*. The potential modal prefix triggers the same rules for changes in the pronominal
prefixes as does *ta-* NEG, as seen in the following:

(5-127) a. ant-ka-tu-r-um
            POT-1SG A-kill-PERF-PL
            'I almost killed them.'

        b. ant-ŋa-tpul-c-um
            POT-1SG O-hit-PERF-PL
            'They almost hit me.'

except that the general third person prefix *pu-* of negative verbs is not
used for verbs with *ant-*.

(5-128) anan-mal
        POT 3SG S-die
        'He almost died.'

    The potential modality indicates events which are viewed by the
speaker as possible events. With future tense or non-perfective aspects,
the meaning is vague as to whether the reading should be the deontic
one ('is permitted/is able to') or the epistemic one ('is possible that'),
much like English *can*.

(5-129) a. ampu-na-wark-kia-nt-nm
            POT 3PL A-DEF-build-NR FUT-PRES-house
            'They can build a house tomorrow.'
            i.e., 'They are able to build a house tomorrow.'
            or 'It is possible that they will build a house tomorrow.'

        b. narmaŋ   irwut   anan-ampa-nt-ut
            woman II SG   mat IX PL   POT 3SG A-weave-PRES-IX PL
            'The woman can weave mats.'
            i.e., 'The woman is able to weave mats.'
            or 'It's possible that the woman will weave mats.'

Sometimes an accompanying expression will disambiguate the meaning.

(5-130) a. m-n   yua-n-tɨ-k-nan
            NR DIST-I SG   good-I SG-do/feel-IRR-OBL
            ant-ka-na-arp-mpi-awt-ɲc-ak
            POT-1SG A-DEF-help-SEQ-get-PRES-SG
            'If he is (a) good (man), it is possible that I will help him.'
            ?'If he is (a) good (man), I will be able to help him.'

  b. ama ampra   kantk-nan
     1SG firewood V PL with-OBL

     ant-ka-na-ampu-nt-ra
     POT-1SG A-DEF-cook-PRES-V PL

     'If I have firewood, I will be able to cook.'
     ?'If I have firewood, it is possible that I will cook.'

With past tense suffixes, and especially with the perfective aspect suffix
-*r*, *ant*- POT is used to indicate events which almost, but did not in
fact, happen.

(5-131) a. ampu-tay-mpi-yawra-t-ak
           POT 3PL A-see-SEQ-take-PERF-SG
           'They almost found him.'

       b. ant-ka-tu-na-nak
          POT-1SG A-kill-NR PAST-SG
          'I almost killed him yesterday.'

Because of this meaning of potential past events which did not occur,
the potential modal prefix is employed in the formation of counterfactual
adverbial clauses (see Section 7.2.3), in both the apodosis and protasis.

(5-132) a. ampi-ya-ntuk-mp-n   ant-ka-wa-ntut
           POT-come-RM PAST-VII SG-OBL POT-1SG A-go-RM PAST
           'If those two had come, I would have gone.'

       b. wanwa   tak m-a   anan-pay-ɲcuk-
          knife IX SG here NR DIST-IX SG POT 3SG S-lie-RM PAST

          mp-n   ant-ka-yawra-ntuk-a
          VII SG-OBL POT-1SG A-take-RM PAST-IX SG

          'If the knife had been here, I would have taken it.'

       c. tuŋkurŋ   ant-ka-tay-kiantuk-mp-n
          eye VI SG   POT-1SG A-see-FR PAST-VII SG-OBL

          ant-ka-tu-kiantuk-nak
          POT-1SG A-kill-FR PAST-SG

          'If I had seen the eyes (of the crocodile), I would have
          killed it.'

The potential modal prefix is properly used in both the apodosis and
protasis, for both encode potential past events which did not occur.

5.2.2.3 Likely Modality

The likely modal prefix *ka*- encodes events which are regarded by the
speaker as likely to occur in the normal course of events. The likely
modal prefix does not normally trigger the same changes in the pronom-

inal prefixes as do *ta-* NEG or *ant-* POT (although is a rarely observed
option). It is simply added to an otherwise normally inflected verb.

(5-133) a. wɲcmpt   mpu-na-ra
           name V PL 3PL-POSS-V PL

           ka-ra-ŋa-taŋ-taw-n
           LIKE-V PL-1SG O-COM-sit-PRES
           'Their names will be mine.'

        b. ka-mpu-ŋa-tput-n
           LIKE-3PL A-1SG O-hit-PRES
           'They are going to hit me.'

        c. ka-mpan-arp-mpi-awl-kt   urakrŋ
           LIKE-1A/2SG O-help-SEQ-get-RM FUT 2 days removed
           'I will help you the day after tomorrow.'

        d. ka-mpan-tu-kr-ŋkt
           LIKE-1A/2SG O-kill-RM FUT-PC
           'We few will kill you.'

ka- LIKE expresses events which are likely to occur, but not regarded
as definite by the speaker. Because of this, *ka-* cannot co-occur in the
near future with *na-* DEF, which implies a much stronger expectation
of occurrence. Both may be used with *-kia* NR FUT but with a subtle
difference in meaning.

(5-134) a. ŋarŋ   ka-n-wa-kia-k
           1 day removed LIKE-2SG S-go-NR FUT-IRR
           (I think it's likely that) you will go tomorrow.'

        b. ŋarŋ   ma-na-wa-kia-k
           1 day removed 2SG S-DEF-go-NR FUT-IRR
           (I am quite sure that) you will go tomorrow.'

Because of its meaning of unrealized, but likely events, *ka-* LIKE
never occurs with past tense suffixes or *-r* PERF (which are favored
by *ant-* POT). It is most common with the present and future tenses,
especially the former. With the future tenses it tends to weaken their
force, indicating likely events, but not definite ones (see 5-134a,b). With
the present tense it expresses an action close at hand that the speaker
thinks will probably come to pass (see also examples 5-133a,c).

(5-135) a. balus-ɲan   ka-ŋkl-ya-ka-arm-n
           airplane-OBL LIKE-3PC S-come-SEQ-board-PRES
           'Those few will board the plane now.'

        b. ma-ra   ama naŋkun ka-ra-taw-n
           other-V PL 1SG toward LIKE-V PL S-sit-PRES
           'The others will stay with me.'

This last example shows that *ya-*, the prefix for classes V, VII, and VIII plural, is realized as *ra-* when following another prefix. As *ka-* LIKE is the only prefix which can precede it, this is the only environment in what *ra-* will appear.

Finally, *ka-* LIKE is completely prohibited from co-occurring with the irrealis. This is explicable in view of the semantic incompatibility of the two: the irrealis expresses events the occurrence of which the speaker expresses no commitment about.

Events which *may* occur are marked by the modal prefix *ant-* POT, while those which *should* occur are marked by *ka-* LIKE. This difference in Yimas is probably best brought out by the following sets of contrastive examples:

(5-136) a. m-n   yua-n-tɨ-k-nan
         NR DIST-I SG   good-I SG-do/feel-IRR-OBL
         ant-ka-na-arp-mpi-awt-ɲc-ak
         POT-1SG A-DEF-help-SEQ-get-PRES-SG
         'If he is (a) good (man), I can help him.'

       b. ŋarŋ   m-ŋa-na-arp-mpi-awl-
          1 day removed   NR DIST-1SG O-DEF-help-SEQ-get-

          kia-nt-mp-n   mnta
          NR FUT-PRES-VII SG-OBL   then

          ka-mpan-arp-mpi-   awl-kt   urakrŋ
          LIKE-1A/2SG O-help-SEQ- get-RM FUT   2 days removed
          'If you help me tomorrow, I'll help you the day after
          tomorrow.'

In the first example, the act of helping is a potential response to the man's good character, but there is no commitment to this, so *ant-* POT is proper in the second clause here. However, the act of one man helping another sets up a reciprocal obligation which within Yimas social customs would be extremely difficult to ignore. Therefore, the act of helping in the second clause in (5-136b) is a highly likely event, given the conditions of the first clause, so that *ka-* LIKE is proper here.

(5-137) a. tawra   kantk-bn   anak
         money IX SG   with-I SG   COP I SG
         kantá anan-wa-n
         but   POT 3SG S-go-PRES
         'He has money, but he isn't going.'

    b. tawra   kantk-n   anak   ka-n-wa-n
       money IX SG with-I SG COP I SG LIKE-3SG S-go-PRES
       'He has money, and he will go.'

In both examples of (5-137), the first clause sets up the condition of having money, and the second predicates the act of going in relation to that condition. The potential prefix has the unmarked reading of a possible event, but one which in the normal course of events will not occur. Hence the presence of the negative in the English translation of (5-136a), not present in the original. The potential prefix *ant-* breaks the expectation of the normal relation between the two clauses. Note the conjunction *kanta* 'but' which informants required here. The likely prefix has none of these negative expectations; it simply indicates that the event of the second clause is a probable event, given the conditions of the first clause.

    Perhaps the most common usage of the likely modal prefix is to form a kind of indirect imperative, an injunction. This construction combines *ka-* LIKE with the imperative/hortative suffix *-n* ~ *-na* (see Section 5.2.3.1) to mean 'let Y do Y'. X must be a third person participant.

(5-138) a. ka-n-pramu-n
          LIKE-3SG S-sleep-IMP
          'Let him sleep.'

       b. ka-n-pay-cmi-ɲa-mpwi
          LIKE-3SG A-first-say-IMP-talk
          'Let him talk first.'

       c. kntm
          body paint VII SG

          ka-mpu-pay-ma-takat-ɲa-mpan-m
          LIKE-3PL A-first-in-touch-IMP-3PL D-VII SG T
          'Let them first put body paint on them inside.'

       d. nmpi   ka-mpu-tra-ya-n
          leaf VII PL LIKE-3PL S-about-come-IMP
          'Let the letters get distributed.'

5.2.3 Mood

Mood is the verbal category which expresses the speech act value of an utterance, i.e., whether it is a statement, question, command, exhortation, wish, etc. The most common mood categories in Yimas, declarative and interrogative, are not morphologically marked. Statements, utterances in declarative mood, are indicated by a sharp final fall in intonation, while questions, the interrogative mood, have a corresponding rise.

(5-139) a.

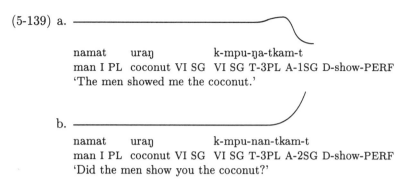

```
namat    uraŋ        k-mpu-ŋa-tkam-t
man I PL  coconut VI SG  VI SG T-3PL A-1SG D-show-PERF
'The men showed me the coconut.'
```

b.

```
namat    uraŋ        k-mpu-nan-tkam-t
man I PL  coconut VI SG  VI SG T-3PL A-2SG D-show-PERF
'Did the men show you the coconut?'
```

Questions can also be indicated by with the sentence final particle *a*, which is always pronounced with a high rising pitch:

(5-140)

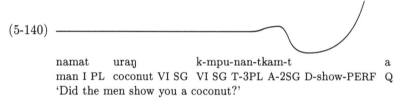

```
namat    uraŋ        k-mpu-nan-tkam-t              a
man I PL  coconut VI SG  VI SG T-3PL A-2SG D-show-PERF   Q
'Did the men show you a coconut?'
```

The other basic mood categories in Yimas, imperatives and hortatives are morphologically indicated by a verbal suffix.

5.2.3.1 Imperative Mood
Verbs in imperative mood are always associated with S or A arguments which are second person (semantically they are agents). The imperative mood always expresses a command which the speaker expects the addressee will carry out. The diagnostic inflections for imperatives are the imperative/hortative suffix -*n* (word-final position) alternating with ~ -*na* (elsewhere), plus one of a set of pronominal prefixes which marks the number of the addressee. If the addressee is singular, it is marked by ∅.

(5-141) a. mi   tak   wi-ŋka-pra-n
           2SG here up-go by land-toward-IMP
           'You come up here!'

       b. mi   ŋa-tput-mpa-n
           2SG 1SG O-hit-IMM-IMP
           'You hit me now!'

If the addressee is dual, the prefix is *naŋk*-.

(5-142) a. kapwa tak   naŋk-wi-ŋka-pra-n
           2DL   here IMP DL-up-go by land-toward-IMP
           'You two come up here!'

b. kapwa naŋk-ŋa-ŋa-mpa-n
   2DL   IMP DL-1SG D-give-IMM-IMP
   'You two give (it) to me now!'

If the addressee is plural the corresponding imperative prefix is *naŋ-* ~ *na-* (the latter before /ŋ/ and optionally before /k/). The final nasal of *naŋ-* occasionally assimilates to a following consonant, so the prefix is realized as *nam-* or *nan-*.

(5-143) a. ipwa tak   naŋ-wi-ŋka-pra-n
            2PL   here   IMP PL-up-go by land-toward-IMP
            'You all come up here!'

       b. ipwa na-ŋa-ŋa-mpa-n
            2PL   IMP PL-1SG D-give-IMM-IMP
            'You all give (it) to me now!'

A paucal addressee is expressed in the same way as a plural one, but with the addition of the paucal suffix.

(5-144) a. paŋkt tak   naŋ-wi-ŋka-pra-na-ŋkt
            2PC   here   IMP PL-up-go by land-toward-IMP-PC
            'You few come up here!'

       b. paŋkt na-ŋa-ŋa-mpa-na-ŋkt
            2PC   IMP PL-1SG D-give-IMM-IMP-PC
            'You few give (it) to me now!'

The prefix forms are found unless there is a following O or D pronominal prefix which is first person non-singular. In these cases all number distinctions are lost, and the addressee is invariably realized by *na-* ~ *ŋa-* (in free variation, but the latter seems favored by *ŋa-* 'give' and by older speakers; the form in /n/ is probably an innovation from *ŋa-* by the diachronic development of the loss of initial /ŋ/, discussed in Section 2.1.1). This is probably the result of neutralization to the plural imperative prefix *naŋ-*, and may reflect a politeness phenomenon.

(5-145) a. mi   na/ŋa-ŋkra-tput-mpa-n
            2SG   IMP-1DL O-hit-IMM-PRES
            'You hit us few now!'

       b. kapwa na/ŋa-kra-ŋa-mpa-na-ŋkt
            2DL   IMP 1-1PL D-give-IMM-IMP-PC
            'You two give (it) to us few now!'

       c. ipwa na/ŋa-kra-tput-mpa-na-ŋkt
            2PL   IMP-1PL O-hit-IMM-IMP-PC
            'You all hit us few now!'

    d. paŋkt na/ŋa-ŋkra-ŋa-n
       2PC   IMP-1DL D-give-IMP
       'You few give (it) to us two!'

It is necessary to note that an imperative verb can only carry one paucal suffix. If both the addressee and the first person O are paucal, then the paucal suffix applies to the latter and an independent paucal pronoun for the addressee must be used.

(5-146) a. paŋkt ŋa-kra-tput-ɲa-ŋkt
       2PC   IMP 1-1PL O-hit-IMP-PC
       'You few hit us few now!'

    b.*ŋa-kra-tput-ɲa-ŋkan-ŋkt
       IMP 1-2PL O-hit-IMP-PC-PC

The allomorph ŋa- is also an alternative to the normal non-singular imperative prefixes when the following pronominal prefix is first singular. Compare the following with the (b) examples in (5-142) through (5-144):

(5-147) a. kapwa ŋa-ŋa-tput-mpa-n
       2DL   IMP-1SG O-hit-IMM-IMP
       'You two hit me now!'

    b. ipwa ŋa-ŋa-ŋa-mpa-n
       2PL   IMP-1SG D-give-IMM-IMP
       'You all give (it) to me now!'

    c. paŋkt ŋa-ŋa-ŋa-mpa-na-ŋkt
       2PC   IMP-1SG D-give-IMM-IMP-PC
       'You few give (it) to me now!'

This, however, does not apply to a singular addressee. It is always realized by ∅, so that the following is ungrammatical (compare with 5-141b):

(5-148)*mi   ŋa-ŋa-tput-mpa-n
       2SG IMP-1SG O-hit-IMM-IMP

So far I have considered imperative verbs which are formally intransitive, i.e., with just an imperative addressee number prefix, or formally transitive, but with only first person O or D participants. It is now necessary to turn to transitive and ditransitive verbs with third person participants. These exhibit some of the more complex structural properties of verbs inflected with *ta-* NEG or *ant-* POT. This may result from the fact that these prefixes all occur in the first prefix slot of the verb and thereby usurp the position for one of the pronominal prefixes (although this explanation is somewhat weakened by the contradictory behavior of *ka-* LIKE). The suffixes which indicate the O of transitive imperative verbs are the same as those used with the modally inflected verbs: the negative number suffixes for human or higher animates and the normal adjectival/ possessive concord suffixes for inanimates.

(5-149) a. awt naŋ-ampu-na-wt
            five IMP PL-burn-IMP-fire O
            'You all light the fire!'

        b. m-uŋ   pay-nŋkrupt-ɲa-uŋ
            NR DIST-X SG first-swallow-IMP-X SG O
            'You swallow that (food) first!'

        c. naŋk-tmi-mpa-na-mpwi
            IMP DL-talk-IMM-IMP-talk O
            'You two talk now!'

        d. kay   naŋ-l-arm-na-ŋkan-i
            canoe VIII SG IMP PL-down-board-IMP-PC-VIII SG O
            'You few board the canoe down below!'

        e. paŋkt naŋ-tput-mpa-na-ŋkan-um
            2PC   IMP PL-hit-IMM-IMP-PC-3PL O
            'You few hit them now!'

        f. nampt   tak   naŋ-wark-na-ra
            house PL   here IMP PL-build-IMP-house PL O
            'You all build houses here!'

The only exception is third person human or higher animate O participants, for which the suffix is -*ak* rather than the expected -*nak*.

(5-150) a. na-ŋa-na-k
            IMP PL-give-IMP-3SG D
            'You all give (it) to him!'

        b. naŋ-tput-mpa-na-ŋkan-ak
            IMP PL-hit-IMM-IMP-PC-3SG O
            'You few hit him now!'

Ditransitive imperative verbs with third person D participants are formed in a similar way. They employ the non-final forms of the dative suffixes because these are followed by the suffixes indicating the theme.

(5-151) a. i-mpa-na-k-mpwi
            tell-IMM-IMP-3SG D-talk T
            'You tell him now!'

        b. i-ɲa-mpan-mpwi
            tell-IMP-3PL D-talk T
            'You tell them!'

        c. na-ŋa-mpa-na-ŋkan-mpan-ra   amtra
            IMP PL-give-IMM-IMP-PC-3PL D-V PL T food V PL
            'You few give them all food now!'

Imperatives are often found with the suffix -*kia*. This commonly indicates an imperative speech act performed at night. But in narrative texts using -*kia* to indicate closer rather than remote events, it is often present in reported direct speech, regardless of the time of day at which the original speech was uttered.

(5-152) naŋ-l-cu-kia-na-k
IMP PL-down-kill-NEAR-IMP-3SG O
'You all kill it down below!'

The original imperative speech act reported in (5-151) was uttered during the day, in mid afternoon, without -*kia*. However, as presented in (5-151), it occurred as reported direct speech in a narrative text describing events which took place a few days previously. The entire text is narrated in the far past rather than remote past, with the tense suffix -*kiantut* FR PAST. Therefore the -*kia* is present in this imperative to mark its closeness to the present as one of the events of the narrative. If the imperative suffix should occur word-finally, it is not realized as the expected -*n* after -*kia*, but instead the irrealis suffix -*k* is found.

(5-153) naŋ-ya-ka-l-ŋka-pu-kia-k
IMP PL-come-SEQ-down-go by land-away-NEAR-IRR
'You two come and go down!'

5.2.3.2 Hortative Mood

The inflection for hortative mood expresses speech acts along a range from true exhortations (e.g., 'let me/us go') to a strong wish to perform an action (e.g., 'I/we want to go). The hortative mood is formed with the same suffix as imperatives, -*n* ~ -*na* IMP, but with a distinct set of hortative pronominal prefixes. Other than this distinct set of prefixes, the formation of hortatives is identical to imperatives. Hortatives are restricted to first person, i.e., the performer of the speech act must at least be a co-performer of the desired act. A similar construction with third person participants is formed with *ka*- LIKE plus -*n* ~ -*na* IMP (see Section 5.2.2.3). The hortative and imperative prefixes are contrasted below:

	IMP	HORT
SG	Ø	anta-
DL	naŋk-	aŋka-
PL	naŋ-	ay-

Some examples of hortative constructions with each of these prefixes follow:

(5-154) a. anta-kntŋaca-kia-na-k
         HORT SG-scare-NIGHT-IMP-3SG O
         'I want to scare him.'
         'Let me scare him.'

      b. wara-t-nti   anta-tɨ-kra-kia-na-ŋ
         what-NFN-act   HORT SG-do-cut-NIGHT-IMP-VI SG O
         'How would I cut it (a rope)?'

      c. anta-pay-wi-ŋka-pu-kia-k   nam-n
         HORT SG-first-up-go by land-away-NEAR-IRR   house-OBL
         'Let me first go up to the house.'

      d. ŋaykum   pu-k   aŋka-pay-cay-ɲa-m
         woman II PL   II PL-PROX   HORT DL-first-see-IMP-3PL O
         'Let us two look at these women first.'

      e. yaɲi   aŋka-pay-tay-kia-na-y
         clay pot VIII SG   HORT DL-first-see-NIGHT-IMP-VIII SG O
         'Let us two first look in the clay pot.'

      f. wut   ay-iranta-irm-kia-k
         night   HORT PL-dance(RED: ira-)-stand-NIGHT-IRR
         'Let us dance tonight.'

      g. awt   ay-ampu-na-wt
         fire   HORT PL-burn-IMP-fire O
         'Let us light a fire.'

For paucal number, the hortative is formed in the usual way, with *ay-*
HORT PL and *-ŋkt* ~ *-ŋkan* PC.

(5-155) a. nmpi   ay-cra-wampak-ɲa-ŋkan-ra
         leaf VII PL   HORT PL-about-throw-IMP-PC-VII PL O
         'Let us few distribute letters.'

      b. awt   ay-ampu-kia-na-ŋkt
         fire   HORT PL-burn-NIGHT-IMP-PC
         'Let us few light a fire.'

The hortative prefix may be followed by a pronominal prefix for
a second person O or D participant, which must be non-singular. As
with the parallel case of imperatives followed by first person O or D
pronominal prefixes, all contrasts of number are lost in the hortative
prefix. But in this case it is the singular hortative, realized as *ant-*,
which generalizes to cover all cases.

(5-156) a. kapa   ant-kul-tput-n
         1DL   HORT-2PL O-hit-IMP
         'Let us two hit you all.'

   b. ipa   patn   ant-ŋkul-ŋa-n
      1PL   betelnut V SG   HORT-2DL D-give-IMP
      'We want to give you both betelnut.'
      'Let us give you both betelnut.'

If the O or D participant is second singular, the portmanteau prefix
ampan- HORT 1A/2SG is the hortative. This is clearly closely related
to the general portmanteau prefix *kampan-* ∼ *mpan-* 1A/2SG.

(5-157) a. kapa   ampan-pay-wut-mpi-ŋa-kia-k
           1DL   HORT 1A/2SG D-first-boil-SEQ-give-NEAR-IRR
           'Let us two first boil and give (them) to you.'

       b. tpuk
          sago pancake X SG

          ampan-pay-caŋ-wura-na-uŋ
          HORT 1A/2SG D-first-COM-get-IMP-X SG T
          'Let me first get a sago pancake for you.'

5.2.3.3 Negative Imperatives and Hortatives

Given the morphological complexity which we have seen associated with
both negatives and imperatives, we might approach the category of negative imperatives with some trepidation. But here, in fact, the language
surprises us, for negative imperatives are quite simply formed. There
are two ways to do so: one, traditional, associated mostly with older
speakers above 40, and a second, innovative, used by younger speakers.
The latter is the simpler and is formed by simply placing *pack* 'don't!'
following a verb inflected with the irrealis suffix. The verb has the same
form as a desiderative (see Section 5.2.1.1) and prohibits any pronominal
affixes.

(5-158) a. mi   yaki   am-ŋ   pack
           2SG   tobacco V PL   consume-IRR   don't
           'Don't smoke!'

       b. ma-mpwi   tmi-k   pack·
          other-talk talk-IRR don't
          'Don't talk any more!'

   The older, traditional way of forming negative imperatives shows
greater similarity to negative constructions than imperatives. The main
difference between an ordinary negative verb and a negative imperative
is the presence of *apu-* NEG IMP in the place of *ta-* NEG. The imperative addressee number prefixes are not used, but rather the normal
pronominal prefixes for second person A/S participants, as in negative
verbs. The only exception is second singular in which the prefix is ∅
like singular imperatives generally. The imperative suffix *-n* ∼ *-na* is

not used with negative imperatives, but is replaced by -*nt* PRES. Third
person O and D participants are referenced by the same suffixes found
in negative verbs and positive imperatives.

(5-159) a. apu-tmi-nc-mpwi   ma-mpwi
           NEG IMP-talk-PRES-talk O other-talk
           'Don't talk any more!'

        b. kapwa apu-ŋkra-kra-nt-ra   yara
           2DL   NEG IMP-2DL A-cut-PRES-V PL O tree V PL
           'Don't you two cut the wood!'

        c. paŋkt apu-nan-kra-nt-ŋkan-ra   yara
           2PC   NEG IMP-2PL A-cut-PRES-PC-V PL O tree V PL
           'Don't you few cut the wood!'

Negative hortatives are only formed with constructions using *pack*
'don't'. There is no parallel to *apu*-.

(5-160) a. ama yaki   am-ŋ   pack
           1SG tobacco V PL consume-IRR don't
           'I don't want to smoke.'
           'Let me not smoke.'

        b. ipa yara   kra-k   pack
           1PL tree V PL   cut-IRR   don't
           'Let's not cut the wood.'

6

The Verb Theme and Clause Structure

6.1 Yimas as a Polysynthetic Language

In this chapter and the next I will deal with what might be called the 'syntax' of Yimas. I put this word in quotes because to a very great extent Yimas lacks the features that we take as diagnostic of syntax in the more familiar languages of Western Europe. Other than the minimal noun phrase discussed in Section 4.6, the syntactic landscape of Yimas strikes a speaker of a western European language as very alien territory indeed, presenting very few analogues to the syntactic constituents we have come to expect.

Like many Amerindian languages, Yimas may be described as polysynthetic. Boas (1911, 74) defined this feature as follows: "a large number of distinct ideas are amalgamated by grammatical processes and form a single word, without any morphological distinction between the formal elements in the sentence and the contents of the sentence." In other words, a word (especially a verbal word) in a polysynthetic language corresponds in the range of distinct ideas expressed in it to what is articulated by a sentence in more familiar languages. To see how this applies to Yimas, consider the following examples (the square brackets indicate the structural level of verb theme, which will be defined later):

(6-1) a. ka-mpu-[pay-ma-takat]-ɲa-mpan-m
LIKE-3PL A-first-in-touch-IMP-3PL D-VII SG T
'Let them first put it (body paint) on them inside.'

b. ya-mpu-[nanaŋ-tacay-ckam]-tuk-mpun
V PL O-3PL A-DUR-see(RED: *tay-*)-show-RM PAST-3PL D
'They were showing those very carefully to them.'

    c. ta-ŋkl-[mampi-tay-mpi-waraca]-k-nak
       NEG-3PC A-again-see-SEQ-return-IRR-3SG
       'Again those few did not see her nor come back.'

    d. paŋkra-[kaykaykay-kwalca-mpi-kulanaŋ-tal]-kia-ntu-ŋkt
       1PC S-quickly-rise-SEQ-walk-start-NIGHT-RM PAST-PC
       'We few got up and quickly started to walk.'

    e. na-n-[mampi-taŋ-tal-kulanaŋ]
       3SG O-3SG A-again-COM-CAUS-walk
       'He made him walk with him again.'

All of these examples constitute single words, yet are translated by sentences in English, in some cases (6-1c,d) by quite complex sentences. That these are single words is clearly supported by a number of facts. First, these sequences are fully coherent and are not interruptible. For example, no word or phrase can come between *kwalca-mpi* arise-SEQ and *kulanaŋ* walk in (6-1d), in spite of the fact that, from the English point of view these would seem to be separate words. Note that in the English translation, the adverb *quickly* occurs between these two verbs; this is not possible in the Yimas form.

Second, the verbal morphology discussed in detail in Chapter 5 applies to these verbal forms as a whole, not individually. Note that the tense suffixes in the above forms occur only once, following the last verb root. Further, the pronominal affixes which mark the core arguments have scope over the whole complex. Thus, in (6-1b) the O and A arguments are indicated by the initial prefixes and the D argument by the final suffix. In (6-1c) the A argument is marked by the second prefix *ŋkl-* 3PC A (immediately following *ta-* NEG), and the O argument by the final suffix *-nak* 3SG. In the corresponding positive sentence, of course, both the A and the O would be indicated by prefixes. Perhaps the most striking case is the long example in (6-1d). Here the S argument is expressed by the initial prefix *paŋkra-* 1PC S, and its number is again referenced by the final suffix *-ŋkt* PC, eight morphemes away!

Third, the ordering of morphemes within these complexes is rigid. For example, in (6-1a,e) any ordering of morphemes other than that given will result in ungrammatical forms. In a very few cases alternative orderings are possible, but with no appreciable difference in meaning.

(6-2) a. na-n-way-mpi-ira-ya-ntut
       3SG O-3SG A-turn-SEQ-ALL-come-RM PAST

     b. na-n-ira-way-mpi-ya-ntut
       3SG O-3SG A-ALL-turn-SEQ-come-RM PAST
       'He turned back and came toward her.'

These sentences are nearly synonymous, and both are regarded as grammatical by native speakers. (There may be a subtle semantic difference between them equivalent to 'He turned and came toward her' (6-2a) versus 'He turned toward her and came (toward her)' (6-2b), but all speakers queried regarded them as practically equivalent. Note that while the two English sentences above have different structures and might be said to have different meanings, they clearly can denote the same event.) The formal difference between the two examples in (6-2) concerns the placement of the allative valence increasing prefix *ira-* 'toward, because of' (see Section 6.2.3.3.3). It is this prefix which sanctions the O prefix *na-* 3SG O for this complex which only contains two intransitive verbs, *way-* 'turn' and *ya-* 'come'. Note that regardless of whether *ira-* ALL is placed immediately before *ya-* (6-3a) or precedes both verb roots (6-3b), it still licenses the appearance of *na-* 3SG O at the beginning of the whole verb, demonstrating its integrity as a single grammatical word.

A final argument in favor of the analysis of the complex expressions in (6-1) as single words concerns the behavior of modifying forms such as those for aspect, modality, and mood. Note that the aspectual marker *nanaŋ-* DUR modifies both verbs in (6-1b), as does the negative prefix in (6-1c). This latter does not mean *'again those few did not see her, but they again came back'. This principle also applies to the scope of *mampi* 'again' in this example: it modifies both verbs. In the text from which (6-1c) is drawn, the expression describes the second time in which someone who has fallen out of a canoe is ignored and the people paddled on. Thus, the intended interpretation: "Again those few did not see her and again those few did not come back (for her)."

These arguments establish fairly conclusively that the constructions in (6-1) are best analyzed as single words. Thus, Yimas is a polysynthetic language. There is a very strong tendency throughout Yimas grammar to reduce complex expressions to single words, as befits its polysynthetic status. In the above examples, clauses and even complex sentences are realized as single words. This tendency also finds articulation in the system of nominals, discussed in Sections 4.4 and 4.6. As pointed out, Yimas productively forms compounds with two nouns, the head noun to the right and the other suffixed with the oblique suffix -*n* ∼ -*nan*.

(6-3) a. num-n   numpram
          village-OBL pig III SG
          'a domesticated pig'

       b. pŋkmp-n   yaw
          guts-OBL   road IX SG
          'intestines'

    c. turuk-n   namarawt
       magic X SG-OBL person I SG
       'magician'
    d. purkmp-n   yaw
       bladder VI SG-OBL road IX SG
       'urethra'

These nominal compounds are further examples of this polysynthetic tendency to reduce complex expressions to single words. That these form single words is indicated by the fact that they may serve as the head of possessive constructions,

(6-4) [ama-na   [num-un   numpram]]
     1SG-POSS village-OBL pig III SG
     'my domesticated pig'

while true noun phrases may not.

(6-5) *[ama-na   [kpa [numpran]]]
     1SG-POSS big pig III SG

These same constraints apply to the tightly knit noun phrases consisting of a modifier plus a noun discussed in Section 4.6. In many ways these too behave as single words. For example, the oblique suffix may occur only once, on the head noun,

(6-6) a. [ma   kay]-ɲan
       other canoe VIII SG-OBL
       'in another canoe'
    b.*ma-nan   kay-ɲan
       other-OBL canoe VIII SG-OBL

while in the loose, scrambling type of nominal constituents, it may occur on both modifier and noun.

(6-7) kay-ɲan   ma-y-ɲan
     canoe VIII SG-OBL other-VIII SG-OBL
     'in another canoe.'

The moral of this discussion of Yimas as a polysynthetic language is that Yimas is one language in which the distinction between the grammatical levels of word and phrase is hazy at best and perhaps nonexistent. (In the next chapter we shall see that a similar haziness applies to the border between clause and sentence.) Basically, it is the genius of Yimas to employ many grammatical devices in a conspiracy to reduce phrase-level units to word-level ones. This is closely related to the fact that Yimas is syntactically a very flat language (see Hale 1983; Blake 1983): that is, the basic relations in Yimas syntactic constructions are syntagmatic, forms following forms in linear sequence, rather than in a

hierarchical arrangement. We shall see many examples of this property
in the next two chapters. One of the results of this resistance to hierarchy is that phrase-level structures are formally rather like words. Thus,
instead of [black[dog]], in which the hierarchical structure is indicated by
the level of bracketing, the Yimas equivalent is rather more like [black-
dog], in which the components are syntagmatically related on the same
level.

Returning now to the examples in (6-1), it will be noted that I have
marked off a sequence of morphemes in each example by enclosing them
within brackets. This simply sets off the verbal morphology discussed
in the previous chapter from the rest of the verb whose structure will
be discussed in this chapter. A verb is made up of the basic verbal
morphology already presented, which corresponds to the *verb periphery*
and what I will term the *verb theme*. Verb themes may themselves be
complex, composed at least of one verb stem plus a set of optional verbal
affixes and incorporated adverbials. For example, in (6-1a) the verb
theme is composed of the verb stem *takat-* 'touch' plus the prefixes *pay-*
'first' and *ma-* 'in'. The verb theme of (6-1c) is composed of two verb
stems *taympi-* 'see' and *waraca-* 'return' plus the incorporated adverbial
mampi- 'again'. A verb stem is in turn composed of no more than one
verb root plus optional derivational affixes. In (6-1e), the verb stem is
composed of the verb root *kulanaŋ* 'walk' and the derivational affixes
taŋ- COM and *tal-* CAUS.

The last chapter dealt with the basic verbal morphology of pronominal affixes: tense, aspect, modality, and mood. These categories form the
basis of the verb periphery and correspond to the morphemes which occur outside the verb theme, those morphological categories which apply
to it as a whole. In this chapter ,I will be concerned with the morphology internal to the verb theme, that complex verbal morphology which
is particularly indicative of Yimas as a polysynthetic language. Because
this morphology is so complex, it is necessary to proceed from the basic
units and build up the morphological structure of the theme, brick by
brick. Thus, we start with the structure of the verb stem and its construction from a verb root and, more specifically, with the question of
the transitivity of Yimas verbs.

6.2 Stem Derivational Processes
6.2.1 The Concept of Transitivity
Yimas is a language in which it is very important to make a clear distinction between the syntactic-semantic notion of the valence of a verb
and the formal morphological idea of transitivity. Very often there is a
mismatch between these two concepts, much more so than in more fa-

miliar languages like English. In Yimas, transitivity is defined formally, by the number of overt pronominal affixes present: an intransitive verb has no more than one pronominal affix, a transitive verb has two, and a ditransitive verb has three. Valence, on the other hand, is a lexical feature of verbs, either basic verb roots or derived verb stems and verb themes. Verbs with one associated core argument are monovalent, those with two are bivalent and those with three are trivalent. Yimas neither allows verbs with more than three pronominal prefixes nor possesses verbs, either basic or derived, with more than three core arguments.

In English and many other languages, there is generally a straightforward correspondence between transitivity and valence: monovalent verbs are intransitive, bivalent verbs are transitive, and trivalent verbs are ditransitive. This is not always transparently so in Yimas. First of all, as pointed out in Section 5.1.6, overt pronominal affixes are not obligatory, but are linked to pragmatic functions like givenness, etc. Hence it is not unusual for a trivalent verb like ŋa- 'give' to appear as an intransitive or simple transitive verb, with only one or two pronominal prefixes.

(6-8) m-n   patn   ka-ŋa-ŋa-n
       NR DIST-I SG betelnut V SG LIKE-1SG D-give-PRES
       'He will give me betelnut.'

Or a bivalent verb like *wampaki* 'throw' can be used intransitively with only a single pronominal affix.

(6-9) nmpi   ay-cra-wampak-ɲa-ŋkt
       leaf VII PL HORT PL-around-throw-IMP-PC
       'Let us few distribute letters.'

Examples like these were discussed earlier in Section 5.1.6, and it was claimed there that they present cases of zero pronominal affixes. With this analysis, the valence and transitivity of these verbs are in a one-to-one correspondence; this is simply disguised by the zero pronominal prefixes. By virtue of the completeness constraint, zero pronominal prefixes are, of course, directly linked to core nominal arguments such as *patn* 'betelnut' or *nmpi* 'leaves', so that all argument slots of these verbs are in fact filled.

More problematic are common cases like those below, in which a verb is marked with more pronominal prefixes than are called for by its valence.

(6-10) a. ta-mp-ant-kia-k-nak-mpwi
          NEG-3 DL A-hear-NIGHT-IRR-3 SG D-talk T
          'Those two did not listen to her.'

b. yampaŋ   k-mpu-ŋa-kra-t
   head VI SG VI SG T-3 PL A-1SG D-cut-PERF
   'They cut my hair.'

The verbs *ant-* 'hear' and *kra-* 'cut' are bivalent, yet the constructions in which they occur are ditransitive, with three core arguments: A, T, and D participants. Note that in neither of these cases is there any valence increasing morphology which would license the extra core argument, although, as we shall see below, there are semantic conditions on when this is permitted (see Section 6.2.3.2). In any case, examples like those of (6-10) and, to a lesser extent, those in (6-9) demonstrate that the relationship between the valence of a verb and its transitivity is somewhat fluid in Yimas.

It is important to note further than the transitivity of a verb is properly a feature of the verb theme. Most commonly, the transitivity of the theme is equivalent simply to the valence of the verb stem with the highest valence index.

(6-11) a. marŋki
          leaf stem VII PL
          kia-ka-nanaŋ-kamal-kula-ntut
          VII PL O-1SG A-DUR-search-walk-RM PAST
          'I walked around looking for leaf stems.'
       b. nawkwantrm   kwarkwa
          chicken III DL today
          tma-mpɨ-ŋkra-na-wut-mpi-ŋa-kia-k
          III DL T-3 DL A-1DL D-DEF-boil-SEQ-give-NIGHT-IRR
          'Tonight those two will boil two chickens and give (them) to us two.'
       c. narm   p-mpu-tpul-kamprak-r-akn
          skin VII SG   VII SG T-3PL A-hit-break open-PERF-3SG D
          'They hit and cut his skin.'

In (6-11a), one verb root *kamal-* 'search' is bivalent while the other, *kula-* 'walk', is monovalent. The bivalent verb root licenses the whole verb theme to be inflected as transitive. (6-11b) again has two verb roots, the bivalent *wul-* 'boil' and the trivalent *ŋa-* 'give'. In this case the verb theme is ditransitive because of the trivalent verb root. Finally, (6-11c) contains two bivalent verb roots, *tpul-* 'hit' and *kamprak-* 'break open', yet the verb theme is formally a ditransitive verb, with three core arguments: A, T, and D. This possibility is sanctioned by the same principles that generated the examples in (6-10) (see the discussion of possessor-raising in Section 6.2.3.2), but note again that the three core arguments are a feature of the entire verb theme, not the individual verb roots.

6.2.2 Verb Stem Derivations: Reciprocal Formation and Valence Decreasing

Yimas has very little in the way of grammatical processes which decrease the valence of a verb. There is in fact only one productive grammatical process which may be viewed as resulting in the reduction of a verb's valence: namely, reciprocal formation. Verbs which are marked with the reciprocal affix are used to express actions in which two or more actors do the same action to each other, e.g., marry (each other), fight (hit each other), or converse (talk to each other). In Yimas, reciprocal verbs are marked by the prefix *ti*- which bears a transparent formal similarity to the verb root *ti*- 'do, feel, become' and may, in fact, be diachronically related to it. The prefix *ti*- RCP always occurs with verb roots which are minimally bivalent.

(6-12) a. m-mpɨ-t-ayk-kr-mp-n   mnta
        NR DIST-3DL S-RCP-marry-RM FUT-VII SG-OBL then

        impa-wa-kt   Madaŋ-nan
        3DL S-go-RM FUT   Madang-OBL

        'If those two get married, they will go to Madang.'

    b. impa-na-kwanan-tɨ-kratk-n
        3DL S-DEF-badly-RCP-fight-PRES
        'It's bad that those two are fighting.'

    c. ta-pu-tɨ-tpul-c-ŋkt
        NEG-3-RCP-hit-PERF-PC
        'Those few did not hit each other.'

    d. impa-na-tɨ-akpi-api-n
        3DL S-DEF-RCP-back V SG-put inside-PRES
        'They both are turning their backs to each other.'

    e. pia-mpɨ-tɨ-i-kia-k
        talk T-3DL A-RCP-tell-NIGHT-IRR
        'They both tell each other.'

The four verb roots in (6-12a–d) are bivalent, yet they may only occur with a single pronominal affix, i.e., they must be formally intransitive. It is in fact, ungrammatical to have two pronominal prefixes, in combination with *ti*-, as (6-13) demonstrates (compare with (6-12b)).

(6-13) *na-n-kwanan-tɨ-kratk-n
       3SG S-3SG A-badly-RCP-fight-PRES

(6-12e) is an example of a trivalent verb in a reciprocal construction. It has two agreement prefixes: a T, *pia-* 'talk' and an A, *mpi-* 3DL A. The missing pronominal affix is that which would express the dative. In the remarks below, for simplicity of exposition I will confine myself to bivalent verb roots, but the same claims apply as well to trivalent verbs; simply alter all the descriptive terms used below for bivalent verb roots to those applicable to trivalent verbs.

While clearly formally intransitive in allowing only one pronominal prefix, reciprocal verbs present a potential problem with respect to the formal status of *ti-* RCP: does this prefix simply stand in place of a core pronominal prefix, so that the verb stem still actually possesses two core argument slots, or does it truly reduce the valence of the verb, making it monovalent, associated only with a single core argument? The way to decide this question, of course, revolves around the role marked by the single pronominal prefix. If it is A or O, this argues that the verb is actually bivalent with only one core argument realized by the pronominal prefix and the other by the prefix *ti-* RCP. If the prefix is the S form, then this supports the claim that the verb is monovalent and occurs with a single core argument, indicated by the S prefix. Unfortunately, the examples above with third person participants are of no help in deciding this question, because as we saw in Chapter 5, the form of third person pronominal prefixes is often determined by linear order, and this relationship disguises their role marking. Rather, we need to consider examples in another person, such as in the following:

(6-14) a. ipa-ti-tpul
       1PL S-RCP-hit
       'We hit each other.'

    b. ipa-nanaŋ-ti-kankantakat-ɲcut
       1PL S-DUR-RCP-ask-RM PAST
       'We were asking each other.'

These examples argue for the second of our two alternatives, i.e., that *ti-* actually reduces the valence of the verb, deriving a monovalent verb stem from a bivalent verb root. In (6-14) the pronominal prefixes are the S forms. As this is the only permissible pronominal prefix, these verbs must be formally intransitive and hence monovalent, with a single core argument. Examples like those in (6-14) with reciprocalization of bivalent verbs, fail to provide evidence as to whether the A or the O is actually lost in the process of reciprocal formation, for there is only a single S prefix in the derived verb form. Trivalent verbs do provide such crucial evidence.

(6-15) a. pia-kay-cɨ-i-kia-k
            talk T-1PL A-RCP-tell-NIGHT-IRR
            'We tell each other.'
        b.*pia-kra-tɨ-i-kia-k
            talk T-1PL D-RCP-tell-NIGHT-IRR

Note that the A prefix form is found in the reciprocal derivative of a trivalent verb, and that the use of the D prefix results in an ungrammatical sentence. This indicates that it is the non-A participant which is suppressed in a reciprocal verb derivation. Looked at in another way, it is the non-A argument which is bound by the A, and not vice versa.

There is still another piece of evidence supporting the analysis of *tɨ*- RCP as a valence decreaser. Yimas has a productive system of nonfinite nominalization (see Section 7.1), and for these constructions, verbal pronominal affixes are entirely prohibited. But these nominalizations can be formed with a verb prefixed by *tɨ*- RCP.

(6-16) karmp-n   tɨ-i-c-mpwi   apiak
        vernacular-OBL   RCP-tell-NFN-talk   COP talk
        'There was talking among them in the vernacular.'

If *tɨ*- is analyzed as an pronominal prefix indicating coreference with a preceding prefix, examples like (6-16), in which there is no other permissible pronominal prefix, become hard to explain. On the other hand, if *tɨ*- RCP is simply a valence decreasing prefix, deriving a bivalent verb stem from the trivalent verb root *i*- 'tell', then (6-16) is unproblematical.

It is common cross-linguistically for reflexive constructions, in which a participant acts upon himself, to be formed in a very similar way to reciprocal constructions, in which two or more participants act upon each other. Yimas departs from this tendency, however, for reflexive and reciprocal constructions in this language actually have little in common. Yimas lacks any coherent way of forming reflexive constructions; a number of seemingly ad hoc devices express this notion. For example, a semantically reflexive verb may be monovalent, as with body action verbs like 'bathe' or 'shave' (as in English),

(6-17) a. na-na-awŋkcpa-n
            3SG S-DEF-bathe-PRES
            'He is bathing (himself).'
        b. ama-na-wantk-n
            1SG S-DEF-dress up-PRES
            'I'm getting dressed up.'

or a normally bivalent verb may be used intransitively, with no overt valence altering morpheme (again, as in English).

(6-18) na-kacakapi
        3SG S-hide
        'He hid (himself).'

Expressing a reflexive notion through intransitive verbs seems to be restricted to cases in which the whole person or body is affected by the action, as in the above examples. More common, perhaps, is the situation where the performer of the action acts upon a part of his body. In such cases, Yimas uses a noun to indicate the body part locus at which the participant acts upon himself, sometimes in association with a possessive complement. The possessor is always expressed by *m-* NR DIST, used as the so-called proximative pronoun, indicating coreference between the possessor of the body part and the performer of the action.

(6-19) a. narm   p-n-warapak-kia-k
           skin VII SG   VII SG O-3SG A-cut skin-NIGHT-IRR
           'She cut herself (her own skin).'

        b. yampaŋ   m-na-ŋ
           head VI SG   NR DIST-POSS-VI SG
           k-n-kra-t-akn
           VI SG O-3SG A-cut-PERF-3SG D
           'He gave himself a hair cut (cut his own hair).'

This is also the way a reflexive relationship between a performer of an action and the possessor of an object is expressed (so-called 'picture' reflexives).

(6-20) a. patn   m-na-kn   na-wayk-t
           betelnut V SG   NR DIST-POSS-V SG   3SG S-buy-PERF
           'He bought his own betelnut (e.g., for himself).'

        b. m-na-∅   na-na-tay-n   pikca
           NR DIST-POSS-IX SG   3SG S-DEF-see-PRES picture IX SG
           'She saw a picture of herself.'

The alert reader may be wondering how does one say 'He saw himself', because in this case there is no particular body part locus around which one can form the construction nor is the expression 'he saw' in a reflexive sense, permissible. The most traditional way to express this is shown below:

(6-21) aŋkaŋkaɲa   m-na-∅   arm-n
        shadow, spirit IX SG NR DIST-POSS-IX SG   water-OBL
        wa-n-tay
        IX SG O-3SG A-see
        'He saw his shadow, spirit in the water.'

In the traditional Yimas world, the only reflecting source was still water, so that (6-21) would be the most natural way to say 'he saw himself'. This is still largely true, for the word for mirror in Yimas is *arm* 'water'. An alternative is to use the empathic pronoun *panawt-(ɲan)* self-OBL discussed in Section 7.1.1.

(6-22) a. panawt-ɲan na-tay   (arm-n)
          self-OBL   3SG S-see (water-OBL)
          'He saw himself (in the water).'

       b. panawt-ɲan na-tu-t
          self-OBL   3SG S-kill-PERF
          'He killed himself.'

This form *panawt(ɲan)* has both contrastive and reflexive uses (see 7.1.1), but these examples only have the reflexive readings, e.g., 'he killed himself', not *'he himself killed him' (see Section 7.1.1). *panawt-ɲan* can only be used in constructions in which the reflexive action affects the whole body or person, not a sub-part of it (compare (6-22) with (6-19). Note that the verbs in these reflexive uses are formally intransitive; this is obligatory, so that the following transitive variants are ungrammatical.

(6-23) a.*panawt-ɲan na-n-tay
          self-OBL   3SG O-3SG A-see

       b.*panawt-ɲan na-n-tu-t
          self-OBL   3SG O-3SG A-kill-PERF

6.2.3 Verb Stem Derivations: Valence Increasing
In contrast to its system of valence decreasing, which is quite impoverished, Yimas has a very rich system of devices for increasing the valence of a verb root. These include causativization, which typically derives a bivalent accomplishment verb stem from a monovalent state, achievement, or activity verb root (Vendler 1967); possessor-raising, which under certain semantic conditions codes the possessor of a core S or O argument as the core D participant of the verb; and oblique promotion, which allows an otherwise adverbial or oblique constituent, marked with *-nan* ~ *-n*, to appear as a core argument of the verb and be indicated by an pronominal affix. I will discuss each of these types in some detail in the following sections.

6.2.3.1 Causativization
Causativization typically derives bivalent verb stems from verb roots which are monovalent. The monovalent verb roots fall into three different semantic classes: states (e.g., *sharp*, *heavy*); achievements, also

called processes (Chafe 1970) (e.g., *lose*, *break*); and activities (*climb*, *arise*). As we shall see, these various semantic types of monovalent verb roots behave differently under causativization. In addition, Yimas possesses three separate formal devices to express causativization: lexical, morphological (i.e., synthetic causatives), and syntactic (i.e., analytical causatives). As befits the status of Yimas as a polysynthetic language, the border between the latter two is rather hazy, so that "syntactic" may not be the best label to use for this last type of causative formation.

6.2.3.1.1 Lexical Causatives. In many languages, a monovalent verb and its corresponding bivalent causative may both be realized by separate lexical verb roots. This is true of some verbs in Yimas as it is in English (e.g., *die*: *kill*). Some examples in Yimas follow:

(6-24) a. na-*mal*
        3SG S-die
        'He died.'

      b. na-n-*tu*-t
        3SG O-3SG A-kill-PERF
        'He killed him.'

Other examples of this type of pairing in Yimas are given below:

	monovalent		*bivalent*
awa-	'burn'	ampu-	'burn'
awkawpc-	'boil'	tumpaŋ-	'boil'
wuray-	'crooked'	tapak-	'make crooked'
aypu-	'lie down'	tɨ-	'lay down'
irm-	'stand'	ta-	'stand up'

Also in this class is the one trivalent causative verb root in Yimas, *tkam*- 'show', and its corresponding non-causative bivalent verb root, *tay*- 'see' (see Foley and Van Valin 1984 on the semantic relationship between 'see' and 'show').

6.2.3.1.2 Non-productive Morphological Causatives. Monovalent achievement verbs enter into a non-productive morphological derivational process with their corresponding bivalent causative accomplishment verbs. The inchoative, the monovalent achievement verb, is marked with -*ara*, and the causative, the bivalent accomplishment verb, with -*aca*. This derivational pattern is no longer productive, rather like the English causative affix -*en*. Often, the verbal root does not occur without one of the derivational suffixes. Consider these examples:

(6-25) a. yan   na-kumprak-*ara*-t
      tree V SG V SG S-split-INCH-PERF
      'The tree split.' (say, along its base and fell over)

   b. yan   na-n-kumprak-*aca*-t
      tree V SG V SG O-3SG A-split-CAUS-PERF
      'He snapped the tree.' (with his hands)

(6-25a) illustrates the inchoative achievement verb stem with -*ara*, while (6-25b) illustrates its causative accomplishment counterpart with -*aca*. The verb in (6-25a) is monovalent and hence intransitive, while in (6-21b) it is bivalent and transitive.

   Interestingly, this is one of the verb roots which can occur without any of these derivational affixes (*kkrak*- 'loosen' and *kamprak*- 'snap' below are others).

(6-26) mi   tanm   ma-kumprak-t?
       2SG bone VII SG 2SG S-break-PERF
       'Did you break any bones?'

The verb in (6-26) is bivalent and causative, but conveys an implication that the event in question did not occur. Thus, the verb root contrasts with the derived form with causative -*aca* in that it is not so strongly completive, i.e., does not imply that accomplishment went through to a notable or successful conclusion.

   Other examples of verb stem pairs in -*ara* INCH and -*aca* CAUS are given below:

	inchoative	*causative*
'loosen'	kkrak-ara-	kkrak-aca-
'tear' (into pieces)	araŋ-ara-	araŋ-aca-
'break open' (along length)	tuak-ara-	tuak-aca-
'burst' (along length)	aplk-ara-	aplk-aca-
'snap' (like a rope)	kamprak-ara-	kamprak-aca-
'break up, open'	pak-ara-	pak-aca-
'open, spread'	apr-ata-	apr-aca-

Commonly, the verb root shows some variation in phonological form between the two stems.

	inchoative	*causative*
'bend'	yapwi-ara-	wapi-ca-
'turn on side'	kapwi-ara-	kap-aca-
'turn over'	taŋkawpi-ara-	taŋkawp-aca-
'stand up'	yamp-ara-	kamp-aca-
'slacken'	wurpi-ara-	wurp-aca-

Note that the inchoative stem in most cases ends in *-i*, which disappears in the causative stem, but there are also irregularities in the initial consonants of the forms for 'bend' and 'stand up'. As the root forms are not predictable they must be entered in the lexicon as variants of each other, depending on the derivational affix chosen.

6.2.3.1.3 Productive Morphological Causatives. The constructions to be treated here are those analogous to English causatives with *make* and *get* (e.g., *She made Ambrose wash the dishes*) in that they are formed using independent verb roots, notably *tal-* 'hold' and *tmi-* 'say'. In a causative construction, the latter is joined with other verb roots in a serial verb construction to form a complex verb theme (see Section 6.3.1 on serial verb constructions). But in its causative use, *tal-* 'hold' already seems to have been reanalyzed as a bound causative morpheme, for it appears in two allomorphs *tar-* ~ *tal-*, with the latter always occurring before /t/ and /y/ and varying freely with the former elsewhere (*tar-* ~ *tal-* contracts to *t-* before verb roots beginning in /ar/, as in *tar-* CAUS + *arpal-* 'exit' > *tarpal-* 'cause to go out').

As might be expected from the basic verb root meanings of *tar-* ~ *tal-* 'hold' and *tmi-* 'say', there is a correlated meaning contrast between them when they are used as causative morphemes. *tar-* ~ *tal-* marks direct causatives, the causing of an event by physically manipulating an object, while *tmi-* is used for indirect causatives, in which the event is brought about through speech, by verbal commands or requests. Consider the following contrast:

(6-27) a. na-ŋa-tar-kwalca-t
            3SG A-1SG O-CAUS-rise-PERF
            'She woke me up.'

        b. na-ŋa-tmi-kwalca-t
            3SG A-1SG O-CAUS-rise-PERF
            'She woke me up.'

While both (6-27a) and (6-27b) are translated as 'she woke me up', they do not actually denote the same event. (6-27a) denotes waking someone up by physical manipulation, say, by shaking, while (6-27b) indicates an event caused by a verbal act, say, by calling someone's name or by yelling. Other examples of causation through physical action, expressed by *tar-* ~ *tal-*, and causation through verbal action, indicated by *tmi-*, follow:

(6-28) Physical action: *tar-* ~ *tal-*
        a. awt tar-mat-ɲa-wt
           fire CAUS-die-IMP-fire O
           'Extinguish the fire!'

    b. yara   ya-mpu-na-tal-kaprapi-n
       tree V PL V PL O-3PL A-DEF-CAUS-collect-PRES
       'They are collecting wood.'

    c. kalakn   na-n-tal-iray
       boy I SG 3SG O-3SG A-CAUS-cry
       'He made the boy cry.' (by hitting him)

(6-29) Verbal action: *tmi-*

    a. kalakn   irpm-un
       boy I SG coconut palm IV SG-OBL

       na-mpu-tmi-wapal
       3SG O-3PL A-CAUS-climb

       'They made the boy climb the tree.'

    b. irwa   ŋaykum   na-mpu-tmi-ampa-t
       mat IX SG woman II PL 3SG O-3PL A-CAUS-weave-PERF
       'The women got her to weave a mat.'

    c. tpuk
       sago pancake X SG

       ku-ka-na-tmi-am-nt-akn
       X SG O-1SG A-DEF-CAUS-eat-PRES-3SG D

       'I made him eat a sago pancake.'

Examples (6-29b,c) are rare examples of bivalent verb roots being causativized. Bivalent verb roots can only be causativized with *tmi-* and even then only sporadically and with great difficulty. Normally, this is expressed by circumlocutions, using jussive complements (Section 7.1.2) like *I told him to eat sago*, or by a sequence of clauses, as in *the woman spoke to him and then he wove a mat* or *after the woman spoke to him, he wove a mat* (see Sections 7.2.3 and 7.3.2). Note that the causee (the performer of the caused event, e.g., 'him' in (6-29c)), is coded as a D participant if the verb contains three pronominal prefixes. Thus, it appears as -*akn* 3SG D in (6-29c) and *ŋa-* 1SG D in the following example:

(6-30) kpa-m   nma-mpu-ŋa-tmi-wark-t
       big-I PL house T-3PL A-1SG D-CAUS-build-PERF
       'The elders made me build a house.'

    Of two causative morphemes, *tar-* ~ *tal-* is clearly the unmarked one, for in unclear or underspecified cases this is the one employed. Consider this example:

(6-31) ama arm   tal-kwalca-k
       1SG water CAUS-rise-IRR
       'I will make the water rise.'

This example comes from a text in which a slain brother will make a flood come to drown the inhabitants of the village as revenge. This is done through magic, which requires both actions and words. Note that *tal-* is the morpheme used. It may also be possible to argue that events accomplished through magic are properly viewed as done by physical action, for, in the Yimas world view, magic is a force raised and brought to bear by a magician's skillful use of ritual. This force may operate through the intermediary of malevolent spirits raised by the magician.

So far I have presented bivalent causative accomplishment verb stems derived from monovalent achievement verb roots (examples in Section 6.2.3.1.2 and example (6-28a) above) and monovalent activity verb roots (examples in (6-27), (6-28b,c), (6-29a), and (6-31)). The only monovalent verb root class not yet treated is that of states. States belong to two different word classes in Yimas: verbs and the small closed class of true adjectives. Both may be causativized.

The true adjectives denote states in their basic root meaning. In order to be causativized, first inchoative forms are derived, which are in turn causativized with the causative prefix *tar-* ~ *tal-*. First, consider some examples of adjectives used as predicates, i.e., in equational sentences.

(6-32) a. maŋkaŋkl   kpa-ŋkl   aklak
arm VI DL big-VI DL COP VI DL
'(His) arms are big.'

b. kumpwi   yua-y   aykk
boy I PL good-I PL COP I PL
'The boys are good.'

These equational constructions are actually composed of two noun phrases, connected optionally by the copula. Note that the adjectives must be suffixed with the proper adjective agreement suffix, converting them to nominals (see Section 4.6).

Inchoative achievement verbs are derived from the true adjectives using the general verb *tɨ-* 'do, feel, become'. Contrast the following with the stative examples in (6-32):

(6-33) a. maŋkaŋkl   kla-kpa-ŋkl-tɨ-ntuk-nakn
arm VI DL VI DL S-big-VI PL-become-RM PAST-3SG D
'His arms became big.'

b. mpa kumpwi   i-ɲa-yua-y-cɨ-n
now   boy I PL I PL S-DEF-good-I PL-become-PRES
'Nowadays the boys are growing up well.'

Note that the adjective and *tɨ-* 'do, feel, become' together form a single verbal stem. The adjective continues to take the proper agreement suffix for the noun it modifies; hence this is properly a type of noun incorporation (see Section 6.2.5). The pronominal affixes and the tense/aspect/mood inflections are, as usual, affixes to the verb theme as a whole. It should be pointed out that incorporation of the adjective is not obligatory. Competing with the examples of (6-33) are (6-34) below:

(6-34) a. maŋkaŋkl   kpa-ŋkl   kla-tɨ-ntuk-nakn
           arms VI DL big-VI DL   VI DL S-become-RM PAST-3SG D
           'Their arms became big.'

       b. mpa kumpwi yua-y   i-ɲa-tɨ-n
          now boy I PL good-I PL I PL S-DEF-become-PRES
          'Nowadays the boys are growing up well.'

There is no discernible meaning difference between constructions with the incorporated nominalized adjective and those without.

When constructions such as those in (6-33) are in turn causativized, the causative prefix *tar-* ~ *tal-* is employed, but there are a few options as to its placement. The most common choice is to place it immediately before *tɨ-* 'become'.

(6-35) a. irpm
          coconut palm IV SG

          mu-ka-kpa-m-tal-cɨ-t
          IV SG O-1SG A-big-IV SG-CAUS-become-PERF
          'I grew the coconut palm to be big.'

       b. kumpwi i-kay-yua-y-cal-cɨ-t
          boy I PL I PL O-1PL A-good-I PL-CAUS-become-PERF
          'We raised the boys to be good.'

The prefix may also occur before the adjective (6-36a) or there may be two occurrences of it, one before the adjective and one before *tɨ-* 'become' (6-36b):

(6-36) a. irpm
          coconut palm IV SG

          mu-ka-tal-kpa-m-tɨ-t
          IV SG O-1SG A-CAUS-big-IV SG-become-PRES
          'I grew the coconut palm to be big.'

       b. irpm
          coconut palm IV SG

          mu-ka-tal-kpa-m-tal-cɨ-t
          IV SG O-1SG A-CAUS-big-IV SG-CAUS-become-PERF
          'I grew the coconut palm to be big.'

This last option is of questionable grammaticality, as it was obtained only in elicitation. I will say no more about it. The difference between (6-35a) and (6-36a) is in the order of derivation. In (6-35a) the causative derivation applies to the stem. The monovalent achievement verb root *ti-* 'become' is first derived to the bivalent causative verb stem by *tar-* ~ *tal-*, and this in turn is joined with the adjective as an incorporated nominal to form the final complex verb theme. This is in keeping with the general pattern of valence-altering devices in Yimas, which derive verb stems from verb roots. (6-36) has the opposite derivational order. First, the adjective derived as a nominal by the proper agreement suffix is joined with *ti-* 'become' to form a verb theme, which is a monovalent achievement predicate. This in turn is causativized by *tar-* ~ *tal-*. Both of the derivational paths are possible, although the first is strongly preferred by most speakers. This is because valence-increasing in this derivation applies at the level of the verb stem, rather than the verb theme, which is the preferred option for this construction in Yimas.

As with the inchoative examples in (6-34), incorporation of the nominalized adjective is not obligatory with these derived causatives. Hence, alternating with the examples in (6-35) and (6-36) we have the following:

(6-37) a. irpm   kpa-m
        coconut palm IV SG   big-IV SG
        mu-ka-tal-ci-t
        IV SG O-1SG A-CAUS-become-PERF
        'I grew the coconut palm to be big.'

     b. kumpwi   yua-y   i-kay-cal-ci-t
        boy I PL   good-I PL   I PL O-1PL A-CAUS-become-PERF
        'We raised the boys to be good.'

Again, there is no meaning difference between these examples without incorporation and the earlier ones with it.

Adjectival nouns such as *tark* 'coldness' and *tamana* 'sickness', used in association with *kantk-* 'with', form inchoatives and causatives in similar ways to true adjectives. The stative uses are also similar in that they commonly employ the copula.

(6-38) a. arm   tark   kantk-rm   aymak
        water   coldness   with-water   COP water
        'The water is cold.'

     b. tamana   kantk-n   amayak
        sickness IX SG   with-I SG   COP 1SG
        'I am sick.'

Note that *kantk-* 'with' is always suffixed with an adjectival agreement suffix for the nominal it modifies.

When these are converted to the corresponding achievement predications, the verb root *ti-* 'become' again appears.

(6-39) a. arm   tark   kantk-rm   ima-na-ti-n
water coldness with-water water S-DEF-become-PRES
'The water is getting cold.'

b. tamana   kantk-n   ama-na-ti-n
sickness IX SG with-I SG 1SG S-DEF-become-PRES
'I'm getting sick.' or 'I'm feeling sick.'

When the monovalent achievement predicates are finally converted to bivalent causatives, the prefix *tar-* ~ *tal-* is added, preceding *ti-*.

(6-40) a. arm   tark   kantk-rm
water coldness with-water

ima-ka-tal-ci-t
water O-1SG A-CAUS-become-PRES
'I made the water cold.'

b. naŋkun   tamana   kantk-n
mosquito V SG sickness IX SG with-I SG

na-ŋa-tal-ci-t
3SG A-1SG O-CAUS-become-PERF
'Mosquitoes made me sick.'

Causative constructions like those in (6-40) can also be formed with some monovalent activity verb roots, specifically, those denoting sounds emanating from the body. In such cases the verb root is nominalized by following it with the postposition *kantk-*.

(6-41) a. iray kantk-n   na-ka-tal-ci-t
cry with-I SG 3SG-1SG A-CAUS-become-PERF
'I made the woman cry.'

b. narmaŋ   panmal   kiaŋ   kantk-nmaŋ
woman II SG man I SG cough with-II SG

na-n-tal-ci-t
3SG O-3SG A-CAUS-become-PERF
'The man made the woman cough.'

The class of adjectival verbs diverges somewhat from true adjectives and adjectival nouns because they are normally monovalent achievement predicates in their root meaning. Thus, adjectival verbs like *urkpwica-* 'black', *wapi-* 'become sharp', and *tŋknt-* 'become heavy' can form inchoative constructions directly, without *ti-* 'become'.

(6-42) a. narm   p-na-urkpwica-n
          skin VII SG   VII SG-DEF-blacken-PRES
          'The skin is turning black.'

    b. wanwa   wa-na-wapi-n
          knife IX SG   IX SG S-DEF-become sharp-PRES
          'The knife is getting sharp.'

    c. kay   i-cŋknt-t   arm-n
          canoe VIII SG   VIII SG O-become heavy-PRES   water-OBL
          'The canoe got heavy from the water.'

The stative predications of these verb roots are none other than finite nominalizations (see Section 7.2.1). They use the irrealis suffix -*k* to indicate an event whose temporal extension is not bound (i.e., a state) and the proper adjectival agreement suffix for the noun modified (the optional copula is most commonly not used here).

(6-43) a. narm   urkpwica-k-m
          skin VII SG   blacken-IRR-VII SG
          'The skin is black.'

    b. wanwa   wapi-k-wa
          knife IX SG   become sharp-IRR-IX SG
          'The knife is sharp.'

    c. kay   tŋknt-k-i
          canoe VIII SG   become heavy-IRR-VIII SG
          aykk
          COP VIII SG VIS
          'The canoe is heavy.'

Interestingly, once these stative predicates are derived by nominalization, it is now possible to form new inchoative constructions with them as incorporated nouns linked to *tɨ*- 'become' in a complex verb theme (as elsewhere, the incorporation is optional).

(6-44) a. narm
          skin VII SG
          p-na-urkpwica-k-m-tɨ-n
          VII SG S-DEF-blacken-IRR-VII SG-become-PRES
          'The skin is turning black.'

    b. wanwa
          knife IX SG
          wa-na-wapi-k-wa-tɨ-n
          IX SG S-DEF-become sharp-IRR-IX SG-become-PERF
          'The knife is getting sharp.'

    c. kay
       canoe VIII SG

       i-cŋknt-k-i-ci̵-t
       VIII SG S-become heavy-IRR-VIII SG-become-PERF

       arm-n
       water-OBL

       'The canoe got heavy from the water.'

The two inchoative constructions for these adjectival verbs, exemplified
in (6-42) and (6-44), are largely synonymous, although the latter seems
to focus especially on the process and be slightly more compatible with
the imperfective aspect while the former looks more to the end state
and is more compatible with perfective. These are only weak tendencies,
though, and, as the above examples show, both aspectual inflections are
available for both constructions.

    Both inchoative construction types for these adjectival verbs may
be causativized to derive bivalent accomplishment predicates. If as
in (6-42) the monovalent achievement verb root itself is the starting
point of the derivation, then *tar-* ~ *tal-* is simply prefixed to the verb
root.

(6-45) a. ikn   antki
          smoke V SG thatch IV PL

          ya-n-tal-urkpwica-t
          IV PL O-3SG A-CAUS-blacken-PERF

          'The smoke blackened the roof.'

     b. wanwa   wa-ka-tar-wapi
        knife IX SG IX SG O-1SG A-CAUS-become sharp

        'I sharpened the knife.'

     c. arm   i-mpu-tal-cŋknt-t
       water VIII SG O-3PL A-CAUS-become heavy-PERF

       kay
       canoe VIII SG

       'The water made the canoe heavy.'

If, on the other hand, the starting point is the construction with the
incorporated nominalized verb joined with *ti̵-* 'become', the causative
derivation is exactly as with a true adjective: *tar-* ~ *tal-* precedes either
ti̵- 'become' or the incorporated nominal, or both, but with the first
choice again very strongly favored.

(6-46) a. tmal   narm
        sun V SG   skin VII SG

        p-n-urkpwica-k-m-tal-cɨ-t
        VII SG O-3SG A-blacken-IRR-VII SG-CAUS-become-PERF

        'The sun darkened my skin.'

     b. marasin   mamam
        medicine V SG   sore VII SG

        p-n-tar-waca-k-m-tɨ-t
        VII SG O-3SG A-CAUS-become small-IRR-VII SG-become-
                                                 PERF

        'The medicine healed the sore.'

     c. ŋaykum
        woman II PL

        i-mpu-tar-kamta-k-i-cal-cɨ-t
        VIII SG O-3PL A-CAUS-become clear-IRR-VIII SG-CAUS-
                                           become-PERF

        anti
        ground VIII SG

        'The women cleared the ground'

Again, incorporation is optional.

(6-47) patn   mama-k-n
        betelnut V SG   bad-IRR-V SG

        na-mpu-ŋa-taŋ-tal-cɨ-t
        3SG O-3PL A-1SG D-COM-CAUS-become-PERF

        'They ruined my betelnut.'

These two causative constructions for adjectival verb roots are synonymous. All speakers queried have explicitly stated this and have been unable to find any context which specifically favors one or the other. It should be pointed out, however, that the former construction, i.e., direct derivation from the root without *tɨ*-, is much more common and is favored by all speakers. The latter construction, i.e., causative derivation from a *tɨ*- derived inchoative, is only spontaneously encountered when the nominalized verb is not incorporated, as in (6-47).

A final point about syntactic causatives concerns the animacy of the causer. Whenever the causer is animate, a causative construction must be used, with the causer functioning as the A participant. However, when the causer is an inanimate object or force, far more common and natural is its appearance as an oblique nominal, with the verb in question being a monovalent inchoative predicate. Compare the following two examples (also note (6-42c) and (6-45c)).

(6-48) a. ikn   antki
          smoke V SG thatch IV PL

          ya-n-tal-urkpwica-t
          IV PL O-3SG A-CAUS-blacken-PERF
          'Smoke blackened the roof.'

     b. ikn-an   antki   ya-urkpwica-t
          smoke V SG-OBL thatch IV PL   IV PL S-blacken-PERF
          'The roof got blackened from the smoke.'

The Yimas alternation is very much parallel to that operative in English, as indicated in the corresponding English translations. The causative construction with the causing force functioning as A, attributes a strong, almost willful, responsibility to the cause in solely bringing about the effect of the roof's blackening. This is in keeping with the coding of the cause as A. On the other hand, the inchoative construction, in which the causing force appears as an oblique, has a somewhat weaker implication. It declares that the roof turned black, and that the reason for that was the smoke, but it does not attribute such a strong and direct responsibility to it, nor does it imply that it was the sole cause. Another example of this type of alternation follows:

(6-49) a. marasin   mamam
          medicine V SG sore VII SG

          p-n-tar-waca-k-m-ti-t
          VII SG O-3SG A-CAUS-become small-IRR-VII SG-become-
                                                               PERF

          'The medicine healed the sore.'

     b. marasin-an   mamam
          medicine V SG-OBL sore VII SG

          p-waca-k-m-ti-t
          VII SG O-become small-IRR-VII SG-become-PERF
          'The sore healed because of the medicine.'

6.2.3.2 Possessor Raising

Possessor raising is a common valence increasing process in Yimas, applicable to both monovalent and bivalent verbs. In possessor promotion constructions, the animate possessor of an absolutive core argument (S or O participant) is realized on its own as a core argument of the verb. It is always coded by a D participant affix. Other than this D pronominal affix, there is no overt indication on the verb; thus, unlike the other valence altering options, there is no specific morpheme to indicate a possessor raising derivation. Possessor raising also diverges from these other constructions in applying at the level of the verb theme, i.e., affecting the verb as a whole. This is the result of the absence of any overt derivational morphology signaling possessor raising. Because of this, there is no motivation for ascribing the derivation to any one verb stem in the verb theme. The other valence altering devices normally derive verbal stems from roots, which in turn can be combined to form a complex verb theme, although, as we have seen earlier and will see again below, there are examples of these applying at the level of the verb theme as well.

Possessor raising is basically restricted to body parts. When possessor raising applies to a monovalent verb, the S argument is realized by an S/O prefix form and the animate possessor by the D affix.

(6-50) a. ŋarwa   wa-ŋa-kwalca-t
         penis IX SG IX SG S-1SG D-rise-PERF
         'I have an erection.'

       b. pamuŋ   irmut
          leg VI SG   shame
          ta-pu-nan-a-ti-kia-nt-ŋ
          NEG-3-2SG D-DEF-feel-NIGHT-PRES-VI SG
          'Your leg has no shame.'

       c. maŋkaŋkl   kla-kpa-ŋkl-ci-ntuk-nakn
          arm VI DL   VI DL S-big-VI DL-become-RM PAST-3SG D
          'His arms have grown big.'

       d. narm   p-kra-nanaŋ-kacakapi-ɲcut
          skin VII SG VII SG S-1PL D-DUR-hide-RM PAST
          'Our skin is deteriorating.'

       e. wampuŋ   mama-k-n   na-ti-k-nakn
          heart V SG bad-IRR-V SG V SG S-feel-IRR-3SG D
          'His heart felt bad.' (i.e., he was angry)

When the base verb theme is bivalent, possessor promotion derives a trivalent verb in which the affected body part is realized by a T prefix and the possessor again by a D affix.

(6-51) a. yampaŋ   k-mpu-ŋa-kra-t
         head VI SG VI SG T-3PL A-1SG D-cut-PERF
         'They cut my hair.'

       b. maŋkaŋ   ka-mpan-kumprak-n
          arm VI SG   LIKE-1A/2SG D-split-PRES
          'I will break your arm!'

c. k-n-pay-mpi-tɨ-kia-k-nakn   yampaŋ
   VI SG T-3SG A-lie-SEQ-lay-NIGHT-IRR-3SG D head VI SG
   'He lay (there) and laid down his head.'
   (talking of a snake coiling up)

d. kikamtaŋ   pu-ŋa-kwanan-tay-kt
   armpit VI SG   3PL A-1SG D-badly-see-RM FUT
   'It's bad if they see my armpit(s).'

e. pŋkmp-n   yaw-n
   guts VII SG-OBL   road IX SG-OBL

   k-n-kaw-kaca-kia-ntuk-nakn
   VI SG T-3SG A-in-swing-NIGHT-RM PAST-3SG D

   muraŋ
   paddle VI SG
   'He swung his paddle down inside its (a crocodile's) guts.'

Note that in all these possessor raising constructions, the entity actually
affected is the possessor, not the body part: it is the possessor's nervous
system which registers the effect. The body part is merely the locus at
which the event occurs and thus is properly coded as the T participant.
The semantics of the T participant in possessor raising constructions
closely parallels that of the T participant of such prototypically trivalent
verbs as *tkam-* 'show' and *ŋa-* 'give' (on the semantics of the theme role
generally, see Foley and Van Valin 1984, Chapter 2). The D participant
of trivalent verbs, whether basic, as for *ŋa-* 'give', or derived, as in (6-51),
properly codes the entity primarily affected by the action.

There is an interesting minor extension of possessor raising beyond
body parts to entities generally residing on or near the skin, and perhaps
viewed as inalienably possessed much like body parts (6-52a,b), and also
to personal characteristics of a person like a name or a voice (6-52c).
Thus, the following are grammatical in Yimas:

(6-52) a. kuran   na-ka-tu-r-akn
          louse V SG   V SG T-1SG A-kill-PERF-3SG D
          'I killed his lice.' (on his own head)

       b. naŋkun   na-ka-tu-r-akn
          mosquito V SG V SG O-1SG A-kill-PERF-3SG D
          'I killed the mosquito on her.'

       c. ta-mpu-ant-kia-k-nak-mpwi
          NEG-3PL A-hear-NIGHT-IRR-3SG O-talk T
          'They didn't listen to her call.'

Treating mosquitoes and lice as body parts is a fascinating bit of ethnolinguistic data telling us something about the local living conditions and how they mold concepts of the body and its space!

6.2.3.3 Promotion to Core

There are six different morphemes which are used to code the core argument status of a constituent which would otherwise have to be an oblique noun phrase or appear in a separate clause. Each of these has a somewhat different semantic function, and most betray a rather close similarity to incorporated adverbials (see Section 6.3.2.1). At least two of them, in fact, must be analyzed as simultaneously an incorporated adverbial and a valence increasing prefix.

6.2.3.3.1 Comitative *taŋ-*.

Comitative participants are those which participate in an event as adjuncts together with its main performer and do so at the same place and in the same time, e.g., *John went with Mary*. In Yimas, comitative participants can be expressed in two ways: as nominals promoted to core argument status by the prefix *taŋ-* COM, or as oblique nominals marked by the postposition *kantk* 'with'.

(6-53) a. ma   ŋarŋ   ipa kantk pu-mampi-wa-k
         other 1 day removed 1PL with   3PL S-again-go-IRR
         'On another day, they went with us.'

      b. ma   ŋarŋ   pu-kra-mampi-taŋ-wa-k
         other 1 day removed 3PL A-1PL O-again-COM-go-IRR
         'On another day, they went with us.'

(6-54) a. impa-n   kantk na-kwalca-t
         I DL-FR DIST with   3SG S-rise-PERF
         'He got up with them both.'

      b. impa-n-taŋ-kwalca-t
         3DL O-3SG A-COM-rise-PERF
         'He got up with them both.'

(6-55) a. ama kantk pu-n-tar-kwalca-t
         1SG with   3PL O-3SG A-CAUS-rise-PERF
         'He woke them up along with me.'

      b. m-n   pu-ŋa-taŋ-tar-kwalca-t
         NR DIST-I SG 3PL O-1SG D-COM-CAUS-rise-PERF
         'He woke them up along with me.'

(6-56) a. ipa kantk ura-mpu-ntak-mpi-ɲa-ntut
         1PL with   IX PL O-3PL A-leave-SEQ-stay-RM PAST
         'They left those (pieces of coconut meat) with us.'

b. ura-mpu-kra-taŋ-ntak-mpi-ɲa-ntut
IX PL O-3PL A-1PL D-COM-leave-SEQ-stay-RM PAST
'They left those (pieces of coconut meat) with us.'

Both the (a) examples with *kantk* 'with' and the (b) examples with *taŋ*- are grammatical, but the latter are the more common and greatly preferred structure in all cases. This is in keeping with the general polysynthetic character of Yimas. Given the choice between coding an event as a clause or as a single word, the latter is generally chosen. There appear to be no meaning differences between these two encodings, beyond the fact that the (a) sentences are far more marked (i.e., much less likely to be uttered spontaneously in a discourse).

Promotion of nominals by *taŋ*- applies to both monovalent and bivalent verb roots, but not to trivalent ones, because Yimas never allows more than three core arguments to a verb. (6-53) and (6-54) illustrate promotion with *taŋ*- applying to monovalent verb roots. In the (a) examples of each, a pronominal appears as an oblique marked by the postposition *kantk* 'with'. In the (b) examples, these pronominals are now realized as core arguments, *kra*- 1PL O and *impa*- 3DL O, as sanctioned by the use of *taŋ*-. With derived bivalent verbs, the constituent promoted by *taŋ*- is always coded by the O prefix form.

Examples (6-55) and (6-56) illustrate bivalent verbs derived into trivalent ones by *taŋ*-. Again, in the (a) examples the pronominal is marked with the postposition *kantk* 'with', but in the (b) examples it is realized as a core argument through promotion by *taŋ*-. Note that with derived trivalent verbs the promoted argument appears in a dative affix form: *ŋa*- 1SG D and *kra*- 1PL D. (6-55b) represents a two step derivation. First, the monovalent activity verb root *kwalca*- 'rise' is derived into a bivalent accomplishment causative verb stem by *tar*- ~ *tal*- CAUS. This stem is then subject to derivation by *taŋ*- COM, which converts it to a trivalent verb stem, licensing the appearance of *ŋa*- 1SG D as a core argument. The ordering of the two prefixes in (6-55b) is free; altering the sequence results in a grammatical sentence with exactly the same meaning.

(6-57) m-n   pu-ŋa-tar-taŋ-kwalca-t
NR DIST-ISG 3PL A-1SG D-CAUS-COM-rise-PERF
'He woke them up along with me.'

(6-56) illustrates *taŋ*- promotion applying at the level of the verb theme. The verb theme here is complex, made up of two verb stems: *ntak*-(*mpi*-) 'leave, abandon' and *naŋ*- 'stay, live' (the final nasal of the stem disappears by nasal truncation). The prefix *taŋ*- immediately precedes *ntak*- 'leave', but it cannot be claimed that it semantically modifies only this verb, for the wrong meaning would result: *'they along with us left those (pieces of coconut meat) which stayed'. Rather, it is clear that *taŋ*- semantically belongs with the second verb *naŋ*- 'stay': 'they left those (pieces of coconut meat), and those stayed with us'. The construction in (6-56b) is the result of applying *taŋ*- promotion at the level of the verb theme: it derives a trivalent verb theme from one which was bivalent, composed of the verb compound *ntak-mpi-naŋ* leave-SEQ-stay, i.e., 'deposit'. Other examples with *taŋ*- follow:

(6-58) a. na-mpan-na-taŋ-ntak-kia-k
            3 SG T-1A/2SG D-DEF-COM-leave-NR FUT-IRR
            'I am going to leave her with you.'

        b. m-n   pia-ŋa-taŋ-tmi
            NR DIST-I SG talk T-1SG D-COM-say
            'He talked with me.'

As pointed out in Section 4.5 and elsewhere, the relationship of possession is commonly predicated through the use of *kantk*- 'with' plus the copula. In such constructions, possession thus is viewed as a comitative relationship between the possessor and the possessed: they accompany each other, and are in the same place and time. This construction with *kantk*- 'with' is most commonly found with objects which may be viewed as alienably possessed, that is, in which the possessive relationship is not an essential, defining, and integral characteristic of possessor and possessed, but rather a relatively transitory and shallow relationship resulting from the vicissitudes of life events. The following are typical examples of alienable possession:

(6-59) a. arm   kantk-n   amyak?
            water   with-I SG   COP 2SG
            'Do you have kerosene?'

        b. tawra   kantk-mampan   aympak
            money IX SG   with-I DL   COP 3DL
            'Those two have money.'

Possession expressed through *kantk*- is also permitted (albeit rather rare) with nouns which are inalienably possessed, such as body parts, names, etc. For these nouns, possession is an essential, defining characteristic of their relation to their possessor, which is thereby a relatively permanent relationship. Examples of inalienably possessed nouns with *kantk*- follow:

(6-60) a. yampaŋ   kantk-n   amayak
            head VI SG   with-I SG   COP 1SG
            'I have a head.'

  b. pamkl kantk-mampan aympak
   leg VI DL with-I DL COP 3 DL
   'Those two have legs.'

  Possessed nominals marked with *kantk-* 'with' in the alienable posses-sion construction are alternatively realizable as core arguments through promotion by *taŋ-* COM. So the examples in (6-59) are paired with the following synonymous examples:

(6-61) a. arm ma-na-taŋ-taw-n?
     water 2SG S-DEF-COM-sit-PRES
     'Do you have kerosene?'

    b. tawra   impa-na-taŋ-taw-n?
     money IX SG 3DL S-DEF-COM-sit-PRES
     'Those two have money.'

taw- 'sit' is the general verb used in predications of possession using *taŋ-* COM. Unlike the (b) examples in (6-53) through (6-56), the exam-ples with *taŋ-* in (6-61) are not preferred over those with *kantk-* 'with' in (6-59). This may be a reflection of the nearly obligatory overt ap-pearance of the possessed noun in the possessive construction, rendering a single-word construction impossible. Possession with *taŋ-* COM in-stead of *kantk-* 'with' is not an available option for inalienably possessed nouns.

  In the previous section, I discussed possessor raising, in which the possessor of an inalienably possessed noun (a body part), could appear as the D participant of the verb, provided the noun was functioning as an S or O participant. *taŋ-* COM licenses an exactly analogous construction for alienably possessed nouns.

  Consider these examples:

(6-62) a. wampunŋ
     sago flour VI SG

     k-mpu-kra-taŋ-mntk-ntut
     VI SG T-3PL A-1PL D-COM-finish-RM PAST
     'They used up all our sago flour.'

    b. impram   p-ŋa-na-taŋ-tat-n
     basket VII SG VII SG T-1SG D-DEF-COM-hold-PRES
     'They seized my basket.'

    c. ma tmat-ɲan na-kay-taŋ-awkura-kr-mpun
     other day-OBL 3SG T-1PL A-COM-get-RM FUT-3PL D
     'Another day, we will get them it (a crocodile).'

d. patn   mama-k-n
   betelnut V SG bad-IRR-V SG
   na-ŋa-taŋ-tal-cɨ-t
   3SG A-1SG D-COM-CAUS-become-PERF
   'He ruined my betelnut.'

These constructions are parallel to the possessor raising constructions
with body parts in that the participant primarily affected by the action
is the animate possessor, coded by the D affix, not the possessed object
coded by the T affix. Further, there is a strong implication that the effect
will be negative (malefactive). This is because in these constructions,
the relationship between the possessor and possessed is terminated by
the action of the verb, with resultant loss or stress on the part of the
possessor. The background context for all the examples above drawn
from texts supports this. The (a) example concerns a scouting party
up in the mountains, with a limited food supply, which was used up by
members of another tribe, resulting in their being hungry. In the (b) example, the speaker's basket and its contents of betelnut were taken from
him, so that he was without betelnut. In (c) the example comes from
a traditional legend concerning a village with a magic totemic crocodile
which endowed them with great strength. Here, the speakers plan to
steal it, to get this strength for themselves, but importantly resulting
in the loss of this strength for the present possessors of the crocodile.
Finally, the (d) example has a transparent negative effect on the speaker
and is self-explanatory.

The other side of this construction, in which positive benefits accrue
to the possessor, is the benefactive use of taŋ- COM. This is actually
just the mirror image of the previous usage, but it is disguised at first by
the structure of English and the English translations. In the benefactive
usage, an actor performs an act which results in the establishment of a
possessive relationship between an object and a possessor, with resultant
benefit to the possessor. Consider these examples:

(6-63) a. uraŋ   k-ka-taŋ-yawra-t-akn
          coconut VI SG VI SG T-1SG A-COM-pick up-PERF-3SG D
          'I picked up a coconut for him.'

       b. upntampiŋ   k-n-taŋ-pampat-ntuk-nakn
          heart VI SG   VI SG T-3SG A-COM-cook-RM PAST-3SG D
          'She cooked the heart for him.'

       c. Mitchell kat   ya-ka-taŋ-wayk-r-akn
          Mitchell card V PL V PL T-1SG A-COM-buy-PERF-3SG D
          'I bought (a pack) of cards for Mitchell.'

    d. tpuk
       sago pancake X SG

       ampan-pay-taŋ-wura-na-uŋ
       HORT 1A/2SG D-first-COM-get-IMP-X SG
       'Let me get sago for you first.'

    e. api,   ŋa-ya-ka-taŋ-apa(n)-na-k
       father I SG   1SG D-come-SEQ-COM-shoot-IMP-III SG
       'Father, come and shoot this (bird) for me.'

In each of these cases, the object comes into the possession of the D participant, who, as the new possessor, derives obvious benefit from the action. An important and fundamental semantic component to all benefactive uses of *taŋ-* is that the actor and the benefactor must be in the same place and time. They are basically viewed as acting together, hence the use of a comitative morpheme. This makes perfect sense within Yimas society and its cultural conception of the self. In this society, a person is not defined individually, as an autonomous source of action, but is viewed as a locus of collective responsibilities, mediated through exchange relations. Thus, as in the above examples, the A and D participants in essence act *together*, in the maintenance of the all important ongoing exchange activities. That this may seem difficult for western readers to grasp at first is simply testimony to the tyrannical hold our ideology may have upon our understanding.

    With possessed body parts, the benefactive use of *taŋ-* COM can contrast with normal possessor raising. Consider these examples:

(6-64) a. narm   p-ka-warapak-r-akn
        skin VII SG   VII SG T-1SG A-cut skin-PERF-3SG D
        'I cut his skin.' (as in treatment for a cold)

       b. narm   p-ka-taŋ-warapak-r-akn
        skin VII SG   VII SG T-1SG A-COM-cut skin-PERF-3SG D
        'I cut his skin for him.' (as a maternal uncle would do for a
        novice in an initiation)

(6-64a) is a straightforward possessor raising construction, but (6-63b) illustrates the benefactive use of *taŋ-* COM. That it is the novice's own skin which is cut follows from the semantic conditions on this use of *taŋ-* COM: the A and D participants must be in the same place and time during the act. Thus, the true possessor of the skin being cut and the beneficiary of the action must be one and the same.

6.2.3.3.2 Benefactive -*ŋa*. The benefactive morpheme -*ŋa* BEN is used to code benefactive core arguments which are not equal exchange participants in a beneficial act because of physical impossibility, due most

commonly to absence from the site of the act. This is the only valence
increasing morpheme which is a suffix and is transparently related to the
verb ŋa- 'give'. It has become specialized in this usage, however, and
must be regarded as a distinct morpheme as the following contrastive
examples demonstrate:

(6-65) a. tpuk   ku-n-awl-mpi-ŋa-r-akn
            sago pancake X SG T-3SG A-take-SEQ-give-PERF-3SG D
            'She took a sago pancake and gave it to him.'

        b. awt ŋa-kra-yawra-mpi-waraca-ŋa-n
            fire IMP 1-1PL D-pick up-SEQ-return-BEN-IMP
            'Bring back fire for us.'

(6-66) a. nawkwantrm
            chicken III PL

            tma-mpɨ-ŋkra-na-wul-mpi-ŋa-kia-k
            III PL T-3DL A-1DL D-DEF-boil-SEQ-BEN-NIGHT-IRR
            'Those two will boil and give two chickens to us two.'

        b. yara   ya-ka-kra-ŋa-r-akn
            tree V PL V PL T-1SG A-cut-BEN-PERF-3SG D
            'I cut trees for him.' (the wood will belong to him)

In the (a) example, ŋa- 'give' is the second member of a serialized verb
construction and has its literal meaning. The A participant performs
the first action and then physically transfers the object manipulated
in or resulting from the action to the recipient. Both the first action
and the transfer are physically realized. In the (b) examples, the A
participant performs an action for the benefit of someone who is not
physically present at the time of the act. Of course, the benefit of any
object produced as a result of the act is predicated to accrue to the
D participant, and this may very likely include physical transfer, but
this is not absolutely necessary, as (6-66b) shows. Rather, what is at
issue with -ŋa BEN is transfer of possession and control of an object
to the benefit of the D participant, in contrast to the serialized use
of the verb ŋa- 'give', for which the actual physical act of transfer is
essential.

As already mentioned, taŋ- COM and -ŋa BEN contrast as to whether
the A and D participants are actually physically present together during
the beneficial act, in the same place and time. The prefix taŋ- COM
requires that they be so, as befits its core comitative meaning, while
the suffix -ŋa BEN does not, which is consistent with the core meaning of physical transfer from one place/person to another of its parent
morpheme, the verb ŋa- 'give'.

(6-67) a. yara   ya-ka-taŋ-kra-t-akn
          tree V PL   V PL T-1SG A-COM-cut-PERF-3SG D
          'I cut (his) trees for him.' or
          'I cut his trees.' (negative effect on him)

       b. yara   ya-ka-kra-ŋa-t-akn
          tree V PL   V PL T-1SG A-cut-BEN-PERF-3SG D
          'I cut trees for him.' (he was absent, maybe too weak to do
          it, but the wood is for him)

(6-68) a. narm   p-ka-taŋ-warapak-r-akn
          skin VII SG VII SG T-1SG A-COM-cut skin-PERF-3SG D
          'I cut his skin for him.' (as in initiation)

       b. narm   p-ka-kan-ŋa-r-akn
          skin VII SG VII SG T-1SG A-COM-pierce-BEN-PERF-3SG D
          'I pierced the skin for him.' (skin of some other creature,
          most likely, an animal)

(6-69) a. awt ŋa-kra-taŋ-yawra-mpi-waraca-n
          fire IMP 1-1PL D-COM-pick up-SEQ-return-IMP
          'Bring back fire for us.' (for those of us present now while
          speaking)

       b. awt ŋa-kra-yawra-mpi-waraca-ŋa-n   = (6-65b)
          fire IMP 1-1PL D-pick up-SEQ-return-BEN-IMP
          'Bring back fire for us.' (for all of us villagers, even those
          absent now)

These three sets of examples put into sharp relief the contrast between
taŋ- COM and -*ŋa* BEN. In (6-67a), for the benefactive reading, the
beneficiary D participant as the potential possessor of the trees cut,
is present and probably cooperating during the act of cutting. Thus,
taŋ- COM must be used. In (6-67b) with *ŋa* BEN the D participant is
absent during the action. Within the Yimas cultural view this situation
would normally arise when the beneficiary was too ill or too old to
participate in the task himself. (6-68a) with *taŋ*- expresses physical and
temporal proximity between the A and D participants during the act of
skin cutting. It is the skin of the D participant which is cut, as part
of the formal ritual cycle of male initiations. The suffix -*ŋa* in (6-68b)
indicates that the D participant cannot be present at the site of the
beneficial act. Hence the skin being pierced must belong to some other
entity. Finally, note the interesting contrast in (6-69). With *taŋ*-, the
group of beneficiaries of the act is restricted to those present when the
command is given, if you like, the class of co-speakers, whereas with *ŋa*-
it includes everyone, even the villagers absent at the time the command
was given. In all cases, *taŋ*- is associated with physical and temporal

proximity between the A and D participants, while *ŋa-* denotes distance between them.

Benefactive nominals are almost invariably coded as core arguments: i.e., realization as oblique constituents, either with -*n* ~ -*nan* OBL or a postposition, is unavailable to them. The sole exception to this generalization occurs when there is no core argument slot available, a situation which arises when a verb is already formally ditransitive. Three core arguments for a verb is the maximum permitted by Yimas; the following are ungrammatical:

(6-70) a.*ya-ka-tkam-ŋa-r-mpan-akn
        V PL T-1SG A-show-BEN-PERF-3PL D-3SG D
        'I showed those to them for him.'

     b.*anti
        ground VIII SG

        k-ka-pul-ŋa-r-ak-mpun
        VIII SG T-1SG A-rub-BEN-PERF-3SG D-3PL D
        'I rubbed dirt on him for them.'

In such cases the benefactive participant must be realized as an oblique constituent, using the allative postposition *nampan* 'towards, because of', to be discussed in more detail in the next section. Thus, the concepts behind the ungrammatical examples of (6-70) would be actually expressed in Yimas as follows:

(6-71) a. ya-ka-tkam-r-mpun   na-nampan
       V SG T-1SG A-show-PERF-3PL D   3SG-because of
       'I showed these to them for him.' (because he asked me to)

     b. anti   i-ka-pul-c-akn
       ground VIII SG   VIII SG T-1SG A-rub-PERF-3SG D

       mpu-nampan
       3PL-because of
       'I rubbed dirt on him for them.' (because they asked me to)

Although sentences like those in (6-71) are grammatical, they are actually quite rare. Such a complex idea is most likely to be expressed in Yimas in more than one predication, i.e., in a complex sentence, such as 'he told me to show those to them, and so I took them, and they saw those'.

6.2.3.3.3 Allative *ira-*. The allative relation is one in which the A participant performs the action in the direction of another participant, which is expressed as the allative nominal. The allative prefix *ira-* parallels *taŋ-* COM in that nominals coded with it enter into a paradigmatic al-

ternation with oblique constituents marked with a postposition. Just as
taŋ- is linked with the postposition *kantk* 'with', *ira-* ALL is associated
with *nampan* 'toward, because of'. Thus, we have the following pairs:

(6-72) a. na-nampan   ka-mpu-wa-n
           3SG-toward LIKE-3PL-go-PRES
           'They can go to him.'

       b. na-mpu-na-ira-wa-n
           3SG O3-PL A-DEF-ALL-go-PRES
           'They are going to him.'

(6-73) a. na-nampan   na-way-mpi-ya-ntut
           3SG-toward 3SG S-turn-SEQ-come-RM PAST
           'He turned back and came toward her.'

       b. na-n-way-mpi-ira-ya-ntut
           3SG O-3SG A-turn-SEQ-ALL-come-RM PAST
           'He turned back and came toward her.'

Although both the (a) and (b) examples above are grammatical, the
constructions with *ira-*, in which the allative nominal is realized as a
core argument, are much more common and greatly preferred. This
is similar to the preference for *taŋ-* COM as opposed to *kantk*, but if
anything, *ira-* is even more favored. The (a) constructions above, while
grammatical, are slightly stilted. In spontaneous ongoing discourse, *ira-*
ALL is nearly invariably found instead of *nampan* 'toward, because of'.
Example (6-73b) is noteworthy because it illustrates the application of
valence increasing by *ira-* at the level of the verb stem inside a complex
verb theme composed of a serial verb construction. The monovalent
verb root *ya-* 'come' is derived into a bivalent verb by *ira-*. This then
combines with the monovalent verb stem *way-mpi* turn-SEQ to form a
verb theme which is itself bivalent and hence occurs with two agreement
affixes *na-* 3SG O and *n-* 3SG A.

Other examples of the use of *ira-* are given below:

(6-74) a. impa-n-ira-kwalca-t
           3DL O-3SG A-ALL-rise-PERF
           'He rose toward those two.' (to meet them)

       b. na-ŋa-ma-ira-ya-kia-k
           3SG A-1SG O-in-ALL-come-NIGHT-IRR
           'She ran toward me inside.'

       c. ira-ya-kia-na-k
           ALL-come-NIGHT-IMP-3SG
           'Come to him!'

    d. ŋarwa   wa-n-ira-wampaki-kia-k-mpn
       penis IX SG IX SG T-3SG A-ALL-throw-NIGHT-IRR-3DL D
       'He sent his penis to those two.'

    e. wut   mi   ka-mpan-na-ira-wapat-n
       night 2SG LIKE-1A/2SG O-DEF-ALL-climb-PRES
       'Tonight, I will come up to you.'

Again, as with *taŋ-* COM when the verb root is monovalent (examples
(6-74a,b,c,e) the added core argument appears with the O affix form as
befits a derived bivalent verb stem. But when the verb root itself is
bivalent, as in (6-74d), the verb stem derived by *ira-* ALL is trivalent,
so the allative participant is coded with a D affix.

So far, I have only considered examples of *ira-* which exhibit a literal
allative meaning, the physical orientation of an action in the direction
of the allative participant. Yimas also has what might be termed a
metaphorical use of *ira-*, generally in association with verbs of emotional
or cognitive state. In these uses, the allative participant represents the
source of the state, but also the entity *toward* which the state is directed.
It is this last component of meaning which accounts for the use of *ira-*.
Consider the following:

(6-75) a. na-n-pay-ira-wampuŋkra-ntut
       3SG O-3SG A-first-ALL-worry-RM PAST
       'He worried over her now.'

    b. nam   wark-t-nti   tia-ka-ira-karnkra-t
       house build-NFN-act act O-1SG A-ALL-dislike-PERF
       'I don't like house building.'

    c. yaŋkuraŋ   k-mp-ira-aykapiŋa-k-nakn
       thoughts VI SG VI SG T-3DL A-ALL-know-IRR-3SG D
       'They both think about her.'

    d. mpu-na-nti   malak-t-nti   wampuŋ
       3PL-POSS-act talk-NFN-act heart V SG
       tia-ŋa-na-ira-kkt-n
       act T-1SG D-DEF-ALL-hurt-PRES
       'What they said angers me.' (literally 'my heart hurts over
       their act of talking.')

In all four examples, the allative nominal is the entity or action toward
which the feelings or thoughts of the A participant flow. In English, entities or actions are often viewed as the cause or source of mental states,
but this does not seem to be the case in Yimas. On the basis of this
linguistic evidence at least, they are seen in this language as the target of
mental states (note especially the last example). (6-75d) is an interest-

ing case of the derivation of a trivalent verb theme from the monovalent root *kkl-* 'hurt'. It becomes a bivalent verb with *ira-*, coding the target of the mental state as a core argument marked on the verb with the class prefix *tia-* 'act'. This then becomes a trivalent verb by possessor raising, coding the possessor of the body part *wampuŋ* 'heart' as a core argument with the prefix *ŋa-* 1SG D (for an analogous bivalent construction see example (6-50e)). The order of application of derivations is irrelevant; either order will give the same result. But because possessor-promotion operates always at the level of the verb theme, I have stated it as the second operation, as this fits with the general system of the language better. Incidentally, (6-75d) is the only example I have ever been able to obtain for possessor raising from an A participant. Note that *wampuŋ* 'heart' is functioning as the A participant, albeit a derived one. This indicates that the proper statement of possessor raising refers to semantic conditions, not syntactic functions. It applies whenever a body part undergoes a change in state with a resulting effect on its possessor.

6.2.3.3.4 Visual *taŋkway-*. This and the following valence increasing prefix do not have post- positional alternatives. The prefix *taŋkway-* VIS is unquestionably an incorporated adverbial in some of its uses (see examples in Section 6.3.2.1.4), but there are also equally clear cases in which it functions as a valence increaser. Consider the contrasts among the following three sentences:

(6-76) a. nmpi   ya-n-na-wampaki-kia-k
           leaf VII PL   VII PL O-3SG A-DEF-throw-NR FUT-IRR
           'He will send letters.'

       b. na-n-ira-wampaki-kia-k-nakn
           V SG T-3SG A-ALL-throw-NIGHT-IRR-3SG D
           'He threw it toward him.' (in his direction)

       c. na-n-taŋkway-wampaki-kia-k-nakn
           V SG T-3SG A-VIS-throw-NIGHT-IRR-3SG D
           'He threw it at him.' (looking at him)

The verb root, *wampaki-* 'throw' is bivalent, as (6-76c) clearly demonstrates. This verb root can be derived into a trivalent verb stem by the use of a valence-increasing affix. In (6-76b), the prefix *ira-* ALL derives a trivalent verb stem and permits the coding of the allative participant as the third core argument, realized as *-nakn* 3SG D. The prefix *taŋkway-* VIS behaves similarly in (6-76c): the verb is formally ditransitive, with the D suffix *-nakn* 3SG D. The prefix *taŋkway-* VIS has an allative meaning in this example, i.e., action directed towards the D participant, but what is crucial is that the A participant is looking at the D participant

when performing the action. It is this which distinguishes *taŋkway-* VIS
from *ira-* ALL. It always expresses that the A participant performs the
action while carefully watching another *animate* participant (O or D).
It commonly implies that the A participant is monitoring the O or D
participant to watch for his reactions. It need not always have an allative meaning and be in contrast with *ira-* ALL; it also contrasts with
taŋ- COM.

(6-77) a. na-n-taŋ-tantaw-k
            3SG O-3SG A-COM-sit(RED: *taw-*)-PERF
            'He sat with him.'

        b. na-n-taŋkway-cantaw-k
            3SG O-3SG A-VIS-sit(RED: *taw-*)-IRR
            'He sat down close to him.' (scrutinizing him)

(*tantaw-* is an irregular reduplication of *taw-* 'sit', rather like *iranta-*
from *ira-* 'dance'). In (6-77a) *taŋ-* COM provides its normal comitative
reading: the A participant sits down jointly with the D. Example (6-
77b) with *taŋkway-* VIS is somewhat different. Rather the A participant
sits down and does so in a way that he can visually monitor the O participant. The act of sitting down need not occur jointly; the O may, for
example, be standing up. Other examples of *taŋkway-* VIS follow:

(6-78) a. na-mpu-taŋkway-iranta-irm-kia-ntut
            3SG O-3PL A-VIS-dance(RED: *ira-*)-stand-NIGHT-RM PAST
            'They danced for her.' (in her honor, watching for responses)

        b. na-n-taŋkway-iray-ɲcut
            3SG O-3SG A-VIS-cry-RM PAST
            'He cried over her.' (looking at her body lying in the canoe)

        c. tpuk
            sago pancake X SG

            ku-n-taŋkway-awl-mpi-ca-kia-k-nakn
            X SG O-3SG A-VIS-take-SEQ-put-NIGHT-IRR-3SG D
            'She took a sago pancake and put it down for him.' (while
            watching him for his responses. The A is the ghost of
            the wife of the D participant.)

In (6-78a) *taŋkway-* VIS has some of the meaning of *ŋa-* BEN. The dance
is done for the benefit of *na-* 3 SG O, in her honor, but she is not expected to join in. She sits back and watches the dance and in turn is
watched for her approval. In (6-78b), the A participant stands over the
body of his wife lying in the canoe and cries while looking at her. In
(6-78c) *taŋkway-* applies at the level of the verb theme: the two bivalent
verb roots, *awl-* 'get' and *ta-* 'put down', are combined in a serial verb

construction to form a complex verb theme. The valence of the verb theme is increased from bivalent to trivalent by the addition of *taŋkway-* which licenses the third core argument, expressed by the D affix *-nakn*.

The prefix *taŋkway-* applies more commonly at the level of the verb theme than do the other valence altering affixes. This is due, no doubt, to the fact that this prefix is simultaneously an adverbial, for the level at which adverbial incorporation occurs is the verb theme (see Section 6.3.2). It is highly likely that all the valence changing affixes are derived diachronically from adverbials (or verbs, the usual source of adverbials in the language). It simply appears that the re-analysis of *taŋkway-* is lagging behind that of *taŋ-* COM or *ira-* ALL. Both in its semantics and morphological combinatorial possibilities, this prefix betrays its adverbial origins.

6.2.3.3.5 Kinetic *pampay-*. The kinetic valence-increasing prefix *pampay-* KIN is associated with the notion of carrying. It is used whenever the core argument participant introduced by valence-increasing is involved as a participant in an act of carrying.

(6-79) a. na-n-pampay-iray-pra-k   (compare 6-77b)
            3SG O-3SG A-KIN-cry-toward-IRR
            'He cried carrying her toward the village.'
            (her dead body lies in the canoe)

        b. na-mpu-pampay-wapal-kia-k
            3SG O-3PL A-KIN-climb-NIGHT-IRR
            'They came up with her.' (carrying her)

The prefix *pampay-* KIN is transparently a fossilized reduplication of the verb root *pay-* 'carry', but the constructions in (6-79) cannot be simply analyzed as the reduplication of this verb root in a serial verb construction. For one thing, the prefix *pampay-* always increases the valence of the verb root to which it is added, which should not be the case if it were simply another verb root linked in a serial verb construction (see Section 6.3.1 on serial verb constructions). Second, the semantic force of *pampay-* is not that of a verb root reduplication. Verb roots, when reduplicated, normally express an iterative action (see Section 6.2.4 on the semantics of verb root reduplication), but this is not necessarily the sense of *pampay-*. Finally, the prefix enters into a system of paradigmatic alternations with the other valence increasing affixes. Compare (6-79a) with (6-78b) and (6-79b) with (6-80) below:

(6-80) na-mpu-taŋ-wapal-kia-k
        3SG O-3PL A-COM-climb-NIGHT-IRR
        'They came up with her.' (she walk along too)

In (6-80) the O participant comes up on her own initiative and by her
own force along with the A participants (hence the use of *taŋ-* COM).
But in (6-79b) she does not. She is carried up by the A participants,
contributing no energy of her own to the event which results in her
change of position. This statement applies even more forcefully to the
corpse lying in the canoe in example (6-79a).

After *taŋ-* COM, *pampay-* is probably the most common of the valence increasing affixes. Some further examples follow:

(6-81) a. na-mpɨ-pampay-arm-kia-k
           3SG O-3DL A-KIN-board-NIGHT-IRR
           'They both boarded with him.' (carried him in the same
           canoe as them)

       b. pu-kay-pampay-cantaw-kia-ntuk-ŋkt   (compare 6-77b)
          3PL O-1PL A-KIN-sit(RED: *taw-*)-NIGHT-RM PAST-PC
          'We sat down with them.' (carried them and sat down
          holding them)

       c. tpwi   i-mp-awkura-pampay-wapal-kia-k
          sago X PL   X PL O-3DL A-gather-KIN-climb-NIGHT-IRR
          'They both were gathering sago and carrying it up with
          them.'

       d. na-mpu-pampay-iranta-tal-k
          3SG O-3PL A-KIN-dance(RED: *ira-*)-start-IRR
          'They started to dance with it.' (carrying it)

The verb *arm-* 'board' is a verb root which can be used monovalently
or bivalently (as in English: *he boarded* or *he boarded the plane*). When
functioning as a bivalent verb, the O is always the site of boarding.
This is typically a canoe within traditional Yimas culture. When the
monovalent verb is further derived by *pampay-*, the O participant is the
entity carried on board, as in (6-81a). In (6-81b), the monovalent verb
stem derived by reduplication of the root *taw-* 'sit' becomes a bivalent
verb by prefixation with *pampay-*. The O argument added denotes the
children carried and sat down with. (6-81) (c) and (d) contrast at the
level of morphological derivation at which valence increasing by *pampay-*
occurs. In (6-81c), the prefix applies at the stem level. The monovalent
verb *wapal-* 'climb' is derived into a bivalent verb stem by *pampay-* ,
and this derived verb stem in turn is combined with the bivalent verb
root *awkura-* 'gather' to form a bivalent complex verb theme. In (6-81d)
the opposite order of derivation applies. First, *iranta-* 'dance' and *tal-*
'hold, start' are joined to form a monovalent complex verb theme, which
in turn is derived by *pampay-* into a bivalent one. Thus, this valence

altering affix, like others, can apply at the level of derivation of either verb stems or verb themes.

6.2.3.3.6 Following *tur-*. This is a rare valence increasing affix and only very few occurrences of it have been encountered. It indicates that the A participant is pursuing the O participant with a view to driving it to the same goal. The following examples illustrate this prefix:

(6-82) a. yura   na-ka-tay   numpram
           dog III SG   III SG O-1SG A-see   pig III SG

           m-na-tur-kulanaŋ
           NR DIST-DEF-FOL-walk

           'I saw the dog which chased the pig.'

      b. pu-n-tur-awramu-ŋ   ma-nan
          3PL O-3SG A-FOL-enter-IRR   male cult house VII SG-OBL

          'He chased them into the male cult house.'

kulanaŋ- 'walk' and *awramu-* 'enter' are monovalent verb roots derived into bivalent verb stems by *tur-* FOL, with the meaning 'walk behind something, causing it to go somewhere', i.e., 'chase'.

The prefix *tur-* FOL is rather like *taŋkway-* VIS in that sometimes it seems to serve like an adverbial, failing to alter the valence of the verb root. The following is an alternative to (6-82a):

(6-83) yura   na-ka-tay   numpran
       dog III SG   III SG O-1SG A-see   pig III SG

       m-na-tal-cur-kulanaŋ
       NR DIST-DEF-CAUS-FOL-walk.

       'I saw the dog which chased the pig.'

Hence the verb root *kulanaŋ-* 'walk' is derived into a bivalent verb stem by the causative prefix *tar-* ~ *tal-*. The prefix *tur-* FOL simply adds the adverbial force of 'behind, following.'

6.2.4 Verb Stem Derivations: Reduplication
The next type of derivation of verb stems from verb roots is reduplication (for the phonology of reduplication, see Section 2.4.). Reduplication typically indicates an iterative action.

(6-84) a. arm   m-um   ima-mpu-nan-nanaŋ-
           water   NR DIST-I PL   water O-3PL A-2SG D-DUR-

           apapi-ŋa-ntut
           put in(RED: *api-*)-BEN-RM PAST

           'They were repeatedly gathering water for you all.'

    b. kaywi
       daughter II SG
       na-iratay-kwalca-kia-ntut
       3SG S-cry(RED: *iray-*)-rise-NIGHT-RM PAST
       '(His) daughter woke up crying and crying.'
    c. pu-kra-nanaŋ-tarat-awram-tut
       3PL A-1PL O-DUR-hold(RED: *tal-*)-enter-RM PAST
       'They were holding (each one of) us, as they entered.'
    d. ya-n-arkark-wampaki-pra-k
       V PL O-3SG A-break(RED: *ark-*)-throw-toward-IRR
       'He repeatedly broke them and threw them as he came.'
    e. na-mpu-wurtwurt-tay-pra-kia-k
       3SG O-3PL A-put down(RED: *wul-*)-try-toward-NIGHT-IRR
       'They kept trying to put it down in the water as they came.'

Reduplication always derives verb stems, never verb themes. Reduplication can be either partial (6-84a,b,c) or full (6-84d), with no apparent difference in meaning. (6-84e) is an especially interesting example in that the verb root *wul-* 'put down' is first reduplicated partially to form the verb stem *wurt-*, which in turn is subject to full reduplication to derive *wurt wurt* 'put repeatedly down'. This extra stage of derivation seems to express an especially strong force of iteration. Given the text from which it comes, the sentence describes an action of putting a depth marker into the river to try to gauge depth, pulling it up, rowing upriver, putting it down in the water again, pulling it up, rowing upriver again, etc.

    The one apparent exception to the statement that partial and full reduplications do not contrast in meaning is *tay-* 'see'. Partial reduplication of *tay-* results in *taray-*, an obligatorily incorporated adverbial (Section 6.3.2.1.5) with the meaning 'free, clear, loose'. The full reduplication, *tacay-*, produces a more literal iteration of 'see', hence 'watch, stare'. Note these two contrastive examples:

(6-85) a. na-n-a-taray-yawra-n?
       3SG O-2SG A-DEF-clear(RED: *tay-*)-pick up-PRES
       'Can you understand him?'
    b. ya-mpu-nanaŋ-tacay-ckam-tuk-mpun
       V PL O-3PL A-DUR-see(RED: *tay-*)-show-RM PAST-3PL D
       'They were showing those to them very well.' (and they
       stared at those)

6.2.5 Verb Stem Derivations: Noun Incorporation
The final type of verb stem derivation to consider is noun incorporation. Noun incorporation is rather rare in Yimas and seems a sporadic pro-

cess which produces idiom-like structures. The only exception to this
is incorporation of nominalized adjectives and adjectival verbs discussed
in Section 6.2.3.1.3, which is fairly common. Yimas noun incorporation
therefore contrasts with that in other polysynthetic languages, both near
(Alamblak: Bruce 1984) and far (Eskimo: Sadock 1980), for which the
process is fully productive, or at least much more so. Examples of noun
incorporation in Yimas follow:

(6-86) a. ampan-pay-pucm-api-n
            HORT 1A/2SG D-first-time VII SG-put in-IMP
            'I will give you time first.' (I will wait)

        b. patn   wayk-r-mpwi
            betelnut V SG   buy-NFN-talk

            pia-ka-na-yaŋkuraŋ-   takat-n
            talk O-1SG A-DEF-thoughts VI SG-   feel-PRES
            'I am thinking about buying betelnut.'

        c. ura-mpu-na-akpi-api-n
            fire O-3PL A-DEF-back V SG-put in-PRES
            'They are putting (their) backs to the fire.' (to warm
            themselves)

All of the incorporated nouns in these examples can serve as independent nouns in their own right: they are not restricted to incorporated
positions (a restriction common with incorporated nominals in other
languages; see Sadock 1980). Further, for most incorporated nominals,
there exist alternative constructions with the same meaning, in which
the noun is not incorporated.

(6-87) akpi   ura-mpu-na-api-n   (compare (6-86c))
        back V SG   fire O-3PL A-DEF-put inside-PRES
        'They are putting (their) backs to the fire.'

Typically, the incorporated noun does not occupy one of the core argument slots of the governing verb root. In other words noun incorporation
does not alter the valence of the verb. Thus, *api-* 'put inside' and *takal-*
'feel' are both bivalent verbs and are formally transitive in (6-86), clearly
demonstrating that the incorporated nouns are not core arguments.

    Verb stems derived by nominal incorporation are subject to other
stem derivational processes, notably valence altering.

(6-88) a. impa-na-t-akpi-api-n
            3DL S-DEF-RCP-back V SG-put in-PRES
            'They are putting their backs to each other.'

b. patn   na-mpu-ŋa-taŋ-mama-k-n-
   betelnut V SG   V SG O-3PL A-1SG D-COM-bad-IRR-V SG-
   tal-cɨ-t
   CAUS-become-PERF
   'They ruined my betelnut.'

In (6-87a) the bivalent verb *api-* 'put in' is derived into a bivalent verb
stem by noun incorporation, yielding *akpi-api-* 'put one's back to'. This
in turn is further derived into a monovalent verb stem by *tɨ-* RCP, yielding *t-akpi-api-* 'put backs to each other.' For (6-87b) the monovalent
basic inchoative verb *tɨ-* 'become' is first causativized with *tal-* ~ *tar-*
CAUS. This produces a bivalent verb stem. The nominalized adjective
mama-k-n bad-IRR-V SG is then incorporated into this bivalent verb
stem. Finally, the complex bivalent verb stem is derived into a trivalent
verb theme with *taŋ-* COM, which codes the negatively affected possessor
of the theme as a core argument.

6.3 Theme Derivational Processes

In the previous section, I discussed the derivation of verb stems from
verb roots. The next level up in the internal structure of Yimas verbs
is that of the verb theme. Verb themes are derived from verb stems in
the same way as verb stems are from verb roots, by the specification of
additional morphological categories. Just as the minimal verb stem is
a verb root, so too the minimal verb theme is a verb stem (which, of
course, may itself, be no more than a verb root). Theme derivational
processes differ from stem derivational processes in that they seem more
'inflectional' than derivational, although as we shall see in Section 6.4,
there are no principled grounds for making this distinction in Yimas.
Theme derivational processes tend to modulate the basic meaning of
the verb, adding specifications for categories such as aspect, place of
action and manner of action, rather than re-orienting the verb, as stem
derivational processes typically do, e.g., altering the number of core
arguments associated with the verb. The difference between stem and
theme derivations, admittedly only impressionistically defined thus far,
will become clearer as the exposition proceeds.

6.3.1 Serial Verb Constructions

The most common type of verb theme derivation in Yimas is that which
results in a serial verb construction. These are an absolutely pervasive
feature of Yimas, as of Papuan languages generally; perhaps the majority
of Yimas verbs in spontaneous, ongoing discourse are composed of serial
verb constructions.

Serial verbs in Yimas fall into two structural types: those connected simply by juxtaposition, with no overt morphological links; and those connected by an overt morpheme, most commonly, -*mpi* SEQ. As would be expected, these two types contrast semantically. The former is used for coding events which are viewed as simultaneous or especially close cause-effect relations (close in both space and time). The latter is used for events which are seen to occur sequentially in the normal progression of events, but with no strong causal link between them.

Serial verb constructions in which the events encoded are in a simultaneous relation commonly occur with the incorporated adverbials *yakal-* CONT or *nanaŋ-* DUR (see Section 6.3.2) or have one of the verb roots reduplicated.

(6-89) a. impa-n-yakal-kulanaŋ-kanta-k
3DL O-3SG A-CONT-walk-follow-IRR
'He was walking following those two.'

b. pu-n-yakal-caŋ-tantaw-malak-ntut
3PL O-3SG A-CONT-COM-sit(RED: *taw-*)-talk-RM PAST
'He was sitting down conversing with them.'

c. marŋki
leaf stem VI PL

kia-kay-nanaŋ-kamat-kula-ntut
VI PL O-1PL A-DUR-search-walk-RM PAST
'We walked around, looking for leaf stems.'

d. impa-iranta-arpal-k
3DL S-dance(RED: *ira-*)-exit-IRR
'They both danced, while coming out.'

e. manpakawrŋki
duck species VI PL

kia-n-kankan-awkura-kiantut
VI PL O-3SG A-shoot(RED: *kan-*)-gather-FR PAST
'He hunted ducks a few days ago.'

Quite commonly, both an incorporated adverbial and reduplication are used:

(6-90) a. wampunŋ
sago flour VI SG

k-mpu-nanaŋ-wurt-am-na-ntut
VI SG O-3PL A-DUR-boil(RED: *wul-*)-eat-DUR-RM PAST
'They were boiling and eating sago flour repeatedly.'

b. apuŋkat
   skink V PL

   na-yakal-apapan-ra-kula-ntut
   3SG S-CONT-shoot(RED: *apan-*)-SIM-walk-RM PAST
   'He walked around, shooting skinks.'

And very occasionally, neither are found:

(6-91) a. ura-n-irm-wampaki-pra-k
          fire O-3SG A-stand-throw-toward-IRR
          'He stood throwing fire toward (them).'

      b. pu-ŋkl-cra-awl-tal-kaprapi-k
         3PL O-3PC A-about-get-hold-gather-IRR
         'Those few grabbed them while collecting them.'

There is an important semantic difference between those juxtaposed serial verb constructions with a reduplicated verb stem and those without. Both types express overall simultaneous actions, but the semantic
force of reduplication is always salient with reduplicated verb stems. In
these cases, repeated occurrences of the action denoted by the reduplicated verb happen within the overall time span of the unreduplicated
stems. Thus in (6-90a) there are repeated acts of boiling within the period devoted to eating, while in (6-89e) the shootings occur within the
time span of gathering food. This even applies to (6-89d), although it
may not be apparent at first, for Yimas dances consist of a short initial chant, followed by dancing and singing for a few minutes, followed
by a short rest, and then the whole sequence is repeated. Thus, (6-
89d) actually expresses iterative acts of dancing within the time span
of exiting. Serial verb constructions without a reduplicated verb are
more straightforward: they simply express overlap—usually total, but
not necessarily—of the time span of the actions denoted by the verb
stems. Thus, in (6-89a) the time span of walking and following, and in
(6-89c) the time span of searching and walking overlap. As I said above,
the overlap need not be complete: for example, (6-89c) could be used
to describe a situation in which a person searched for an object while
walking along, but then gave up and continued to walk along. Thus,
while the time span of searching is contained within that of walking, the
converse is not true: the period of walking is not contained within the
act of searching.

The semantic difference between simultaneous serial verb constructions with and without reduplicated verb stems can be diagrammed as
follows, using an A and B for the actions of the first and second verb
stems respectively,

Not reduplicated:
$$\cdots \quad \overline{\text{A}} \quad \cdots$$
$$\overline{\text{B}}$$

Reduplicated:
$$\overline{\text{A}} \quad \overline{\text{A}} \quad \overline{\text{A}} \quad \overline{\text{A}}$$
$$\overline{\text{B}}$$

where the dots in the first diagram indicate the potential extension of duration of action A.

The other type of serial verb constructions formed with simple juxtaposition expresses a very close cause-effect relationship between the two actions denoted by the verb roots. In this case, the effected result must follow directly and immediately after the causing event; there can be no period of time separating the time spans of the causing event and the resulting state. In fact, they should partially overlap, so that these examples may be viewed as a type of simultaneous serial verb constructions, with the temporal relations diagrammed as follows:

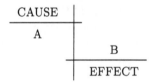

CAUSE

A

B

EFFECT

Serial verb constructions with this type of temporal relationship are not very common, but the following are examples:

(6-92) a. narm   pu-tpul-kamprak-r-akn
         skin VI SG   3PL S-hit-break-PERF-3SG D
         'They hit and broke his skin.'

       b. nawn   ya-ŋa-awa-ta-n
         who   V PL-1SG D-excrete-put-PRES
         'Who is urinating on me?'

The (a) example describes a hazing event during the rituals for male initiations. The boys are beaten, causing large skin welts to rise on the skin. The welts rise immediately from the impact of the blows, and further, given that the boys are beaten for an extended period, the time span of the beating and the rising of the welts actually overlap. (6-92b) is similar. It might be paraphrased as 'who is urinating, causing it to be put on me?' Again the second event follows immediately as the effective result of the first causing event, and overlap of the time span of the two events is likely: given a full bladder and the force of gravity, one would be expected to be still urinating when it begins to reach the unfortunate victim below. The causative relationship in (6-92b) is perhaps rather strained: what seems more important to the use of this simple juxtaposed serial verb construction is the temporal overlap of the two events, so perhaps these might be best viewed as a sub-type of simultaneous constructions.

Yimas also possesses a morpheme -*ra* SIM which can be used to link verb stems in a serial verb construction expressing a simultaneous relation. This morpheme does not contrast semantically with simple juxtaposition but does seem to suggest complete overlap of the time span of the two events denoted by the verb roots.

(6-93) a. na-n-munta-ra-wapal-k
    3SG O-3SG A-call-SIM-ascend-IRR
    'She called out to him while going up.'

  b. yarayŋkat
    lizard V PL

    na-yakal-apapan-ra-kula-ntut
    3SG S-CONT-shoot(RED: *apan*-)-SIM-walk-RM PAST

    'He was shooting lizards while walking around.'

In (6-93b), for example, the repeated acts of shooting and the act of walking are completely contemporaneous: when the A ceases walking, he ceases shooting. In (6-93a) the speech called out in this instance is a longish utterance, plausibly viewed as occupying the same time span as the act of ascending.

The majority of serial verb constructions in Yimas denote actions in a sequential relationship. The temporal spans of the events in a sequential relationship may not overlap. They may be a gap between the span of one event and that of the following, or they may follow each other immediately, one after the other, but in the latter case no necessary cause-effect relationship is predicated between them. Thus, two events in a sequential relationship may be diagrammed as follows,

where the dotted section of the lines indicate the acceptable extension of the duration of the events.

Verb stems which denote actions in a sequential temporal relationship cannot be simply juxtaposed to form a serial verb construction. Rather, they must be linked together, with the morpheme -*mpi* SEQ joined as a suffix to the first verb stem.

The suffix -*mpi* SEQ is not restricted to serial verb constructions: It also marks dependent verbs in Yimas. Dependent verbs are a common feature of Papuan languages, as are serial verbs (see Foley 1986, 178–80). Dependent verbs are termed thus because they are dependent on the following fully inflected independent verb for specifications of tense and mood (see Section 7.3.1 for further discussion on dependent verb constructions). Dependent verbs and serialized verbs share a number of similarities, but they are different constructions and it is important to be clear about the differences between them, especially as they both employ -*mpi* in Yimas.

Consider the following examples:

(6-94) a. arm-n   kay
          water-OBL   canoe VIII SG
          i-ka-ak-mpi-wul
          VIII SG O-1SG A-push-SEQ-put down
          'I pushed the canoe down into the water.'

      b. kay   ak-mpi   i-ka-wul
          canoe VIII SG   push-SEQ   VIII SG O-1SG A-put down
          arm-n
          water-OBL
          'I pushed the canoe and put it into the water.'

(6-94a) is a serial verb construction; the two verbs are connected by -*mpi*. (6-94b) illustrates a dependent verb marked simply by -*mpi*, followed by a fully independent verb, with pronominal affixes and tense inflection (in this case the ∅ allomorph of the perfective after a segment linked to the autosegment F). The difference between these two can be summed up very simply: (6-94a) is one clause, but (6-94b) is two. This is reflected in the English translations of the two examples. The serial verb construction encodes a single, yet complex event, while a dependent-independent verb sequence expresses two separate events, one followed in time by another.

The contention that serial verb constructions constitute a single clause and encode one event, but the verbs in dependent-independent chains comprise separate clauses and encode multiple events is well supported by a number of structural factors. Given that serial verb constructions are one clause, the verbs within them together form one predication, one verb theme. Hence, there can only be a single set of pronominal affixes for the verb, as in (6-94a). But as dependent verbs function as the predicates of separate clauses, they should be able to co-occur with their own set of pronominal affixes, and, indeed, they can.

(6-95) kay   i-ka-ak-mpi   arm-n
        canoe VIII SG   VIII SG O-1SG A-push-SEQ water-OBL
        i-ka-wul
        VIII SG O-1SG A-put down
        'I pushed the canoe and put it into the water.'

As verbs in a serial verb construction form a single, albeit complex, verb theme, they constitute a single grammatical word. Hence, other words should not be able to be inserted between them, breaking the integrity of the word. This predication is indeed borne out (compare the example below with (6-94a)).

(6-96) a.*kay   i-ka-ak-mpi   arm-n
          canoe VIII SG VIII SG O-1SG A-push-SEQ water-OBL
          wul
          put down
      b.*i-ka-ak-mpi   kay   wul
          VIII SG O-1SG A-push-SEQ canoe VIII SG put down
          arm-n
          water-OBL

Such insertions, however, should be no problem in a dependent verb chain, for each verb constitutes a separate word. This is, in fact, the case.

(6-97) a. kay   ak-mpi   arm-n
          canoe VIII SG push-SEQ water-OBL
          i-ka-wul
          VIII SG O-1SG A-put down
          'I pushed the canoe and put it into the water.'
      b. ak-mpi   kay   i-ka-wul
          push-SEQ canoe VIII SG VIII SG O-1SG A-put down
          arm-n
          water-OBL
          'I pushed the canoe and put it into the water.'

Note that the fundamental structural contrast between the ungrammatical structures of (6-96) and the grammatical ones in (6-97) is the placement of the pronominal affixes. If they occur on the first verb root but not the second, the structure is interpreted as a serial verb construction; if on the second but not the first, it is recognized as a dependent verb chain. The reason has to do with the linking of pronominal affixes to tense inflection; the tense inflection licenses their appearance. Thus, in (6-96) the tense inflection occurs on the second verb root, forcing a structural interpretation of this and the previous verb root as a single unit, i.e., a serial verb construction. Because this sequence is interrupted by the intrusion of other words, these examples are ungrammatical. But in (6-97) the verb inflected for tense also co-occurs with the pronominal affixes, establishing only this as a coherent unit. The previous verb is therefore determined to be a dependent verb, not an element in a serial verb construction, and hence the two verbs may be freely separated by other words.

Another formal difference between serial verb constructions and dependent verb chains is in their behavior under negation. Serial verb constructions can only be negated as a whole, as befits their semantic function of encoding a single event. The semantic scope of the negative can be restricted to only one verb stem in the serial structure, or may negate all verb stems; negation with serial verb constructions is ambiguous. But only one occurrence of the negative prefix is allowed, at the beginning of the entire verb.

(6-98)   arm-n   kay
            water-OBL   canoe VIII SG
            ta-ka-ak-mpi-wul-c-i
            NEG-1SG A-push-SEQ-put down-VIII SG
            'I did not push the canoe down into the water.' (I pulled it) or
            'I did not push the canoe down into the water.' (I pushed it
            onto the ground) or
            'I did not push the canoe down into the water.' (I was sleeping
            and did nothing to the canoe, and so it is still on the ground)

Because dependent verb chains constitute separate clauses which encode distinct events, one would expect that *ta-* NEG could occur separately on the verb stems. This is true, but it must occur on the independent verb, the one that carries tense.

(6-99)   kay   ak-mpi   arm-n
            canoe VIII SG   push-SEQ   water-OBL
            ta-ka-wul-c-i
            NEG-1SG A-put down-PERF-VIII SG
            'I didn't push the canoe or put it into the water.'
            (I did neither act)

Note that the scope of *ta-* NEG is still over both verbs in (6-99), even though it only occurs on the second, independent verb. In order to block this, the first verb must be an independent verb, either in a subordinate (6-100a) or coordinate (6-100b) linkage (see Sections 7.2.3 and 7.3.2).

(6-100) a. kay   i-ka-ak-r-mp-n
           canoe VIII SG   VIII SG O-1SG A-push-PERF-VII SG-OBL
           arm-n   ta-ka-wul-c-i
           water-OBL   NEG-1SG A-put down-PERF-VIII SG
           'Although I pushed the canoe, I did not put it into the
           water.' (I pushed it onto the ground.)
        b. kay   i-ka-ak-t   arm-n
           canoe VIII SG   VIII SG O-1SG A-push-PERF   water-OBL
           kanta ta-ka-wul-c-i
           but   NEG-1SG A-put down-PERF-VIII SG
           'I pushed the canoe, but did not put it into the water.' (I
           pushed onto the ground.)

Further, it is ungrammatical to have *ta-* NEG on the first, dependent
verb.

(6-101)*kay   ta-ak-mpi   arm-n
        canoe VIII SG NEG-push-SEQ   water-OBL
        i-ka-wul
        VIII SG O-1SG A-put down

The reason for the ungrammaticality of a sentence like (6-101) is the fact
that *ta-* NEG has scope over both verbs in a dependent verb chain, but
that its scope is only interpretable as spreading to the left (this is a general feature of languages like Yimas in which the head of constructions
are generally on the right (see Reesink 1986)). Given these two conditions, the above structure is uninterpretable and hence ungrammatical.
The idea behind (6-101) needs to be expressed using two independent
verbs in a coordinate linkage.

(6-102) kay   ta-ka-ak-r-i   kanta
        canoe VIII SG   NEG-1SG A-pull-PERF-VIII SG   but
        i-ka-wul
        VIII SG O-1SG A-put down
        'I didn't push the canoe, but I put it into the water.'
        (I pulled it.)

Other verbal inflectional categories like tense or mood parallel negation in that it is equally impossible to specify a dependent verb for these
separately from an independent verb. A dependent verb must take its
specifications for tense and mood from a following independent verb;
they may not even be inflected for these categories. A dependent verb
chain is distinguished from a serial verb construction as follows: since
the serial verb construction constitutes the core of a verb theme, it is

inflected for tense and aspect as a unit, while a dependent verb takes no inflections for these categories, which are supplied by the specifications on the following independent verb. Consider the difference between the following serial verb construction and dependent verb chain in the imperative mood.

(6-103) a. arm-n   kay
           water-OBL canoe VIII SG
           naŋk-ak-mpi-wut-ɲa-y
           IMP DL-push-SEQ-put down-IMP-VIII SG O
           'You two, push the canoe down into the water!'

       b. kay   yawra-mpi   arm-n
           canoe VIII SG pick up-SEQ water-OBL
           naŋk-wut-ɲa-y
           IMP DL-put down-IMP-VIII SG
           'You two, pick up the canoe and put it into the water!'

Note that the serial verb construction (6-103a) takes the imperative inflections as a whole, the prefixes *naŋk-* IMP DL and the suffix -*na* IMP, flanking the serial construction functioning as the verb theme. In (6-103b), exemplifying a dependent verb chain, the imperative affixes occur only on the second (independent) verb. However, the first (dependent) verb is also imperative in mood, as seen by the English translation.

Serial verb constructions with -*mpi* SEQ in which the events coded stand in a sequential temporal relationship, are very common in Yimas. Most narrative texts contain dozens of examples. The majority of these contain only two verb stems. Below are some examples of these:

(6-104) a. nawkwantrm
           chicken III PL
           tma-mpɨ-ŋkra-na-wul-mpi-ŋa-kia-k
           III DL T-3DL A-1DL D-DEF-boil-SEQ-give-NR FUT-IRR
           'They both will boil two chickens and give them to us two.'

       b. awt ŋa-kra-awl-mpi-waraca-ŋa-n
           fire IMP 1-1PL D-get-SEQ-return-BEN-IMP
           'Bring back fire for us!'

       c. ya-ka-tpat-n
           come-SEQ-descend-IMP
           'Come down!'

       d. pu-wapal-mpi-kaprapi-k
           3PL S-climb-SEQ-gather-IRR
           'They came up and gathered.'

The suffix -*ka* SEQ is a special morpheme which replaces -*mpi* SEQ following the basic motion verbs *wa-* 'go' and *ya-* 'come'. Serial verb constructions composed of three verb stems are less common, but are by no means rare.

(6-105) a. ya-n-park-mpi-kapik-mpi-wark-t
             V PL O-3SG A-split-SEQ-break-SEQ-tie-PERF
             'He split them, broke them into pieces and tied them together.'

         b. num-n   na-way-mpi-waraca-mpi-ya-ntut
             village-OBL   3SG S-turn-SEQ-return-SEQ-come-RM PAST
             'He came back to the village.'

         c. pu-kra-awl-mpi-ayn-pi-ya-kia-k-ŋkt
             3PL A-1PL O-get-SEQ-put in-SEQ-come-NIGHT-IRR-PC
             'They got us few and put us inside (a canoe) and came back'.

         d. pla-n-ma-awkura-mpi-kacakapi-mpi-tɨ-pra-k
             VII PL O-3SG A-in-gather-SEQ-hide-SEQ-lie down-toward-
                                                              IRR
             'He got those two (flutes) and hid them and lay them down inside.'

A serial verb construction consisting of more than three verb stems has never been encountered. This sharply distinguishes Yimas serial verb constructions from dependent verb chains in Arafundi, Enga, or the languages of the central highlands, in which long chains of such verbs, often more than a dozen, are not uncommon.

As mentioned in the previous section, some of the verb stem derivational processes discussed there can also apply at the level of the verb theme. In fact, when the verb theme is composed of a serial verb construction, it is most commonly the case that the valence altering derivational processes apply to it as a whole. Examples of this were presented in Section 6.2, to which the reader is advised to refer. I provide a few further examples now.

(6-106) a. na-mpu-tɨ-kaprak-mpi-ŋa-k
             V SG O-3PL A-RCP-cut up-SEQ-give-IRR
             kalk
             sago pudding V SG
             'They shared the sago pudding.'

         b. uraŋknut
             coconut meat IX PL

ura-mpu-kra-taŋ-ntak-mpi-ɲa-ntut
IX PL O-3PL A-1PL D-COM-leave-SEQ-stay-RM PAST

'They left the coconut meat with us.'

c. na-mpu-taŋkway-iranta-irm-kia-ntut
3SG O-3PL A-VIS-dance(RED: *ira-*)-stand-NIGHT-RM PAST
'They danced for her.'

d. na-kay-pampay-arpal-mpi-cantaw-ntut
3SG O-1PL A-KIN-exit-SEQ-sit(RED: *taw-*)-RM PAST
'We carried them out and sat down.'

In each of these examples, the valence altering morpheme applies to a
verb theme made up of a serial verb construction. In (6-106a) the verb
theme is trivalent because of the presence of the trivalent root *ŋa-* 'give',
so that when *ti-* RCP reduces the valence by one argument the formal
result is a transitive verb. The other three examples illustrate valence-
increasing. The prefix *taŋ-* COM in (6-106b) derives a trivalent verb
theme from one composed of a bivalent verb root *ntak-* 'leave' and a
monovalent one *naŋ-* 'stay'. In (6-106c), the prefix *taŋkway-* VIS derives
a bivalent verb theme from one composed of two monovalent verb stems
iranta- 'dance' and *irm-* 'start'. Finally, the kinetic prefix *pampay-* KIN
in (6-106d) applies to a verb theme made up of two monovalent verb
stems, *arpal-* 'exit' and *tantaw-* 'sit down', to derive a bivalent verb
theme.

6.3.1.1 Specializations in Serial Verb Constructions: Modality

The verbs *tal-* 'hold' and *tay-* 'see' have specialized uses when appearing
as the last member in a serial verb construction. They and the previous verb must be linked by simple juxtaposition; the verb stem linking
morphemes are prohibited in these uses.

The verb *tal-* in this usage has the meaning 'start'. Consider these
examples:

(6-107) a. tumpntut tpwi
morning   sago pancake X PL

naŋk-apapi-tal-kia-na-i
IMP DL-fry(RED: *api-*)-start-NR FUT-IMP-X PL

'Tomorrow morning, you both start to fry sago pancakes.'

b. paŋkra-kaykaykay-kwalca-mpi-kulanaŋ-tal-kiantu-ŋkt
2PC S-quickly-rise-SEQ-walk-start-FR PAST-PC
'We few got up quickly and started to walk.'

In (6-107a) the verb root *api-* 'put inside, fry' is reduplicated to mark
iteration and then joined to *tal-* 'start' with the overall meaning of 'start
to repeatedly fry'. Example (6-107b) presents a more complex serial verb

construction, with three verb roots and using the sequential morpheme
-*mpi* SEQ as a linker. Because the meaning of a sequential temporal
relation in Yimas is one of an event finishing and then being followed
by another, the interpretation of *tal*- 'start' is one in which it modifies
only the immediately preceding verb, to which it is linked only by juxtaposition. Thus, the meaning of the verb theme in (6-107b) is 'get up
quickly and then start to walk' in which the first act of rising is followed
sequentially in time by starting to walk. If *tal*- 'start' were to modify
both verbs in the sequential relationship, the interpretation would be
nonsensical: *'starting to rise and then walk.'

The verb root *tal*- 'hold' is unique in Yimas in that it can be used in
a specialized way both before and after a verb root, but with a difference
in meaning.

(6-108) a. na-ka-tal-kwalca-t
   3SG O-1SG A-CAUS-rise-PERF
   'I woke him up.'

   b. na-kwalca-tal
   3SG S-rise-start
   'He started to get up.'

Before the verb root, *tal*- 'hold' is, of course, nothing but the causative
prefix *tar*- ~ *tal*-, but after the root it has a specialized meaning
'start'.

The other verb root used in a specialized way in serial verb constructions to express modality is *tay*- 'see'. It has the meaning 'try' in these
cases.

(6-109) a. ya-n-a-armarm-tay-n
   VIII PL O-3SG A-DEF-board(RED: *arm*-)-try-PRES
   kacmpt
   canoe VIII PL
   'He tries to board the canoes.' (one after another)

   b. na-mpɨ-kwalca-tay-ɲcut
   3SG O-3DL A-rise-try-RM PAST
   'They both tried to wake him up.'

Note that *tay*- 'try' differs from its English equivalent in that in these
constructions it is not necessary that the person trying and the person
performing the following act are one and the same. Example (6-109b)
could be well paraphrased as 'they both tried him and he got up'. Note
that (6-109b) is formally transitive: this is sanctioned not by *kwalca*-
'rise', which is monovalent, but by *tay*- 'try' which is a bivalent verb
root, as demonstrated by its literal meaning 'see'.

It is important to note that although these two verbs have specialized meanings in serial verb constructions, such readings are not obligatory. Although they, of course, must have their literal meanings after -*mpi* SEQ (6-110a), this is also possible if they are joined simply by juxtaposition (6-110b).

(6-110) a. na-mpu-wampaki-mpi-tay-k
　　　　　3SG O-3PL-throw-SEQ-see-IRR
　　　　　'They threw it and watched it.'

　　　　b. impa-mpu-yakal-irm-tay-ɲcut
　　　　　3DL O-3PL A-CONT-stand-see-RM PAST
　　　　　'They were standing up and watching those two.'

6.3.1.2 Specializations in Serial Verb Constructions:
　　　　ti- 'do, feel, become'
The verb root *ti*- 'do, feel, become' is used in serial verb constructions in two specialized ways. In both these uses, it occurs as the first verb in the serial structure and is only linked to the following verb by simple juxtaposition. In the first of these uses, *ti*- 'do, feel, become' is always employed in combination with the verbal prefix *tia*- 'act, deed' (or its suffixal variant -*nti*) to emphasize that an action is accomplished to a greater extent than is usually expected. This is most common with verbs of motion, as these examples illustrate:

(6-111) a. tia-n-t-arm-mpi-wa-k
　　　　　act O-3SG A-do-board-SEQ-go-IRR
　　　　　'He boarded (the canoe) and went for good.'

　　　　b. tia-kay-c-arpal-kiantu-ŋkt
　　　　　act O-1PL A-do-exit-FR PAST-PC
　　　　　'Those few came outside completely.'

　　　　c. tia-n-taŋ-ti-wa-kia-ntuk-nakn
　　　　　act O-3SG A-COM-do-go-NIGHT-RM PAST-3SG O
　　　　　'He went with her for good.'

Notice that, in some ways, *ti*- 'do, feel, become' functions in these examples as a valence increaser, to derive bivalent verb themes from monovalent verb roots of motion. It is treated here as a specialized use of a serial verb construction rather than as a valence increasing prefix because it is completely restricted to a single introduced participant, coded by the agreement prefix *tia*- 'act'. As this prefix is transparently related to the semantics of the verb root *ti*- 'do, become, feel', it seems on balance more justified to treat this construction as a specialized serial verb construction, although, I do admit, the boundary between specialized serial verb constructions and, say, constructions with *pampay*- KIN is not a sharp one. The last example above (6-111c) is an interesting one. Although the core lexical verb root *wa-* 'go' is monovalent, the whole verbal construction is formally ditransitive. This is because serialization with *ti-* 'do' derives a bivalent verb theme and requires the presence of *tia-* 'act'. This in turn is derived into a trivalent verb theme by *taŋ-* COM, which licenses the appearance of *-nakn* 3SG D.

Related to this first specialized use of *ti-* 'do, feel, become' is the second one involving the interrogative adverbial *waratnti* 'how, in what way'. Consider first the following example:

(6-112) takmpi   tia-kay-ɲanaŋ-ti-ntut
         like this act O-1PL A-DUR-do-RM PAST
         'We used to do it like this.'

Since *ti-* 'do, feel, become' is a bivalent verb in this usage, it is associated with two pronominal affixes: *kay-* 1PL A and, filling the O slot, *tia-* 'act', so (6-112) literally means 'we used to do the act like this' The interrogative *waratnti* adverb contains the suffixal equivalent of *tia-* 'act' which is *-nti*. When this interrogative word is used in a clause, it typically is linked to the verb *ti-* 'do, feel, become', joined by juxtaposition as the first member of a serial verb construction. The adverb *waratnti* 'how' is formally a noun (it has the nominal concord suffix *-nti* 'act'), and is regarded as a core argument (note that it has no oblique suffix). Just as *ti-* 'do, feel, become' requires *tia-* 'act' in (6-111), it sanctions *waratnti* in the examples below:

(6-113) a. waratnti   tia-kay-ɲanaŋ-ti-kra-ntut
            how   act O-1PL A-DUR-do-cut-RM PAST
            'How did we used to cut (it)?'

        b. waratnti   anta-ti-kra-kia-na-ŋ?
            how   HORT SG-do-cut-NIGHT-IMP-V SG
            'How will I cut this?'

        c. waratnti   pia-mpu-ti-ant-kia-kt?
            how   talk O-3PL A-do-hear-NIGHT-RM FUT
            'How will they understand?'

        d. waratnti
            how
            ya-ka-na-ti-l-awt-mpi-kawra-kia-k?
            V PL O-1SG A-DEF-do-down-get-SEQ-stub-NR FUT-IRR
            'How am I getting (these) and stubbing (toes)?'

Although formally all the verbs in (6-113) are transitive, matching the bivalent specifications of their verb stems, they are actually trivalent, for the third core argument is *waratnti* 'how'. This is possible because of the use of *ti-* 'do, feel, become' in all the above examples, which links to *waratnti* 'how' in much the same way as it did to *tia-* in (6-112). This is transparently the case in (6-113a) in which the prefix *tia-* is overtly present and appositionally linked to *waratnti*.

6.3.2 Adverbial Incorporation

A second common process of derivation in Yimas which derives verb themes from verb stems is adverbial incorporation. Yimas possesses two types of adverbials: those which are base adverbials and can only appear incorporated as part of the verb theme and those which are derived from other word classes, notably adjectives and adverbs, and normally can appear either as incorporated elements or as independent words. As an example of the first type, consider *pay-* '(at) first, right now'. A sentence in which it appears as an incorporated element of the verb theme (6-114a) is grammatical, but one in which it appears as an independent word (6-114b) is not.

(6-114) a. na-mpu-pay-kulanaŋ-tay-ɲcut
 V SG O-3PL A-first-walk-see-RM PAST
 'They walked around and looked at it first.'

 b.*pay na-mpu-kulanaŋ-tay-ɲcut
 first V SG O-3PL A-walk-see-RM PAST

But *mampi* 'again' is a member of the second class. It is derived from the adjective root *ma-* 'other' plus the adverb derivational suffix *-mpi* and can appear either as incorporated element (6-115a) or as an independent word (6-115b).

(6-115) a. na-n-mampi-ira-wampuŋkra-ntut
 3SG O-3SG A-again-ALL-angry-RM PAST
 'He was angry with her again.'

 b. mampi na-n-ira-wampuŋkra-ntut
 again 3SG O-3SG A-ALL-angry-RM PAST
 'He was angry with her again.'

Obligatorily incorporated adverbials commonly, but not exclusively, express aspectual or temporal notions, while optionally incorporated adverbials denote the manner in or degree to which an action is carried out. I will first take up the discussion of the former.

6.3.2.1 Obligatorily Incorporated Adverbials

6.3.2.1.1 Continuative *yakal-*. This morpheme and the next one to be discussed are the most common of incorporated adverbials. The continuative *yakal-* (sometimes contracted to *kal-*) expresses that an action or event continues uninterrupted over an extended period and is translatable by the Tok Pisin usage *i wok long*. It is commonly found in combination with verbs denoting actions. It may only be used in past and future tenses; in the present, its function is usurped by *na-* DEF + *-nt* PRES.

Examples of *yakal-* follow:

(6-116) a. impa-yakal-cmi-kiantut
            3DL S-CONT-say-FR PAST
            'Those two were talking.'

      b. na-mpɨ-yakal-ca-mpi-yampara-pu-k
            V SG O-3DL A-CONT-put up-SEQ-erect-away-IRR
            'Those two were putting it up and erecting it while going.'

      c. pu-n-yakal-caŋkway-cantaw-malak-ntut
            3PL O-3SG A-CONT-VIS-sit(RED: *taw-*)-converse-RM PAST
            tak
            here
            'He was sitting here, talking with them to their faces.'

The position of incorporated adverbials is fixed. The obligatory incorporation of adverbials always occurs at the level of the verb theme and, thus, follows the derivation of a complex verb theme through verb serialization (6-116b) or valence altering (6-115c). Any other order of the morphemes in (6-116b,c) is ungrammatical.

6.3.2.1.2 Durative *nanaŋ-*. This morpheme expresses an event or, more commonly, a state which endures over an uninterrupted span of time. In contrast to *yakal-* CONT, *nanaŋ-* DUR is more commonly associated with verbs denoting states or conditions, and is typically translated by the Tok Pisin preverbal particle *se* HAB. Verbs marked by *nanaŋ-* DUR are typically viewed as extending over a longer period of time than those with *yakal-* CONT, hence the correlation of *nanaŋ-* with the Tok Pisin habitual particle. It is transparently related to the verb *naŋ-* 'live, stay' by partial reduplication, but the meaning is now quite divergent, and it must be regarded as a separate morpheme. A relationship between stance verbs like 'stay' or 'sit' and a durative/progressive morpheme is a common feature of Papuan languages (Foley 1986). The adverbial *nanaŋ-* DUR is also commonly found in combination with the aspectual suffix *-na(ŋ)* DUR (see Section 5.2.1.6.2).

Examples of *nanaŋ* DUR are:

(6-117) a. kay   na-nanaŋ-yamat-ɲa-ntut
            canoe VIII SG   3SG S-DUR-carve-DUR-RM PAST
            'He was making a canoe.'

THE VERB THEME AND CLAUSE STRUCTURE

    b. wampunŋ
       flour VI SG

       k-mpu-nanaŋ-wurt-am-na-ntut
       VI SG O-3PL A-DUR-put down(RED: *wul-*)eat-DUR-
                                 RM PAST
       'They were boiling and eating our sago flour.'

    c. tpwi   i-mpu-nanaŋ-pampay-cut-ɲcut
       sago X PL X PL O-3PL A-DUR-KIN-cross-RM PAST
       'They were carrying the sago across.'

As with *yakal-* CONT, *nanaŋ-* DUR is added at the level of the verb theme, after serialization (6-117b) and valence alternations (6-117c).

    The two adverbials *yakal-* CONT and *nanaŋ-* DUR are close in meaning, but there is a regular contrast between them. Consider this pair of examples:

(6-118) a. na-ka-yakal-cantaw-tay-ɲcut
         3SG O-3SG A-CONT-sit(RED: *taw-*)-RM PAST
         'I was sitting down, watching him.'

      b. na-ka-nanaŋ-tantaw-tay-ɲa-ntut
         3SG O-1SG A-DUR-sit(RED: *taw-*)-see-DUR-RM PAST
         'I was sitting down and saw him.'

yakal- CONT expresses actions which continue over a relatively short period and is associated with verb roots denoting actions or events. Thus, in (6-118a) it is the event predicate *tay-* 'see' which is largely modified by *yakal-* CONT; the meaning of the verb is paraphrasable as 'He was sitting down and he was engaged in staring at him'. In contrast, *nanaŋ-* DUR denotes an event which occurs over a longer period, so that the event is viewed as habitual or almost a state or condition. It tends to be associated with verb roots denoting states or conditions, such as *tantaw-* 'sit (down)'. Thus, in (6-118b) it is the stance verb stem *tantaw-* which is mainly modified by *nanaŋ-* DUR, so that the sentence is perhaps best paraphrased as 'He was engaged in sitting down, and he saw him'.

6.3.2.1.3 *pay-* 'at first, right now'. This incorporated adverbial is straightforward: it marks events happening immediately or to be carried out right away or as the first act in a sequence of acts. It is most commonly found with imperative or hortative verbs (see examples in Section 5.2.3).

(6-119) a. na-n-pay-ira-wampuŋkra-ntut
         3SG O-3SG A-first-ALL-angry-RM PAST
         'He was angry right then at her.'

      b. ɲa-mpwi   anta-pay-api-ɲa-mpwi
         other-talk HORT SG-first-put in-IMP-talk
         'Let me first put in more talk.' (i.e., record)

6.3.2.1.4 Visual *taŋkway-*. As mentioned in Section 6.2.3.3.4, in addition
to its uses as a valence increaser, *taŋkway-* VIS also functions as an
incorporated adverbial. While functioning as an adverbial it is best
translated by 'carefully' in English, for it expresses that the action being
accomplished is being carefully monitored by vision. Examples follow:

(6-120) a. ya-n-taŋkway-wampaki-pra-k
          V PL O-3SG A-VIS-throw-toward-IRR
          'He threw those down carefully.' (watching their fall)

       b. pu-kra-nanaŋ-taŋkway-cakat-kula-ntut
          3PL A-1PL O-DUR-VIS-feel-walk-RM PAST
          'They cared for us, as we walked around.' (watched over us)

Both examples in (6-120) are transitive, and the valence of their verb
themes is bivalent; clearly *taŋkway-* does not function as a valence-
increaser in these examples. Rather it supplies the adverbial notion of
manner of an action, action done with visual monitoring. Note that (6-
120b) contains two incorporated adverbials, *nanaŋ-* DUR and *taŋkway-*
VIS; this ordering is obligatory. Whenever an aspectual/temporal adverbial and a manner adverbial occur together, the sequence aspect-manner,
as in (6-120), is rigid. There are also rare, sporadic examples of the use
of other valence increasing affixes as incorporated adverbials, as seen in
the example below:

(6-121) aympanuŋ   ku-mp-ira-yawra-k
       heavy pounding stick X SG X SG O-3DL A-ALL-pick up-IRR
       'They both fetched a heavy pounding stick.'

As *yawra-* 'pick up' is a bivalent verb root, *ira-* ALL, simply adds the
adverbial meaning 'toward' and does not increase the valence of the verb.

6.3.2.1.5 *taray-* 'free, clear, loose'. As mentioned in Section 6.2.4, this
adverbial is a partial reduplication of *tay-* 'see'. In some uses it has clear
adverbial functions, parallel to the four morphemes just discussed.

(6-122) na-n-a-taray-yawra-n?
       3SG O-3SG A-DEF-clear-pick up-PRES
       'Can you understand him?'

However, *taray* 'clear' parallels *taŋkway-* VIS in that it too can function
as a valence increaser. In this usage it has a causative meaning 'let free,
clear, loose', as in these examples:

(6-123) a. ya-mpɨ-taray-mul-kia-k
            V PL O-3DL A-clear-run away-NIGHT-IRR
            'They both let them loose and ran away.'

        b. na-mpɨ-taray-wapat-ɲcut
            3SG O-3DL A-clear-ascend-RM PAST
            'Those two let him loose and went up.'

Both verb roots in (6-123) are monovalent, yet the full verbs are formally transitive. This is due to *taray-*, which in such cases derives a bivalent verb stem from the monovalent verb root, adding the meaning 'let loose'.

This valence increasing use of *taray-* 'clear' explains another anomaly that it shares with *taŋkway-* VIS in contrast with the other obligatorily incorporated adverbials. Only these two can be added at the level of the verb stem, inside a complex verb theme such as a serial verb construction, a property typical of the valence altering prefixes. This is possible with *taray-* even when it functions clearly as an adverbial rather than a valence increasing prefix. Examples of *taray-* 'clear' being added inside a complex verb theme follow:

(6-124) a. k-n-kra-mpi-caray-ca-k
            VI SG O-3SG A-cut-SEQ-clear-put up-IRR
            'He cut it and put it aside.' (cut it and put it up clear)

        b. ɲct   ya-n-awa-taray-ca-kia-k
            urine V PL   V PL-3SG A-excrete-clear-put up-NIGHT-IRR
            'She urinated right on him.' (she dropped it and it fell clear on him)

Note that in (6-124), *taray-* 'clear' is unquestionably functioning as an adverbial, for *ta-* 'put up' is already a bivalent verb and the examples are simple transitives. If *taray-* 'clear' did function as a valence increaser here, the examples should be ditransitive.

One might ask why, in view of the fact of the great similarity between *taŋkway-* VIS and *taray-* 'clear', the former was discussed in the section on valence increasing and the latter was not. To a certain extent, such decisions are arbitrary, but the primary criterion was the fact that *taray-* 'clear' more commonly functions as an incorporated adverbial rather than a valence increaser, while the ratio for *taŋkway-* VIS is the other way around. Also, *taray-* 'clear' has a transparent relationship to a verb stem *tay-* 'see', a feature diagnostic of many adverbials, particularly the optionally incorporated ones, while *taŋkway-* VIS, like the valence increasing morphemes generally, is synchronically unanalyzable (although the single exception to this generalization, *pampay-* KIN, is, like *taray-* 'clear', also transparently related to a verb root, *pay-* 'carry').

What this demonstrates is the rather fuzzy nature of the boundaries between certain morpheme classes in Yimas, in this case, verbs, adverbials, and valence altering affixes.

6.3.2.1.6 *kwanan-* 'badly, incorrectly, aimlessly'. This morpheme expresses that an action has no purpose, either in itself or because it is performed badly or incorrectly. In this meaning it occurs with *na-* DEF.

(6-125) a. ya-mpu-na-kwanan-tay-n
V PL O-3PL A-DEF-badly-see-PRES
'It's bad that they see them.' (without having the right by being initiated)

b. paŋkra-na-kwanan-kulanaŋ
1PC S-DEF-badly-walk
'We are walking about aimlessly.'

c. impa-na-kwanan-tɨ-kratk-n
3DL S-DEF-badly-RCP-fight-PRES
'Those two are fighting each other for no reason.'

(6-125c) is a further example of adverbial incorporation following verb stem derivation by a valence altering affix, in this case *tɨ-* RCP. With verbs in one of the future tenses, *kwanan-* 'badly' expresses that things will turn out badly if the event expected to occur in the future does eventuate.

(6-126) a. ŋaykum   tia-mpu-kwanan-tay-kt
woman II PL   act O-3PL A-badly-see-RM FUT
'It will be bad if women see this custom.'

b. kampra   ama-kwanan-tɨ-kt
hunger IX SG   1SG S-badly-feel-RM FUT
'It will be bad if I feel hungry.'

6.3.2.1.7 *kwanti-* 'now, today'. This incorporated adverbial clearly is historically derived, albeit irregularly, from the temporal word, *kwarkwa* 'today' (probably a reduplication) plus *-ɲti* 'act'. Synchronically, however, these two must be viewed as unconnected because there are no productive morphological processes to connect them. *kwanti-* 'now' expresses that an event is now coming to completion or has just done so. It contrasts with *pay-* 'first, right now' in being oriented to completed or about to be completed actions, rather than ongoing acts or those not yet begun. Examples follow:

(6-127) a. paŋkra-na-kwanti-ya-kia-k
3PC S-DEF-now-come-NEAR-IRR
'We few just arrived now.'

b. yampaŋ   k-n-a-kwanti-kacakapi-n
head VI SG VI SG O-3SG A-DEF-now-hide-PRES
'He hid his head just then.'

6.3.2.1.8 *pwi-* 'later, then'. This incorporated adverbial indicates that
an event occurred or will occur after another important event. It is not
common, but some examples are given below:

(6-128) a. ama ta-pwi-ya-n
1SG NEG-then-come-PRES
'I won't come then.'

b. na-mpu-pwi-cu-k
3SG O-3PL A-then-kill-IRR
'They killed him then.'

6.3.2.1.9 *mamaŋ-* 'slowly'. This is a very straightforward incorporated
adverbial: it expresses that an object in motion is proceeding slowly.
Interestingly, its opposite *kaykaykay* 'quickly' is only an optionally incorporated adverbial. Examples of *mamaŋ-* 'slowly' follow:

(6-129) a. kacmpt   ya-kay-mamaŋ-arkat-ɲcut
canoe VIII PL VIII PL O-1PL A-slowly-paddle-RM PAST
'We paddled the canoes slowly.'

b. pu-na-l-mamaŋ-ira-pra-n
3PL S-DEF-down-slowly-dance-toward-PRES
'They are dancing as they come slowly down.'

6.3.2.1.10 *kaykaykay-* 'quickly'. This is the opposite of *mamaŋ-* 'slowly'.
It expresses that an object in motion is proceeding quickly. This is only
an optionally incorporated adverbial, but is presented here because of
its paradigmatic contrast with *mamaŋ-* 'slowly'. Thus, the following two
sentences are equivalent in meaning:

(6-130) a. aŋka-kaykaykay-cu-impu-pu-n
HORT DL-quickly-out-go by water-away-IMP
'Let us go outside quickly.'

b. kaykaykay aŋka-tu-impu-pu-n
quickly   HORT DL-out-go by water-away-IMP
'Let us go outside quickly.'

The (a) example illustrates the optionally incorporated adverbial *kaykaykay* 'quickly' as an incorporated element, and (b) exemplifies it as an
independent word.

6.3.2.2 Optionally Incorporated Adverbials

With the exception of *kaykaykay* 'quickly', all optionally incorporated adverbials are derived from adjective or verb roots. Although there are some irregular forms (presented below), these adverbials are derived from the root by the suffix *-mpi*. This suffix is clearly related to the morpheme *-mpi* SEQ used in serial and dependent verb constructions, and is no doubt an historical development from it, but must be analyzed as a separate morpheme. It does not have a sequential temporal meaning as is always present in the case of *-mpi* SEQ. Rather, the form it derives is simply an adverbial modifying the verb or clause in which it appears.

As already mentioned, optionally incorporated adverbials can be derived from either adjective or verb roots. Adjective roots derive adverbials as follows:

Adjective		*Adverbial*	
kpa	'big'	kpanti	'in a big way, strongly'
yua	'good'	yuanti	'well'
mama	'bad'	mamanti	'badly, poorly'
ma	'other'	mampi	'again'

Of these only *mampi* 'again' is regularly derived by the suffixation of *-mpi* ADV. The others have an affix *-nti*, possibly a fossilized use of *-nti* 'act'. Examples of adverbials derived from verbs follow:

Verb		*Adverbial*	
makɲc-	'walk quietly'	makcmpi	'quietly, stealthily'
pramuŋ	'sleep'	praŋkampi	'sleepily, with eyes closed'
kalc-	'strong, hard'	kalcmpi	'strongly, with force'
pampaŋ-	'correct'	pampaŋpi	'correctly'

Again, the first two show irregularities in the derivation, though *-mpi* is used in all cases. Although all of these adverbials belong to the optionally incorporated class, i.e., have the option of appearing as independent words, it is certainly the case that they more commonly occur incorporated as part of the verb theme. Some examples in which they are incorporated are given below:

(6-131) a. karŋ
  glans penis VI SG

  k-n-mampi-malakmalak-
  VI SG O-3SG A-again-converse(RED: *malak*)-

  awram-kia-k-nakn
  enter-NIGHT-IRR-3SG D

  'He talked on and inserted his penis again.'

THE VERB THEME AND CLAUSE STRUCTURE

b. na-mpɨ-mampi-pucm-api-k
3SG O-3DL A-again-time VII SG-put in-IRR
'They both gave him time again.'

c. wurmpl   pla-mpu-makcmpi-wuntampwi-k
flute VII DL   VII DL O-3PL A-quietly-blow on-IRR
'They played the flutes quietly.'

d. impa-n-taŋ-praŋkampi-aypu-kia-k
3DL O-3SG A-COM-with eyes closed-recline-NIGHT-IRR
'He slept with them both.'

Adverbial incorporation always applies at the level of the verb theme, after any formation of a complex verb theme by serialization. Hence, the scope of an incorporated adverbial is potentially ambiguous when preceding a serial verb construction, as in the following:

(6-132) na-mpɨ-mampi-kwalca-mpi-tay-ɲcut
3SG O-3DL A-again-rise-SEQ-see-RM PAST
'They both got up again and saw him' or
'They both got up and saw him again.'

Out of context, example (6-132) is necessarily ambiguous; *mampi* 'again' could modify either verb root in the serial verb construction. The only way to disambiguate (6-132) would be to break it up into two separate clauses, with *mampi* 'again' attached to only one of the verbs.

Adverbial incorporation can co-exist in the same verb form with nominal incorporation. Example (6-131b) above is an example of this. In such cases, the adverbial always precedes the nominal: this is the result of the respective levels of derivation. Nominal incorporation is a stem derivational process, while adverbial incorporation is a theme derivational process, so the incorporated nominal must always occur closer to the verb root than the incorporated nominal. This applies whether the incorporated nominal is a basic noun, as in (6-131b), or a nominalized adjective or adjectival verb. The latter are found, for example, in the inchoative and causative constructions discussed in Section 6.2.3.13, and illustrated again (but this time with incorporated adverbials) in (6-133).

(6-133) a. mamam
       sore VII SG

       p-na-kaykaykay-waca-k-m-tɨ-n
       VII SG S-DEF-quickly-small-IRR-VII SG-become-PRES
       'The sore is becoming small quickly.'

b. irpm   mu-ka-kaykaykay-kpa-m-
coconut palm IV SG IV SG O-1SG A-quickly-big-IV SG-
tal-ci̵-t
CAUS-become-PERF
'I made the coconut palm big quickly.'

In these examples, the order of morphemes is rigid: the incorporated adverbial must precede the verb theme, consisting of the nominalized adjective (6-133b) or adjectival verb (6-133a) (with its appropriate concord marker) plus the main verb ti̵- 'become' and associated prefixes, such as tal- CAUS in (6-133b). If the causative construction is formed directly on an adjectival verb root (i.e., without the use of ti̵- 'become', and concomitant nominalization), there is more flexibility.

(6-134) a. arm   kay
         water   canoe VIII SG
         i-mpu-mampi-cal-cŋknt-t
         VIII SG O-3PL A-again-CAUS-heavy-PERF
         'The water made the canoe heavy again.'

     b. arm   kay
         water   canoe VIII SG
         i-mpu-tar-mampi-cŋknt-t
         VIII SG O-3PL A-CAUS-again-heavy-PERF
         'The water made the canoe heavy again.'

These two examples differ only in the placement of the adverbial *mampi* 'again'; it occurs before *tal-* CAUS in (6-134a) but after it in (6-134b). The former is by far the more common type and is preferred by all speakers. It represents the normal derivation sequence. The prefix *tal-* CAUS derives a bivalent verb stem from the monovalent adjectival verb root *tŋknt-* 'become heavy'. Then at the theme level, adverbial incorporation applies, adding *mampi* 'again'. Example (6-134b) represents a marked pattern of derivation with causativization applying unusually at the level of the verb theme after adverbial incorporation has occurred. This is an anomaly, but we have seen earlier cases of valence derivation applying at the theme level. In any case, it is a rather rare situation in Yimas when an incorporated adverbial appears closer to a verb root than a morpheme of a stem derivational process.

Having discussed obligatorily and optionally incorporated adverbials in some detail, I must now mention the small class of obligatorily unincorporated adverbials. These are four in number and are derived from the class of deictic words.

	Deictic		*Adverbial*
tak	'here'	takmpi	'in this way'
mnti	'there'	mntmpi	'in that way'
taŋka	'where'	taŋkampi	'to where'
wara	'what'	waratnti	'how'

These four can only appear as independent words; incorporation is completely ungrammatical for them.

(6-135) a. mntmpi   paŋkra-ta(w)-war-ŋkt?
in that way 2PC S-sit-HAB-PC
'Do you few live like that?'

b.*paŋkra-mntmpi-ca(w)-war-ŋkt
2PC S-in that way-sit-HAB-PC

Other examples of these obligatorily unincorporated forms are provided below:

(6-136) a. waratnti namarawt   pu-n-awkura-naŋ?
how   person I SG 3PL O-3SG A-gather-DUR
'How is this person getting them?'

b. taŋkampi kapwa-na-mampi-arm-pi-wa-n?
to where   2DL S-DEF-again-board-SEQ-go-PRES
'Where are you both boarding (the canoe) to go to again?'

6.3.3 Elevationals/Directionals

This next set of morphemes is a pervasive feature of Yimas discourse. Just as the tense inflections of Yimas verbs express the temporal position of the narrated event with respect to the time of the ongoing speech act, so the elevational/directional morphemes indicate the spatial coordinates of the described event, either with respect to the place of the speech act or the place of other events in the discourse. These morphemes indicate either the vertical position of the described event (the elevationals: up versus down) or its direction (the directionals: in, out, in a straight line, in many directions). The actual morphemes in Yimas are given below:

Elevationals		*Directionals*	
wi-	'up'	ma-	'in, inside'
l-	'down'		(the bush, lakes, house)
		kaw-	'in, inside' (a canoe, canal, house)
		tu-	'out, outside'
		kawku-	'straight across, in a straight line'
		tra-	'about, in many directions or places'

These morphemes can be used to mark the location of events which occur in a stationary locale, in which case they are used alone, or can indicate the direction of motion of a moving event, in which case they commonly co-occur with the motion suffixes -*pu* 'motion away' or -*pra* 'motion toward'. I will consider their use for stationary events first.

As already mentioned, the elevationals/directionals locate the position of the described event with respect to the spatial position of the speech act or some other event or some participant in the discourse. Some examples of orientation with respect to the place of the speech act follow:

(6-137) a. pu-na-wi-am-n
             3PL S-DEF-up-eat-PRES
             'They are eating up there.'

        b. kay   i-na-l-ampu-n
             canoe VIII SG   VIII SG S-DEF-down-float-PRES
             'The canoe is down there.'

        c. arm   pay-l-ap-mpi-awkura-n
             water first-down-put in-SEQ-gather-IMP
             'Fetch water down there first!'

Examples (6-137a,b) are statements concerning an event occurring elsewhere. The elevational in each case locates this event or state with respect to the position of the speech act. The last example is a command. In this case, the elevational morpheme indicates the location of the place in which the command is to be executed. The location is specified with respect to the place where the command is given, the location of the speech act. Note further that (6-137c) contains both an incorporated adverbial *pay-* 'first' and an elevational *l-* 'down' in that order. Both of these are morphemes added at the level of the verb theme (note that the verb theme is complex, also containing a serial verb construction), but this ordering is typical.

Elevationals/directionals can also be used to orient a stationary event with respect to other events or participants in the discourse.

(6-138) a. nampt   ya-mpu-tra-wark-k
             house PL   house PL O-3PL A-about-build-IRR
             'They built their houses about.' (in different places)

        b. kntm   ka-mpu-pay-ma-takat-ɲa-mpan-m
             paint VII SG   LIKE-3PL A-first-in-feel-IMP-3PL D-VII SG T
             'They can paint them all inside first.'

    c. patn   pu-na-ma-kpuct-pay-n
       betelnut V SG 3PL S-DEF-in-chew(RED: *kpuc-*)-lie-PRES
       'They are lying down inside, chewing betelnut.'

(6-138a) locates the places in which houses were built with respect to the site of the village which is the topic of the section of the narrative from which this example was drawn. It states that the houses were distributed widely, in different directions, all over the village site. Examples (6-138b,c) both locate the events they are describing within the male cult house, which is the central prop in this narrative about traditional male initiations. The directional *ma-* 'in' expresses that the events reported occurred inside the male cult house as opposed to other described events which took place outside of it.

    The direction of moving events can also be specified by the elevational/directional morphemes. If the verb involved is inherently one involving motion, the elevationals/directionals can be used alone.

(6-139) a. kra-kawku-arm-ŋ
        3PL S-straight-board-IRR
        'Those few went straight and boarded.'

    b. nmpi   ay-cra-wampak-ɲa-ŋkt
       leaf VII PL HORT PL-about-throw-IMP-PC
       'Let us few send notices around.' (in different directions)

Otherwise, the motion suffixes *-pu* 'motion away' and *-pra* 'motion toward' are used, although these are commonly employed even if the verb denotes motion. The place toward which or away from which the motion is directed can be either the place of the speech act (i.e., the speaker) or the site of Yimas village, depending on context. These two suffixes are added at the end of the verb theme, after specialized uses of verb roots such as *tay-* 'try' or *tal-* 'start' and the valence increasing suffix *-ŋa* BEN, and before any tense or aspect suffixes. While these two suffixes mostly co-occur with the elevational/directional prefixes, they can be used alone, as in these examples:

(6-140) a. na-n-pampay-iray-pra-k
        3SG O-3SG A-KIN-cry-toward-IRR
        'He cried carrying her toward the village.'

    b. na-mpu-wurtwurt-tay-pra-kia-k
       3SG O-3PL A-put down(RED: *wul-*)-try-toward-NIGHT-IRR
       'They kept trying to put it down in the water as they came toward the village.'

Note that in (6-140b) the meaning component of motion is supplied strictly by -*pra* 'motion toward', the verb roots in the theme expressing other types of actions.

Most commonly, -*pu* 'motion away' and -*pra* 'motion toward' are found in combination with an elevational/directional prefix, which more specifically indicates the direction of the movement.

(6-141) a. nmpaŋki   kia-mpɨ-kawku-ta-pu-k
           fish trap VI PL   VI PL O-3DL A-straight-put-away-IRR
           'They both put the fish traps straight down.'

       b. kapa-l-way-mpi-mul-pra-kia-k
          1DL S-down-turn-SEQ-run-toward-NIGHT-IRR
          'We turned around and ran down here.'

       c. paŋkra-kaw-ŋka-pu-kiantu-ŋkt
          1PC S-in-go by land-away-FR PAST-PC
          'We few went inside.'

       d. anta-pay-wi-ŋka-pu-kia-k   nam-n
          HORT-first-up-go by land-away-NR FUT-IRR   house-OBL
          'Let me go up to the house first.'

       e. na-tu-arpal-pu-ntut
          3SG S-out-exit-away-RM PAST
          'He went outside.'

In each of these examples -*pu* and -*pra* specify 'motion away' or 'motion toward', respectively, while the various choices of the elevationals/directionals add the specific directions, 'up', 'down', 'straight', and so forth.

The elevational/directional prefixes are one of the few grammatical features of Yimas that show a clear ergative-absolutive alignment. With intransitive verbs, they indicate the relative position/direction of the S argument.

(6-142) a. kay   i-na-l-ampu-n
           canoe VIII SG   VIII SG S-DEF-down-float-PRES
           'The canoe is down there.'

       b. ka-mpu-tra-ya-n
          LIKE-3PL S-about-come-PRES
          'They can get distributed.'

With transitive verbs, it is always the position of the O argument that is specified by the prefixes. With many transitive verbs, of course, the A and O are in the same place, but for those verbs where this is not the case, it is the location of the O argument which is indicated.

(6-143) irmpŋ   na-nan-l-ant-kia-ntut?
        slit drum V SG   V SG O-2PL A-down-hear-NIGHT-RM PAST
        'Did you all hear the slit drums down below?'
        *'Did you all down below hear the slit drums?'

The verb root *ant-* 'hear' is a perception verb for which typically the
perceiver (A participant) and the source of noise (the O participant)
are in a different place. In (6-143) the elevational prefix *l-* 'down' can
only be interpreted as indicating the location of the slit drum (the O
participant), not the perceivers.

Transitive verbs of motion where the A participant moves toward the
O argument or where the O participant itself moves are parallel: it is
the location or the direction of movement of the O participant which is
coded by the elevational/directional prefixes.

(6-144) a. kay   naŋ-l-arm-na-ŋkan-i   (compare 6-142a)
           canoe VIII SG   IMP PL-down-board-IMP-PC-VIII SG
           'You all board the canoe below.'
           *'You all below board the canoe.'

        b. nmpi   ay-cra-wampak-ɲa-ŋkt   (compare (6-142b)
           leaf VII PL   HORT PL-about-throw-IMP-PC
           'Let us few distribute messages.'
           *'Let us few around send messages.'

        c. nampt   ya-mpu-tra-wark-k
           house PL house PL O-3PL A-about-build-IRR
           'They built their houses about.'

In (6-144a), the A participant moves toward the O participant, the position of which is specified by *l-* 'down' as below the point of origin for
the movement. Example (6-144b) illustrates the setting in motion of the
O participant by an action of the A participant. Again, it is the direction of the O (in this case, many directions) which is expressed by the
elevational/directional prefix *tra-* 'about'. Finally, (6-144c) illustrates a
case where through the action of the A participant, the O participant
actually comes into being. Again, the directional prefix *tra-* 'about' indicates the location of these created objects (O participant) not that of
the creators (A participant).

The final question to be addressed in this section is the placement
of elevational/directional inflections in the morphological derivation of
a verb. They have been treated here as morphemes added at the level
of the verb theme and this analysis works well for the great majority of cases. For example, an elevational/directional prefix usually

appears before a serial verb construction, just as with incorporated adverbials.

(6-145) a. impa-na-kaw-ya-ka-pay-n
      3DL S-DEF-in-come-SEQ-lie-PRES
      'They are both coming and lying down inside.'

    b. pla-n-ma-awkura-mpi-kacakapi-mpi-ci-pra-k
      VII PL O-3SG A-in-gather-SEQ-hide-SEQ-put down-toward-
                                IRR
      'He brought these two and hid them and put them inside.'

    c. kapa-l-way-mpi-mul-pra-kia-k
      1DL S-down-turn-SEQ-run-toward-NIGHT-IRR
      'We turned around and ran down here.'

In each example of (6-145), an elevational/directional prefix precedes a complex verb theme which is of a serial verb construction. And in each case, the prefix actually semantically modifies the last verb root in the serial construction, the one farthest removed from it. Clearly, by these examples, elevationals/directionals must be analyzed as morphemes added at the level of the verb theme, parallel to incorporated adverbials.

However, there are problems with this claim, for there exist examples where the prefixes occur inside serial verb constructions, like stem derivational affixes.

(6-146) a. ka-mpan-a-ya-ka-l-awkura-kia-k
      LIKE-1A/2SG O-DEF-come-SEQ-down-get-NR FUT-IRR
      'I will come and get you down there tomorrow.'

    b. na-n-ya-ka-ma-ta-mpi-cantaw-kia-k
      V SG O-3SG A-come-SEQ-in-put-SEQ-sit(RED: taw-)-
                               NIGHT-IRR
      'He came and put it and sat down inside.'

    c. paŋkra-kwalca-mpi-cu-ŋka-pu-kiantu-ŋkt
      1PC S-rise-SEQ-out-go by land-away-FR PAST-PC
      'We few got up and came outside.'

    d. pu-ŋa-tmi-wi-impu-pra-t
      3PL A-1SG O-say-up-go by water-toward-PERF
      'He made me come upriver toward the village.'

These exceptions fall into two clearly defined types. In the first type, the elevational/directional follows the basic motion verbs wa- 'go' and ya- 'come' joined in a serial construction by -ka SEQ, as illustrated in (6-146a,b). It may be that serialization of these two verbs using -ka SEQ is a later stage in the derivation, itself a derivation at the verb theme level. In other words, in (6-146b) a complex verb theme is first composed by serializing the verb root *ta-* 'put' and the verb stem *tantaw-* 'sit down'. To this verb theme is then added the directional prefix *ma-* 'in'. Finally, this complex theme is then serialized again at the theme level with *ya-* 'come' to form the final complex serial verb construction. This analysis finds some plausibility in that it is strictly lexically governed by the two basic motion verbs; it needs to be stipulated as an option restricted to these verbs in the grammar. This construction however, is only optional and is not obligatory as example (6-145a) clearly demonstrates, for there *kaw-* 'inside' precedes *ya-* 'come' + -*ka* SEQ in a serial construction.

The second two examples illustrate the other type of exception, which involves the verb roots, *ŋka-* 'go by land' and *impu-* 'go by water'. These exceptions are explained by the fact that the elevational/directional prefixes are probably already associated lexically with these verb roots, so that the prefix plus root should be regarded as a single verb stem. This explanation is immediately confirmed by the observation that it is possible to use two elevational/directional prefixes with these verbs, one before the root and joined at the stem level, and one at the level of the verb theme, preceding the serial verb construction.

(6-147)   ipa-na-ma-kulanaŋ-ma-ŋka-pu-n
        1PL S-DEF-in-walk-in-go by land-away-PRES
        'We are walking, going inside.'

Having established that the elevational/directional prefixes are morphemes added at the level of the verb theme, we need to consider their ordering constraints with the other morphemes added at this level, incorporated adverbials. Although these morphemes function at the same level their sequential order is rigid; the adverbial must precede the elevational/directional (see also examples (6-138b) and (6-141d)).

(6-148)   kia-mpɨ-mampi-ma-tay-pu-k
        VI PL O-3DL A-again-in-see-away-IRR
        'They both saw those and went inside again.'

There is only one exception to this rule in my entire corpus, which is given below:

(6-149)   pu-na-l-mamaŋ-ira-pra-n
        3PL S-DEF-down-slowly-dance-toward-PRES
        'They are dancing as they came down slowly.'

In this one case, the elevational precedes the adverbial, but no explanation is available for the anomaly.

6.4 An Explicit Account of Yimas Verbal Morphology

In the last chapter and the previous sections of this chapter, I have presented a detailed discussion of the structure and categories of Yimas verbal morphology. Within the verb, I have distinguished three levels of structure: root, stem, and theme, and I have shown how the morphemes of these three levels interact. I have also attempted a fairly careful description of the meanings and functions of the morphemes in the various morphological categories, such as tense suffixes, pronominal affixes and valence altering affixes, etc. In this section, I will try to draw all this together and present a fairly explicit and coherent account of Yimas verbal morphology.

Perhaps the primary bifurcation in the Yimas verb is that reflected in the division of material between this chapter and the previous one. This is the split between the categories within the verb theme, e.g., adverbials, serialized verbs, valence altering affixes, and those outside of it, e.g., pronominal affixes, aspect, tense, and mood. In more traditional terms, this corresponds·to the difference between derivational and inflectional morphology, respectively. Derivational morphology is normally described as that belonging properly to the lexicon, generating a new complex form from a simplex base form, while inflectional morphology is held to belong to the clause as a whole, specifying semantic and syntactic categories at this level. Derivational morphology is usually optional, while some categories of inflectional morphology in a language are often obligatory. While this distinction can be drawn in Yimas (as I just did above), I do not believe it is of any great value in the description of the language. I believe that ultimately all of the verbal morphology in Yimas is produced as the result of derivational processes. There is no sudden switch in the structural behavior of the verbal morphology when one passes from inside of the verb theme to outside, so there are no motivated grounds for drawing a distinction between two types of morphology at this boundary. Rather the whole structure of a Yimas verb is the result of ordered processes of morphological derivation, as I will demonstrate below.

But before proceeding to this, let me first dispose of the argument that the verbal morphology should be produced via syntactic rules. I cannot consider all classes of morphology here, so let me consider what might be the most promising cases—valence altering. There are a couple of compelling arguments for treating valence changing as a lexical derivation process and not a case of a syntactic rule. First, note that although Yimas has numerous productive valence increasing affixes, the final output of these derivations can never be more than a trivalent verb stem, the maximum permitted for underived verb roots like ŋa- 'give' or *i-* 'tell'. In other words, the result of the valence increasing rules must be the equivalent of the valence of a base lexical item. This constraint makes sense if the valence increasing rules occur in the lexicon, but does not if they are independent syntactic processes.

Now let me consider the second argument. Remember, as noted in earlier sections, that valence increasing prefixes may have alternate constructions involving postpositions, as in the following examples, repeated from previous sections.

(6-150) a. ipa   kantk pu-mampi-wa-k
         1PL with   3PL S-again-go-IRR
         'They went with us.'

      b. pu-kra-mampi-taŋ-wa-k
         3PL A-1PL O-again-COM-go-IRR
         'They went with us.'

(6-151) a. na-nampan   na-way-mpi-ya-ntut
         3SG-toward 3SG S-turn-SEQ-come-RM PAST
         'He turned back and came toward her.'

      b. na-n-way-mpi-ira-ya-ntut
         3SG O-3SG A-turn-SEQ-ALL-come-RM PAST
         'He turned back and came toward her.'

In the (a) examples, a participant in the event appears as an oblique phrase, while in the (b) examples, it is a core argument. Thus, oblique nominals marked by the postpositions *kantk* 'with' and *nampan* 'toward' correspond to core nominals coded by the valence increasing prefixes *taŋ-* COM or *ira-* ALL, respectively. From the structural alternations and the paraphrase equivalences between the (a) and (b) examples above, one may conclude that there is a convincing case for a productive syntactic process in Yimas which promotes oblique nominals to core arguments, much as dative shift constructions are commonly analyzed in English: *he gave a book to Mary* becomes *he gave Mary a book*.

This analysis, however, runs into immediate problems when we consider the entire range of valence increasing affixes in Yimas. For most of these, unlike *taŋ-* COM and *ira-* ALL, there is simply no alternative construction in which the core argument licensed by the valence increasing prefix appears as an oblique nominal. In other words, there are no paraphrase equivalents such as the (a) examples in (6-150) and (6-151) for these examples:

(6-152) a. na-n-taŋkway-iray-ɲcut
         3SG O-3SG A-VIS-cry-RM PAST
         'He cried over her.' (looking at her body)

b. na-n-pampay-iray-pra-k
   3SG O-3SG A-KIN-cry-toward-IRR
   'He cried carrying her toward the village.'

The ideas behind the examples in (6-152) can only be expressed in this way; alternatives with oblique nominals do not exist (although paraphrases employing two clauses are possible). This casts grave doubt on the productive syntactic analysis of valence increasing in Yimas. There are no plausible underlying syntactic constructions from which the examples in (6-152) can be derived. Rather one must conclude that they (and, by extension (6-150b) and (6-151b)) are base generated. Further, because the sequence of valence affix plus verb root forms a single verb stem, this base generation must be accomplished by morphological rules and most likely accomplished in the lexicon.

Having established the morphological basis of such processes as valence changing, it is now time to turn to a more detailed account of the derivation of Yimas verb forms. This model of Yimas verbal morphology means that the entire polysynthetic structure of a verb, with all its elaborate morphological specifications, is produced by a complex, ordered series of derivations. The morphological rules which accomplish these derivations are located in a component of the lexicon. It will be the task of the remainder of this section to elucidate explicitly the internal structure of this derivational process in its various stages.

The starting point, of course, for all Yimas verbs is a verb root: these are all entered separately in the lexicon. Let us represent a verb root with the symbol V_0.

The next state is the derivation of verb stems from verb roots. The verb stem is represented by V_1. There are a number of processes which derive verb stems, i.e., convert V_0 to V_1: reduplication, noun incorporation, and valence altering. These processes are themselves hierarchically arranged. The most basic, i.e the one applied first, is reduplication. Reduplication seems to be the most lexicalized of all derivational processes: there are two bits of evidence to support this. First, there is a special dissimilation rule that applies to reduplicated forms that does not apply elsewhere in the grammar (rule (2-7)). This removes the F autosegment from a reduplicated segment, so that *wul-* 'put in water' reduplicated is *wurt-*, not **wult-*. This is a specialized phonological rule, something to be expected for a highly lexicalized process. Second, Yimas has some irregular reduplicated forms: *ira-* 'dance' reduplicated is *iranta-*, not **irata-*. This, again, would be expected of a highly lexicalized process. So, applying reduplication to two representative verb roots, we have the following derivations:

(6-153)

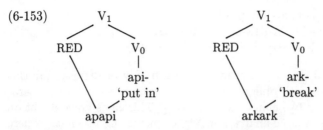

This derivation can be stated as the lexical rule $V_1 = (RED) + V_0$.

The next stem-level derivational process is noun incorporation. As mentioned in Section 6.2.5, this is a sporadic process which often results in idiomatic constructions, a feature diagnostic of a highly lexicalized process. The only productive type is incorporation of nominalized adjectives. Diagrammatic examples of noun incorporation are given below:

(6-154)

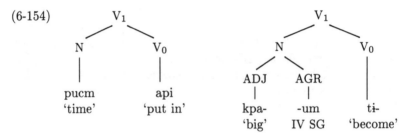

Combining reduplication and noun incorporation in one lexical rule, we have $V_1 = (N) + (RED) + V_0$.

Finally, we turn to the most common and most varied type of verb stem derivation: valence alterations. All valence changing processes but possessor raising and ŋa- BEN are possible at the level of the verb stem. A couple of examples illustrating valence changing inside serial verb constructions (hence on the level of the verb stem) follow:

(6-155) a. na-n-way-mpi-ira-ya-ntut
3SG O-3SG A-turn-SEQ-ALL-come-RM PAST
'He turned and came toward her.'

b. tpwi   i-mp-awkura-pampay-wapal-kia-k
sago X PL X PL O-3DL A-gather-KIN-ascend-NIGHT-IRR
'They both were gathering sago and carrying it up with them.'

Valence altering affixes not uncommonly co-occur with the other two derivational categories of the verb stem, reduplication and noun incorporation.

(6-156)

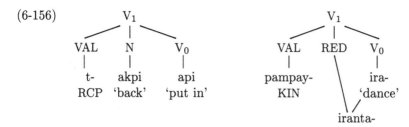

With incorporated nominalized adjectives or adjectival verbs, there is some variation in the placement of the causative prefix. As pointed out in the discussion of examples (6-35) and (6-36) the causative prefix *tar- ~ tal-* can occur either before the incorporated nominal or the inchoative verb *ti-* 'become'. These possibilities can be represented as follows:

(6-157)

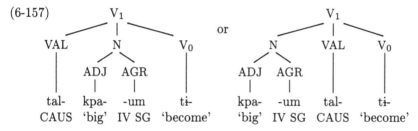

Alternations like that in (6-157) are not possible for any other valence changing affix, nor is it even possible for *tar- ~ tal-* CAUS with any other morpheme type other than an incorporated nominalized adjective. Thus in addition to the general rule for lexical derivation of verb stems,

(6-158) $V_1 = (VAL) + (N) + (RED) + V_0$

we will need the following optional sub-rule:

(6-159) If VAL = CAUS,
         VAL + N ⇒ N + VAL (optional)

Having treated the derivation of verb stems, I now turn to the verb theme. The core of all complex verb themes is the serial verb constructions. Structurally, there are two types of serial verb construction: those in which the verb stems are joined by simple juxtaposition and those where they are linked by overt morphemes *-ra* SIM or *-mpi* SEQ, as illustrated below:

(6-160) a. wampuŋ
            sago flour VI SG

k-mpu-nanaŋ-wurt-am-na-ntut
VI SG O-3PL A-DUR-boil(RED: *wul-*)-eat-DUR-RM PAST
'They were boiling and eating sago flour repeatedly.'

b. na-n-munta-ra-wapal-k
3SG O-3SG A-call-SIM-climb-IRR
'She called out to him while going up.'

c. pu-kra-awl-mpi-ayn-pi-ya-kia-k-ŋkt
3PL A-1PL O-get-SEQ-put in-SEQ-come-NIGHT-IRR-PC
'They got us few and put us few inside (a canoe) and came back.'

d. paŋkra-kwalca-mpi-kulanaŋ-tal-kiantu-ŋkt
1PC S-rise-SEQ-walk-start-FR PAST-PC
'We few got up and started to walk.'

As the (c) and (d) examples indicate, serial verb constructions are not limited to just two verb stems. This possibility must be handled in the explicit derivational rule, as must the alternation between simple juxtaposition and the usage of morpheme linkers. I suggest the following formula:

(6-161) $V_2 = ([V_1 + [\{ {}^{-mpi}_{-ra} \}]]^n) + V_1$

where n can be either one or two. This will provide the following structures for the verb themes of (6-160a) and (6-160d):

(6-162) a.

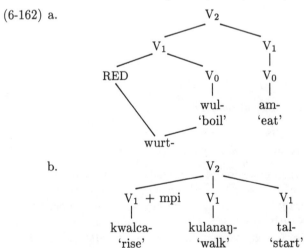

b.

Similar structures are found when a valence altering affix applies at the stem level within a serial verb construction. The following structure is the verb theme of example (6-150b).

(6-163)

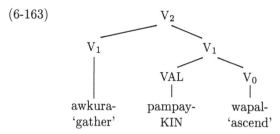

Following the formation of serial verb constructions, valence changing may apply again, this time at the level of verb theme. I repeat a few examples of this below:

(6-164) a. uraŋknut
coconut meat IX PL

ura-mpu-kra-taŋ-ntak-mpi-ɲa-ntut
IX PL T-3PL A-1PL D-COM-leave-SEQ-stay-RM PAST
'They left the coconut meat with us.'

b. na-mpu-taŋkway-iranta-irm-kia-ntut
3SG O-3PL A-VIS-dance(RED: *ira-*)-stand-NIGHT-RM PAST
'They danced for her.'

c. na-kay-pampay-arpat-mpi-cantaw-ntut
3SG O-1PL A-KIN-exit-SEQ-sit(RED: *taw-*)-RM PAST
'We carried them out and sat down.'

d. awt ŋa-kra-yawra-mpi-waraca-ŋa-n
fire IMP 1-1PL D-pick up-SEQ-return-BEN-IMP
'Bring back fire for us.'

Note that, as (6-164d) demonstrates, valence increasing with *ŋa-* BEN applies here, although possessor raising still does not. To handle valence changing at the theme level, rule (6-161) must be expanded as follows:

(6-165) $V_2 = (VAL) + ([V_1 + [\{{}^{-mpi}_{-ra}\}]]^n) + V_1 + (VAL)$

Applying this rule and rule (6-158) to the verb themes in (6-164) we get the following structural descriptions:

(6-166) a.

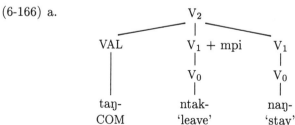

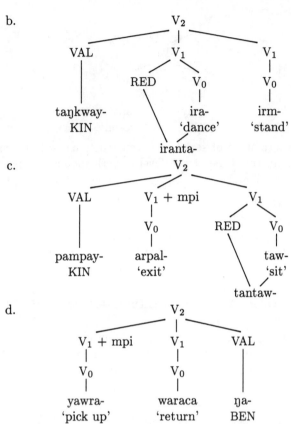

b.

c.

d.

The next stage in the derivation introduces the elevationals/directionals. Remember that these correspond to two order classes of morphemes: the elevational/directional prefixes such as *l-* 'down', and the motion suffixes, *pu-* 'away' and *pra-* 'toward'. Adding these order classes to rule (6-165) we now derive the following:

(6-167) $V_2 = (ELEV)+(VAL)+([V_1+[\{^{-mpi}_{-ra}\}]]^n)+V_1+(VAL)+(MOT)$

which generates the following structures:

(6-168) a. V_2 = (6-141b)

b.   = (6-138c)

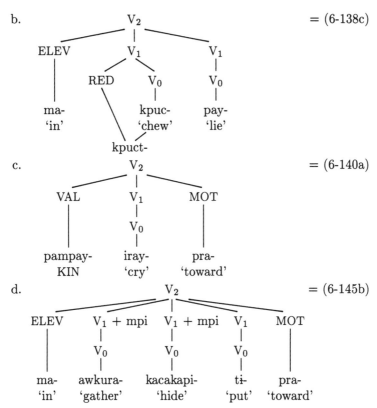

c.   = (6-140a)

d.   = (6-145b)

As mentioned briefly in Section 6.3.3, elevationals/directionals can occasionally appear inside serial verb constructions, usually when the previous verb root is either *wa-* 'go' or *ya-* 'come' linked by *ka-* SEQ. In
other words, V₂ constituents can occasionally be joined recursively with
other V₂ constituents (when V₀ = *wa-* 'go'/*ya-* 'come') to form another
V₂, as in the following:

(6-169)   V₂   = (6-146a)

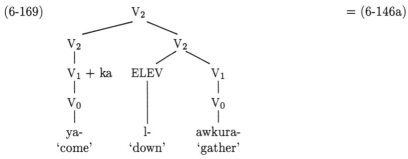

This recursive property for V₂ can be expressed formally as follows:

(6-170) $V_2 = V_2$ $(V_0 = wa\text{-}/ya\text{-}) + V_2$

The first V_2 must be a minimal V_2, i.e., can only consist of V_0 plus the linking morpheme $-ka$ SEQ. The second V_2 is not so constrained (see (6-146b)).

The final derivational process of the verb theme is adverbial incorporation, both obligatory and optional (optionally incorporated adverbials will have already been derived from adjectives and verbs elsewhere by lexical rules). The language permits more than one incorporated adverbial in a single V_2 constituent (see example (6-120b)). The normal position for incorporated adverbials is as the first morpheme of the verb theme, so that (6-167) should be amended as follows:

(6-171) $V_2 = ((\text{ADV})^n) + (\text{ELEV}) + (\text{VAL}) + (\,[V_1 + [\{{}^{-\text{mpi}}_{-\text{ra}}\}]\,]^n) + V_1$
$+ (\text{VAL}) + (\text{MOT})$

The first three classes of morphemes generally appear in the order given, as in these examples:

(6-172) a.

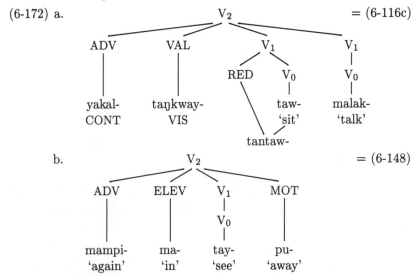

(6-172) a. V_2 = (6-116c)

ADV   VAL V_1 V_1

RED V_0 V_0

yakal-   taŋkway-   taw-   malak-
CONT   VIS   'sit'   'talk'

tantaw-

b. V_2 = (6-148)

ADV   ELEV V_1 MOT

V_0

mampi-   ma-   tay-   pu-
'again'   'in'   'see'   'away'

But there are very occasional examples such as the following where the ordering among the morphemes is other than that generated by (6-171), which suggests there is some flexibility of ordering. For example, both of the following examples are grammatical (although the former is preferred), and both are offered when the sentence is elicited:

(6-173) a. na-mpu-mampi-caŋ-wa-t
        3SG O-3PL A-again-COM-go-PERF
        'They went with him.'

b. na-mpu-taŋ-mampi-wa-t
3SG O-3PL A-COM-again-go-PERF
'They went with him.'

And the following structure was encountered in a text:

(6-174) V_2 = (6-149)

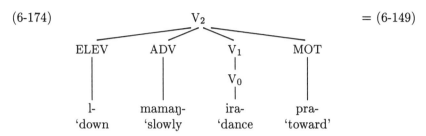

ELEV   ADV V_1 MOT
                                          |
                                         V_0

l-   mamaŋ-   ira-   pra-
'down   'slowly   'dance   'toward'

Although structures like (6-174) and (6-173b) do exist in Yimas, they are much less common than those of (6-173a) and (6-172), so I see no reason to alter rule (6-171). One should just note some acceptable permutations among the first three morpheme classes.

With incorporated adverbials we reach the border of the verb theme and pass into the morphology of the verb proper. Let me represent a fully inflected Yimas verb simply by V. The only obligatory inflection of a Yimas verb is tense (IMP functions as a tense suffix in imperatives and hortatives). Preceding the obligatory tense suffixes are the optional aspect suffixes and the multifunctional -*kia*. Preceding V_2 is the prefix *na*- DEF. Thus, the next stage in the derivation of a Yimas verb is specification for these categories as follows:

(6-175) $V = (na\text{-}) + V_2 + (\text{ASP}) + (\text{-}kia) + \text{TNS}$

This rule together with (6-169) and (6-156) generate the following structures:

(6-176) a.   V   = (6-69b)

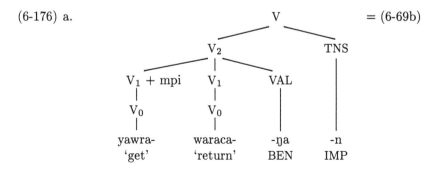

V_2 TNS

$V_1 + \text{mpi}$ V_1 VAL
   | |
  V_0 V_0

yawra-   waraca-   -ŋa   -n
'get'   'return'   BEN   IMP

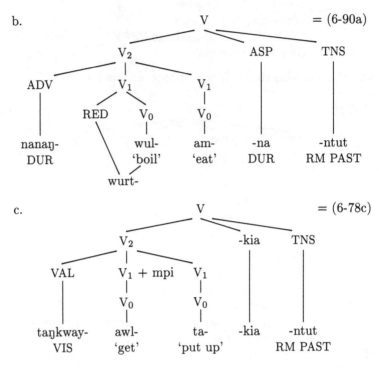

b.   V   = (6-90a)

c.   V   = (6-78c)

Following derivation with the tense and aspect suffixes, the pronominal affixes are added. The valence of V_2, the verb theme, determines the number of possible pronominal affixes. The valence of the verb theme in turn is derived from the valences of the individual verb roots plus the effect of any valence changing affixes. This is also the place in the derivation of a verb where possessor raising applies. By this process the animate possessor of a body part will be coded by a dative affix. A Yimas verb can have up to three pronominal affixes, realized by three prefixes or a combination of prefixes and suffixes. There may be no pronominal affixes at all. A paucal suffix may also appear to indicate the paucal number of a first or second person participant. By including the stage of the addition of the pronominal agreement affixes to (6-175) we get the following,

(6-177) $V = ((PRO)^n) + (na\text{-}) + V_2 + (ASP) + (\text{-}kia) + TNS$
$+ (PC) + ((PRO)^{3-n})$

where n can be any number from one to three, though if it is three, the second PRO constituent must be zero. Rule (6-177) will generate these structures:

(6-178) a.   = (6-1b)

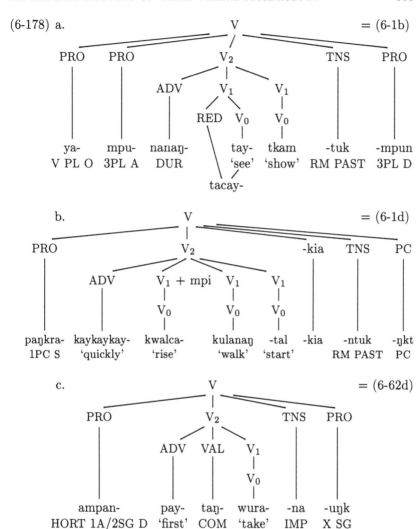

The final stage in the lexical derivation of a Yimas verb is the addition of the modal prefixes. As discussed in detail in Section 5.2.2, this commonly results in a realignment of the pronominal affixes, so that the prefix which would appear first in the word in normal forms appears as a final suffix in the modally inflected form. This can be expressed explicitly as follows:

(6-179) $\text{MOD} + (\text{PRO})^n + \ldots \#$

       $\Rightarrow \text{MOD} + (\text{PRO})^{n-1} + \ldots + \text{PRO} \#$

With rule (6-179) in mind, we can revise rule (6-177) to its final form:

(6-180) $V = (MOD) + ((PRO)^n) + (na\text{-}) + V_2 + (ASP) + (\text{-}kia)$
          $+ TNS + (PC) + ((PRO)^{3-n})$

This will generate structures like the following:

(6-181) a. $= (6\text{-}1a)$

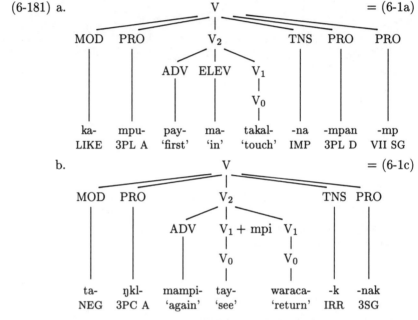

ka-	mpu-	pay-	ma-	takal-	-na	-mpan	-mp
LIKE	3PL A	'first'	'in'	'touch'	IMP	3PL D	VII SG

b. $= (6\text{-}1c)$

ta-	ŋkl-	mampi-	tay-	waraca-	-k	-nak
NEG	3PC A	'again'	'see'	'return'	IRR	3SG

I have reduced the statement of the morphological generation of Yimas verbs to three separate phrase structure like rules, although it appears that each of these rules contain a number of steps, which I have discussed in some detail. I repeat the rules for sake of easy reference below.

(6-182) $V = (MOD) + ((PRO)^n) + (na\text{-}) + V_2 + (ASP) + (\text{-}kia)$
          $+ TNS + (PC) + ((PRO)^{3-n})$

$V_2 = ((ADV)^n) + (ELEV) + (VAL) + ([V_1 + [\{{}^{\text{-mpi}}_{\text{-ra}}\}]]^n) + V_1$
          $+ (VAL) + (MOT)$

$V_1 = (VAL) + (N) + (RED) + V_0$

$V_0 = $ lexical verb root

As a final illustration of how these rules operate to generate Yimas verbal structures, let me consider in detail the derivation of the following Yimas verb:

(6-183) pu-kay-yakal-caŋ-tantaw-malakmalak-kia-ntuk-ŋkt
        3PL O-1PL A-CONT-COM-sit(RED: *taw*-)-talk(RED: *malak*-)
        -NIGHT-RM PAST-PC
        'We few were sitting down conversing with them.'

To the verb roots given below,

$$V_0 = \textit{taw-} \text{ 'sit' and } \textit{malak-} \text{ 'talk'}$$

we apply the following rule:

$$V_1 = (VAL) + (N) + (RED) + V_0$$

This applies to both examples of V_0 deriving the following structures:

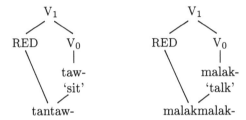

The next stage applies the rule for the level of V_2. First, a serial verb construction at V_2 from both examples of V_1 is formed.

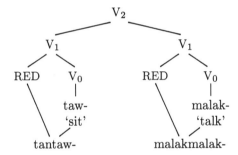

Then, VAL is added.

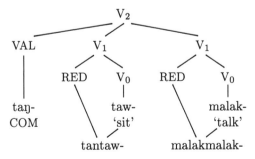

The final derivation at V_2 is adverbial incorporation.

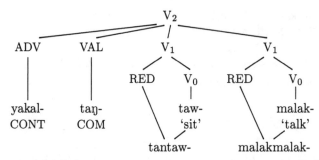

This gives the full expansion for this verb at the level of V_2, as permitted by the expansion rule for V_2 given again below.

$$V_2 = ((\text{ADV})^n) + (\text{ELEV}) + (\text{VAL}) + ([V_1 + [\{{}^{-mpi}_{-ra}\}]]^n) + V_1 \\ + (\text{VAL}) + (\text{MOT})$$

Now we consider the level of V. The first stage of derivation at V is TNS and associated categories. Supplying these, we generate the following:

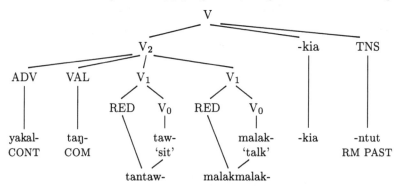

Finally, we add the pronominal affixes giving the following, complete structure for (6-183).

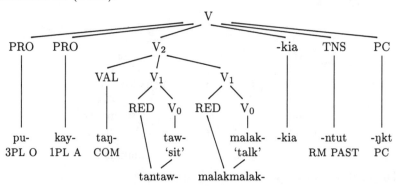

The categories above V_2 are all added by the rule expanding V given below:

$$V = (\text{MOD}) + ((\text{PRO})^n) + (na\text{-}) + V_2 + (\text{ASP}) + (\text{-}kia)$$
$$+\text{TNS} + (\text{PC}) + ((\text{PRO})^{3-n})$$

6.5 Yimas Clause Structures

Yimas clauses present a stark contrast to the highly structured and hierarchically ordered pattern of its verbal morphology. Yimas clauses have very little structure and certainly none that could be called hierarchical, analogous to the levels of V_0, V_1, V_2, and V in the verb. Yimas is an excellent exemplar of a non-configurational language at the clausal level (Chomsky 1981; Hale 1983): word order is free and clausal constituents largely correspond to the word. Let me examine these claims in more detail.

The only obligatory constituent of a clause in Yimas is a verb. In fact, the great majority of clauses consist of just a verb. If other constituents are present, they are arranged loosely around the verb, in no obligatory order, although locationals and temporals tend to be located at the clause periphery. Thus, in addition to examples like (6-184a,b) with verb-final word order, the language also possesses the fully acceptable variants in (6-184c,d).

(6-184) a. marmp-n   kay
      river VII SG-OBL canoe VIII SG
      i-ka-ak-mpi-wul
      VIII SG O-1SG A-push-SEQ-put down
   b. kay   marmp-n
      canoe VIII SG river VII SG-OBL
      i-ka-ak-mpi-wul
      VIII SG O-1SG A-push-SEQ-put down
   c. kay   i-ka-ak-mpi-wul
      canoe VIII SG VIII SG O-1SG A-push-SEQ-put down
      marmp-n
      river VII SG-OBL
   d. marmp-n   i-ka-ak-mpi-wul
      river VII SG-OBL VIII SG O-1SG A-push-SEQ-put down
      kay
      canoe-VIII SG
      'I pushed the canoe into the water.'

A clause with both nominals following the verb (i.e., a verb-initial structure) is perfectly grammatical, but is a bit more marked pragmatically than the above examples.

(6-185) i-ka-ak-mpi-wul   kay
         VIII SG O-1SG A-push-SEQ-put down   canoe VIII SG
         marmp-n
         river VII SG-OBL
         'I pushed the canoe into the river.'

Examples (6-184a,b) correspond to what may be called the unmarked word order, i.e., with the verb last. A verb is associated in Yimas with a falling intonation contour at its end, which in (6-184a,b) also functions to mark the end of the clauses. This falling verbal intonation contour also occurs in (6-184c,d), but in these cases, another separate falling intonation pattern occurs on the final constituents. This falling intonation pattern is no more prominent on core arguments (6-184c) than oblique constituents (6-184d). It may be that these final nominal constituents correspond to a kind of afterthought phenomenon, as indicated by the separate intonation contour, but these must not be equated with afterthought constructions in English. Yimas clauses like (6-184c,d) have none of the marked pragmatic force of afterthought constructions in English: postverbal constituents in Yimas are slightly more contrastive than preverbal ones and thus (6-184c,d) are somewhat more marked than (6-184a,b), but this difference is nowhere near as emphatic as that between *John went to Berlin last weekend* and *He went to Berlin last weekend, John did.* It is also important to note that in examples like (6-184a,b), the core argument *kay* 'canoe' is already rather contrastive in that it is encoded both as an independent noun and as a pronominal *i-* VIII SG O. The most neutral version of (6-184a) with no contrastive reading at all on *kay* 'canoe' would lack the independent noun altogether (see Section 5.1.5). It should be pointed out that afterthought constructions with a core argument such as (6-184d) commonly code the argument simultaneously with a pronominal affix. This suggests that what is happening pragmatically in these cases is that the speaker first codes the argument as an established referent with a pronominal affix, but having done so, then decides that this coding is insufficient either because there are multiple potential referents for that affix, or because the referent is too far removed in the discourse, or because it is simply not emphatic enough. He then repeats the full constituent preverbally, producing an afterthought construction like (6-184d). The potential weakness in this argument is that afterthought constructions with core arguments (6-184d) are not more marked phonologically or frequency-wise than those with oblique nominals (6-184c), for which no verbal coding with a pronominal affix is available. This further suggests that these afterthought constructions in Yimas are not highly marked pragmatically, but represent weakly contrastive variants from the unmarked versions.

The same comments apply to examples with more than one overt core argument, as shown below:

(6-186) a. panmal   kay   i-n-yamal
        man I SG canoe VIII SG VIII SG O-3SG A-carve

     b. kay   panmal   i-n-yamal
        canoe VIII SG man I SG VIII SG O-1SG A-carve

     c. panmal i-n-yamal   kay
        man I SG VIII SG O-3SG A-carve canoe VIII SG

     d. kay   i-n-yamal   panmal
        canoe VIII SG VIII SG O-3SG A-carve man I SG

     e. i-n-yamal   panmal   kay
        VIII SG O-3SG A-carve man I SG canoe VIII SG

        'The man made a canoe.'

If one asks a Yimas speaker to translate 'the man made a canoe', one is most likely to get (6-186a) as the equivalent (with (6-186b) a close second). In this sense one could claim the word order of (6-186a), i.e., actor-object verb (SOV), as the unmarked word order of Yimas. However, this claim is actually a chimera of elicitation, for in actual Yimas discourse, examples like (6-186a) are quite rare. This is due largely to the fact that clauses with two overt nominals functioning as core arguments are very uncommon in Yimas, a highly marked structure; but even when this does occur, it is by no means the case that a structure like (6-186a) is statistically more frequent than (6-186b), or, for that matter, (6-186c) or (6-186d). In this sense, the notion of unmarked word order in Yimas corresponds more to an idealization of the linguist than anything actually in the grammatical patterns of the speakers of the language. Thus, both (6-186a) and (6-186b) can fairly be taken as being roughly equivalent as to unmarked realizations of 'the man made a canoe', with the proviso that both structures are in actuality highly marked for having two overt nouns as core arguments.

Given the fact that the base structures (6-186a,b) are already quite marked, it should come as no surprise that the afterthought constructions (6-186c,d) are not much more so. In fact, constructions like (6-184d), in which the noun functioning as the A participant of a transitive occurs as an afterthought constituent, are probably the most common of all afterthought constructions, and statistically would be more common in Yimas texts than constructions like (6-186a,b). Sentences like (6-186d) occur commonly in texts when the actions jump back and forth sequentially between two or more central A participants. Often when the A participant changes, the speaker first encodes the new A with an overt deictic or just a pronominal affix or both, but he then decides that this marking was insufficient and thus additionally express it as an afterthought noun. Example (6-186e), like (6-184) earlier, is the most marked of these alternatives, because it is difficult to imagine a context in which it would be appropriate, given the pragmatic force of contrastiveness associated with afterthought nominals.

Yimas clauses are normally just a string of words. (Phrasal constituents are relatively rare in Yimas and will be discussed below.) Other than the verb, the words usually belong to the class of nominals and there may be more of them than allowed by the valence of the verb, as in this example:

(6-187) aŋkayapan patn   ama-na-kn   mama-k-n
         afternoon betelnut V SG 1SG-POSS-V SG bad-IRR-V SG
         kalakn   na-n-kpuc-t   nam-n
         boy I SG V SG O-3SG A-chew-PERF house-OBL
         'In the afternoon, the boy chewed my rotten betelnut in the house.'

This verb contains a bivalent verb root *kpuc-* 'chew' which functions formally as a transitive verb with two pronominal affixes, *na-* V SG O and *n-* 3SG A. Associated in the same clause are a temporal *aŋkayapan* 'afternoon' and five nominals, one oblique *nam-n* house-OBL 'in the house' and the rest core, *kalakn* 'boy', *patn* 'betelnut', *ama-na-kn* 1SG-POSS-V SG 'mine' and *mama-k-n* bad-IRR-V SG 'bad'. The four core nominals must be linked to the two core argument slots of the verb for this sentence to be grammatical (by the completeness constraint; see Section 5.1.5).

A sentence like (6-187) is generated around the verb; all other constituents are paratactically linked to it. The verb emerges from the lexical and morphological derivational rules of the previous section fully formed. It is a transitive verb, with two core arguments, one specified as class V SG and the other as third person singular.

$$\text{na - n -kpuc-t}$$

$$\begin{bmatrix} V \\ SG \\ O \end{bmatrix} - \begin{bmatrix} 3 \\ SG \\ A \end{bmatrix} \text{-chew-[PERF]}$$

The pronominal prefixes can now be linked to nominals with the same specifications. The feature cluster

$$\begin{bmatrix} 3 \\ SG \\ A \end{bmatrix}$$

is easily matched to *kalakn* 'boy' which is third singular and, being animate, is the only possible noun that could be linked to the *n-* pronominal prefix. The other prefix with the feature cluster

$$\begin{bmatrix} V \\ SG \\ O \end{bmatrix}$$

has three possible nominals that may be linked to it: *patn* 'betelnut', *ama-na-kn* 1SG-POSS-V SG 'mine', and *mama-k-n* bad-IRR-V SG 'bad'. Because all of these are direct nominals, i.e., neither affixed with *-n* ~ *-nan* OBL nor in a postpositional phrase, they must all be linked to this one pronominal affix, or by the completeness constraint, the sentence will be ungrammatical. This linkage is possible because all of them have the same feature specifications as the pronominal prefix.

$$\begin{bmatrix} V \\ SG \\ O \end{bmatrix}$$

The nominals *ama-na-kn* 1SG-POSS-V SG 'mine' and *mama-k-n* bad-IRR-V SG bear a similar kind of loose paratactic relationship to the noun *patn* 'betelnut' (in this case, commonly termed apposition) that *patn* 'betelnut' and *kalakn* 'child' bear to the pronominal prefixes. Finally, the oblique nominal *nam-n* house-OBL 'in the house', functioning as a locational, and the temporal *aŋkayapan* 'afternoon' can be freely added, for not being direct nominals, they need not be linked to the verb. Such oblique and peripheral constituents modify the clause as a whole. The structure of (6-187) can be diagrammatically represented as shown below:

(6-188)

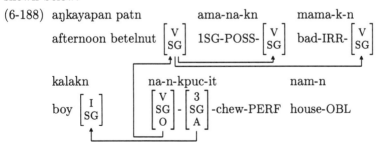

'In the afternoon, the boy chewed my rotten betelnut in the house.'

As mentioned above, clausal constituents are generally words. The only phrasal constituents that exist at the clause level are noun phrases and postpositional phrases. As discussed in Section 4.6, Yimas has a very restricted category of noun phrase, consisting of no more than two words and generated by the following rules, repeated below for convenience (where N = true nouns, independent pronouns and deictics, as well as nominalized adjectives and verbs).

(6-189)   NP   →   (M) + N

M   → $\begin{Bmatrix} \text{POSSR} \\ \text{ADJ} \end{Bmatrix}$

NPs can be either direct (as in 6-190a) or oblique, taking the oblique suffix as a single constituent (6-190b).

(6-190) a. ama-na   patn
            1SG-POSS betelnut V SG
            'my betelnut'

       b. ma   pucmp-n
            other time-OBL
            'at another time'

Postpositional phrases parallel noun phrases in that the head always occurs to the right; in this case, it is the postposition. Unlike noun phrases which are highly restrictive in only allowing a single modifier to occur before the head noun, postpositional phrases allow a number of prehead modifiers, which correspond to nominals.

(6-191) a. makaw   mawnta   kantk
            fish (sp) IX SG fish (sp) V SG with
            'with makaw and catfish'

       b. kumpwi   kpa-y   kpa-y   kantk
            boys I PL big-I PL   big-I PL   with
            'with grown up boys'

The modifiers may even constitute a noun phrase,

(6-192) ama-na   matn   kantk
          1SG-POSS brother I SG   with
          'with my brother'

or they may be no more than a pronoun.

(6-193) a. ama-naŋkun
            1SG-toward
            'to my house'

b. mpu-nampan
3PL-toward
'toward them'

The two rules for generating postpositional phrases are therefore as follows:

(6-194)   PP   →   O + P
           O   →   (NP)^n

Applying these rules to (6-191b) we get the phrase structure:

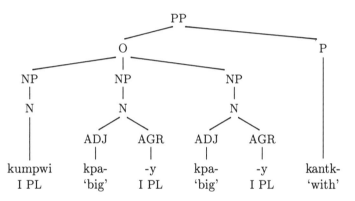

As already discussed, at the actual clause level there are no hierarchical structure or ordering constraints among the constituents. Adapting the convention of Gazdar et al. (1985) of using a comma for constituents freely ordered, we can write the following rule for generating Yimas clauses:

(6-195) S → (NP)^n, (PP)^n, (X)^n, V

where X indicates words belonging to minor word classes, such as temporals and locationals.

Applying this rule and those in (6-189) and (6-194) to example (6-196) we generate the phrase structure (6-197).

(6-196) ŋarŋ   ama-na   matn   na-wa-nan   mi
         1 day removed 1SG-POSS brother 3SG S-go-NR PAST 2SG
         kantk
         with
         'Yesterday my brother went with you.'

(6-197)

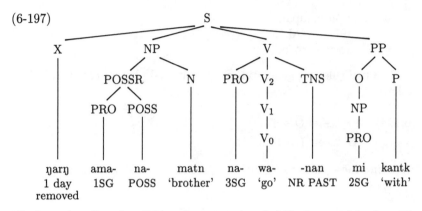

ŋarŋ	ama-	na-	matn	na-	wa-	-nan	mi	kantk
1 day removed	1SG	POSS	'brother'	3SG	'go'	NR PAST	2SG	'with'

The branches directly off S can be rotated and shifted around freely with
no change in meaning, but this is not true of the next level of branches,
those corresponding to the phrasal units and the V. We have already
seen that the internal structure of the V is highly complex and hierarchically ordered. It may be that the very simple structure of the clause
level in Yimas compensates for the highly elaborate structure at lower
levels, especially inside the V. It is a commonplace among modern linguistic theories that internal hierarchical structure is a universal feature
of language. This may be true, but languages like Yimas demonstrate
that such a structure need not be manifested at the clause level, where
it is commonly expected, but may show up elsewhere, where it is less
expected, for example, in the internal structure of the words. It may be
a truism that polysynthetic languages like Yimas choose to elaborate the
internal structure of words in contradistinction to phrases and clauses.

If one glances back at the phrase structure rules in (6-189) and (6-
194), an obvious generalization about Yimas emerges: the heads of constructions always occur to their right. The question then arises as to
what is the head of a clause. The only obligatory constituent of a clause
is, of course, the verb, and the rightmost obligatory constituent of a
verb is the tense morpheme. I suggest then that we consider TNS as the
head of its clause. In other words, as a noun phrase is defined by its
head noun and a postpositional phrase by its head postposition, so is
the category S defined by the tense morpheme.

7

Interclausal Relations

Most of the syntactic constructions in Yimas which join two or more
clauses together involve the process of nominalization. There are two
basic types of nominalizations in Yimas: non-finite, rather like infinitives
or gerunds in English; and finite, equivalent to English relative and
subordinate clauses. · The former always makes use of the non-finite
suffix -*ru*, while the latter are commonly formed around the near distal
deictic stem *m*-.

7.1 Non-Finite Nominalizations
7.1.1 The Suffix -*ru* and Agentive Nominalizations
Non-finite nominalizations are formed by the suffix -*ru* NFN. This occurs in the normal TNS slot and usurps all tense inflections. Suffixal
positions before TNS (i.e., ASP and -*kia*) can be specified in a non-
finite nominalization, as can all categories of the verb theme. But suffixal categories following TNS and all prefixal categories of the V (i.e.,
MOD, PRO, and *na*-) are completely prohibited in non-finite nominalizations. Thus, one could briefly state that nominalization applies at the
level of the verb theme (V_2), plus a couple of inner V categories. It is
most common, however, to find -*ru* NFN being added to a simple verb
root (V_0).

The suffix -*ru* NFN is subject to some phonological rules, so that it
exhibits considerable formal variation. The /u/ of -*ru* NFN is especially
subject to loss, first as a result of unstressed /u/ deletion (rule (2-9)).

(7-1) /wayk-ru-mat/   >   *waykrmat*
      buy-NFN-M PL   'buyers'

      /ampa-ru-maŋ/   >   *amparmaŋ*
      weave-NFN-F SG   'weaver'

But the /u/ of -*ru* is subject to deletion in a couple of other environments
as well, and in these cases the deletion is specific to this morpheme, not

part of a general rule of unstressed /u/ deletion. First, it always deletes
when the following suffix begins with a vowel or the semivowel *w*.

(7-2)   /wayk-ru-awt/   >   *waykrawt*
        buy-NFN-M SG   'buyer'

        /tu-ru-awt/   >   *turawt*
        kill-NFN-M SG   'killer'

        /tu-ru-wal   >   *tutwal*
        kill-NFN-manner   'killing'

It also deletes when the following suffix begins with /n/. This typically
occurs when the suffix is *-nti* 'act', and the deletion of /u/ anticipates
the following rule of liquid strengthening which will produce a stop-
homorganic nasal-stop cluster, a favored phonotactic structure of Yimas
(see Section 2.1.2). A few examples of this follow:

(7-3)   /tar-kwalca-ru-nti/   >   *tarkwalcatnti*
        CAUS-rise-NFN-act   'waking someone up'

        /kra-ru-nti/   >   *kratnti*
        cut-NFN-act   'cutting'

Finally, it obligatorily deletes in verb plus noun compounds (see Section
4.4). This is a morphologically, rather than phonologically, conditioned
environment.

(7-4)   /pan-ru-impram/   >   *pant impram*
        pound sago-NFN-basket VII SG   'basket for holding
                                          pounded sago'

The /r/ of *-ru* is also subject to specific, as well as general phonological rules. For example, the general rules of /r/ strengthening (rules
(2-4) through (2-6)) apply to it.

(7-5)   /ira-ru-awt/   >   *iratawt*
        cry-NFN-M SG   'cry baby'

        /wayk-ru-nti/   >   *wayktnti*
        buy-NFN-act   'buying'

It is always realized as *t* following nasals.

(7-6)   /pan-ru-awt/   >   *pantawt*
        pound sago-NFN-M SG   'sago worker'

        /tkam-ru-wal/   >   *tkamtuwal*
        show-NFN-manner   'showing'

Following the loss of /u/ before /w/, the /r/ of *-ru* is always realized
as *t*.

(7-7) /ŋa-ru-wal/   >   *ŋatwal*
give-NFN-manner   'giving'
/ayk-ru-wal/   >   *ayktwal*
marry-NFN-manner   'marriage customs'

The second examples in (7-6) and (7-7) provide an interesting contrast: in both cases, the /r/ of *-ru* is realized as *t*, but the /u/ is deleted in the latter and not the former. In the former example, /r/ of *-ru* becomes *t* following the preceding nasal. If the /u/ were now to be deleted, it would produce an impermissible cluster for Yimas, **mtw*. Even assuming for the sake of argument that /u/ deletion should occur here, vowel insertion would certainly be required to break up the cluster. But the inserted vowel could not go between *m* and *t* because this is a nasal plus stop cluster, which may not be broken up in Yimas. Rather it would have to be inserted between *t* and *w* and would, of course, be realized as *u* before *w*. So the end result of this putative derivation with /u/ deletion is the same as if it never occurred: a phonetic *u* appears nonetheless.

The second example in (7-7) is different in that the *t* results from the deletion of the underlying /u/ of *-ru*. The resulting cluster **ktw* is also impermissible, but so is **kt*. Hence, vowel insertion applies to break up **kt*, leaving *tw* intact. A closely parallel form is given below:

(7-8) /tuk-ru-wal/   >   *tukutwal*
wash sago-NFN-manner   'washing sago'

This is identical to the second example in (7-7) except that the V inserted by vowel insertion becomes *u* by R-spreading (rule (2-8)) as follows:

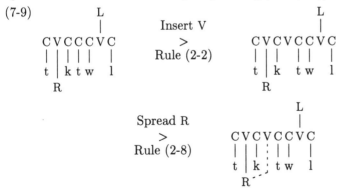

(7-9)

The /r/ of *-ru* is also subject to palatalization, but then always is realized as *c*. This seems to indicate an intermediate stage of *t*, which is well justified, as the realization *c* generally appears in most of the same environments as *t* except that it follows a segment associated with the autosegment F.

(7-10) /i-ru-nti/   >   *icnti*
        tell-NFN-act   'telling'

        /wapi-ru-wampuŋ/   >   *wapicwampuŋ*
        sharpen-NFN-desire   'want to sharpen'

In both the examples in (7-10), the /r/ of -*ru* would appear as *t* if it were
not for the adjoining high front vowel. This simply causes palatalization
of *t* to *c*. Note that, unusually, palatalization does not spread rightward
in the first example from *c* to the adjoining *n* and *t*.

There are other cases in which the /r/ appears as *c* without benefit
of an intermediate stage *t*, for in these examples, if it were not for the
presence of a segment with the F autosegment, the *r* would remain
unchanged.

(7-11) /i-ru-awt/   >   *icawt*
        tell-NFN-M SG   'teller'

versus

        /ŋa-ru-awt/   >   *ŋarawt*
        give-NFN-M SG   'give'

Other examples of /r/ appearing as *c* follow:

(7-12) /api-ru-awt/   >   *apicawt*
        put inside-NFN-M SG   'cover'

        /tay-ru-wal/   >   *taycuwal*
        see-NFN-manner   'seeing'

        /awl-ru-mat/   >   *awlcumat*
        get-NFN-M PL   'gatherers'

Note that in this last example, the general rule of unstressed /u/ deletion
is blocked. The morpheme specific rule for -*ru* NFN converting /r/ to
c after a segment associated with F takes precedence and after it has
applied, the environment for the general rule no longer exists.

The final variation to mention for the segment /r/ in -*ru* is in verb
plus noun compounds. In these constructions it is invariably realized
simply as *t*.

(7-13) /mawrun tu-ru iŋkay/   >   mawrun tut iŋkay
        enemy kill-NFN spear V PL   'spears for killing enemies'

The suffix -*ru* NFN is used as the basic derivational suffix in all sorts
of nominalization constructions. These are very common in Yimas, for
they correspond to the general embedded or complement constructions
of other languages. Perhaps the most straightforward kind of nominalization is agentive nominalization, equivalent to English -*er*. There
are seven different morphemes to indicate agentive nominalizations in
Yimas, a distinct masculine and feminine form for each of the three

numbers, singular, dual and plural, and a paucal form, undifferentiated
for gender, as in the following:

	M	F
SG	-awt	-maŋ
DL	-mampan	-mprump
PC	-ŋkt	
PL	-mat	-nput

With the exception of -*awt* M SG and -*mat* M PL, these forms are closely
related to the adjectival concord suffixes for classes I and II. Forms with
these suffixes are all subject to the phonological rules discussed above:
in addition, the /u/ of -*ru* NFN regularly deletes before -*ŋkt* PC.

(7-14) /ampa-ru-ŋkt/   >   *amparŋkt*
         weave-NFN-PC   'a few weavers'

The feminine suffixes for agentive nominalizations are only used in the
non-singular to refer to groups which are exclusively female: mixed
groups are denoted by the masculine suffixes. The masculine forms
are also used for animals and inanimate objects. Examples of agentive
nominalizations follow:

(7-15) a. kpanti-pramuŋ-tu-mat
          big-sleep-NFN-M PL
          'people who sleep too much'

       b. irut   ampa-r-maŋ
          mat IX PL   weave-NFN-F SG
          'a mat weaver (F)'

       c. pacuk-r-awt
          copulate-NFN-M SG
          'a promiscuous man'

       d. taŋkway-cakal-cu-mprum
          VIS-feel-NFN-F DL
          'the two women that look after (the children)'

       e. namtamparawt-ɲan   api-c-awt
          foot IX DL-OBL   put in-NFN-M SG
          'a sock'

These agentive nominalizations always carry a habitual meaning: they
denote an object or person (or group of people) which typically performs the action of the nominalized verb root. This habitual or typical
meaning is readily apparent in all of the above examples, but perhaps
especially clear are (7-15a,e). If one wishes to form an agentive nominalization to express a non-habitual performer of an action, a finite relative
clause must be used (see Section 7.2.1). Note that agentive nominal-

izations in Yimas are commonly associated with nouns or adverbials, much like those of English: *dishwash-er*, *story tell-er*, *hard work-er*. In both languages such nouns may never function as A participants, but are typically O or T arguments. The last example (7-15e) with the oblique suffix *-n* ~ *-nan*, illustrates an agentive nominalization that has actually been realized as the head noun of a noun plus noun compound (see Section 4.4), much like English *blackboard erase-r*. As with English *dishwasher* versus *dish maker*, the boundary in Yimas between compounds and agentive nominalizations is rather fuzzy.

These suffixes have a number of other uses besides marking agentive nominalizations. Some of these involve subordinate clauses and will be discussed in the relevant sections on relative clauses (see Section 7.2.1) and temporal adverbial clauses (see Section 7.2.3); here I will confine myself to word-level uses. These suffixes can be added to locative words with or without the oblique suffix *-n* ~ *-nan* to express a person or people associated with that place.

(7-16) a. num-n   num-n-mat
           village-OBL   village-OBL-M PL
           'in the village'   'villagers'

       b. Tamprakmal   Tamprakmal-mat
           native name of Yimas village   Yimas village-M PL
           'Yimas'   'Yimas people'

       c. Wamut   Wamut-ɲum-n-awt
           name for stretch of   Wambramas-village-OBL-M SG
           river where Wambramas   'a Wambramas man'
           village lies
           'Wambramas'

The oblique suffix plus *-awt* M SG, etc. can be added to Tok Pisin words denoting other areas of Papua New Guinea and, indeed, the world, to indicate the inhabitants of that area.

(7-17) a. Kavieŋ-n-awt
           Kavieng-OBL-M SG
           'a man from Kavieng'

       b. Chimbu-n-mat
           Chimbu-OBL-M PL
           'Chimbu people'

       c. Ostrala-n-awt
           Australia-OBL-M SG
           'an Australian'

These suffixes are also added to a stem *pan-* (of no separate meaning, but probably related to *panmal* 'man'), to derive contrastive pronouns 'myself', 'yourself', 'himself', 'themselves', etc. Consider these examples:

(7-18) a. ama pan-awt   na-ka-tu-t
       1SG self-M SG 3SG O-1SG A-kill-PERF
       'I killed him myself.'

      b. pan-put   kalk
       self-F PL sago pudding V SG

       na-mpu-nanaŋ-kwayŋ-na-ntut
       V SG O-3PL A-DUR-turn-DUR-RM PAST

       'They (the women) stirred the sago pudding themselves.'

      c. m-n   pan-awt-mpwia   "ama paympan
       NR DIST-I SG self-M SG-QUOTE 1SG   eagle

       tampan"
       NEG COP

       'He himself said "I am not an eagle." '

These contrastive pronouns sometimes occur with the oblique suffix but with no apparent difference in usage or meaning. Compare (7-19) below with (7-18a):

(7-19) m-n   pan-awt-ɲan   trmantak
       NR DIST-I SG self-M SG-OBL spear V SG

       na-n-awkura-ntut
       V SG O-3SG A-get-RM PAST

       'He got a spear himself.'

These pronoun forms are contrastive in that they indicate that the performer of the action is exhaustively defined by their referent, i.e., 'it is they and no one else who X-ed'. Thus these forms always denote agentive participants. This explains to a certain extent their morphological formation. The suffixes -*awt* M SG, etc., are of course most commonly used to derive agentive nominalizations. Because of the meaning of *pan-*, it varies between a purely contrastive and a reflexive usage. Consider these examples:

(7-20) a. m-n   pan-awt   na-n-tu-t
       NR DIST-I SG self-M SG 3SG O-3SG A-kill-PERF
       'He killed him himself.'
       *'He killed himself.'

      b. m-n   pan-awt-ɲan   na-tu-t
       NR DIST-I SG self-M SG-OBL 3SG S-kill-PERF
       'He killed himself.'
       *'He killed him himself.'

The verb in (7-20a) lacks any valence decreasing affix so, being a bivalent verb, it must be associated with two core arguments, an A *n-* 3SG A and an O *na-* 3SG O. The contrastive pronoun *panawt* 'self' must be linked to the A participant above, deriving the meaning 'he killed him himself'. The verb in the reflexive example (7-2b), while semantically bivalent, is formally intransitive. Further, *pan-* is marked with the oblique suffix so may not function as a core argument. Thus, the single core argument *m-n* 'he' is an S acting on himself, and hence the reflexive reading of the construction.

As can be gleaned from the preceding examples, these contrastive pronouns only mark gender and number. Person must be expressed through an appositional independent pronoun or deictic (*mi pan-maŋ* 2SG self-F SG 'you, yourself'; *kapa pan-mampan-an* 1DL self-M DL-OBL 'both of us, ourselves'; *m-um pan-put* NR DIST-II PL self-F PL 'those, themselves'). The pronoun or deictic can be left out if the referent is clear from the immediate context, and in any case, deictics are commonly omitted with the contrastive pronouns. If a contrastive pronoun occurs alone (7-18b), it is normally interpreted as third person unless contextual features determine otherwise.

7.1.2 Complementation

Complementation is one of the most interesting and elaborated parts of Yimas grammar, and is remarkably different in a number of ways from the system of complements in many other languages, including other Papuan languages. Complements are not all that common in Yimas formal narrative discourse, but in everyday speech and conversation they are frequently encountered.

Complements in Yimas are typically nominalizations and are formed with *-ru* NFN. In other words, in order for a clause (the complement) to function as an argument of another clause (the main or matrix clause), it must be made non-finite through the process of nominalization. Complement nominalizations are like nouns and nominals generally in being affixed with suffixes to mark noun class; we have already seen this with the suffixes *-awt* M SG, etc. It is these class suffixes which indicate the different types of complements. In addition to the agentive nominalizations marked by *-awt* M SG, etc., there are four types of complements in Yimas: complements of speech or language, marked by *-mpwi*; complements of desire (*-wampuŋ*), complements of action (-nti), and complements of customary action (*-wal*). The semantics of each type will be discussed below, but first I wish to present the general syntactic features of Yimas complementation structures.

The first point about Yimas nominalized complements is that they have the basic syntactic structure of compounds. Remember that Yimas possesses a productive means of forming verb plus noun compounds using the -*t* allomorph of -*ru* NFN (see Section 4.4).

(7-21) a. ayk-t   yaw   yua-∅   yak
           marry-NFN   road IX SG good-IX SG   COP IX SG
           'That's a proper match of marriage partners.'

       b. am-t   tpuk   ku-n-kacapal
           eat-NFN   sago pancake X SG X SG O-3SG A-forget
           'He forgot his sago for eating.'

The compounds in (7-21) are very close to complements. If we replace the head noun of the compound in (7-21b) with complement markers and specifically that of the complement of desire, -*wampuŋ* (nothing but the class V noun meaning 'heart'), we derive a parallel complementation structure of almost morpheme-for-morpheme similarity.

(7-22) tpuk   am-tu-wampuŋ   na-n-kacapal
        sago pancake X̱ SG   eat-NFN-heart V SG V SG O-3SG A-forget
        'He lost interest in eating sago.'

In (7-22) the head noun of the compound is *wampuŋ* 'heart', the indicator of a complement of desire. This is what is marked on the verb as the O participant by *na-* V SG O, the class and number specifications for *wampuŋ* 'heart'.

It is also possible for class markers by themselves to function as the heads of verb plus noun compounds either with or without an overt coreferential noun.

(7-23) a. tpuk   am-t-uŋ   ku-n-kacapal
           sago pancake X SG   eat-NFN-X SG   X SG O-3SG A-forget
           'He forgot his sago for eating.'

       b. am-t-uŋ   ku-n-kacapal
           eat-NFN-X SG   X SG O-3SG A-forgot
           'He forgot his (sago) for eating.'

Example (7-23a) differs from (7-21b) in that the order of verb plus noun has been altered, changing the embedding structure of modifier plus head to one of two appositional nominals of the same class and number, the second being headed by the class marker -*uŋ* X SG. This alternation is no different from that involving possessors or adjectives.

(7-24) a. ama-na   matn
           1SG-POSS   brother I SG
               versus
           matn   ama-na-kn
           brother I SG   1SG-POSS-I SG
           'my brother'

b. kpa   kay
   big   canoe VIII SG
   versus
   kay   kpa-y
   canoe VIII SG   big-VIII SG
   'a big canoe'

Example (b) in (7-23) is simply the second nominal in the appositional arrangement of (7-23a) standing on its own. This clause would be used whenever the context makes it clear what referent denoted by a class X SG noun is being talked about (expressed by the suffix -*uŋ* X SG), just as *kpa-y* big-VIII SG would generally be all that is necessary in a discourse about canoes.

   The examples in (7-23) are again very closely paralleled by complement structures.

(7-25) a. tpuk   am-tu-mpwi   pia-n-kacapal
          sago pancake X SG   eat-NFN-talk   talk O-3SG A-forget
          'He forgot to eat sago.'

     b. am-tu-mpwi   pia-n-kacapal
        eat-NFN-talk   talk O-3SG A-forget
        'He forgot to eat.'

In (7-25) the class marker -*mpwi* 'talk' is used to mark a nominalized complement of speech; the complements could express the A participant's thoughts (thoughts are regarded as internal speech in Yimas), or could paraphrase an order or exhortation directed to the A which was forgotten. The class marker -*mpwi* 'talk' functions as the head of these nominalized complements, so that in fact they have the syntactic structure of verb plus noun compounds. Since compounds have the following syntactic structure,

(7-26)

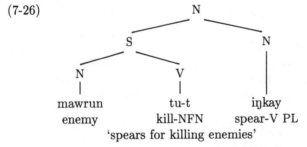

'spears for killing enemies'

nominalized complements can be represented in rather the same way. The complement in (7-22) has the structure (7-27), and (7-25) that of (7-28).

(7-27)

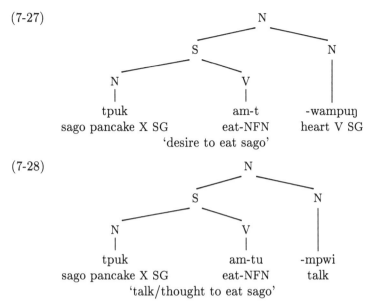

'desire to eat sago'

(7-28)

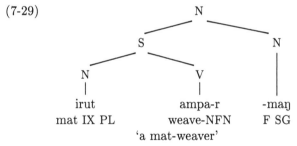

'talk/thought to eat sago'

Incidentally, this structure can also be applied to the agentive nominalizations discussed in Section 7.1.1. An example is given below:

(7-29)

N

S N

N V

irut ampa-r -maŋ
mat IX PL weave-NFN F SG

'a mat-weaver'

Having now established the internal syntactic structure of these nominalized complements, it is necessary now to turn to the syntactic relationship between them and the main clause. We have already seen that Yimas clauses are very loosely structured, with nominals paratactically arranged around their governing verb and linked to it through the pronominal affixes. The same loose, paratactic link applies between the verb of the main clause and its complement; Yimas complements unlike their English counterparts are not really embedded. Yimas complements can function in all core argument roles except A and D; these are forbidden because A and D participants must typically be higher animates and preferably humans, features complements typically lack (agentive nominalizations, however, can freely function as A or D participants). In the

following examples which illustrate complements functioning in various
core argument roles, the complements are linked to the verb through
pronominal affixes agreeing in class and number with the head of the
complement.

(7-30) complement functioning as S:

    a. yaki   am-t-wal   mama-k-n
       tobacco V PL eat-NFN-custom V SG bad-IRR-V SG

       anak
       COP V SG

       'Smoking tobacco is bad.'

    b. tar-kwalca-t-nti   mpu-na-nti   mama-nti antiak
       CAUS-rise-NFN-act 3PL-POSS-act bad-act   COP act
       'Their waking me up was bad.'

(7-31) complement functioning as O:

    a. yaki   am-tu-wal   ntak-na-k
       tobacco V PL eat-NFN-custom V SG leave-IMP-V SG
       'Stop smoking!'

    b. tpwi   am-tu-mpwi
       sago pancake X PL eat-NFN-talk

       ta-pu-na-yaŋkuraŋ-   takal-war-mpwi
       NEG-3-2SG A-DEF-thought- feel-HAB-talk

       'You never think about eating sago.'

    c. nam   wark-t-nti   tia-ka-ira-karŋkra-t
       house build-NFN-act act O-1SG A-ALL-tired-PERF
       'I'm tired of building houses.'

(7-32) complement functioning as T:

    a. patn   wayk-ru-mpwi pia-ka-i-mpi-cay-
       betelnut V SG buy-NFN-talk   talk T-1SG A-tell-SEQ-

       c-mpun
       see-PERF-3PL D

       'I tried to tell them to buy betelnut.'

    b. ŋaykum   irut   ampa-t-wal
       woman II PL mat IX PL weave-NFN-custom

       tia-mpu-na-tkam-t-mpun
       act T-3PL A-DEF-show-PRES-3PL D

       'The women are teaching them how to weave mats.'

These complements are all linked to their matrix verb in just the way
that nouns in the same roles would be linked—through the coreferential pronominal affixes. The complements, which of course are formally

nominals, are not in an embedded subordinated relationship to the matrix verb any more than a noun argument of the verb would be. It is the pronominal affixes which fill the argument slots of the verb, and any associated nominals, including complements, are paratactically linked to these. As an example, consider (7-31c). The verb root here is the monovalent *karŋkra-* 'be tired, bored'. This verb root is derived into a bivalent verb theme by *ira-* ALL, so that the verb occurs with two pronominal prefixes *tia-* act O and *ka-* 1SG A. The matrix verb could certainly stand on its own as a complete sentence, with the meaning 'I'm tired of these actions', with the referent of *tia-* act O supplied from context. However in (7-31c), its referent is actually overtly present in the sentence in the form of the nominalized complement, paratactically linked to the syntactic structure of (7-31c) and can be represented as follows:

(7-33)

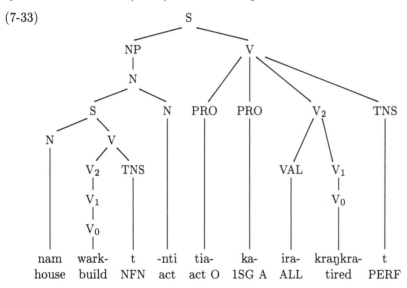

nam	wark-	t	-nti	tia-	ka-	ira-	kraŋkra-	t
house	build	NFN	act	act O	1SG A	ALL	tired	PERF

Because the verbal pronominal affixes are optional (their presence or absence governed by the pragmatic principles discussed in Section 5.1.6), it is not uncommon for a nominalized complement to be linked to a verb without any coreferential agreement affix. Consider the following pairs of examples:

(7-34) a. impram   pay-cu-mpwi   na-kacapal
           basket VII SG carry-NFN-talk   3SG S-forget

       b. impram   pay-cu-mpwi   pia-n-kacapal
           basket VII SG carry-NFN-talk   talk O-3SG A-forget
           'He forgot to carry the basket.'

(7-35) a. patn   wayk-ru-mpwi na-yaŋkuraŋ-takal
          betelnut V SG   buy-NFN-talk 3SG S-thought-feel

       b. patn   wayk-ru-mpwi pia-n-yaŋkuraŋ-takal
          betelnut V SG   buy-NFN-talk talk O-3SG A-thought-feel
          'He thought to buy betelnut.'

The formal difference between the (a) and (b) examples is simply the
absence versus presence of the prefix *pia-* 'talk' for the O argument.
This formal difference correlates with a consistent, albeit subtle, semantic contrast. The (b) examples, with the prefix, express a situation in
which the A participant states verbally to some other participant that
he is going to carry the basket or get betelnut (but in (7-34b) he sub-
sequently forgets to do so). The (a) examples, without the prefix, do
not require that A state his intention verbally to someone else; he may
simply have the intention as an idea in his mind (again (7-34a) indicates
that the intention slips his mind). Note that the use of the pronominal agreement prefix here very closely reflects its pragmatic function
with noun phrases generally. With the prefix, the intention expressed
by the complement has been stated explicitly; it is very much established information in the context of the discourse. Without it, the complement is simply an intention in the A participant's mind, and not
stated explicitly, and hence not clearly established information in the
discourse.

    In the examples presented so far, the complements have always pre-
ceded the matrix verbs. This is probably the most common order, but
is by no means the only one. Complements can follow the matrix verb,
as in these examples:

(7-36) a. pu-ŋa-tkam-t   patn
          3PL A-1SG D-show-PERF   betelnut V SG
          kpuc-t-wal
          chew-NFN-custom V SG
          'They showed me how to chew betelnut.'

       b. tia-ka-na-aykapiŋa-n   God-na   anti
          act O-1SG A-DEF-know-PRES   God-POSS   ground VIII SG
          papk-t-wal
          carve-NFN-custom V SG
          'I know how God made the world.'

       c. mama-k-n   anak   mntmpi   ti-t-wal
          bad-IRR-V SG   COP V SG   like that do-NFN-custom V SG
          'It is bad to do that.'

There seems to be no meaning difference between the two orders, complement-matrix or matrix-complement: they are interchangeable, although the former is preferred. This flexibility, interestingly, also applies to nominals inside the complement. These too can be transposed outside of the complement.

(7-37) (see (7-31a))

    a. am-tu-wal   yaki   ntak-na-ra
       eat-NFN-custom V SG tobacco V PL leave-IMP-V PL

    b. am-tu-wal   ntak-n-ra   yaki
       eat-NFN-custom V SG leave-IMP-V PL tobacco V PL

       'Stop smoking!'

(7-38) (see (7-36a)

    a. na-mpu-ŋa-tkam-t   kpuc-t-wal
       V SG T-3PL A-1SG D-show-PERF chew-NFN-custom V SG

       patn
       betelnut V SG

    b. patn   na-mpu-ŋa-tkam-t
       betelnut V SG V SG T-3PL A-1SG D-show-PERF

       kpuc-t-wal
       chew-NFN-custom V SG

       'They showed me how to chew betelnut.'

These sentences are generated by shifting a core argument of the complement outside of the embedded S. Note that the moved core arguments of the embedded S are now coded as core arguments of the main verb, by -ra V PL in (7-37) and na- V SG T in (7-38). In other words both of the movements in the following structure are acceptable:

(7-39)

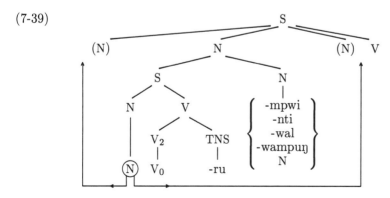

The complement as a whole, of course, can appear among the various
core nominals associated with the matrix verb, but so can its shifted
core argument.

Consider the following examples:

(7-40) a. ŋaykum   irut   ampa-t-wal
        woman II PL   mat IX PL   weave-NFN-custom V SG

        ŋaykump-n   kumpwi
        woman II PL-OBL   child I PL

        tia-mpu-na-tkam-t-mpun
        act T-3PL A-DEF-show-PRES-3PL D

   b. ŋaykum   ŋaykump-n   kumpwi   irut
       woman II PL   woman II PL-OBL   child I PL   mat IX PL

       ampa-t-wal
       weave-NFN-custom V SG

       tia-mpu-na-tkam-t-mpun
       act T-3PL A-DEF-show-PRES-3PL D

   c. ŋaykum   irut   ŋaykump-n   kumpwi
       woman II PL   mat IX PL   woman II PL-OBL   child I PL

       ampa-t-wal
       weave-NFN-custom V SG

       tia-mpu-na-tkam-t-mpun
       act T-3PL A-DEF-show-PRES-3PL D

   'The women are teaching the girls how to weave mats.'

The matrix verb in (7-40), being ditransitive, is linked to three nominal
arguments: the A, *ŋaykum* 'women', the D, *ŋaykump-n kumpwi* 'girls',
and the complement *irut ampa-t-wal* 'how to make mats' functioning
as T. The complement only has the single overt nominal argument,
irut 'mats', functioning as O. The entire complement can appear between the other noun arguments of the matrix verb (7-40a) or following
them (7-40b). Further, the single noun argument of the complement,
irut 'mats', can appear among the arguments of the matrix verb, as
in (7-40c).

Perhaps the most salient morphological difference between matrix
and complement verbs, other than the suffix -*ru* NFN, is the use of
pronominal affixes with the former and their obligatory absence in the
latter. The lack of pronominal affixes for complement verbs is correlated with restrictions on associated nominal arguments. An S or A
argument of a complement verb (the subject of the verb in the sense
of the term used in English grammar) cannot appear as a simple core

argument of the verb, but must be suffixed with *na* POSS and linked to the complement as a whole (especially its head), rather than the governing verb.

Look at these examples:

(7-41) a. mpu-na-nti   malak-t-nti   wampuŋ
      3PL-POSS-act converse-NFN-act heart V SG

      tia-ŋa-na-ira-kkt-n
      act O-1SG D-DEF-ALL-hurt-PRES

      'I'm angry because of their conversation.'

    b. tia-ka-na-aykapiŋa-n   God na   anti
      act O-1SG A-DEF-know-PRES God POSS ground VIII SG

      papk-t-wal
      carve-NFN-custom

      'I know how God made the world.'

    c. patn   kpuc-t-wal   mpu-na-kn
      betelnut V SG chew-NFN-custom 3PL-POSS-V SG

      pu-ŋa-tkam-t
      3PL A-1SG D-show-PERF

      'They showed me how they chew betelnut.'

    d. Stephen na   yaki   am-tu-wal
      Stephen POSS tobacco V PL eat-NFN-custom

      mama-k-n   anak
      bad-IRR-V SG COP V SG

      'It is bad for Stephen to smoke.'

These examples show that the S or A arguments of the complement verb are clearly coded as possessor nouns, unlike the other core arguments which simply appear as normal unaffixed arguments of the verb. The S or A arguments can appear in either of two ways: as a possessor of the complement as a whole, taking the complement as its head in a tightly knit NP construction (7-41b,d); or as a separate NP on its own in a juxtaposed structure, with its head being a possessive concord suffix agreeing with that of the complement (7-41a,c). (Alternatively the proper concord suffix can be replaced for all complement types by *-kn* the class V singular possessor concord suffix). The first, the closely knit type, is illustrated in the following diagram of (7-41b), while the second appositional structure appears in the diagram of (7-41c). These structures, and indeed complement structures generally, require some revisions to the phrase structure rules presented in Section 4.6, which generate noun phrases.

(7-42)

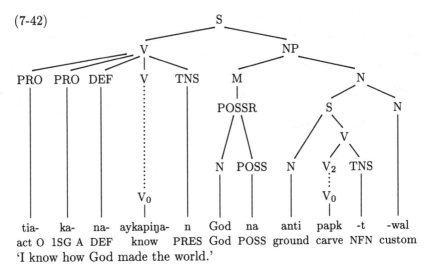

tia- ka- na- aykapiŋa- n God na anti papk -t -wal
act O 1SG A DEF know PRES God POSS ground carve NFN custom

'I know how God made the world.'

(7-43)

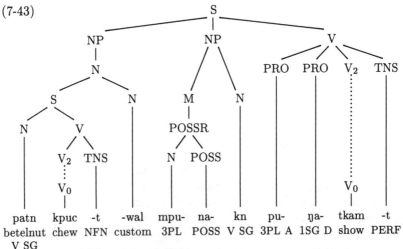

patn kpuc -t -wal mpu- na- kn pu- ŋa- tkam -t
betelnut chew NFN custom 3PL POSS V SG 3PL A 1SG D show PERF
V SG

'They showed me how they chew betelnut.'

Complements in Yimas are clearly noun phrases, but are more complicated exemplars of this constituent type than those discussed previously, particularly the one illustrated in (7-42). Let me concentrate on revising the rules to account for this example, as this illustrates the most complex type of NP in Yimas. This example differs from the simpler types discussed in Section 4.5, in that its head is itself complex rather than a single noun or concord affix. Thus, the first rule of (4-75) can remain unchanged.

(7-44)   NP   →   (M) + N

As well, the possible fillers of M are unaltered, so the next rule also remains unchanged,

(7-45)   M   → $\begin{Bmatrix} \text{POSSR} \\ \text{ADJ} \end{Bmatrix}$

although the class of fillers permitted by this rule is now, of course, extended to S or A arguments of complement verbs, as in (7-41b,d). Interestingly, the language also allows adjectives to modify a complement within the noun phrase (7-46a), although a juxtaposed structure is strongly preferred, as in (7-46b):

(7-46) a. kpa pacuk-t-wampuŋ   ama-na-tɨ-n
           big copulate-NFN-heart V SG 1SG S-DEF-feel-PRES
       b. pacuk-t-wampuŋ   kpa-n   ama-na-tɨ-n
          copulate-NFN-heart V SG big-V SG   1SG S-DEF-feel-PRES

          'I am feeling very randy.' (literally, 'I feel a big desire to copulate.')

What does need to be added is a rule expanding the N in rule (7-44)/(4-75). This must generate the structures presented in (7-26) through (7-29) above and in numerous other examples. Reflecting the consistent head-to-the-right pattern of Yimas, this rule should be as follows,

(7-47)   N   →   (S)   + N
                     [NFN]

where N, of course, can be a noun, but can also be any of the agentive nominalization or complement marking suffixes. Finally, the non-finite S is expanded as follows:

(7-48)   S   →   (NP)^n +   V
          [NFN]   [NFN]

(7-49)   V   →   V$_2$ + TNS: -ru NFN
          [NFN]

If the reader glances back now at example (7-42), it will be immediately clear that rules (7-44) through (7-49) directly and straightforwardly generate the complement structure.

While some complements do have overt S or A arguments as generated by the above rules, the large majority do not, i.e the S or A argument is simply missing. These complements fall into two types. In the first, the referent for the S or A participant is simply unknown or left open, that is, it could correspond to more than one referent depending on different interpretations of the discourse context. I will call these uncontrolled complement structures, and these are now illustrated. Complements functioning as S are always uncontrolled in Yimas.

(7-50) a. yaki   am-tu-wal   mama-k-n
          tobacco V PL   eat-NFN-custom V SG   bad-IRR-V SG
          anak
          COP V SG
          '(My, your, someone's) smoking tobacco is bad.'

     b. patn   wayk-r-mpwi   i-r-mpwi   ama-na-mpwi
        betelnut V SG   buy-NFN-talk tell-NFN-talk 1SG-POSS-talk
        mama-mpwi apiak
        bad-talk   COP talk
        'It was bad for me to tell (you, him, them) to buy betelnut.'

But it is also possible (albeit rarely) for a complement in O or T function to be uncontrolled.

(7-51) kalakn   tpwi   pan-tu-wal
        boy I SG   sago X PL   pound sago-NFN-custom V SG
        ta-pu-na-aykapiŋa-nt-nti
        NEG-3-DEF-know-PRES-act
        'The boy does not know how (one, we, they) pound sago.'

In the other type of complement with a missing A or S argument, its referent must be one of the typically animate participants of the matrix clause, either the A or the D. This type I will call a controlled complement structure. Complements functioning as O or T are generally controlled. The argument in the matrix clause which corresponds to the missing S or A participant in the complement is called the controller. Whether the controller is the A or D participant depends on the valence and the semantics of the verb. If the matrix verb is bivalent and the complement is functioning as O, then the controller is obviously the A participant.

(7-52) a. tpuk   am-tu-wampuŋ   na-na-tɨ-n
          sago X SG   eat-NFN-heart V SG 3SG S-DEF-feel-PRES
          'He feels like eating sago.'

     b. patn   wayk-r-mpwi   pia-ka-kacapal
        betelnut V SG buy-NFN-talk talk O-1SG A-forget
        'I forgot to buy betelnut.'

     c. impram   pay-cu-mpwi   ta-pu-n-yaŋkuraŋ-takal
        basket   carry-NFN-talk NEG-3-2SG S-thought-feel
        'You didn't remember to bring a basket.'

    d. tpuk   am-tu-mpwi   na-tmi
       sago X SG eat-NOM-talk 3SG S-say
       'He is talking about eating sago.'

It is important to note that verbs like *kacapal-* 'forget' and *yaŋkuraŋtakal* 'think, remember' only take obligatorily controlled complements in one of their uses, that corresponding to the equivalent English verbs with infinitive complements, e.g., *forget/remember/think to eat*. In Yimas, constructions parallel to English *that* clause complements, such as *forget/remember/thought that she ate*, there is no issue of control. Compare these examples with (7-52b,c):

(7-53) a. pia-ka-kacapal   patn
       talk O-1SG A-forget betelnut V SG

       na-n-wu-t
       V SG O-2SG A-get-PERF

       'I forgot that you got betelnut.'

      b. pia-ka-yaŋkuraŋ-takal   narmaŋ   impram
       talk O-1SG A-thought-feel woman II SG basket VII SG

       p-n-pay
       VII SG O-3SG A-carry

       'I think that the woman brought a basket.'

Yimas does not possess embedded *that* clauses like English. The structures in (7-53) are again paratactic. The clauses are just juxtaposed: one is not embedded in the other. The two clauses can occur in either order. Unlike (7-52b) in which the complement is linked to the pronominal prefix *pia-* 'talk' on the matrix verb as a nominal in apposition to it, the juxtaposed clauses in (7-53) are linked together as equals. The second clause does not bear an appositional relationship to the prefix *pia-* 'talk' in (7-53), but to the clause as a whole. So, (7-53a) roughly might be paraphrased as 'I forgot (some) talk/idea: you got betelnut'. Perhaps a more natural English sentence with a similar structure would be: *I forgot: did you get betelnut or not?* Note that, as mentioned briefly above, thought is treated as language. Thinking is conceived by the Yimas as simply internal talking. The semantic contrast in Yimas between a nominalized complement and a juxtaposed clause with 'think' and 'forget' is very much like that between the English equivalents of an infinitive complement versus a *that* clause. The nominalized complement expresses an event which should have occurred or failed to occur, *as a result of* the cognitive act denoted by the matrix verb. The juxtaposed clause, on the other hand, encodes an event which either occurred or failed to occur, but which the cognitive act denoted by the matrix verb had no role in effecting. The matrix verb simply registers the content of the consciousness of the A participant with respect to that event.

Turning now to trivalent verbs in which the complement functions as T, it is immediately apparent that these represent the most complex case, for now either the A or D participant of the matrix verb is eligible as controller. Which of these is the controller is determined by the semantics of the matrix verb, in exactly the way the universal theory of control presented in Foley and Van Valin (1984, 307–11) predicts. Complement-taking trivalent verbs which denote directive speech acts, i.e., attempts by the speaker to get the addressee to do something, always have the D participant as controller; otherwise the controller is the A. The verb roots *i-* 'tell' and *kankantakal-* 'ask' are the prototypical verbs expressing directive speech acts, in Yimas and in other languages. Both of these have D participant control.

(7-54) a. tpuk   am-tu-mpwi   pia-mpu-ŋa-i
            sago X SG eat-NFN-talk talk T-3PL A-1SG D-tell
            'He told me to eat sago.'

       b. impram   pay-cu-mpwi   na-kra-kankantakal
            basket VII SG carry-NFN-talk 3SG A-1PL D-ask
            'He asked us to carry a basket.'

The only way to avoid obligatory D control with directive verbs like *i-* 'tell' is not to use a complement structure at all, but to employ a juxtaposed structure like those of (7-53) with the equivalent of the complement expressed as a direct quote. (Yimas like many Papuan languages lacks indirect speech constructions.) Compare (7-55) with (7-54a):

(7-55) pia-mpu-ŋa-i   "ipa tpuk   am-ŋ"
          talk T-3PL A-1SG D-tell   1PL   sago X SG   eat-IRR
          'They told me: "We want to eat sago." '

In (7-55), *ipa* 'me' in the direct quote is, of course, coreferential with the A participant of the matrix verb, *mpu-* 3PL A, not the D, *ŋa-* 1SG D. The same remarks concerning the structure of juxtaposed clauses made above with respect to (7-53) apply to (7-55) as well.

Trivalent verbs which do not denote directive speech acts have A participant control. Contrast these examples with (7-54):

(7-56) a. kay   yamal-cu-mpwi
            canoe VIII SG carve-NFN-talk
            pia-mpu-ŋa-taŋ-tmi
            talk T-3PL A-1SG D-COM-say
            'They talked with me about their building a canoe.'

    b. tpuk   am-tu-mpwi   pia-mpu-ŋa-taŋkway-cmi
       sago X SG eat-NFN-talk talk T-3PL A-1SG D-VIS-say
       'He told me (looking at me) about his eating sago.'
    c. ŋaykum   irut   ampa-t-wal
       woman II PL mat IX PL weave-NFN-custom

       ŋaykump-n   kumpwi
       woman II PL-OBL child I PL

       tia-mpu-na-tkam-t-mpun
       act T-3PL A-DEF-show-PRES-3PL D
       'The women showed/taught the girls how to weave mats.'

Unlike the inherently directive and trivalent verb of saying *i*- 'tell', the verb *tmi*- 'say' is non-directive and is bivalent. In (7-56a,b) the bivalent verb root *tmi*- 'say' is derived into a trivalent verb theme by the valence increasing prefixes *taŋ*- COM and *taŋkway*- VIS. Although the verb themes in (7-56a,b) are trivalent verbs of saying, they do not express directive speech acts, so that the controller is the A participant. The difference in semantics between these verbs and those in (7-54) explains why these have A control, while those in (7-54) have D control.

The final example in (7-56) is especially interesting in that, in a certain sense, there is some ambiguity as to the controller. If the sentence simply denotes a situation in which women are weaving mats and girls are watching in order to learn the skills, the controller is unquestionably the A participant. If, however, the girls are actively weaving at the same time as part of or as a result of the women's instruction, then in a sense the girls must be regarded as co-agents of the complement. In this situation, the D participant of the matrix verb is at least the co-controller of the complement. But note that this latter scenario is very close semantically to the directive speech act verbs. In (7-56c) the A participants of the matrix verb (the women) perform an action (showing, teaching) to get the D participants (the girls) to do the action of the complement (weaving). This is semantically completely analogous to directive speech acts, in which the speaker through the critical speech act tries to get the addressee to perform the action of the complement.

To close out this section I wish to discuss in more detail the different semantic and morphological features of the four types of complements. Complements associated with the use of language, either external (speech) or internal (thought) are invariably marked with -*mpwi* 'talk'. This is linked to the pronominal prefix *pia*- (or its variants) on the matrix verb. This may be the unmarked form for Yimas complements, for occasionally a complement which is semantically one of the class of desire complements will be realized morphologically as an -*mpwi* 'talk' com-

plement. For example, both of the following are encountered, although
the former is much more common and accepted by native speakers as
'correct' Yimas:

(7-57) a. yaki   am-tu-wampuŋ   na-na-tɨ-n
          tobacco V PL eat-NFN-heart V SG 3SG S-DEF-feel-PRES
       b. yaki   am-tu-mpwi na-na-tɨ-n
          tobacco V PL eat-NFN-talk 3SG S-DEF-feel-PRES

       'He wants to smoke.'

Both examples in (7-57) contain complements of desire, yet only the
(a) example is marked in the usual way, with -*wampuŋ* 'heart'. The (b)
example uses -*mpwi* 'talk', but is in fact completely identical in meaning
to (a). Other examples of complements with -*mpwi* 'talk' can be found
in (7-52), (7-54) and (7-56) as well as earlier in this section.

The examples in (7-57) may suggest that complements of desire
marked by -*wampuŋ* 'heart' are losing ground to -*mpwi* 'talk' complements and may ultimately be replaced by the latter. Of the four types
of complements, those in -*wampuŋ* are undoubtedly the least common
in texts. Most examples I have are complements of a single verb of internal sensation, *tɨ*- 'feel' (which does have meanings other than that
of internal sensation, like 'do' and 'become'), but other possible matrix
predicates are *kacapal*- 'forget' (example (7-22)) or *mama*- 'bad'. The
complement marked by -*wampuŋ* 'heart' expresses an event that the A of
the matrix predicate or the speaker or addressee of the whole utterance
wishes to happen. It is, thus, a complement of desire, a desire of one of
the main participants of the speech act or of the A of the matrix verb.
Complements with -*wampuŋ* 'heart' do not normally co-occur with a
coreferential pronominal affix on the verb, but if there is any agreement,
it must be of the form for a class V singular noun, the morphological features of the independent noun *wampuŋ* 'heart'. A couple of additional
examples of -*wampuŋ* 'heart' complements follow:

(7-58) a. tpuk   am-tu-wampuŋ   kpa-n
          sago X SG   eat-NFN-heart V SG big-V SG
          ama-na-tɨ-n
          1SG S-DEF-feel-PRES
          'I've got a big yen to eat sago.'
       b. yaki   am-tu-wampuŋ   mama-k-n
          tobacco V PL eat-NFN-heart V SG bad-IRR-V SG
          anak
          COP V SG
          'It is bad to like smoking.'

The final types of complements denote actions and are rather like English gerunds. There are two types of these: those which denote habitual actions, skills or customs and are marked by the suffix -*wal* 'custom', plausibly related to the tense suffix -*war* HAB; and those which denote a single event occurring at a point in time and are indicated by the suffix -*nti*.

The verbal prefix linked to both of these complement types is *tia*- 'act' (and its variants), but complements in -*wal* also have the option of agreeing as a class V singular noun (see example (7-30a)). This is, in fact, the required pattern when the complement is in agreement with adjectives or adjectival verbs (see examples (7-14c,d). The semantic contrast between these two action complement types is clearly brought out in the following:

(7-59) a. tpuk   am-t-nti   yua-nti   antiak
              sago X SG eat-NFN-act good-act COP act
              '(Your) eating sago is good.'

      b. tpuk   am̃-tu-wal   yua-n   anak
              sago X SG eat-NFN-custom good-V SG COP V SG
              'Eating sago is good.'

The first example would be uttered, say, by someone who approached someone else who had recently been too sick to eat but was now sitting down eating sago. The sentence expresses the speaker's view that present act of eating by the previously sick person is good in this particular context. Maybe it will build up the sick person's strength. The second example simply expresses the idea that the basic custom of the Yimas people (and of lowland Sepik villagers generally) of eating sago is good in general. It is their traditional food, it has made them strong, etc. Clearly then, -*nti* 'act' complements express specific, context-bound actions, while -*wal* 'custom' complements denote general practices.

Complements in -*wal* 'custom' are quite common; there have been numerous examples earlier in this section (such as (7-31a), (7-32b), (7-36), and (7-40)). Complements with -*nti* 'act' are rarer, but representative examples presented previously include (7-30b), (7-31c), and (7-41a).

Verbs in all complement types strongly tend to be simpler morphologically than matrix verbs. As can be gleaned from the above examples, they are usually just a verb root plus -*ru* NFN. It is possible to have more complex complement verbs, although they occur rarely. A complement verb can consist of a verb theme rather than just a verb root, as in (7-60).

(7-60) mŋkawŋ   yara-mpi-wul-cu-mpwi
        post X SG   pick up-SEQ-put down-NFN-talk
        pia-ka-i-c-mpun
        talk T-1SG A-tell-PERF-3PL D
        'I told them to erect the post.'

Here, the complement verb consists of a verb theme formed by a serial verb construction consisting of two verb roots, *yara-* 'pick up' and *wul-* 'put down'.

7.1.3 Purpose Clauses

Purpose clauses share a number of the grammatical properties of complements, but contrast with the latter in that they never function as a core argument of the matrix verb. Rather, they function somewhat like oblique constituents of the matrix verb, expressing the intended goal of the action of the matrix verb. Purpose clauses are like complements in that they are non-finite: they never occur with pronominal agreement affixes or true tense suffixes (only the irrealis suffix). Purpose clauses are always controlled: the A or S of a purpose clause can never be overtly expressed and is always coreferential with a human core argument of the matrix verb. Normally this is the S or A participant, but if the verb has more than one human participant, it is possible for the O or D to be the controller. (See example (7-61c) below.) The verb in a purpose clause is marked by the irrealis suffix $-k \sim -\eta k$, as in these examples:

(7-61) a. ma   ŋarŋ   waŋkia   awl-k
          other   1 day removed rafters IX PL get-IRR
          ipa-wa-ntut
          1PL S-go-RM PAST
          'Next day we went to get (wood for) rafters.'
       b. wut   am-kia-k
          night eat-NIGHT-IRR
          na-ma-ŋka-pu-kia-k
          3SG S-in-go by land-away-NIGHT-IRR
          'At night he went inside to eat.'
       c. ŋaykum   m-ŋa-wampak-c-um   kumpwi
          woman II PL   NR DIST-1SG O-throw-PERF-3PL   child I PL
          taŋkway-cakal-k
          VIS-grasp-IRR
          'It was the women who sent me to look after the children.'

In (7-61a,b) the matrix verbs are monovalent verbs of motion with only an S participant, which is then the controller of the purpose clause. Note further the presence of -*kia* in both the matrix verb and that of the purpose clause. Its presence on both verbs is obligatory. True complements diverge here in prohibiting -*kia*. Example (7-61c) has a bivalent main verb with two human arguments, an A, *ŋaykum* 'women', and an O, *ŋa-* 1SG O. The controller of the purpose clause must be the O participant: witness the above translation. (7-61c) cannot have A control (*"it was the women who sent me so that they could look after the children').

The irrealis suffix -*k* ∼ -*ŋk* is the general and common marker of purpose clauses, but in one specific context there is an alternative to it. If the act denoted by the purpose clause is to be carried out directly and immediately as the result of a directive speech act, such as a request or an order, then the marker for a complement of speech -*mpwi* 'talk' plus the immediate aspect clitic *mpan* IMM may be used. Compare (7-62) with (7-61c) above:

(7-62) ŋaykum   m-ŋa-wampak-c-um   kumpwi
        woman II PL NR DIST-1SG O-throw-PERF-3PL child I PL

        taŋkway-cakal-cu-mpwi mpan
        VIS-grasp-NFN-talk   IMM

        'It was the women who sent me to look after the children.'

Examples (7-61c) and (7-62) are very close in structure and meaning. They structurally contrast in that (7-61c) has the irrealis suffix -*k* ∼ -*ŋk* while (7-62) has the form of a complement with -*ru* NFN plus -*mpwi* 'talk' and the clitic *mpan* IMM. The meaning difference is that (7-62) requires an immediately prior verbal order or request to someone that they look after the children. This is not the case in (7-61c); although this scenario is possible, others are also, such as an arrangement made days earlier or a pre-established custom that one does regularly. It needs to be noted that not all speakers make this contrast. For some speakers the contrast is one of immediacy; for them purpose clauses in -*mpwi* *mpan* need to follow directly from the action of the matrix verb. Other speakers seem to use the two ways of forming purpose clauses interchangeably. And even some speakers who make it in some contexts do not make it in others. It appears to be a semantic distinction well on its way to being lost.

7.1.4 Non-Finite Relative Clauses

Yimas has two types of constructions corresponding to English relative clauses. A relative clause is a clause-level construction (or more formally, an S) which modifies a noun, such as *the dog [which chased the cat]*, in which the relative clause *which chased the cat* modifies the noun *dog*, generally called the head of the relative clause. This relative clause is embedded as a constituent within the whole noun phrase, so that the constituent structure is [*the dog* [*which chased the cat*]]. Both of the Yimas relative clause types differ from English relative clauses in that they are *never* embedded, but are simply nominalized forms of verbs appositionally linked to a noun they modify, their 'head noun', rather like juxtaposed possessive nominals. The two types of relative clauses in Yimas contrast as to whether they are tensed or not. Non-finite relative clauses are prohibited from occurring with tense suffixes and instead have -*ru* NFN plus one of the set of suffixes which mark agentive nominalizations (for head nouns referring to humans) or one of the possessive/adjectival concord suffixes (for non-humans). Finite relative clauses, which will be discussed in detail in Section 7.2.1, are formed with or without the stem *m*- NR DIST, but require a true tense suffix. This difference correlates closely with a meaning difference. Non-finite relative clauses denote traits or characteristic actions of the noun modified, while finite relative clauses denote states which hold or actions which occur within the time frame denoted by the tense suffix on their verbs. Consider this contrast in the following examples:

(7-63) a. namarawt   [awt   pampay-kulan-t-awt]
             person I SG   fire   KIN-walk-NFN-M SG
             'the person who tends the fire' (as his job)

        b. namarawt   [awt   m-na-pampay-kulaŋ]
             person I SG   fire   NR DIST-DEF-KIN-walk
             'the person who is tending the fire' (right now, others may
             do so at other times)

The glosses in (7-63) clearly bring out the meaning contrast between the non-finite (7-63a) and the finite (7-63b) relative clauses. The non-finite relative clause expresses a long duration characteristic action, hence the reading of the action as a job, while the finite relative clause denotes the action as occurring within the time frame of the tense suffix, 'right now', as the tense in (7-63b) is present imperfective. A similar contrast can be found with states.

(7-64) a. namarawt   [tamana   ti-r-awt]   na-mal
             person I SG   sickness IX SG   feel-NFN-M SG   3SG S-die   ·
             'The person who was always sick died.'

        b. namarawt   [tamana   kantk-n]   na-mal
             person I SG   sickness IX SG   with-I SG   3SG S-die
             'The sick person died.'

The non-finite relative clause in (7-64a) denotes a typical characteristic state. The copula *anak* COP 3SG has been deleted in (7-64b), leaving just the postpositional phrase inflected with the concord suffix -*n* I SG as the finite relative clause (the copula could be inserted, but it is better to omit it). Again, the finite relative clause is bounded in time, denoting a temporary, transitory state of illness.

The syntax of non-finite and finite relative clauses is nearly identical and because the latter are the more common type, I will discuss the syntax of relative clauses in detail in Section 7.2.1. The one significant difference between the two types is in the range of core argument positions which are relativizable (Keenan and Comrie 1977). The relativized noun is that obligatorily missing argument of the relative clause which must be coreferential with the noun modified, the 'head'. Any core arguments plus locationals and temporals are relativizable with a finite relative clause, but the relativized nouns in non-finite relative clauses are restricted to S or A arguments. This is readily explicable, because non-finite relative clauses are nothing but agentive nominalizations in apposition to some nominal (the 'head noun'). Hence the noun which they relativize must belong to the same general class as agentive nominalizations, i.e., either S or A. Interestingly, as (7-65c) shows, it is possible to use a non-finite relative clause to relativize a nominal which is a non-agentive S. Examples of non-finite relative clause are provided below:

(7-65) a. m-ŋkt   pu-k   namat
       NR DIST-3PC 3PL-PROX person I PL

       pu-ŋkl-awl-k   [nampt   wark-r-mat]
       3PL O-3PC A-get-IRR house PL build-NFN-M PL

       'Those few got these people who build houses.'

    b. pu-n   [Macanum-n   taw-r-mat]
       3PL-FR DIST village name-OBL sit-NFN M PL

       manpa   Wansatmal
       crocodile III SG name

       pu-nanaŋ-wurt-ira-ntut
       3PL S-DUR-put down(RED: wul-)-dance-RM PAST

       'Those who lived at Macanum put down the crocodile Wansatmal while dancing.'

    c. mŋkawŋ   yampara-t-uŋ
       post X SG   stand-NFN-X SG

       ku-ka-pay-pu-t
       X SG O-1SG A-carry-away-PERF

       'I took the post for standing up.'

A slight morphological peculiarity of non-finite relative clauses (one they share with non-finite oblique clauses to be discussed in the next section) concerns singular class III and V nouns functioning as 'heads'. Instead of the expected concord suffix -*n* III/V SG in this case, what is actually found is the agentive nominalization suffix -*awt* M SG, as in this example:

(7-66) kakam   [awt yara-t-awt]
        tree (sp) V SG   fire pick up-NFN-M SG
        'a (piece of *kakam*) wood for picking up fire'

Other inanimate nouns are regular, in that the proper concord suffixes are used.

(7-67) awruk   [awt yara-t-uŋ]
        torch X SG   fire pick up-NFN-X SG
        'a torch for picking up fire'

In addition to the positive non-finite relative clauses exemplified thus far, Yimas also possesses negative non-finite relative clauses, which express the lack of a state or characteristic action. These are formed with the postposition -*kakan* 'without' which behaves morphologically like the attributive *kantk*- 'with'. (See example (7-64b)), except that it uses the agentive nominalization suffixes for human 'head' nouns. There is even a further exception to this last generalization: for the singular of classes I, III, and V, -*kakan* actually uses a zero morpheme, rather than either the expected -*awt* M SG or -*n* I, III, V SG.) Consider these examples:

(7-68) a. wik   mpa-n   [yaki   am-kakan-mat]
           week V SG   one-V SG   tobacco   eat-without-M PL
           na-kay-caw-ntut
           V SG O-1PL A-sit-RM PAST
           'We stayed one week without smoking tobacco.'

(This is an interesting example with the normally monovalent verb being used transitively, with two pronominal agreement prefixes.)

       b. kumpwi   ka-i-kra-taŋ-naŋ-n
           boy I PL LIKE-I PL A-1PL O-COM-stay-PRES
           [api-kakan-i]?
           put inside-without-I PL
           'Will the boys stay with us, without being put inside?'

       c. namla-mpu-ŋa-tkam-t
           house DL T-3PL A-1SG D-show-PERF
           mntk-kaka-nml
           finish-without-house DL
           'They showed me two unfinished houses.'

The noun modified by the non-finite relative clause in (7-66b) is *kumpwi* 'boys'. This is marked on the relative clause by the concord suffix -*i* I PL. Example (7-68a) lacks an overt independent 'head' noun for the relative clause. Rather it is simply represented by the pronominal agreement prefix *kay-* 1PL A, and this in turn is linked to the coreferential concord suffix -*mat* following -*kakan* 'without' in the relative clause. The final example illustrates a negative non-finite relative clause modifying an inanimate noun, in this case, *houses* DL, indicated by the proper concord suffixed -*nml* 'houses' DL following -*kakan* 'without' (with loss of its final /n/ before the initial /n/ of -*nml* houses DL).

Negative non-finite relative clauses contrast with positive ones in that they are not restricted to S or A participants as the relativized noun. Rather they permit any core argument to function as such, and this often results in ambiguity.

(7-69) wakn   na-mpu-ŋa-tkam-t
        snake V SG   V SG T-3PL A-1SG D-show-PERF
        [namat   tu-kakan-∅]
        person I PL   kill-without-V SG

        'They showed me the snake $\begin{cases} \text{that doesn't kill people.'} \\ \text{that people don't kill.'} \end{cases}$

The first reading in (7-69) comes from taking the relativized noun to be the A argument of the relative clause, while the second takes it as the O. Further examples of this ambiguity are in the examples of (7-68): in the (a) example the relativized noun is the A participant, while in (b) it is the O.

7.1.5 Non-Finite Oblique Clauses

One of the most common features of Yimas narratives is a type of non-finite clause whose function is rather like English participles in -*ing* in examples like *sitting in the chair, he saw the mouse underfoot*. As with English participles, the corresponding Yimas constructions are not inflected for tense but are assigned the same tense as the following fully inflected main verb. The Yimas construction also has much the same meaning as English -*ing* participles: to express an event basically simultaneous with that of the main verb.

Non-finite oblique clauses are formed like most non-finite clauses in Yimas, with -*ru* suffixed to a verb. This is followed by one of the concord suffixes. This codes the number and gender or class of the S or A participant of the oblique clause, which may or may not be overtly present. Finally comes the oblique suffix, -*n* ~ -*nan*. The oblique suffix always takes the form -*ɲan* following the suffixes ending in /t/ indicating that

the underlying forms of these suffixes actually terminate in palatals. But
as the oblique suffix is the only morpheme to follow them there is no
independent way to ascertain this. Also, the final /ŋ/ of the suffix -maŋ
F SG is always lost before the oblique suffix.

Consider the following examples:

(7-70) a. ama Bil   kantk taw-kia-r-awt-ɲan
        1SG Bill with   sit-NEAR-NFN-M SG-OBL

        pia-mpt-ŋa-i-kia-ntut
        talk T-3DL A-1SG D-tell-NEAR-RM PAST
        'While sitting with Bill, they told me.'

    b. wark-r-mat-ɲan   nam   kumpwi mnta
        build-NFN-M PL-OBL house boy I PL and then

        numa-mpu-ntak-t
        village O-3PL A-leave-PERF
        'While building a house, the boys left the village.'

    c. m-uŋ   tantaw-am-kia-r-awt-ɲan
        NR DIST-X SG sit(RED: taw-)-eat-NIGHT-NFN-M SG-OBL

        m-rm   maɲckrm   tma-mpɨ-kra-k
        NR DIST-3DL binding V DL V DL O-3DL A-cut-IRR
        'While (he was) sitting down eating it (sago), those two cut
        the two bindings.'

    d. mampi pay-cu-mprump-nan mpa kwantayn
        again   lie-NFN-F DL-OBL   now far

        ima-l-ŋka-pu-tapi
        water S-down-go-away-COMP
        'While (they both were) sleeping again, the water receded
        completely.'

    e. arm   nampt   ya-mpu-tawɲcak-kia-k
        water   house PL house PL O-3PL A-flood-NIGHT-IRR

        m-um   pay-kia-r-mat-ɲan
        NR DIST-I PL lie-NIGHT-NFN-M PL-OBL

        num-n-mat
        village-OBL-M PL
        'The water flooded the houses while they, the villagers,
        slept.'

As with all the other non-finite constructions in Yimas, these non-finite
oblique clauses are again nominalizations, for only nominals may be
suffixed with the oblique suffix. In each of these examples the agentive
nominalization suffixes mark the number of the S (examples (7-70a,d,e),

or A (examples (7-70b,c) argument of the oblique clause, which otherwise may be completely lacking, as is the case in all the above examples, except (7-70a,e). Verbs in non-finite oblique clauses may be suffixed with -*kia*; this is in fact obligatory if the main verb is marked with -*kia*, as in examples (7-70a,c,e). It is not uncommon for -*kia* in these non-finite oblique clauses to be followed immediately by -*k* IRR and then -*ru* NFN, as in the following example:

(7-71) mpa irm-kia-k-r-ŋkt-ɲan
       now stand-NEAR-IRR-NFN-PC-OBL

       paŋkra-na-ma-ŋka-pu-kia-k
       1PL S-DEF-in-go by land-away-NEAR-IRR

       'Standing now, we few walked inside.'

Constructions like (7-71) plus its use in purpose clauses and elsewhere (to be discussed in Section 7.2.2) suggest that the irrealis is well on its way to being re-analyzed as a non-finite marker. Another point in support of this view is that -*k* IRR can sometimes replace -*ru* NFN altogether in these constructions as in (7-72) below. (Note that verbs in non-finite oblique clauses can and commonly do consist of a serial verb construction forming a complex verb theme. One such example is (7-70c).)

A very important point of contrast between non-finite oblique clauses and the other non-finite constructions discussed in this chapter is that they are never *obligatorily* controlled. As we have seen, the S and A participants of these clauses can be freely omitted, but if this is done, they are not always completely recoverable within the sentence. For example, the A participant of (7-70b) need not be *kumpwi* 'boys'. It could just as easily, and perhaps more likely, be *ipa* 'we', with the sentence meaning 'while we were building a house, the boys left the village'. Note also that in examples (7-70c,d) the S and A participants of the non-finite oblique clause correspond to no core argument of the main clause of the sentence which contain them. They are, however, equivalent to core participants in previous sentences. As a further example of these discourse-controlled missing S/A participants in non-finite oblique clauses, consider the following example:

(7-72) tay   mpa pia-ka-i-kia-ntuk-mpn
       then now talk T-1SG A-tell-NEAR-RM PAST-3DL D

       "awt   ay-ampu-kia-na-ŋkt.   Ama
       fire   HORT PL-light-NEAR-IMP-PC. 1SG

       kampra   kpa-n   ama-na-tɨ-kia-k".
       hunger V SG big-V SG 1SG S-DEF-feel-NEAR-IRR

Tay   mpa   taw-kia-k-ŋkt-ɲan   tay
then   now   sit-NEAR-IRR-PC-OBL   then

mpa   Kayan   na-na-ma-impu-pra-kia-k
now   name   3SG S-DEF-in-go by water-toward-NEAR-IRR

na-ka-amkay-kia-ntut
3SG O-1SG A-call-NEAR-RM PAST

'And right then I told those two "Light a fire! I'm very
hungry." Then while we were sitting, Kayan paddled in
toward us and I called out to him.'

In this example, the S participant of the non-finite oblique clause consisting of *tay mpa taw-kia-k-ŋkt-ɲan* 'while sitting down' is 'we', never
mentioned explicitly in the discourse, but is the group consisting of the
speaker and companions. The speaker, of course, was the A participant
of the previous clause and his companions that of the clause before.
That the speaker and his companions are the S of the non-finite oblique
clause is simply established by inference of the hearer.

While the above examples establish that the referent of a missing S
or A participant need not be in the sentence containing the non-finite
oblique clause, it is, of course, the case that they may be. More often
than not, the referent is a core argument of the main clause joined to
the non-finite clause. Example (7-71) above illustrates this. The S of
the main clause is also the S of the non-finite oblique clause. Further
examples are in (7-73) in which the referent is the A (7-73a) or the D
(7-73b) in the main clause.

(7-73) a. pu-ŋa-tay   wi-impu-pra-ru-mat-ɲan
          3PL A-1SG O-see up-go by water-toward-NFN-M PL-OBL
          'While paddling up toward me, they saw me.'

       b. taw-kia-r-ŋkt-ɲan
          sit-NEAR-NFN-PC-OBL

          pia-kra-i-kia-ntuk-ŋkt
          talk T-1PL D-tell-NEAR-RM PAST-PC

          "nan-pay-taw-kia-na-ŋkt   balus
          IMP PL-first-sit-NEAR-IMP-PC   airplane V SG

          m-n   mpa   na-na-tmuk-kia-k"
          NR DIST-V SG now   V SG S-DEF-fall-NEAR-IRR
          'While (we were) sitting, (they) told us "Wait first. The
          airplane is landing now." '

Because the referent of the missing S or A argument can be coreferential with any core argument or indeed none at all, sentences containing

them can be ambiguous, if the agreement suffixes are right. Consider
the following examples:

(7-74) pu-kra-ant-t   pan-t-mat-ɲan
        3PL A-1PL O-hear-PERF   pound sago-NFN-M PL-OBL
        'They heard us when pounding sago.' (either they or we could
        be pounding sago)

The verb in the non-finite oblique clause is coded as having a plural S
argument by the suffix -*mat* M PL. But both core arguments of the main
clause are plural, so that both can serve as referents for the missing S
argument, resulting in the sentence being ambiguous.

Yimas also possesses negative non-finite oblique clauses in addition
to the positive ones. Like the negative non-finite relative clauses, these
are formed with -*kakan* plus agentive nominalization or class concord
suffixes, which again mark the number and gender or noun class of the S
or A argument of the oblique clause, which may or may not be overt. Following this comes the oblique suffix -*n* ∼ -*nan*, exactly as with their positive counterparts. As we have seen, positive non-finite oblique clauses
express states which hold or events which occur within the time frame
of the main verb, i.e., they must be simultaneous. Negative non-finite
oblique clauses are simply the converse of this: they express states or
events which may not occur during the time frame of the main verb.
The practical effect of this is to produce a conditional sentence 'if not X,
then Y' (for more detailed discussion on conditionals, see Section 7.2.3).
Consider these examples:

(7-75) a. ŋaykum   ya-kakan-put-ɲan
            woman II PL   come-without-F PL-OBL

            ta-ka-na-way-mp-i-waraca-mpi-wa-n
            NEG-1SG S-DEF-turn-SEQ-return-SEQ-go-PRES

            'If the women aren't coming, I'm not going back.'

        b. balus   ya-kakan-∅-an   ipa   wara
            airplane V SG come-without-V SG-OBL   1PL   what

            ipa-na-am-n?
            1PL S-DEF-eat-PRES

            'If the plane doesn't come, what do we eat?'

        c. m-n   mala-k   ant-kakan-∅-an
            NR DIST-I SG   talk-IRR   hear-without-I SG-OBL

            yampaŋ   mnta   k-kay-ɲa-tput-nc-ak
            head VI SG   then   VI SG T-1PL A-DEF-hit-PRES-3SG D

            'If he doesn't listen, we'll hit him in the head.'

All three examples are in the present tense, as indicated by the tense suffix on the main verb. This is typical of negative oblique clauses. The non-finite oblique clauses are within the same time frame as the main clause and express events whose non-occurrence right now is responsible for the circumstances holding in the main clause. Thus, in (7-75a) the speaker's decision not to return is contingent on whether the women come or not. If they do not come, the situation of the main clause will eventuate. Similar remarks apply to (7-75c). The middle example (7-75b) is perhaps the most interesting. The failure of the plane to arrive will leave the speaker and his group without food. This situation is thus summed up in the query which forms the main clause, 'what do we eat?'.

An interesting difference between positive and negative non-finite oblique clauses concerns word order possibilities. While core arguments of positive non-finite oblique clauses can occur after the verb, as examples (7-70b,e) demonstrate, this is not possible with negative non-finite oblique clauses. So (7-76) is ungrammatical.

(7-76) *ya-kakan-∅-nan   balus   ipa   wara
       come-without-V SG-OBL airplane V SG 1PL   what
       ipa-na-am-n
       1PL S-DEF-eat-PRES

This may indicate that *-kakan* 'without', like *kantk* 'with', is a postposition and governs an NP constituent preceding, blocking any possible extraction from it.

7.2 Finite Nominalizations

Finite nominalizations contrast with non-finite ones in that they require a tense suffix and never take *-ru* NFN. Pronominal affixes may also occur on verbs in finite nominalizations. Another typical morphological feature of finite nominalizations, albeit not a universal one, is the near distal deictic stem *m-*. The verbs of finite nominalizations commonly occur suffixed to this stem, replacing the normal class and number concord suffixes, with the whole forming a complex nominal not unlike *m-n* NR DIST-I SG 'he'. The use of distal deictics to mark relative clauses is common in Papuan languages (Reesink 1987; Olson 1981) and elsewhere (note English *that*). In most languages, this occurs at the boundary of the relative clause, but in Yimas it is a form bound, like a prefix, to the inflected verb of the relative clause. This again reflects the polysynthetic nature of the language; a relative clause will commonly consist of nothing but a fully inflected verb, suffixed to *m-* NR DIST. A clause is again realized as a word-level unit. Finite nominalizations have a similar range of functions to their non-finite counterparts, except that they are never used as complements. Their most common functions are as relative and oblique (i.e., adverbial) clauses.

7.2.1 Finite Relative Clauses

Finite relative clauses are not an infrequent feature of Yimas discourse. The verbs in finite relative clauses share a good deal in their morphological formation with modally inflected verbs, the discussion of which the reader may care to review (see Section 5.2.2). Finite relative clauses are typically marked by *m-* NR DIST, to which the fully inflected verb is suffixed. (There is a sub-type of finite relative clauses which does not employ *m-* NR DIST, and this will be discussed in detail later in this section.) The stem *m-* NR DIST functions much like the *wh* word or *that* in English—to mark the whole relative clause as a definite referring expression. The other obligatory morpheme marking a finite relative is a class and number concord suffix. These are the adjectival concord suffixes for the various noun classes and occur as the final suffix of the verb, except that human nouns do not distinguish class, i.e., masculine and feminine nouns take the same set of suffixes, those found with modally inflected verbs (see Section 5.2.2).

(7-77) a. krayŋ   [m-na-taw-nt-ŋ   tak-ɲan]
             frog VI SG   NR DIST-DEF-sit-PRES-VI SG   rock-OBL
             'the frog sitting on the rock'

        b. krayŋ   [m-ka-tu-r-ŋ]
             frog VI SG   NR DIST-1SG A-kill-PERF-VI SG
             'the frog which I killed'

        c. krayŋ   [m-ŋa-tay-nc-ŋ]
             frog VI SG   NR DIST-1SG O-see-PRES-VI SG
             'the frog watching me'

The suffix *-ŋk* VI SG (*-ŋ* in word final position) occurs on each of the verbs in these relative clauses, marking the class and number of these nominalizations and hence indicating what noun is modified by them, i.e., what are their head nouns. The same class and number concord suffix is used regardless of the participant role of the relativized noun: S in (7-77a), O in (7-77b), and A in (7-77c). This is typical of lower animate and inanimate nouns, but higher animate and especially human nouns are more complicated. It will be necessary to discuss relativization on the differing participant role types separately.

The basic rule is that the noun which is being relativized is marked only once, by the final class and number concord suffix. The relativized noun may be defined as the noun coreferential to the 'head', but obligatorily absent in the relative clause. Thus, in all three examples in

(7-77) the relativized noun is *krayŋ* 'frog', the same as the 'head', but it is obligatorily absent in these relative clauses and only traced by the concord suffix agreeing with it in number and class. Relative clauses in which the relativized noun functions as S are the simplest case, so let's start there. The only agreement suffix permitted on a verb in a relative clause with the S as the relativized noun is the final concord suffix; the S *cannot* be also coded by a pronominal prefix. Consider these:

(7-78) a. namarawt   [m-ya-t-∅]
            person I SG   NR DIST-come-PERF-3SG
       b.*namarawt   [m-n-ya-t-∅]
            person I SG   NR DIST-3SG S-come-PERF-3SG
            'the person who came'

The relativized noun in both of these is the S participant, *namarawt* 'person'. This is, of course, the same as the head noun, and is marked by the concord suffix ∅. (Human singular nouns and singular nouns of classes III and V are irregular in that instead of the expected concord suffix -*n*, a zero morpheme is found. This is parallel to the usage with modally inflected verbs.) Example (7-78b) is ungrammatical because the S is coded twice on the verb, once by the concord suffix and also by the pronominal agreement prefix *n*- 3SG S. The latter is completely prohibited by the blanket rule against double marking of the relativized noun.

When the relativized noun is an A argument, the resulting structure is similar to that with relativization on an S. The verb can contain pronominal agreement prefixes in addition to the obligatory concord suffix, but these must code an O or D participant, *never* the A. The morphology for marking a relativized A is identical to that for S.

(7-79) a. namarawt   [narmaŋ   m-tpul-∅]
            person I PL   woman II SG   NR DIST-hit-3SG
            'the person who hit the woman'
       b. Elias
            name

            [m-kra-pay-pra-kia-ntuk-ŋkt-∅
            NR DIST-1PL O-carry-toward-NEAR-RM PAST-PC-3SG
            mota-nan]
            outboard motor-OBL

            'Elias who brought us few with his outboard motor'
       c. ŋaykum   [irut   m-na-ampa-nt-um]
            woman II PL   mat IX PL   NR DIST-DEF-weave-PRES-3PL
            'the women who are weaving the mats'

Pronominal agreement prefixes for O or D are only permissible if their person is first or second: third person prefixes are prohibited. So (7-80a) is grammatical, but (7-80b) is not.

(7-80) a. namat   [m-ŋa-tpul-c-um]
        person I PL   NR DIST-1SG O-hit-PERF-3PL
        'the people who hit me'

      b.*namat   [m-pu-tpul-c-um]
        person I PL   NR DIST-3PL O-hit-PERF-3PL
        'the people who hit them'

The reason for this restriction is probably to eliminate ambiguity. Because the third person pronominal prefixes do not actually distinguish participant roles as do those of the first and second persons, but vary in form according to their word position, a form like (7-80b) would be ambiguous as to whether *pu-* codes A or O. In fact, a string like (7-80b) can only have the meaning where *pu-* functions as the A.

When the relativized noun is O, pronominal agreement prefixes of any person are permitted on the verb to code the A participant. Consider these examples:

(7-81) a. napntuk   [m-kay-ɲanaŋ-tmi-awŋkcpa-ntuk-uŋ]
        chant X SG NR DIST-1PL A-DUR-say-bathe-RM PAST-X SG
        'the chant which we sing while bathing'

      b. anti   [God m-n-papk-ntuk-i]
        land VIII SG God NR DIST-3SG A-carve-RM PAST-VIII SG
        'the world which God made'

      c. tpwi
        sago palm IV PL

        [m-mpɨ-nanaŋ-pan-tuk-i]
        NR DIST-3DL A-DUR-pound sago-RM PAST-IV PL
        'the sago palms which they both were pounding'

Singular human nouns (and nouns of class III and V which behave morpho- logically like them) have a special concord suffix -*nak* used when the relativized noun is in O function.

(7-82) a. [Macprak m-n-wu-ntuk-nak]   kaywi
        name   NR DIST-3SG A-take-RM PAST-3SG O girl II SG
        'the daughter which Macprak adopted'

      b. wakn   [namat   m-mpu-tu-r-ak]
        snake V SG person I PL NR DIST-3PL A-kill-PERF-V SG O
        'the snake which the people killed'

This is the only concord suffix for relative clauses that actually codes the participant role of the relativized noun. All others are oblivious to this.

As with the evidence from the modally inflected verbs, the anomaly
of -*nak* 3SG O illustrates a nominative-accusative bias in this part of
Yimas grammar. Note that, when relativized, S and A participants
of these specific class and number features are coded alike, with ∅ ~
-*n*, while O participants are treated differently, requiring -*nak*. The
following examples make this very clear:

(7-83) a. namarawt   [m-na-taw-n-∅   mnti]
           person I SG   NR DIST-DEF-sit-PRES-3SG   there
           'the person who is sitting there'

        b. namarawt   [narmaŋ   m-tpul-∅]
           person I SG   woman II SG NR DIST-hit-3SG
           'the person who hit the woman'

        c. namarawt   [narmaŋ   m-n-tpul-c-ak]
           person I SG   woman II SG NR DIST-3SG A-hit-PERF-3SG O
           'the person whom the woman hit'

It is difficult to explain the reason for this form. It cannot be to eliminate
ambiguity, for the obligatory absence of any third person pronominal
prefixes in A relativization versus their presence in O relativization is
sufficient to accomplish this. Further this is exactly how disambiguation
is accomplished in the dual and plural which use the same concord suffix
regardless of the participant role of the relativized noun.

(7-84) a. namat   [m-na-taw-nt-um   mnti]
           person I PL   NR DIST-DEF-sit-PRES-3PL   there
           'the people who are sitting there'

        b. namat   [ŋaykum   m-tpul-c-um]
           person I PL   woman II PL NR DIST-hit-PERF-3PL
           'the people who hit the women'

        c. namat   [ŋaykum   m-mpu-tpul-c-um]
           person I PL   woman II PL NR DIST-3PL A-hit-PERF-3PL
           'the people whom the women hit'

Relativization of the T argument of a ditransitive verb is simplest
if the D participant is first or second person and hence marked by a
pronominal prefix. Then, the concord suffix for the relativized T noun
simply follows the tense suffix.

(7-85) a. nmprm   ŋarŋ
           leaf VII SG 1 day removed
           [m-mpu-ŋa-ŋa-na-m]
           NR DIST-3PL A-1SG D-give-NR PAST-VII SG
           'the letter they gave me yesterday'

    b. impram
    basket VII SG
    [m-nan-a-ampa-ŋa-nt-m]
    NR DIST-2SG D-DEF-weave-BEN-PRES-VII SG
    'the basket which she is weaving for you'

If the D is third person and thus a suffix, the concord suffix for the relativized T follows it, causing the D suffix to appear in its non-word-final form.

(7-86) a. nmprm   [ŋarŋ
        leaf VII SG   1 day removed

        m-mpu-ŋa-na-k-m]
        NR DIST-3PL A-give-NR PAST-3SG D-VII SG
        'the letter they gave to him yesterday'

     b. nmprm   [ŋarŋ
        leaf VII SG   1 day removed

        m-ka-ŋa-na-mpan-m]
        NR DIST-1SG A-give-NR PAST-3PL D-VII SG
        'the letter he gave to them yesterday'

Relativization of D participants presents a special problem. The m- NR DIST stem always occupies one of the verbal pronominal prefix positions potentially usurping the position for the prefix for the T participant. The pronominal affixes for third person D participants are suffixes following the tense suffix, and this is the position for the concord suffix marking the class and number features of the noun modified by the relative clause. Both of these present morphological difficulties for relativization of D participants, and this is generally avoided in the language. I have never encountered an example in spontaneous usage, but in elicitation sessions I have been able to get speakers to produce examples like the following, although given the context in which they were obtained, it is probable that they are fairly stilted.

(7-87) kalakn   [ŋaykum   amtra
      boy I SG   woman II PL food V PL

      ya-mpu-na-ŋa-nt-akn]   nam-n
      V PL-3PL A-DEF-give-PRES-3SG D house-OBL

      na-na-iray-n
      3SG S-DEF-cry-PRES

      'The boy that the women gave food to is crying in the house.'

The relative clause in (7-87) has no unambiguous concord suffix nor m- NR DIST. The verbal pronominal suffix in this example does double duty as both the relative clause concord marker and the affix for a third person singular D participant. The stem *m-* NR DIST is completely prohibited because of *ya-* V PL T. In fact, the modified noun plus the relative clause looks like a main clause, and (7-87) is ambiguous between a construction with a relative clause and one consisting of two conjoined clauses with the meaning 'The women gave the food to the boy in the house and he is crying.' What, in fact, can discriminate between these two are word order constraints. If the first clause is simply one of two conjoined clauses, then *kalakn* 'boy' can occur anywhere within it, say between *ŋaykum* 'women' and *amtra* 'food'. If, however, it is the external modified noun of a relative clause, this is not possible. It must always occur outside of the relative clause, either before it, as in (7-87), or after it.

Yimas does not restrict relativization to core arguments only. The language allows relative clauses to be formed by relativizing locationals (and temporals, as well, but these will be discussed in Section 7.2.3). When a locational is relativized, the clause describes the place at which an event occurs, but locative relative clauses contrast with those formed for core arguments in that they never permit a true head noun, although a locational word or deictic may be present, as following examples illustrate:

(7-88) a. maramara   mnti   ya-n-ta-t
            goods V PL   there V PL O-2SG A-put-PERF
            [yan   m-n-a-irm-t-a-n]
            tree V SG   NR DIST-V SG S-DEF-stand-PRES-IX SG-OBL
            'You put the goods there where the tree stands.'

        b. mawn [m-um
            above   NR DIST-I PL
            m-mpu-kaprak-war-a-n]
            NR DIST-3PL A-cut skin-HAB-IX SG-OBL
            'up there where they cut their skin'

The relative clause in the (a) example can only be construed as modifying *mnti* 'there', but the class-number concord marker on the verb is *-a* IX SG. This is the typical class-number marker for referring to places or areas and may reflect a now lost noun referring to this concept (much as *-mpwi* 'talk' and *-nti* 'act' probably do). This may be related to the prefix *ta-* found on the other locational deictics *ta-k* 'here' and *ta-n* 'there' or even more likely to the interrogative stem *-ŋka* 'where', both of which end in *-a* and on phonological grounds are plausible members of class IX. In any case, the relative clause is marked as modifying a

class IX singular noun which clearly cannot be the locational deictic.
Rather we must assume some obligatorily missing noun of this class and
number specification which, in turn, is in apposition to the deictic. Similar remarks apply to (7-88b), with the locational word *mawn* 'above'.
Sometimes there is not even a deictic or locational word to act as a stand
in head for a locative relative clause; they simply occur on their own as
in (7-89):

(7-89) a. [maramara   m-mpu-ti-r-a-n]
          goods V PL NR DIST-3PL A-lay down-PERF-IX SG-OBL

          m-ra   ya-kay-ɲa-tacay-kulanaŋ
          NR DIST-V PL V PL-1PL A-DEF-see(RED: *tay-*)-walk
          'Where they laid out the goods, we walked around looking
          at them.'

     b. [paspot
        passport V SG

        m-mpu-pampan-takal-war-a-n]
        NR DIST-3PL A-correct-touch-HAB-IX SG-OBL

        kapa-wa-kia-ntut
        1DL S-go-NEAR-RM PAST
        'We both went to where they fix passports.'

Negative finite relative clauses are formed in the same way that
tensed clauses generally are negated, with the verbal prefix *ta-* NEG
(this obligatorily replaces *m-* NR DIST). In relative clauses, however,
ta- creates some problems because the morphological effect of negation
on a verb is very much like that of relativization: both require participants normally coded by pronominal prefixes to appear as suffixes.
This can result in negative relative clauses being ambiguous (note that
the same result obtains with negation by *-kakan* 'without' used with
non-finite relative clauses).

(7-90) namarawt   [narmaŋ   ta-pu-n-tpul-c-ak]
       person I SG woman II SG NEG-3-3SG A-hit-PERF-3SG O
       'the person that {the woman did not hit.' / did not hit the woman.'}

The suffix *-nak* 3SG O could be either the result of negation or relative
clause formation. If the latter, it would identify the relativized noun as
in O function and thus require the first of the two possible readings. This
is, in fact, the preferred reading. If *-nak* 3SG O derives from negation,
then no conclusions are possible concerning the role of the relativized
noun and the relative clause is therefore compatible with a reading of it
being the A participant (the second meaning above). The only way to

force a reading of the A as being the relativized noun is not to code the O by a verbal affix at all.

(7-91) namarawt   [narmaŋ   ta-pu-tpul-∅]
        person I SG   woman II SG   NEG-3-hit-3SG
        'the person who hit the woman'

Here the bivalent verb *tpul-* 'hit' is formally intransitive, with just a single participant coded by *pu-...-∅*. The fact that the concord suffix on the verb is ∅ rather than *-nak* indicates that the relativized noun must be A. Hence, this example is not ambiguous.

The placement of a relative clause (finite or non-finite) with respect to its 'head' noun is free. It can precede the 'head' noun,

(7-92) [Macprak m-n-wu-ntuk-nak]   kaywi
         name   NR DIST-3SG A-take-RM PAST-3SG O   girl II SG
         'the daughter which Macprak adopted'

or follow it.

(7-93) Elias [m-kra-pay-pra-kia-ntuk-ŋkt-∅]
        Elias   NR DIST-1PL O-carry-toward-NEAR RM PAST-PC-3SG
        mota-nan]
        outboard motor-OBL
        'Elias who brought us few with his motor'

It need not even adjoin it, in fact most commonly does not.

(7-94) a. napntuk   ku-k   kawk
            chant X SG   X SG-PROX   COP X SG VIS
            [m-kay-ɲanaŋ-tmi-awŋkcpa-ntuk-uŋ]
            NR DIST-1PL A-DUR-say-bathe-RM PAST-X SG
            'It was this chant which we sang while bathing.'
       b. manpawi   pu-ŋa-tkam-t
            crocodile III PL   3PL A-1SG D-show-PERF
            m-mpu-tu-r-um]
            NR DIST-3PL A-kill-PERF-3PL
            'They showed me the crocodiles they killed.'

And, if the 'head' is already well established in the discourse it is possible to omit it entirely.

(7-95) na-mpu-ŋa-tkam-t
        III SG T-3PL A-1SG D-show-PERF
        [m-pu-tu-r-ak]
        NR DIST-3PL A-kill-PERF-3SG O
        'They showed me the one they killed.' (i.e., a crocodile)

Admittedly, this last possibility, while grammatical, is not common. Relative clauses normally function to provide definite descriptions for an entity just being introduced in order to help the hearer identify it. To provide the definite description but omit the noun to which it applies is pragmatically very odd and requires quite a marked context to be acceptable. Example (7-95) belongs in a narrative context discussing crocodiles, where the entity described by the relative clause is already well established. The relative clause then functions contrastively, to select a particular set of crocodiles out of the class which is already the topic.

The freedom of movement of relative clauses and their very weak links to their 'head' nouns is fully in keeping with the analysis adopted here that they are independent nominals in their own right, but appositionally linked to their head. Unlike other nominals, though, finite relative clauses are full clauses and partake of the grammatical features of clauses. As discussed in Section 6.5, Yimas clauses are very loosely structured, with nominals (core and oblique) occurring in any order with respect to the verb. Structurally, a Yimas clause is flat, with the verb and nominal clauses all on the same level, as first order branches of S. Relative clauses have the same basic structure, and are just as free in their word order possibilities. Thus, (7-96a,b) are both fully grammatical.

(7-96) a. irmpŋ   [m-na-taw-n   nam-n
          slit drum I SG   NR DIST-DEF-sit-PRES   house-OBL
          maymp-n]
          side-OBL
          'the slit drum which is next to the house'

       b. namarawt   [m-n-tpul-c-ak   narmaŋ]
          person I PL NR DIST-3SG A-hit-PERF-3SG O   woman II SG
          'the person that the woman hit'

Relative clauses can assume any function in the main clause: core arguments, obliques, or even constituents of possessive NPs. Most commonly they are linked to 'head' nouns in these functions and thus assume the same functions, although the 'heads' can be missing, with the relative clauses bearing these functions on their own. Examples of relative clauses in various functions follow:

(7-97) a. Relative clause as S:
          [Macprak   m-n-wu-ntuk-nak]   kaywi
          name   NR DIST-3SG A-take-RM PAST-3SG O   girl II SG
          na-mal-kia-ntut
          3SG S-die-NIGHT-RM PAST
          'The daughter which Macprak adopted died.'

b. Relative clause as A:

namarawt   [m-ya-t-∅]   manpa
person I SG   NR DIST-come-PERF-3SG   crocodile III SG
na-n-tu-t
III SG O-3SG A-kill-PERF
'The person who came killed a crocodile.'

c. Relative clause as O:

tpwi
sago IV PL

[m-mpɨ-nanaŋ-pan-tuk-i]
  NR DIST-3DL A-DUR-pound sago-RM PAST-IV PL
i-mp-nanaŋ-pampay-arkat-ɲcut
IV PL O-3DL A-DUR-KIN-paddle-RM PAST
'They both paddled, carrying the sago which they were
working.'

d. Relative clause as T:

irpm   mu-ka-tkam-r-mpun
coconut palm IV SG   IV SG T-1SG A-show-PERF-3PL D
[m-n-wut-ɲcuk-um]
  NR DIST-2SG A-put down-RM PAST-IV SG
'I showed them the coconut palm you planted.'

e. Relative clause as D:

panmal   patn   na-ka-ŋa-r-akn
man I SG   betelnut V SG   V SG T-1SG A-give-PERF-3SG D
[manpa   m-tu-t-∅]
  crocodile III SG   NR DIST-kill-PERF-3SG
'I gave betelnut to the man who killed the crocodile.'

f. Relative clause as oblique:

mawn [m-um
above   NR DIST-3PL
m-mpu-kaprak-war-a-n]   ipa-awramu-ŋ
NR DIST-3PL A-cut skin-HAB-IX SG-OBL 1PL-enter-IRR
'We go inside upstairs where they cut skin.'
(as in initiation rituals)

g. Relative clause as possessor:

[awt m-nanaŋ-pampay-caw-na-ntut]   na
fire NR DIST-DUR-KIN-sit-DUR-RM PAST   POSS

       kalakn   na-n-tay-mpi-yara-k
       boy I SG   I SG O-3SG A-see-SEQ-pick up-IRR
       'The son of he who was tending the fire found it.'
   h. Relative clause as possessed:
       manm   p-ka-tay   m-ɲa
       male cult house VII SG VII SG O-1SG A-see 2SG-POSS
       [m-mpu-tkam-r-m]
       NR DIST-3PL A-show-PERF-VI SG
       'I saw the cult house, yours which they showed.'

Relative clauses can also function as arguments of embedded clauses, such as complements and purpose clauses.

(7-98) a. tia-ka-na-aykapiŋa-n   anti
       act O-1SG A-DEF-know-PRES land VIII SG

       papk-t-wal   [God
       carve-NFN-custom   God

       m-n-papk-ntuk-i]
       NR DIST-3SG A-carve-RM PAST-VIII SG
       'I know how God made the world.'

     b. pu-ŋa-tmayk-t   wakntt   tay-cu-mpwi
       3PL A-1SG O-summon-PERF snake V PL see-NFN-talk
       mpan [kalakn   m-n-a-tu-nt-um]
       IMM   boy I SG NR DIST-3SG A-DEF-kill-PRES-3PL
       'They summoned me to see the snakes the boy is killing.'

Note that in both of these examples, the relative clause follows the nonfinite verb (it is possible for them to precede).

The above facts clearly demonstrate that finite relative clauses have all the syntactic features and privileges of nouns, including class and number, but at the same time remain full finite clauses, with tense realized on the verb. They must be analyzed in the most basic terms as an N realized as a clause. There are two morphological exponents of these nominal features—*m*- NR DIST and the final concord suffixes—and so the question arises as to which of these is the head of the construction, i.e., that morpheme which actually makes the sentential constituent into a noun phrase. This would be difficult to decide if it was not for one small piece of evidence, and that is the concord suffix -*nak* 3SG O. This actually codes the function of the relativized noun, which is a clause-internal constituent, not that of any constituent in the main clause. Thus, its behavior is like that of a verbal pronominal affix within the relative clause. This leaves *m*- NR DIST to assume the function of the head of the relative clause, and suggests a more formal structure like the following:

(7-99)

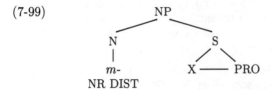

This structure is anomalous in having its head on the left, because Yimas otherwise is a consistent head to the right language. However, this discrepancy must be faced with the deictics generally; consider the following deictic forms for class I SG:

(7-100) na-k   m-n   na-n
        I SG-PROX   NR DIST-I SG   I SG-FR DIST
        'this'   'that near you'   'that yonder'

Regardless of whether we choose the concord suffix or the deictic stem as the head in these forms, at least one form will be anomalous. Sticking to the majority head to the right pattern of Yimas, we can analyze the proximal and far deictic forms as consisting of modifier + head, with the head being the deictic stem. Applying this then to the near distal form, we identify *m*- NR DIST as its head. This is unusual because the head is on the left, but it does independently vindicate the structure (7-100) suggested for relative clauses.

The stem *m*- NR DIST is not equivalent to the head noun of an English relative clause such as *the man who killed the crocodile*. It is equivalent rather to the main clause noun to which the relative clause as a whole is paratactically linked.

Consider the structure of example (7-97a), which is diagrammed below in (7-101). Because *m*- is a form bound to the verb, noun arguments of the relative clause occur before it, represented by the line branching from the S of the relative clause and crossing over the vertical line from the N of the relative clause. The concord suffix on the verb of the relative clause marks the class and number (and the participant role) of the relativized noun. These features are transferred to *m*- NR DIST, much as -*m* on English *who-m* identifies that the relativized noun is an object. Since *m*- NR DIST is the head of the noun phrase, these features are also those of the noun phrase as a whole. These finally are matched up to the features of the noun *kaywi* 'girl' which is thereby established as the noun modified by the relative clause.

(7-101)

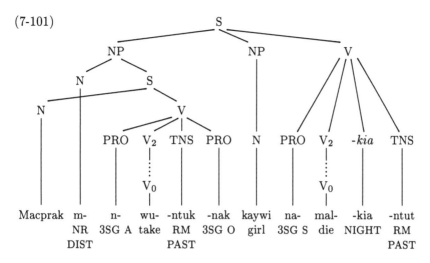

This analysis of relative clauses, headed by *m-* NR DIST is further supported by the behavior of those without *m-*. Because they lack *m-*, it is impossible to argue that they are headed by anything but the concord suffix. This claim is buttressed by the fact that finite relative clauses without *m-* take exactly the same concord suffixes as adjectives or possessives. The suffix *-nak* 3SG O which marks role as well as person and number in relative clauses with *m-* is not available for those without it. This indicates that the final suffixes in relative clauses without *m-* are just concord suffixes, like those terminating juxtaposed adjectives or possessives, and not pronominal affixes to the verb. Thus, the *m-* less relative clause in (7-102a) has the structure in (7-102b):

(7-102) a. wul-k-n
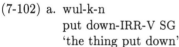
put down-IRR-V SG
'the thing put down'

b.

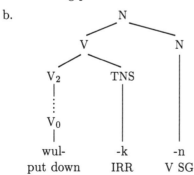

The constituents of these relative clauses are highly restricted. They can never be more than a verb theme (generally just a verb root) plus a tense suffix (including -*kia*). No pronominal prefixes nor nominal arguments are permitted. These constructions are very much parallel to English nominalized adjectives or participles in -*ed* such as *the dead* or *the cooked*. These finite relative clauses without *m*- NR DIST are the patient-oriented counterpart to the agentive nominalizations. Whereas agentive nominalizations denote the agent or effective cause of an action, these patient-oriented nominalizations describe the object affected or produced by the action. Note these semantic contrasts between the two nominalizations, using the same verb roots.

(7-103) Agentive: -*ru* + -*awt* M SG, etc.
         Patientive: verb + TNS + AGR

      a. tu-r-awt   tu-t-$\emptyset$
         kill-NFN-M SG   kill-PERF-I SG
         'killer'   'someone killed'

      b. kalc-r-awt   kalc-k-n
         strengthen-NFN-M SG   strengthen-IRR-I SG
         'hard worker'   'a strong person'

      c. yarac-r-awt   yarac-k-n
         color-NFN-V SG   color-IRR-I SG
         'kind of paint'   'white man'

      d. amp-r-awt   amp-$\emptyset$-ra
         kindle-NFN-M SG   kindle-PERF-V PL
         'fire lighter'   'firewood'

As mentioned earlier, agentive nominalizations operate on a nominative-accusative basis in that the participant role played by the derived nominal with respect to the verb root must be S or A. Patientive nominalizations conversely are ergative-absolutive in orientation, for the derived nominal holds an S, O, T, or even oblique role to the verb root, but never A or, indeed, D. Compare the following patterns of derivations.

(7-104) Agentive nominalizations

      a. as S:
         na-na-iray-n   ⇒   ira-c-awt
         3SG S-DEF-cry-PRES   cry-NFN-M SG
         'He is crying.'   'crybaby'

      b. as A:
         na-n-tu-t   ⇒   tu-r-awt
         3SG O-3SG A-kill-PERF   kill-NFN-M SG
         'He killed him.'   'killer'

(7-105) Patientive nominalizations

    a. as S:

        na-mal   ⇒   mal-k-n

        3SG S-die   die-IRR-I SG

        'He died.'   'a corpse'

    b. as O:

        na-n-tu-t   ⇒   tu-t-∅

        3SG O-3SG A-kill-PERF   kill-PERF-I SG

        'He killed him.'   'someone killed'

    c. as T:

        na-n-ŋa-r-mpun   ⇒   ŋa-t-∅

        V SG T-3SG A-give-PERF-3PL D   give-PERF-V SG

        'He gave it to them.'   'a gift'

    d. as oblique:

        kay-ɲan   ama-wa-kia-k

        canoe VIII SG-OBL   1SG S-go-NEAR-IRR

        'I'll go by canoe.'

                              ⇒   wa-kia-k-ra

                                  go-NEAR-IRR-V PL

                                  'means/route of going'

Interestingly, Yimas allows non-finite nominalizations rather like agentive nominalizations to be formed for locationals. These are identical in form to other non-finite nominalizations except that they require the concord marker -a IX SG and the oblique suffix. These describe a place which exists specifically for the purpose of performing the action described by the relative clause, as in these examples:

(7-106) a. awŋkcpaŋ-t-a-n

        bathe-NFN-IX SG-OBL

        'bathing place'

    b. wok-nanaŋ-t-a-n

        work-DUR-NFN-IX SG-OBL

        'work place'

        (*nanaŋ-* DUR is used here in a typical way in modern Yimas: by adding it to Tok Pisin words, new Yimas verb roots are derived.)

    c. mawrun   tu-r-a-n

        enemy I SG kill-NFN-IX SG-OBL

        'place for killing enemies'

These finite relative clauses without *m-* NR DIST quite commonly function alone without being linked as a modifier to any other noun in the clause. This has led in some cases to their being re-analyzed as noun stems.

(7-107) wa-n   [amp-∅-ra]   yara-k
         go-IMP   kindle-PERF-V PL   pick up-IRR
         'Go collect firewood!'

The main verb in this example is in the imperative mood, yet the tense of the nominalization is perfective. These two are contradictory, of course, the imperative corresponding to actions yet to be done, and the perfective to those already completed. This contradiction is possible simply because nominalizations like *ampra* 'firewood' or *amtra* 'food' are now nouns in their own right and are no longer seen as the result of a productive nominalization process, rather like *the dead* in English.

The only relative clauses without *m-* NR DIST which commonly do have an overt modified 'head' noun are those functioning like English adjectives to express qualities or states. As pointed out in Sections 3.3 and 6.2.3.1.3, most Yimas roots corresponding to English adjectives are actually verbs denoting processes, the so-called adjectival verbs. When these translate English adjectives, i.e., denote states or qualities, they are nothing but these *m-* less finite relative clauses, most commonly found with the tense suffix -*k* IRR to describe an unbounded temporal duration, although other tense suffixes are possible (7-108c).

(7-108) a. teŋ   [kamta(k)-k-ŋ]   akk
            tank VI SG   become empty-IRR-VI SG   COP VI SG INVIS
            'The water tank is empty.'

        b. kay   [tŋknt-k-i]   i-awŋki
            canoe VIII SG become heavy-IRR-VIII SG   VIII SG S-sink
            'The heavy canoe sank.'

        c. mampayŋki   [krk-r-ŋki]   kumpwi
            banana VI PL   ripe-PERF-VI PL   boy I PL

            kia-mp-awl
            VI PL O-3PL A-get
            'The boys took the ripe bananas.'

A final point to consider here is the meaning contrast associated with the presence versus absence of *m-* NR DIST in finite relative clauses. The structural difference is represented in (7-99) versus (7-102b). To illustrate the contrast, consider (7-109a,b), diagrammed as (7-110a,b):

(7-109) a. m-n-wul-k-nak
            NR DIST-3SG A-put down-IRR-3 SG O
            'that which he put down'

b. wul-k-n
put down-IRR-I/V SG
'someone/something put down'

(7-110) a.

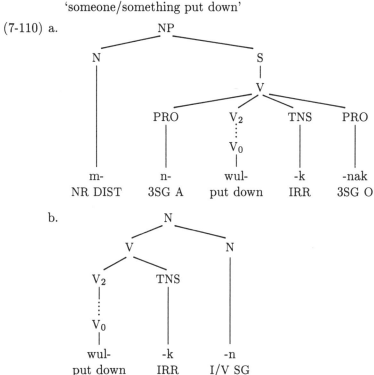

b.

Finite relative clauses with *m*- NR DIST are obligatorily associated with a definite, established, modified 'head' noun as their referent, while those without *m*- are not, often having a vague class of referents as possible referents (e.g., means of going (7-105d)). This is, of course, fully in keeping with the presence versus absence of the definite near distal stem. Further, a finite relative clause with *m*- often has established nominal participants, reflected in the verbal pronominal affixes, while those without *m*- never do. They obligatorily lack all expression of nominal participants, either as independent words or pronominal affixes.

A common use of finite relative clauses with *m*- NR DIST is in cleft constructions. These are equational sentences in which certain identifying or descriptive features of a focused noun are provided by a relative clause. The semantics of clefts thus prohibits them from occurring with relative clauses without *m*- NR DIST. English examples are *it was John who sheared the sheep* and *John was the one who sheared the sheep*. Yimas clefts consist of a noun plus a modifying relative clause plus an

optional copula. The relative clauses in both Yimas and English clefts
present information which is already known or presumed from the context of the speech act. The function of a cleft construction is to use this
information to identify the proper referent of the noun of the cleft or
at least to predicate something important and relevant about it. Thus
the relative clause in both examples, *who sheared sheep*, provides relevant information about the head noun of these cleft constructions, *John*.
Yimas clefts are exactly parallel.

(7-111) a. Elias
       name
       [m-kra-pay-pra-kia-ntuk-ŋkt-Ø]
       NR DIST-1PL O-carry-toward-NEAR-RM PAST-PC-3SG
       'It was Elias who brought us few.'
    b. ŋaykum   [m-ka-tpul-c-um]   pu-k
       woman II PL   NR DIST-1SG A-hit-PERF-3PL II PL-PROX
       apuk
       COP PL
       'These are the women that I hit.'

Clefts are important in Yimas because they play a central role in
content questions, otherwise known as *wh* questions. Note that in questions like *Who sheared the sheep?* or *What did he shear the sheep with?*,
the action of shearing sheep is presupposed and established and what is
at issue is who did the action or what was used to perform it. Thus, the
pragmatic force of the non-*wh* component of these questions is identical
to that of a relative clause in a cleft, and so it is really no surprise that
some *wh* questions in Yimas take the forms of clefts. If the *wh* word
is functioning as S, then a cleft construction is obligatory; to use an
ordinary clause structure is ungrammatical.

(7-112) a. nawn   m-na-ya-n?
       who SG NR DIST-DEF-come-PRES
    b.*nawn   na-na-ya-n?
       who SG 3SG S-DEF-come-PRES
       'Who is coming?'

(7-113) a. wara   m-na-tmuk-nt-ra?
       what NR DIST-DEF-fall-PRES-V PL
    b.*wara   ya-na-tmuk-n?
       what V PL S-DEF-fall-PRES
       'What is falling down?'

Note that *wara* 'what' is assigned the class and number specifications V
PL; *nawn* 'who' is I SG.

When the interrogative word functions as A, a cleft construction is again required as long as the O participant is first or second person.

(7-114) a. nawm   m-kul-cpul-um
            who PL   NR DIST-2PL O-hit-PL
            'Who hit you all?'

        b. wara   m-ŋa-am-ra?
            what   NR DIST-1SG O-eat-V PL
            'What bit me?'

But if the O participant is third person, a cleft construction is not used. Instead an ordinary main clause is found, with a verbal pronominal prefix cross-referencing the question word.

(7-115) a. nawn   pu-n-tpul?
            who SG   3PL O-3SG A-hit
            'Who hit them?'

        b. nawn   impa-n-tpul?
            who SG   3DL O-3SG A-hit
            'Who hit those two?'

        c. nawrm   na-mpɨ-tpul
            who DL   3SG O-3DL A-hit
            'Who hit him?'

        d. nawm   na-mpu-tpul
            who PL   3SG O-3PL A-hit
            'Who hit him?'

For core arguments other than S or A, cleft constructions are never permissible. Further, the interrogative word cannot be cross referenced on the verb by a pronominal affix. It is the obligatory absence of an affix which distinguishes the case in which the interrogative word is O and the A third person from the converse case above in (7-115). Contrast (7-116) with (7-115):

(7-116) a. nawn   pu-tpul   /*na-mpu-tpul
            who SG   3SG S-hit   / 3SG O-3PL A-hit
            'Who did they hit?'

        b. nawn   impa-tpul   /*na-mpɨ-tpul
            who SG   3PL S-hit   / 3SG O-3DL A-hit
            'Who did they both hit?'

        c. nawrm   na-tpul   /*impa-n-tpul
            who DL   3SG S-hit   3DL O-3SG A-hit
            'Who did he hit?'

d. nawŋkt   pu-tpul   /*kra-mpu-tpul
who PC   3PL S-hit   3PC O-3PL A-hit
'Who did they hit?'

Other examples of interrogative words in core argument positions follow:

(7-117) a. wara   ipa-na-am-n?   (as O)
           what   1PL S-DEF-eat-PRES
           'What are we going to eat?'

     b. wara   pu-ŋa-na-ŋa-n?   (as T)
        what   3PL A-1SG D-DEF-give-PRES
        'What are they going to give me?'

However, when an interrogative word is the relativized noun of a relative clause in O function, it may be marked by an pronominal affix within the relative clause.

(7-118) nawn   ma-tay   [ŋaykum
        who SG   2SG S-see   woman II PL

        m-mpu-na-tput-ɲc-ak]?
        NR DIST-3PL A-DEF-hit-PRES-3SG O
        'Did you see who the women are hitting?'

The fascinating thing about this example is that the relative clause would not be grammatical if it was a normal interrogative cleft construction.

(7-119)*nawn   [ŋaykum
        who SG   woman II PL

        m-mpu-na-tpul-ɲc-ak]?
        NR DIST-3PL A-DEF-hit-PRES-3SG O
        'Who are the women hitting?'

Interestingly, question words functioning as D participants are obligatorily followed by *na* POSS.

(7-120) a. nawn   na   na-ŋkra-na-ŋa-n
           who SG   POSS   V SG T-1DL A-DEF-give-PRES
           patn?
           betelnut V SG
           'Who are we both going to give betelnut to?

     b. irpm   nawn   na
        coconut palm IV SG   who SG   POSS
        mu-mpu-na-tkam-n?
        IV SG T-3PL A-DEF-show-PRES
        'Who are they going to show the coconut palm to?'

What distinguishes *nawn* 'who' in the D role from its use as a possessor
is the presence of a class and number concord suffix in the latter.

(7-121) pu-n   nawn na-ŋ   pu-kra-t?
       I PL-FR DIST who   POSS VI SG   3PL S-cut-PERF
       'Whose (hair) did they cut?'

7.2.2 Perception Complements

Perception complements describe an event which is the object of an act
of perception such as seeing or hearing. These are expressed in three
different ways in Yimas. The most straightforward of these parallels
English constructions like *I saw him shearing the sheep*. The S or A
participant of the perceived event is expressed as the O participant of
the main verb of perception, and the perceived event is expressed in
a finite relative clause with *m-* NR DIST, linked to this O participant.
These perception complements contrast with true relative clauses in that
they do not have free choice of tense. Regardless of the tense of the
main clause, that of the perception complement must be imperfective,
morphologically realized by *-nt* PRES or, optionally, *-kia-k* NEAR-IRR.
Consider these examples:

(7-122) a. pu-ka-tay
          3SG O-1SG A-see

          m-na-wi-impu-pra-nt-um
          NR DIST-DEF-up-paddle-toward-PRES-PL
          'I saw them paddling up toward me.'

     b. pu-ŋa-ant-t
          3SG O-1SG O-hear-PERF

          m-na-pan-kia-k-∅
          NR DIST-DEF-pound sago-NEAR-IRR-SG
          'They heard me working sago.'

     c. impa-ka-tay   nam   m-na-wark-nt-rm
          3DL O-1SG A-see   house   NR DIST-DEF-build-PRES-DL
          'I saw them both building a house'

The restricted tense possibilities in perception complements, practically
marking relative tense rather than absolute tense (imperfective = simultaneous with the time of the main verb rather than with the time
of the speech act), essentially makes these perception complements like
non-finite constructions. It is predictable, then, that an alternative construction for perception complements are true non-finite constructions.
Replacing the finite relative clauses in the examples of (7-122) are non-
finite oblique clauses.

(7-123) a. pu-ka-tay   wi-impu-pra-r-mat-ɲan
            3SG O-1SG A-see up-paddle-toward-NFN-M PL-OBL
            'I saw them paddling up toward me.'

        b. pu-ŋa-ant-t   pan-t-awt-ɲan
            3SG A-1SG O-hear-PERF   pound sago-NFN-M SG-OBL
            'They heard me working sago.'

        c. manpa   na-mpu-tay   arm-n
            crocodile III SG III SG O-3PL A-see water-OBL

            ampu-r-awt-ɲan
            float-NFN-III SG-OBL
            'They saw a crocodile floating in the water.'

There seems to be no meaning difference between the finite relative
clauses in (7-122) and the non-finite oblique clauses in (7-123). Both
constructions are equally common and acceptable.

    The third construction for perception complements is finite, but oc-
curs with the suffixes -nti 'act' or -wal 'custom', the markers for non-
finite action complements (see Section 7.1.2) or finite manner clauses
(see Section 7.2.3). Consider these examples:

(7-124) a. na-ka-tay   mnta wa-t-nti
            3SG O-1SG A-see then   go-PERF-act
            'I saw him go.'

        b. ta-ŋkl-cay-kia-k-nak   mnti kacakapi-k-nti
            NEG-3PC A-see-NEAR-IRR-3SG O there hide-IRR-act
            'Those few did not see him disappear.'

This construction is not common and has only been encountered with
tay- 'see'. As with the other perception complement constructions, its
S or A is realized as the O of the main verb. The verb of the perception
complement is finite in the sense that it has a tense suffix, but its tense
specification must be identical to that of the main verb. These perception complements may be finite, but they are completely prohibited
from bearing verbal pronominal affixes for core arguments, rather like
non-finite complements. Although these constructions look superficially
like non-finite complements of action they cannot be analyzed as such.
The conjunction mnta 'then' is only allowed when clauses are joined; it
is prohibited in true non-finite complement constructions. The effect of
the suffixes -nti 'act' or -wal 'custom' is to nominalize the perception
clause, just as m- NR DIST does. The semantic force of this construction in comparison to the other two types of perception complements
is illustrated by the English glosses. The -nti construction looks at the
perceived event as a punctual, completed act, while the other two con-

structions focus on it as an ongoing, still perceived event. This is not unlike the difference in English between *I saw him disappear* (also *I saw his disappearance*) (*-nti*/*-wal* construction) and *I saw him disappearing* (finite relative clause with *m-* NR DIST or non-finite oblique clause). This semantic difference in English is discussed in some detail in Kirsner and Thompson 1976.

7.2.3 Finite Oblique Clauses

These correspond to English adverbial clauses, i.e., those subordinate clauses beginning with *when, if, because, although, after*, etc. In Yimas these are all formally the same construction, the semantic difference between them being carried by the choices for tense and modal affixes. Like their non-finite counterparts, the verbs of finite oblique clauses all terminate in the oblique suffix *-n* ∼ *-nan*. Just as non-finite oblique clauses are non-finite relative clauses plus the oblique suffix, a similar pattern holds for finite oblique clauses. Consider these examples:

(7-125) a. m-n-awram-r-mp-n   mpa-n
          NR DIST-3SG A-enter-PERF-VII SG-OBL   one-I SG

          namarawt   anak
          person I SG   COP I SG

          'When he went in, he went alone.'

      b. m-ka-na-wa-kia-nt-mp-n
          NR DIST-1SG A-DEF-go-NEAR-PRES-VII SG-OBL

          ŋarŋ
          1 day removed

          ta-ka-mampi-waraca-mpi-ya-kt
          NEG-1SG A-again-return-SEQ-come-RM FUT

          'When I go tomorrow, I won't come back again.'

As with finite relative clauses, the verbs in these oblique clauses begin with *m-* NR DIST. The concord suffix *-mp* VII SG, following the tense suffix and preceding the oblique suffix, is that for the understood noun *pucm* 'time', having its class and number specifications. This is the understood noun modified by the relative clause, so that these finite oblique clauses really mean something like 'at the time that X', but, in fact, the noun never appears overtly. Its only indication is the final concord suffix *-mp* VII SG, much like the understood noun for 'place' in the locational relative clauses is referenced by *-a* IX SG. In essence these finite oblique clauses with adverbial meaning and locational relative clauses are the same type of construction: i.e., clausal nominalizations functioning in oblique roles in the main clause and linked to no overt modified noun.

Finite oblique clauses function like temporal words in the way that locational relative clauses act like locationals.

While locational relative clauses are the only means of expressing
clauses functioning in an oblique locational role, this is not true of temporal clauses. In addition to the temporal relative clauses of (7-125),
it is also possible to add the oblique suffix directly to a clause. This
option is much less common and tends to be used if the verb is an adjectival verb, or lacks pronominal affixes or if the clause in question is
equational. Miscellaneous examples of this follow:

(7-126) a. kunampwi pay-k-nan   ampan-a-tu-n
         axe V SG   carry-IRR-OBL   HORT 1A/2SG O-DEF-kill-IMP
         'If I had an axe, I would kill you!'

      b. mampayŋki   krk-kt-ŋki-ɲan
         banana VI PL   ripe-RM FUT-VI PL-OBL
         kia-mp-awl-kt
         VI PL O-3PL A-get-RM FUT
         'When/if the bananas ripen, they will take them.'

      c. ampra   kantk-n-an
         firewood V PL   with-I SG-OBL
         ant-ka-na-ampu-nt-ra
         POT-1SG A-DEF-light-PRES-V PL
         'If I had firewood, I would light a fire.'

The optional copula is missing in the oblique clause of the above
example.

      d. ama tak   taw-r-mpwi   i-k-nan   mnta
         1SG here sit-NFN-talk tell-IRR-OBL then
         ant-ka-na-taw-n
         27POT-1SG S-DEF-sit-PRES
         'If (they) tell me to stay here, I can stay.'

What semantically distinguishes these oblique clauses formed with just
the oblique suffix from the temporal relative clauses is their overall
vagueness. Note that three of the four examples use vague tense markers
like the irrealis or the remote future in the oblique clause (and (7-126c)
would too, if the copula was present), and in the last example even the
A participant is left unspecified. This construction is limited to setting
relatively vague background conditions for the event in the main clause;
temporal relative clauses tend to be rather more specific and bound to a
clearer time interval, although with a gradient semantic dimension like
this it is difficult to be too precise about when to use one or the other
construction.

As mentioned above, these oblique finite clauses have a fairly wide semantic range to cover, corresponding to all types of English subordinate clauses except manner clauses. The semantic contrast between English subordinating conjunctions like *when* and *if* is carried in Yimas by different choices of tense suffixes or modal prefixes, because Yimas lacks subordinating conjunctions of any kind. I will discuss these semantic differences in turn.

The simplest and most common usage of oblique finite clauses is as temporal adverbial clauses. The temporal relationship between the oblique clause and the main clause can be either simultaneous or sequential. However, finite oblique clauses with a simultaneous temporal relationship to the main clause are quite unusual, for this is the proper semantic domain of the non-finite oblique clauses (see Section 7.1.4). They do occur, but only in a meaning of partial temporal overlap; complete overlap requires the non-finite construction.

(7-127) a. m-mpu-ŋa-na-tay-ɲc-mp-n
         NR DIST-3PL A-1SG O-DEF-see-PRES-VII SG-OBL

         pu-ka-apan-kt
         3PL O-1SG A-spear-RM FUT

         'When they see me, I will spear them.'

    b. stua-n   m-n-a-irm-t-mp-n
       store-OBL   NR DIST-2SG S-DEF-stand-PRES-VII SG-OBL

       yaki-ɲmprm   ŋa-wu-ŋa-n
       tobacco-leaf VII SG 1SG D-get-BEN-IMP

       'When you are at the store, buy me some tobacco!'

    c. ama Ostrala-nan
       1SG Australia-OBL

       m-ka-tantaw-ntuk-mp-n
       NR DIST-1SG A-sit(RED: *taw-*)-RM PAST-IX SG-OBL

       nma-mpu-araŋaca-ntut   maramara
       house O-3PL A-tear-RM PAST   goods-V PL

       ama-na-ra   mnta
       1SG-POSS-V PL   then

       ya-mpu-makacmpi-awt-ɲcut
       V PL O-3PL A-stealthily-take-RM PAST

       'While I was in Australia, some people broke into my house and stole my belongings.'

In these examples there is only partial overlap between the actions of the two clauses. In (7-127a), seeing will precede spearing, but of course, will coincide partly with it. For (7-127b), the act of buying tobacco will occur sometime in the time span of being in the store, but the latter will certainly extend beyond that. Similarly for (7-127c), my stay in Australia had a much longer duration than the burglary of my house, but did overlap with it. As the first two examples demonstrate, a finite oblique clause in a simultaneous temporal relation can be marked with the imperfective regardless of the tense of the main clause. This choice shows relative tense, i.e., simultaneous with respect to the tense of the main verb, which registers the actual absolute tense of the overall sentence. In (7-127c), the verb of the oblique clause shows remote past, the absolute tense, and is identical with that of the main verb. (7-127b) is also interesting in that the scope of the imperative does not operate over the oblique clause. This is universally the case: oblique clauses are invariably declarative; no other illocutionary force specification is possible for them. This is because they encode presupposed background information (Haiman 1978).

It should be noted in the above examples that the finite oblique clauses precede the main clause. This is generally the case because Yimas discourse is highly iconic: the order of the clauses reflects the order in the real world of the events described by the clause. Because finite oblique clauses describe presupposed background information and because established presupposed information is generally temporally prior in narratives to new asserted information, it follows then that the finite oblique clauses should precede their main clauses. This constraint predictably is most rigid with finite oblique clauses in a sequential temporal relation, e.g., those which express an event which is temporally prior to that of the main event. Examples of these follow:

(7-128) a. m-nan-a-tmuk-kia-nt-ŋkan-mp-n
         NR DIST-2PL S-DEF-fall-NEAR-PRES-PC-VII SG-OBL

         Mosbi-ɲan   pampan-takal-kia-nt-ŋkt
         Moresby-OBL   correct-grasp-NEAR-PRES-PC

         'After you few land in Moresby, they will fix you few up.'

      b. na-mpu-taŋ-awkura-mpi-mul-k-mp-n
         III SG O-3PL A-COM-gather-SEQ-run away-IRR-VII SG-OBL

         tay   m-um   Kamrat   taw-r-mat   mnta
         then NR DIST-I PL   place name   sit-NFN-M PL   then

         na-mpu-pampay-iranta-tal-k
         III SG O-3PL A-KIN-dance(RED: *ira-*)-start-IRR

         'After they stole it (their crocodile), they, the inhabitants of Kamrat, started to dance, carrying it.'

c. turis
tourist I PL

ya-mpu-na-pay-kulanaŋ-tay-ɲc-mp-n
V PL O-3PL A-DEF-first-walk-see-PRES-VII SG-OBL
ma-ra   ya-mpu-na-wayk-n
other-V PL   V PL O-3PL A-DEF-buy-PRES
'After the tourists first walk around looking at them, they
buy the goods.'

d. tampin   m-n-ya-kr-mp-n   mnta
   later   NR DIST-3SG S-come-RM FUT-VII SG-OBL   then
   na-ŋa-tay-kt
   3SG A-1SG O-see-RM FUT
   'After he comes, he will see me.'

The reader will have noticed that examples (7-128b,c) lack the stem *m*-
NR DIST. This simply is due to the morphological constraint against
having *m*- precede two pronominal prefixes; both of these examples have
an O and an A prefix. In all of these examples, the tense specification
of the oblique clause is identical to that of the main clause. This is not
actually required, but is almost always the case. This morphological feature distinguishes these sequential oblique clause from the simultaneous
ones, which allow a present tense, regardless of the tense of the verb of
the main clause.

In the absence of any other markers, a sequential temporal relationship is always entailed between a finite oblique clause and the main
clause. This is illustrated in (7-128a). There are no morphemes which
specifically express the sequential temporal relationship between the
clauses; this is simply the force of the construction. However, the other
three examples do have overt morphemes to indicate sequentiality. In
(7-128b) the conjunctions *tay* and *mnta* both mean 'then' and indicate
that the clause preceding the one in which they are found describes
events which are temporally prior. Example (7-128c) has the temporal
morpheme in the oblique clause. This is the incorporated adverbial *pay*-
'first' which indicates that the clause containing it describes events occurring before those of the clause following. Finally, the finite oblique
clause in (7-128d) contains the temporal *tampin* 'after, later, behind',
which has much the same function as its English translation equivalent.
This last form is very likely a calque on the equivalent use of the Tok
Pisin adverb *bihain* 'after', and I suspect it is not traditional usage.

Yimas has no overt and distinct way of expressing adverbial clauses
equivalent to English causal clauses with *because* or *since*. This meaning

is just an additional contextually based inference drawn from a finite
oblique clause in a sequential relationship to the main clause. A good
example is the following:

(7-129) m-mpu-na-malak-nt-mp-n
         NR DIST-3PL S-DEF-converse-PRES-VII SG-OBL

         pu-na-tɨ-kratk-n
         3SG S-DEF-RCP-fight-PRES
         'When/because they are arguing, they fight each other.'

A simple sequential temporal relational—they argue and then they
fight—is all that is necessarily entailed by this example. But given
the nature of the events of the two clauses, arguing and fighting, in
the real world, there is a very high likelihood that there is more than
this temporal relationship between them. More precisely, it would almost certainly be the case that the arguing led to the fighting as a
causal force. This is not entailed by (7-129), but it is clearly a very
favored inference. Of course, how strongly favored this causal inference
would be varies with the events encoded, but it is potentially available
to any finite oblique clause and main clause in a sequential temporal
relationship.

Conditionals and counterfactuals are also expressed in Yimas by the
same kind of construction. What distinguishes these from sequential
and simultaneous temporal clauses is the presence of verbal affixes associated with unreal events, such as the irrealis suffix or modal prefixes.
Finite oblique clauses functioning as conditional clauses express events
which have not yet occurred, but which will lead, if they do occur, to the
consequential events described in the main clause. Hence, the tenses of
the main clause must be those of events not yet realized: imperfective,
near/remote future, irrealis, or the imperative mood. The tense of the
conditional clause can be identical to that of the main clause, marking
absolute tense (although the imperative, of course, is blocked in embedded clauses); irrealis, indicating indefinite time; or either imperfective
or perfective, marking relative tense. Imperfective in the conditional
clause indicates simultaneity with the main clause (7-130a); perfective
indicates that the event of the conditional clause occurs prior to that of
the main clause (7-130b).

Consider these examples:

(7-130) a. apwi   m-ɲa-kn
           father I SG 2SG-POSS-I SG

           m-n-a-pan-t-mp-n
           NR DIST-3SG S-DEF-pound sago-PRES-VII SG-OBL

       mnta   arp-mpi-awt-ɲa-k
       then   help-SEQ-get-IMP-3 SG O
       'If your father is working sago, help him!'
  b. m-n   m-n-tay-c-mp-n
       NR DIST-I SG NR DIST-2SG A-see-PERF-VII SG-OBL
       mnta   na-kra-i-ɲa-mpwi
       then   IMP 1-1PL D-tell-IMP-talk
       'If you see him, tell us!'
  c. m-mpu-ya-kr-mp-n
       NR DIST-3PL S-come-RM FUT-VII SG-OBL

Wamur-mat	mampayŋki	wunt	kantk
Wambramas-M PL	banana VI PL	sago grub V PL	with

pay-pra-kt	ama-na-ra
carry-toward-RM FUT	1SG-POSS-V PL

       'If the Wambramas people will come, they can bring
       my bananas and sago grubs.'
  d. kunampwi pay-k-nan   ampan-a-tu-n
       axe V SG   lie-IRR-OBL   HORT 1A/2SG O-DEF-kill-PRES
       'If I had an axe, I would kill you'

Examples (7-130a,b) illustrate relative tense in the conditional clause, imperfective (simultaneous with main clause) or perfective (prior to main clause). Example (7-130d) shows irrealis for the conditional clause; this indicates a general, not temporally bounded condition for the event of the main clause. Finally, example (7-130c) has the remote future in both the main and the conditional clause.

    Conditionals contrast with counterfactuals in that while the former are concerned with events which have not yet occurred, the latter describe situations which might or might not have occurred and then expound the consequences of this. While the main clauses following conditionals are marked with tenses for unrealized events, those following counterfactuals have the tenses of realized events, the multiple past tenses (and the irrealis, if used as a legendary past) and the perfective and imperfective. In addition, the main clauses with counterfactuals are invariably prefixed with *ant-* POT, the modal prefix encoding potential, but probably unrealized actions (except for the negative copula verbs *tampan* and *kayak* which do not permit this prefix). The verb of oblique counterfactual clauses is also usually prefixed with *ant-* POT, but it may be omitted, especially if the verb has no pronominal prefixes (7-131c). *ant-* POT, of course, displaces *m-* NR DIST. Consider these examples of counterfactual clauses:

(7-131) a. tuŋkurŋ   ant-ka-tay-c-mp-n
           eye VI SG   POT-1SG A-see-PERF-VII SG-OBL

           ant-ka-tu-r-ak
           POT-1SG A-kill-PERF-III SG O

           'If I had seen the eye (of the crocodile), I would have killed it.'

     b. kiap   m-n
         patrol officer I SG   NR DIST-I SG

         anan-ya-ntuk-mp-n   ipa-na-kn
         POT 3SG S-come-RM PAST-VII SG-OBL 1PL-POSS-V SG

         taw-t-wal   mama-k-n   anak
         sit-NFN-custom V SG   bad-IRR-V SG   COP V SG

         'If the patrol officer had not come, we would not live well.'

     c. ampra   kantk-n-an
         firewood V PL   with-I SG-OBL

         ant-ka-na-ampu-nt-ra
         POT-1SG A-DEF-light-PRES-V PL

         'If I had firewood, I would light a fire.'

     d. Tamprakal-mat paŋka
         Yimas-M PL   spear V PL

         ampu-na-wampak-ɲcuk-mp-n
         POT 3 PL A-DEF-throw-RM PAST-VII SG-OBL

         m-um   anti   kayak
         NR DIST-I PL   land VIII SG   not have

         'If the Yimas did not fight, they would not have land'

Note that the potential modal prefix *ant-* can have either positive or negative force in the corresponding English translation. Compare (7-131a,b): the verbal forms are morphologically very similar, yet the former is translated as a positive verb in English and the latter as a negative. This is because the semantic force of a counterfactual depends on the actual status in the real world of the event in the clause. Thus, in the first example the eye was in fact not seen, so in the counterfactual the clause is positive; but in the second, the patrol officer did indeed come, so the counterfactual clause is negative.

Note that the tenses in the counterfactual clauses of all these examples correspond to those of realized events: perfective (7-131a), remote past (7-131b,d), and imperfective (7-131c). Counterfactual clauses are of two semantic types. The first type are those which describe potential events which failed to happen, with the main clause expressing the consequential events which would have occurred if the events of the counterfactual clause had eventuated. Examples (7-131a,c) illustrate this type. In (7-131a) the speaker would have killed the crocodile if he had seen the eye, but because he failed to see it, he therefore did not kill the crocodile. For (7-131c), the speaker would have lit a fire if he had firewood, but because he has none, no fire is lit.

The second type of counterfactual clauses are those which describe actual real events which occurred, but pose the hypothetical, counterfactual situation of them not happening, with the event of the main clause being the consequence of their non-occurrence. Examples (7-128b,d) illustrate this type. The patrol officer did indeed come to Yimas, so the counterfactual clause does express an actual event. But it poses the counterfactual situation of his not coming, with the situation described in the main clause being the result of his non-appearance. Similarly, in (7-128d) the Yimas did indeed fight fiercely and have an abundance of rich land. But the counterfactual clause posits the hypothetical situation of their not fighting, and conjectures the result would be a lack of land.

The final semantic category of subordinate clauses formed on this pattern are concessives. These are quite rare in Yimas and are formed with the finite oblique clause in the sentence being positive and the main clause negative.

The following example is illustrative:

(7-132) kay   i-ka-ak-r-mp-n
         canoe VIII SG   VIII SG O-1SG A-push-PERF-VII SG-OBL
         arm-n   ta-ka-wul-c-i
         water-OBL   NEG-1SG A-put down-PERF-VIII SG
         'Although I pushed the canoe, I did not put it down into the
         water.'

There is one final type of finite oblique clause to consider, manner clauses, but these are formed quite differently from those treated far. Rather than with -*mp* VII SG and -*n* ∼ -*nan* OBL, finite manner clauses are formed using the suffix -*nti* 'act'.

Consider these examples:

(7-133) a. tay mpa anta-tɨ-kia-na-nti
           so   now   HORT SG-do-NIGHT-IMP-act
           apiamparut-nan   m-kay-cɨ-wat-nti
           mat at hearth IX PL-OBL   NR DIST-1PL A-do-HAB-act
           'So I will now do as we do on the mats of the hearth.'

   b. mntmpi   m-n-ti-wa-k-nti   mntmpi
      like that NR DIST-3SG A-do-go-IRR-act like that

      na-ya-k
      3SG S-come-IRR

      'He came just like he went.'

   c. irut   ipa-na-ampa-n   ma-nput
      mat IX PL 1PL S-DEF-weave-PRES other-II PL

      m-mpu-t-ampa-wat-nti
      NR DIST-3PL A-do-weave-HAB-act

      'We are weaving mats,like others (women) weave them.'

   d. nampt   apwiam
      house PL father I PL

      m-mpu-ti-wark-ntuk-nti   mnta
      NR DIST-3PL A-do-build-RM PAST-act   then

      ya-mpu-wark-wat
      house PL-3PL-build-HAB

      'They build houses like their fathers built houses.'

Note that the verb root *ti-* 'do, become feel' is always used in combination with *-nti* 'act' in the verb of the manner clause. This function is undoubtedly like that with *waratnti* 'how', to allow the suffix *-nti* 'act' to code a core argument (see Section 6.3.1.2). As with temporal and locational relative clauses, these manner clauses are finite relative clauses without external modified nouns, their only indication being the final suffix *-nti* 'act'. The manner clause of (7-133d), for example, may be more literally glossed as '(like) the act(s) which their fathers did building houses'. Although these manner clauses are oblique constituents (they are manifestly not core arguments of the main clauses), they differ from all others in never being suffixed with *-n* ~ *-nan*. This is a unique feature of them. There is, however, an alternative construction available employing relative clauses without *m-* NR DIST and the postposition *nampayn* 'like' which overtly marks the manner clause as oblique.

(7-134) a. mal-k-n   nampayn ma-na-pay-n
           die-IRR-I SG like   2SG S-DEF-lie-PRES
           'You are sleeping like a corpse.'

        b. kiaŋ   kantk-n   nampayn na-na-malak-n
           cough with-I SG like   3SG S-DEF-converse-PRES
           'He is talking like he has a cold.'

7.3 Clause Chaining and Coordination

In addition to the rich array of nominalized structures I have described in the previous sections of this chapter, Yimas also possesses several types of conjoined clause structures. One of these, clause chaining, is very common in Papuan languages (Foley 1986, 175–98) and I will take this up first.

7.3.1 Clause Chaining and Dependent Verbs

Clause chaining is accomplished in Papuan languages through the use of dependent verbs. The difference between dependent verbs and serialized verbs was discussed and illustrated in Section 6.3.1. To recapitulate, dependent verbs are the predicates of full but dependent clauses, which obligatorily take their specifications for tense and mood from the following fully inflected verbs of the independent clause. Consider these examples from Iatmul of the middle Sepik River region (Staalsen 1972):

(7-135) a. vɨ-sɨmpla yə-wɨn
        see-SIM   come-1SG
        'I saw it while coming.'

     b. vɨ-laa   yə-wɨn
        see-SEQ come-1SG
        'Having seen it, I came.'

The first of the verbs in these two examples is the dependent one, while the second is independent. The independent verb is inflected for the person/number of its S argument (-wɨn 1SG), past tense ($\emptyset$), and declarative mood (also $\emptyset$). The dependent may have none of these inflections. It simply takes a suffix -sɨmpla SIM or -laa SEQ which indicates the temporal relationship between it and the following independent verb. Dependent clauses are not in a subordinate or embedded relationship to the independent clause. The structural relationship is one of coordination (see Foley and Van Valin 1984, 239–44), yet dependence. The difference between chained dependent clauses and coordinated independent clauses is simply that in the former the specifications for some semantic features such as tense and mood are taken from the independent clause, while in the latter the clauses are separately specified for these same features.

Iatmul dependent verbs obligatorily take their specification for their subjects (S or A argument) from the following independent verb. If the subjects are different, two independent verbs in a coordinate structure must be used.

(7-136) klə-ntɨ   maa yə-ntɨ
       get-3SG DR   come-3SG
       'He₁ got (it) and he₂ came.'

This constraint is not operative in many other Papuan languages. In these other languages, dependent verbs are marked for switch reference, which monitors whether their subjects are the same or are different from that of the following verb, such as in these Kewa examples (Franklin 1971):

(7-137) a. ní réko-a   ágaa lá-wa
         1SG stand-SEQ talk   say-1SG NR PAST
         'I stood up and spoke.'

       b. ní réka-no   ágaa lá-a
         1SG stand-DR.1SG   talk   say-3SG NR PAST
         'I stood up and he spoke.'

In (7-137a), the dependent verb *reko-* 'stand' has the same subject as the following independent verb and so is simply suffixed with -*a* SEQ to mark its temporal relationship. In (7-137b), the subjects of the independent and dependent verb are different; hence the dependent verb receives the suffix -*no* to indicate that its own subject is first singular, but that that of the next verb will be different.

Dependent verbs in Yimas are always marked with -*mpi* SEQ and express a sequential temporal relationship between it and the following verb (those in a simultaneous relationship must use other constructions, like non-finite oblique clauses). Normally, they take no other inflections but -*mpi* SEQ, although it is possible for them to co-occur with -*kia* NIGHT/NEAR and -*k* IRR. This is yet another example of the common usage of -*k* IRR as a non-finite suffix. They take their specifications for tense and mood from the following verb, but unlike the Iatmul examples above, it is not necessary that their S or A argument be coreferential with that of the independent verb (there is no switch reference system).

Consider these examples:

(7-138) a. kalakn   ŋayuk   tay-mpi na-na-kuck-n
         boy I SG mother II SG see-SEQ 3SG S-DEF-happy-PRES
         'The boy, having seen his mother, is happy.'

       b. irpm   nam-n   antmta-mpi
         coconut palm IV SG house-OBL   cross-SEQ
         mu-na-irm-n
         IV SG S-DEF-stand-PRES
         'The coconut palm is leaning against the house.'

    c. wayk-mpi mnta ka-n-na-awramu-n
       buy-SEQ then LIKE-3SG S-DEF-enter-PRES
       'He can buy (them) and then come inside.'

    d. kaprak-mpi yaŋi-ɲan   na-mp-ayŋ
       cut up-SEQ pot VIII SG-OBL V SG O-3PL A-put in
       'Having cut (it) up, they put it in a pot.'

    e. tmal   l-ŋka-p-mpi   kumpwia
       sun V SG down-go by land-away-SEQ flying fox VIII PL
       mnta wa-ka-tay
       then VIII PL O-1SG A-see
       'The sun having set, then I saw flying foxes.'

    f. tmal   kray-mpi ya-kay-am-wat   amtra
       sun V SG dry-SEQ V PL O-1PL A-eat-HAB food V PL
       'The sun having dried it, we always eat the food.'

    g. pampan-tat-mpi   mnta narmaŋ
       pound sago(RED: *pan-*)-start-SEQ then woman II SG
       ŋka-pra-k-mp-n
       go by land-toward-IRR-VII SG-OBL
       pia-n-i-k-nakn
       talk T-3SG A-tell-IRR-3SG D
       'He started pounding sago, and then when (his) wife comes
       toward (him), she tells him ...'

These examples typify the range of uses of dependent verbs in Yimas. The first four examples exhibit the typical pattern of same subject dependent verbs in other Papuan languages: in each case the S or A participant of the dependent verb is the same as the S or A participant of the following independent verb. The last three examples demonstrate the divergence of Yimas from this wider pattern: in each case the S or A participant of the dependent verb is different from that of the independent verb, but the actual morphology of the dependent verb remains unchanged from the previous cases.

Let me take each example in turn. Example (7-138a) has the A participant of the dependent verb identical to the S participant of the independent verb. The shared participant *kalakn* 'boy' actually occurs in the dependent clause and is only coded in the independent clause by the verbal prefix *na-* 3SG S. The (b) example is similar: the shared noun between the dependent and independent clauses *irpm* 'coconut palm' is in S function in both clauses and again appears overtly in the dependent clause and as the verbal pronominal prefix *mu-* IV SG in the independent clause. Example (7-138c) is especially interesting: note that the modal

prefix *ka-* LIKE obligatorily has scope over both the independent and
dependent verbs. The typical way to prevent this would be to recast
(7-138c) as (7-139) below, with the dependent clause as a finite oblique
clause:

(7-139) ya-n-wayk-r-mp-n   mnta
         V PL O-3SG A-buy-PERF-VII SG-OBL   then

         ka-n-na-awramu-n
         LIKE-3SG S-DEF-enter-PRES

         'He bought them and now can come inside.'

The A argument of the dependent verb in (7-138c) is identical to the
S argument of the independent clause as in the previous two examples,
but unlike these, it is not indicated in the dependent clause, its sole
formal indication being the pronominal prefix on the independent verb,
n- 3SG S. Similar remarks apply to (7-128d). In this case, the dependent
and independent clauses share all core arguments, but there is no overt
indication of these in the dependent clause. Its core arguments are
coded by the pronominal prefixes, *na-* V SG O and *mpu-* 3PL A, on the
independent verb.

Now let me turn to the last three cases, in which the S or A argument
of the dependent verb is not equivalent to that of the independent verb.
Consider (7-138e), in which the dependent clause has the S argument
tmal 'sun', while the independent verb has an A argument *ka-* 1SG A
and an O argument *kumpwia* 'flying foxes'. Note that the dependent
and independent clauses share no core arguments. Further, Yimas has
no switch-reference system. The dependent verbs which share an S or
A argument with the following independent verb (7-138a,b,c,d), and
those which do not (7-138e,f,g), have exactly the same morphological
formation.

In (7-138f), the dependent clause has an A participant *tmal* 'sun' and
the independent clause an A *kay-* 1PL A. They do, however, share an
O participant *amtra* 'food' which appears as a noun in the independent
clause as well as the pronominal prefix *ya-* V PL O.

Finally, the dependent clause in (7-138g) is followed by both a finite
oblique clause and an independent clause. The A argument of the dependent clause is *panmal* 'man' understood from the previous sentence
in the text. The A argument of the independent clause (and the S argument of the finite oblique clause) in turn is *narmaŋ* 'woman'. In this
example it is the D participant *-nakn* 3SG D of the independent clause
which is coreferential with the S *panmal* 'man' of the dependent clause.
To summarize then, (7-138e) has no core arguments in common between
the dependent and independent clauses; in (7-138f) they share their O

arguments; and in (7-138g) the S argument of the dependent clause is coreferential with the D participant of the independent clause. Clearly, Yimas does not impose constraints as to shared core arguments in the formation of dependent clauses.

Yimas narrative texts typically show an abundance of dependent clauses. Together with finite oblique clauses, these can be strung together to form sentences of considerable length, as in this example:

(7-140) _A[yaŋi   ma-y   mnta   i-mp-awl-k]_A
        pot VIII SG other-VIII SG then   VII SG O-3PL A-get-IRR

        _B[kpa-y   mnta   warapak-mpi-ca-k-mp-n
        big-VIII SG then   flay-SEQ-put-IRR-VII SG-OBL

        yaŋi-ɲan   wul-k-mp-n
        pot VIII SG-OBL   put down-IRR-VII SG-OBL

        wut-mpi   na-mpu-tɨ-krapak-mpi-ŋa-k]_B
        put down-SEQ   3SG O-3PL A-RCP-divide-SEQ-give-IRR

        _C[kalk   na-mpu-wul-k]_C
        sago pudding V SG V SG O-3PL A-put down-IRR

        'They got another pot, a big one, and then having flayed
        and put (her) in the pot, having put (her) down there,
        they took their share, and they made sago pudding.'

This sentence begins with an independent clause within the labelled brackets A which is coordinated to those bracketed and labeled B and C. B is internally quite complex: it consists of two finite oblique clauses in a row, followed by a dependent clause and then the independent clause. The coordination of these is marked by the conjunction *mnta* 'then' used with independent verbs. Coordination of clauses and the use of conjunctions like *mnta* is the topic of the next section.

7.3.2 Clause Coordination

Clause coordination, as used here, differs from clause chaining in that the clauses so linked all contain fully specified independent verbs. Such structures are more common in Yimas than in other Papuan languages, such as those of the highlands, in which clause chaining patterns are heavily predominant. In Yimas clause chaining and clause coordination are roughly of the same frequency.

Coordinated clauses always contain independent verbs, but they are also often linked by one of the two conjunctions in Yimas, *mnta* 'then' and *kanta* 'but'. As the English glosses indicate, *mnta* 'then' expresses the idea that the event described by the clause containing it follows that of the previous clause in time, while *kanta* 'but' indicates that the event or situation described by its clause is contrary to the expectations of the speaker, as built up on the information provided in the previous clause. The former can be used to link any two clauses regardless of their structural relationship, i.e., subordination, clause chaining or clause coordination, as these examples demonstrate:

(7-141) a. Subordinate clause/main clause

apwi   m-ɲa-kn
father I SG   2SG-POSS-I SG

m-n-a-pan-t-mp-n
NR DIST-3SG-DEF-pound sago-PRES-VII SG-OBL

mnta   arp-mpi-awt-ɲa-k
then   help-SEQ-get-IMP-3 SG O

'If your father is working sago, help him.'

b. Clause chaining: dependent clause/independent clause

tmal   l-ŋka-p-mpi   kumpwia
sun V SG   down-go by land-away-SEQ   flying fox VIII PL

mnta   wa-ka-tay
then   VIII PL O-1SG A-see

'The sun having set, then I saw flying foxes.'

c. Coordinated clauses: dependent clause/independent clause

balus   na-tmuk-t   *mnta*
plane V SG V SG S-fall-PERF   then

na-mama-k-n-tɨ-t
V SG S-bad-IRR-V SG-become-PERF

'The plane landed and then crashed.'

kanta 'but' contrasts with *mnta* in that it seems only to be used with coordinated clauses.

(7-142) impa-l-ŋka-pra-kia-k   parwa-n
3DL S-down-go by land-toward-NIGHT-IRR dock IX SG-OBL

kanta kamta-k-wa   impa-tay-kia-k
but   empty-IRR-IX SG   3DL S-see-NIGHT-IRR

'They both came down to the dock, but saw that it was empty.'

One interesting structural property of these two conjunctions is their position: both have a strong tendency to occur after the first non-verbal word of their clause. In clauses consisting of just a verb, the conjunctions simply precede it (i.e., they may never follow the verb of their clause). This rule is not absolutely binding but is statistically extremely significant. The following examples illustrate this common positioning of the conjunctions in Wackernagel's (i.e., second) position:

(7-143) a. tumpntut *mnta* ipa-wa-ntut   Pakanan
         morning then 1PL S-go-RM PAST place name
         'Then in the morning we went to Pakanan.'

      b. tmal   l-ŋka-p-mpi   kmpwia
         sun V SG down-go by land-away-SEQ flying fox VIII PL

         mnta wa-ka-tay
         then   VIII PL O-1SG A-see

         'The sun having set, then I saw flying foxes.'

      c. pu-na-wapat-n   napntuk   *mnta*
         3PL S-DEF-climb-PRES   chant X SG then

         ku-mpu-na-yawra-wapat-n
         X SG O-3PL A-DEF-pick up-climb-PRES

         'They came up, and then they came up chanting.'

      d. tantukwan takmpi   kapa-taw-wat   anti
         alone   like this 1DL S-sit-HAB   land VIII SG

         kanta waca-k-i-ɲan   kapa-taw-wat
         but   small-IRR-VIII SG-OBL   1DL S-sit-HAB

         'We two live by ourselves like this, but we live on little land.'

In each of these examples, the conjunction follows the first word of the clause which contains it. If the clause consists of just the verb, the conjunction immediately precedes this:

(7-144) amtra   ya-n-awl-mpi-waraca-t   *mnta*
        food V PL V PL O-3SG A-get-SEQ-return-PERF   then

        ya-n-kaprak-t   *mnta* ya-n-am-t
        V PL O-3SG A-cut-PERF   then   V PL O-3SG A-eat-PERF

        'He got and returned with the food, cut it up and ate it.'

In a number of cases, the clause boundaries are not sharp and it is not clear whether the conjunctions are in clause initial or second position. This is because of the common feature of the language in permitting nominals to follow the verb, especially focused core arguments and obliques. Consider the placement of the second occurrence of *mnta* 'then' in (7-140) and that of *kanta* 'but' in (7-142). Taking the second example first note that the conjunction follows *parwa-n* 'on the dock' which seems to belong to the preceding clause. If it belonged to the clause containing *kanta* it should lack the oblique suffixes, as does its modifier in this clause *kanta-k-wa* 'empty', although it is possible to analyze it as an oblique constituent of the second clause, with the meaning 'empty (place) at the dock'. Thus, it is rather indeterminate as to whether *parwa-n* belongs to the first or second clause in this sentence, with the result that it is equally indeterminate as to whether *kanta* is in clause-initial or clause-second position. Similar remarks apply to (7-140) with respect to the status of *kpa-y* 'big'. It could modify either occurrence of *yaŋi* 'pot' in this sentence and thus be assigned to either the clause governed by the verb preceding it or the one following it. If the former is chosen, *mntn* occurs clause-initially; if the latter, in clause-second position. Examples like (7-140) and (7-142) are quite common in Yimas and demonstrate the rather hazy nature of the boundaries of coordinated clauses and the overall looseness of structure in sentence formation.

In addition to *mnta* 'then' and *kanta* 'but', there is one other conjunction in Yimas. This is *tay* 'so, then'. This differs from the other two in that it is primarily the introducer of a sentence rather than a clause linker, although it does occasionally occur internally to a sentence (see (7-128b)). As a sentential introducer, it most commonly occurs in combination with *mpa* 'now, already'.

(7-145) a. tay   mpa anta-tɨ-kia-na-nti
            then   now HORT SG-do-NIGHT-IMP-act

            apiamparut-nan   m-kay-cɨ-wat-nti
            mat at hearth IX PL-OBL NR DIST-1PL A-do-HAB-act

            'So I will now do as we do on the mats of the hearth.'

          b. tay   mpa   ma   tmat-ɲan   *mnta*
             then now   other sun/day V SG-OBL   then

             pia-kay-cmi-kiantut
             talk O-1PL A-say-FR PAST

             'And now on another day we said.'

          c. tay   mpa ya-kia-k-mpi   m-rm   upnk-n
             then now come-NEAR-IRR-SEQ NR DIST-I PL lake-OBL

             wa-r-mpwi   impa-yakal-cmi-kiantut
             go-NFN-talk 3DL S-CONT-say-FR PAST

             'Having then arrived, they both were talking about going to the lake.'

Unlike many Papuan languages, Yimas lacks a morphological system of switch-reference. Two clauses with a change in S or A participants can be freely conjoined with no morphemes specifically indicating this change, the verbal pronominal affixes commonly being sufficient for this purpose:

(7-146) a. pu-ka-tpul   pu-ŋa-apaniŋ-t
         3PL O-1SG A-hit   3PL A-1SG O-spear-PERF
         'I hit them and they speared me.'

       b. pia-kay-i-c-mpun   mnta   pu-taw-t
         talk T-1PL A-tell-PERF-3PL D   then   3PL S-sit-PERF
         'I told them and they stayed.'

In (7-146a), there is a mirror image shifting of participant roles between the two clauses: the A of the first clause becomes O in the second and vice versa. This change is simply handled by the verbal pronominal prefixes, *ka-* 1SG A to *ŋa-* 1SG O (the switch of *pu-* from O to A arises then by default). The (b) example shows the D of the first clause becoming the S of the second. Again, the verbal morphology is sufficient to express this: *-mpun* 3PL D to *pu-* 3PL S.

The above two examples are typical of Yimas. However, in narrative texts with multiple third person participants, the language does occasionally signal a change in S or A participants with forms of *m-* NR DIST. This is certainly not obligatory, nor even the majority pattern. Further, these deictic forms are not restricted to S or A participants; with the right context they can easily refer to O or D participants. But their use to signal a change in S or A is not an uncommon feature of Yimas narrative texts, as this bit of text illustrates:

(7-147) a. impa-wi-campulanta-pu-k
         3DL S-up-run away-IRR

       b. impa-mpu-yakal-irm-tay-k
         3DL O-3PL A-CONT-stand-see-IRR

       c. m-rm   impa-na-ma-tampulanta-pu-k
         NR DIST-I DL   3DL S-DEF-in-run-away-IRR

       d. m-n   impa-tay-mpi-kwalca-k   paympan
         NR DIST-I SG   3DL O-see-SEQ-rise-IRR   eagle III SG
         'They both ran up and away. They stood watching them
         both. They both ran away inside. He, the eagle, saw
         them both and took off.'

The S argument *impa-* 3 DL S of the (a) clause becomes the O (*ipa-* 3DL O) of the (b) clause, which has a (non-coreferential) A argument *mpu-* 3PL A. This change is only indicated by the verbal pronominal prefixes. In passing from clause (b) to (c), the O participant of (b) is now the S participant of (c). This participant is coded not only by the verbal prefix *impa-* 3 DL S, as occurred in the transition between the previous two clauses, but also by the coreferential deictic form *m-rm* NR DIST-I DL 'those two'. A deictic form also occurs in clause (d). The S argument of clause (c) becomes the O of (d), and yet another A participant appears.

This A participant is not coded by a verbal pronominal prefix at all: it appears as the postverbal noun *paympan* 'eagle' and the deictic form *m-n* NR DIST-I SG 'that'. It is instructive to compare the transition between clauses (a) and (b) with (c) and (d). In both cases, the S argument of the first clause becomes the O argument of the second, which in turn has a different A argument. Clearly, the use of deictics to monitor the change of S or A participants between clauses is only sporadic at best. The primary participant tracking derived in the language is unquestionably the verbal pronominal affixes.

Reference Matter

Appendix: Yimas Texts

Text 1: Origins of Yimas Village
This text was given by Stephen Mambi in 1978.

1. m-rm   Tat   Kampunawkwan m-rm
   NR DIST-I DL   name   name   NR DIST-I DL

   tantukwan   impa-nanaŋ-pay-ɲcut   anti-ɲam-n,
   alone   3DL S-DUR-lie-RM PAST   land VIII SG-house-OBL

   Malwampi   anti-ɲam-n
   place name   land VIII SG-house-OBL

   'Tat and Kampunawkwan lived alone in a cave, a cave (called)
   Malwampi.'

2. tay   m-n   Yaŋkay tantaw-r-awt
   then   NR DIST-I SG   name   sit(RED: *taw-*)-NFN-M SG

   anak   Macnumun
   COP 3SG   place name

   'And there was Yaŋkay, an inhabitant of Macnumun.'

3. tay   ikn   mnta   na-n-tay-ɲa-k-mpn
   then   smoke V SG   then   V SG T-3SG A-see-DUR-IRR-3DL D

   m-rm   tumpntut imp-arpat-mpi-cantaw-k
   NR DIST-I DL   morning   3DL S-exit-SEQ-sit(RED: *taw-*)-IRR

   'He watched their smoke, (when) they came out and sat down
   in the morning.'

4. tay   mpa   impa-yakal-cantaw-k
   then   now   3DL S-CONT-sit(RED: *taw-*)-IRR

   na-mpɨ-na-mamakn-kwalca-mpi-tay-n
   3SG O-3DL A-DEF-bad-rise-SEQ-see-PRES

457

"namarawt m-n   anak   m-na-ya-n"
person I SG   NR DIST-I SG   COP 3SG   NR DIST-DEF-come-PRES

'And (while) they both were living there, they stood up surprised and saw him, "There is someone coming." '

5.   m-rm   kwalca-mpi anti-ɲam-n
      NR DIST-I DL   rise-SEQ   land VIII SG-house-OBL

      imp-awram-pi-cantaw-k
      3DL S-enter-SEQ-sit(RED: *taw*-)-IRR

      'They both got up and went inside and stayed inside the cave.'

6.   irpuŋ   k-mp-awl-k   wantakampa nampayn
      stone VI SG   VI SG O-3DL A-get-IRR   door IX SG   like

      k-mp-antmta-k
      VI SG O-3DL A-cross-IRR

      'They both got a stone and used it like a door.'

7.   tay   mpa m-n   wapat-mpi
      then   now NR DIST-I SG   climb-SEQ

      pia-n-a-tmi-n   "yanawntrm, kapwa taŋka-mpi
      talk O-3SG A-DEF-say-PRES friend I DL   2DL   where-ADV

      kapwa-wa-t?   awt ura-k   awrak.   ikn
      2DL S-go-PERF   fire fire-PROX   COP fire   smoke V SG

      na-ŋkul-cay-ŋa-t   taŋka-mpi
      V SG T-2DL D-see-BEN-PERF   where-ADV

      kapwa-n-arm-pi-wa-n?"
      2DL S-DEF-board-SEQ-go-PRES

      'And he came up and said "Friends, where have you gone? This fire is here. I saw your smoke. Where are you going?" '

8.   m-rm
      NR DIST-I DL

      na-mpɨ-yakal-cantaw-ant-ntut
      3SG O-3DLA-CONT-sit(RED: *taw*-)-hear-RM PAST

      anti-ɲam-n
      land VIII SG-house-OBL

      'They both sat listening to him in the cave.'

9.   tay   mpa kay   mnta i-n-arm-ŋ
      then   now canoe VIII SG   then   VIII SG O-3SG A-board-IRR

way-mpi   na-wa-k
turn-SEQ   3SG S-go-IRR

'And so he then boarded his canoe, turned around and went back.'

10. tay   ma   ɲarŋ   aŋkayapan
    then   other   1 day removed   afternoon

    na-n-tay-kia-k-mpn   ikn
    V SG T-3SG A-see-NEAR-IRR-3DL D smoke V SG

    "impa-n   aympak"
    I DL-FR DIST COP 3DL

    'And the next afternoon he saw their smoke "That's them over there." '

11. ma   ŋarŋ   tumpntut mnta
    other   1 day removed   morning then

    na-na-way-mpi-ya-n
    3SG S-DEF-turn-SEQ-come-PRES

    'And next morning he came back.'

12. tay   na-mpɨ-mampi-kwalca-mpi-cay-ɲcut   "ŋarŋ
    then   3SG O-3DL A-again-rise-SEQ-see-RM PAST yesterday

    m-ya-nan   m-n   anak
    NR DIST-come-NR PAST   NR DIST-I SG COP 3SG

    na-na-mampi-ya-n"
    3SG S-DEF-again-come-PRES

    'They got up and saw him again "The one who came yesterday is coming again." '

13. m-rm   kwalca-mpi impa-tpat-ɲcut
    NR DIST-I DL   rise-SEQ   3DL S-descend-RM PAST

    anti-ɲam-n.   wantakampa
    land VIII SG-house-OBL door IX SG

    wa-mp-awt-ɲcut   wa-mp-antmta-ntut
    IX SG O-3DL A-get-RM PAST IX SG O-3DL A-cross-RM PAST

    'They got up and went down inside the cave. They got a door and closed it.'

14. tay   mpa   m-n   wapat-mpi
    then   now   NR DIST-I SG   climb-SEQ

    impa-n-a-mampi-munta-n   "yanawntrm,
    3DL O-3SG A-DEF-again-call out-PRES friends I DL

ikn   na-ŋkul-cay-ŋa-t.   tay   taŋka-mpi
smoke V SG V SG O-2DL D-see-BEN-PERF   then   where-ADV

kapwa-na-mampi-arm-pi-wa-n?"
2DL S-DEF-again-board-SEQ-go-PRES

'He came up and called out to them again: "Friends, I saw your
smoke. Where are you going?" '

15.   mnta tia-n-t-arm-pi-wa-k
      then act O-3SG A-do-board-SEQ-go-IRR
      'He went back.'

16.   tay   mpa k-n-ira-aykapi-k-mpn   "kratut
      then now VI SG T-3SG A-ALL-know-IRR-3DL D   twilight

      kapwa ŋkut-ɲa-ira-kwalca-kia-k   ŋarŋ."
      2DL   2DL O-DEF-ALL-rise-NR FUT-IRR 1 day removed

      'Then he figured them out: "At twilight tomorrow morning I
      will come up on you." '

17.   tay   mpa kratut   mnta impa-n-ira-kwalca-k
      then now twilight then 3DL O-3SG A-ALL-rise-IRR
      'Then before dawn he came up on them.'

18.   mpa kay   arm-pi   na-ya-k
      now canoe VIII SG board-SEQ 3SG S-come-IRR
      'He boarded a canoe and came.'

19.   tay   m-rm   awt impa-n-arpat-mpi-ampu-n
      then NR DIST-I DL   fire 3DL S-DEF-exit-SEQ-light-PRES
      'They came outside and lit a fire.'

20.   awt arpat-mpi-ampu-r-mampan-an   tktntrm
      fire exit-SEQ-light-NFN-M DL-OBL   chair V DL

      tma-mp-awt-ɲcut.
      V DL O-3DL A-get-RM PAST
      'While coming outside and lighting a fire, they got two chairs.'

21.   tantaw-r-mampan-an   m-n   mpa
      sit(RED: taw-)-NFN-M DL-OBL   NR DIST-I SG   now

      impa-n-a-munta-n   "yanawntrm a,
      3DL O-3SG A-DEF-call out-PRES   friend I DL   VOC

mntmpi kapwa-taw-wat?"
like that 2DL S-sit-HAB

'While they were sitting down, he called out to them
"Friends, do you live like that?" '

22. na-mpɨ-tmi-k   "yanaw   a,   ya-ka-wapat-n
     3SG O-3DL A-say-IRR friend I SG VOC come-SEQ-climb-IMP

     kapa takmpi kapa-taw-wat"
     1DL   like this 1DL S-sit-HAB

     'They said to him "Friend, come up here. We live like this." '

23. tay   mpa tkt   na-mpɨ-ŋa-k-nakn
     then   now chair V SG V SG O-3DL A-give-IRR-3SG D

     na-mpɨ-tmi-cantaw-k   tpuk
     3SG O-3DL A-say-sit(RED: *taw*-)-IRR sago pancake X SG

     ku-mpɨ-ŋa-k-nakn
     X SG O-3DL A-give-IRR-3SG D

     'They gave him a chair and told him to sit down, and they
     gave him some sago.'

24. n-am-k-mp-n   patn
     3SG S-eat-IRR-VII SG-OBL betelnut V SG

     na-mpɨ-ŋa-k-nakn   yaki
     V SG O-3DL A-give-IRR-3SG D tobacco V SG

     na-mpɨ-ŋa-k-nakn
     V SG O-3DL A-give-IRR-3SG D

     'He having eaten, they gave him betelnut and they gave him
     tobacco.'

25. am-pi   pia-n-i-k-mpn   "kapwa kanta
     eat-SEQ talk T-3SG A-tell-IRR-3DL D 2DL   but

     takmpi kapwa-taw-wat?"
     like this 2DL S-sit-HAB

     'Having smoked, he asked them "you always live like this?" '

26. "kapa takmpi kapa-taw-wat   tantukwan. namarawt
     1DL   like this 1DL S-sit-HAB alone   person I SG

     kayak   kapa kantk taw-r-awt.   anti   kanta
     not have 1DL   with   sit-NFN-M SG land VIII SG but

waca-k-i-ɲan   kapa-taw-wat"
small-IRR-VIII SG-OBL   1DL S-sit-HAB

' "We live alone like this. There is no one to live with us. We
live on only a little land." '

27. mnta pia-n-i-k-mpn   "aŋkurmpwimp-n mpan
    then talk T-3SG A-tell-IRR-3DL A   name-OBL   IMM

    ya-k   wara
    V PL-PROX   what

    m-ŋkul-caŋ-apica-mpi-irm-wa-ra?"
    NR DIST-2DL O-COM-hang-SEQ-stand-HAB-V PL

    'Then he asked them "What is this Aŋkurmpwimpn which
    is hanging up above you both?" '

28. "anti   aykk   kanta namarawt
    land VIII SG COP VIII SG VIS but   person I SG

    kapa-kamal-wat anti   kra-t-awt"
    1DL S-find-HAB land VIII SG cut-NFN-M SG

    ' "That's land, but we're still searching for someone to cut
    the land loose." '

29. "na-k   kapwa na-ŋkran-a-aykapiŋa-n
    I SG-PROX   2DL   3SG O-2DL A-DEF-know-PRES

    yawkawp-n   marŋ   k-k   kra-t-awt?"
    rope V SG-OBL stem VI SG VI SG-PROX cut-NFN-M SG

    ' "Do you two know he who can cut this rope?" '

30. "kapa ta-ŋkra-na-aykapiŋa-nt-ak"
    1DL   NEG-1DL A-DEF-know-PRES-3SG O

    ' "We don't know him." '

31. nmpi   mnta ya-ŋkl-wampaki-k,   ma-m
    leaf VII PL then   VII PL O-3PC A-throw-IRR other-VII SG

    Kapakmat-n   mnta p-ŋkl-wampaki-k
    Wambramas-OBL   then   VII SG O-3PC A-throw-IRR

    ma-m   Marianan   p-wa-k   ma-m
    other-VII SG   place name VII SG S-go-IRR, other-VII SG

    Kwaran   num-n   p-wa-k   ma-m
    place name village-OBL   VII SG S-go-IRR other-VII SG

Yuprajumn   p-wa-k
village name   VII SG S-go-IRR

'And so they sent letters, they sent one to Wambramas, another
went to Marianan, another to the village at Kwaran
and another to Yuprajumn village.'

32. tay   m-m   wu-mpi
    then   NR DIST-VII SG   get-SEQ

    ya-mpu-tay-k-mp-n
    VII PL O-3PL A-see-IRR-VII SG-OBL

    pia-mpu-tmi-k   "ipa   ta-kay-ɲa-aykapiŋa-nti
    talk O-3PL A-say-IRR   1PL   NEG-1PL A-DEF-know-act

    m-ŋ   kra-t-wal"
    NR DIST-VI SG   cut-NFN-custom

    'And when they got it, after having seen them, they said
    "We don't know how to cut it." '

33. m-n   Wankn   num-n   Pampak
    NR DIST-I SG   place name   village-OBL   name

    p-n-mampi-wu-mpi-cay-k-mp-n
    VII SG O-3SG A-again-get-SEQ-see-IRR-VII SG-OBL

    pia-n-tmi-k   "tak   nan-wampak-ɲa-m
    talk O-3SG A-say-IRR   here   IMP PL-throw-IMP-VII SG O

    Tampjumn   Kikay   ka-n-tu-kwalca-n   m-n
    place name   name   LIKE-3SG S-out-rise-IMP   NR DIST-I SG

    tia-n-a-aykapiŋa-n"
    act O-3SG A-DEF-know-PRES

    'When Pampak in the village at Wankn received another one,
    he said "Send one here to Tampjuman; Kikay can come;
    he knows how to do that." '

34. Kikay   mnta   na-tu-kwalca-k   Tamprakmak   m-rm
    name   then   3SG S-out-rise-IRR   name   NR DIST-I DL

    kantk   Tukmpian   apakrm   Wakuntapnŋ   m-rm
    with   name   sister-II DL   name   NR DIST-II DL

    Alajcŋmay
    name

    'Kikay left with Tamprakmak and Tukumpian and two sisters
    Wakuntapnŋ and Alajcŋmay.'

35. mnta   kra-tu-kwalca-k-mp-n   kra-arpal-k
    then   3PC S-out-rise-IRR-VII SG-OBL   3SG S-exit-IRR

arpat-mpi   Pampak   pia-n-i-k-ŋkan
exit-SEQ   name   talk T-3SG A-tell-IRR-3PC D

"kay   i-ɲa-l-ampu-n.
canoe VIII SG VIII SG S-DEF-down-float-PRES

kay   nan-l-arm-na-ŋkan-i
canoe VIII SG IMP PL-down-board-IMP-PC-VIII SG O

kapŋ   m-n   anak   Mampukut-kapŋ
cloth V SG   NR DIST-V SG   COP V SG   name of cloth V SG

na-na-l-ampu-n   kanta   pampak
V SG S-DEF-down-float-PRES   but   fastening stick V SG

mpa-n   ta-kul-ŋa-kr-ŋkan-ak
one-V SG   NEG-2PL D-give-RM FUT-PC-3SG T

ama-na-kn   anak"
1SG-POSS-V SG   COP V SG

'After they came out (of the village), while they were leaving,
Pampak said to them: "There is a canoe down below. Board
the canoe down below. There is a cloth for cleaning canoes,
Mampukutkapŋ is there. But I won't give you a stick for
tying up the canoe; that's mine." '

36. tay   mpa mamaŋ-tul-c-ŋkt-ɲan   Wakuntapnŋ   mnta
    then now slowly-cross-NFN-PC-OBL   name   then

    na-taŋ-awŋkwi-k-ŋkan
    3SG S-COM-sink-IRR-3PC D

    'And while they were slowly crossing (the lake), Wakuntapnŋ
    fell overboard.'

37. tay   ta-ŋkl-mampi-cay-mpi-waraca-k-nak
    then NEG-3PC A-again-see-SEQ-return-IRR-3SG O

    m-n   kanta na-ŋkl-cay-mpi-ntak-k
    NR DIST-II SG   but   3SG O-3PC A-see-SEQ-leave-IRR

    'They didn't see her and turn back; they just left her behind.'

38. mpa l-mpu-pra-t-ŋkt-ɲan   Alaɲcɲan
    now down-go by water-toward-NFN-PC-OBL place name

    Alaɲcŋmay mnta na-mampi-awŋkwi-k
    name   then 3SG S-again-sink-IRR

    'While they were coming toward Alaɲcɲan, Alaɲcŋmay also
    fell overboard.'

39. tay   mpa tia-ŋkl-cɨ-ya-kia-k   num-n
    then now act O-3PC S-do-come-NIGHT-IRR   village-OBL

wapal-kia-k-mpi   m-rm
climb-NIGHT-IRR-SEQ NR DIST-I DL

na-mpɨ-tay-kia-k
3SG O-3DL A-see-NIGHT-IRR

'And then they came straight to the village and came ashore,
and they both [the villagers] saw him [Kikay].'

40. tay   mpa impa-ŋkl-wapat-mpi-kankantakal-kia-k
     then   now 3DL O-3PC A-climb-SEQ-ask-NIGHT-IRR

     "kapwa kanta mntmpi   kapwa-taw-wat?"
     2DL   but   like that 2DL S-sit-HAB

     'And they asked them both "Do you two live like this?" '

41. "kapa takmpi   kapa-taw-wat anti   kayak"
     1DL   like this 1DL S-sit-HAB land VIII SG not have

     ' "We live like this; we have no land." '

42. m-rm   mnta impa-n-wampaki-kia-k
     NR DIST-I DL   then 3DL O-3SG A-throw-NIGHT-IRR

     Tamprakmak m-rm   Tukmpian
     name   NR DIST-I DL   name

     impa-way-mpi-wa-k
     3DL S-turn-SEQ-go-IRR

     'He sent them both away, Tamprakmak and Tukmpian
     returned.'

43. m-n   mnta impa-n-kankantakal-kia-k
     NR DIST-I SG   then 3DL O-3SG A-ask-NIGHT-IRR

     "wara-ti-nti   anta-tɨ-kra-kia-na-ŋ?
     what-NFN-act   HORT SG-do-cut-NIGHT-IMP-VI SG O

     pampukapan?"
     middle

     'Then he asked them both "How shall I cut it? In the
     middle?" '

44. tay   m-n   na-mampi-yaŋkuraŋ-kamal-kia-k
     then NR DIST-I SG   3SG S-again-thought-search-NIGHT-IRR

     "tay ama m-ŋ
     then 1SG NR DIST-VI SG

     m-ka-na-kra-kia-nt-mp-n   ama
     NR DIST-1SG S-DEF-cut-NIGHT-PRES-VII SG-OBL 1SG

tay yaw   kayak   wa-kia-k-ra   mpa tak
then road IX SG not have go-NIGHT-IRR-V PL   now here

ama-taw-kt"
1SG S-sit-RM FUT

'Then he pondered "If I cut this, I won't have a way to go back;
I'll have to stay here." '

45. tay   mpa kaŋ
     then now kina shell VI SG

     k-n-wura-kia-k   yakut-n
     VI SG O-3SG A-remove-NIGHT-IRR   netbag V SG-OBL

     mact mnta k-n-kra-mpi-caray-ca-kia-k
     top   then VI SG O-3SG A-cut-SEQ-clear-put-NIGHT-IRR

     yakawp-n   marŋ   mnta iratak-mpi-tmuk-kia-k
     rope V SG-OBL stem VI SG then shake-SEQ-fall-NIGHT-IRR

     anti
     land VIII SG

     'And then he took out a kina shell from a netbag and cut the
     rope clear at the top and the land shook and fell down.'

46. k-n-kra-kia-k-mp-n   m-rm
     VI SG O-3SG A-cut-NIGHT-IRR-VII SG-OBL   NR DIST-I DL

     ta-mpɨ-tay-kia-k-nak   mnti kacakapi-k-nti
     NEG-1DL A-see-NIGHT-IRR-3SG O there hide-IRR-act

     mnta tia-n-tɨ-wa-kia-k   Tampɲumun
     then   act O-3SG A-do-go-NIGHT-IRR   place name

     'When he cut it, they both did not see him disappear there;
     he went back to Tampɲumun.'

47. m-rm   mnta pia-mpɨ-tmi-kia-k
     NR DIST-I DL   then   talk T-3DL A-say-NIGHT-IRR

     "namat   kayak   mnti taw-r-mat   anti
     person I PL not have there sit-NFN-M PL   land VIII SG

     ma-m   kantk taw-r-i   kawŋkawn-i
     other-I PL with   sit-NFN-VIII SG this sort-VIII SG

     aykk.   nmpi
     COP VIII SG VIS   leaf VII PL

     aŋka-tra-wampaki-ɲa-ra.
     HORT DL-about-throw-IMP-VII PL O

ka-mpu-tra-ya-n"
LIKE-3PL S-about-come-IMP

'Then they both said "There are no people living there. This
sort of land is for living with others. Let's send letters
around. They can come from various places." '

48. m-um   mnta pu-tra-ya-k
    NR DIST-I PL then   3PL S-about-come-IRR

    Ambiantumpan-an m-taw-k-um   Yacmpt-nan
    Angriman-OBL   NR DIST-sit-IRR-I PL Yesimbit-OBL

    m-taw-k-um   Kapakmat-n
    NR DIST-sit-IRR-I PL Wambramas-OBL

    m-taw-k-um   Marianan   taw-r-mat
    NR DIST-sit-IRR-I PL place name sit-NFN-M PL

    Marawn   taw-r-mat   mnta
    place name sit-NFN-M PL then

    pu-mpi-tra-awl-tal-kaprapi-k
    3PL O-3DL A-about-get-CAUS-gather-IRR

    'And they came from various directions: those who lived at
    Angriman, those who lived at Yesimbit, those who lived at
    Wambramas, the inhabitants of Marianan, the inhabitants of
    Marawn; they got them from various directions and made
    them gather.'

49. tay   mpa nampt
    then   now house PL

    ya-mpu-tra-wark-k-mp-n   wark-mpi
    house PL-3PL A-about-build-IRR-VII SG-OBL build-SEQ

    irmpŋ   mnta na-mpu-kawŋ-kia-k
    slit drum V SG then   V SG O-3PL A-beat-NIGHT-IRR

    'After they had built houses about, they beat the slit drum.'

50. mnta pu-kaprapi-kia-k-mp-n
    then 3PL S-gather-NIGHT-IRR-VII SG-OBL

    pia-ŋkl-cmi-kia-k   "ipa   ŋarŋ
    talk O-3PC A-say-NIGHT-IRR 1PL 1 day removed

    amtra   awl-k   ipa-na-wa-kia-k"
    food V PL get-IRR 1PL S-DEF-go-NR FUT-IRR

    'Then after they assembled, some of them said "Tomorrow
    we will go to get food." '

51. tay   ma   ŋarŋ   amtra   awl-k   mnta
    then   other 1 day removed   food V PL get-IRR then

    pu-wa-k
    3PL S-go-IRR

    'And next day they went to get food.'

52. m-n   Parampt-paympan   Kanaymanan   tan
    NR DIST-V SG   name-eagle V SG   place name OBL   there

    nanaŋ-taw-na-ntut
    DUR-sit-DUR-RM PAST

    'And he Parampitpaympan (totemic eagle) was living at
    Kanayman.'

53. m-um   mnta   pu-n-tay-mpi-kwalca-k
    NR DIST-I PL   then   3PL O-3SG A-see-SEQ-rise-IRR

    awkura-mpi   pu-n-api-k   man-an
    collect-SEQ 3PL O-3SG A-put in-IRR   male cult house-OBL

    'Then he saw them and flew up and collected them and put
    them inside (his) male cult house.'

54. ma-m   ma   ŋarŋ   mnta
    other-I PL   other 1 day removed   then

    pu-ŋkl-mampi-wampaki-k
    3PL O-3PC A-again-throw-IRR

    'Another day, they sent some more people.'

55. m-um   pu-n-mampi-awkura-mpi-api-k
    NR DIST-I PL   3PL O-3SG A-again-collect-SEQ-put in-IRR

    paympan
    eagle V SG

    'Again he, the eagle, collected them and put them inside.'

56. tay   ma   ŋarŋ   mnta   pia-ŋkl-cmi-k
    then   other 1 day removed   then   talk O-3PC A-say-IRR

    "m-n   wara   ti-mpi   namarawt
    NR DIST-I SG   what   do-SEQ   person-I SG

    pu-n-awkura-naŋ?   wara-t-nti
    3PL O-3SG A-collect-DUR   what-NFN-act

    ay-ci-takat-ɲa-ŋkan-ak?"
    HORT PL-do-touch-IMP-PC-3SG O

    ' "What is he doing, this person collecting them? What are we
    to do with him?" '

57. muntawktn   plum   mu-ŋkl-al-k
    at first   tree (sp) IV SG   IV SG O-3PC A-cut-IRR
    at-mpi   mu-ŋkl-yamal-k   kal
    cut-SEQ   IV SG O-3PC A-carve-IRR   canoe VIII DL
    waca-k-l   mpɨ-nampayn
    small-IRR-VIII DL   3DL-like
    'First they cut a *plum* tree and carve it like two small canoes.'

58. tay   mu-ŋkl-wanalca-mpi-wul-k   kanta
    then IV SG O-3PC A-push-SEQ-go down-IRR   but
    mu-awŋkwi-cantaw-k
    IV SG S-sink-sit(RED: *taw-*)-IRR
    'Then they pushed it down (into the water), but it sank.'

59. tay   m-rm   mnta pia-mpɨ-tmi-k   Kayan
    then NR DIST-I DL   then   talk O-3DL A-say-IRR   name
    Paput m-rm   mnta pia-mpɨ-tmi-k   "kapa
    name   NR DIST-I DL   then   talk O-3DL A-say-IRR   1DL
    ŋa-ŋkra-yamiŋ-pi-api-n.   yampnuŋ
    IMP-1DL O-make magic-SEQ-put in-IMP   tree (sp) X SG
    Tamprakmat-n   ayŋk-n   m-na-irm-t-uŋ.
    place name-OBL   side-OBL   NR DIST-DEF-stand-PRES-X SG
    yampnuŋ   ku-k   ay-at-ɲa-ŋkt"
    tree (sp) X SG   X SG-PROX   HORT PL-cut-IMP-PC
    'Then Kayan and Paput said "You must make magic for us
    two. There is a *yampnuŋ* tree standing at the side of
    Tamprakmal. Let's cut this tree." '

60. yampnuŋ   mnta ku-ŋkl-al-k
    tree (sp) X SG   then X SG O-3PC A-cut-IRR
    'And then they cut the *yampnuŋ* tree.'

61. ku-ŋkl-al-k-mp-n   kaykaykay mnta
    X SG O-3PC-cut-IRR-VII SG-OBL   quickly   then
    ku-ŋkl-mampi-yamal-k
    X SG O-3PC A-again-carve-IRR
    'After they cut it, they quickly hollowed it out.'

62. kamarawŋkawl   maɲckrm   ula-ŋkl-tɨ-k
    canoe half IX DL   twine piece V DL   IX DL O-3PC A-put-IRR
    'They tied the two canoe halves together with two pieces of
    twine.'

63.   mnta   pia-ŋkl-cmi-k   "apa
      then   talk O-3PC A-say-IRR   OK

      naŋk-arm-pi-aypu-n   Kayan   mawŋkwat   Paput
      IMP DL-board-SEQ-lie-IMP   name   other side   name

      mawŋkwat"
      other side

      'And they said "OK, you two get in now, Kayan on one side,
      Paput on the other." '

64.   tay   muntawktn impa-arm-pi-aypu-k   parmpantrm
      then at first   3DL S-board-SEQ-lie-IRR   bow V DL

      yakutnmpl   kaŋkl   kantk
      netbag VII DL   kina shell VI DL   with

      pla-ŋkl-wanalca-k
      VII DL O-3PC A-push-IRR

      'Then they both first boarded the canoe, and they shoved
      them off off with two bows, two netbags and two kina shells.'
      (the prefix *pla-* VII DL O refers to an unmentioned but
      understood noun, *pucmpl* piece of wood VII DL, which refers
      to the two halves of the canoe in which the two men are lying)

65.   pla-wi-ŋka-pu-k   Waŋan
      VII DL O-up-travel-away-IRR   small lake near village

      awntumki
      lizard VI PL

      kia-mpɨ-wi-apapan-ta-pu-k
      VI PL O-3DL A-up-shoot(RED: *apan-*)-put-away-IRR

      'They both went up to Waŋan, and they both shot lizards as
      they went up.'

66.   pia-mpɨ-tmi-k   "mpa   kwarkwa
      talk O-3DL A-say-IRR   now   today

      na-ŋkra-na-apan-ŋ"
      V SG O-1DL A-DEF-shoot-IRR

      'They both said "We both will shoot him today." '

67.   arm-pi   mnta   impa-mamaŋ-tampulanta-pu-k
      board-SEQ   then   3DL S-slowly-run-away-IRR

      'They boarded and came slowly.'

68.   tay   Kayan   antkmpt-ɲan   Tamprukn   tapnk-n
      then name   sago leaf VII DL-OBL   lake name   canal-OBL

tan   impa-pay-cat-mpi-yampara-k
there   3DL S-first-hold-SEQ-stand-IRR

'Kayan first fasten themselves to two sago leaves there in the
canal to Tamprukn.'

69. m-um   num-n-mat   Kampramanan
     NR DIST-I PL   village-OBL-M PL   place name

     wapal-cap-mpi   yampara-k
     climb-COMP-SEQ   stand-IRR

     'The villagers all climbed Kampramanan and stood there.'

70. m-rm   mpa tan   impa-ampu-mpi-awl-k
     NR DIST-I DL   now   there 3DL S-float-SEQ-get-IRR

     'They both floated and rested for a while there.'

71. ampu-mpi-awl-k-mp-n   mnta tia-mpɨ-tɨ-wa-k
     float-SEQ-get-IRR-VII SG-OBL   then   act O-3DL A-do-go-IRR

     upunk-n
     lake-OBL

     'After resting, they both went all the way to the lake.'

72. impa-mpu-yakal-irm-tay-ɲcut
     3DL O-3PL A-CONT-stand-see-RM PAST

     'They stood watching them both.'

73. wayway-kulanaŋ-kia-k-r-mampan   m-n
     turn(RED: way-)-walk-NEAR-IRR-NFN-M DL   NR DIST-V SG

     impa-tay-mpi-kwalca-k   paympan
     3DL O-see-SEQ-rise-IRR   eagle V SG

     'While they were both drifting around, he, the eagle, saw them
     both and took off.'

74. impa-n-tay-mpi-kwalca-k   muntawktn
     3DL O-3SG A-see-SEQ-rise-IRR   at first

     impa-n-tu-awkura-pra-k
     3DL O-3SG A-out-collect-toward-IRR

     'He saw them both and took off at first; he came out to collect
     them both.'

75. pla-kulkara-mpi-awŋkwi-k-nakn
     VII DL S-drop-SEQ-sink-IRR-3SG D

     'They both drop from him and fall into the water.'

76. pia-mpu-tmi-k   "ka-ŋkul-awkura-mpa-n.
     talk O-3PL A-say-IRR   LIKE-2DL O-collect-IMM-IMP

     naŋk-walɲa-n."
     IMP DL-light-IMP

     'They (the villagers) said "He must collect you now. You must
     be light." '

77. tay   na-mampi-kaŋkaŋ-pi-tampulanta-k
     then 3SG S-again-turn(RED: *kaŋ-*)-SEQ-run-IRR

     na-tu-ŋka-pra-k   pla-n-awkura-k
     3SG S-out-travel-toward-IRR   VII SG O-3SG A-collect-IRR

     pla-n-wampak-mpi-api-k
     VII SG O-3SG A-throw-SEQ-put in-IRR

     'Then he turned and came again; he came out and collected
     them both and threw them both inside (his male cult house).'

78. tay   mpa   wut   am-kia-k
     then now   night eat-NEAR-IRR

     na-ma-ŋka-pu-kia-k
     3SG S-in-travel-away-NIGHT-IRR

     'Then that night he went inside to eat.'

79. aypu-t-ut   wut   pia-n-i-kia-k-nakn
     lie-NFN-night night talk T-3SG A-tell-NIGHT-IRR-3SG D

     "ŋay, ama tpuk   am-t-wampuŋ
     mama 1SG sago pancake X SG   eat-NFN-desire

     ama-na-tɨ-kia-k"
     1SG S-DEF-feel-NIGHT-IRR

     'During the night time for sleeping, he said "Mama, I feel like
     eating sago." '

80. "tmalŋkat-n   tpwi   am-t-mpwi
     day/sun V PL-OBL   sago pancake X PL   eat-NFN-talk

     ta-pu-n-yaŋkuraŋ-takal-wat"
     NEG-3-2SG S-thought-feel-HAB

     ' "During the day you never think about eating sago." '

81. tpuk   ku-n-ŋa-kia-k-nakn
     sago pancake X SG   X SG O-3SG A-give-NIGHT-IRR-3SG D

     'She gave him a sago pancake.'

82. ku-n-am-kia-k-mp-n   ma-uŋ
     X SG O-3SG A-eat-NIGHT-IRR-VII SG-OBL   other-X SG

tantaw-am-kia-r-awt-ɲan   maɲckrm
sit(RED: *taw-*)-eat-NIGHT-NFN-M SG-OBL   twine V DL

tma-mpɨ-kra-kia-k.
V DL O-3DL A-cut-NIGHT-IRR

'After he ate it, while sitting and eating another one, they both cut the two pieces of twine.'

83. pia-mpɨ-t-i-kia-k   "mi   tanm
     talk O-3DL A-RCP-tell-NIGHT-IRR   2SG   bone VII SG

     ma-kumprak-t?"   "ama tanm ta-ka-kumprak-t"
     2SG S-break-PERF   1SG   bone   NEG-1SG S-break-PERF

     "ama kayak."
     1SG no

     'They said to each other "Did you break any bones?" "I didn't break any bones." "Me neither." '

84. tay   maɲckrm   mnta   tma-mpɨ-kra-kia-k
     then   twine V DL   them   V DL O-3DL A-cut-NIGHT-IRR

     'Then they both cut the two pieces of twine.'

85. kapuk   ku-pay-kia-k
     noise X SG   X SG S-carry-NIGHT-IRR

     'A noise came up.'

86. pia-mp-i-kia-k-nakn   "manm
     talk O-3DL A-eat-NIGHT-IRR-3SG D   male cult house VII SG

     kapuk   p-na-ma-pay-kia-k.   mi
     noise X SG   VII SG S-DEF-in-carry-NIGHT-IRR   2SG

     kpa-nti   maramara   muntak
     big-ADV   things V PL   many

     ma-awkawkura-api-wat."
     2SG S-collect(RED: *awkura-*)-put in-HAB

     'They both (his parents) tell him (the eagle) "There is a noise inside your male cult house. You collect too many things inside there." '

87. m-rm   impa-arpat-mpi-yampara-kia-k   Kayan
     NR DIST-I DL   3DL S-exit-SEQ-stand-NIGHT-IRR   name

     Paput   m-rm
     name   NR DIST-I DL

     'Kayan and Paput came out and stood up.'

88. ma-n   payŋkan-awt ma-n   ampan-awt
    other-I SG left-M SG   other-I SG right-M SG

    'One man on the left, the other on the right.'

89. tay mpa pia-mpɨ-t-i-kia-k
    then now talk O-3DL A-RCP-tell-NIGHT-IRR

    'They both were talking (over plans).'

90. parmpantrm
    bow V DL

    tma-mp-api-kan-kia-k-mp-n
    V DL O-3DL A-put in-shoot-NIGHT-IRR-VII SG-OBL

    mundawktn mpawŋ   impa-yampara-kia-k
    at first   together 3DL S-stand-NIGHT-IRR

    'After they both loaded and drew their bows, they stood up together.'

91. wa-mpɨ-mayn-pi-tay-kia-k-mp-n
    IX SG O-3DL A-fit-SEQ-see-NIGHT-IRR-VII SG-OBL

    "kayak, mi mawŋkwat yampara-kia-k.   ama mawŋkwat."
    no   2SG other side stand-NIGHT-IRR 1SG other side

    'They both try their positions, "No, you stand on one side, me on the other." '

92. mawŋkwara   mawŋkwara   mnta impa-yampara-kia-k
    other side PL other side PL then 3DL S-stand-NIGHT-IRR

    'They both stand side by side.'

93. tay m-n   pia-mp-i-kia-k-nakn
    then NR DIST-V SG talk T-3DL A-tell-NIGHT-IRR-3SG D

    apucaprm   "mi mpa ma-ŋka-pu-kia-k   kapa
    parents I DL 2SG now in-travel-away-NIGHT-IRR 1DL

    mpa aypu-kia-k"
    now lie-NIGHT-IRR

    'And then his parents tell him "You go inside now; we want to sleep now." '

94. m-rm   impa-pampan-takat-mpi-yampara-kia-k
    NR DIST-I DL 3DL S-correct-touch-SEQ-stand-NIGHT-IRR

    'They both stand up straight.'

95. m-n   mpa n-awram-kia-k
    NR DIST-V SG now   3SG S-enter-NIGHT-IRR
    'He came inside.'

96. awram-pi   na-tantaw-kia-k
    enter-SEQ 3SG S-sit(RED: *taw-*)-NIGHT-IRR
    'He came in and sat down.'

97. pucmp-n   muntawktn tma-mp-art-kia-k
    time VII SG-OBL at first   V DL O-3DL A-draw-NIGHT-IRR
    'At this time, they first drew (their bows).'

98. art-mpi   tar-kia-k
    draw-SEQ hold-NIGHT-IRR
    'They drew them and held them.'

99. tampin mnta na-mp-apan-kia-k
    after   then   3SG O-3DL A-shoot-NIGHT-IRR
    'Then they shot him.'

100. na-mp-apan-kia-k   parmpantrm
     3SG O-3DL A-shoot-NIGHT-IRR bow V DL

     tma-mp-ak-tar-kia-k
     V DL O-3DL A-pull-hold-NIGHT-IRR
     'They both shot him; they pulled and held their bows.'

101. irmpŋ   na-mp-awl-kia-k   Kapiatmal
     slit drum V SG V SG O-3DL A-get-NIGHT-IRR name

     yura   mampi Kapiatmal
     dog III SG again   name
     'They both took a slit drum Kapiatmal, also a dog, Kapiatmal.'

102. mpa impa-iranta-arpal-kia-k   "kapa Kayan
     now   3DL S-dance(RED: *ira*)-exit-NIGHT-IRR 1DL   name

     Paput m-rm"
     name   NR DIST-I DL
     'They both came outside now dancing. "We are Kayan and
     Paput." '

103. mpa impa-l-ŋka-pra-kia-k   parwa-n
     now   3DL S-down-travel-toward-NIGHT-IRR dock IX SG-OBL

     kanta kamta-k-wa   impa-tay-kiak   kay
     but   empty-IRR-IX SG 3DL S-see-NIGHT-IRR canoe VIII SG

ta-pu-wura-kia-k-um
NEG-3-tie up-NIGHT-IRR-PL

'They both came down, but saw an empty dock. They didn't tie up a canoe there.'

104. mpa tay-mpi mnta impa-ira-pu-kia-k
   now see-SEQ then 3DL S-dance-away-NIGHT-IRR

'Seeing this, they both left dancing.'

105. na-mpi-yakal-ca-mpi-yampara-pu-ntut   mnta
   V SG O-3DL A-CONT-put-SEQ-stand-away-RM PAST then

impa-yakal-irm-ira-ntut
3DL S-CONT-stand-dance-RM PAST

'They both put (the slit drum) down and stood up and then danced.'

106. mpa tay-mpi impa-ira-pu-k   numpk-n
   now see-SEQ 3DL S-dance-away-IRR mountain V SG-OBL

parmpan kantk iŋkay irmpŋ   yura
bow V SG with spear V PL slit drum V SG dog III SG

mnti ya-mpi-taray-mul-kia-k
there V PL O-3DL A-clear-flee-NIGHT-IRR

'Then they went away dancing, and there on the mountain they left behind a bow, spears, the slit drum and the dog.'

107. mnti pia-mpi-tmi-kia-k   "mpa
   there talk T-3DL A-say-NIGHT-IRR now

mntmpi nan-taw-n. kapa mpa kay
like that IMP PL-sit-IMP 1DL now canoe VIII SG

ta-pu-nan-wura-t-um."
NEG-3-2PL S-tie up-PERF-PL

'There they said "Now you can stay as you are. You didn't tie up a canoe for us." '

108. tay m-n   apwi m-na-kn   Kaplmal
   then NR DIST-V SG father I SG 3SG-POSS-I SG name

na-kwalca-mpi-campulanta-k mntmpi
3SG S-rise-SEQ-run-IRR   like that

impa-n-yakal-kulanaŋ-kanta-ntut
3DL O-3SG A-CONT-walk-follow-RM PAST

'Then his father Kaplmal got up and came; he was following them both.'

109. tay   m-n   Paɲanman
      then   NR DIST-I SG   name

      na-yakal-cuku-ntut   na-n-kankantakal-k
      3SG S-CONT-wash sago-RM PAST   3SG O-3SG A-ask-IRR

      "impa-n   aympak   impa-na-ira-pu-n.
      3DL-FR DIST   COP 3DL   3DL S-DEF-dance-away-PRES

      impa-n-tay?"
      3DL O-2SG A-see

      'Then Paɲanman was washing sago, and he asked her "Those
      two who are going away dancing, did you see them?" '

110. kanta m-n   na-tu-k   Kaplmal
      but   NR DIST-I SG   3SG S-kill-IRR   name

      'But Kaplmal killed her.'

111. na-tu-k-mp-n   mnta   na-waraca-k
      3SG S-kill-IRR-VII SG-OBL   then   3SG-return-IRR

      'He killed her and went back.'

112. m-n   paympan   tan   na-tmuk-k
      NR DIST-V SG   eagle V SG there 3SG S-fall-IRR

      Kaywal-ɲan   numkat-n
      Kaiwaria-OBL   village PL-OBL

      'The eagle fell down there in the villages at Kaiwaria.'

113. tanpat   tan   ya-mpu-pampay-caw-war-akn
      bone VII PL   there VII PL O-3PL A-KIN-sit-HAB-3SG D

      'They still hold his bones there.'

114. mpa pia-k   apiak
      now talk-PROX   COP talk

      'This story is enough.'

Text 2: The Flood
This text was given in 1985 by Stephen Mambi.

1.   m-rm   Yapalmay m-rm   Mampalmay
     NR DIST-II DL   name   NR DIST-II DL   name

     m-rm   impa-nanaŋ-taw-ntut   matn   kantk
     NR DIST-II DL   3DL S-DUR-sit-RM PAST   brother-I SG with

Yampwiŋkawi
name

'Yapalmay and Mampalmay lived with their brother
Yampwiŋkawi.'

2. yaŋi-ɲan   na-mpɨ-nanaŋ-kacakapi-takat-ɲcut
   clay pot VIII SG-OBL 3SG O-3DL A-DUR-hide-touch-RM PAST

   'They hid him in a clay pot.'

3. tay   ma   tmat-ɲan   pan-ŋ   impa-wa-k
   then other sun/day V SG-OBL pound sago-IRR 3DL S-go-IRR

   'One day they both went to work sago.'

4. pan-ŋ   impa-wa-k-mp-n   matn
   pound sago-IRR 3DL S-go-IRR-VII SG-OBL   brother I SG

   m-n   n-arpal-k-mp-n   num-n-mat
   NR DIST-I SG   3SG S-exit-IRR-VII SG-OBL village-OBL-M PL

   mnta na-mpu-tu-k   matn   m-rm
   then 3SG O-3PL A-kill-IRR brother I SG NR DIST-II DL

   mpɨ-na-kn   Yampwiŋkawi
   3DL-POSS-I SG   name

   'After they both went to work sago, the brother came outside
   and then the villagers killed him, the brother of those two,
   Yampwiŋkawi.'

5. tay   wapal-kia-k-mpi
   then climb-NIGHT-IRR-SEQ

   pia-mpu-i-kia-k-mpn   "ipa numpran
   talk T-3PL A-tell-NIGHT-IRR-3DL D   1PL pig III SG

   ipa-na-takat-n   am-kia-k   num-n
   1PL S-DEF-touch-PRES   eat-NIGHT-IRR   village-OBL

   numpran   na-kay-cu-t."
   pig III SG III SG O-1PL A-kill-PERF

   'When they both returned (in the afternoon), they told them
   both "We have a pig to eat. We killed a domesticated pig." '

6. m-rm   pia-mpɨ-tmi-kia-k   "ipwa
   NR DIST-II DL talk O-3DL A-say-NIGHT-IRR   2PL

   nan-wurt-am-kia-na-k"
   IMP PL-put down(RED: wul-)-eat-NIGHT-IMP-III SG O

   'They both said "you boil and eat it." '

7. tay   mpa mnta pia-mpɨ-tmi-kia-k
   then   now   then   talk O-3DL A-say-NIGHT-IRR

   "yaɲi   aŋka-pay-cay-kia-na-y"
   clay pot VIII SG HORT DL-first-see-NIGHT-IMP-VIII SG O

   'They both said "let's first check the clay pot." '

8. tay   yaɲi   i-mpɨ-tay-kia-k
   then clay pot VIII SG VIII SG O-3DL A-see-NIGHT-IRR

   kanta kamta-k-i   impa-tay-kia-k
   but   empty-IRR-VIII SG   3DL S-see-NIGHT-IRR

   'They both checked the clay pot, but they both saw it was
   empty.'

9. pia-mpɨ-tmi-kia-k   "tak
   talk O-3DL A-say-NIGHT-IRR   here

   na-mpu-wura-mpi-cu-k"
   3SG O-3PL A-take-SEQ-kill-IRR

   'They both said "They took him and killed him." '

10. m-rm   impa-iray-kia-k
    NR DIST-II PL   3DL S-cry-NIGHT-IRR

    'They both cried.'

11. tay   waca-k-nmaŋ   mnta n-aypu-kia-k   mnta
    then small-IRR-II SG   then   3SG S-sleep-NIGHT-IRR   then

    pia-n-ŋa-kia-k-nakn   tac-t-nti-ɲan
    talk T-3SG A-give-NIGHT-IRR-3SG D   dream-NFN-act-OBL

    "kapwa ŋarŋ   tpwi   tumpntut
    2DL   1 day removed sago pancake X PL   morning

    naŋk-apapi-tal-kia-na-y.   ama
    IMP DL-put in(RED: api-)-start-NEAR-IMP-X PL O   1SG

    arm   tal-kwalca-k"
    water CAUS-rise-IRR

    'The little sister was sleeping, and he gave her this in a dream
    "Tomorrow morning you both start frying sago pancakes. I will
    raise the water." '

12. kpa-nmaŋ   mnta pia-n-kwalca-mpi-i-kia-k-nakn
    big-II SG   then   talk T-3SG A-rise-SEQ-tell-NIGHT-IRR-3SG D

    "kapa ŋarŋ   tia-k   kapa-na-tɨ-kia-k
    1DL   1 day removed act-PROX   1DL S-DEF-do-NR FUT-IRR

arm   kpa-rm   tal-kwalca-r-awt   anak
water big-water CAUS-rise-NFN-M SG COP 3SG

num-n-mat   pu-k   mal-capi-k."
village-NFN-M PL I PL-PROX die-COMP-IRR

'Then she got up and told her big sister "We will do this
tomorrow: he will be the one who raises the flood. All these
villagers will die." '

13. tay   m-n   kpa-nmaŋ
     then NR DIST-II SG   big-II SG

     ta-pu-n-ant-mpi-ca-kia-k-nak-mpwi
     NEG-3-3SG A-hear-SEQ-put-NIGHT-IRR-3SG D-talk

     pia-n-ant-kia-k-nakn
     talk O-3SG A-hear-NIGHT-IRR-3SG D

     'The big sister did not ignore her; she listened to her.'

14. mnta i-mp-apapi-tal-kia-k
     then X PL O-3DL A-put in(RED: *api-*)-start-NIGHT-IRR

     aŋkayapa   wa-ta-kia-k-mp-n
     afternoon IX SG IX SG S-put-NIGHT-IRR-VII SG-OBL

     waŋkantrm
     ring for climbing coconut palm V DL

     tma-mpɨ-tɨ-kia-k
     V DL O-3DL A-do-NIGHT-IRR

     'Then they both started to fry them (sago pancakes); when
     afternoon came, they made two rings for climbing coconut
     palms.'

15. wut   mnta impa-wapat-mpi-cantaw-kia-k
     night then 3DL S-climb-SEQ-sit(RED: *taw-*)-NIGHT-IRR

     irpmut-ɲan
     coconut palm IV DL-OBL

     'Then during the night they climbed up and sat atop two
     coconut palms.'

16. impa-wapat-mpi-cantaw-kia-k   m-rm
     3DL S-climb-SEQ-sit(RED: *taw-*)-NIGHT-IRR NR DIST-water

     arm   mnta ima-kwalca-kia-k
     water then water S-rise-NIGHT-IRR

     'They climbed and sat down and then the water rose.'

17. mpa mpa m-rm   arm   ima-kwalca-kia-k
     now now NR DIST-water   water water S-rise-NIGHT-IRR

     nampt   ya-mpu-tawɲca-kia-k-mp-n
     house PL house PL O-3PL A-flood-NIGHT-IRR-VII SG-OBL

     m-um   pay-kia-k-r-mat-ɲan
     NR DIST-I PL lie-NIGHT-IRR-NFN-M PL-OBL

     num-n-mat
     villages-OBL-M PL

     'The water still rose after it flooded the houses, while the
     villagers slept.'

18. tay mpa taw-ru-mprump-nan muntawktn uraŋ
     then now sit-NFN-F DL-OBL   at first   coconut VI SG

     k-mpɨ-yawra-mpi-wampaki-kia-k   kanta warpayn
     VI SG O-3DL A-get-SEQ-throw-NIGHT-IRR but   near

     k-taŋ-awŋkwi-k-mp-n   arm
     VI SG O-COM-sink-IRR-VII SG-OBL   water

     ta-pu-n-ara-mpa-nt-rm
     NEG-3-DEF-dry-IMM-PRES-water

     'Then while the two were waiting, they both first got and
     threw a coconut, but it hit the water nearby, so the water
     wasn't dry yet.'

19. mampi pay-cu-mprump-nan ma-ŋ
     again   lie-NFN-F DL-OBL   other-VI SG

     k-mpɨ-wampak-k   mpa
     VI SG O-3DL A-throw-IRR now

     ima-na-l-ŋka-pu-n   ma   kwantayn
     water S-DEF-down-travel-away-PRES other distant

     k-awŋkwi.
     VI SG S-sink

     'While they both still waited, they both threw another one; now
     the water had gone down and it hit the water further away.'

20. tay mampi pay-cu-mprump-nan mpa kwantayn
     then again   lie-NFN-F DL-OBL   now distant

     ima-l-ŋka-pu-tapi
     water-down-travel-away-COMP

     'While they both waited the water went down nearly completely.'

21. tay   pay-cu-mprump-nan plcaŋplcaŋ   pay-cu-rm-nan
     then lie-NFN-F DL-OBL   water to ankles lie-NFN-water-OBL

     k-mpɨ-wampak-k   mpa ima-n-ara-tapi
     VI SG O-3DL A-throw-IRR   now water S-DEF-dry-COMP

     'While they both waited, with water at the level of one's ankles,
     they both threw one, and now the water was completely dry.'

22. tay   ma-ŋ   k-mpɨ-yawra-mpi-wampak-k
     then other-VI SG VI SG O-3DL A-get-SEQ-throw-IRR

     'Then they both got and threw another one.'

23. ant-ɲan   k-tmuk-k   mpa anti
     land VIII SG-OBL   VI SG S-fall-IRR now land VIII SG

     aykk
     COP VIII SG VIS

     'It fell to the ground; now there was land.'

24. tay   mpa tpaɬ-cu-mprump-nan   tmal   mpa
     then now descend-NFN-F DL-OBL   sun/day V SG now

     na-na-kiakiak-aypu-n
     VI SG-DEF-dawn-lie-PRES

     'When they both came down, the sun came out.'

25. tpat-mpi   m-num   num   marm
     descend-SEQ   NR DIST-village   village smell V SG

     mama-k-n   numa-na-wampaki-n
     bad-IRR-V SG   village S-DEF-throw-PRES

     'When they both came down, the village smelled bad.'

26. m-rm   arm-pi   Yampwiɲcaŋkuntmpanan
     NR DIST-II SG   board-SEQ   Masindanai

     impa-wa-k
     3DL S-go-IRR

     'They both boarded (a canoe) and went to Masindanai.'

27. mpa mnti   impa-taw-k
     now there 3DL S-sit-IRR

     'They both stayed there.'

28. mpa pia-k   apiak
     now talk-PROX   COP talk

     'This story is enough.'

Text 3: How Men's Penises Got Shortened

This text was given in 1978 by Stephen Mambi.

1.   Aympt Barati m-rm   tan   impa-nanaŋ-taw-ntut
    name   name NR DIST-II DL there 3DL S-DUR-sit-RM PAST

    'Aympt and Barati lived there.'

2.   tay   m-n   Awkuri Taŋkiampun kay
    then NR DIST-I SG name   place name   canoe VIII SG

    na-nanaŋ-yamat-na-ntut
    3SG S-DUR-carve-DUR-RM PAST

    'Awkuri was making a canoe at Taŋkiampun.'

3.   tay   wurŋkat-n   mnta ŋarwa
    then night PL-OBL   then   penis IX SG

    na-nanaŋ-ira-wampaki-kia-ntuk-mpn   kika
    3SG S-DUR-ALL-throw-NIGHT-RM PAST-3DL D rat III SG

    nampayn
    like

    'During the nights he used to send his penis to them both like a rat.'

4.   tay   kika-n   arŋk-n
    then rat III SG-OBL mosquito net VI

    ku-mpɨ-nanaŋ-yawra-kia-ntut   "ki, ki, ki, ki"
    X SG O-3DL A-DUR-get-NIGHT-RM PAST

    'Under the guise of a rat they would get it (*paɲawŋ* X SG 'scrotum') in the mosquito net. "ki, ki, ki, ki." '

5.   tay   m-rm   kwalca-mpi
    then NR DIST-II DL rise-SEQ

    pia-mpɨ-nanaŋ-tmi-kia-ntut   "tmalŋkat-n
    talk T-3DL A-DUR-say-NIGHT-RM PAST sun/day V PL-OBL

    panmal   kantk-nprum ta-ŋkra-taw-wa-rm   tay
    man-I SG with-II DL   NEG-1DL S-sit-HAB-DL then

    wurŋkat-n   panmal   kantk-nprum kapa-tɨ-kia-wat
    night PL-OBL man I SG with-II DL   1DL S-do-NIGHT-HAB"

    'After getting up, they both said "During the day we don't have a man; at night we have a man." '

6.   tay   ma   wut   mampi
    then other night again

wa-n-ira-wampaki-kia-k-mpn   mnta
IX SG O-3SG A-ALL-throw-NIGHT-IRR-3DL D   then

wa-mpɨ-yawra-awram-kia-ntut   "ki, ki, ki, ki"
IX SG O-3DL A-get-enter-NIGHT-RM PAST

'Then the next night he again sent it to them both, and they took it and it goes inside "ki, ki, ki, ki." '

7.   tay   m-rm   kwalca-mpi
     then   NR DIST-II DL   rise-SEQ

     pia-mpɨ-nanaŋ-tmi-kia-ntut   "tmalŋkat-n
     talk T-3DL A-DUR-say-NIGHT-RM PAST   sun/day V PL-OBL

     panmal   kantk-nprum   ta-ŋkra-taw-wa-rm   tay
     man-I SG   with-II DL   NEG-1DL S-sit-HAB-DL   then

     wurŋkat-n   panmal   kantk-nprum kapa-tɨ-kia-wat"
     night PL-OBL   man I SG   with-II DL   1DL S-do-NIGHT-HAB

     'After getting up, they both said "During the day we don't have a man; at night we have a man." '

8.   tay   ma   tmat-ɲan   mnta
     then   other   sun/day V SG-OBL   then

     k-mp-ira-aykapi-k-nakn
     VI SG-3DL-ALL-know-IRR-3SG D

     'Then next day they both figured him out.'
     (*yaŋkuraŋ* VI SG 'thought(s)')

9.   aympanuŋ   mnta ku-mp-ira-yawra-k
     heavy pounding stick X SG   then   X SG O-3DL-ALL-get-IRR

     'They got a heavy pounding stick.'

10.   ku-mp-ira-yawra-k-mp-n   mnta
     X SG O-3DL A-ALL-get-IRR-VII SG-OBL   then

     ku-mpɨ-pampantakat-mpi-cɨ-k   tmat-ɲan
     X SG O-3DL A-fix-SEQ-put-IRR   sun/day V SG-OBL

     'After they both got it, they fixed it up and put it aside during the day.'

11.   wut   mnta wa-n-ira-wampaki-kia-k-mpn
     night   then   IX SG O-3SG A-ALL-throw-NIGHT-IRR-3DL D

     m-n   Barati pia-n-i-kia-k-nakn   Aympt
     NR DIST-II SG   name   talk T-3SG A-tell-IRR-3SG D   name

"mi tal-kia-na-uŋ,   kpa-nmaŋ."
2SG hold-NIGHT-IMP-X SG big-II SG

'Then that night he sent it to them both, and Barati told
Aympt "You hold it, big sister." '

12. m-n   Aympt mnta ku-n-tal-kia-k
    NR DIST-II SG name   then   X SG O-3SG A-hold-NIGHT-IRR

    'Aympt held it.'

13. mpa mnta k-n-mampi-malakmalak-awram-kia-k-nakn
    now   then   VI SG O-3SG A-again-converse(RED: *malak*-)enter-
                                          NIGHT-IRR-3SG D

    'He talks and enters his (glans penis) again.'
    (*karŋ* VI SG 'glans penis')

14. Aympt yawra-kia-k-mpi   mnta
    name   get-NIGHT-IRR-SEQ then

    k-n-tmpaŋaca-kia-k-nakn   mnta
    VI SG O-3SG A-cut in half-NIGHT-IRR-3SG O then

    wa-akak-mpi-cantaw-kia-k-nakn
    IX SG S-pull(RED: *ak*-)-SEQ-sit(RED: *taw*-)-NIGHT-IRR-3SG D

    'Aympt got it (stick), and then she cut it (penis) in two, and
    then his (penis) pulled up short.'

15. tay   m-n   mat-mpi tan
    then NR DIST-I SG   die-SEQ   there

    tia-n-t-awŋkwi-kia-k   Ayparatantaŋn
    act O-3SG A-do-sink-NIGHT-IRR place name

    'Then he died and sank completely at Ayparatantaŋn.'

16. m-rm   Waklŋkat kay   mnta
    NR DIST-II DL name   canoe VIII SG then

    i-mp-arm-kia-k
    VIII SG O-3DL A-board-NIGHT-IRR

    'They both boarded a canoe, Waklŋkat.'

17. m-rm   matntrm   Papakum m-rm   mnta
    NR DIST-II DL brother I DL name   NR DIST-I DL then

    impa-mpɨ-taray-mul-kia-k
    3DL O-3DL A-clear-run away-NIGHT-IRR

    'They both left the two brothers Papakum behind.'

18. tay   m-rm   Awn   taɲcak Pukrmarmpn
    then NR DIST-II DL place name here   Karawari River

tan   kratŋ-pi   impa-wa-kia-k
there straight-ADV 3DL S-go-NIGHT-IRR

'They went straight from Awn here to the Karawari River.'

19. taɲcan impa-arpal-kia-k   mnta
     there 3DL S-exit-NIGHT-IRR   then

     na-mpɨ-mpmta-kia-k
     3SG O-3DL A-travel along-NIGHT-IRR

     'They came out there and traveled along it.'

20. m-rm   narmprum   yua-nprum   wampwiatanpi
     NR DIST-II DL   woman II DL good-II DL face and eye V PL

     yua-ra   tak-nprum
     good-V PL   with-II DL

     'They were two good women with pretty faces.'

21. tay m-n   ma-n   taŋkarawat   Yampun
     then NR DIST-I SG   other-I SG   young man I SG Sepik River

     numkat-n   mnta
     village PL-OBL then

     na-mpɨ-tay-mpi-yawra-pu-kia-k
     3SG O-3DL A-see-SEQ-get-away-NEAR-IRR

     pia-mpɨ-tmi-kia-k   "kapa payum
     talk T-3DL A-say-NEAR-IRR   1DL   man I PL

     kapa-na-kamat-kulanaŋ. kapa tantukwan kapa-taw-wat.
     1DL S-DEF-search-walk 1DL   alone   1DL S-sit-HAB

     panmal   kayak"
     man I SG not have

     'Then they both went and found a young man in the villages
     of the Sepik River. They both said "We both are looking for
     husbands. We are alone. We don't have a husband." '

22. m-n   mnta impa-n-ayk-kia-k
     NR DIST-I SG   then 3DL O-3SG A-marry-NEAR-IRR

     'He married them both.'

23. mpa pia-k   apiak
     now talk-PROX   COP talk

     'This story is enough.'

Bibliography

Abbott, S. 1978. Murik Verb Morphology. Unpublished manuscript. Summer Institute of Linguistics, Ukarumpa, Papua New Guinea.

Bateson, G. 1936. *Naven*. Cambridge: Cambridge University Press.

Becker, A., and I. Oka. 1974. Person in Kawi: Exploration of an Elementary Semantic Dimension. *Oceanic Linguistics* 13:229–256.

Blake, B. 1983. Structure and Word Order in Kalkatungu: The Anatomy of a Flat Language. *Australian Journal of Linguistics* 3:143–76.

Boas, F. 1911. Introduction. *Handbook of American Indian languages*, 1–83. Bureau of American Ethnology Bulletin 40.1.

Bresnan, J., and S. Mchombo. 1987. Topic, Pronoun and Grammatical Agreement in Chichewɲa. *Language* 63:741–82.

Bruce, L. 1984. *The Alamblak Language of Papua New Guinea (East Sepik)*. Pacific Linguistics, vol. C.81. Canberra: Australian National University.

Capell, A. 1951. Languages of the Bogia District, New Guinea. *Oceania* 22:130–47,178–207,314.

Chafe, W. 1970. *Meaning and the Structure of Language*. Chicago: University of Chicago Press.

Chomsky, N. 1981. *Lectures on Government and Binding*. Dordrecht: Foris.

Clements, N., and K. Ford. 1979. Kikuyu Tone Shift and its Synchronic Consequences. *Linguistic Inquiry* 10:179–210.

Comrie, B. 1985. Causative Verb Formation and Other Verb-deriving Morphology. In *Language Typology and Syntactic Description, vol. 3: Grammatical Categories and the Lexicon*, 312–48, ed. T. Shopen. Cambridge: Cambridge University Press.

DiSciullo, A., and E. Williams. 1987. *On the Definition of a Word*. Cambridge MA: MIT Press.

Dixon, R. M. W. 1977. Where have all the Adjectives Gone? *Studies in Language* 1:19–80.

Dixon, R. M. W. 1979. Ergativity. *Language* 55:59–138.

Elson, B., and V. Pickett. 1962. *An Introduction to Morphology and Syntax.* Santa Anna, CA: Summer Institute of Linguistics.

Foley, W. 1986. *The Papuan Languages of New Guinea.* Cambridge: Cambridge University Press.

Foley, W. 1988. Language Birth: the Processes of Pidginization and Creolization. In *Linguistics: The Cambridge Survey, vol. 4: Language: the Socio-cultural Context,* 162–84, ed. F. Newmeyer. Cambridge: Cambridge University Press.

Foley, W. 1991. Language Change and Language Allegiance in the Sepik. In *Innovation, Variation and Synthesis in the Sepik,* ed. A. Forge and S. Lindenbaum. Washington: Smithsonian Press.

Foley, W., and R. Van Valin. 1984. *Functional Syntax and Universal Grammar.* Cambridge: Cambridge University Press.

Foreman, V. 1974. *A Grammar of Yessan-Mayo.* Language Data, Asian-Pacific Series 4.

Franklin, K. 1971. *A Grammar of Kewa, New Guinea.* Pacific Linguistics, vol. C.19. Canberra: Australian National University.

Franklin, K. 1975. Comments on Proto-Engan. *Pacific Linguistics* C38:263–75.

Gazdar, G., E. Klein, G. Pullum and I. Sag. 1985. *Generalized Phrase Structure Grammar.* Oxford: Basil Blackwell.

Gewertz, D. 1983. *Sepik River Societies.* New Haven: Yale University Press.

Goldsmith, J. 1979. *Autosegmental Phonology.* New York: Garland Publishing.

Goldsmith, J. 1985. Vowel Harmony in Khalkha Mongolian, Yaka, Finnish and Hungarian. In *Phonology Yearbook 2,* 253–76, ed. C. Ewen and J. Anderson. Cambridge: Cambridge University Press.

Haiman, J. 1978. Conditionals are Topics. *Language* 54:564–89.

Hale, K. 1983. Warlpiri and the Grammar of Non-configurational Languages. *Natural Language and Linguistic Theory* 1:5–47.

Harrison, S. 1989. Cultural Efflorescence and Political Evolution on the Sepik River. In *Innovation, Variation and Synthesis in the Sepik,* ed. A. Forge and S. Lindenbaum. Washington: Smithsonian Press.

Humboldt. W. 1836. *Über die Verschiedenheit des Menschlichen Sprachbaues und Ihren Einfluss Auf die Geistige Entwickelung des Menschengeschlechts.* Berlin: Köningliche Akademie der Wissenschaften.

Keenan, E., and B. Comrie. 1977. Noun Phrase Accessibility and Universal Grammar. *Linguistic Inquiry* 8:63–100.

Kiparsky, P. 1968. Linguistic Universals and Linguistic Change. In *Universals in Linguistic Theory*, 171–202, ed. E. Bach and R. Harms. New York: Holt, Rinehart, Winston.

Kiparsky, P. 1981. Lexical Morphology and Phonology. In *Linguistics in the Morning Calm*, 3–91, ed. I. Yang. Seoul: Hanshin.

Kiparsky, P. 1985. Some Consequences of Lexical Phonology. In *Phonology Yearbook 2*, 85–138, ed. C. Ewen and J. Anderson. Cambridge: Cambridge University Press.

Kirsner, R., and S. Thompson. 1976. The Role of Pragmatic Inference in Semantics: A Study of Sensory Verb Complements in English. *Glossa* 10:200–40.

Klima, E. 1964. Negation in English. In *The Structure of Language*, 246–323, ed. J. Fodor and J. Katz. Englewood Cliffs, NJ: Prentice-Hall.

Lang, A. 1973. *Enga Dictionary, with English Index*. Pacific Linguistics, vol. C.20. Canberra: Australian National University.

Laycock, D. 1959. Fieldnotes on the Angoram Language. Unpublished.

Laycock, D. 1965. *The Ndu Language Family (Sepik District, New Guinea)* Pacific Linguistics, vol. C.1. Canberra: Australian National University.

Mead, M. 1935. *Sex and Temperament in Three Primitive Societies*. New York: Morrow.

Mead, M. 1938. The Mountain Arapesh: An Importing Culture. *American Museum of Natural History Anthropological Papers* 36:139–349.

Nida, E. 1949. *Morphology*. Ann Arbor: University of Michigan Press.

Olson, M. 1981. *Barai Clause Junctures*. PhD thesis, Australian National University.

Palmer, F. 1984. *Grammar*. Harmondsworth: Penguin.

Pawley, A. 1966. *The Structure of Kalam: A Grammar of a New Guinea Highlands Language*. PhD thesis, University of Auckland.

Payne, J. 1985. Negation. In *Language Typology and Syntactic Description, vol. 1: Clause Structure*, 197–242, ed. T. Shopen. Cambridge: Cambridge University Press.

Reesink, G. 1986. Being Negative can be Positive. In *Pragmatics in Non-Western Perspective*, 115–42, ed. G. Huttar and K. Gregersen. Dallas: Summer Institute of Linguistics.

Reesink, G. 1987. Structures and their Functions in Usan, a Papuan Language of New Guinea. *Studies in Language Companion Series 13*. Amsterdam: Benjamins.

Sadock, J. 1980. Noun Incorporation in Greenlandic: a Case of Syntactic Word Formation. *Language* 56:300–19.

Schmidt, J. 1953. *Vokabular und Grammatik der Murik-Sprache in Nordost-Neuguinea*. Micro-Bibliotheca Anthropos 3.

Silverstein, M. 1976. Hierarchy of Features and Ergativity. In *Grammatical Categories in Australian Languages*, 112–71, ed. R. Dixon. Canberra: Australian Institute of Aboriginal Studies.

Silverstein, M. 1980. Of Nominatives and Datives: Universal Grammar from the Bottom Up. Unpublished manuscript, University of Chicago.

Staalsen, P. 1972. Clause Relationships in Iatmul. *Pacific Linguistics* A31:45–69.

Swadling, P. 1984. Sepik Prehistory. Presented at Wenner-Gren Symposium 95: Sepik Research Today: the Study of Sepik Cultures in and for Modern Papua New Guinea. Basel, Switzerland, August 1984.

Tuzin, D. 1974. Social Control and the Tambaran in the Sepik. In *Contention and Dispute: Aspects of Law and Social Control in Melanesia*, 317–51, ed. A. Epstein. Canberra: Australian National University.

Vendler, Z. 1967. *Philosophy in Linguistics*. Ithaca: Cornell University Press.

Wurm, S. 1982. The Papuan Languages of Oceania. *Acta Linguistica 7*. Tübingen: Gunter Narr.

Z'graggen, J. 1971. *Classificatory and Typological Studies in the Languages of the Madang District*. Pacific Linguistics, vol. C.19. Canberra: Australian National University.

Library of Congress Cataloging-in-Publication Data

Foley, William A.
The Yimas language of New Guinea / William A. Foley.
    p.   cm.
Includes bibliographical references.
ISBN 0-8047-1582-3
1. Yimas language—Grammar. 2. Yimas language—Usage. 3. Yimas
language—Noun phrase. 4. Language and culture—Papua New Guinea.
5. Sociolinguistics. I. Title.
PL6621.Y55F6 1991
499'.12—dc20   91-17261
                                                            CIP